Netherlands Yearbook of International Law

Volume 45

More information about this series at http://www.springer.com/series/8913

Mónika Ambrus · Ramses A. Wessel
Volume Editors

Netherlands Yearbook of International Law 2014

Between Pragmatism and Predictability: Temporariness in International Law

ASSER PRESS
CAMBRIDGE UNIVERSITY PRESS
Springer

Volume Editors
Mónika Ambrus
Department of International and Constitutional Law
University of Groningen
Groningen
The Netherlands

Ramses A. Wessel
Centre for European Studies
University of Twente
Enschede
The Netherlands

ISSN 0167-6768 ISSN 1574-0951 (electronic)
Netherlands Yearbook of International Law
ISBN 978-94-6265-059-6 ISBN 978-94-6265-060-2 (eBook)
DOI 10.1007/978-94-6265-060-2

Library of Congress Control Number: 72-623109

This Volume is also available as a journal product, either as part of the subscription to Volume 61 of the Netherlands International Law Review, or as a stand-alone journal, both through Cambridge University Press. In addition to the electronic version published on http://www.springerlink, the Yearbook is also available online through the Cambridge Journals Online service.

Published by T.M.C. ASSER PRESS, The Hague, The Netherlands www.asserpress.nl
Produced and distributed for T.M.C. ASSER PRESS by Springer-Verlag Berlin Heidelberg

Printed on acid-free paper

Springer Science+Business Media B.V. Dordrecht is part of Springer Science+Business Media (www.springer.com)

Board of Editors

Aims and Scope

The Netherlands Yearbook of International Law (NYIL) was first published in 1970. As a double-blind peer-reviewed publication, the NYIL offers a forum for the publication of scholarly articles of a conceptual nature in a varying thematic area of public international law. In addition, each Yearbook includes a section *Dutch Practice in International Law*. The NYIL is published under the auspices of the T.M.C. Asser Instituut.

T.M.C. Asser Instituut

Located in the 'international zone' of The Hague—the City of Justice, Peace and Security, The T.M.C. Asser Instituut is a leading, inter-university research institute operating in the broad field of international law.

Founded in 1965, the Institute's international community of scholars is engaged in research, postgraduate training and dissemination of knowledge in furtherance of the purposes and principles of international law. This inter-university institute cooperates closely with and supports the Dutch universities' activities in the relevant disciplines. The academic fields covered by the Institute are Private International Law, Public International Law, Law of the European Union, International Commercial Arbitration, International Humanitarian Law, International Criminal Law and International Sports Law.

The Institute enjoys an excellent reputation at national and international level for its development, organisation and hosting of conferences and academic meetings, demand-driven postgraduate programmes and training. Its ancillary websites and data collections all contribute to a coherent and integral strategy in the area of knowledge transfer.

The Institute has its own publishing house, T.M.C. Asser Press. The T.M.C. Asser Press not only serves the publishing needs of the T.M.C. Asser Instituut, but also those of academics and practitioners worldwide in the fields of International and European Law.

T.M.C. Asser Instituut
Institute for Private and Public International Law
International Commercial Arbitration and European Law

Institute Address:
R.J. Schimmelpennincklaan 20–22
2517 JN, The Hague
The Netherlands

Mailing Address:
P.O. Box 30461
2500 GL The Hague
The Netherlands
Tel.: +3170 342 0300
Fax: +3170 342 0359
Email: NYIL@asser.nl
Internet: www.asser.nl

Contents

Part I Between Pragmatism and Predictability: Temporariness in International Law

1 Between Pragmatism and Predictability: Temporariness in International Law ... 3
Mónika Ambrus and Ramses A. Wessel
1.1 Introduction ... 4
1.2 Forms of Temporariness ... 5
1.2.1 Temporary Objects ... 6
1.2.2 Temporary Subjects ... 8
1.3 International Law and Change ... 9
1.3.1 Temporary Objects and International Law ... 9
1.3.2 Temporary Subjects and International Law ... 13
1.4 Conclusion: All Relative? ... 15
References ... 16

2 Temporariness and Change in Global Governance ... 19
Rene Uruena
2.1 Introduction ... 20
2.2 International Law in a Constant Present ... 21
2.3 Change and Temporariness ... 26
2.3.1 Change and Temporariness in a Global Regulatory Space ... 28
2.3.2 Thinking About Change in the Constant Present ... 32
2.4 Normative Challenges ... 33
2.5 Conclusion ... 37
References ... 38

3 Temporary International Legal Regimes as Frames for Permanent Ones ... 41
Jean Galbraith
3.1 Introduction ... 42
3.2 Why Use Temporary International Legal Regimes? ... 44
3.2.1 Factors Favouring the Use of Temporary Regimes ... 44
3.2.2 Sources of Strength for Temporary Regimes ... 47
3.3 Temporary Regimes as Foundations for Permanent Regimes ... 48
3.3.1 Causes ... 49
3.3.2 Implications ... 51
3.4 Case Studies ... 54
3.4.1 Refugee Law ... 54
3.4.2 International Criminal Law ... 58
3.4.3 Climate Change ... 61
3.5 Conclusion ... 63
References ... 63

4 The International Rule of Law Time After Time: Temporary Institutions Between Change and Continuity ... 67
Sofia Ranchordás
4.1 Introduction ... 68
4.2 The (International) Rule of Law as a Source of Legal Certainty ... 71
4.2.1 The Rule of Law: Here, There and Everywhere? ... 71
4.2.2 The International Rule of Law and Time ... 76
4.2.3 The International Rule of Law as a Law of Lasting Rules? ... 78
4.3 Temporary Rules, Institutions and Measures ... 82
4.3.1 Temporary Legislation and the Rule of Law at Home ... 82
4.3.2 International Temporary Institutions, Rules and Measures ... 85
4.4 Conclusion ... 87
References ... 89

5 International Law and Time: A Reflection of the Temporal Attitudes of International Lawyers Through Three Paradigms ... 93
Christian Djeffal
5.1 International Law in Time: The Familiar Stranger ... 94
5.2 Paradigm Shifts ... 96
5.2.1 The Temporalisation of International Law ... 97
5.2.2 The Flexibilisation of International Legal Time? ... 104
5.3 General Conclusions ... 115
References ... 117

6 (Inter)Temporal Considerations in the Interpretative Process of the VCLT: Do Treaties Endure, Perdure or Exdure? . . . 121
Panos Merkouris
6.1 Introduction . . . 122
6.2 Definitional Issues . . . 125
6.2.1 Endurantism, Perdurantism, and Exdurantism . . . 125
6.2.2 Intertemporal Law . . . 128
6.2.3 Principle of Contemporaneity and Evolutive/Dynamic Interpretation . . . 129
6.3 Silence Can Speak Volumes: The Lack of Explicit References to Intertemporal Considerations in the VCLT . . . 134
6.3.1 Pre-VCLT Considerations on the Topic . . . 134
6.3.2 Rejection of Explicit Incorporation of the Doctrine of Intertemporal Law in the VCLT: Draft Article 56 . . . 135
6.3.3 Rejection of Explicit Solutions to Intertemporal Considerations Through the Backdoor of Article 31 . . . 137
6.4 Points of Entry of Intertemporal Considerations in Article 31 VCLT . . . 139
6.4.1 Direct Point of Entry . . . 139
6.4.2 Indirect Point of Entry . . . 144
6.5 Limits . . . 150
6.6 Conclusion . . . 151
References . . . 152

7 Shifting Demands in International Institutional Law: Securing the United Nations' Accountability for the Haitian Cholera Outbreak . . . 157
Kate Nancy Taylor
7.1 Introduction . . . 158
7.2 The Responsibility of the UN for the Cholera Outbreak . . . 159
7.3 The UN's Jurisdictional Immunity . . . 161
7.4 Alternative Modes of Dispute Settlement . . . 164
7.4.1 The UN's Obligation to Settle Private Law Disputes . . . 164
7.4.2 Would the Cholera Claims Fall Within the Scope of the UN's Liability? . . . 165
7.4.3 Dispute Settlement Mechanisms in UN Peacekeeping Operations . . . 169
7.5 Shifting Demands in the Law of International Organisations . . . 172
7.5.1 Would a Domestic Court Be Willing to Adjudicate the Cholera Claims? . . . 172
7.5.2 Elevating the Cholera Claims to an International Level . . . 176
7.5.3 The Rule of Law in the UN and the Handling of the Cholera Claims . . . 178
7.5.4 The Human Rights Imperative . . . 180
7.5.5 Demands for the Enhanced Accountability of the UN . . . 183

7.6 Permanent Versus *Ad Hoc* Solutions 187
7.6.1 Theorising Permanent Solutions 187
7.6.2 *Ad Hoc* Solutions: A Revised Role for Domestic Courts? 189
7.7 Conclusion 191
References 192

8 Protecting Human Rights During Emergencies: Delegation, Derogation, and Deference 197
Evan J. Criddle
8.1 Introduction 198
8.2 The Resilience of Derogation Standards 201
8.3 Derogation Standards as Delegations 206
8.4 Deference for an Altruistic Regime 212
8.5 Conclusion 218
References 219

9 Temporary Protection: Hovering at the Edges of Refugee Law 221
Jean-François Durieux
9.1 Introduction 222
9.2 Time in the International Legal Regime 226
9.2.1 Time as 'Attachment' 226
9.2.2 Time as Deadline 227
9.2.3 A Clash of Times 230
9.3 Temporary Protection in Europe, 1992–2001 232
9.3.1 A Time of Crisis 233
9.3.2 After the Crisis 240
9.4 Hovering on 244
9.5 Conclusion: Time for a Showdown 249
References 252

10 Between the Devil and the Deep Blue Sea: Enhancing Flexibility in International Climate Change Law 255
Harro van Asselt
10.1 Introduction 256
10.2 Flexibility in the United Nations Climate Change Regime 258
10.2.1 Delegated Law-Making 259
10.2.2 Scientific Input 260
10.2.3 Review and Amendment 262
10.2.4 Entry into Force, Reservations and Withdrawal 265
10.2.5 Differentiation 266
10.2.6 Implementation 268
10.2.7 Compliance 269
10.2.8 Flexibility in the Climate Change Regime: Advances and Limitations 271

10.3 A Pluralist Approach to International Climate Change Law as an Alternative Model 272
10.3.1 The Virtues of a Pluralist Approach. . . . 273
10.3.2 The Baby and the Bathwater 276
10.4 Enhancing Flexibility in International Climate Change Law 278
10.5 Conclusions 281
References. . . . 282

11 Commissions of Inquiry: Flexible Temporariness or Permanent Predictability? 287
Christian Henderson
11.1 Introduction 288
11.2 Commissions of Inquiry as Temporary Adjudicative Bodies of International Law. . . . 289
11.3 The Impact of Temporary Commissions of Inquiry Upon International Legal Adjudication 295
11.3.1 The Formality of International Legal Adjudication. . . . 295
11.3.2 The Principle of Non-intervention. . . . 300
11.3.3 Procedural Fairness 303
11.4 Concluding Remarks: A Permanent Commission of Inquiry?. . . . 307
References. . . . 310

12 Special Temporary Measures and the Norm of Equality 311
Adeno Addis
12.1 Introduction 312
12.2 The Nature of Special Temporary Measures 317
12.2.1 Special Rights and Special Measures 317
12.2.2 The Nature of Special Measures 318
12.3 Equality and Special Measures 321
12.3.1 Equality as Non-discrimination (Equality of Treatment) 321
12.3.2 Equality as Equality of Opportunity 322
12.4 Temporariness and Predictability: The Issue of Durational Limit . . . 325
12.5 Temporariness and Predictability: The Virtue of Candor. . . . 327
12.6 Conclusion 329
References. . . . 330

13 Paradise Postponed? For a Judge-Led Generic Model of International Criminal Procedure and an End to 'Draft-as-You-Go' 331
Michael Bohlander
13.1 Introduction 332
13.2 A Case in Point: The STL 337
13.3 The Conceptual Framework: Purpose, Fairness and Efficiency . . . 341
13.3.1 Characteristics of Domestic Procedures 341

13.3.2 Problems of International Procedure: Geo-Politics, Mass Atrocities and Creation of a Historical Record... 342
13.3.3 Sources of International Criminal Procedure: The Limited Role of Human Rights Law............ 343
13.3.4 International Criminal Procedure and General Sources of International Law............................ 344
13.3.5 Efficiency in Fairness: The Path Forward........... 345
13.4 Preferring the Judge-Led Model: Reasons and Parameters..... 346
13.4.1 Romantic Views of the Role of the Judge in the Adversarial Trial.......................... 346
13.4.2 Absence of the Dichotomy Between Spheres of Professional and Lay Adjudication.............. 347
13.4.3 Efficiency Aspects: Adversarial Versus Judge-Led Model.............................. 348
13.5 Conclusion.. 354
References... 355

Part II Dutch Practice in International Law

14 Platforms, Protestors and Provisional Measures: The *Arctic Sunrise* Dispute and Environmental Activism at Sea...................... 359
Richard Caddell
14.1 Introduction.. 360
14.2 The *Arctic Sunrise* Dispute............................ 362
14.2.1 Jurisdiction of the Tribunal....................... 365
14.2.2 Non-participation of the Respondent State.......... 368
14.2.3 Prompt Release and Provisional Measures.......... 370
14.3 Platforms and Protest Activism.......................... 374
14.3.1 Offshore Installations and the Law of the Sea........ 374
14.3.2 Freedom of Speech at Sea....................... 378
14.4 Concluding Remarks.................................. 382
References... 383

Table of Cases.. 385

Index.. 387

Part I
Between Pragmatism and Predictability: Temporariness in International Law

Chapter 1
Between Pragmatism and Predictability: Temporariness in International Law

Mónika Ambrus and Ramses A. Wessel

Abstract One of the key functions or purposes of international law (and law in general for that matter) is to provide long-term stability and legal certainty. Yet, international legal rules may also function as tools to deal with non-permanent or constantly changing issues, and rather than stable, international law may have to be flexible or adaptive. *Prima facie*, one could think of two main types of temporary aspects relevant from the perspective of international law. First, the nature of the object addressed by international law or the 'problem' that international law aims to address may be inherently temporary (*temporary objects*). Second, a subject of international law may be created for a specific period of time, after the elapse of which this entity ceases to exist (*temporary subjects*). These types of temporariness raise several questions from the perspective of international law, which are hardly addressed from a more conceptual perspective. This volume of the *Netherlands Yearbook of International Law* aims to do exactly that by asking the question of how international law reacts to various types of temporary issues. Put differently, where does international law stand on the continuum of predictability and pragmatism when it comes to temporary issues or institutions?

Keywords Temporariness · Temporary objects · Temporary subjects · Predictability · Pragmatism · Legal certainty · Change

---

Mónika Ambrus is lecturer in public international law, Department of International and Constitutional Law, University of Groningen, The Netherlands. Ramses A. Wessel is Professor of International and European Institutional Law at the University of Twente, Enschede, The Netherlands.

M. Ambrus
Department of International and Constitutional Law, University of Groningen, Groningen, The Netherlands
e-mail: m.ambrus@rug.nl

R.A. Wessel (✉)
Centre for European Studies, University of Twente, Enschede, The Netherlands
e-mail: r.a.wessel@utwente.nl

M. Ambrus and R.A. Wessel (eds.), *Netherlands Yearbook of International Law 2014*,
Netherlands Yearbook of International Law 45, DOI 10.1007/978-94-6265-060-2_1

Contents

1.1 Introduction 4
1.2 Forms of Temporariness 5
1.2.1 Temporary Objects 6
1.2.2 Temporary Subjects 8
1.3 International Law and Change 9
1.3.1 Temporary Objects and International Law 9
1.3.2 Temporary Subjects and International Law 13
1.4 Conclusion: All Relative? 15
References 16

1.1 Introduction

One of the key functions or purposes of international law (and law in general for that matter)[1] is to provide long-term stability and legal certainty. Indeed, when adopting conventions, drafting treaties, making regulations generally the idea is not that those rules will elapse. Think, for instance, of human rights conventions the endurance of which is ensured by rather general formulations. Yet, international legal rules may also function as tools to deal with non-permanent or constantly changing issues, and rather than stable, international law may have to be flexible or adaptive. Hersch Lauterpacht discussed this question in terms of a struggle between change and stability and justice and security. And he pointed out that '[e]xperience teaches that in this struggle the element of change is not always victorious, for the simple reason that stability and security are in themselves a powerful constituent element of justice.'[2] In his view, '[a]t present international law is more static than any other law not only because of the absence of an international legislature, but principally because it regulates relations which are not in themselves liable to be affected in a decisive manner by economic and other changes.'[3] Whether this observation still holds true today is one of the main questions that is addressed in this volume of the *Netherlands Yearbook of International Law*. According to Lauterpacht, one of the reasons for the insistence by international law on *status quo* is the absence of an international legislature which could deliberately change this situation. So far no such legislature has been created[4], which then raises the question how could international law, if at all, still react to or be influenced by changes, thus temporary issues. More concretely, what are the tools at the disposition of international law through which temporariness is dealt with.

Prima facie, one could think of two main types of temporary aspects relevant from the perspective of international law. First, the nature of the object addressed

[1] Provided that 'law' is driven by the rule of law and not by undemocratic or authoritarian ideas.

[2] Lauterpacht 2011, at 256.

[3] Ibid., at 257–258.

[4] Apart perhaps from the fact that international organizations are increasingly seen as contributing to 'international legislation'. See Wessel 2015.

by international law or the 'problem' that international law aims to address may be inherently temporary (*temporary objects*). While the object of regulation itself does not cease to exist, its features are bound to change throughout time. These changes are generally unknown or difficult to predict. In these cases regulations aim to address moving targets. Examples of this type of temporariness are abundant: climate change, migration, developing countries, belligerent occupations and so on. Oftentimes this type of temporariness is studied through concepts that are aimed to deal with changes and uncertainty, such as risk management and regulation, precaution or resilience.

Second, a subject of international law may be created for a specific period of time, after the lapse of which this entity ceases to exist (*temporary subjects*). These subjects mainly concern the establishment of institutions or certain entities. Examples of such temporary institutions are also ample in international law: territorial administrations, states in transition, the International Criminal Tribunal for Rwanda and for the former Yugoslavia and so on. The mainstream discussion with regard to this type of temporariness seems to focus on questions of justice, fairness and accountability.

In addition to the above-mentioned approaches, these types of temporariness raise several questions from the perspective of international law, which are hardly addressed from a more conceptual perspective. This volume of the *Netherlands Yearbook of International Law* aims to do exactly that, including the following questions. How does international law deal with matters that are non-permanent? What happens to international law when the originally temporary creatures become permanent? What is the effect of temporary regulations on matters that are permanent? How does temporariness affect legal certainty? These and related questions are addressed in the contributions of this volume of the *Yearbook* from various perspectives in order to explore the impact of temporariness on international law, namely how international law reacts to various types of temporary issues. Put differently, where does international law stand on the continuum of predictability and pragmatism when it comes to temporary issues or institutions?

Rather than providing a summary of each contribution, this introduction places the chapters within the above indicated framework of the two main forms of temporariness. After introducing these forms of temporariness as addressed in this volume, this chapter will discuss how these forms relate to and what effect they have or can have on international law. In order to gain further insights into the nature of temporariness, the chapter also highlights the main concepts associated or contrasted with the notion of temporariness in the concluding chapter.

1.2 Forms of Temporariness

This section introduces these two main forms of temporariness as addressed in the chapters without exploring their impact on international law, which is the subject of the next section.

1.2.1 Temporary Objects

An outstanding example of temporary objects is climate change, which is explored in van Asselt's chapter. This object is temporary in the sense that, as the name already indicates, the climate is undergoing certain changes; i.e. its nature varies or might vary from time to time, which is influenced, among others, by technological advances, socio-economic conditions and demographic developments. In addition, due to developments and shifts in scientific insights the manner in which climate change is seen is also prone to changes. Put differently, from time to time this problem needs to be tackled differently—i.e. a solution at a given moment in time might not work at another moment. Accordingly, a particular mechanism addressing the problem is quasi *per definitionem* temporary.

Another widely known example of a temporary object in international law is the situation of refuge-seekers. While refugees are generally seen as subjects of international law, the problem surrounding them can rather be described as the object of regulation. As Durieux's chapter describes, the nature of refugee protection is inherently temporary, though in a somewhat different manner than that of climate change: the general purpose of this regime is to re-establish the relationship between the original state of nationality and provide a temporary solution until then—thus regarding the regime as an 'exception'. I.e. the problem is generally seen as temporary, while in the case of climate change the problem has become temporary due to the changes involved. Nevertheless, the refugee protection regime is also subject to changes—making it temporary in a different manner. Namely, the refugees change, the number of refugees to be 'tackled' at a certain point in time is also subject to change, and obviously the domestic situation in the receiving state as well as in the state of origin also varies in many respects—which might also have impact on the way in which temporary protection can and will be provided to those who are escaping from their state of origin.

As explained in Criddle's chapter, national crises or emergencies are also temporary 'problems' that in general justify the somewhat reduced protection of human rights, i.e. the adoption of human right derogations. Put differently, the temporary problem here is the lower level of protection of human rights, which depends on the particular circumstances of the emergency situation. Similarly to refugee protection, the problem here is inherently and strictly temporary. As soon as the crisis or emergency ends, derogations should be eliminated too.

As opposed to human rights derogations, affirmative action measures rather provide a higher level of protection, as discussed in Addis' chapter. When affirmative actions or positive action measures are needed, the problem that needs to be addressed is inequality that stems from past discriminatory treatment. In other words, affirmative action measures aim to heal the consequences of a differential treatment adopted in the past, which has resulted in an unequal situation in the present. Nevertheless, they are similar to human rights derogations in that they will need to cease to exist after a period of time, namely when equal opportunities have been created.

Questions like these relate to an overarching objective of international law: a stable rule of law. If one perceives the international rule of law as the framework to provide stability and fairness (following domestic democratic notions based on that idea), the question is to what extent it can be combined with temporary issues. Ranchordás answer to this is that temporary institutions and rules can actually promote the international rule of law, providing more flexible solutions for the long-term achievement of a stable rule of law. In fact, as she argues, 'temporary certainty can contribute to thicker definitions of the rule of law including long-standing justice and protection of human rights.'[5]

In a way, this reveals that, international law itself (or at least parts of it) could also be regarded as an object of temporariness. In fact, one could argue that some temporariness is inherent in the sources of international law. Considering the main ones: custom is inherently fluid and allows international law to change according to adapted practices and legal opinions. While the objective of written law is to overcome uncertainties and provide 'fixed' interpretations, treaties are often seen as 'living instruments', the interpretation of which may follow new insights and developments. In fact, as the contribution of Merkouris indicates, treaty law itself allows for change over time. In the law of treaties 'subsequent practice', 'subsequent agreements', 'relevant rules' and 'supplementary means' play an essential role and discussions often relate to the tension between the intentions of the drafters and the ways in which these play out later.

As legal scholars, we are not merely observers of changes in international law. Scholarly insights are equally temporary and obviously contribute to changes in the international rules. The 'shift from eternity (natural law) to temporality (changeable law)' is man-made. In his contribution, Djeffal points to the influence of paradigm changes over time. The question raised in his contribution is whether in the dialectal process from atemporality to temporality, we can see a new paradigm termed 'fluxus': asserting that the law is necessarily moving and changing and hardly ascertainable. 'Under such an assumption, predicting the law generally means to predict the next decision. The temporal focus is, therefore, on the next moment.'[6]

Similarly, international law, as object of temporariness, may be challenged to remedy flaws in its system. When structural solutions are out of sight due to, for instance, political controversies, temporary solutions may be in order, and acceptable to the international community. The present collection offers ample examples of such temporary 'repairs', including the establishment of *ad hoc* tribunals. An example that has received quite some attention of the past years concerns the immunity of international organisations. As an almost inherent element of the international system, structural changes are not to be foreseen in the immediate future. Yet, international organisations change and are increasingly active in rule-making that has effects on individuals. Taylor's contribution points to

[5] Ranchordás 2015.

[6] Djeffal 2015.

accountability gaps in this regard, in particular in relation to private claims. The question then is whether unpreferred consequences of systemic choices can be remedied by allowing for temporary solutions (in this concrete case: dealing with 5000 private law claims which emerged in response to the allegedly negligent importation of cholera into Haiti by UN peacekeepers).

1.2.2 Temporary Subjects

An outstanding example of temporary subjects is the so called commissions of inquiry (CoIs). As explored in Henderson's chapter, these subjects are being established as a reaction to an incident in an *ad hoc* manner. It seems that, in addition to the political difficulties involved in negotiating the establishment of a permanent (quasi-)judicial body, the nature of the incidents justifies the creation of such *ad hoc* mechanisms. These commissions are established for investigating (mainly) the facts of a specific international incident involving two or more states. As Henderson explains,

> [t]hese contemporary CoIs, while not producing legally binding outcomes, nonetheless carry out various adjudicative functions, from determining applicable legal frameworks and the scope of the legal rules and norms in question to determining whether particular acts amount to violations of these rules and norms.[7]

He even indicates that CoIs

> offer what may be the only, or at least most formal, treatment of the legal issues raised in the context of a particular conflict or crisis, and perhaps represent an important shift in the *modus operandi* of the international community in seeking at least some accountability for violations of international law.[8]

Temporariness of subjects of international law can also take a different form, as illustrated in Bohlander's chapter. Although there is a permanent court for punishing those responsible for the most serious crimes, international criminal justice still seems to favour temporary solutions, as Bohlander points out. More specifically, he argues that the present criminal tribunals have been set up in an *ad hoc* manner, resulting in not-well-thought-through procedural rules and thus representing a mix of the two main systems, namely the adversarial and the judge-led models. This approach leaves quite some room for judicial trial and error—reflecting another temporary dimension of these institutions. In this case, temporariness relates to the functioning of specific institutions, or put differently, temporariness is visible in the main legal features of the operation of these institutions. The institutions themselves might be established on a permanent basis, but the manner in which they carry out their work is characterised by temporary elements.

---

[7] Henderson 2015.

[8] Ibid.

Galbraith, at a more theoretical level, examines the impact of temporary institutions, or more broadly, temporary regimes on international law. Two of her examples can be seen as addressing temporary objects (refugee law as well as climate change), while the example of international criminal law can be related to temporary subjects. In this regard, her contribution shows that these two aspects of temporariness can clearly be compared as to their general effect on permanent regimes. She examines through different theories (rational design approach, historical institutionalism, constructivism and behavioural international law) the reasons behind these temporary 'regimes' as well as the manner in which they shape permanent ones.

Last but not least, Uruena's chapter approaches the question of temporariness in a somewhat different manner. Rather than looking at the temporary subjects as defined above, he analyses the so-called 'permanent subjects'. In his view, even though many of the subjects of international law are established as permanent 'institutions', this permanency does not mean that they are static, i.e. that they do not change. Put differently, even permanent institutions can be seen as temporary ones, given their dynamic existence that is steered by interaction among the various actors/subjects of international law. Such a dynamic is, however, difficult to be discovered given the constant present used in international law. This dynamic also implies that the permanence of institutions is relational: 'international norms and institutions are "permanent" or "provisional" in comparison to *other* international norms and institutions.'[9]

1.3 International Law and Change

Both temporary objects and subjects have an interesting relationship with international law. This section looks at this relationship through the lenses of the chapters in this volume.

1.3.1 Temporary Objects and International Law

The chapters addressing temporary objects of international law essentially focus on the relationship between these objects and international law: how does international law enable the regulation of these objects, what is the role of permanent institutions in this regard, and how does a temporary measure impact upon a general norm?

Concerning climate change as a temporary object of international law, van Asselt's chapter argues that the 'changing circumstances make it challenging to govern the problem of climate change through a single set of rules fixed in time,

[9] Uruena 2015 (emphasis in original).

and therefore point to the need for a flexible, dynamic and adaptive legal system.' He, however, also admits that '[a]t the same time, the flexibility necessary to address the temporary nature of the subject matter may well challenge one of the core rationales of legal norms: to provide legal certainty and predictability and, more broadly, to uphold the rule of law.'[10] In other words, a changing problem needs legal answers that can adjust to the extent the problems require. To put it bluntly, temporary problems require temporary solutions. Such temporary solutions, so the argument goes, can be 'produced' if certain flexibility mechanisms are built into the legal regime. His chapter examines to what extent the regime of climate change can be regarded as flexible. Analysing its various aspects, he finds that 'flexibility has been the rule rather than the exception in the *design* of the United Nations climate change regime.'[11] Nevertheless, he admits that in practice the regime still faces certain challenges. In his view, 'the adaptability of the climate regime is limited in at least two important respects: the evolution of commitments in accordance with changing national circumstances and changing the overall ambition in light of new scientific evidence.'[12] All in all, the chapter suggests that international law has tried to cope with the fact that climate change is an object that requires temporary solutions, i.e. flexibility. Accordingly, the temporary object did have a significant impact on the design and functioning of the international legal regime that regulates this object, and thus this regime can be characterised as pragmatic, which nevertheless ensures predictability.

As far as migration or refuge, another temporary object in international law, is concerned, Durieux's chapter explores how international law reacted to the temporary problem of 'refuge time'. The international legal regime on refugee protection includes several 'temporal' aspects as a reaction to the special nature of the refuge situation. First, over time the position of the refugee should be brought closer to that of citizens. Second, a deadline is set as to until when the refugee can be regarded as refugee, in order to avoid that this status last longer than desirable. As Durieux explains

> [t]he management of "refuge time" is the source of an obvious tension within the 1951 Convention regime. Premature return to a continuing situation of persecution or violence is clearly prohibited by the *non-refoulement* principle. … Meanwhile, attachment leads to integration, which becomes the default solution.[13]

In the 1980s the focus was on the free will of the refugee to return. However, in the 1990s the question of what the host state can do in order to 'convince' the refugee to return home ('promote voluntary repatriation') has become rather urgent, given the crisis in Yugoslavia. This has led to the emergence of the concept of 'temporary protection' in Europe. This concept has tried to solve the tension between the focus on return and integration by placing a strong focus on the return aspect.

---

[10] van Asselt 2015.

[11] Ibid. (emphasis in original).

[12] Ibid.

[13] Durieux 2015.

Indeed, it was defined as 'a return-oriented protection mechanism'. While in Europe temporary protection has been regulated, within the UN it was only loosely referred to. So one can see an interesting parallel development here: while at the UN level the emerging crisis did not lead to any formal or practical changes in the approach towards refugees, at the EU level a new approach was adopted and applied. In the latter case the temporary problem has had a huge impact on the manner in which the refuge problem was treated and actually shifted the focus from finding a balance towards promoting return, while in the former case the problem did not lead to much visible change thus creating some tensions concerning large-scale influx of refugees. Put in more abstract terms, at the European level a concrete crisis has induced the adoption of a specific approach towards all refuge situations, while at the international level it was not possible to create an exception even for such a crisis. One might say that Europe has adopted a more pragmatic approach as opposed to the international level's seeming focus on predictability.

Emergency or crisis situations can also be addressed by adopting temporary measures that allow for certain derogations from human rights. The leading human rights agreements formulate such derogation possibilities in a rather broad manner, though generally enshrining that certain steps need to be followed. The question can then be raised how these broad standards can be translated into rules. An increasingly frequently emerging response to this question is '[t]he idea that international law needs to develop more concrete rules for human rights derogation'.[14] However, this has so far not happened, and most probably will not happen soon. How can then these standards be seen? 'Should derogation standards be understood primarily as delegations of rule-making authority to international courts and commissions? Or should they be construed as delegations to states to develop "rules adapted to their special needs"?'[15] In simple and more general terms, the question that is raised with regard to human rights derogations in Criddle's chapter is the following: who is authorised under international law to decide on the concrete temporary measures? The underlying idea behind this allocation of authority can be related to the point made in van Asselt's chapter, namely flexibility or pragmatism. Emergency situations vary per situation and per country. Accordingly, they also require a response that can be fit to the particular case, thus the possibility to derogate from human rights needs to be adaptable to this case, hence requiring flexibility. Based on the case-law of the most relevant human rights international adjudicative bodies, Criddle's chapter identifies that international human rights law (HRL) essentially 'entrusts states with [the] primary responsibility to determine what measures are necessary to protect and fulfil human rights for their people during national crises.'[16] I.e. international law considers states as the most appropriate actors to adopt measures that are suitable for addressing an emergency.

[14] Criddle 2015.

[15] Ibid.

[16] Ibid.

'Broad derogation standards are the mechanisms HRL employs to structure its jurisprudence of altruism, empowering states to design temporary human rights regimes that are tailored to the specific exigencies of particular national crises.'[17] Nevertheless, human rights courts provide the final guarantee 'that states do not abuse their discretionary power'.[18] While in general, given this role of states, a deferential approach is adopted by international courts, the judicial deference should be 'conditioned upon the state serving as a faithful trustee for its people',[19] so the argument goes. Essentially one could then conclude that international law through laying down a broad standard as well as judicial deference ensures that there is ample flexibility when the adoption of emergency measures is needed, whereby it can be qualified as an example of a pragmatic approach, which at the same time aims to ensure predictability.

One might conceive affirmative actions as comparable to human rights derogations, given that on the face of it, they also seem to deviate from the general rules, in this specific case from the idea of equality, in the sense that they entitle a group to special protection. However, as Addis' chapter argues, 'the analogy with emergency exceptions is misplaced and the worry that these measures will undercut the very coherence of the norm of equality is unwarranted.'[20] In other words, affirmative actions do not 'undermine the coherence and predictability of the norm itself.'[21] 'They suspend non-discrimination in its narrow and formal sense while preparing the ground for a broader and more robust notion of equality.'[22] I.e. they actually 'do not leave the general norm of equality in suspension for a temporary period.'[23] In a more general sense, Addis' chapter clearly illustrates that a temporary measure can have a long-term effect on a general concept under international law, namely it can change and complement its meaning, thus contributing to its predictability even though the measure itself might be regarded as a pragmatic one.

As noted above, predictability may also be assured by structurally including 'temporality' in an international legal regime. As we have seen, international treaty law—as analysed by Merkouris—forms a good example of a legal regime allowing for change. Treaties, as key objects of international law, are meant to stabilise the system and provide legal certainty. Yet, treaty law allows for temporary solutions and dynamic interpretations over time. The reason for this is obvious: by not allowing 'time' to affect the interpretation of international agreements, they would run the risk of becoming dead letters rather than accepted bases for international cooperation. A similar notion lies behind the flexible solutions described by Ranchordás, where she points to the fact that, in the end, these contribute to a

[17] Ibid.

[18] Ibid.

[19] Ibid.

[20] Addis 2015.

[21] Ibid.

[22] Ibid.

[23] Ibid.

stable rule of law, as well as a further promotion and consolidation of the rule of law. Taylor's chapter, while highlighting their caveats, also suggests that temporary solutions could contribute to closing, at least to a certain extent the accountability gap regarding international organisations.

1.3.2 Temporary Subjects and International Law

The chapters looking at temporary subjects essentially focus on the relationship between these subjects and international law: how does international law facilitate or enable the creation of such subjects; how do they affect international law in a more general sense; and how does international law actually accommodate these subjects or their temporary features?

Henderson's chapter argues that international law, and more specifically certain features of international adjudication, makes it possible or facilitates the creation of and reliance on these institutions. Put differently, this chapter looks into the question how permanent subjects of international law actually enable or even promote the emergence of such commissions. In his view, there are at least three features of international law that can be 'blamed' for such a promotion: the formality of international adjudication, the principle of non-intervention, and procedural fairness. CoIs are such temporary institutions that can avoid falling in the trap of these features. Temporariness can thus be seen as providing correction to some negative impacts of permanent institutions, thus their existence might be best explained by a pragmatic approach.

In a somewhat different manner, Bohlander's chapter explores the impact of temporary criminal justice solutions on international (criminal) law. He argues that the so called 'draft-as-you-go' approach, thus the application of temporary solutions, rather than well-thought-through models as well as the room provided through this approach for judicial trial and error,

> open[…] the building of the administration of justice up to intruders with separate agendas and to political negotiations that would appear to fit and fix the temporary emergency and to fill the temporary gaps in the law needed for the fixing.[24]

Such an approach, in other words, can have serious consequences as far as the legitimacy of these permanent institutions and legal certainty are concerned—so the argument goes. I.e. embedding in the main features of international criminal law systems such temporary solutions clearly has a negative impact on international criminal justice. Accordingly, the pragmatic approach adopted in this case clearly has a negative impact on the predictability of international law.

As indicated above, Uruena's chapter argues that even the so-called 'permanent' institutions and rules are constantly in the process of change, even though the language of international law suggests a constant present: 'international law approaches

[24] Bohlander 2015.

norms and institutions as though they had always been there. Once change occurs, it approaches new (or changed) norms and institutions as if *those* norms had always been there.'[25] He suggests then to think about change, thus temporariness, in a somewhat different manner. As indicated above, he argues that the permanency of these institutions and norms is relational, which enables us 'to think of norms, not as discrete utterances, but rather as part of a wider landscape in which the temporal and the permanent help define each other.'[26] Accordingly, he suggests that we use the notion of 'global regulatory space' in which various forces exert different pulls. So permanence is impossible, 'which is triggered by the constant movement of all the objects in the global regulatory space.'[27] And the result of this interaction between the various actors is a particular state of art in international law. Put differently, he aims to discover the underlying ideas behind, or, as he calls it, the 'deep grammar' of change in international law, even though this theory would not change the perception of seeing norms and institutions as 'static' or as 'discrete events'. The theory of incremental change based on the proposed 'gravitational pull', however, has its own caveats or challenges, namely tunnel vision and regulatory capture. The former implies that '[t]alking in terms of a "gravitational force" creates the risk of losing sight of an overarching narrative of a "good" society.' The latter danger is that the global regulatory space makes it possible for private actors to exert influence on the decision-making relying on gravitational pull. Such influence could have desired as well as negative impact. In order to avoid these caveats, Uruena's suggestion is to set up a normative framework based on which one could devise a 'vocabulary to perform a critique of the reasons behind such a powerful pull'.[28] Whether or not it is necessary to assess the 'appropriateness' of the extent of 'pull' of certain norms and institutions is up for debate. Nevertheless, such a pull can be seen as incorporating pragmatism in the permanent institutions in a manner that might negatively impact predictability, given the fact that they are difficult to identify and foresee. In any event it is of utmost importance to have a vocabulary for exploring the nature of changes even in permanent institutions that are inherently also temporary given the workings of the various pulling forces. In light of the other chapters, the question could be raised how are then so-called temporary institutions and rules different from the so-defined 'permanent ones' other than the basic rules establishing them?

Similarly to Bohlander's chapter, Galbraith's contribution also examined the impact of concrete temporary subjects on permanent ones (or on international law in a broader sense) but from a more theoretical perspective. She examined how four different theories of state behaviour would and could explain the impact these temporary regimes might have on future permanent regimes. All theories she studied indicate that the impact of temporary regimes on permanent ones is not

25 Uruena 2015 (emphasis in original).

26 Ibid. (emphasis in original).

27 Ibid. (emphasis in original).

28 Ibid.

negligible. First, 'a rational design approach suggests that states can iron out mistakes or adjust to new conditions in ways that are not overly influenced by the structure of the temporary regime.'[29] Second, '[u]nder a historical institutionalist perspective, one would expect the design choices made for temporary regimes to have outsized influence in some but not all contexts.' Probably this theory provides the best explanation as to the creation of commissions of inquiry, as described in Henderson's chapter. Third, the constructivist approach suggests that 'the power of the temporary regimes is largely in strengthening the norms of governmental and other actors in favour of the objective of the regime.' The 'pull' discussed in Uruena's chapter concerning the changes in permanent institutions could be best explained based on this theory. Last, 'a behavioural international law approach would suggest that temporary regimes are always sticky, with the magnitude varying based on the extent to which these regimes serve as defaults or reference points.'[30] This last one is actually the point made by Bohlander. Interestingly, all these theories seem to try to find a balance between pragmatism and predictability—change is necessary, but certain elements need to be added in order to ensure predictability. They suggest that actually no choice should be made between pragmatism and predictability, as they can be both facilitated and maintained at the same time.

All in all, we can conclude that temporariness (or permanency) is relational. Nevertheless, this temporal element of either the objects or the subjects of international law has impact on international law. While it seems that concerning temporary objects there is an underlying aim to ensure both predictability and at the same time being pragmatic, as far as temporary subjects are concerned a pragmatic approach might turn out to have a negative impact on predictability. This difference might be explained by the difference between objects and subjects as such. Subjects of international law have 'independent' living and functioning, and they oftentimes want to set up their own approaches, mechanisms etc. Objects of international law, however, are subject to regulation, which most likely will ensure predictability when addressing a problem.

1.4 Conclusion: All Relative?

A popular view on temporariness in international law may be that it potentially harms the already quite shaky international legal order. Indeed, as we argued in our introduction to this chapter, one of the key functions or purposes of international law is to provide long-term stability and legal certainty. In analysing the different views on temporariness, we may conclude that this element is certainly

29 Galbraith 2015.

30 Ibid.

present, but that the opposite is also visible. Depending on whether positive or negative meanings are associated with temporariness, a particular expectation is created, thus having an impact on the response provided, too.

With regard to temporary objects where the issue or object is changing (and is thus temporary), this change is simply seen as a given that needs to be addressed in one way or another; i.e. the association with temporariness is definitely not negative. The general response to this change is the need for having 'flexibility' mechanisms built into the system. The system then can be criticised if it lacks or does not sufficiently embed such mechanisms. In addition, temporariness is also seen in this context as a phenomenon that can provide meaning, thus influence the interpretation of otherwise permanent concepts—as, for instance, illustrated in Addis' chapter.

Unlike temporary objects, the temporary subjects of international law are associated with both positive and negative features. As far as the positive features are concerned, it has been highlighted that temporary institutions can be seen as correcting, at least to a certain extent, the deficits of so-called permanent institutions. Moreover, temporariness is also contrasted with being static, through which temporariness is essentially seen as a form of flexibility or dynamism. However, Bohlander's chapter, for instance, also highlights the dangers of '*ad hocism*' as a form of temporariness as opposed to well-thought-through regimes. In this latter case, temporariness thus obtains a negative association.

It is the search for this balance between pragmatism and predictability that seems to form the thread through our analysis of the different perspectives. At the same time these two notions should not always be contrasted, as, for instance, illustrated by Criddle's chapter. Under certain circumstances, pragmatism may contribute to predictability as the latter is not only based on static international law, but may require dynamism and change to remain relevant. The chapters in the present volume underline that change is not something that we should see as an exception; in many cases it is a structural or systemic part of the international legal system.

References

Addis A (2015) Special temporary measures and the norm of equality. Netherlands Yearbook of International Law 45:311–331

Bohlander M (2015) Paradise postponed? For a judge-led generic model of international criminal procedure and an end to 'draft-as-you-go'. Netherlands Yearbook of International Law 45:333–357

Criddle EJ (2015) Protecting human rights during emergencies: delegation, derogation and deference. Netherlands Yearbook of International Law 45:197–220

Djeffal C (2015) International law and time: a reflection of the temporal attitudes of international lawyers through three paradigms. Netherlands Yearbook of International Law 45:93–119

Durieux J (2015) Temporary protection: hovering at the edges of refugee law. Netherlands Yearbook of International Law 45:221–253

Galbraith J (2015) Temporary international legal regimes as frames for permanent ones. Netherlands Yearbook of International Law 45:41–65

Henderson C (2015) Commissions of inquiry: flexible temporariness or permanent predictability. Netherlands Yearbook of International Law 45:287–310

Lauterpacht H (2011) The function of law in the international community. Oxford University Press, Oxford

Merkouris P (2015) (Inter)temporal considerations in the interpretative process of the VCLT: do treaties endure, perdure or exdure? Netherlands Yearbook of International Law 45:121–156

Ranchordás S (2015) The international rule of law time after time: temporary institutions between change and continuity. Netherlands Yearbook of International Law 45:67–91

Taylor K (2015) Shifting demands in international institutional law: securing the United Nation's accountability for the Haitian cholera outbreak. Netherlands Yearbook of International Law 45:157–195

Uruena R (2015) Temporariness and change in global governance. Netherlands Yearbook of International Law 45:19–40

van Asselt (2015) Between the devil and the deep blue sea: enhancing flexibility in international climate change law. Netherlands Yearbook of International Law 45:255–286

Wessel RA (2015) Revealing the publicness of international law. In: Molenaar EJ, Nollkaemper PA, Nouwen S, Rijngaert C (eds) What's *wrong* with international law? What's wrong with *international* law? Martinus Nijhoff Publishers, Leiden, Boston (forthcoming)

Chapter 2
Temporariness and Change in Global Governance

Rene Uruena

El amor es eterno mientras dura.
Luis Cardoza y Aragón.

Abstract A crucial aspect of international law is to provide long-term stability and legal certainty. This function presumes that international law-making creates discrete norms and institutions that remain static until they are changed (or replaced) by other discrete institutions. This paper adopts a different point of departure to think about 'temporariness'. It suggests a dynamic of norm creation and institutional change in global governance. Neither norms nor institutions remain static once they become 'permanent'. They adapt, evolve and transform. This contribution argues that this process of change is driven by interaction among institutions and actors, which is the default technology of post-national rule-making. How to start thinking about such interaction? What is the added value of focusing on the process of interaction and not on the allegedly static characteristics of actors themselves? How can this approach provide a different normative and critical framework to think about debates on global governance? In answering these questions, this chapter will explore the interaction between international institutions in order to develop the central tenets of a methodology to think about institutional change in post-national rule-making.

Keywords Change · Global governance · Temporariness · International law · Global regulatory space

R. Uruena (✉)
Director of the Master's Program in International Law,
Universidad de Los Andes, Bogotá, Colombia
e-mail: rf.uruena21@uniandes.edu.co

M. Ambrus and R.A. Wessel (eds.), *Netherlands Yearbook of International Law 2014*,
Netherlands Yearbook of International Law 45, DOI 10.1007/978-94-6265-060-2_2

Contents

2.1 Introduction 20
2.2 International Law in a Constant Present 21
2.3 Change and Temporariness 26
2.3.1 Change and Temporariness in a Global Regulatory Space 28
2.3.2 Thinking About Change in the Constant Present 32
2.4 Normative Challenges 33
2.5 Conclusion 37
References 38

2.1 Introduction

An important role of international law is to provide long-term stability and legal certainty. This function presumes that international law-making creates discrete norms and institutions that remain static until they are changed (or replaced) by other discrete institutions. This paper adopts a different point of departure to think about 'temporariness'. It suggests a dynamic view of norm creation and institutional change in global governance. Neither norms nor institutions remain static once they become 'permanent'. They adapt, evolve and transform. This chapter argues that the idea of temporariness implies a certain theory of change, and that this process of change is, in turn, driven by interaction among institutions and actors. Such interaction, the chapter argues is the default technology of post-national rule making.

While some efforts have been made to explain the role of interaction in the creation of the normative value of international law,[1] much of the literature trying to re-think the overall legal architecture of global governance seems to be oblivious of the important role of inter-institutional interaction in legal change. This article is an effort to start thinking about change in such terms. What is the added value of focusing on the process of interaction and not on the allegedly static characteristics of norms and institutions? How can this approach provide a different normative and critical framework to think about debates on global governance?

To address these questions, the text proceeds as follows. The ability to distinguish between permanent and provisional is crucial to thinking about international law. This ability is based on a particular view of change, which is explored in Sect. 2.2. Section 2.3 contains the central contribution of the article, and explores the dynamics of change in a global regulatory space. Then, Sect. 2.4 explores some of the challenges that this reading of change faces. Finally, Sect. 2.5 concludes.

[1] See, for example, Toope and Brunnée 2010.

2.2 International Law in a Constant Present

As hinted at above, temporariness and permanence are crucial elements of the vocabulary of international law. Some international norms are expressly temporal in their design; for example, most international courts have the *prima facie* jurisdiction to order provisional measures that, most evidently, are intended to be applicable for a limited span of time.[2] On the other side of the spectrum, there are institutions intended to be permanent: international organizations are a good example. States create organizations to stabilise a particular bargain of interests, thus creating a centralized and independent structure that enhances state interaction and the effectiveness of operational activities.[3] These advantages are gained if the organization is permanent (or at least if it is expected to be permanent). To be sure, institutions do change and are dynamic; however, the expectation of their permanence is crucial—otherwise, if the bargain is perceived as temporal, the organization will suffer in its ability to centralise activities, hence affecting its independence and, ultimately, its potential influence.

The ability to make the distinction between 'permanent' and 'provisional' in international law is based on a particular view of change. The idea of 'permanence' implies a negation of change—or at least its pause for a considerable amount of time. Temporariness, on the other hand, suggests the potential of change—'this is temporal' means this is 'subject to change'. Permanent, in contrast, means, closed for change.

To be sure, the idea of permanence as 'closed to change' does not imply total immutability. It is clear that permanence requires certain adjustment and adaptation: the field of organizational ecology as applied to international organizations has developed key insights on the role of marginal adaptation for resilience.[4] And, in a more trivial sense, institutions are actually changing all the time: staffs come and go, budgets rise and diminish, and headquarters open and close. The measure, then, is one of degree: while some change is always present, permanence seems to imply the absence of core change. In the extreme, defining as 'permanent' an international institution whose constituent document, institutional structure, and actual name changes every day is non-sensical.

But this begs the question: when does change stop being marginal? This question points to the central challenge. Despite its importance, the underlying concept of change in international law is hopelessly under-theorized. The first challenge is, then, where to start looking for the deep grammar that makes the idea of temporariness intelligible in international law. For that purpose, it is useful to build on a distinct trend in legal scholarship exploring the idea that an underlying consciousness can be read between the lines of discrete legal rules. Such is the notion of

[2] See generally Rosenne 2005.

[3] Abbott and Snidal 1998.

[4] For example, Abbott et al. 2013.

langue, as taken by Duncan Kennedy from Saussarian semiotics.[5] Kennedy argues that specific legal rules in a given moment are not discrete occurrences, but are rather connected by an underlying link. The key concept here is the difference between *parole* and *langue*: *parole* is the specific utterance, which may be understood as 'sound bites', while *langue* is the set of resources available at any particular moment to compose such utterances. In a subsequent text, Kennedy refers to *langue* as the legal consciousness of a given time, as a 'vocabulary of concepts and typical arguments'[6] that underlie the 'specific, positively enacted rules of the various countries'.[7]

The purpose here is not to discuss in depth the structuralist insight that meaning is produced by the relations among linguistic terms themselves (and not by an underlying connection to factual history, which lies at the heart of the langue/parole distinction).[8] Instead, this mindset is useful here as it opens another level of engagement with the question of temporariness in international law. While Kennedy's description of succeeding legal consciousness proposes neither an idea of the concept of change within each moment, nor an idea of the process of change from one moment to the next, the notion of legal consciousness allows us to start looking for the deep grammar that defines the frontier of possibilities in international law. The langue/parole distinction opens a space of inquiry where, this article argues, the notion of change lies. Such will be the space explored in what remains of this text.

The *langue* of international law features a particular view of change, according to which, ultimately, there is *no change* in international law. That is to say, international law approaches norms and institutions as though they had always been there. Once change occurs, it approaches new (or changed) norms and institutions as if *those* norms had always been there. The underlying idea is that international norms and institutions are discrete events that occur linearly over time, and can be thought not of as continuum, but rather as a collection of discrete points in time that have little interaction with what happened earlier, or later.

This is not to say the langue of international law is based upon the idea that all norms pre-exist their time of creation. On the contrary: the time before the moment of creation (legal enactment, entry into force, and so forth) seems irrelevant for international law. All that matters is what exists now: what came earlier and was changed in order to have what we have now either disappears, or exists as

---

[5] Kennedy 2000, at 1175.

[6] Kennedy 2006, at 23. The notion of legal consciousness can be traced back to the 1975 manuscript *The Rise and Fall of Classical Legal Thought,* especially Chapter One: 'Legal Consciousness'. The manuscript was reformatted and published as D. Kennedy, *The Rise and Fall of Classical Legal Thought* (2006), which included the version of Chapter One published as D. Kennedy, Toward a historical understanding of legal consciousness: the case of classical legal thought in America 1850–1940, 3 *Research in Law and Sociology*, 1980.

[7] Kennedy 2006, at 45.

[8] For an introduction to the basic distinction in the context of linguistics, see Lyons 1968. For a map of the different possible implication in legal reasoning, see Kennedy 1985, at 248–270.

currently existing norms that are either in conflict, or are exceptions, or somehow complement the other parts of the currently existing legal landscape.

That is, though, not an accurate description. International law often has to make sense of change. When forced to do that, the answers remain mostly *ad hoc,* focused on thinking about the norm as, again, permanent *for now*. The issue of change emerges in some of the most traditional areas of international law. A succinct look at some *paroles* should give us a sense of international law's underlying *langue* for change. Consider, for instance, the problem of treaty revision, particularly multilateral treaties. As is well known, the Vienna Convention on the Law of Treaties (VCLT) establishes subsidiary rules regulating the amendment of a treaty (Articles 39–41).[9] The VCLT reflects international law's standard approach to change: once an amendment is adopted, it has to be approved by all parties to the treaty. However, under Article 40(4) VCLT, the 'amending agreement does not bind any State already a party to the treaty which does not become a party to the amending agreement'. As a consequence, the revised treaty will coexist with the unrevised treaty, and will be applicable only to those parties that approved it. In contrast, the unrevised treaty remains in force among parties that did approve the revision.[10] To be sure, this solution makes sense from the perspective of state sovereignty and the need for state consent. However, it also shows that the VCLT reflects a theory of *non-change*: it considers the new treaty as a norm that had always existed; and the old treaty as well. The issue is thus framed as a problem of treaty conflict,[11] and not as an issue of temporality.

Sometimes, treaties change outside the standard process of revision. Here, again, international law features a theory of non-change. A clear example is the debate on subsequent practice as a tool of treaty interpretation. Under Article 31(3)(b) VCLT, interpretation of a treaty can refer to 'any subsequent practice in the application of the treaty which establishes the agreement of the parties regarding its interpretation'. This clause was used by the International Court of Justice (ICJ) in *Namibia*, to explain that the meaning of the term 'concurring vote' included in Article 27(3) UN Charter had changed. The ICJ understood that abstentions in the context of the UN's Security Council should not be regarded as the absence of a concurring vote. Therefore, the abstention of a veto member amounted, in practice, to a concurrent vote.[12] In the Court's words:

> The proceedings of the Security Council extending over a long period supply abundant evidence that presidential rulings and the positions taken by members of the Council, in particular its permanent members, have consistently and uniformly interpreted the practice of voluntary abstention by a permanent member as not constituting a bar to the adoption of

[9] 1969 Vienna Convention on the Law of Treaties, 1155 UNTS 331 (hereinafter VCLT).

[10] See Yee 2000; Bowman 1995.

[11] Klabbers 2009a.

[12] *Legal Consequences for States of the Continued Presence of South Africa in* Namibia *(South West Africa) notwithstanding Security Council Resolution 276 (1970)*, ICJ, Advisory Opinion, 21 June 1971, at 16.

> resolutions. By abstaining, a member does not signify its objection to the approval of what is being proposed; in order to prevent the adoption of a resolution requiring unanimity of the permanent members, a permanent member has only to cast a negative vote.[13]

To be sure, this interpretation implies an important change of the applicable norm. Beyond the discussion of whether the words are capable of sustaining the Court's interpretation,[14] the relevant point for our purposes here is that, according to the Court's own narrative, this change did not occur at a given moment in time. It was, rather, *incremental*: some state practice would not have sufficed, but the accumulation of state practice (the 'proceedings of the Security Council extending over a long period') triggered this change. However, the Court fails to explain how that changed occurred, or when the scale was tipped. Instead, the ICJ thinks of the new rule ('abstention is not non-concurrence') as if it had existed always. Once again, there is no idea of change here: there is the identification of a norm, without a temporal dimension.

One last illustration can be found in customary international law. One interesting challenge in the construction of custom is the possibility of a subsequent objector; that is, a state that objects the formation of a customary rule *after* the rule has been established. This possibility, however, is closed. While the idea of a persistent objector is accepted on the basis of the required state consent,[15] the possibility of a state opting-out of an established customary rule is generally rejected.[16] For the International Law Association,

> [t]here is fairly widespread agreement that, even if there is a persistent objector rule in international law, it applies only when the customary rule is in the process of emerging. It does not, therefore, benefit States which came into existence only after the rule matured, or which became involved in the activity in question only at a later stage … In other words, there is no 'subsequent objector' rule.[17]

The problem appears when a state decides to opt-out of an established rule (say, Norway opting out of the rule that establishes a 10 nautical miles closing line for bays) and slowly succeeds in gaining the acquiescence of others state—which was the approach actually taken by the ICJ in the *Anglo-Norwegian Fisheries Case*. Two possibilities appear at that point: first, states acquiesce to the sole objector's opt-out of the norm (and hence we have a persistent objector); or, second, the other states join the objector, triggering new practice that points to the emergence of a new customary rule. In the latter case, are we facing a breach, or a new norm? International law has no vocabulary to tackle with that moment in the middle.

---

[13] Ibid., at 22.

[14] For doubting that they do, see Brownlie 2008, at 187.

[15] *Anglo–Norwegian Fisheries Case (United Kingdom v. Norway)*, ICJ, Judgment of 18 December 1951.

[16] Shaw 2008, at 91.

[17] International Law Association, Committee On Formation Of Customary (General) International Law, Statement of principles applicable to the formation of general customary international law, 2000, at 27.

Either it reads it as a breach, hence assuming that the old customary rule is permanent; or it reads it as a new customary norm, that will coexist with the old one, thus triggering a network of legal relations similar to the case of treaty revision discussed earlier. Once again, the point here is not that the new rule is preferable to the old rule,[18] or that the possibility of a 'subsequent objector' is a threat for the international rule of law.[19] The point is rather that the vocabulary of international law fails to recognize the process of incremental change. It takes two discrete moments of the process, and frames each as permanent. If conflicts arise, they are conflicts of norms, and not moments in a continuum.

It is possible to think differently of international law in terms of dynamic change. This article is an effort in that direction. The problem, though, is that the current international legal consciousness seems to build on the idea of the constant present. As can be seen in the above examples, the problem is not that the *langue* of international law lacks a theory of change. Many disciplines are struggling with the same challenge; in international relations, for example, realists believe that the only relevant source of change is the relative capability of states, while liberals and constructivists point to other sources of change, such as knowledge and culture, among others.[20] So, the problem is not an absence of a theory of change. The problem is that international law *does* have a specific theory of change that, like is often the case with the deep grammar of law, remains unspoken. According to this theory, change is the sudden and complete replacement of the old by the new, which in turn implies the complete disappearance of the old. As a result of change, then, all looks as if nothing had ever changed: the norms and institutions that we have now look permanent, and completely unconnected to what came before them. Ultimately, international law's theory of change is one of a constant present.

This narrative has at least three distinct consequences. First, international law accommodates change by acknowledging new normative utterances as permanent. There is, in this sense, an important political dimension to this constant present: if change is the complete replacement of the old by the new, then it becomes relevant to explore who decides on the replacement. That is, there is very little guidance in the norms that are being replaced, or in the ones that replace them, on how or why the process of replacement should occur. International legal change becomes, then, a conceptual problem similar with a structure parallel to the right/exception dichotomy in human rights, which has been discussed widely by critical scholars.[21] Just as there is no inherent normative guidelines to decide when an exception should apply instead of the rule (making the issue *political*, by definition), so does the complete replacement of a norm by a 'posterior' norm implies a political question that needs to be considered.

---

18 Bradley and Gulati 2010.

19 Cogan 2006.

20 Holsti 2004, at 4–14.

21 Koskenniemi 2001, at 84–85; Kennedy 2002, at 118–119. The key insight is, of course, Schmittian: 'Sovereign is he who decides on the exception.' Schmitt 2005, at 5.

Second, the narrative of constant present makes it difficult to normatively engage with change in international law. In a constant present, it is hard to question the pathways that brought the current *status quo*, and ask: what were the forces that triggered these changes? Is it normatively desirable that, for example, power or economic pressure trigger the changes that create the current international system? What kind of standards can we use to judge whether a change is good or bad, fair or unfair? These kinds of questions are occluded by international law's theory of change, which forces us to remain on a descriptive mode. To be clear, the constant present does not imply that the langue of international law builds on the notion of pre-existing norms or institutions. Rather, it posits that norms are discrete utterances that occur in a given moment in time (a basic positivist tenet) and, *at the same time,* it treats such utterances as outside time once (unless otherwise explicitly provided). They become part of the constant present, until they disappear. Such is the paradox that occludes the questions posed above.

The third effect of this constant present is that it obscures the complex colonial heritage of international law. A now robust body of scholarship has shown that international law that we have today is part of the complex institutional and ideological offspring of the colonial encounter.[22] Thinking in terms of a constant present obscures the relevance of this heritage, and neutralises the critical power of shedding lights on such lineage.

2.3 Change and Temporariness

As a result of this theory of (non-)change, it is quite difficult to grasp the dynamics of temporariness in international law. In an awkward turn, what is temporal is also part of the constant present. Provisional norms and institutions are, by definition, temporal, but they exist *today* as if they were permanent. It is as if we were taking photos of a column of smoke, one each hour, for three hours. When we look at the photos, the smoke exists in each photo as permanent—even though it is, by definition, temporal.

Thinking about temporariness requires, then, to think differently about change in international law. To do that, a useful starting point is to underscore that, in the long term, everything (a norm, an institution, a building or a state) is *always* provisional. Nothing is truly permanent—all decays and ultimately disappears. This is, of course, obvious. However, when we think of temporality in international law, we are not thinking in those terms. The point of reference is not *time* as such: short term or long term thinking is, in this context, irrelevant. Rather, the notion of permanence in international law seems to be relational: international norms and institutions are 'permanent' or 'provisional' in comparison to *other* international norms and institutions.

---

[22] See Koskenniemi 2012a and Anghie 2005.

This relational quality means that temporariness in international law is neither objective, nor completely subjective. On the one hand, it does not refer to an objective standard that differentiates permanent from provisional. While international instruments do refer constantly to an institution being 'permanent' or 'provisional', these statements seem to provide very little insight as to the temporal dynamics of international law. For example, one would be mistaken to write off the Provisional Protocol for the Application of the General Agreement on Trade and Tariffs (GATT) as 'provisional', thus failing to recognize the temporal implications of it giving legal stability to almost fifty years of trade negotiations.[23] However, temporariness is not just in eye of the beholder; it is not wholly based on perception. While it does seem reasonable for individuals to think of temporariness as perception-based ('The Beatles have been here forever'—'no, they have not'), this subjective character is less straightforward in the case of international law. It would make little sense to think, for instance, of the International Criminal Tribunal for the Former Yugoslavia (ICTY) as 'permanent' in the same sense as the International Criminal Court (ICC) is 'permanent'. Even if the ICTY can be perceived by one person as 'permanent' (it is surely perceived as 'permanent' by Milomir Stakić, who was sentenced to forty years in prison),[24] it is still 'provisional' from the perspective of the vocabulary of international law. From this latter perspective, comparison (and not perception, nor 'facts') is the key to think about temporariness. We will refer to this idea as the *comparative* concept of temporariness.

The comparative concept of temporariness means that norms and institutions are provisional relative to other norms and institutions. In this context, it starts making sense to speak of the ICJ's provisional measures as 'temporary', because they are so in comparison to, say, the decision on merits. If we take this line of reasoning one step further, we find that all institutions are provisional. Indeed, if it is true that temporariness is relative, then it becomes a relevant question to ask whether there are any truly permanent norms or institutions. The comparative concept of temporariness suggests there are none: there will always be other institutions or norms that can be read as more permanent, thus making all institutions provisional. This, I suggest, is not only a way of giving content to the concept of temporariness in international law, but also the point of entry for an alternative theory of change.

---

[23] See Hansen and Vermulst 1988. The GATT 1947 was temporal, but somehow stable, as it provided the framework for the reduction of tariffs across the board for five decades. Temporariness in international law is neither objective, nor completely subjective, but rather is relational. As will be discussed later on, the point is not that all of international law is temporary, but rather that some norms and institutions are more temporary than others—hence, the *comparative* concept of temporariness proposed here.

[24] See *Prosector v. Stakic (Prijedor)*, Appeals Chamber, Judgment, Case No. IT-97-24, 22 March 2006, at 141.

2.3.1 Change and Temporariness in a Global Regulatory Space

A central advantage of the comparative concept of temporariness is that it makes us think of international norms and institutions in reference to *other* norms and institutions. This is particularly valuable, because it leads us to think of norms, not as discrete utterances, but rather as part of a wider landscape in which the temporal and the permanent help define each other. What is the shape of this wider landscape? After more than a decade of debates about fragmentation[25] and regime-collision in international law,[26] it seems clear that the structure of the international legal system is one of overlapping normativity. Scholarship that recognises such proliferation seem focused, though, on considering them as discrete actors that compete, cooperate or dominate each other—a dynamic that has been observed in international relations,[27] transnational business governance,[28] environmental governance,[29] and domestic regulation.[30] Even critical work that underscores the importance of hegemony still depicts each regime as a self-standing unit eager to dominate other self-standing regimes.[31]

However, these norms and institutions do not appear in a vacuum; they are not discrete utterances of law. Quite on the contrary, they are expressions, and form part, of a changing global regulatory space, in which they interact. This approach, I suggest, provides the basis for a different conceptualisation of change in international law, which will in turn help us think differently about temporariness in international law.

Perhaps the best way to think about it is by clarifying the image of a global regulatory space. The notion of a 'regulatory space' was suggested as a reaction to the narrow reading of the (domestic) regulatory process in terms of a conflict between public authority and private interests.[32] Against this view, the regulatory process within the nation state can be better understood as a 'space', where it becomes possible to explore the 'complex and shifting relationships between and within organizations at the heart of economic regulation.'[33] The key is 'to understand the nature of this shared space: the rules of admission, the relations between occupants, and the variations introduced by differences in markets and issue arenas.'[34]

---

[25] Koskenniemi and Leino 2002.

[26] Teubner and Fischer-Lescano 2004.

[27] Abbott et al. 2013.

[28] Eberlein et al. 2014.

[29] Oberthür and Gehring 2011.

[30] Uruena 2012a.

[31] Koskenniemi 2012b.

[32] Hancher and Moran 1989.

[33] Ibid.

[34] Ibid.

These dynamics can be observed in global governance. Global interactions can be seen as part of an emergent 'global administrative space', which has been defined as 'a space, distinct from the space of inter-state relations governed by international law and the domestic regulatory space governed by domestic administrative law, although encompassing elements of each.'[35]

This image of a 'regulatory space' aptly captures some of the dynamic interactions between international norms and institutions that characterise global governance. Most important for our purposes, it is also useful to think differently about change in international law. As was discussed earlier, international law fails to register the process of incremental change. Instead, it focuses on discrete events occurring in particular moments of time, and frames each of them as permanent. Incremental change, then, is the notion that the *langue* of international law is unable to express. I suggest that the idea of a 'regulatory space' helps to think about the process of incremental change. To do so, we must engage in a thought experiment. Let us imagine for a minute that norms and institutions exist in the global regulatory space, much like planets and other great masses exist in the actual physical space. To be sure, we can think of each planet independently; we often do, and such is our usual practice. However, many of the realities that affect our daily life are not just the mere product of our independent planet, but are rather a function of *other* planets and masses in space. For instance, think of seasons, or sea tides: Earth spins in one way and not another, at a certain angle and not the other, not only because events that happen on Earth, but rather due to the relative equilibrium of gravitational forces around it, which include, of course, its own mass and gravitational force.

This is just an image. My argument is not that the global regulatory space is an actual space with actual forces.[36] It is useful, though, to illustrate the kind of dynamics triggered by institutional interaction in the global regulatory space, and its impact in our idea of change. International norms and institutions seem to have a 'mass' that exerts a certain pull towards them. This 'pull' has been observed before. A similar 'pull', exerted by international norms, has been famously discussed by Thomas Frank, in his theory of legitimacy. In his groundbreaking study, Franck understood legitimacy as

> a property of a rule or rule-making institution which itself exerts a pull towards compliance on those addressed normatively, because those addressed believe that the rule or institution has come into being and operates in accordance with generally accepted principles of right process.[37]

---

[35] Kingsbury et al. 2005.

[36] But see Hornstein 2005. The image of the international legal architecture as a 'universe' with 'planets' has been explored earlier in Simma and Pulkowski 2006. Their argument, though, is an intervention in the fragmentation debate, and proposes a narrative of multiple self-contained regimes that exist at the same moment of time, and clash against each other. This narrative is part of the 'constant present' consciousness in international law, which this article critically engages with.

[37] Franck 1990, at 25.

This pull is only marginally related to our discussion: Franck's agenda with legitimacy is to walk the road between positivism and naturalism that is able to explain the puzzle of compliance with international legal norms. However, it is useful to think in terms of degree in international law, and not of mere binaries. To do that, Franck engages with Anthony D'Amato and denounces the stark division between law and non-law in the international legal order. Instead of focusing on the enforcement issue (the so-called 'Austinian challenge'), Franck proposes that the key issue is whether the subjects of a given rule believe themselves obliged, despite their countervailing self-interest, to act in accordance with the law. This is where legitimacy enters the scene: the problem is not law/non-law, Franck would say, it is the independent pull to compliance that matters.[38] Compliance pull is a matter of degree; that is, while a rule simply is or is not binding, it may be more or less legitimate.[39]

My goal here is not to discuss the question of legitimacy and Franck's almost psychological explanation for it. His 'pull', though, is useful here to see the kind of dynamics that my own explanation seeks to describe. We can think of the pull that international norms and institutions exert over each other in similar terms, without going into the discussion of legitimacy. Each norm and institution draws toward it whatever is around: it exerts a sort of 'gravitational pull' that attracts other norms and institutions. The situation of norms and institutions in the global regulatory space is, therefore, the result of a relative equilibrium of all the 'gravitational pulls', as exerted by each and all norms or institutions.

One example of this process is the World Trade Organization. It is a well-established institution and carries considerable weight in the global regulatory space. Other regimes and institutions tend to gravitate towards it. Thus, environmental norms have been pulled towards it: a well-known example is the precautionary principle, which the WTO has failed to apply (and then applied) on several occasions.[40] This issue has been framed as a problem of fragmentation, and is also part of the wider 'trade and environment' debate, which is now part of the mainstream of international legal scholarship.[41] However, these readings seem to imply that the WTO has remained static, 'colliding' with environmental values, whereas in fact the WTO has changed its approach to the precautionary principle: while the Appellate Body in *EC—Hormones* expressly rejected the status of precautionary principle as a binding customary international rule,[42] it incrementally changed its position.[43] While its weight has attracted the issue towards its dispute resolution mechanism, the WTO has also changed as it interacted with the precautionary principle.

---

[38] Ibid., at 47.

[39] Ibid., at 49.

[40] Cheyne 2007. See generally Sustein 2005.

[41] For a summary of the debate, see Howse 2002.

[42] *European Communities—Measures Concerning Meat and Meat Products*, Appellate Body Report, WT/DS26/AB/R, WT/DS48/AB/R, 16 January 1998, adopted by DSB 13 February 1998 (hereinafter *EC—Hormones*).

[43] For the patterns of incremental change since *EC—Hormones*, see Wirth 2013.

Not only formal inter-governmental organizations such as the WTO exert a 'gravitational pull'. Also less structured regimes of governance, such as international investment law, exert their own pull. International investment law regime has grown to be a crucial part of the framework of global governance. A tightly-knit net of almost 5500 international investment agreements (IIA) covers the planet.[44] An important aspect of the current IIA wave is its decentralised nature. Unlike the WTO, investment deals are commonly stricken on a bilateral basis: there is no single decision-making centre to follow. However, the sheer amount of international investment agreements,[45] on the one hand, and the impacts (both financial and reputational) that an arbitration award may have on a host state,[46] on the other, make adjudication by investment tribunals a matter of importance of domestic constituencies.

The investment regime features a specialized set of norms, a distinct institutional architecture (including courts), a distinct epistemic community and a particular rationale. It can, therefore, be read as independent enough as to exert a pull on its own right. As a result, many other norms and institutions have been attracted to the investment regime. Most evidently, this attraction has been felt by human rights and environmental standards, but also by international law of armed conflict,[47] among others. These regimes have been influenced by the very existence of the international investment regime: in their interaction with the latter, human rights, environmental law and the law of armed conflict have been transformed. Once again, the point here is not fragmentation, but rather that the investment regime carries a weight in the regulatory space, and that such a weight pulls other norms and institutions towards it. The investment regime, in turn, is not let unaffected by this dynamics: its approach to human rights rules, for example, may change over time as the interaction continues,[48] particularly under the ever-changing form of the fair and equitable standard.[49]

Thinking about the architecture of international law in these terms allows us to think about interaction when collusions occur, and also when collusions are not occurring. Most of legal scholarship that factors in the challenges of the multiplicity of legal orders in international law seems to be biased towards focusing on events of conflict; that is, when two international norms provide conflicting solutions to similar cases, or when two institutions collide when exercising their powers.[50] It assumes that the principle is non-interaction, and the exception is interaction, which triggers collision and incoherence. This bias is understandable, as instances of collision are clearer, and seem more politically important. Against

44 UNCTAD, Developments in international investment agreements in 2005, 2006, at 1.

45 See Elkins et al. 2008.

46 Khamsi and Alvarez 2009.

47 Hernández 2013.

48 Dupuy 2009.

49 Kingsbury and Schill 2009.

50 See, for example, Pauwelyn 2003.

this view, I suggest that the opposite is true: international norms and institutions are *all the time* in interaction with each other. While collisions do exist, they tell us little of the day-to-day workings of international law. In contrast, thinking in terms of a global regulatory space allows us to consider the interactions that result, not in conflict, but rather in the practice of international law.

2.3.2 Thinking About Change in the Constant Present

The idea of a global regulatory space where international norms and institutions exercise different gravitational forces is useful to conceptualise change and temporariness in international law differently. To do so, one might start by considering the relative 'weights' of the different norms and institutions that interact, which in turn will determine their own pull, and ability to resist the pull of other norms or institutions. This starting point is crucial, considering that the dynamics of the global regulatory space is not governed by a notion of sovereign equality. Quite on the contrary, the last couple of decades have seen the emergence of global regulation without the medium of treaties, treaty-based institutions, international customary law, or, more fundamentally, the traditional expression of state consent. Regulatory networks (such as the Basel Committee on Banking Supervision),[51] public-private entities (such as the International Organization for Standardization (ISO)),[52] and purely private entities (such as the Fédération Internationale de Football Association (FIFA))[53] or privatised public utilities at the transnational level,[54] among many others, have become crucial players in determining the distribution of global regulatory power today. Domestic agencies, such as the US Environment Protection Agency, also emerged as influential actors in regulating issues which are of global concern. These networks, entities and agencies reveal a transformed global regulatory landscape that features, for instance, private actors exercising public powers, informal norms that carry the weight equivalent to that of formally binding instruments, and decentralised networks of regulation. However, their weight is not equal: some have more 'mass' than others, and therefore exert more pull than others.

Relative differences in weight, and the dynamics of the 'gravitational pull', imply that the possibility of permanence in international law stops making sense. The global regulatory space is dynamic: each and all norms and institutions are exerting their pull over the others. Each norm and institution is always 'moving' towards others, or is remaining still because it is resisting the pull of others. The point is that the principle of the global regulatory space is movement and change; there is nothing static, only constant movement.

---

[51] Slaughter and Zaring 2006.

[52] See Klabbers 2005.

[53] See Casini 2010.

[54] See Morgan 2011.

The idea of permanence becomes, in that context, difficult to maintain. Even the most permanent of institutions (say, the United Nations) is exerting its pull; thus moving, or resisting moving, in dynamic terms. Note, however, that the impossibility of permanence is not related to the idea of the long-term as a time horizon. The argument is not that nothing is permanent because in the long term all will be gone: such was the starting point for our exploration. The argument made here is that institutions that *right now* seem permanent are actually moving, and thus cannot be thought of as permanent in any significant sense. The opposite, however, is not true. Thinking in these terms does not make the 'temporal' become 'permanent'. The reasoning here is focused on the impossibility of permanence—which is triggered by the constant movement of all the objects in the global regulatory space.

2.4 Normative Challenges

Thinking about change in these terms does not imply a radical transformation of the *langue* of international law. This view of change is not a rebuttal of the 'constant present' view discussed earlier. The deep grammar of international law will still consider norms and institutions as discrete events. However, this view of change helps to unpack each of these discrete norms, and looks for the dynamic in what is presented as static. By doing so, it allows us to destabilize the sense that what seems permanent right now is a necessity. In contrast, it suggests that the 'permanent' is only one particular point of incremental change. The advantage, then, is that thinking of change in terms of the global regulatory space forces us to consider the *process* of constant change.

This view poses an important normative challenge, because it risks perpetuating the *status quo*. When thinking about the pull that one norm or institution exerts over others, one is simply describing such movement. However, this view provides no vocabulary to perform a critique of the reasons behind such a powerful pull, or a normative standard to discuss whether the fact that one institution or norm carries so much weight is appropriate or not. In this sense, the description that is proposed here could be subject to critique in terms of ideology, understood as 'the ways in which meaning serves to establish and sustain relations of domination.'[55] Thus understood, ideology is part of the legal consciousness of a given time or, more precisely, the legal consciousness of a given time uses ideology to perpetuate the *status quo* it represents. In our case, the idea of incremental change could sustain an unequal distribution of power by occluding the normative dimensions of the 'gravitational pull'. Specifically, there are at least two normative challenges in thinking in terms of incremental change in the global regulatory space: (a) tunnel vision; and, (b) regulatory capture.

[55] John Thomson, *Ideology and modern culture*, Polity, Cambridge, 1990, at 56, quoted in Marks 2001, at 110.

First, the suggested view of change seems to lack an overarching narrative of the public good in the global regulatory space. Perhaps the main challenge is the issue of 'tunnel vision'.[56] Each institution and norm acting in the global regulatory space has a particular mandate, or exists in order to regulate a certain area of global politics or production; that is, they are only concerned with that specific issue, and not necessarily with wider societal concerns. The climate change regime will be concerned with climate change and not with, say, the rights of women. And human rights regime institutions will be focused on that specific issue, and not on economic development, or the environment. Each of these institutions may talk in terms of 'common good'; however, when these norms and institutions 'pull' towards them, they pull towards their own structural bias[57]—leaving the common good to be sorted out by the competition among norms and institutions in the global regulatory space. Talking in terms of a 'gravitational force' creates the risk of losing sight of an overarching narrative of a 'good' society.

Moreover, international norms and institutions are not static objects to be found in nature. Instead, they are put together in order to achieve a goal that is not given by the norm or institutions in itself, but rather by external political forces that see international law as one more of their tools to achieve their needs.[58] An international norm or institution will most likely play the part intended for it by the powerful. What is more, institutions themselves may have hegemonic ambitions, in the sense that they seek to expand their world-view, placing their goal as more important (or universal) in detriment of the goals of others. Thinking about change in these terms could obscure important differences of power and, in fact, could perpetuate as neutral the structure of the global regulatory space, which is a specific creation of those in power. This move, in turn, could end up empowering the narrowly defined experts that decide what the objective of the norm or institutions is. Because the mindset of regimes is wholly instrumental, a certain transnational elite that acts outside democratic or legal checks of accountability could end up being empowered by global specialized regimes.[59] Thus, the idea of neutral 'gravitational forces' could play into this expert-power base, legitimizing as 'change' what is only the result of the (functional) agenda of domination.

A second important normative challenge is regulatory capture. Framing the dynamics of change in terms of 'gravitational pulls' in the global regulatory space opens spots for private parties to engage actively with the decision-making process in the regulatory space. Private parties will use the different patterns of influence and change among institutions as a tool to achieve their goal. This, in turn, could have normatively desirable results, or could further empower global actors that are already mighty, as they hold the expertise to read the patterns of influence and 'gravitational pulls' described in this contribution.

---

56 Teubner and Korth 2012, at 37.

57 Koskenniemi 2005, at 600.

58 See, generally, Koskenniemi 2007; Uruena 2012b, at 74–77.

59 See Kennedy 2005.

An example of a desirable outcome is the engagement of activists with the human rights regulatory space. As has been explored by Kathryn Sikkink, transnational networks of activists have played a fundamental role in the transformation of human rights governance in Latin America.[60] During the era of massive human rights violations and authoritarian regimes, Sikkink explains, local activists learned to use a 'boomerang effect' where non-state actors, faced with repression at home, would seek help in international courts and organizations, in order to bring pressure to their respective government from above. The goal of activism in this context was to bypass the failed domestic judiciary, and get a hierarchically superior order by the IACtHR against a state.[61] In this way, global human rights activists achieve their desired political output, and they also transform the structure of the regulatory space applicable to human rights, bringing new layers of complexity and opportunity.

In contrast, thinking in terms of change and the 'gravitational pull' could end up opening spaces for powerful private actors to take over the regulatory process. An example is dairy regulation. Dairy regulation is an exercise of global governance, characterized by interaction between several institution, and bodies of norms: the WTO, the Organization for Economic Cooperation and Development (OECD), the World Health Organization (WHO), the International Organization for Standardization (ISO), the World Organization for Animal Health (OIE), among many others. Each of these institutions carries a particular weight, exerting a particular pull over the others. The International Dairy Federation (IDF), in turn, is a private industrial organization that represents the dairy sector worldwide, by providing a source of scientific expertise in support of the development of quality milk and dairy products.[62] IDF is well known for its scientific expertise, and often provides background information and scientific support to different international organizations.

In the universe of possibilities, the IDF engages with several institutions in different ways. However, the key issue in regulation is food standards. Thus, when the IDF entered the space of global dairy regulation, it was attracted by the Codex Alimentarius Commission, which is the institution that carries more weight in that area of regulation.[63] The attraction grew to be quite close, and the IDF ended

60 Sikkink and Booth Walling 2007; Sikkink 2002; Sikkink 2005.

61 Sikkink and Risse 1999; Sikkink and Keck 1998.

62 See www.fil-idf.org. Accessed 5 July 2014.

63 Part of the Codex's 'weight' derives, in turn, from its close contact with the World Trade Organizations. Article 3 of the WTO's SPS Agreement provides, in essence, that domestic food regulations that conform to international standards are presumed to be in compliance with that Agreement and GATT; in contrast, WTO members that depart from international standards must provide scientific justification to do so. Section 3(a) of Annex A of the SPS Agreement, in turn, defines international standards for food safety as those created by Codex Alimentarius, among others. Therefore, member states of the WTO that comply with the (voluntary) standards of the Codex are presumed to comply with the (mandatory) dispositions of the SPS Agreement and the GATT. In practice, such reference to the Codex, as included in the SPS Agreement, implies that States have an important incentive to follow the Codex: although remaining formally voluntary, adopting the Codex does substantially reduce the risk of WTO litigation. Livermore 2006.

embedded into the Codex itself. The purpose of the Codex is to protect consumers and facilitate fair practices in the trade of food through the definition of detailed product specifications and minimum requirements.[64] The governing body of the Codex is the Codex Alimentarius Commission, which features an Executive Committee, seven Commodity Committees, and nine General Subject Committees. The point of entry for the IDF to the regulatory space was the Codex Committee on Milk and Milk Products, hosted by New Zealand. The IDF became the only private organization formally recognized in the Codex Procedural Manual as being responsible for providing first drafts of Codex standards for a group of food commodities; similarly, it also contributes expert input throughout the development of new standards until their final adoption and monitors all the other Codex Committees that influence the dairy sector. The IDF thus became an integral part of the global space of dairy regulation.

Neither of these examples shows a particularly exceptional dynamics: the IDF is an industrial organization seeking to influence regulatory standards applicable to its sector. In turn, human rights activists are trying to achieve their own goal. But consider these examples from the perspective of the architecture of regulation applicable to dairy, or to human rights. From that perspective, we see a group of different institutions that have overlapping power over a particular issue, or a particular set of products. Private parties then enter the regulatory space—first as target to the regulation, but then become part of the regulatory process. This dynamic is not only a matter for lobbyists, but also transforms the architecture of the regulatory process that is being influenced. They are trying to influence such institutions but, by doing so, they lend more weight to some institution over the others. At the end, the weight of each institution or set of norms (the Codex Commission, or the Inter-American System of Human Rights) is changed, boosted by the 'gravitational pull' of private institutions such as of the IDF or human rights NGOs.

All of these are important challenges. A way to address them is to think of an overarching normative criterion to assess the patterns of certain 'gravitational' pulls. This approach would use the advantages of thinking in dynamic terms about change in international law, and at the same time steer clear of a reading that simply perpetuates the *status quo*. One example of such normative criteria could come from Thomas Franck's work, for whom the normative pull that characterises legitimacy in the community of states features four indicators: (a) determinacy, meaning the literary (text-based) quality of a rule that 'makes its message clear';[65] (b) symbolic validation, that occurs when 'a signal is used as cue to elicit compliance with a command';[66] (c) coherence, meaning the attribution whereby 'distinctions in the treatment of "likes" be justifiable in principled terms';[67] and, finally, (d) adherence, referring to the 'quality of being validated by an infrastructure of

[64] FAO/WHO, Codex Alimentarius Commission procedural manual, 2004.

[65] Franck 1990, at 52.

[66] Ibid., at 92.

[67] Ibid., at 144.

rules about rules.'[68] Or we could consider Benedict Kingsbury's attempt to fill a parallel void, by arguing that not all practices of global governance can be interpreted as 'law'.[69] Instead, only those practices that fulfill the requirement of 'publicness' can be considered law, and thus entitled to the benefits of using such language (publicness, for his purpose, is 'the claim made for law that it has been wrought by the whole society, by the public, and the connected claim that law addresses matters of concern to the society as such').[70] Finally, one last strategy could be along the lines of global constitutionalism; that is, evaluating interaction among institutions and their 'gravitational pull' through the prism of certain core legal standards, just as a national constitution limits the exercise of authority in a domestic setting.[71]

Many other options are available. It seems important, though, to underscore that this contribution's suggestion of reading change in dynamic terms requires a normative standard that complements this enhanced description of the mechanics of global governance. Such standard, in turn, is also part of the global regulatory space, and carries weight as well, thus attracting other norms and institutions towards it. Note, however, that this normative standard needs not to be the source of validity of the other norms or institutions in the global regulatory space—it is not a *Grundnorm*. It just needs to carry enough weight, and thus enough 'gravitational pull'. The greater the weight it carries, the more successful it will be in serving as true normative standards in global governance.

2.5 Conclusion

The notion of temporariness is central in international law. However, its deep grammar assumes that international law-making creates discrete institutions that remain static until they are changed (or replaced) by other discrete institutions. As was discussed, change is the complete replacement of the old by the new. As a result of change, then, all looks as if nothing had ever changed: the norms and institutions that we have now look permanent, and completely unconnected to what came before them. International law's theory of change is one of a constant present.

This chapter proposes a different approach, focusing on the dynamics of change in the global regulatory space. This approach has certain advantages, as it helps us communicate the constant movement of 'permanent' norms and institutions, providing a vocabulary to describe the incremental change that remains hidden in the standard view of change in international law. The challenge, though, is that this new vocabulary may be lacking in critical potential—it may end up working as an

---

[68] Ibid., at 184.

[69] Kingsbury 2009.

[70] Ibid., at 31.

[71] For a description of the trends, see, generally, Klabbers 2009b.

ideological device that justifies the reality it describes. This, I think, is no reason to reject it. It is not the case that the phenomena it describes will stop occurring because we have no conceptual way of grasping it. However, this challenge does point to the need to think of ways to enhance the incipient vocabulary of change in global governance. But we need to build that vocabulary in the first place. This chapter is an effort to that effect.

References

Abbott KW, Snidal D (1998) Why states act through formal international organizations. J Confl Resolut 42:3–32

Abbott KW, Green JF, Keohane RO (2013) Organizational ecology and organizational strategies in world politics. Harvard Kennedy School of Government Discussion Paper 13–57

Anghie A (2005) Imperialism, sovereignty and the making of international law. Cambridge University Press, Cambridge

Bowman MJ (1995) The multilateral treaty amendment process—a case study. Int Compar Law Q 44:540–559

Bradley C, Gulati M (2010) Withdrawing from international custom. Yale Law J 120:202–275

Brownlie I (2008) Principles of public international law, 7th edn. Oxford University Press, Oxford

Casini L (2010) Il diritto globale dello sport. Giuffrè Editore, Milano

Cheyne I (2007) Gateways to the precautionary principle in WTO law. J Environ Law 19:155–172

Cogan JK (2006) Noncompliance and the international rule of law. Yale J Int Law 31:189–210

Dupuy P-M (2009) Unification rather than fragmentation of international law? The case of international investment law and human rights law. In: Dupuy P-M, Francioni F, Petersmann E-U (eds) Human rights in international investment law and arbitration. Oxford University Press, Oxford, pp 45–62

Eberlein B, Abbott KW, Black J, Meidinger E, Wood S (2014) Transnational business governance interactions: conceptualization and framework for analysis. Regul Gov 8:1–21

Elkins Z, Guzman AT, Simmons B (2008) Competing for capital: the diffusion of bilateral investment treaties, 1960-2000. Univ Ill Law Rev 2008:265–304

Franck TM (1990) The power of legitimacy among nations. Oxford University Press, New York

Hancher L, Moran M (1989) Organizing regulatory space. In: Hancher L, Moran M (eds) Capitalism, culture, and economic regulation. Clarendon Press, Oxford, pp 271–299

Hansen M, Vermulst E (1988) The GATT protocol of provisional application: a dying grandfather. Columbia J Transnatl Law 27:263–308

Hernández GI (2013) The interaction between investment law and the law of armed conflict in the interpretation of full protection and security clauses. In: Baetens F (ed) Investment law within international law: integrationist perspectives. Cambridge University Press, Cambridge, pp 21–50

Holsti KJ (2004) Taming the sovereigns: institutional change in international politics. Cambridge University Press, Cambridge

Hornstein DT (2005) Complexity theory, adaptation, and administrative law. Duke Law J 54:913–960

Howse R (2002) Appellate Body rulings in the *Shrimp/Turtle* case: a new legal baseline for the trade and environment debate. Columbia J Environ Law 27:491–521

International Law Association—Committee On Formation Of Customary (General) International Law (2000) Statement of principles applicable to the formation of general customary international law. International Law Association, London

Kennedy D (1980) Toward an historical understanding of legal consciousness: the case of classical legal thought in America, 1850–1940. Res Law Sociol 3:3–24

Kennedy D (1985) Critical theory, structuralism and contemporary legal scholarship. New England Law Review 21:209–290

Kennedy D (2000) A semiotics of critique'. Cardozo Law Rev 22:1147–1189

Kennedy D (2002) The international human rights movement: part of the problem? Harv Hum Rights J 15:101–125

Kennedy D (2005) Challenging expert rule: the politics of global governance. Syd Law Rev 27:5–28

Kennedy D (2006) Three globalizations of law and legal thought. In: Trubek DM, Santos A (eds) The new law and economic development: a critical appraisal. Cambridge University Press, Cambridge, pp 19–73

Khamsi K, Alvarez J (2009) The Argentine crisis and foreign investors: a glimpse into the heart of the investment regime. Yearb Int Invest Law & Policy 2008–2009:379–478

Kingsbury B (2009) The concept of 'law' in global administrative law. Eur J Int Law 20:23–57

Kingsbury B, Schill S (2009) Investor-state arbitration as governance: fair and equitable treatment, proportionality and the emerging global administrative law. New York University Public Law and Legal Theory Working Papers. http://lsr.nellco.org/nyu_plltwp/146. Accessed 3 Aug 2014

Kingsbury B, Stewart RB, Krisch N (2005) The emergence of global administrative law. Law and Contemp Probl 68:15–61

Klabbers J (2005) Reflections on soft international law in a privatized world. Finnish Yearb Int Law 16:313–328

Klabbers J (2009a) Treaty conflict and the European Union. Cambridge University Press, Cambridge

Klabbers J (2009b) Setting the scene. In: Ulfstein G, Peters A, Klabbers J (eds) The constitutionalization of international law. Oxford University Press, Oxford, pp 1–44

Koskenniemi M (2001) Human rights, politics and love. Mennesker & Rettigheder 4:33–45

Koskenniemi M (2005) From apology to utopia: the structure of international legal argument, 2nd edn. Cambridge University Press, Cambridge

Koskenniemi M (2007) The fate of public international law: between technique and politics. Modern Law Rev 70:1–30

Koskenniemi M (2012a) A history of international law histories. In: Fassbender B, Peters A, Peter S, Högger D (eds) The Oxford handbook of the history of international law. Oxford University Press, Oxford, pp 943–971

Koskenniemi M (2012b) Hegemonic regimes. In: Young M (ed) Regime interaction in international law: facing fragmentation, Cambridge: Cambridge University Press, Cambridge, pp 305–323

Koskenniemi M, Leino P (2002) Fragmentation of international law? Postmodern anxieties. Leiden J Int Law 15:553–579

Livermore MA (2006) Authority and legitimacy in global governance: deliberation, institutional differentiation, and the Codex Alimentarius. N Y Univ Law Rev 81:766–801

Lyons J (1968) Introduction to theoretical linguistics. Cambridge University Press, London

Marks S (2001) Big brother is bleeping us—with the message that ideology doesn't matter. Eur J Int Law 12:109–123

Morgan B (2011) Water on tap: rights and regulation in the transnational governance of urban water services. Cambridge University Press, Cambridge

Oberthür S, Gehring T (2011) Institutional interaction: ten years of scholarly development. In: Oberthür S, Schram Stokke O (eds), Managing institutional complexity: regime interplay and global environmental change, MIT Press, Cambridge, Massachusetts, pp 25–58

Pauwelyn J (2003) Conflict of norms in public international law: how WTO law relates to other rules of international law. Cambridge University Press, Cambridge

Rosenne S (2005) Provisional measures in international law: the International Court of Justice and the International Tribunal for the Law of the Sea. Oxford University Press, Oxford

Schmitt C (2005) Political theory: four chapters on the concept of sovereignty. University of Chicago Press, Chicago
Shaw MN (2008) International law, 6th edn. Cambridge University Press, Cambridge
Sikkink K (2002) Human rights advocacy networks and the social construction of legal rules. In: Dezalay Y, Garth B (eds) Global prescriptions: the production, exportation and importation of a new legal orthodoxy. University of Michigan Press, Ann Arbor, pp 37–64
Sikkink K (2005) The transnational dimension of the judicialization of politics in Latin America. In: Sieder R, Schjolden L, Angell A (eds) The judicialization of politics in Latin America. Palgrave Macmillan, New York, pp 263–292
Sikkink K, Booth Walling C (2007) The justice cascade and the impact of human rights trials in Latin America. J Peace Res 44:427–445
Sikkink K, Keck M (1998) Activists beyond borders. Cornell University Press, Ithaca, New York
Sikkink K, Risse T (1999) The socialization of international human rights norms into domestic practices. In: Risse T, Sikkink K, Ropp S (eds) The power of human rights: international norms and domestic politics. Cambridge University Press, Cambridge, pp 1–38
Simma B, Pulkowski D (2006) Of planets and the universe: self-contained regimes in international law. Eur J Int Law 17:483–529
Slaughter A-M, Zaring D (2006) Networking goes international: an update. Ann Rev Law Soc Sci 2:211–229
Sunstein CR (2005) Laws of fear: beyond the precautionary principle. Cambridge University Press, Cambridge
Teubner G, Fischer-Lescano A (2004) Regime-collisions: the vain search for legal unity in the fragmentation of global law. Michigan J Int Law 25:999–1046
Teubner G, Korth P (2012) Two kinds of legal pluralism: collision of transnational regimes in the double fragmentation of the world society. In: Young M (ed) Regime interaction in international law: facing fragmentation. Cambridge University Press, Cambridge, pp 23–54
Toope SJ, Brunnée J (2010) Legitimacy and legality in international law: an interactional account. Cambridge University Press, Cambridge
Uruena R (2012a) The rise of the constitutional regulatory state in Colombia: the case of water governance. Regul Gov 6:282–299
Uruena R (2012b) No citizens here: global subjects and participation in international law. Martinus Nijhoff Publishers, Leiden
Wirth D (2013) The World Trade Organization dispute over genetically modified organisms: the precautionary principle meets international trade law. Vermont Law Rev 37:1153–1188
Yee S (2000) The time limit for the ratification of proposed amendments to the constitutions of international organizations. Max Planck Yearb UN Law 4:185–213

Chapter 3
Temporary International Legal Regimes as Frames for Permanent Ones

Jean Galbraith

Abstract This chapter explores the footprint that temporary international legal regimes can leave on international law. Drawing on four different theories of state behaviour, it considers how temporary regimes can shape future permanent regimes. Under a rational design approach, temporary legal regimes influence future permanent regimes largely because they provide valuable experiences from which state actors learn. Under other theories of behaviour—historical institutionalism, constructivism, and behavioural international law—temporary legal regimes can have even more influence on permanent ones. Although these other three theories have important differences, all suggest that temporary regimes strongly shape the real and perceived possibilities for future permanent design choices. This chapter then looks at how these different theoretical approaches play out in case studies in refugee law, international criminal law, and international environmental law. While these case studies do not solely support any one theoretical account, collectively they demonstrate that temporary regimes can have outsized influence on permanent ones. This in turn has important implications for negotiators involved in regime design.

Keywords Temporary international legal regimes · Rational design · Historical institutionalism · Constructivism · Behavioural international law

I am grateful for comments received from Roger Clark, Cary Coglianese, Jen Daskal, participants at the Junior International Law Scholars Association workshop at New York Law School, two anonymous reviewers, and the Editorial Board of the *Netherlands Yearbook of International Law*.

J. Galbraith (✉)
University of Pennsylvania Law School, Philadelphia, PA, USA
e-mail: jgalbraith@law.upenn.edu

M. Ambrus and R.A. Wessel (eds.), *Netherlands Yearbook of International Law 2014*,
Netherlands Yearbook of International Law 45, DOI 10.1007/978-94-6265-060-2_3

Contents

3.1 Introduction ... 42
3.2 Why Use Temporary International Legal Regimes? ... 44
  3.2.1 Factors Favouring the Use of Temporary Regimes ... 44
  3.2.2 Sources of Strength for Temporary Regimes ... 47
3.3 Temporary Regimes as Foundations for Permanent Regimes ... 48
  3.3.1 Causes ... 49
  3.3.2 Implications ... 51
3.4 Case Studies ... 54
  3.4.1 Refugee Law ... 54
  3.4.2 International Criminal Law ... 58
  3.4.3 Climate Change ... 61
3.5 Conclusion ... 63
References ... 63

3.1 Introduction

In a sense, all international legal regimes are temporary—or can be. The failure of the League of Nations and the 'Permanent' Court of International Justice drove home the reality that all international organizations can end, even those intended to last forever. Nonetheless, states approach the creation of different international regimes with different intentions as to their permanence. Sometimes states build regimes that are clearly temporary, either because they have an explicitly limited duration or because they deal with a discrete, temporally bounded problem. In these instances, the decisions to make regimes that are temporary are deliberate, and often bargained-for consequences of the negotiating processes.

But interestingly, these temporary regimes often have great influence on the permanent shape of international law. They frequently serve as the blueprints for permanent international legal regimes. Sometimes this is because states choose to make temporary regimes permanent, as when the 1951 Refugee Convention, which was originally applicable only to previously displaced refugees, was broadened by the 1967 Protocol to cover all refugee crises. And sometimes this is because states choose to use temporary regimes as models for permanent regimes, as the ad hoc international criminal tribunals served as models for the International Criminal Court (ICC).

This chapter considers how temporary regimes can shape later, permanent ones. It engages with the puzzle of why, after initially insisting on temporary regimes, states later become willing to develop permanent ones along the same lines. To do so, it draws on four theories of behaviour found in the international law and international relations literature: rational design theory, historical institutionalism, constructivism, and behavioural international law.[1]

Under each of these theories, there are conditions under which states would choose to design permanent regimes based on temporary ones. But these conditions differ importantly across the different theories. From a rational design perspective, temporary regimes influence states' later design choices largely because states learn from their experiences with temporary regimes and this learning shapes their decision whether to build a permanent regime. As a leading scholar of this approach puts it, states 'may choose to make their initial agreement of finite duration, and then … use the information they have gained through their experience under the agreement to realign the division of gains in the renegotiated agreement.'[2]

The other three theories mentioned—historical institutionalism, constructivism, and behavioural international law—suggest an even greater effect of temporary regimes on permanent ones. Under each of these approaches, temporary regimes shape the real and perceived possibilities for future design choices in ways that go well beyond the merits of their content. Put broadly, a temporary regime serves to frame the debate around the creation of a permanent regime. The permanent regime can differ from the temporary one, but such departures require vision and effort to obtain.

While all three of these approaches would predict some degree of framing, they differ among themselves as to why framing occurs and how strong its effects are. From a historical institutionalist approach, framing occurs primarily because of path dependency: the existence of a temporary regime considerably heightens the costs of making different design choices for a later, permanent regime. From a constructivist approach, by contrast, framing operates mainly because the temporary regime has changed norms and preferences. Finally, from a behavioural international law approach, framing operates largely because actors involved in the negotiations for the permanent regime have a bias in favour of preserving the *status quo*, as represented by the temporary regime.

---

[1] My discussion of these theories is necessarily brief and omits many nuances. For one thing, scholars within each approach have different views of the contours of the approach, but I only identify what I view as the most conventional accounts of each approach. Additionally, some mechanisms can be common to multiple theories, but here I describe these mechanisms only under the theory which I view as most emphasizing them. To give a few examples, rational design scholars might acknowledge the importance of transaction costs (which I describe under historical institutionalism); historical institutionalists and constructivists have close connections and may further consider their approaches supported by behavioural mechanisms; and accounts drawn from behavioral economics often use rational design approaches as a starting point. Ryan Goodman and Derek Jinks, for example, posit a theory of state behaviour that draws on both constructivist and behavioural principles. Goodman and Jinks 2004, at 626–630. Finally, these theories are not the only accounts of state behaviour. But they cover a considerable swathe of the field and thus are helpful in conceptualizing the influence of temporary regimes.

[2] Koremenos 2001, at 293.

After discussing what these four different theories of state behaviour would suggest about the relationship between temporary regimes and permanent ones, this chapter considers some case studies of initially temporary regimes and their relationship to later permanent regimes. Specifically, it looks at developments in refugee law, international criminal law, and climate change negotiations and discusses them in light of the four theories. Although the conclusions that can be drawn from a few case studies are necessarily limited, the case studies suggest that temporary international legal regimes serve as frames for later permanent ones in ways that go beyond what a rational design theory would predict, and that each of the other approaches may have something to contribute as to why. The chapter concludes by considering the implications of these findings for those involved in international regime design. Most importantly, these findings suggest that deliberately short-term solutions may sometimes be the best way to develop strong, long-term global governance mechanisms.

The themes explored here are broad ones, and the chapter necessarily leaves many issues unaddressed. At the level of theory, it treats the four theories of state behaviour discussed here with a very broad brush and provides little in the way of background. At the level of application, it is similarly brief in its consideration of the three case studies offered. Finally, with regard to content, it focuses only on instances where legally binding temporary regimes give rise to legally binding permanent regimes. It does not discuss soft law regimes or regional regimes, and it barely touches on the important question of how regimes evolve informally. The central argument of this chapter—that temporary regimes may have outsized effects on the permanent shape of international law—is one that may also have implications for these other contexts.

3.2 Why Use Temporary International Legal Regimes?

This section considers why states sometimes choose to create international legal regimes that are temporary rather than permanent. It suggests that the temporary nature of these regimes can encourage states to make stronger commitments than they would make to permanent regimes.

3.2.1 Factors Favouring the Use of Temporary Regimes

Broadly speaking, there are two main reasons states might create a temporary regime rather than a permanent one. First, states might prefer a temporary regime due to the particular context at issue. These state preferences might stem from rational interests, as a rational design approach would suggest, or might reflect a mixture of rational calculations and biases on the part of relevant actors, as a behavioural international law approach would suggest.[3] Second, the process for creating a temporary regime may be less cumbersome than the process for creating a permanent one.

A rational design approach to state behaviour provides a useful starting point for thinking about when and why states might prefer temporary regimes. As Barbara Koremenos and co-authors explain, the basic premise underlying this approach is that 'states construct and shape institutions to advance their goals' and that the use of different institutional designs for different regimes is 'the result of rational, purposive interactions among states and other international actors to solve specific problems.'[4] Temporality is one such design feature, and so states will sometimes have good reason to build temporary regimes rather than permanent ones.[5]

One reason states might prefer a temporary regime is if they are addressing what they perceive as a discrete and short-term need. Crises arising from humanitarian emergencies are good examples. At a high level of generality, one can define the problems of war, mass atrocities, and natural disasters as recurrent ones. But the manifestations of these problems are rare and unpredictable enough that temporary institutions can reasonably deal with specific instances. The field of international criminal law provides many examples, including the International Military Tribunals following World War II, the International Criminal Tribunal for the former Yugoslavia (ICTY), and the International Criminal Tribunal for Rwanda (ICTR). All these were temporary tribunals designed to deal with specific crises and with corresponding jurisdictional limits.[6]

States may also sometimes prefer temporary regimes for issues that are ongoing and continuous. They are not always willing to develop permanent solutions to permanent problems, even when they are fully aware that these problems will endure. Koremenos explains this largely by reference to uncertainty.[7] Given lack of clarity about a problem's scope, distributional effects, or best solution, states may prefer to address these problems through temporary commitments. The negotiators of the Nuclear Non-Proliferation Treaty, for example, initially wrote a twenty-five year duration period into the treaty because, as one of them put it, they were afraid of an 'iron corset, which could not be adjusted to the changing

[3] The theories of historical institutionalism and constructivism discussed in Sect. 3.3 speak less strongly to initial design choices than they do to subsequent design choices, and so I omit discussion of them in this section.

[4] Koremenos et al. 2001, at 762.

[5] Of course, not all states share the same preferences. Sometimes certain states might prefer permanent regimes and other states prefer temporary ones. My discussion here focuses on what might motivate those states that prefer temporary regimes; the next sub-section considers how states that prevail on their preferred temporality might therefore be induced to make concessions on other issues, such as the depth of their commitments.

[6] Crises can also trigger the establishment of permanent regimes. See, e.g., Katzenstein 2014 (discussing how crises can further the formation of international courts).

[7] Koremenos 2001, at 291. See also Meyer 2010, at 382–84; Bilder 1981, at 49–51.

conditions of history.'[8] Other examples of temporary regimes aimed at persistent issues include the Kyoto Protocol, which committed the developed countries that ratified it to emissions reductions for a fixed period of years, and commodities treaties like the International Cocoa Agreement, which regulates the international cocoa market and currently applies for a default period of ten years. As Jacob Gersen has observed regarding temporary domestic legislation, this approach 'allocat[es] enactment costs to the sunset period, [unlike] permanent legislation [which] concentrates them in the initial time period.'[9]

The discussion so far assumes that states are making rationally instrumental choices in preferring temporary regimes. But these preferences could also have origins that are not explained by a rational design approach. Some additional explanations could be drawn from the developing field of behavioural international law, which considers whether states and other international actors might be subject to heuristic biases similar to those demonstrated in behavioural economics research.[10] Among other things, this research shows that individuals tend to overvalue goods already in their possession relative to potential future gains, a finding known as the endowment effect, and to be overoptimistic about their ability to control the future.[11] For example, one interesting study finds that 'individuals value options in a way that is different from the expected value of these options, and, in particular, that decision makers overvalue their options and are willing to overinvest to keep these options from disappearing.'[12] If applicable to states and their agents, such biases could be another reason for states to prefer temporary regimes to permanent ones, since temporary regimes appear to foreclose fewer options in the future.

A further reason that states may use temporary regimes is that these regimes can face fewer procedural barriers to establishment. Permanent international legal regimes grounded on legally binding commitments tend to be done as treaties that require domestic ratification by every state party. Temporary regimes may also require the treaty form and domestic ratification but sometimes, particularly at moments of crisis, they can be formed through less cumbersome ways. Thus, the President of the United States committed the United States to the General

---

[8] Koremenos 2001, at 289 (quoting Italian negotiator Roberto Caracciola).

[9] Gersen 2007, at 264. For an interesting discussion of how temporary regimes can disrupt existing equilibria, see Ginsburg et al. 2014.

[10] Existing work in behavioural international law at the theoretical level includes Aaken 2014 and Braude 2015. Empirical work suggests that state decision-makers are indeed subject to behavioural biases in at least some international legal contexts. Galbraith 2013 (showing that states tend to embrace optional ICJ jurisdictional clauses in treaties only where these clauses are presented as the default option); Poulsen 2014 (describing the power of reference points in negotiations over bilateral investment treaties); cf. Weyland 2005, at 281–294 (showing how peer effects influence states' legislative decision-making).

[11] See Aaken 2014, at 426–435 (reviewing the literature on these and other biases).

[12] Shin and Ariely 2004, at 584.

Agreement on Tariffs and Trade (GATT) without obtaining the advice and consent of the U.S. Senate in part on the grounds that the GATT was a stopgap measure.[13] The ICTR and the ICTY were created by the UN Security Council under Chapter VII, thus requiring neither the explicit consent of the states to whom they most directly applied—Rwanda and the states of the former Yugoslavia—nor domestic ratification by any other state. (Indeed, Rwanda cast a vote in the Security Council against the establishment of the ICTR.[14]) Because such abbreviated processes create fewer veto points, they can be employed more easily and more swiftly.

3.2.2 Sources of Strength for Temporary Regimes

The discussion above theorises conditions under which states might choose temporary regimes over permanent ones. Such choices can also be understood as one aspect of the well-recognised trade-off between form and substance in international institutional design.[15] Specifically, the use of temporary regimes can lead to states embracing deeper commitments than they would accept in permanent regimes.

As noted earlier, temporary legal regimes require states to surrender less control than do comparable permanent regimes. With a temporary regime, a state can feel confident that in due course it will be legally absolved of whatever obligations it has entered into. Therefore, it may be willing to accept greater obligations with temporary regimes than with permanent ones. (To be sure, states have ways out of permanent regimes as well, some lawful and some unlawful,[16] but the costs are usually greater and the possibility for continued influence are reduced.) With temporary regimes, a state may also be willing to delegate more power to central decision-makers. To use Albert Hirschman's formulation, a temporary regime offers greater ease of 'exit' and therefore states may accept having less 'voice'.[17]

States may be particularly willing to accept robust temporary regimes where these regimes are aimed at specific, short-term crises. As discussed earlier, such crises lend themselves well to the use of temporary regimes. The need for swift and vigorous action in these settings is apparent. States may therefore be willing to take on deep though temporary commitments and also to delegate

---

[13] Hobin 1964, at 337–340.

[14] UNSC Res. 955, 8 April 1994. Voting record available at http://unbisnet.un.org:8080/ipac20/ipac.jsp?session=P397X40999794.25610&profile=voting&uri=full=3100023~!482018~!48&ri=6&aspect=power&menu=search&source=~!horizon. Accessed 18 July 2014.

[15] E.g., Raustiala 2005, at 593–594; Coglianese 2000.

[16] See Helfer 2005, at 1591 (describing denunciation clauses as providing 'a hedge against uncertainty that … enables states to negotiate more expansive or deeper substantive treaty commitments *ex ante*'); Gersen 2007; Meyer 2010; Coglianese and Nicolaidis 2001.

[17] Hirschman 1970.

decision-making authority to actors within international organizations. In order to deal with the refugee crisis set off by World War II and its aftermath, for example, states both accepted significant substantive obligations to refugees and entrusted powerful decision-making authority to the UN High Commissioner for Refugees.

Strong substantive obligations and powerful delegations will be even more likely where the temporary regimes have comparatively low procedural hurdles to establishment and where the states that design the temporary regimes are not the states most affected by them. The ad hoc international criminal tribunals are a good example. Their establishment by the Security Council as opposed to through a treaty process not only meant that it was easier for them to be established, but also that they could be imbued with powers they might never otherwise have obtained. These powers doubtless also owed something to the fact that they were set up to focus on prosecuting persons from the former Yugoslavia and Rwanda, not on persons from Security Council states that voted for their establishment.[18]

Although temporary regimes can inspire deeper commitments by states, it is important to recognise that other trade-offs are also available. For example, deeper substantive commitments might also be obtainable by choosing soft law commitments over hard law commitments, by prioritising the depth of the commitments over the number of states likely to join the regime, and by allowing grace periods before commitments take effect.

3.3 Temporary Regimes as Foundations for Permanent Regimes

Temporary regimes often give rise to permanent ones. This is interesting in and of itself. It suggests a change in position on the part of states: having once deliberately chosen temporary regimes, they later come to embrace lasting ones. High-profile examples include the 1967 Protocol removing the temporal limits on the Refugee Convention of 1951 and the decision of the parties to the Nuclear Non-Proliferation Treaty to extend it indefinitely. Temporary regimes can also serve as models for permanent regimes, as the ICTY and ICTR did for the ICC.

This section draws on several distinct theories of state behaviour to consider the causes and implications of such shifts. It considers the two perspectives mentioned in the prior section—rational design and behavioural international law. In addition, it considers two other perspectives—historical institutionalism and constructivism—that offer insights into how institutions, once they have been created, can shape future design choices. This section shows that under the last three of these perspectives, the initial design choices for the temporary regime have an outsized

[18] Although NATO countries did become involved in the conflict in Kosovo (which developed after the establishment of the ICTY), the ICTY Prosecutor chose not to investigate allegations regarding the actions of NATO.

effect on the shape of the future regime. These choices serve as frames for the real or perceived possibilities of the permanent regime. This stickiness has a double-edged character from the prospective of robust regime-building.

3.3.1 Causes

When and why do temporary regimes become blueprints for permanent regimes? Different theories of state behaviour offer different explanations, which are often complementary but also can be in tension with each other.

Rational Design. From a rational design perspective, a central reason why temporary regimes might develop into permanent ones is learning on the part of states. Looking at how initially temporary regimes like the Nuclear Non-Proliferation Treaty are ultimately made permanent by their state parties, Koremenos argues that learning explains much of the answer.[19] Uncertainty about the future and a desire to avoid risks make states unwilling to make permanent commitments at first. But then states see that the temporary regimes seemed to work reasonably well and become willing to embrace them permanently. With regard to the Nuclear Non-Proliferation treaty, by the time its initial duration was drawing to a close, interview evidence suggests that 'essentially all of the parties … favor[ed] extension, a fact that itself provides powerful evidence of learning.'[20]

Historical Institutionalism. Broadly speaking, historical institutionalists consider 'the way in which institutional configurations … often shape political outcomes by facilitating the organization of certain groups while actively disarticulating others.'[21] A major feature of this analysis is a focus on the sequencing of events and how this sequencing can give rise to path-dependent results.[22] From a historical institutionalist perspective, temporary regimes are likely to influence permanent regimes in ways that go beyond the functional value of the temporary regime. This influence partly stems from predictable aspects of renegotiation processes. Once a temporary regime is established, there are reduced costs to building a permanent regime off of the temporary regime instead of starting from scratch. In addition, proposals to take a different approach may make other countries suspicious that these proposals are simply attempts to advance the interests of the proposers at the expense of others. Besides these factors, other case-specific aspects of the temporary regime may also lead it to leave a strong mark on the

[19] Koremenos 2001, at 310–312, 314–15 (also discussing the Arctic Treaty).

[20] Ibid., at 312.

[21] Thelen 2002, at 92.

[22] Fioretos 2011, at 371 and 376. See also Pierson 2000, at 251 (emphasising the need to understand path dependency in terms of marked increases in the cost of change at later times); Sverdrup 2002, at 123–127 (exploring the role played by sequencing in the context of the conferences leading to the Amsterdam and Nice Treaties).

permanent one. For example, the very existence of the temporary regime may mobilize constituencies focused on making it permanent. Such constituencies could include both domestic political actors and the international civil servants involved in the temporary regime.

Constructivism. Central to constructivist accounts is the view 'that the meanings in terms of which action is organized arise out of interaction.'[23] Where for scholars of rational design preferences are for the most part exogenously determined, constructivists consider that preferences are heavily shaped by interactions. Martha Finnemore and Kathryn Sikkink suggest that new international norms develop through the efforts of particular, persuasive individual and group actors, and then typically 'become institutionalized in specific sets of international rules and organizations.'[24] The norms then 'cascade' more broadly around the globe until they are widely internalised.[25] A constructivist approach would suggest that temporary international legal regimes can themselves institutionalise and strengthen norms, thus shifting the preferences of relevant domestic and international actors to further favour the objects of the temporary regimes. By helping shift preferences, the temporary regimes therefore make it more likely that states will support permanent regimes.

Behavioural International Law. A behavioural approach would also suggest that temporary regimes have an outsized effect on shaping later permanent ones. A key finding of behavioural research is that actors tend to favour default options (due to factors like the endowment effect and loss aversion) and to make use of reference points more powerfully than pure instrumental rationality would predict.[26] This has implications for the renegotiation of agreements. In a working paper studying the renegotiation of contracts, for example, Fabian Herweg and Klaus Schmidt propose that the 'initial contract sets the reference point that causes feelings of loss if the contract is renegotiated.'[27] Rather than achieving rationally optimal outcomes in renegotiation, parties are likely either simply to continue the original contract or to renegotiate in a way that hues closer to the original contract than is optimal.[28] Applied to international regime design, this approach suggests that the design choices for temporary regimes will prove sticky for reasons that go beyond the increased transaction costs that come with making changes. Because these temporary regimes embody the *status quo* and/or serve as reference points, state representatives will have biases in favour of continuing them as is. This creates a bar to renegotiation that, while not surmountable, is higher than it would be for purely rational states.

---

[23] Wendt 1992, at 403. For a recent overview of the field, see Brunnée 2013.

[24] Finnemore and Sikkink 1998, at 900. For considering how international organisations can serve as a fora for competing norms, see Hurd 2005, at 502–503.

[25] Finnemore and Sikkink 1998, at 902–905.

[26] For reviewing the literature on these biases, see Aaken 2014. For showing that states favour default options in ICJ jurisdictional clauses in treaties, see Galbraith 2013, at 329–336.

[27] Herweg and Schmidt 2013, at 2; see also Bartling and Schmidt 2012.

[28] Herweg and Schmidt 2013, at 2.

3.3.2 Implications

The theories of state behaviour described above can all explain why temporary regimes will sometimes be made permanent. But these theories emphasise different mechanisms and thus have different (though often complementary) implications for the question of how to approach the initial design of temporary international legal regimes. Table 3.1 sets forth these differences in emphasis at a high level of generality.

Table 3.1 The influences of temporary regimes on permanent ones

Theory	How temporary regimes influence future ones	Implications for negotiators of initial regimes
Rational design	States learn from their experiences with temporary regimes	Be aware that temporary regimes' successes or failures will be factors for consideration in future negotiations
Historical institutionalism	Temporary regimes trigger path dependency and build constituencies in favor of their permanence	Note that the very existence of temporary regimes furthers the likelihood of future permanent ones
		Make design choices with the awareness that they are likely to be fairly sticky for the long term, especially if permanent regimes can be established by the same processes used for temporary ones
Constructivism	Temporary regimes further the spread of the norms that they reflect and therefore increase support for permanent regimes	Expect that by helping the norms they stand for to spread, temporary regimes may make it easier in the future to create permanent and robust regimes
		Anticipate that models can play an important role in spreading norms
Behavioural international law	States and other relevant actors use temporary regimes as reference points and can have status quo biases in favor of their features and continuation	Consider that initial temporariness may enable unusually deep commitments and delegations, as states may overvalue apparent exit
		Make design choices with the awareness that they are likely to be quite sticky for the long term, even if these initial regimes are only models

If a rational design approach accurately predicts state behaviour, then the focus for negotiating an initial temporary regime should simply be on getting a good temporary regime. This is because temporary regimes may not be as sticky under a rational design approach as they are under the other theories of state behaviour considered here. Just as states can find reasons to make temporary regimes permanent under a rational design approach (such as learning that they work and deciding to make them lasting) so they could also find reasons to alter or abandon these temporary regimes (such as from learning that these temporary regimes do not work too well). If there are permanent solutions that are better for all the state parties, then these will be implemented. Even permanent solutions that are better for only some of the parties can be obtained, if the restructuring process does not require the consent of all state parties or if side-deals are an option. And if permanent solutions are not obtainable under these conditions, then the temporary regime will simply expire without replacement. In other words, a rational design approach suggests that states can iron out mistakes or adjust to new conditions in ways that are not overly influenced by the structure of the temporary regime.

If any of the other three approaches more accurately predicts state behaviour, however, then temporary regimes will have a greater effect on the existence and shape of permanent ones. The choices made in temporary regimes are especially likely to be entrenched, and negotiators can sometimes use the very fact of initial temporariness to promote choices they perceive as desirable. Although this general point holds across all three approaches, they give rise to different conclusions as to (1) how strongly the temporary regime influences the existence and scope of the permanent one; (2) how this effect manifests itself; and (3) the extent of the effect in situations where the temporary regime is a model or is established without the full panoply of procedures that the permanent regime would require.

Under a historical institutionalist perspective, one would expect the design choices made for temporary regimes to have outsized influence in some but not all contexts. The effect will be strongest where the temporary regimes have the same reach as the proposed permanent regimes and were created through the same procedural mechanisms. Under these conditions, the constituencies developed by the temporary regime increase the likelihood that a permanent regime will be established, and the increased costs that come with making changes raise the likelihood that the permanent regime will closely track the temporary one. Negotiators should thus expect that their initial design choices will be sticky, whether these choices are good or bad. The effect is likely to be much weaker, however, where the temporary regime is simply a model rather than broadly applicable, or where it is set up through easier procedures. In these instances, some renegotiation is inevitable—particularly if a new international regime will be set up—and different actors and constituencies will be involved. These factors invite reconsideration of initial design choices and thus reduce the likelihood of path dependent actions.

Under a constructivist approach, the power of the temporary regime is largely in strengthening the norms of governmental and other actors in favour of the objective of the regime. If this approach is accurate, negotiators might place greater emphasis on simply creating the temporary regime, with the expectation that the regime will cause actors' commitments to deepen and perhaps to cascade. Once commitment has deepened, negotiators could seek both to create a permanent regime and to strengthen this regime in comparison to the temporary one. A constructivist approach thus might worry less than a historical institutional approach about specific design features of the temporary regime, due to the expectation that the regime could be improved following broader acceptance of the norm. Also in contrast to a historical institutionalist approach, a constructivist approach would suggest that temporary regimes could have a strong effect on shaping permanent ones even if these temporary regimes are simply models or were established through easier procedures. This is because norms can be shaped by models and from regimes established through stopgap procedures.

Finally, a behavioural international law approach would suggest that temporary regimes are always sticky, with the magnitude varying based on the extent to which these regimes serve as defaults or reference points. As with a historical institutionalist approach, a behavioural approach suggests that temporary regimes will prove influential in shaping permanent regimes when they have the same reach and are created through the same procedural mechanisms. Indeed, a behavioural approach would predict an even stronger influence than a historical institutional approach, because of potential cognitive biases in favour of the *status quo* and the use of the temporary regime as a reference point. Similar to a constructivist approach, a behavioural approach would predict that temporary regimes will influence the creation of permanent ones even where these temporary regimes are only models or were subject to lessened procedural barriers. Models do not represent the *status quo* with regard to states not subject to the models, but they can still serve as reference points. Finally, a behavioural approach would predict that the specific design features of the temporary regime would serve as important templates for the permanent regime. In sum, a behaviouralist approach predicts a particularly powerful influence of the temporary regime on the permanent one. Based on this approach, negotiators of initial regimes should be constantly aware that their choices are likely to have effects that outlast the temporary regime, whether for good or for ill. Negotiators could also try to strategically harness behavioural biases. For example, those interested in strong, permanent institutions—especially ones where significant power is delegated to civil servants—could seek to establish models or other temporary regimes subject to lessened procedural hurdles in order to establish reference points for future regime-building.

The different theories of state behaviour thus hold different implications for the negotiators of temporary regimes. These theories may also have significance for negotiators deciding whether and how to make a permanent regime given the existence of a temporary one. From rational design and historical institutionalist approaches, the effects of the temporary regime are primarily just existing factors to work with, but constructivist and behavioural international law approaches suggest that the rhetorical use of these temporary regimes may matter. Negotiators who value the temporary regime and wish to make it permanent should emphasise the norm created by the regime and strive to describe the regime as embodying the *status quo* and setting the reference point. By contrast, negotiators who think that the temporary regime has problems should strive to minimise the framing effects caused by it. One way would be to emphasise different frames, such as competing models or templates.[29]

3.4 Case Studies

Which of the four approaches given above most accurately describes why and how temporary regimes can become permanent regimes? As just discussed, the answer could hold important implications for how negotiators should approach the design of temporary regimes. Unfortunately, this is a hard question to answer. Under all four theories temporary regimes can be made into permanent ones; and, comparably, under all four theories temporary regimes can be abandoned or, if made permanent, substantially modified. The difference between these theories is primarily one of the locus and degree of stickiness. Moreover, it is possible and in fact likely that aspects of several or even all of these theories are at work, perhaps to different extents in different contexts.

This section does not pretend to offer a final answer, but, through the exploration of case studies, it seeks to tease out some initial insights. I look here at three initially temporary regimes and their permanent implications in three areas of law: refugee law, international criminal law, and climate change. Collectively, they suggest that temporary regimes do indeed leave a strong footprint on future permanent ones, for reasons that go well beyond learning.

3.4.1 Refugee Law

In the wake of World War II, a refugee crisis swept Europe and other parts of the world. In December 1950, the General Assembly (GA) passed a resolution and an accompanying statute creating the Office of the UN High Commissioner for Refugees (UNHCR).[30] These contained both temporary and permanent elements: on the one hand, the High Commissioner was given competence over all refugees regardless of when they became refugees, but on the other hand the Statute contained a presumption that the Office of the High Commissioner would have only a

[29] Larrick 2009, at 466. See also Soll et al. 2013, at 7. Compromise drafts drawn up by a single state, for example, can sometimes have striking influence in negotiations. E.g., Letts et al. 1993 (describing the role of the Australian draft in the Chemical Weapons Convention negotiations).

[30] UNGA Res 428 and Annex, 14 December 1950. Prior to this, there were protections for some refugees embodied in certain international agreements and there were also some predecessor organizations, including the International Refugee Organization (IRO), which was involved in the drafting of the Refugee Convention. Discussion of these predecessors is beyond the scope of this chapter. For background, see Loescher 2001, at 21–49; Holborn 1956.

three-year lifespan.[31] The High Commissioner was entrusted with responsibility for 'providing international protection, under the auspices of the United Nations, to refugees who fall within the scope' of the Statute, and states were called upon to cooperate with the High Commissioner.[32] Then, in the summer of 1951, delegates from 26 mostly western countries gathered in Geneva to finalise a new Refugee Convention. This Convention contained substantial state obligations towards refugees, including the principle of *non-refoulement*, and also committed them to 'undertake to cooperate' with the UNHCR.[33]

The UNHCR Statute and the Refugee Convention quite consciously created a temporary, crisis-specific regime. The Statute established the position of the High Commissioner on a temporary basis and did so using a less rigorous process (a vote of state parties in the UN) than a formal treaty would require. The Refugee Convention then cemented the powers of the High Commissioner and states' obligations towards refugees, but it did so only as a temporary regime. For the Refugee Convention applied not to all refugees, but only to persons who became refugees prior to January 1, 1951—and states had the further option of limiting their obligations to encompass only refugees within Europe.[34] This temporal limit was critical to the negotiations, as some states were willing to accept the substantial commitments of the Convention only with respect to the refugee crisis at hand. While certain negotiators were hopeful that this would shine the way to a broader approach to refugee issues,[35] delegates from some states were deeply wary of any permanent regime.[36]

Yet, this once-temporary regime became the foundation for something permanent. The GA kept extending and re-extending the mandate of the UN High Commissioner,[37] and, in 1965, a group of legal scholars assembled with the encouragement of UNHCR to consider how to resolve the tension between the temporal reach of the Convention and the realities of post-1951 refugees.[38] This

[31] UNGA Res. 428, Annex at 5, 6B, 14 December 1950. Throughout, I use the term 'refugees' as shorthand for those persons covered by the subject-matter provisions of the respective instruments, i.e., those with a well-grounded fear of prosecution on certain specified grounds.

[32] UNGA Res. 428, 14 December 1950, at 2; UNGA Res. 428, Annex, 14 December 1950, at 1.

[33] Articles 33 and 35 of the 1951 Convention Relating to the Status of Refugees, 189 UNTS 150.

[34] Article 1(A) and (B) 1951 Convention Relating to the Status of Refugees, 189 UNTS 150.

[35] The Final Act of the Conference did express the aspiration that the Convention would 'have value as an example exceeding its contractual scope.' Final Act of UN Conference of Plenipotentiaries on the Status of Refugees and Stateless Persons, 189 UNTS 37, para E.

[36] Fitzpatrick 1996, at 232. He indicates that 'this limitation reflected the negotiators' reluctance to accept an open-ended obligation and their preference for an ad hoc solution to problems posed by persons displaced in Europe by the Second World War and the onset of the Cold War.' See also Loescher 2001, at 44–46.

[37] This continued until the early twenty-first century, when the General Assembly decided to make the post of High Commissioner permanent 'until the refugee problem is solved.' UNGA Res. 58/153, 24 February 2004.

[38] This conference was organized by the Carnegie Endowment with the collaboration of Switzerland and UNHCR. Weis 1967, at 40.

group decided not to seek 'the preparation and adoption of a new Convention … [as] such a procedure would, in the opinion of the participants, be too lengthy and cumbersome to meet the need for urgency.'[39] Instead, the group proposed a Protocol that simply removed the temporal and geographic limitations of the Refugee Convention, leaving its substantive and structural provisions virtually untouched.[40] In promoting this approach to states, the High Commissioner

> pointed out in [a] paper that such a Protocol, dealing with a most pressing need, i.e., that of removing the dateline, would not, from a long-term point of view, in any way prevent States from proceeding to a revision of the Convention.[41]

In 1967, the GA took note of the Protocol and made it available for accession, despite the concerns of some states that the GA and its relevant committees had engaged in very little discussion and review of the Protocol. The representative from the Philippines, for example, said that despite his vote favouring moving the Protocol forward within the GA process, 'he would in future insist that the articles of important international instruments should be considered in detail.'[42] Although states thus had little input into the content of the Protocol, they proved willing over time to accede to it. Today the Protocol has 146 parties.[43]

Given the initial reluctance of states to accept a permanent refugee regime, it is striking that they came to embrace a Protocol that made the Convention permanent—and did so without weakening either the Convention's strong substantive provisions or the power it gave to the High Commissioner. It is possible to understand this shift by drawing on each of the four approaches to state behaviour discussed above, but these approaches differ in how well they can explain it.

The negotiation of the Protocol and its referral by the General Assembly for state accession seem least related to a rational design approach. Of course, there is a plausible reason why the Protocol would be desirable from a rational design perspective: states could have rationally found the Refugee Convention to work sufficiently well that they wanted to have the opportunity to make it applicable to all future refugees with no additional changes. But if the Protocol were the product of rational and purposeful state design, one would expect states to have played more of a role in its formation—especially given how important the removal of the temporal and geographic limits of the Convention was. Yet, states seemed largely

---

[39] Ibid., at 43.

[40] Ibid., at 43. In its final form, the Protocol provided that state parties would 'undertake to apply articles 2 to 34 inclusive of the Convention' with the removal of its temporal limit and the removal (subject to prior reservations) of the geographic limit. The remaining Final Clauses of the Protocol closely tracked those of the Convention, but unlike the Convention it did permit states to reserve out of International Court of Justice jurisdiction. See generally Protocol Relating to the Status of Refugees, 31 January 1967, 606 UNTS 267.

[41] Weis 1967, at 44.

[42] Ibid., at 47.

[43] UN Treaty Collection, Depository Status for the Protocol Relating to the Status of Refugees, https://treaties.un.org/Pages/ViewDetails.aspx?src=TREATY&mtdsg_no=V-5&chapter=5&lang=en. Accessed 17 October 2014.

passive participants, as they did not play a direct role in its drafting, and they discussed it only lightly in the GA.

The creation of the Protocol can broadly fit under a constructivist account. The Convention had strengthened the norm of protection for refugees, and now non-state actors sought to cement that norm by developing a permanent Protocol. Nonetheless, this approach does little to help understand why the creators of the Protocol did not seek further advances. By 1965, it was apparent that many displaced persons in critical need of help failed to meet the technical definition of refugee and could only receive help from UNHCR through the High Commissioner's good offices.[44] The drafters of the Protocol, however, deliberately chose simple extension over more elaborate revisions.

The development of the Protocol fits fairly well with both a historical institutionalist and a behavioural international law perspective. The impetus behind the Protocol came less from states than from the UNHCR and its supporters—and, as historical institutionalists would observe, this community's very existence depended on the existing temporary regime. Moreover, as a behavioralist would note, what this community chose to propose was in essence an extension of the *status quo*. This choice seems to have stemmed from the concern that further reforms would have been 'cumbersome' to develop,[45] perhaps because states would then have demanded a more active role in the Protocol's creation and content. By contrast, states proved passive in a process aimed at continuing the legal standards and procedures that were already in place. Despite the importance of the issue of temporal and geographic limits, states proved comfortable with letting the Protocol go through the GA without much debate.

Whatever the precise mechanism, it seems clear that the current permanent refugee regime is due in large part to the temporary regime that preceded it. This has brought benefits to refugee law, not only substantively but also in terms of the power of UNHCR. Once states had delegated sizeable power to the High Commissioner in a temporary context, they became willing to make this approach permanent. In contrast, in instances where states have begun with permanent regimes, they have often proved more reluctant to cede enforcement power to independent actors. The permanent treaties in human rights law, for example, have not created any independent figure with comparable power—unlike the High Commissioner for Refugees, the authority of the High Commissioner for Human Rights comes only out of the General Assembly.[46] On the other side of the coin,

---

[44] Loescher 2001, at 109–114 (describing how the High Commissioner increasingly used his good offices in the 1960s); Barnett and Finnemore 2004, at 91–93. The 1969 regional convention drawn up by the Organisation of African Unity did come to include a broader definition of refugee. See Loescher 2001, at 126.

[45] Weis 1967, at 43.

[46] See UNGA Res. 48/141, 20 December 1993.

however, the permanent regime remains formally limited by the constraints set down in the original, temporary regime, most notably the fact that the definition of refugee does not apply to large numbers of displaced persons.[47] In short, for all its temporary origins, the Refugee Convention has proved astonishingly durable in both its strengths and its limits.

3.4.2 International Criminal Law

International criminal law also originated through crisis-specific regimes. The ICTY and the ICTR, like the IMTs before them, dealt with particular events and were established through relatively swift procedures. Their scopes were designed in such a way that they would mainly impact countries with very little international clout—the states of the former Yugoslavia and Rwanda for the ad hoc tribunals, and the defeated countries of World War II for the IMTs. Their implementation did not require the domestic ratification or even the consent of many countries (including the countries whose citizens they were likely to try).[48] These factors encouraged and enabled the states involved in their creation to entrust these institutions with a great deal of power, including providing the prosecutors with the authority to decide whom to investigate and prosecute.

The crisis-specific nature of the ICTY and ICTR, then, seemed essential to the robust powers with which they were vested. Yet, in 1998, states gathered at the Rome Conference and negotiated a full-fledged treaty for a permanent international court whose strength would be roughly comparable to the ad hoc tribunals. The Rome Statute is much longer than the ICTY and ICTR Statutes and differs from them in many particulars.[49] But its existence and shape nonetheless owes much to the *ad hoc* tribunals. As the second ICTY Prosecutor, Richard Goldstone, put it bluntly: 'Absolutely, without the ICTR and ICTY there would not have been an ICC. Had the tribunals not been established, or worse, had they

[47] The administrative flexibility of UNHCR goes some way – but far from all the way – in relaxing these constraints. E.g., Goldenziel 2014.

[48] The ICTY and ICTR were established by the Security Council. UNSC Res. 827, 25 May 1993; UNSC Res. 955, 8 April 1994. The IMTs were also established through streamlined processes; for example, the London Charter setting up the Nuremberg IMT did not receive advice and consent from the U.S. Senate.

[49] Compare the Statute of the ICTY with the Rome Statute of the International Criminal Court. UNSC S/25704, Report of the UN Secretary-General pursuant to para 2 of Security Council Resolution 808 (1993), 3 May 1993; 1998 Rome Statute of the International Criminal Court, 2187 UNTS 90 (hereinafter Rome Statute). To give only one of the many differences, pursuant to the principle of complementarity as enshrined in Article 17 Rome Statute, the ICC can only exercise jurisdiction in cases where the relevant states are unwilling or unable to prosecute. See Burke-White 2008.

been established and failed substantially, [the Rome Conference] would not have even been held.'[50]

Perhaps the most contested issue at the Rome Conference was the Prosecutor's power to initiate investigations. The International Law Commission's (ILC) draft statute had limited the Prosecutor to bringing cases following state party complaints or a Security Council Resolution, on the grounds that the international legal system was not ready to support an independent Prosecutor.[51] As the preparatory work for the Rome Conference went on, however, actors began to urge giving the Prosecutor an independent power to open investigations and '[i]n particular it was argued that the Prosecutor of the two existing ad hoc Tribunals was granted *ex officio* powers and there was therefore no reason to deny the same power to the Prosecutor of the Court.'[52] This approach ultimately prevailed at the Rome Conference. And while the most powerful and populous countries still remain outside the ICC, to date 122 nations have become parties to the Rome Statute.[53]

While the influence of the ad hoc tribunals is apparent, the reason or reasons for this influence is less obvious. Once again, each of the approaches to state behaviour discussed above would emphasise a different reason. A rational design perspective would focus on the learning that states gained from the experience of the ad hoc tribunals; a historical institutional perspective would note how the *ad hoc* tribunals created a community of supporters for the permanent court; a constructivist perspective would draw upon how the *ad hoc* tribunals increased the normative preferences of states in favour of international criminal justice; and a behavioural international law perspective would consider how the *ad hoc* tribunals may have served as a reference point, both for the principle of international criminal justice and for the specific structural choices made for the ICC, in a way whose influence reached well beyond an account based on rational instrumentality.

Once again, each of these explanations has some plausibility. Yet, again, the rational design perspective does not seem to have as much explanatory power as the other three perspectives. The trouble with a rational design approach here is that the ad hoc tribunals had not been in operation long enough for states to learn

---

50 R Goldstone, Interview on obstacles in international justice, 2009, http://hir.harvard.edu/rethinking-finance/obstacles-in-international-justice. Accessed 5 July 2014. See also Katzenstein 2014, at 192 (drawing on additional sources in explaining '[w]ithout the example of these tribunals, governments would have been unwilling to create an independent criminal court').

51 De Gurmendi 1999, at 175–176.

52 Ibid., at 178. The NGO Coalition for the ICC, an influential umbrella group for NGOs, was one of the entities emphasizing this parallel. Pejic argues that 'there is no compelling justification for the difference in the "trigger mechanism"' between the ICTY and ICTR Prosecutor and the future ICC Prosecutor. (Pejic 1996.) Those attempting to counter this argument suggested that the ICTY and ICTR Prosecutors should be viewed not as having true *proprio moto* powers, but rather as having received a Security Council referral to investigate the situation in the former Yugoslavia and Rwanda. See de Gurmendi 1999, at 180.

53 UN Treaty Status, Depository information for the Rome Statute of the International Criminal Court, https://treaties.un.org/pages/ViewDetails.aspx?src=TREATY&mtdsg_no=XVIII-10&chapter=18&lang=en. Accessed 17 October 2014.

much or to have confidence that what immediate lessons there were would hold true for the long term. By 1998, the *ad hoc* tribunals were still quite young, had only a modest number of suspects in custody, and between them had completed one trial and no appeals.[54] There were certainly some insights to gather from the tribunals' experience to date, such as the fact that, in practice, even an independent prosecutor is substantially dependent on state cooperation. Yet, if learning was the main mechanism of the tribunals' influence, it is surprising that states seemed to rely so heavily on the tribunals' limited experience.

A historical institutionalist account helps explain why the ad hoc tribunals might have mattered in ways apart from their merits. These tribunals strengthened the community of advocates for an international criminal court, and there were lower transaction costs to drawing on the ICTY and ICTR Statutes in constructing the Rome Statute. But it is still surprising how much influence these models had, given that the Rome Conference itself offered a chance to step away from a path-dependent course. There was great opportunity for alternative input at the Rome Conference (and no shortage of input offered), and there was a need for the resulting treaty to clear domestic state ratification processes in a way that had not been required for *ad hoc* tribunals established by the Security Council. Yet, states were willing to draw substantially—though far from completely—on the ICTY and ICTR template, including on the deeply contentious issue of the Prosecutor's independent powers.

A constructivist approach goes further in suggesting why many states would become so much more willing to embrace a permanent international criminal court after the establishment of the ICTY and ICTR. For constructivists, the establishment of the *ad hoc* tribunals helped shift the normative preferences of states and their agents (and the networks that work with their agents) in favour of greater international criminal justice.[55] The concept of such a norms shift helps explain why so many states that had little if any direct involvement with the creation or operation of the ad hoc tribunals would come to back the broader, permanent project. But shifts in norms at a broad level do not fully demonstrate why the specific features of the ICTY and ICTR cast such a strong shadow on the negotiations at Rome.

Finally, a behavioural international law approach would anticipate that the ad hoc tribunals both would make states more willing to embrace a permanent international criminal court and would significantly influence its ultimate shape. The fact that the *ad hoc* tribunals were out there—that international criminal justice was being pursued through international courts somewhere in the world—changed the reference points of states and other relevant actors in a way that caused them to become more comfortable with the broader project. Similarly, the particulars of the *ad hoc* tribunals were important frames for the negotiations at the Rome Conference, not so much because these particulars worked well as because they

54 See Galbraith 2009, at 145–153 (providing charts with custody, trial, and appeals dates).

55 See Ralph 2009, at 141–143.

were a reference point. Of course, the tribunals were not the only reference points—others included the ILC's draft statute and, for each state, its own set of expectations about how courts should function, including views about civil law and common law approaches.

In sum, the ICTY and ICTR proved crucial to the development of the ICC in its present form. Although it is difficult to pin down exactly why this influence was so substantial, the answer seems to go well beyond rational learning on the part of states. Indeed, the power of this influence may have caught some actors by surprise. Had the United States foreseen how strongly the ICTY and ICTR Prosecutors would be viewed as models for the ICC Prosecutor, for example, it might well have tried to have the Security Council draft somewhat different prosecutorial powers into the Statutes of the *ad hoc* tribunals. As in the refugee context, initial temporariness played a crucial role in furthering the emergence of a permanent executive figure with considerable independent authority.

3.4.3 Climate Change

Coordinated state action on climate change began not with models or temporary regimes, but rather with a permanent framework treaty. The 1992 UN Framework Convention on Climate Change established commitments with regard to the process of further negotiations, but did not clearly set up specific legally binding emissions limits.[56] Five years later, the Kyoto Protocol committed the developed countries that ratified it to certain specified emissions reductions for the temporary commitment period of 2008-2012.[57] 'The expectation was that this first commitment period would be followed by a second commitment period, a third, and so on, indefinitely into the future.'[58]

The Kyoto Protocol was developed as a full-fledged treaty, subject to domestic ratification, and thus could not build in the greater depth that can come with more abbreviated processes. In addition, unlike the crisis-born rise of refugee law, negotiators at the time of the Kyoto Protocol understood that climate change would be an ongoing and continuous problem. In their design choices, negotiators imported some structural features from the Montreal Protocol on Substances that Deplete the Ozone Layer—the strongest reference point for many negotiators—without fully considering whether design choices aimed at protecting the ozone

[56] Article 4(2) of the 1992 UN Framework Convention on Climate Change, 1771 UNTS 107 (hereinafter UNFCCC). For discussing the ambiguities, see Bodansky 1993, at 516–517. As noted in its preamble, the UNFCCC came after some GA resolutions and other soft law actions on climate change. For further details, see Bodansky 1993, at 461–474.

[57] Article 3(1) of the 1997 Kyoto Protocol to the United Nations Framework Convention on Climate Change, 2303 UNTS 148. While the Protocol itself is not temporary, this commitment period is.

[58] Bodansky 2011, at 697.

layer would prove appropriate for the greater and more diffuse challenge of climate change.[59]

The regime set up under the Kyoto Protocol has been far from adequate. The commitment period does not apply to the majority of emitters—including the United States, which never ratified the Protocol, and developing countries like China and India, which are not subject to the Protocol's emissions reductions provisions. Climate change and its resulting problems continue at an alarming pace, and there is widespread recognition that a better solution is needed. Yet, so far a legally binding replacement has proved elusive. The story of the continuing negotiations is far too extensive to recount, but so far one piece of these negotiations has been an agreement to create a second commitment period under the Kyoto Protocol.[60] This agreement, which would run to 2020, has yet to enter into force, and some important developed countries have made clear that they will not take on this second commitment period.[61] The Kyoto Protocol thus serves as an example of a temporary regime that has been extended but that (so far) has yet to give rise to a permanent, or more permanent replacement.

Looking ahead, the different theories of behaviour discussed here would give rise to varying predictions as to the effect that the Kyoto Protocol will have on the future climate change regime. Both a rational design approach and a constructivist approach offer some bases for optimism going forward. From a rational design perspective, one would expect that states will learn from the inadequacies of the Protocol and improve on it. If there are solutions that are better for all states, these will be embraced, and even solutions that are better overall but not better for all states can be reached with side-payments. From a constructivist perspective, one might anticipate that the Protocol will build norms in favour of addressing climate change—norms that would lead to stronger and better efforts going forward.[62] In the United States, for example, some local governmental actors have used the Kyoto Protocol as a rallying point even though the national government has failed to adopt it.[63]

For historical institutionalists and behavioral international law scholars, the example of the Kyoto Protocol highlights how temporary regimes can potentially have downsides as well as benefits for permanent international law. Historical institutionalists might emphasise how the process of climate change negotiations, from the framework convention on, has generated a focus on universal state participation and emission-cap commitments and has crowded out other, potentially more effective solutions.[64] From a behavioural international law perspective, these

---

[59] Victor 2011, at 215–224. He observed critically that '[m]ore than any other model, the herd looked to Montreal'. Ibid., at 220.

[60] Doha Amendment to the Kyoto Protocol, 8 December 2012 (not yet in force).

[61] See http://unfccc.int/files/kyoto_protocol/application/pdf/kp_doha_amendment_english.pdf (noting the decisions of Canada, Japan, Russia, and New Zealand). Accessed 14 October 2014.

[62] Brunnée suggests that the design of the Kyoto Protocol's compliance mechanisms may foster a norm of compliance. Brunnée 2003, at 261–262, 278–280.

[63] Osofsky and Levit 2008, at 410.

[64] See Victor 2011, at 203–240.

design features are also likely to prove far more resilient than is rationally optimal, as international actors are accustomed to them. In addition, because of the endowment effect, parties to the Kyoto Protocol may be more reluctant than is rational to make further concessions in future agreements. Improvements can occur where a temporary regime is a poor fit as a long-term solution or model, but these improvements require extra effort to achieve.

3.5 Conclusion

Paradoxically, the best way to get to robust, long-term global governance may be to begin with short-term, situation-specific fixes. Once short-term regimes are developed, they can have outsized influence on the development of later, permanent regimes, even when these short-term regimes were established through less rigorous processes than required for the permanent regimes. The nature and degree of this influence depends on how international actors behave, and much work needs to be done to improve predictive models. In the meantime, negotiators of initial regimes should be aware that their choices may prove exceptionally sticky.

References

Barnett M, Finnemore M (2004) Rules for the world: international organizations in global politics. Cornell University Press, Ithaca

Bartling B, Schmidt K (2012) Reference points in (re)negotiation: the role of contracts and competition. Working Paper. http://ssrn.com/abstract=2123387. Accessed 5 July 2014

Bilder R (1981) Managing the risks of international agreement. University of Wisconsin Press, Madison

Bodansky D (1993) United Nations Framework Convention on Climate Change: a commentary. Yale J Int Law 18:451–558

Bodansky D (2011) A tale of two architectures: the once and future U.N. climate change regime. Ariz State Law J 43:697–712

Braude T (2015) Behavioral international law. University of Pennsylvania Law Review 163:(forthcoming)

Brunnée J (2003) The Kyoto Protocol: a testing ground for compliance theories? Heidelb J Int Law 63:255–280

Brunnée J (2013) Constructivism and international law. In: Dunoff J, Pollack M (eds) Interdisciplinary perspectives on international law and international relations: the state of the art. Cambridge University Press, New York, pp 119–145

Burke-White B (2008) Proactive complementarity: the International Criminal Court and national courts in the Rome system of justice. Harv Int Law J 49:53–108

Coglianese C (2000) Globalization and the design of international institutions. In: Nye J, Donahue J (eds) Governance in a globalizing world. Brookings Institution Press, Washington, pp 297–318

Coglianese C, Nicolaidis K (2001) Securing subsidiarity: the institutional design of federalism in the US and Europe. In: Nicolaidis K, Howse R (eds) The federal vision: legitimacy and levels of governance in the US and the EU. Oxford University Press, Oxford, pp 277–299

de Gurmendi SAF (1999) The role of the international prosecutor. In: Lee R (ed) The International Criminal Court: the making of the Rome Statute. Kluwer Law International, The Hague, pp 175–216
Finnemore M, Sikkink K (1998) International norm dynamics and political change. Int Org 52:887–917
Fioretos O (2011) Historical institutionalism in international relations. Int Org 65:367–399
Fitzpatrick J (1996) Revitalizing the 1951 Refugee Convention. Harv Hum Rights J 9:229–254
Galbraith J (2009) The pace of international criminal justice. Mich J Int Law 31:79–156
Galbraith J (2013) Treaty options: towards a behavioral understanding of treaty design. Va J Int Law 53:309–363
Gersen J (2007) Temporary legislation. Univ Chic Law Rev 74:247–298
Ginsburg T, Masur J, McAdams R (2014) Libertarian paternalism, path dependence, and temporary law. Univ Chic Law Rev 81:291–359
Goldenziel J (2014) Regulating human rights: international organizations, flexible standards, and international refugee law. Chic J Int Law 14:453–492
Goodman R, Jinks D (2004) How to influence states: socialization and international human rights law. Duke Law J 54:621–703
Helfer L (2005) Exiting treaties. Va Law Rev 91:1578–1648
Herweg F, Schmidt K (2013) Loss aversion and inefficient renegotiation. http://www.nottingham.ac.uk/economics/documents/seminars/senior/sass-19-02-14-schmidt.pdf. Accessed 15 Aug 2014
Hirschman A (1970) Exit, voice, and loyalty. Harvard University Press, Cambridge, MA
Hobin P (1964) GATT, the California Buy American Act, and the continuing struggle between free trade and protectionism. Calif Law Rev 52:335–349
Holborn L (1956) The International Refugee Organization. Oxford University Press, Oxford
Hurd I (2005) The strategic use of liberal internationalism: Libya and the UN sanctions. Int Org 59:495–526
Katzenstein S (2014) In the shadow of crisis: the creation of international courts in the twentieth century. Harv Int Law J 55:151–209
Koremenos B (2001) Loosening the ties that bind: a learning model of agreement flexibility. Int Org 55:289–325
Koremenos B, Lipson C, Snidal D (2001) The rational design of international institutions. Int Org 55:761–799
Larrick R (2009) Broaden the decision frame to make effective decisions. In: Locke EA (ed) Handbook of principles of organizational behavior. Wiley and Sons, Chicester, pp 461–480
Letts M, Mathews R, McCormack T, Mortaitis C (1993) The conclusion of the Chemical Weapons Convention: an Australian perspective. Contemp Sec Policy 14:311–332
Loescher G (2001) The UNHCR and world politics: a perilous path. Oxford University Press, New York
Meyer T (2010) Power, exit costs, and renegotiation in international law. Harv Int Law J 51:379–426
Osofsky H, Levit J (2008) The scale of networks?: local climate change coalitions. Chic J Int Law 8:409–436
Pejic J (1996) The need for an independent prosecutor. Int Crim Court Monitor 1996:8
Pierson P (2000) Increasing returns, path dependence, and the study of politics. Am Polit Sci Rev 94:251–267
Poulsen L (2014) Bounded rationality and the diffusion of modern investment treaties. Int Stud Quart 58:1–14
Ralph J (2009) Anarchy is what criminal lawyers and other actors make of it: international criminal justice as an institution of international and world society. In: Roach S (ed) Governance, order, and the International Criminal Court. Oxford University Press, Oxford, pp 133–153
Raustiala K (2005) Form and substance in international agreements. Am J Int Law 99:581–614

Shin J, Ariely D (2004) Keeping doors open: the effect of unavailability on incentives to keep options viable. Manage Sci 50:575–586

Soll J, Milkman K, Payne J (2013) A user's guide to debiasing. http://opim.wharton.upenn.edu/~kmilkman/Soll_et_al_2013.pdf. Accessed 15 Aug 2014

Sverdrup U (2002) An institutional perspective on treaty reform: contextualizing the Amsterdam and Nice Treaties. J Eur Publ Policy 9:120–140

Thelen K (2002) The explanatory power of historical institutionalism. In Mayntz R (ed), Akteure-Mechanismen-Modelle, Max Planck Institute, pp 91–107

van Aaken A (2014) Behavioral international law and economics. Harv J Int Law 55:421–481

Victor D (2011) Global warming gridlock. Cambridge University Press, New York

Weis P (1967) The 1967 Protocol relating to the status of refugees and some questions of the law of treaties. Br Yearb Int Law 42:39–70

Wendt A (2002) Anarchy is what states make of it: the social construction of power politics. Int Org 46:391–425

Weyland K (2005) Theories of policy diffusion: lessons from Latin American pension reform. World Polit 57:262–295

Chapter 4
The International Rule of Law Time After Time: Temporary Institutions Between Change and Continuity

Sofia Ranchordás

Abstract The rule of law has emerged both on the domestic and international levels as a promise of longstanding democracy, economic development and peace. On both levels, the rule of law is often associated with the longstanding character of institutions and the predictability of rules, meaning that 'citizens are entitled to laws that are neither murky nor uncertain'. However, does this always mean in practice that the rule of law can only be concretized by laws and legal institutions that last forever? More specifically in the international context, can we guarantee the consolidation of the international rule of law through the coexistence of both permanent and temporary institutions and instruments? In this chapter, I analyse the meaning of the rule of law at the domestic and international levels and discuss its complex relationship with time. I argue that the past, present and future of the rule of law can be, in some cases, united by the use of temporary institutions such as international criminal tribunals or truth commissions, rules and measures. Temporariness can be essential to react swiftly to humanitarian crises, provide transitory justice, gradually concretize the rule of law in fragile democracies, and adapt legal orders to evolving economic and political circumstances.

Keywords Rule of law · International rule of law · Temporary legislation · Temporary institutions · International criminal tribunals · Legal certainty · Predictability · Transitory justice · Sunset clauses · Truth commissions · Time and law

---

Sofia Ranchordás is Assistant Professor at Tilburg Law School, The Netherlands. She would like to thank the Editorial Board of the *Netherlands Yearbook of International Law* and the anonymous reviewers for useful comments and insights.

S. Ranchordás (✉)
Tilburg University, Tilburg, The Netherlands
e-mail: S.H.Ranchordas@uvt.nl

M. Ambrus and R.A. Wessel (eds.), *Netherlands Yearbook of International Law 2014*, Netherlands Yearbook of International Law 45, DOI 10.1007/978-94-6265-060-2_4

Contents

4.1 Introduction 68
4.2 The (International) Rule of Law as a Source of Legal Certainty 71
4.2.1 The Rule of Law: Here, There and Everywhere? 71
4.2.2 The International Rule of Law and Time 76
4.2.3 The International Rule of Law as a Law of Lasting Rules? 78
4.3 Temporary Rules, Institutions and Measures 82
4.3.1 Temporary Legislation and the Rule of Law at Home 82
4.3.2 International Temporary Institutions, Rules and Measures 85
4.4 Conclusion 87
References 89

4.1 Introduction

In times of far-ranging social upheavals, Arab Springs that accelerate the arrival of turbulent summers in neighbouring countries, and terrorist groups that submerse recent and fragile democracies in winters of religious intolerance never experienced before, international law seeks to offer certainty, stability, and predictability. In both times of war and peace, international law aims to provide a balance between the need to guarantee stability at different levels and the urge to react to crises, evidencing what human life is about: 'a *permanent* struggle between good and evil, between our capacities of self-improving and self-harming', between the need to hold on to the past and the desire to move forward.[1] This desire to achieve or reinforce the legal certainty and predictability of international rules implies, first of all, the submission of national legal orders to law. In the past few decades, international law seems to have joined forces with the rule of law—a once domestic political/legal ideal that is now being globally promoted and has acquired an important role in the international area, notably in the context of democratic transitions.[2]

The rule of law has emerged in the international context as the necessary means to support economic development,[3] peace and security and as a crucial component of the administration of justice.[4] The definitions of the rule of law vary between its perception as a safeguard against arbitrary governance, the requirement that a government exercises its power through the application of general rules to the defence of property rights.[5] The meaning and application of the rule of law in the international arena are still contested nowadays. However, the international rule of law may open the path to peace in post-conflict scenarios, enhance the primacy of

[1] Alott 2005, at 7.

[2] Peerenboom 2005, at 809; Appicciafuoco 2010, at 741. See also Nollkaemper et al. 2012.

[3] Krever 2011, at 287.

[4] Sannerholm 2009, at 15.

[5] Waldron 2009, at 15; Tamanaha 2004.

human rights over dubious domestic arrangements and offer the political and legal stability and consensus that are missing elsewhere.[6]

International law is often regarded as a source of longstanding rules. Temporary rules and institutions have nonetheless been used over time, namely in exceptional circumstances. Think of the temporary peace operations in Kosovo or in East Timor, the international criminal tribunals from Nuremberg to Yugoslavia or even the multiple transitory justice programmes designed to promote the rule of law internationally. Temporary institutions and rules offer an alternative to an all-or-nothing solution, which may be a realistic option for developing countries and post-conflict states.

The Nuremberg Military Tribunal was one of the first examples. This temporary institution was generally seen as 'an experiment, almost an improvisation' that went beyond existing legal provisions and treaties, requiring 'international law to be written backwards' to incorporate the war-making acts of the Nazi government and the crimes perpetrated against the German people by the dictatorship and the extermination of citizens on grounds of race.[7] Instead of remaining bound to the past and the principle that 'a man must not be punished for an act which did not constitute a crime at the time when it was committed',[8] the Tribunal established a new and temporary relationship with the past for the sake of justice. The Nuremberg Tribunal ensured that the perpetrators of the mentioned crimes were judged and convicted, not allowing them to hide behind a distorted curtain of legality.

The legitimacy of the Nuremberg Tribunal and other international criminal tribunals is often explained by the analogy with military tribunals and the fact that the international arena requires different rules from the ones applied on the domestic level.[9] In addition, temporary tribunals are exceptional solution-providers conceived to provide relief to victims of often unforeseeable crimes. Despite these arguments, one may wonder whether the temporariness of these tribunals and the possibility to 'write law backwards' are not contrary to the idea of legal stability. Or are temporary institutions in fact essential to build a lasting international rule of law, particularly in post-war scenarios?

The Geneva Convention of 12 August 1949 relative to the protection of civilians in time of war appears to be one of the legacies of the Nuremberg Trials. However, the ability of these temporary institutions to consolidate the rule of law in more recent post-war scenarios has also been criticized. In some cases, temporary institutions are deemed to remain limited to 'the spaceship effect': 'they arrive, do their

6 Chesterman 2008, at 331.

7 Overy 2003, at 1, 14–15.

8 Ibid., at 1 and 23.

9 Crawford 2003, at 109 and 129. The topic of the legitimacy of international criminal courts was raised before the ICTY in the *Tadic* case. *Prosecutor v. Tadic*, Appeals Chamber, Decision on the Defense Motion for Interlocutory Appeal on Jurisdiction, Case No. IT-94-I-AR72, 2 October 1995.

business, and take off', leaving the domestic population confused as what to do next.[10] While this may be congruent with the (international) rule of law if the demand for justice is merely temporary—as in the case of Nuremberg—in other cases, where there might be a more longstanding demand for the rule of law, it might be important to ask whether permanent institutions should be preferred.

In this chapter, I acknowledge the above-raised dilemmas regarding the complex relationship between temporary institutions and the idea of stability that flows throughout international law. I argue nevertheless that, with the resemblance of what happens on the domestic level, temporary institutions and rules *can* actually promote the international rule of law, providing at first transitory solutions for the long-term achievement of a stable rule of law. To wit, the temporary certainty offered by transitory institutions can be a more solid alternative to the dream of a Western rule of law that might take years to arrive or be built on pillars of sand.

They can do so not only for the sake of justice in the specific case of criminal tribunals but also to ensure that the promotion of the rule of law in post-conflict scenarios can be adapted to local circumstances. Under such circumstances, the establishment of temporary institutions can be beneficial since they can be easily evaluated and reshaped according to the evolving local political and social circumstances. This can avoid, for example, a pure transplant of a Western rule of law to countries that are still struggling to establish a stable democracy.

This chapter aims mainly to explore how the international rule of law is affected by the existence and creation of temporary rules and institutions: are they a threat to the rule of law or rather a necessary element to ensure that the rule of law continues to evolve together with society? In this chapter, I argue that in exceptional circumstances such as in post-conflict scenarios, temporary institutions and temporary rules may assist not only the promotion but also the consolidation of the rule of law. I also discuss the challenge of finding the different dimensions of the promotion of a global rule of law and the need to achieve a compromise formula for the implementation of the rule of law. This 'formula' would combine temporariness with the ability to welcome the response and feedback from recipients, thus providing room for learning and adaptability to the evolving circumstances.[11]

My line of argument fits the body of literature that has criticised institutional transplants of the rule of law deprived of any effort to customise it to the local political and social environment.[12] I start out by analysing first the meaning of the rule of law and the international rule of law (Sect. 4.2.1) and the role of time in international law (Sect. 4.2.2). The relationship between time and law permeates the whole discussion: in international law, the past is a decisive element for obtaining consensus in the present and future.[13] Time and international law have a multifaceted

[10] Stromseth 2009, at 87 and 88.

[11] Nollkaemper et al. 2012, at 2.

[12] Carothers 2006. For a thorough analysis, see Sannerholm 2009. See also Kleinfeld 2012.

[13] More generally, on the relationship between time and law, see Ost 1999.

relationship: time can be a building block in the case of customary law, an interpretation and consensus-gathering tool, but 'what comes afterwards' is also an important dimension of temporariness that might justify the suspicion against temporary rules and institutions. Although international tribunals or, for example, interim measures are temporary, their decisions are definitive and will endure after the extinction of these institutions. The focus of the paper shall not be placed specifically on international tribunals—which are only here referred to as illustrations of the main arguments—but rather on the contribution of temporary institutions to the concretization of the international rule of law. I relate the first part of this chapter to an important element of the rule of law on both the domestic and international levels: legal certainty (Sect. 4.2.3). There is a widespread consensus that the rule of law must offer continuity and predictability in order to be effective and meaningful. But should this always be the case? 'One size fits all' solutions might be undesirable when it comes to the promotion of the rule of law abroad and offering swift responses to humanitarian crises. In Sect. 4.3, I discuss the importance of temporary rules and institutions for the development of the rule of law and argue that temporariness can be a stepping stone to the future concretization of a solid domestic and international rule of law.

4.2 The (International) Rule of Law as a Source of Legal Certainty

4.2.1 The Rule of Law: Here, There and Everywhere?

Both at the national and international levels, the rule of law has been used for different purposes, in war, peace and post-war scenarios and given uncountable definitions. However, the rule of law appears to be everywhere and is often prescribed as the remedy for all ills. At the international level, we witness that the concept of the rule of law 'is more easily invoked than understood': although states seem to invoke it, this has not precluded them from turning their backs to it when it no longer suited their interests, revealing a lack of understanding of what the rule of law truly entails.[14] This has occurred so often and so incoherently that the rule of law risks becoming meaningless.[15]

The 'colours of the flag of the rule of law' have flown over the UN field workers in different countries in Africa, symbolising an effort to 'drive off spectres of civil strife and criminal autocracy, to rescue peoples from the rhythm of revenge and bring them back into the law's delay of freedom and human rights'.[16] In some

[14] Allain 2000, at 1.

[15] Nelson and Cabatingan 2010, at 2.

[16] Eijsbouts 2001, at 3.

cases this flag was erected too quickly, without considering the post-war scenario and its inherent complexities. In other cases this flag was a mere symbol to which little value was attached. The (international) rule of law—even if it is in many cases a mere symbol—is worth discussing, promoting and keeping since although the ideal of an international rule of law might not bring immediate international order, it confers substance and 'attractive force' to international law.[17]

4.2.1.1 The Rule of Law at Home and Abroad

The idea of the rule of law has multiple translations with more or less equivalent significations (*Rechtsstaat*, *État de droit*, *stato di diritto*, *Estado de Direito*). The German term *Rechtsstaat*, for example, refers to a theoretical and ideological trajectory from enlightened absolutism to a self-governed society under law.[18] The Anglo-American term 'rule of law'—which shall be used throughout this chapter—concentrates rather on the executive top of the state, with its bureaucracy and methods, placing more focus on parliamentary sovereignty.[19] The rule of law encompasses multiple dimensions, concepts and levels that imply significant institutional complexity both at the international and domestic levels.[20] Dicey's classic study on the rule of law at the domestic level refers to three dimensions: 'the absolute supremacy or predominance of regular law as opposed to the influence of arbitrary power', 'equality before the law' including the sovereign, and 'the general principles of the constitution [that] are with us the result of judicial decisions determining the rights of private persons in particular cases brought before the courts'.[21]

Although the rule of law might sound like a tautological concept, its meaning is far from being self-evident and remains highly contested, varying from thin and thick conceptions. A basic conception of the rule of law conceives it as the idea of a 'system in which law is able to impose meaningful restraints on the state and individual members of the ruling elite.'[22] Beyond this concept, the rule of law can be reduced to thin and instrumental perceptions of the rule of law as the 'law – good or bad – that works'. However, if we reduce the rule of law to procedures of law rather than to its substance, are we accepting that the rule of law can be a non-democratic principle, compatible with extreme poverty, as long as it allows law enforcement to work? Or should the rule of law be freighted with values?[23]

---

[17] Georgiev 1993, at 4.

[18] Frankenberg 2014.

[19] For a distinction between Rechtsstaat and rule of law, see Blaam 1990, at 76.

[20] Nagle 2008, at 3.

[21] Dicey 1885.

[22] Peerenboom 2005, at 809.

[23] For a discussion of the different perceptions of the rule of law, see Humphreys 2010. See also Raz 2001.

These questions take us to the 'thicker conception' of the rule of law that incorporates notions of political morality, fairness, gender roles, social justice and human rights.

The thicker conception of the rule of law is a key element in sustainable political and economic development, promoting justice, and rendering ruling bodies institutionally and normatively accountable and compatible with international governance structures. Some of the different roles of the rule of law may be more accentuated 'at home' than abroad: while at the domestic level, this idea is an *end* in itself; at the international level, the promotion of the rule of law can be qualified as a *means*.[24] It is a *means* to guarantee prosperity, stability in peace, namely in developing countries and post-conflict scenarios. The promotion of the rule of law has been mainly translated into technical assistance, for example, from the World Bank to these countries to ensure the development of an effective legal system, non-violent mechanisms for resolving political disputes, and the promotion of human rights.[25] The promotion of the rule of law in the international arena aims to develop 'an international model for nonviolent, effective system-building and conflict resolution'.[26]

A great number of actors have been involved in the active promotion of the rule of law in developing and post-conflict states.[27] In the last decades, the World Bank has worked in the development of governance structures for these countries, insisting that 'the rule of law promotes effective and sustainable economic development and good governance … and economic growth.'[28] Rule of law promotion normally implies a multitude of promoters who may advocate a number of different institutions and rules.

Arguably, the successful promotion of the rule of law means refusing a 'one size fits all' recipe for the implementation of the rule of law, and suggests a compromise formula, which considers the response and feedback from recipients, opening the door to learning possibilities.[29] In order to achieve this compromise, it is important to understand the rule of law dynamics, *i.e.*, the 'distinct but interrelated processes of rule of law promotion (the promoter perspective) and the rule of law conversion (the recipient perspective), and the modalities, mechanisms, and processes that link the two (the diffusion perspective).'[30] This process of promotion, conversion and diffusion means that the concretization of the rule of law is a multi-staged process. New rules and institutions aiming to guide the country

---

[24] Humphreys 2010, at 9–10.

[25] Chesterman 2008, at 331.

[26] Kötter and Schuppert 2014, at 71.

[27] Carothers 2006, at 15.

[28] World Bank Legal Vice Presidency, Initiatives in Legal and Judicial Reform 3 (World Bank 2004), http://www-wds.worldbank.org/servlet/WDSContentServer/WDSP/IB/2004/03/01/000012009_20040301142827/Rendered/PDF/250820040Edition.pdf. Accessed 15 September 2014. On the specific role of the World Bank in the promotion of the rule of law, see Krever 2011, at 287.

[29] Nollkaemper et al. 2012, at 2.

[30] Ibid., at 4.

towards the rule of law are—and perhaps should always be—established gradually. This perspective of the promotion of the rule may allow rules to evolve and develop over time. This is congruent with the perspective that the rule of law has its own dynamics: as, Nollkaemper, Peerenboom and Zürn point out, rarely is anything adopted without adaptation or implemented without resistance.[31]

A mere reduction of the rule of law to the idea of the supremacy of law or the idea that agents exercising public authority should be bound by law is not sufficient to evidence its different dimensions. The rule of law has different groups of addressees: on the one hand, it imposes legal obligations upon government officials. On the other, the rule of law limits and coordinates the behaviour of citizens who are expected to obey the rules that apply to them.[32] While this second dimension might be straightforward, the first constitutes an additional complexity to the concretisation of the rule of law in the international arena. As Jeremy Waldron observes

> the applicability of the ideal we call 'the Rule of Law' in international law is complicated by (1) the fact that there is no overarching world government from whom we need protection (of the sort that the rule of law traditionally offers) and … (2) the fact that international law affects states, in the first instance, rather than individuals (for whose sake we usually insist on rule of law requirements).[33]

States can nevertheless repudiate the application of an international rule of law even by arguing that they are 'law-imbued entities' that already constrain the conducts of their officials with rules of their own. As Waldron points out, any attempt to resist international law 'should be based on legality rather than the repudiation of legality'.[34] In addition, this resistance to the rule of law based on national rules cannot be easily offered by developing countries characterised by high levels of corruption and post-conflict turbulence where the rule of law barely exists. Is it thus possible to talk about a true international rule of law? And what are we talking about?

4.2.1.2 The International Rule of Law

The meaning of the rule of law in the international arena is still contested both in the context of the promotion of this idea to new democracies and in the international community. The implementation of 'an international rule of law' is complicated, amongst other things, by the fact that, contrary to the traditional concept of the rule of law, international law presumes a horizontal relationship between sovereign states. In the international realm, the rule of law is not meant to protect legal subjects from the state government or the law itself. Instead, as Jeremy Waldron observes, this ideal can be conceived here as a protection of corporations against

[31] Ibid., at 5.

[32] Tamanaha 2011, at 4; Waldron 2009, at 16.

[33] Waldron 2011, at 315.

[34] Ibid.

states, or states from other states at the international level.[35] The starting point of the domestic rule of law is rather a vertical relationship between the sovereign and its citizens, where the rule of law aims to submit the sovereign to the rule of law.[36]

Controversies aside, the rule of law appears to be alive and well at the domestic level and its magic persuasiveness is being exported to non-Western countries.[37] More recently, the aspiration that the international community will live the dream of the rule of law has grown exponentially. We might not have an almighty world government lording it over all social, cultural, economic, and political activity in the world, but we still have international law, its actors and institutions.[38]

In the international arena, the rule of law has been defined in 'thick terms' by the Secretary-General of the United Nations as

> [a] principle of governance in which all persons, institutions and entities, public and private, including the State itself, are accountable to laws that are publicly promulgated, equally enforced and independently adjudicated, and which are consistent with international human rights norms and standards. It requires, as well, measures to ensure adherence to the principles of supremacy of law, equality before the law, accountability to the law, fairness in the application of the law, separation of powers, participation in decision-making, legal certainty, avoidance of arbitrariness and procedural and legal transparency.[39]

The international rule of law has been promoted at the international level through international treaties and organizations and is deeply embedded in the Charter of the United Nations and in different UN resolutions, such as the Millennium Declaration.[40] Another example is Resolution 61/39 adopted on December 4, 2006, where the General Assembly 'requests the Secretary-General to prepare an inventory of the current activities of the various organs, bodies, offices, departments, funds and programmes within the United Nations system devoted to the promotion of the rule of law at the national and international levels.'[41]

The international rule of law encompasses elements that are essential for state to state relationships. However, beyond this perception of the international rule of law as the application of rule of law principles to the relationship between states and other subjects of international laws, other definitions are also available in the literature. Simon Chesterman refers to the 'rule of international law' as the rule that privileges international law over domestic legal arrangements, namely the primacy of human rights or even the perception of the rule of law in the international arena as a 'global rule of law'.[42]

---

[35] Ibid.

[36] Waldron 2014.

[37] The path to the rule of law might however be long in some cases. See Peerenboom 2002.

[38] Waldron 2011, at 316.

[39] UN Secretary-General, The rule of law and transitional justice in conflict and post-conflict societies, 2004, http://www.unrol.org/files/2004%20report.pdf. Accessed 15 September 2014.

[40] UNGA Res. 55/2, 18 September 2000.

[41] UNGA Res. 61/39, 4 December 2006.

[42] Chesterman 2009, at 67.

The international rule of law is thus not a constraint of 'a super government', but rather an ideal of international law that provides predictability and stabilises social relationships, protecting the freedom of the different actors in the international realm.[43] As Mattias Kumm explains, the rule of law acts as an additional limit to the domestic level, contributing to the protection of individuals, enhancing

> the checks and balances of a constitutional system, [complementing] domestic separation of powers. An effective institutionalization, international legality also has the tendency to limit the options of the executive branch to claim foreign affairs prerogatives and thereby shift power to the executive branch in a way that endangers and potentially destabilizes democracy on the national level.[44]

Although there is a widespread international consensus regarding the value and importance of the rule of law, this consensus is not always translated into real significance. Words do not often mean much in post-war scenarios when many leaders will promise to restore law and order, but only few of them will actually implement the rule of law agenda.[45] In addition, the international rule of law is challenged by the constantly changing circumstances: novel and unexpected threats to human rights and international peace, and more destructive forms of using force. Can the international rule of law face these challenges by responding with temporary instruments that accommodate these changes or is the international rule of law rather 'a law of lasting rules'?

4.2.2 The International Rule of Law and Time

The relationship between time and the (international) rule of law has been a highly overlooked topic in the literature. This subject is nonetheless essential at a time of dramatic changes as the ones we are witnessing today in the international realm. Understanding how time influences law can also help us to understand how we can promote and maintain the rule of law over time in recent democracies and post-conflict scenarios.

Laymen often see law as a source of immutability and rigidity. Law is nonetheless in permanent movement. And this is also true for international law. Nonetheless, law follows a different pace and does not change at the same speed as other realities around us do. Law is—either thanks to amendments or statutory interpretation—adaptive, but it is also bound by a sense of continuity that is at the origin of the principle of legal certainty.[46] Law—also international law—can be conceived as a process over time, which is not only reflected in the time span between the beginning of negotiations between states and the implementation of international legal

---

[43] Kumm 2003, at 19–32.

[44] Kumm 2004, at 909.

[45] Carothers 2006, at 19.

[46] Marauhn 2011, at 52.

obligations but also in its consequent mutations. This process of change is visible in the evolution of rules after their entry into force, in the amendments to treaties, the room for a modern interpretation of treaty clauses and even their termination.[47] The Treaty of Paris of 1951 establishing the European Coal and Steel Community was an illustration of a treaty that was clearly influenced by the recent past and designed to build a peaceful present and future. This treaty—to which we will come back later—came into force in 1952 and expired exactly fifty years later, after having achieved its mission of producing economic and political stability in Western Europe.

The fifty years of this treaty's existence do not seem to have threatened the continuity of this European alliance and the reestablishment of the rule of law after the Second World War. Law must have a minimum of stability but reducing law either to a state of 'absolute stability' or to an 'instrument of change' seems too simplistic.[48] A certain degree of continuity is desired since a high mutability of law could endanger the foreseeability that flows from the rule of law.[49]

The (international) rule of law has an ambivalent relationship with time: the rule of law must be characterised by sufficient stability and live longer than the 'men who make the laws' but, in order for law to rule, 'it must be responsive and indeterminate, capable of extending to the infinite variety that confronts it … and be saturated in temporality.'[50] This core of stability does not change the fact that if law is meant to fulfil its function as a supreme instrument of social order, it has to respond to social change and adapt to it.[51]

In international law, time or the past is a 'building block': in the case of customary international law, for example, it is clear that the past is a decisive element in building the present and the future. Customary law—the doctrine of instant custom aside—is the most vivid example of this function of time: since custom is not written, its meaning and validity have to be traced back to its genesis and the fulfilment of the requirements of state practice and *opinio juris*.[52] It is 'a constant and uniform usage, accepted as law'.[53] However, one of the most contested aspects in customary law is the period of time that is necessary to establish or change a customary rule, and which, according to the *North Sea Continental Shelf* cases does not need to be an extended one. Instead, there is no specific time requirement for the formation of customary international law as long as the practice has sufficient density.[54] Therefore, the period of time that goes by does not necessarily make 'the building block' bigger or more relevant to international law.

---

47 Ibid., at 54.

48 Ost 1998, at 14.

49 Eyer 2008, at 666.

50 Fitzpatrick 1998, at 185.

51 Friedman 1959, at ix.

52 Kammerhofer 2011, at 62.

53 *Asylum case* (*Colombia/Peru*), ICJ, Judgment of 2 November 1950.

54 Guzman 2005, at 158.

In this context, it is clear that the nature and functions of some institutions established to consolidate the rule of law cannot have a temporary character. Temporariness is not available to every single institution and treaty. In its report 'The Rule of Law and Transitional Justice in Conflict and Post-conflict Societies', the Security Council emphasises that despite the need 'to act directly for the protection of human rights ... where conflict has eroded or frustrated the domestic rule of law, in the long term, no ad hoc, temporary or external measures can ever replace a functioning national justice system.'[55] It is important to emphasise here the use of the expression 'in the long term', from which we can conclude that transitory measures and institutions may be allowed at an early stage as long as they are later replaced by permanent ones.

Temporary institutions can be essential to solve transitory problems, but they do not always offer a solution for the future. A distinction must be made here between rule of law institutions and measures that can have a temporary character and are in fact a first step in developing the consolidation of the rule of law, and those institutions that represent the pillars of a legal order and must have a permanent character. In the first case, we can think of truth commissions, international criminal tribunals, or interim measures designed to provide temporary relief. Domestic courts and independent administrative bodies are however examples of institutions that require a 'longer life' in order to guarantee the independence and accountability of the judiciary.

In addition to the mentioned distinction, the establishment of temporary institutions might leave us with accountability problems that must be solved if temporary institutions are to be employed on a broader basis in the international arena. This might happen, for example, if international tribunals and organizations behave as 'spaceships' that land, promote the rule of law or enforce international criminal law, and leave, leaving also behind the effects of more or less problematic trials. International tribunals that act like spaceships come, see, but they do not conquer. And the international rule of law is precisely about conquering a legal order and ensuring its 'submission' to the rules of (international) law either 'for good' or for at least a stable period of time.

4.2.3 The International Rule of Law as a Law of Lasting Rules?

The rule of law has been traditionally associated with a source of predictability, particularly for developing economies and democracies in transition. The rule of law is nourished by lasting rules: in a dynamic world where we see constant changes, the rule of law is 'the steady-centre around which events and ideas foment'.[56]

---

[55] UN Security Council, The rule of law and transitional justice in conflict and post-conflict societies, S/2004/616, 23 August 2004.

[56] Allott 2005, at 13.

This is true for the rule of law 'at home' and 'abroad': the rule of law is a principle that deems to confer legal certainty to the relationship between citizens and the states, individuals among themselves, and also between states. 'At home', legal certainty and the rule of law can almost be conceived as two sides of the same coin. In civil law countries, the principle of legal certainty is derived from the German concept of *Rechtsstaat* (see above) and is regarded as a shield against the arbitrariness of public administration.[57]

In common law countries, legal certainty also refers to predictability and consistency, but it plays a more important role in safeguarding business activity and the calculation of legal risks.[58] In addition, here legal certainty is not expected to confer as much determinacy as in civil law countries.[59] However, regardless of where 'your home' is located, there are two important aspects regarding the relationship between legal certainty and the rule of law: first, legal certainty is a source of the continuity, consistency and predictability of laws and a safeguard against arbitrary and retroactive decisions; second, uncertainty is an enemy of the rule of law.[60]

Legal certainty and the rule of law also seem to walk hand in hand at the international level. First, in developing countries and post-conflict scenarios, the promotion of the rule of law is expected to facilitate economic transitions to the market model, conferring legal and institutional predictability and efficiency in a variety of areas, which are essential for the operation of a market economy.[61] Second, a 'true rule of law' in the international realm is expected to enhance social stability, but this can only be guaranteed if a certain degree of predictability, continuity and consistency underlie the actions, reactions, or interactions of states.[62]

Although legal certainty can be deconstructed in several dimensions, more attention shall be devoted to continuity. This element seems to be inherent in the international rule of law since time is a building block in international law. On the one hand, it might take centuries of social struggle, long-lasting state practice, and intellectual effort to establish one principle commonly accepted by a number of actors within the international community or within a given society. Continuity translated into years of consistent state practice appears to enable the construction of a certain coherence regarding rules and principles. On the other hand, law and particularly international law aims to bring stability and certainty back to a world characterised by permanent change and a lack of consensus. International law lives

57 For a thorough analysis of the principle of legal certainty, see Popelier 1997; Oldenziel 1998.

58 See Bayern 2012, at 53.

59 For a comparative legal study analysis of the principle of legal certainty, see Maxeiner 2006, at 541.

60 Scalia 1989, at 1175.

61 Carothers 2006, at 17.

62 Allott 2005, at 13.

between an unstable balance between continuity and change. And although law is expected to keep up with an evolving society, 'law cannot be infinitely flexible and custom's social role is precisely unwarranted, hasty change.'[63]

There is a common perception that continuity matters more in international law than at the municipal level. Continuity in international law may refer to the roots of the whole system of international law, its norms and institutions, principles, structures or conceptions.[64]

Continuity is also a key element when reflecting upon the implementation of the rule of law and what binds new political officials to honour existing rules and institutions. Should the instruments of the rule of law be made out of 'laws of and for the living', as Thomas Jefferson advocated in 1789 in a letter to James Madison?[65] Or should they be perpetual? Nowadays, there is no doubt that laws should endure beyond the ravages of time: this continuity confers authority on law, and offers predictability and 'reckonability' to law.[66] In fact, in spite of this perception, one of the problems that often arises at the domestic level is the difficulty or even inability to bind new political officials to existing rules. This difficulty constitutes a fundamental barrier to the establishment of the rule of law. As Barry Weingast explains,

> no matter how attractive are today's institutions or rights, they are no good in the long term if tomorrow's regime can alter them at will. This issue is intimately tied to the issue of creating a perpetually lived state, a state whose characteristics and institutions do not depend on the identity of leaders or dominant coalition.[67]

The power to undo institutions has been a threat throughout history (e.g. Nazi Germany, Venezuela under Hugo Chavez) and explains why continuity plays an important role in the context of the rule of law. Institutional instability strengthens the ideal that there should be a 'rule of law' that lives beyond and—sometimes—in spite of the rule of men. In this context, it is also worth noting that the rule of law cannot be created by open access orders. The rule of law requires institutions to provide for the law and a set of credible commitments that protect those institutions and ensure that they survive. The absence of perpetuity makes it very difficult for states to commit to long-term rules, institutions and policies.[68] The certainty of law should therefore mean that laws survive the people that adopted them.

From the perspective of the history of international law, it is difficult to define what a period of continuity is, notably as far as the continuity of norms and

---

[63] Koskenniemi 2006.

[64] Steiger 2011, at 13 and 34.

[65] Thomas Jefferson, Letter to James Madison, 6 September 1789, www.thefederalistpapers.org. Accessed 15 September 2014. In this letter, the Founding Father refused 'perpetual constitutions' and argued that 'no society can make a perpetual constitution or even a perpetual law. The earth belongs to the living. [Therefore] every constitution ... and every law naturally expires at the end of thirty-four years.'

[66] Referring to K. Llewellyn, see Scalia 1989, at 56. See also Strauss 2008, at 997.

[67] Weingast 2010, at 29.

[68] Ibid., at 39.

institutions is concerned.[69] Continuity can refer to the existence of lines of structures, principles and ideas. Continuity is a retrospective concept, but it does not exclude the possibility of evolution and the need to welcome necessary changes. The rise and fall of states is one of the inevitable realities that imposes a certain discontinuity in the international legal order. Also, for instance, the balance between territorial integrity and the need to guarantee the self-determination of peoples reflects this bridge between continuity and necessary change.[70] 'International law as a legal order itself asks fundamental questions of continuity and discontinuity … [for example] colonization, a basic structure of the law of nations over centuries, no longer exists.'[71]

Continuity and certainty in international law can be conceived as real barriers in the way of responses to future changes of popular sentiment. However, sometimes the popular sentiment does not want continuity. Without wishing to open the Pandora's box of the clash between justice and legal certainty, it is important to remember that rupture might be necessary to guarantee justice. In the international realm 'there is antagonism between modern, policy-oriented international law and a concept of democracy which gives primacy … to what the people want now.'[72] However, is the coherence of international law always achieved by the above-described continuity, or rather by a mix of continuity, temporary rupture and the modernisation of existing structures conceivable?[73] As Barry Weingast observes, although certainty is essential for the promotion of the rule of law, this ideal requires not only the supremacy of the law but also a dynamic component by which the law holds not only today but also in the future.[74] As Cassesse recently pointed out, 'realizing utopia' in international law might imply reconciling the need for certainty and change through the implementation of different instruments than the ones that the international order has used so far.[75]

We can also question whether the continuity of law and institutions is always essential to gather consensus as to controversial topics in the international community, or whether temporary solutions might be more consensual because they do not last forever. This approach has been visible, namely at domestic levels in the case of counterterrorism policies, where sunset clauses have been adopted in periods of high risk of terrorist attacks.

What is more, *ad hoc* or temporary measures might be essential in order to enable international environmental policies designed to support sustainable development,

---

[69] Steiger 2011, at 13 and 35.

[70] See, for example, Declaration on principles of international law concerning friendly relations and co-operation among states in accordance with the Charter of the United Nations, G.A. res. 2625, Annex, 25 UN GAOR, Supp. (No. 28), U. N. Doc. A/5217, 1970, at 121.

[71] Steiger 2011, at 13 and 36.

[72] Daintith 2001, at 115 and 119–120.

[73] Steiger at 13 and 16.

[74] Weingast 2010, at 50.

[75] See Cassesse 2012.

economic growth, or even adapt domestic asylum policies in order to allow governments to prioritize humanitarian crises when necessary and to decide more rapidly on the cases of, for example, environmental migrants.[76] All of these are examples of temporary rules, measures and institutions that have been employed in different countries and that seem to be compatible with a sound concretization of the rule of law.

4.3 Temporary Rules, Institutions and Measures

While continuity can be conceived as the 'bridge between the present and the past' of international law, it presupposes 'a certain kind of identity' which is basic in its essence and must admit mutations to adapt to new challenges.[77] In the last decades, international law has faced numerous challenges to its continuity. Revolutions, unprecedented changes in politics, the economy (e.g. the economic crisis in countries such as Argentina) and society, the need to prosecute war criminals quickly and effectively and to solve urgent humanitarian situations have shaken the international legal order. Similar phenomena have been experienced at the domestic level, forcing governments to enact emergency legislation or to adopt sunset clauses. Both at the international and national levels, the pressure of change has led to the creation of temporary institutions, rules and measures that aim to address specific topics such as war crimes or inherently temporary situations such as high levels of counterterrorism.

4.3.1 Temporary Legislation and the Rule of Law at Home

Temporary legislation is an overreaching term used to refer to different forms of temporary legislation and regulations at the domestic level, such as temporary-effects legislation, emergency legislation, sunset clauses, and experimental legislation.[78] Temporary legislation refers to laws that terminate at the end of a beforehand established period, except if the legislator decides otherwise.[79] Ad hoc and temporary rules and measures are often used at the domestic level to respond to national and international crises. Temporary measures can be adopted to allow policymakers to decide more flexibly, within a shorter period of time and on a casuistic basis on matters such as immigration resulting from environmental catastrophes. Environmental

---

[76] Omeziri and Gore 2014, at 43.

[77] Steiger 2011, at 13 and 15.

[78] Gersen 2007, at 247.

[79] Ibid.

migrants like those fleeing the ravages of the 2010 earthquake in Haiti required Canada to adopt a number of ad hoc and temporary measures in order to prioritize humanitarian help over its 'usual' immigration rules.[80]

Temporary rules are not adopted on a systematic basis in most countries but, in the past years, national legislators have become more interested in dispositions that allow them to evaluate the effectiveness of new regulations and terminate unnecessary rules.[81] Temporary legislation has also been used as a consensus-gathering mechanism, which has allowed legislators to win over the opposition and public opinion on complex and controversial matters such as significant limitations of fundamental rights in the context of counterterrorism policies.

Although terrorism is not necessarily a temporary problem, this threat knows different levels of risk and might therefore require the adoption of exceptionally stringent measures. In addition, the forms and techniques employed by terrorists evolve rapidly, obliging states to review their approach to combating terrorism. The USA Patriot Act[82] is an example of the use of sunset clauses to respond to a situation of a higher level of terrorist threat.

Sunset clauses are dispositions that establish that an institution (e.g. an agency), a policy programme or a law will be extinguished after a certain period, except if the sunset clause is renewed.[83] The sunset clauses adopted in the USA Patriot Act referred to the possibility to limit significantly the fundamental rights of alleged terrorists. Although these clauses were successively renewed and have influenced other countries to adopt temporary measures to fight terrorism, this has remained controversial. In Germany, the adoption of sunset clauses was suggested in 2002 in the *Terrorismusbekämpfungsgesetz*. This Act introduced various temporary limitations to fundamental rights based on the need to safeguard national security.[84]

A similar attempt was made in the Netherlands, where the Dutch Council of State argued that temporary rules should be added to the bill on counterterrorism.[85] This Bill on Administrative Measures concerning National Security (*Wet Bestuurlijke Maatregelen Nationale Veiligheid*) included extraordinary measures and competences to be used in the prevention of terrorist attacks.

The adoption of a sunset clause in the context of an international treaty or convention on terrorism might sound in abstract unrealistic, but a temporary provision

---

80 Omeziri and Gore 2014, at 44.

81 See Ranchordás 2014a.

82 Uniting and strengthening America by providing appropriate tools required to intercept and obstruct terrorism (USA PATRIOT) Act of 2001, 18 USC 1, Public Law 107–56, 26 October 2001.

83 Davis 1981, at 383.

84 Gesetz zur Bekämpfung des internationalen Terrorismus (Terrorismusbekämpfung), *Bundesgesetzblatt*, Teil I, Nr. 3, 9 January 2002, at 361. See also Ranchordás 2014a, at 64–65.

85 Regels inzake het opleggen van beperkende maatregelen aan personen met het oog op de bescherming van de nationale veiligheid (Wet bestuurlijke maatregelen nationale veiligheid), Opinion of the Dutch Council of State and ministerial report, *Kamerstukken* II, 30 566, nr. 4, 2005–2006, at 12.

could be used to gather consensus on the employment of stricter measures at times of higher international terrorism alert.

Sunset clauses create more room for political bargains and have been chosen as a means to achieve social or political consensus. Opponents of a specific law or provision may be more willing to adopt it if there is a guarantee that the previously existing *status quo* will return after the sunset expires.[86] This occurs, for example, when there is a conflict of multiple interests or when information as to the potential (negative) effects of law might be lacking. The adoption of sunset provision increases the probability that political opponents will support new laws due to the 'promise' of a future evaluation or revision.[87]

Although temporary legislation is often perceived as a 'necessary evil' for problems that permanent legislation would not be able to solve, temporary rules do not necessarily constitute a threat to the rule of law and legal certainty. Instead, they can further the principle of legal certainty, granting citizens temporary certainty (for example, with a two or three-year sunset clause) instead of a situation of permanent uncertainty and constant amendments to permanent legislation.[88] Moreover, sunset clauses ensure a more frequent review of legislation, reducing the risk of obsolete and unnecessary rules. These provisions also provide clarity as to the duration of an extraordinary or transitory policy.[89]

Sunset clauses could be used in the quest for the promotion of the rule of law 'abroad'. In post-conflict scenarios, the implementation of permanent institutions and programmes is unrealistic. The lack of political, economic and social stability requires the customisation of solutions. In addition, the imposition of Western rule of law institutions might in many cases be too early for recently established legal orders or systems still trying to recover from the ravages of war.

A broader employment of temporary legislation accompanied by the duty to regularly evaluate the effects of these new rules and institutions could contribute to the development of the rule of law. Sunset clauses force legislators to reconsider the need for existing legislation and allow them to adapt it to changing circumstances. Temporary provisions could also be a way of limiting the powers of the executive, guaranteeing a more frequent legislative oversight particularly of measures which may only be necessary for a short period.

Laws are instruments that offer determinability as to the citizens' rights and duties *in concreto*, but this certainty shall only endure if laws remain permeable to future possibilities of change.[90] Recently established democracies that are being introduced to the ideal of the rule of law would benefit from these instruments of change. Of course, one could argue that there is the risk that temporary institutions and regulations will not bind officials in the same way as permanent laws do.

[86] Ginsburg et al. 2013, at 42.

[87] Maltzman and Shipan 2008, at 255.

[88] Ranchordás 2014b.

[89] For arguments that judicial sunsets promote the rule of law, see Gentithes 2014, at 411–412.

[90] Popelier 1997, at 115.

Moreover, once the international actors leave the country, national officials could also be tempted to allow sunset clauses to expire without providing a dignified follow-up to the establishment of the rule of law in the country. These are risks which are inherent in any legislative or policy intervention: we can always erase the legacy of our predecessors. This is valid both for temporary and permanent rules.

Temporary institutions, measures and rules offer the advantage of taking into account the different stages of economic and political development of the country. This can guarantee that policies and laws reflect a real-time situation and provide the instruments that the country needs in order to be 'ruled by law'.

4.3.2 International Temporary Institutions, Rules and Measures

One of the menaces for the international rule of law could be, from a theoretical point of view, the use of temporary commissions, operations and institutions such as the UN operations in Kosovo or East Timor or the international tribunals, respectively.[91] In the mentioned areas of conflict, the UN had direct responsibility for the administration of justice, the training and control of the police and prison services, and the (re-)establishment of the rule of law. These temporary initiatives—although well intended—have been criticised due to the lack of accountability of international officials towards the local populations,[92] limited time-frames and the limited jurisdiction of temporary and hybrid tribunals, and deficient judicial systems that fail to observe rules of criminal proceedings.[93] Although the Yugoslav Tribunal, resembling Nuremberg or Tokyo, is a temporary court, the effects of incidents of individuals being mistakenly detained and wrongly accused might last longer than the temporary operations and institutions.[94]

At the international level, temporary institutions and rules might be even less common than at the municipal level. However, there are some cases of temporary measures, operations and commissions worth noting. Truth commissions are examples of official, temporary and non-judicial bodies which are established to address past human rights abuses and collect facts regarding violations of human rights perpetrated over a certain period. These commissions were established for example in El Salvador, Guatemala, Chile, East Timor and Sierra Leone.[95] These commissions do not aim to replace courts or to provide justice themselves, but rather to make justice possible. Instead, some of these commissions exist side by side with courts. Think of the Yugoslav Truth and Reconciliation Commission, which was created to assist the

---

[91] Chesterman 2008, at 331.

[92] Ibid.

[93] Stromseth 2009, at 90.

[94] Allain 2000, at 126.

[95] UN Security Council, The rule of law and transitional justice in conflict and post-conflict societies, S/2004/616, 23 August 2002.

International Criminal Court for Former Yugoslavia. This truth commission aimed to provide not only the 'big picture' of Yugoslav society and war scene but also to recommend legislative, judicial, administrative, and policy reforms that could contribute to changing the environment and eliminating the structures that fostered impunity.[96]

At the level of rulemaking, the drafting and ratification of complex treaties may take years. This can be, in principle, incompatible with the adoption of short-term sunset clauses. However, the adoption of sunset clauses in the international realm is not an unknown phenomenon: in fact parties to bilateral or multilateral treaties may choose to include a termination clause (a 'sunset clause'). This can be relevant, for example, in bilateral investment treaties which are often perceived by developing countries as being more favourable to foreign investors. The employment of a sunset clause can allow the country to terminate the treaty if a brighter future for its economy can be anticipated.[97] Temporariness can thus be valuable in the international arena to ensure adaptability to changing political and economic circumstances and guarantee that developing countries do not remain lost forever in the translation of bilateral treaties.

Temporary dispositions, *in concreto* sunset clauses, can also be used at the international level to limit the powers of international organizations. A well-known example of an international treaty containing a sunset clause is the already mentioned European Coal and Steel Community Treaty, where this provision was included to limit the powers of the Commission. With a fifty-year sunset clause, member states felt reassured when granting extraordinary powers to the Commission since this temporary institution would not be able to erode member state authority in the long-term future.[98]

Another potential room for the creation of temporariness in the international realm refers to international criminal tribunals. According to the Nuremberg principles, crimes against humanity and genocide give rise to a duty to prosecute on the part of the international community as a whole.[99] The Nuremberg trials were 'an experiment' with a temporary institution that deemed to treat the perpetrators of aggression differently at that time. In addition, this tribunal—resembling similar tribunals that would later emerge—was confronted with the additional complexity of the rather unspecified and evolving nature of the crimes. Nuremberg had to write international law backwards, giving rise to multiple questions as to the observance of the principle of legality. Nuremberg extended the application of international law to individuals due to their link to the State, suspending sovereign immunity in order to enforce international criminal law effectively.[100]

[96] Peijic 2001, at 2.

[97] For example, in March 2014, Indonesia announced the intention to terminate 60 bilateral investment treaties with multiple countries. The country would only remain bound for another 15 years to the Netherlands due to a sunset clause in the bilateral treaty with the latter, see http://www.ft.com/cms/s/0/3755c1b2-b4e2-11e3-af92-00144feabdc0.html#axzz3FrFPpbmN. Accessed 15 September 2014.

[98] Alter and Steinberg 2007.

[99] Broomhall 2003, at 19–20 and 56.

[100] Ibid., at 21.

International criminal tribunals should be expected to be seen as legitimate and comply with the standards for the rule of law which we also expect from national criminal justice systems. However, as James Crawford points out, this complexity may be enhanced by the question of whether an international criminal tribunal that operates on an occasional basis can be at the same time be 'established by law'—in the sense of compliance with the principle of legality—and observe the rule of law.[101] The establishment of international criminal courts such as Nuremberg and Tokyo was haunted by the phantom of the rule of law and the crucial question of whether these courts had been established by law. Their temporary status was not the main concern here. Instead, their legacy was. These and other more recent temporary tribunals—at the resemblance of international operations—have often been regarded as 'spaceships' (see above) that are established ad hoc to enforce international criminal law but do not establish a continuum of justice between the past, the present and the future.[102] Temporary institutions themselves are not incompatible with the idea of the continuity of the rule of law. However, it is important to guarantee that there is a subtle transition between the rule of temporary international institutions and the rule of domestic courts.

In conclusion, 'temporariness' appears to be left out of the traditional concept of the international rule of law since it is contrary to the stability and continuity that international law aims to build. However, the rule of law is not blind to humanitarian crises, the need to adapt rules to support economic development or the consolidation of democracies. In such contexts, temporary institutions, measures and rules can in fact contribute to a more effective establishment of this ideal, allowing for the development of a tailored 'rule of law suit' that fits the international community and the current situation of specific States. In addition, temporary institutions and regulations both at home and abroad constrain extraordinary powers that might be necessary, for example, in times of crisis. This can ensure enhanced oversight and reduce the risks of arbitrariness of institutions. Although temporary institutions are not a panacea and should not affect the core of international law that must remain permanent for the sake of its validity, temporariness can advance the rule of law.[103]

4.4 Conclusion

'The rule of law is a cornerstone of a contemporary constitutional democracy', it has a decisive role in 'cementing the recent transitions from authoritarian or totalitarian regimes to constitutional democracy in Eastern Europe and elsewhere.'[104] However,

---

[101] Crawford 2003, at 109 and 125.

[102] Stromseth 2009, at 87 and 88.

[103] For a framework and the limits of the application of temporary legislation at the domestic level, see Ranchordás 2014a.

[104] Rosenfeld 2001, at 1307.

the rule of law can only fulfil its function if the nature and complexity of problems are correctly and effectively approached and adequate instruments are used.

The promotion of the rule of law has been a complex task in the last decades: developing countries, recent democracies and post-conflict states lack stable entrenched institutions, financial means, material and human resources, and trained legal officials. These circumstances will nonetheless evolve in most cases. Therefore, the instruments required for the construction of the rule of law might need to be adapted later. As far as the international rule of law is concerned, it is important to mention that despite its core of predictability and continuity, this ideal is also compatible with the use of temporary institutions such as international criminal tribunals that can ensure the effectiveness of international law.

In this chapter, I advocate the use of temporary institutions for two reasons. First, temporary institutions such as temporary ad hoc international criminal tribunals are essential to re-establish the rule of law in a post-conflict scenario and ensure justice. This was already visible with the Nuremberg and Tokyo Tribunals, and has also been more recently pursued by multiple truth commissions. Second, an adequate promotion of the rule of law in post-conflict states might benefit from a temporary approach to institutions and rules. In countries 'lost in translation' between war and peace, temporary rules and institutions may do more for the consolidation of the rule of law than inflexible and standard rule of law instrument remedies.

Temporary institutions are an important element of the adequate promotion of the rule of law since they can be easily adapted and terminated, considering new economic and political circumstances. These institutions fit the 'rule of law dynamics', which implies that there is a long way to go before the rule of law is adequately established. As the country changes, so should a part of the institutions. In addition, the evaluation and sunset of temporary institutions facilitates the accommodation of the rule of law instruments to the local characteristics. Although the rule of law might have a core which a number of us will agree upon, its concretization may vary time after time from time to time, and from place to place. What is relevant to isolated territories in the Pacific may have no application to rural areas in Africa.[105] Mere institutional transplants usually fail to promote the rule of law when institutions are imposed from the outside with little consideration of the political and social environment of the target country.[106] Customised and temporary solutions might fit the context of the law and development project of legal pluralism and constitute an alternative to a uniform implementation of the rule of law.[107]

Time plays a decisive role in the construction of the international rule of law. However, 'this time' does not need to be indefinite. Rather, temporary institutions and rules can also contribute to the advancement of the rule of law. Temporary

[105] Tamanaha 2011, at 2.

[106] See Guthrie 2013, at 1175–1180.

[107] Tamanaha 2011, at 11.

certainty might be better than lasting uncertainty, the attribution of powers limited by the force of time and evaluations can reassure states when ratifying treaties, and temporary rules allow countries to adapt to 'thicker' forms of the rule of law.

Temporary institutions and rules are not a panacea, but they are compatible with the core of legal certainty pertaining to the (international) rule of law. While the beat of an international and one day, a world rule of law goes on,[108] we are reminded in this chapter that international law does not need to sprint toward this goal. Instead it can crawl towards it safely but steadily with the help of temporary rules, time after time.

References

Allain J (2000) A century of international adjudication: the rule of law and its limits. T.M.C Asser Press, The Hague

Allott P (2005) Towards the international rule of law: essays in integrated constitutional theory. Cameron May, Folkestone

Alter KJ, Steinberg D (2007) The theory and reality of the European Coal and Steel Community. In: Meunier S, McNamara K (eds) European integration and institutional change in historical perspective. Oxford University Press, Oxford

Appicciafuoco L (2010) The promotion of the rule of law in the Western Balkans: the European Union's role. Ger Law J 11:741–768

Bayern SJ (2012) Against certainty. Hofstra Law Rev 41:53–90

Blaam LC (1990) The Rechstaat idea compared with the rule of law as a paradigm for protecting rights. S Afr Law J 107:76–96

Broomhall B (2003) International justice and the International Criminal Court: between sovereignty and the rule of law. Oxford University Press, Oxford

Cabatingan L, Nelson R (2010) A preface and an introduction. In: Cabatingan L, Heckman J, Nelson RL (eds) Global perspectives on the rule of law. Routledge, London, pp 1–13

Carothers T (2006) Promoting the rule of law abroad: in search of knowledge. Carnegie Endowment for International Peace, New York

Cassesse A (ed) (2012) Realizing utopia: the future of international law. Oxford University Press, Oxford

Chesterman S (2008) An international rule of law? Am J Comp Law 56:331–362

Chesterman S (2009) I'll take Manhattan: the international rule of law and the United Nations Security Council. The Hague J Rule Law 1:67–73

Crawford J (2003) The drafting of the Rome Statute. In: Sands P (ed) From Nuremberg to The Hague: the future of international criminal justice. Cambridge University Press, Cambridge

Daintith T (2001) Is international law the enemy of national democracy? In: Reestman AJA, Vandamme T (eds) Ambiguity in the rule of law: the interface between national and international legal systems. Europa Law Publishing, Groningen, pp 114–122

Davis A (1981) Review procedures and public accountability in sunset legislation: an analysis and proposal for reform. Adm Law Rev 33:393–413

Dicey A V (1885) Introduction to the study of law of the constitution. 8th reprint, Liberty Fund, Oxford

Eijsbouts W (2001) Introduction. In: Vandamme TAJ, Reestman JH (eds) Ambiguity in the rule of law: the interface between national and international legal systems. Europa Law Publishing, Groningen, pp 3–10

[108] Van Wynen and Thomas 1975.

Eyer KE (2008) Administrative adjudication and the rule of law. Adm Law Rev 60:647–682
Fitzpatrick P (1998) Law in the antinomy of time: a miscellany. In: Ost F, Van Hoecke M (eds) Temps et droit. Bruylant, Brussels
Frankenberg G (2014) Political technology and the erosion of the rule of law: normalizing the state of exception. Edward Elgar, Cheltenham
Friedman WG (1959) Law in a changing society. University of California Press, Los Angeles
Gentithes M (2014) Sunsets on constitutionality and Supreme Court efficiency. Va J Soc Policy Law 21:373–421
Georgiev D (1993) Politics of rule of law: deconstruction and legitimacy in international law. Eur J Int Law 4:1–14
Gersen JA (2007) Temporary legislation. Univ Chic Law Rev 74:247–298
Ginsburg T, Mansur J, McAdams R (2013) Libertarian paternalism, path dependence, and temporary law. Coase-Sandor Institute for Law and Economics Working Paper No. 645 (2d Series) Public Law and Legal Theory Working Paper No. 431, www.ssrn.com. Accessed 15 Sept 2014
Guthrie BJ (2013) Beyond investment protection: an examination of the potential influence of investment treaties on domestic rule of law. N Y Univ J Int Law & Polit 45:1151–1180
Guzman AG (2005) Saving customary international law. Mich J Int Law 27:115–176
Humphreys S (2010) Theatre of the rule of law: transnational legal intervention in theory and practice. Cambridge University Press, Cambridge
Kammerhofer J (2011) Uncertainty in international law: a Kelsenian perspective. Routledge, London
Kleinfeld R (2012) Advancing the rule of law abroad: next generation abroad. Carnegie Endowment for International Peace, Washington
Koskenniemi M (2006) From apology to utopia: the structure of international legal argument. Cambridge University Press, Cambridge
Kötter M, Schuppert G (2014) Applying the rule of law to contexts beyond the state. In: Barenbom P, Silkenat J, Hickey J Jr (eds) The legal doctrines of the rule of law and the legal state (*Rechtsstaat*). Springer, Heidelberg, pp 71–89
Krever T (2011) The legal turn in late development theory: the rule of law and the World Bank's development model. Harv Int Law J 52:287–319
Kumm M (2003) International law in national courts: the international rule of law and the limits of the internationalist model. Va J Int Law 44:19–32
Kumm M (2004) The legitimacy of international law: a constitutionalist framework of analysis. Eur J Int Law 15:907–931
Maltzman F, Shipan CR (2008) Change, continuity, and the evolution of the law. Am J Polit Sci 42:252–267
Marauhn T (2011) The relevance of culture in framing international law. In: Marauhn T, Steiger H (eds) Universality and continuity in international law. Eleven International Publishing, The Hague, pp 45–59
Maxeiner J (2006) Legal certainty: a European alternative to American legal indeterminacy? Tulane J Int Comp Law 15:541–607
Nagle L (2008) On armed conflict, human rights, and preserving the rule of law in Latin America. Penn State Int Law Rev 27:1–44
Nollkaemper A, Peerenboom R, Zürn M (eds) (2012) Rule of law dynamics: in an era of international and transnational governance. Cambridge University Press, Cambridge
Oldenziel HA (1998) Wetgeving en rechtszekerheid: een onderzoek aar de bijdrage van het legaliteitsvereiste aan de rechtszekerheid van de burger. Kluwer, Alphen aan den Rijn
Omeziri E, Gore C (2014) Temporary measures: Canadian refugee policy and environmental migration. Refuge 29:43–53
Ost F (1998) L'instantané ou l'institué? L'institué ou l'instituant? Le droit a-t-il pour vocation de durer? In: Ost F, Van Hoecke M (eds) Temps et droit. Bruylant, Brussels, pp 14–30
Ost F (1999) Le temps du droit. Éditions Odile Jacob, Paris

Overy R (2003) The Nuremberg trials: international law in the making. In: Sands P (ed) From Nuremberg to The Hague: the future of international criminal justice. Cambridge University Press, Cambridge

Peerenboom R (2002) China's long march toward rule of law. Cambridge University Press, Cambridge

Peerenboom R (2005) Human rights and rule of law: what's the relationship? Georget J Int Law 36:809–946

Pejic J (2001) The Yugoslav Truth and Reconciliation Commission: a shaky start. Fordham Int Law J 25:1–22

Popelier P (1997) Rechtszekerheid als beginsel van behoorlijke wetgeving. Intersentia, Antwerp

Ranchordás S (2014a) Constitutional sunsets and experimental legislation: a comparative perspective. Edward Elgar, Cheltenham

Ranchordás S (2014b) Sunset clauses and experimental legislation: blessing or curse for legal certainty? Statute Law Rev, Advance Access, 11 Feb 2014

Raz J (2001) The rule of law and its virtue. In: Dyzenhaus D, Ripstein A (eds) Law and morality. University of Toronto Press, Toronto, pp 210–230

Rosenfeld M (2001) The rule of law and the legitimacy of constitutional democracy. South Calif Law Rev 74:1307–1352

Sannerholm RZ (2009) Rule of law after war: ideologies, norms and methods for legal and judicial reform (Doctoral Dissertation). Örebro Studies in Law, Örebro

Scalia A (1989) The rule of law as a law of rules. Univ Chic Law Rev 56:1175–1181

Steiger H (2011) Universality and continuity in international public law? In: Marauhn T, Steiger H (eds) Universality and continuity in international law. Eleven International Publishing, The Hague

Strauss DA (2008) On the origin of rules (with apologies to Darwin): a Comment on Antonin Scalia's the rule of law as a law of rules. Univ Chic Law Rev 75:997–1013

Stromseth J (2009) Justice on the ground: can international courts strengthen domestic rule of law in post-conflict societies? Hague J Rule Law 1:87–97

Tamanaha BZ (2004) On the rule of law: history, politics, theory. Cambridge University Press, Cambridge

Tamanaha BZ (2011) The rule of law and legal pluralism in development. Hague J Rule Law 3:1–17

Van Wynen TA, Thomas AJ Jr (1975) A world rule of law: prospects and problems. SMU Press, Dallas

Waldron J (2009) The rule of international law. Harv J Law & Publ Policy 30:15–30

Waldron J (2011) Are sovereigns entitled to the benefit of the international rule of law? Eur J Int Law 22:315–343

Waldron J (2014) The rule of law in public law. New York University Public Law and Legal Theory Working Papers. Paper 481, http://lsr.nellco.org/nyu_plltwp/481. Accessed 15 Sept 2014

Weingast BR (2010) Why developing countries prove so resistant to the rule of law. In: Cabatingan L, Heckman J, Nelson R (eds) Global perspectives on the rule of law. Routledge, London

Chapter 5
International Law and Time: A Reflection of the Temporal Attitudes of International Lawyers Through Three Paradigms

Christian Djeffal

Abstract What is the relation between law and time? How do international lawyers conceive law in time? This chapter aims to answer the question of how international law is situated in time in a paradigmatic fashion. Looking at social time—the common perception of time in society as opposed to individual or astronomical time—the law is an institution defining time but also relying on a temporal conception. The chapter establishes three basic paradigms of how international law has been situated temporally: the paradigm of atemporality, depicting law as eternal and unchangeable; the paradigm of temporality, defining law as ascertainable but changeable; and the paradigm of fluxus, defining the law as necessarily changing, unsteady and moving. The chapter shows how the understanding of international lawyers shifted from the paradigm of atemporality to the paradigm of temporality. It reviews the treatises of international legal scholars and the notion of peace in peace treaties from the 17th to the 20th century. The chapter then goes on to discuss whether there has been a second paradigm shift from the paradigm of atemporality to the paradigm of fluxus. For this purpose three cases are explored: the evolutive interpretation of the notion of security, the changing customary law on state immunities and the principle of sustainable development. The chapter concludes with the outlook of transcending the paradigmatic approach with a cubistic look at the relationship between law and time.

Keywords International law in time · Temporality · Natural law · Positivism · Realism · Evolutive interpretation

---

The author received his PhD from the Humboldt-University of Berlin and is currently a law clerk at the Higher Regional Court of Frankfurt.

C. Djeffal (✉)
Darmstadt, Germany
e-mail: Christian.djeffal@gmail.com

M. Ambrus and R.A. Wessel (eds.), *Netherlands Yearbook of International Law 2014*,
Netherlands Yearbook of International Law 45, DOI 10.1007/978-94-6265-060-2_5

Contents

5.1 International Law in Time: The Familiar Stranger 94
5.2 Paradigm Shifts 96
5.2.1 The Temporalisation of International Law 97
5.2.2 The Flexibilisation of International Legal Time? 104
5.3 General Conclusions 115
References 117

5.1 International Law in Time: The Familiar Stranger

Time is a 'familiar stranger'.[1] This paradox was expressed by St. Augustine as follows: 'What then is time? If no one asks me, I know; if I want to explain it to a questioner, I do not know.'[2] The interesting point is that the understanding of time and representations of time are part of our daily routine. However, time is still a mystery and many questions in relation to it are far from being solved. One important way of structuring our understanding of time is the distinction between astronomical time, i.e., the time ascertainable through methods from natural sciences—personal time, i.e., the time as it is perceived by individuals—and social time, i.e., the time as it is conceived in society.[3] Our understanding of time is, at the same time, evolving. Concerning individual time, the perception of a human being changes during her/his lifetime. With regard to astronomical time, the theory of relativity has shown that time is not a stable value but subject to the speed with which a body travels.[4] The fact that social time varies is evident from the fact that cultures sometimes have specific concepts of time[5] or their own calendar.[6] There are ongoing debates about the nature and the concept of time in physics, literature,

[1] This is the title of Fraser 1987.

[2] Augustinus, *Confessiones*, Lib XI, XIV, (17). For the translation, see Augustine 2006, at 242. The Latin original reads: 'quid est ergo tempus? si nemo ex me quaerat, scio; si quaerenti explicare velim, nescio.'

[3] For this distinction, see Sorokin and Merton 1937.

[4] For an explanation, see Russel 1926.

[5] So, for example, in ancient Greek, there were concepts of *chronos* and *kairos*, one denoting time as enduring while the other designating something like the right point in time. See Smith 1969.

[6] See, for example, the different calendars in China or many Islamic countries. A very famous switch of calendar systems was made by the catholic church replacing the Julian calendar by the Gregorian calendar according to Aloysius Lilius' plans. For the evolution of calendars, see Kinnebrock 2014, at 37–39.

sociology, psychology and in particular in philosophy.[7] The same applies in the field of jurisprudence. Lawyers and legal scholars frequently have to deal with temporal questions: there are questions of temporal applicability, dates, deadlines, time periods; legal principles like frustration, delay and *estoppel* can directly depend upon certain periods of time. Irrespective of the great importance of time, the general question of how the law is situated in time has rarely been addressed.[8]

In society, there is a need for agreed time standards. An agreed time standard is explicitly or implicitly based upon a concept of time. This chapter argues that the concept of law is based on temporal assumptions particularly concerning the changeability of the law. Like the conception of time, the concepts of law and in particular international law in time have varied. This chapter summarises those conceptions as three paradigms, namely the paradigm of atemporality, under which law is seen as eternal and unchangeable, the paradigm of temporality, under which law is seen as changeable but generally stable and the paradigm of fluxus under which law is seen as an unstable set of decisions. The chapter shows in an exemplary fashion how the temporal concepts of international law have shifted from the paradigm of atemporality to the paradigm of temporality and it discusses whether there might be a third shift to the paradigm of fluxus with the help of three case studies, each relating to a specific question concerning the different formal sources of international law, i.e. international treaties, customary international law and general principles.

Law is related to time in several ways: it relies on a conception of social time and also enforces it. In many jurisdictions, the time system is regulated by law. Paragraph 4 of the German Code on Measurement Units and Measurement of Time provides that '[l]egal time is the middle European time'. The concept of legal time means that whenever German law refers to time, middle European time and the underlying Coordinated Universal Time are to be applied. This Coordinated Universal Time is currently regulated in the form of a recommendation of the International Telecommunications Union (ITU).[9] The international standards of time are never absolute, and there is a constant effort to improve them.[10]

The concept of law is also based on a certain temporal understanding. This is evident in relation to the question whether law or its most important norms can ever change. Time has often been associated with change.[11] Change is important for the measurement of time, which is true for every timekeeper from the sundial to the atomic clock. The question of the law in time is also the question

[7] For an interdisciplinary bibliography, see Das 1990.

[8] One rare example is Husserl 1955. In his great treatment of time and law, Günther Winkler also expresses an obvious lack of reflection of international law and time. Winkler 1995.

[9] Recommendation ITU-R TF.460–6.

[10] Currently, discussions are going on as to whether leap seconds are to be abolished as they could threaten computer systems. See McMillan 2015.

[11] See, for example, the following quote: 'It is a commonplace that time, not space, is the dimension of change.' Le Poidevin and MacBeath 1993, at 1.

whether and how law is subject to change. This question is part of the temporality of the law. Like the concept of time, the temporality of law, and of international law in particular, has never been defined in an absolute manner but only by relying on workable concepts. Workable concepts are agreed collective assumptions of time, which are necessary for all parts of society. A concept of time underlies the concept of law. These underlying concepts shall be referred to as paradigms, which are taken to be assumptions common to all relevant (legal) actors.[12] As Thomas Kuhn has shown, such paradigms underlie scientific discourse even in the natural sciences.[13] Whether ideas, claims and propositions are to be conceived as true and acceptable is often dependent upon the prevailing paradigms. In cases of competition, a shift of paradigms might occur, which results in a scientific revolution leading to a different view of the very same matter. The present contribution aims to apply this approach to temporal paradigms in international law.

5.2 Paradigm Shifts

As a hypothesis, three temporal paradigms are laid out. They will be called atemporality, temporality and fluxus. They describe the basic stances that international lawyers can take in relation to the temporal dimension of international law. The paradigm of atemporality represents the idea that international law is eternal and unchangeable. Under this paradigm, international law is totally independent and separate from and not affected by time. The paradigm of temporality expresses the stance that international law is ascertainable and changeable but that it also endures for a fixed and specified amount of time. It endures for a certain time, mostly until it is changed. The paradigm of fluxus is based on the idea that international law is necessarily unsteady, moving and changing. Those paradigms can be traced in the scholarly reflection of international law as well as in international legal practice. The creation of international law as we know it coincided with a shift from atemporality to temporality. As of now, the temporal paradigm is competing with fluxus, but it is not clear which paradigm will prevail. Before engaging with this question, we will revisit the first paradigm shift from the paradigm of atemporality to the paradigm of temporality that is called the temporalisation of international law.

[12] The use of the word ‘paradigm’ can be misleading as even Kuhn, who coined the phrase in this context, did not use the term consistently and later even dropped it. This is why this term is used only in one of the many potential meanings.

[13] Kuhn 1996.

5.2.1 *The Temporalisation of International Law*

5.2.1.1 Scholarly Approaches

The concept of *ius gentium* has evolved substantially over time.[14] Cicero's definitions are considered to be the earliest available systematic definitions of this term, the Latin equivalent to the term law of nations.[15] Cicero did not generally restrict *ius gentium* to a class of actors or just to the relations of different peoples. His conception came very close to natural law and was basically the law attaching to human nature applying between individuals as well as peoples. This also had significant temporal consequences. In the discourse in *de republica*, Cicero laid down a concept of the *lex aeterna* entailing a particular temporal vision:

> True law is right reason in agreement with nature; it is of universal application, unchanging and everlasting … It is a sin to try to alter this law, nor is it allowable to attempt to repeal any part of it, and it is impossible to abolish it entirely. We cannot be freed from its obligations by senate or people, and we need not look outside ourselves for an expounder or interpreter of it. And there will be different laws at Rome and at Athens, or different laws now and in the future, but one eternal and unchangeable law will be valid for all nations and all times …[16]

This is a definition of the *lex aeterna*, establishing the basic idea that there is an eternal and unchangeable law. This law was binding upon all nations, thus the concept of *lex aeterna* encompasses the concept of international law. On another occasion, Cicero explicitly associated the *ius gentium* with natural law and described it as being applicable among all nations.[17]

The same thought can be found in the great codification of Roman law, the *Corpus Iuris Civilis*. In its definition of *ius gentium*, it focused on the laws in existence in all jurisdictions.[18] Later in the text, the temporality of at least a part of the *ius gentium* was explicitly addressed:

> Now, natural laws, which are followed by all nations alike, deriving from divine providence, remain always constant and immutable: but those which each state establishes for itself are liable to frequent change whether by the tacit consent of the people or by subsequent legislation.[19]

This part of the tekst opposes a universal *lex aeterna* with the law in specific nations that is subject to change. The idea of the *lex aeterna* was explicitly relied upon by Augustine and Thomas Aquinas; the defining feature of *ius gentium* was that it was directly deduced from natural law.[20]

---

[14] For a conceptual analysis of the term, see Steiger 1992; Djeffal 2013.

[15] For a general treatment of the notion of *ius gentium* see Kaser 1993, at 14–20.

[16] Cicero, *De Republica*, III, 33. Translated by Grewe 1995, at 173.

[17] Cicero, *De Officiis* 3, 17, 69.

[18] *Codex Iustianus*, I, 2, 1; translation by Grewe 1995, at 169.

[19] Ibid., I, 2, 11; translation by Grewe 1995, at 172.

[20] Thomas Aquinas, *Summa theologica*, Book I, at 95 a. 4 co. For an interpretation of this section, see Schilling 1919, at 18–29. See also Grewe 2000, at 85–86.

They reinforced the general idea that natural law was valid irrespective of place and time and no human law could conflict with it and remain valid.[21] This could be considered the peak of the paradigm of atemporality in international law.

Authors like Suárez, Grotius, Wolff and Vattel contributed to a shift from this atemporal paradigm towards temporality. This temporalisation[22] of international law coincided with what is frequently referred to as the creation of classical international law. It was succinctly being seen as positive and not exclusively natural law. It is interesting that the first modern authors of international law explicitly addressed the temporality of law in general and of international law in particular. With his treatise *de lege*, Francisco Suárez laid down a general jurisprudence that also included some revolutionary thoughts about international law. He distinguished between divine and human law and explained that human law was temporal whereas divine law was eternal.[23] A great achievement of Suárez was to situate the law of nations in a completely new way by setting it apart from natural law. He compared natural law and the law of nations in their spatial and temporal dimension and arrived at common as well as distinctive features. Spatially, natural law and the law of nations were both universal in the sense that they applied to all nations. Regarding their temporality, natural law was unchangeable and eternal while the law of nations was subject to changes like all human law.[24] So while there was an eternal law, Suárez regarded the law of nations as human and therefore, temporal, and changeable.

Hugo Grotius upheld the idea that there was a law of nature that 'is unchangeable,–even in the sense that it cannot be changed by God'.[25] Even though he remained in the tradition of the *lex aeterna*, he allowed for several exceptions: despite its perpetuity, the conditions of its operations were subject to change. So, in a different setting, the law of nature was to be interpreted differently. Yet, international law belonged to the category of human law, which Grotius explicitly distinguished from natural law.[26] Citing *Dio Chrysostom*, he observed that the law of nations 'is the creation of time and custom'.[27] The law of nations was created in time, it was changeable and it was human. International law was not eternal but temporal in that it could change over time.

---

[21] See the summary by Grewe 2000, at 85.

[22] The term 'temporalisation' is borrowed from Koselleck 1997. He used this term to exemplify the basic tenants of conceptual history.

[23] Suárez 1944 [1612], at 172 (Book II, Chapter IV, 8).

[24] Suárez grounded this observation in the fact that natural law was directly derived from the good and evil nature of things while the law of nations was not necessarily attached to such categories. It 'does not forbid evil acts on the ground that they are evil, but renders [certain] acts evil by prohibiting them.' Ibid., at 342 (Book II Chapter XIX 2).

[25] Grotius 1925, at 40 (Book I, Chap I, X, 5).

[26] Ibid., at 44 (Book I, Chap I, XIV, 1–2).

[27] Ibid.

A very categorical and explicit treatment of the problems of temporality can be found with Christian Wolff in his treatise *Jus Gentium Methodo Scientifica Pertractum*. He developed a categorisation of the law of nations based on its sources. He denoted the category of the law of nations that also belonged to natural law as the 'necessary law of nations', and defined as 'law of nature applied to nations'.[28] The defining characteristic of the necessary law of nations was that it is immutable, which he explicitly derived from the immutability of the law of nations.[29] The 'voluntary law of nations', forming the second category, could be directly deduced from the necessary law of nations.[30] It provided for the general legal institutions and principles allowing for the operation of the legal system. The voluntary law rests on the assumed consent of all nations. The third category is the 'stipulative law of nations' resting on the express consent and the customary law of nations that stems from the implied consent of nations. The stipulative and customary law of nations were changeable and, therefore, temporal. So, Wolff provided for a gradual system distinguishing between natural and positive law. This refined system of the categories and sources of the law of nations allowed a permanent and perpetual foundation combined with durable but also changeable elements that comes very close to the current doctrine of sources. The category of voluntary law stands between natural and positive law. It is derived from natural law by an assumed consensus between all states and provides the basis for positive international law. All in all, Wolff combined atemporal and temporal notions are combined in his system.

Emer de Vattel followed the exposition of his teacher and relied on the same categories and explicitly stated that states could not change the necessary law of nature.[31] Even though he rendered the voluntary law of nations much more concrete by using the society of states as the basis of state sovereignty and the freedom of states resulting from it,[32] Vattel clearly emphasised that states were bound by the necessary law of nations just as individuals and that this law was immutable just as natural law.[33]

The scholars who have been reviewed so far partly departed from the paradigm of atemporality and included temporal elements. They based positive international law on an eternal and unchangeable core. Christian Wolff provided for a general categorisation with temporal as well as atemporal elements. The eternal *nucleus* left in his conception of international law was questioned by positivists who

[28] Wolff 1934, at 4 (Book 1 Prolegomena para 4).

[29] Ibid., at 10 (Book 1 Prolegomena para 5).

[30] Ibid., at 17–18 (Book 1 Prolegomena para 22).

[31] Vattel 1995 [1916], at 49–57 (Preliminaries, paras 1–57).

[32] Wolff stressed the collective of states much more, which he described as *civitas maxima*. Wolff 1934, at 11.

[33] Vattel 1995 [1916], at 50–51 (Preliminaries, paras 8–9).

furthered conceptions solely based on the paradigm of temporality.[34] Johan Wolfgang Textor, for example, departed from a strict separation of *ius gentium* and natural law. While he thought that they had a common ground in natural reason, he emphasised that they

> differ[ed], however, in the manner of their development; for the Law of Nature issues direct from Natural Reason, whereas the Law of Nations issues through the medium of international usage, upon which the varying conditions and relations of human life have exercised a preeminent influence.[35]

The positive approach was also translated into the temporal construction of the law of nations: as it was based upon the usage of states, the later usage would replace and override the former so that the law of nations could develop and change.[36]

Richard Zouche founded the law of nature and the law of nations in right reason but separated them as to their sources[37]: the law of nature was derived by the right conclusion from the first principles of nature, while the law of nations rested on the consent of states. He interestingly observed that right reason could reveal itself in the long-standing and universal agreement of nations. Right reason was, however, in Zouche's thinking not a necessary condition for the validity of a norm of international law. To use his own words,

> besides common customs, anything upon which single nations agree with other single nations, for example by compacts, conventions and treaties, must also be deemed to be law between nations, since the solemn promise of a state establishes law, and whole peoples, no less than single persons, are bound by their own consent.[38]

The positivist tradition in international law[39] could clearly be considered as the ruling paradigm at the beginning of the 19th century.[40] Together with this shift towards a positivist view of international law came its temporalisation. The temporalisation in international legal scholarship happened gradually. While Christian Wolff developed a system including an unchanging part of the law that he framed

---

[34] For an overview of the positivistic scholarship in international law, see Nussbaum 1958, at 164–185.

[35] Textor 1916 [1680], at 4 (Chapter 1, para 11).

[36] Ibid., at 5 (Chapter 1, para 15). It is very interesting that natural law rather indirectly breaks into his line of argument when he states that '[t]his is especially so in view of the frequent mutations of human life, in which Right Reason finds the justification of dictating now one and now another law to States.' Ibid. As previously stated, right reason was in Textor's conception the common basis for the law of nature and the law of nations. It has to be acknowledged that the quoted passage restricts right reason to a general justification for changes and not the element triggering change.

[37] Zouche 1916 [1650], at 1 (Part 1, Sect. 1, para 1).

[38] Ibid., at 1 (Part 1, Sect. 1, para 1).

[39] For the purposes of the present inquiry, it does not seem to be necessary to look at the scholars denying the legal nature of international law such as Austin and Spinoza. If international law is not considered as law, no issue of its temporality can arise.

[40] Grewe 2000, at 502.

necessary law, other authors such as Johann Wolfgang Textor separated the law of nations categorically from natural law and established that the law of nations was temporal and changeable.

5.2.1.2 Practice of Peace Treaties: The Temporalisation of Eternal Peace

This general shift from atemporality to temporality can also be shown in state practice. One good point of reference in that regard is the notion of peace in peace treaties. It is obvious from the very name of a peace treaty that the *telos* of such a treaty is peace. From the classical authors mentioned above, there was also a clear understanding that there were generally two sets or—to use a rather modern term—regimes of international law: the law of war and the law of peace. Many books have relied on this as the most fundamental distinction and it is telling that we find this in the title of Grotius' most famous book *De jure belli ac pacis*. From this we can conclude that the notion of peace was central for scholars of international law, but it was also essential to practice:

Peace treaties have been concluded throughout human history. Yet, they have entailed different notions of peace: a normative vision of perpetual or eternal peace or a rather factual vision defining peace as the absence of violence which could be broken at any time if it conflicted with the *raison d'état*. There is evidence that the notion of peace in peace treaties was being temporalised in the sense that it moved away from the idea of general and eternal peace to a rather temporal notion of peace functioning as a factual description. The difference between the two notions is very well expressed in Immanuel Kant's famous *Perpetual Peace*, which he wrote in the form of an international treaty accompanied by a commentary. The project was aimed at outlining the requirements of a general and perpetual peace, and he began by setting out six articles that should immediately be observed, which he called preliminary articles. The first of those is that no peace treaty ought to be concluded with a hidden reservation for future war.[41] In this section, Kant interestingly argued that the very term perpetual peace ought to be regarded as a pleonasm since an unperpetual peace ought to be regarded merely as a cessation of hostilities and not as peace as such. From this it can be inferred that in his definition the perpetuity was a necessary criterion for the very notion of peace. A mental reservation as to the perpetuity of peace was enough for Kant to void the peace treaty. At the end of this article, Kant remarked that if one were thinking in terms of *raison d'état*, his idea would seem rather remote and pedantic. So Kant himself admitted that his idea would not appeal to realists. Such a mind frame opposed to Kant's could be found with Carl von Clausewitz, who argued that the reasons for peace were that states either satisfied their interest for which they had started the war or ceded hostilities to wait for a

[41] Kant 1796, first preliminary article.

better opportunity.[42] The Clausewitzian vision of war was instrumental; the pursued object justified breaches of the peace.[43] This means in turn that the end of a war is by no means absolute, but is seen by the conquered state as a 'passing evil' that can be changed later.[44]

The historian Jörg Fisch conducted a study on peace treaties throughout history.[45] His quantitative analysis shows that peace treaties were steadily concluded for an unlimited period of time, but that the notion of peace changed from a qualitative and more precisely temporal point of view: it became less important and more relative. Some examples will illustrate his observations. The importance of the eternal concept of peace is particularly obvious when it is included in the name of the treaty such as in the case of the Eternal Peace of 1686 between Russia and Poland. The importance of eternal and perpetual peace derived from the preambles to the treaties but also from general or specific provisions in the treaties. This can be very well shown by looking at the Peace of Treaty of Osnabrück (*Instrumentum Pacis Osnabrugensis*), which is one of the two treaties representing the Westphalian Peace ending the Thirty Years War.[46] The preamble to this treaty tells the story of the peace process and how the parties decided to negotiate on a universal peace (*de pace universali*), which in that context meant a peace including all parties to the conflict. Article I of the treaty set out a general obligation of keeping the peace and clearly emphasised the temporal dimension of peace as perpetual.[47] The same article stipulates that the treaty ought to further utility, honour and advantages for all parties in order to achieve a true peace. The basis of the perpetual peace is enshrined in Article II, which grants a general and perpetual amnesty. Another interesting feature is enshrined in Article XVII of the treaty stipulating in its second section that the treaty ought to be perpetually enshrined in the constitution of the Holy Roman Empire (*perpetua lex et pragmatica imperii sanctio*) that was to be implemented on the next occasion as constitutional law and that ought to be recognised by all relevant actors within the Holy Empire for all times (*tanquam regula quam perpetuo sequantur*). This is very interesting since the treaty did not only foresee its own perpetuity but also the perpetuity of the implementation into the constitution of the Holy Roman Empire. This matched with a general trend from the Westphalian Peace to the 19th century: the perpetuity of the notion of peace was accompanied by the explicit perpetuity of provisions of the treaty enshrining the peace as well as this treaty as a whole. Even when the Westphalian

---

[42] See von Clausewitz 1832–1834, Chapters 1 and 13.

[43] Ibid., Chapters 1 and 2.

[44] Ibid., Chapters 1 and 9.

[45] Fisch 1979, at 333. In line with the methodological limitations as set out above, the present study shall be confined in its historical sections to the relations between European states, which leaves the Sublime Port, China and colonial relations out of the picture.

[46] On the temporality of peace in the peace treaties of Westphalia, see Duchhardt 2004, at 49. For a general description, see Fassbender 2012b.

[47] The phrase used in Latin reads '*pax sit christiana, universalis, perpetua*'.

Peace was violated in the Franco-Dutch War of 1672–78, the Peace Treaty of Nijmingen between the Emperor and France stipulated not only a 'Christian, Universal, True and Sincere Peace' but extended this also temporally to their 'heirs and successors'.[48] In Article II, the parties also founded their agreement in the Treaty of Muenster and, therefore, reinstalled the Westphalian Peace.

This development can be contrasted with developments in the 19th century during which perpetual peace was generally included in the treaties, while the context indicated that eternal peace was not really envisaged. This can be interpreted as a shift as the term 'eternal' has a religious connotation and is also even extensive in that it extends time without beginning or end whereas perpetual can have the meaning of extending without end into the future but not into the past. As an example for such a treaty, one could look at the Peace Treaty Concerning the Termination of the Crimean War of 1856/Paris.[49] It included in Article I the general reference to perpetual peace, extending the obligation to 'heirs and successors … in perpetuity'. Other than the Treaty of Osnabrück, the amnesty clause in Article II contained no perpetual reference. Article VIII provided for an obligation of allowing mediation before resorting to the use of force. This provision was aimed at preserving peace, yet, the fact that it made the use of force only dependent upon compliance with a formal requirement also indicated that the treaty at least envisaged further hostilities. This might be considered a realistic and open provision. It embraced peace, but it generally accepted the possibility of future wars, which cannot be reconciled with a general obligation to keep the peace. In the Prusso-Austrian Peace Treaty of 1866, the only perpetual reference is again the prolongation of the treaty 'to heirs and successors … henceforth and forever' in Article I; apart from this, no other reference to perpetual peace was included. These two treaties exemplify the diminished importance of the notion of peace in peace treaties. Another trend substantiating the finding of a change in the notion of peace is that mutual guarantees of peace vanished, instead unilateral guarantees of peace were made subject to the condition of the fulfilment of obligations in the treaty such as the payment of reparations.[50]

Another good example is the Congress of Berlin of 1878 which led to the Treaty of Berlin 1878. When the Russian representative, Gortschakow, asked for a guarantee by all parties to the treaty to enforce it also with forceful means, Bismarck, acting as a mediator at this conference, stepped in. He explained that he did not believe that there was a formula that could save Europe and protect it with absolute certainty from repeating the incidents that stirred it up.[51] The Congress could only do what men do and which was subject to the ups and downs of history. Therefore, Bismarck discarded the idea that a general and lasting peace could be created and secured.

---

[48] Grewe 1988, at 205.

[49] Reprinted in Grewe 1992, at 19.

[50] Steiger 2004, at 91.

[51] Geiss 1979, at 151.

As commentators have pointed out, the commitment to perpetual peace diminished substantially.[52] This is another indication that the relationship was temporalised in the sense that peace was limited temporally to the next use of force. The notion of peace temporalised. It moved from a Kantian idea of perpetual peace to a limited peace as envisaged by Clausewitz. The temporalisation of peace as fleshed out here reinforces the general shift that was pointed out before from atemporality to temporality.

5.2.2 The Flexibilisation of International Legal Time?

Under the paradigm of fluxus the law is seen as necessarily developing and moving. The question that is asked in this chapter is whether fluxus has become the main paradigm in international legal scholarship and practice. Whereas atemporality regards the law as unchangeable and temporality sees it as steady for a limited duration, the notion of fluxus emphasises that there is not even limited steadiness.[53] Under the paradigm of fluxus, law is viewed as unsteady and continuously changing. In support of this contention it could be argued that there is an increasing trend towards such abrupt changes. To give one example concerning the continental shelf, two authors have observed that important general norms of international law such as the law of territory can change from one day to another.[54] There are different ways to explain this general observation: either by sticking to temporality and explaining the new perception by a circumstantial acceleration in law and society, or by rethinking the relationship between law and time in order to adjust it to the constant changes in the law. The latter would result in claiming the paradigm of fluxus.

Sticking to temporality, one could contend that law still endures for a limited amount of time, but due to internal and external necessities, changes just happen more frequently. This can be explained with new legal mechanisms and procedures that facilitate norm creation in international law, such as mechanisms for producing the secondary law of international organisations. But there might also be external triggers for such a development. In sociology, a continuing trend towards social acceleration has been identified which is triggered by societal, technological and personal developments.[55] This acceleration in some parts of society would then require other areas, such as law, to react in an ever quicker manner to the new challenges.

Yet, it would also be possible to replace the paradigm of temporality and its underlying assumptions with another temporal concept of international law that is more in tune with its frequently occurring changes. An influential theory

[52] Neff 2005, at 177; Fisch 1979, at 366–367. For an account that peace clauses were much briefer but still contained a reference to a normative vision of peace, see Steiger 2004, at 82.

[53] This is again an ideal-typical definition aimed at clearly bringing out the important features of the general paradigm in its purest form.

[54] Crawford and Viles 1994.

[55] For an overview, see Rosa 2003.

emphasised that international law ought to be viewed rather as a process than a system of rules.[56] This stream of international legal thinking was inspired by American legal realism as well as similar views in international relations.[57] The major shift was to focus on decisions of legal actors rather than on rules.[58] Rosalyn Higgins, for instance, defined international law as a 'continuing process of authoritative decisions.'[59] For her, rules 'are just past decisions' and not abstract and general entities from which certain results are to be deduced.[60] International legal process scholarship then either just empirically described the decisions taken by international legal actors or complemented them with a normative value framework that ought to guide the policy decisions of the actors. Irrespective of whether a normative approach is pursued, the construction of international law as a process has serious consequences for its temporal construction. If there is no preconceived rule having a separate existence and no essence, it would also be hard to attribute a general duration to any rule. When a competent person has to decide, this can be done in line with previous decisions or by departing from them. The decision-maker has the choice. This is the first challenge to the paradigm temporality. Another problem is that there might be patterns of behaviour but those can change and they are never exactly the same either.[61] A decision might be situated in very similar circumstances as compared to previous decisions. But they are never exactly the same. This means that by necessity the law is changing. Seeing law as a process, every legal decision is at least a possibility to alter previous decisions. What is more, no decision occurs in exactly the same circumstances, which is why every decision entails something new. From this point of view, abstract and enduring rules are an *ex post facto* construction that does not really capture what the law is about. Decisions, however, only occur at certain points in time. They are singular acts instead of general enduring rules.

To see international law as a process means that the concept of temporality can no longer be upheld. In current international legal discourse, this is, however, far from agreed. The paradigms of temporality and fluxus currently compete. The three case studies that follow aim at testing the potential of the competing paradigms to explain norms in time and to point to the possible consequences of employing one paradigm or the other. Every case study highlights one particular problem in the field of the three accepted formal sources of international law and will illustrate how questions of temporality play out in international law and where international law stands now in relation to the competing paradigms. Concerning

---

56 General overviews of scholarly discourse can be found in O'Connell 1999; Koh 1997. For a recent attempt stressing the rules rather than the process, see d'Asprémont 2011.

57 Falk 1995, at 1991.

58 McDougal 1956, at 55.

59 Higgins 1968, at 58–59.

60 Higgins 1994, at 3.

61 McDougal 1956, at 63.

the law of treaties, the first case study will briefly explain evolutive interpretations of the notion of peace and security in the United Nations Charter (Sect. 5.3.1). In the field of customary international law, we will look at the role of domestic courts creating exceptions to state immunity (Sect. 5.3.2). Regarding the general principles, we will look at the principle of sustainable development and its impact as a material international legal principle.

5.2.2.1 Evolutive Interpretation of the Notion of Security

To bring out the temporal implications of static and evolutive interpretations, we will focus on one of the most important terms in international law: security. The rise of the notion of security can be very well observed in the inter-war years between 1918 and 1945. In this period, security entered the academic discourse, the discipline of security studies was invented.[62] The League of Nations International Committee of Intellectual Cooperation organised a two-year collective research effort resulting in the 7th and 8th International Studies Conference on the topic 'collective security'. There were contributions by the leading international lawyers of the time, such as Hersch Lauterpacht, René Cassin and Georges Scelle.[63]

One indicator for the increased importance of the term 'security' can be derived from a content analysis determining the frequency of its use in the Charter. While the term 'security' is mentioned only once in the preamble to the Covenant of the League of Nations, it is mentioned 143 times in the Charter of the United Nations (UN Charter) and could be considered as the substantial concept[64] that is the most frequently used in the Charter.[65] The importance of security in the UN Charter rests not only on quantitative observations; the Preamble mentions peace and security as an end: the first purpose mentioned in Article 1(1) UN Charter is to maintain international peace and security. Articles 39, 42 and 43 empower the Security Council to take forceful measures to maintain or restore international peace and security. The fact that the main organ of the United Nations vested with the greatest legal powers is itself called the Security Council as opposed to the 'Peace Council' or the like again reinforces the central importance of security in the Charter. Yet, the notion of security has evolved substantially over time. All of those changes occurred after the end of the cold war.

Traditionally, security was conceived as the security of states. In 1994, the United Nations Development Programme released a Human Development report that included, amongst other things, the new concept of human security. One of its

[62] McDonald and Brollowski 2012, para 7.

[63] Bourquin 1936.

[64] By this, I mean words apart from auxiliary words like 'or' 'the' or 'and'.

[65] Actually, eight words are used more frequently, those are 'the' 'of' 'and' 'to' 'in' 'shall' 'article' and 'council'. The phrase 'security' is either used in the context of 'peace and security' or regarding the 'Security Council', save for Article 83(3) UN Charter.

defining features was to shift from a state-centric notion of security to a notion of security that focused on people.[66] This understanding has been underlying other developments in the notion of security as well. While security was originally constructed internationally with a focus on cross-border action,[67] it was later claimed that it transcended the international and also relates to national and transnational actions. It is not only about cross-border actions from states but also from non-state actors such as terrorists: the Security Council has recently stipulated that 'terrorism in all forms and manifestations constitutes one of the most serious threats to international peace and security'.[68] Another important trend is that the threats that security protects against have proliferated. In 1992, Secretary-General Boutros Boutros Ghali redefined security as follows:

> The concept of peace is easy to grasp; that of international security is more complex, for a pattern of contradictions has arisen here as well. … Technological advances are altering the nature and the expectation of life all over the globe. The revolution in communications has united the world in awareness, in aspiration and in greater solidarity against injustice. But progress also brings new risks for stability: ecological damage, disruption of family and community life, greater intrusion into the lives and rights of individuals.[69]

The Report of the High-Level Panel on Threats, Challenges and Change that was summoned by the Secretary-General also looked towards poverty, infectious diseases and environmental degradation and transnational organised crime.[70]

In summary, security has substantially evolved from an international outlook focusing on physical violence between states on a large scale to national and transnational dangers for human beings involving many threats that must have seemed rather remote to the drafters of the Charter. Can this remarkable evolutive interpretation be explained by the paradigm of temporality or does it rather point to fluxus? To answer this question, we have to look at how the relevant actors construct this evolutive interpretation. The Secretary-General Boutros Boutros Ghali stressed that the United Nations, being 'a gathering of sovereign states', depended on the 'common ground' that the states accepted among themselves.[71] He then went on to observe a 'changing context' in which he situated the new meaning of security.[72] This line of argumentation can be seen even more clearly in the High-Level Panel Report: after describing the new security threats mentioned above, the Panel stated that the 'central challenge for the twenty-first century is to fashion a

[66] United Nations Development Programme, Human development report, 1994, at 22–23.

[67] Report of the High-Level Panel on Threats, Challenges, and Change, A more secure world. Our shared responsibility, 2004, at 1 and 9.

[68] UNSC Res. 2119, 17 December 2013.

[69] Quoted by McDonald and Brollowski 2012, § 10.

[70] Report of the High-Level Panel on Threats, Challenges, and Change, A more secure world. Our shared responsibility, 2004, at 24–27.

[71] UN Secretary-General, An agenda for peace. Preventive diplomacy, peace-making and peace-keeping, A/47/277–S/24111, 31 January 1992, para 2.

[72] Ibid., para 8 ff.

new and broader understanding, bringing together all these strands, of what collective security means.'[73] The way in which such a new understanding is to be fashioned has been described as 'a new security consensus'.[74] The Panel did not make any efforts to link its findings to the drafters of the Charter,[75] but looked for a new consensus in the face of changed circumstances. Those circumstances are described in the most dramatic fashion speaking about 'Different worlds: 1945 and 2005'.[76] The impact of these changes had to be fully understood, while they indicated a 'fundamentally different security climate'.[77]

How is such a development possible under general international law? Such questions are frequently formulated as a choice between static and dynamic interpretation. They arise when the meaning of a provision in a treaty is changed through interpretation. Evolutive interpretation has attracted a great deal of attention[78] since there is a trend towards evolutive interpretation in international law.[79] Under international law, questions of stasis and evolution are to be determined according to the rule of interpretation as enshrined in the Vienna Convention on the Law of Treaties (VCLT), in particular Articles 31 and 32. Under certain circumstances, the interpreter is competent to attest a changing meaning of the text of a treaty such as the notion of peace and security. The changing interpretation of the concept of peace and security is based on flexibility pointing towards the paradigm of fluxus. It seems that the understanding of the term by particular actors, in the present case actors such as the Security Council, the Secretary-General or the High-Level Panel, are determinative. Those actors decide based upon present challenges and compromises; the outcome of their decisions often has a new quality that is very far from the original understanding.

Yet, the evolutive interpretation of the notion of peace and security can also be understood from the perspective of the paradigm of temporality. The High-Level Panel Report looked for a 'new security consensus'. From the perspective of temporality, the consensus is something ascertainable that, once it is reached, endures to the next consensus and is, therefore, an expression of the temporality in the field of the interpretation of international treaties. On the other hand, one could also point to the fluidity of the concept itself, and to the fact that it largely depends on what states think at a certain point in time. From this perspective, one could question whether and to what extent a consensus reached on the interpretation could

---

[73] Report of the High-Level Panel on Threats, Challenges, and Change, A more secure world. Our shared responsibility, 2004, at 9 and 11.

[74] Ibid., at 11 and 15.

[75] For such an enterprise, see Abbott 2002.

[76] Report of the High-Level Panel on Threats, Challenges, and Change, A more secure world. Our shared responsibility, 2004, at 10.

[77] Ibid., at 14.

[78] See the respective parts of the three reports reprinted in Nolte 2013. See also Fitzmaurice 2008, 2010; Linderfalk 2011; Venzke 2012; Bjorge 2014. See also Djeffal 2015.

[79] Nolte 2012, at 1679.

really and substantially programme the way in which security is looked at in the future. This observation would again point towards fluxus. Both paradigms offer explanations as to how the meaning of the term security has been changed, yet both frame the process of that evolution in a very particular way. Fluxus focuses on the actions of the interpreters whereas temporality aims at ascertaining the content through legal method.

5.2.2.2 Changing Custom and Domestic Courts: New Exceptions to State Immunities

Article 38(1)(b) of the Statute of the International Court of Justice (ICJ Statute) defines the source of customary international law as 'international custom, as evidence of a general practice accepted as law'. In the mainstream methodology as well as in international legal practice, from this definition two criteria were deduced, namely *consuetudo* or state practice and *opinio iuris sive necessitatis*.

Legal practice as well as mainstream methodology requires evidence of those two elements. An interesting problem in this regard would be to look at custom formation as well as changes in customary law from a temporal perspective. Textor asked the question of 'what amount of time' was necessary for the formation of customary law.[80] He interestingly came up with a solution, which we would conceive today as being quite modern: he thought that 'any interval or period of time is enough for the introduction' of customary international law.[81] For him, every state had to engage in the custom, but it would be enough to engage once. The idea of instant custom was foreseen by Textor. His conception of custom could be considered to be in the middle of two extreme temporal conceptions of customary international law: the idea that custom ought to be practised over a substantial period of time to become binding on others, and the idea that custom can be changed at any time by courts. The first view is strongly related to the actual practice of the participants forming the custom. If the main focus lies on mere actions, it takes some time to stabilise the expectations so that the custom is ascertainable. Examples for such approaches can be found within traditional doctrine, especially during the period of the existence of the League of Nations.[82] Common law represents the other extreme since it is not really related to the actions of the legal subjects but is rather determined by courts and their system of judicial precedent. It is interesting to see that common law originated from a customary order being based on the practice of the King's court,[83] but then went on to emancipate itself. Such a customary system would be very

---

80 Textor 1916 [1680], at 6 (Chapter 1, para 20).

81 Ibid., at 6 (Chapter 1, para 21).

82 See with further references Verdross and Simma 1984, at 361.

83 Plucknett 2001 [1956], at 313.

close to the paradigm of fluxus because the judicial actors, if they are not bound by precedent, could at any time change the respective law. Is international law moving in this direction? To provide an answer to this question in an exemplary fashion, we will look at the role national that courts play in the determination of exceptions to state immunity.

State immunity is an expression of the sovereign equality of all states which was already articulated in the *maxim par in parem non habet imperium,* which can be traced back to *Bartolus de Sassoferato*. It has been customary that no state could exercise jurisdiction over another state. Any incident in which the actions of another state are determined by foreign domestic courts against its will used to amount to violations of customary international law. At the end of the 19th century, there was a significant trend to create limits to the doctrine of state immunity by distinguishing the nature of the acts of states. While *acta iure imperii* or sovereign acts were still immune from the jurisdiction of other states, *acta iure gestionis* or commercial acts did not fall under state immunity. It is interesting that this trend was created by domestic courts, starting in Italy and then followed by the Belgian, Egyptian, Austrian and English courts.[84]

Domestic courts can play an important role in the ascertainment of customary international law as they are organs of the state and judicial bodies at the same time.[85] They adjudicate in the name of the people, which means the people in their respective state but they are also independent bodies determining the law in a neutral and objective manner. This Janus-headedness could be conceived as giving them a special competence to change customary law to a larger extent as compared to international courts since they combine the authority of being an organ of a state with the status of being a neutral and objective interpreter and applier of international law. This could be an argument for the special status of domestic courts when it comes to customary international law. An attempt to alter the law was made by the Italian Corte di Cassazione, which held that the doctrine of state immunity was not applicable in cases of a violation of *ius cogens* norms,[86] i.e. the court purported to have found another exception to state immunity. It thereby purported to modify an institution of customary international law. The case came before the International Court of Justice (ICJ) and the question was whether lifting the immunity and admitting the case to be heard before an Italian court violated Germany's right to immunity. The ICJ stuck to the traditional method of validating changes in customary international law and denoted the decision of the Italian

[84] For a detailed analysis, see the ILC's Draft Convention on the Law of State Immunities, reprinted in Watts 1999, at 2052.

[85] Roberts 2011, at 60.

[86] Ferrini Corte di Cassazione (Sezioni Unite), Judgment, No 5044, 6 November 2003, registered 11 March 2004, 87 Rivista diritto internazionale (2004) 539. It should be mentioned that the Corte Constitutionale followed the ICJ in its determination of customary international law, but went on to establish the supremacy of the Italian constitution over international law. For this latter aspect, see Corte Constitutionale 238/2014.

courts as isolated practice that was considered to be illegal.[87] Regarding the status of *ius cogens*, the ICJ held that there was no norm conflict between the law of state immunity and preceding violations of *ius cogens*. It is also significant that the ICJ looked at state practice, and especially the practice of national courts also in this regard.[88] The judgment of the ICJ cannot be understood as accepting the notion of fluxus, and the court rather adhered to a temporal vision of customary international law. It can change quite quickly, but changes will always have to be related to actions of states and no changes will be made until sufficient uniformity is achieved.[89] Customary international law generally endures as long as it is not abrogated by contrary practice.

To ascertain changing custom is, nevertheless, not free from questions challenging the paradigm of temporality. Firstly, breaches could be subsequently legalised if other participants replicate the violation. Today's lawbreaker can become tomorrow's lawmaker. If a substantial number of states follow a state breaking the custom, this could lead to a state of fuzziness in which it is not clear whether states have actually changed the custom, whether the old custom is still in existence or whether the rule has become obsolete. The ICJ took a very clear stance on both issues. Its method took a clear temporal stance. According to the immunities case, the practice reviewed by the Court reinforces the temporal paradigm as custom is still rooted in the actions of the participants, i.e. the states. Domestic courts are viewed primarily as organs of the state, they are not accepted as authoritative decision-makers, rather their practice is through the traditional method of finding customary international law. The method employed by the Corte di Cassatione would point more towards fluxus. A different assessment of the law based on the non-derogable status of *ius cogens* could generally lead to more dynamism and the independent assessment of the law by single actors. The traditional method as used by the ICJ is more in line with the paradigm of temporality than with fluxus as it looks for a consensus in the practice of states. As long as the consensus is there, the law endures. The law cannot be changed by single actors in a rather spontaneous manner.

5.2.2.3 Sustainable Development and the Materialisation of International Law

Article 38(1)(c) ICJ Statute also mentions 'the general principles of law recognized by civilized nations' as a source of law. Examples of such general principles include good faith and *estoppel*. These are all rather general or technical principles. From the outset, it was not clear whether Article 38(1)(c) ICJ Statute would

87 *Jurisdictional Immunities of the State (Germany v. Italy: Greece intervening)*, ICJ, Judgment of 3 February 2012, paras 69–74, 83–89, 96.

88 Ibid., para 96.

89 Lepard 2010, at 35–36; Villiger 1997, at 24–25.

only import principles shared amongst all legal systems into the international sphere or whether there were also principles that were genuine to international law.[90] The text can be read either way: this recognition could be internal within the legal systems of the member states or external in the sense that states accepted them in the international sphere. During the drafting process of the Statute of the Permanent Court of International Justice, which contained a provision with almost the same text, Delegate La Pardelle remarked that principles could be based on principles in the national legal order (‘*principes qui sont à la base du droit national’*), while Delegate Fernandez remarked that they could also be based on international consensus thereon (‘*principes de droit supérieurs de tote controverse*’).[91] This difference has partly been captured by distinguishing between principles of law and principles of international law.[92]

Yet, principles are not necessarily only a source of law, they can also be seen as a category of norms that have features which are different from other categories such as rules.[93] Whereas sources confer legal validity on norms, categories of norms describe certain common features shared by norms (formal principles). Under certain conditions, norms have the status of a norm in international law (material principles). Among existing international legal norms are such that could be described as principles. They are described as flexible standards that influence the law rather indirectly and do not function in an all or nothing fashion.[94] In cases of intersections between different material principles, they would need to be weighed and balanced against each other. Principles as a category of norms can also be enshrined in treaties or customary international law. Article 2 UN Charter contains principles, such as sovereign equality and the peaceful settlement of disputes, which guide the actions of the organisation and its members. In this sense, there might be material principles of international law irrespective of which actual formal source they stem from.[95] One principle belonging to this category is the principle of sovereignty.[96] While the principle of sovereignty has a long tradition, the idea of principles as a category of norms is gaining ground in international legal scholarship and practice also in other areas of international law.[97] Borrowing a phrase from Max Weber, this development could be described as the ‘materialisation of international law’ as the law is not only based on formal rules but is enriched with material principles. This tendency also affects the way in which

---

[90] Schlüter 2010, at 74–86.

[91] Verdross and Simma 1984, at 383–384.

[92] For a detailed analysis with further references see Raimondo 2008, at 41.

[93] Ibid., at 41–42.

[94] Dworkin 1978, at 24–25.

[95] A major textbook based on this idea was written by the late Brownlie 2008, at 18–19.

[96] For a recent general treatment, see Crawford 2012. For a discussion of the similar notion of sovereign equality, see Fassbender 2012a.

[97] See, for example, Letsas 2004; Simma and Alston 1988–1989.

international law is conceived temporally, which shall be shown using the example of sustainable development.

The content as well as the *problematique* of sustainable development is best described by the definition of the World Commission on Environment and Development (the Brundtland Commission), which denoted sustainable development as 'development that meets the needs of the present without comprising the ability of future generations to meet their own needs'.[98] Three points of this formulation ought to be highlighted. First, the formal source of the principle of sustainable development is unclear. Second, sustainable development has a general temporal connotation in that it balances considerations of the present with considerations of the future which could also indicate something of the underlying temporal vision. Third, a general problematic feature of legal principles is that their legal effects vary to a significant extent.

Sustainable development has been mentioned in soft law instruments as well as in international treaties.[99] The normative status of the principle is, however, not clear. 'Is it an objective, or a process, or a principle or all of those things', a commentator once asked.[100] The ICJ described it in the *Gabčíkovo–Nagymaros* case as a concept and left its normative status open.[101] It was denoted as a legal principle in the *Iron Rhine* arbitration.[102] The arbitral tribunal interestingly decided not to enter into the controversies concerning the sources but went on to make the following statement:

> Importantly, these emerging principles now integrate environmental protection into the development process. Environmental law and the law on development stand not as alternatives but as mutually reinforcing, integral concepts, which require that where development may cause significant harm to the environment there is a duty to prevent, or at least mitigate, such harm … This duty, in the opinion of the Tribunal, has now become a principle of general international law. This principle applies not only in autonomous activities but also in activities undertaken in implementation of specific treaties between the Parties.[103]

It is significant that the tribunal established sustainable development as a principle between those two sentences. It found a common core of all 'emerging principles' and deduced from this that sustainable development has become a principle of general international law. It is remarkable that in the determination of the validity

---

[98] World Commission on Environment and Development, Our common future, 1987, at 43. See also United Nations Conference on Environment and Development, Rio Declaration on Environment and Development, 2–14 June 1992, principle 3.

[99] For an extensive overview, see Schrijver 2008.

[100] Sands 1995, at 305.

[101] *Gabčíkovo-Nagymaros Project* (*Hungary/Slovakia*), ICJ, Judgment of 25 September 1997, para 140.

[102] For details, see Djeffal 2011, at 579–585.

[103] *Iron Rhine Arbitration* (*Belgium/Netherlands*), Arbitral Tribunal, Judgment of 24 May 2004, para 59.

of this legal principle, the tribunal went beyond the ordinary doctrine of sources and deduced sustainable development from emerging principles.[104]

Regarding the content of the norm, the tribunal defined it as 'conservation, management, notions of prevention and of sustainable development, and protection for future generations'.[105] It stressed the environmental aspect of the principle. The ICJ gave the principle a slightly different meaning in the *Pulp Mills* case as it held that 'the balance between economic development and environmental protection … is the essence of sustainable development'.[106] It would also be possible to emphasise another aspect of the principle, namely the development in less developed states. One could also reconceptualise this tension as competing notions of inter-generational and intra-generational justice. The development of states seeks to achieve justice so that all human beings living together on Earth have a roughly equivalent status (intra-generational justice). Yet, sustainable development also seeks to achieve justice between current and future generations living on Earth (inter-generational justice). This means that sustainable development aims to marry different considerations in the way of balancing. It is not only a principle competing with other principles but a principle parts of which compete with each other internally:[107] applied to a problem separately, sustainability and development might point in different directions. This creates a tension within the notion of sustainable development that has to be resolved. From the perspective of temporality, one would say that the principle appears in different shapes at different times, stressing either intra-generational or inter-generational justice, but there is an abstract content as described above. From the perspective of fluxus, one would say that this principle is vague so that it is determined by different decision-makers. They set the priorities differently.

The flexibility inherent in the principle of sustainable development is all the more interesting in our context as it has a strong temporal aspect: development partly focuses on changing the present state of affairs by putting states on a more equal footing. The environmental aspect enshrined in the concept of sustainability is concerned with the future and aims at preserving Earth for future generations. Sustainable development is therefore an institutionalised balancing process between the needs of the present and the needs of the future. As a legal principle it functions as a temporal meta-norm as it imports assumed considerations of future generations into today's law. The evolution of the concept exemplifies the general problem of this principle as described above: it aims at

[104] Ibid., para 58.

[105] Ibid., para 58.

[106] *Pulp Mills on the River Uruguay* (*Argentina v Uruguay*), ICJ, Judgment of 20 April 2010, para 179.

[107] This is quite different from formal principles like the precautionary principle or proportionality. These latter principles are formal in that they require a balancing of the different material considerations in the respective situations. In contrast, sustainable development contains the two competing normative considerations.

marrying divergent considerations on which there has never been agreement. Therefore, it remains to be seen whether the principle will evolve in a way that it can be conceptualised as incrementally developing over time in a certain direction or whether it will be a flexible tool in the hands of different decision-makers. This flexibility can be of great benefit for international disputes especially in the so-called hard cases, as Dworkin has shown.[108] The principle of sustainable development might be well explained by the paradigm of fluxus since its content can currently be determined to a large extent by the person competent to render the decision based on the principle. All in all, the use of principles as a category of norms makes the legal system more flexible but harder to ascertain legal norms. Especially in the case of sustainable development, which is not only indeterminate but is composed of diametrically conflicting parts, it becomes clear that principles are pointing towards the temporal paradigm of fluxus.[109]

5.3 General Conclusions

The present article inquired into how the concept of time in society (social time) and, in particular, international lawyers have been seeing time. Three temporal paradigms have been assumed and substantiated in the present article: atemporality (unchangeabilty of the law), temporality (changeability and durability for specific periods of the law) and the paradigm of fluxus (moving, instable and changing character of the law). The paradigm shift from atemporality to temporality (the temporalisation of international law) was exemplified by several voices from legal scholarship and the different construction of the notion of peace in international peace treaties from the Treaty of Osnabrück to treaty practice in the 19th century. The idea of an eternal law vanquished, the notion of eternal peace was far less prominent in later treaty practice. Is there another paradigm shift from temporality to fluxus, as some voices viewing law as a process suggest? Three case studies looked into which paradigm can best explain specific problems relating to the sources of international law. A disputed question was whether there ought to be another exception to the law of state immunity in cases in which breaches of *ius cogens* norms are at issue. Such an exception was called for by certain domestic courts, which posed the question whether domestic courts ought to be regarded as more independent. The ICJ stuck to the traditional method that is much closer to the paradigm of temporality. The principle of sustainable development has already been applied as a legal principle in international law and aims at mitigating development considerations with environmental concerns. Those normative considerations are both included in this legal principle which makes its application very flexible. It is hard to predict which of the two elements of the principle will prevail in any specific case which is

[108] Dworkin 1975.

[109] This might not be true for every legal principle.

why this principle can be aptly explained by the paradigm of fluxus. The evolutive interpretation of the notion of security in the United Nations Charter can be explained from the perspective of both temporal paradigms, the paradigm of temporality and the paradigm of fluxus. It has changed substantially over time, which again points to fluxus. Yet, the relevant actors seem to believe that their consensus establishes its meaning. Such a consensus would endure for a limited time, which points towards temporality. Both paradigms can explain the evolutive interpretation of the term security, yet the respective paradigms show the meaning of the term and its changeability in a different light. All in all, the case studies suggest that the question whether there has been or will be a paradigm shift towards fluxus is open.

The paradigms that were introduced as hypotheses were framed in an ideal-typical manner. They served to illustrate certain approaches to time that were held in international legal scholarship and practice. The fact that we do not know how our general knowledge about time evolves poses another question: will international legal scholarship continue to analyse international law in this paradigmatic fashion that also produces certain general assumptions about time or is another mode of inquiry possible? Such an inquiry beyond the paradigmatic approach would not take a definite stance but try to view the problems from the perspective of different paradigms at the same time. The approaches of Christian Wolff and Emer de Vattel are examples of such a combination concerning the paradigm of atemporality and the paradigm of temporality. The result of such an analysis would be equivalent to a cubistic picture uniting different standpoints regarding one problem. It would result not only in a combination of the perspectives but transcending them. The inquiry would aim at showing all aspects of the problem at the same time. The method would then be different from the case study conducted above; it would not try to identify one fitting paradigm but would look at the cases through the lenses of all paradigms at the same time. What, then, is time? A cubistic enterprise would not answer this question but keep asking. Atemporality, temporality and fluxus would all be part of the picture (Table 5.1).

Table 5.1 Summary: the three temporal paradigms in international law

	Atemporality	Temporality	Fluxus
Concept of law	Natural law	Positivism	Post-positivism
How to find the law	Recognition	Ascertainment	Construction
Temporal state	Eternal	Measurable and Durable	Necessarily moving
Changeability	Unchangeable	Changeable	Changing
Temporal dimensions	Past, present and future	Present	Next moment
Construction of temporality	Transcendent	Immanent	Contingent

References

Abbott DW (2002) The United Nations and intrastate conflict: a legislative history of article 39 of the United Nations Charter. UC Davis J Int Law Policy 8:275–345

Augustine (2006) Confessions (trans: Sheed FJ, Foleytrs MP (ed)). 2nd edn. Hackett Publishing Company, Indianapolis

Bjorge E (2014) The evolutionary interpretation of treaties. Oxford University Press, Oxford

Bourquin M (ed) (1936) Collective security. A record of the seventh and eighth international studies conferences, Paris 1934—London 1935. International Institute of Intellectual Co-Operation, Paris

Brownlie I (2008) Principles of public international law. Oxford University Press, Oxford

Cicero MT (1995) De re publica: selections (Zetzel EG (ed)). Cambridge University Press, Cambridge

Crawford J (2012) Sovereignty as a legal value. In: Crawford J, Koskenniemi M (eds) The Cambridge companion to international law. Cambridge University Press, Cambridge, pp 117–133

Crawford J, Viles T (1994) International law on a given day. In: Ginther K, Hafner G, Lang W, Neuhold P, Sucharipa-Behrmann L (eds) Völkerrecht zwischen normativem Anspruch und politischer Realität. Festschrift für Karl Zemanek zum 65. Geburtstag, Duncker und Humblot, Berlin, pp 45–68

D'Aspremont J (2011) Formalism and the sources of international law. Oxford University Press, Oxford

Das TK (1990) The time dimension: an interdisciplinary guide. Preager, New York

de Vattel E (1995 [1916]) The law of nations or the principles of natural law (Droit des gens ou principes de la loi naturelle, appliqués à la conduite et aux affaires des nations et des souverains) (translation of the edition of 1758). W.S. Hein, Buffalo

Djeffal C (2011) The 'Iron Rhine' case—a treaty's journey from peace to sustainable development. ZaöRV 71:569–586

Djeffal C (2013) Critical theory, structuralism and contemporary legal scholarship. New England Law Review 21:209–290

Djeffal C (2015) Static and evolutive interpretation of international treaties: a functional reconstruction. Cambridge University Press, Cambridge (forthcoming)

Duchhardt H (2004) From Westphalia to the revolutionary era. In: Lesaffer R (ed) Peace treaties and international law in European history. From the late middle ages to world war one. Cambridge University Press, Cambridge, pp 45–58

Dworkin R (1975) Hard cases. Harv Law Rev 88:1057–1109

Dworkin R (1978) Taking rights seriously. Harvard University Press, Cambridge

Falk R (1995) Casting the spell: the New Haven school of international law. Yale Law J 104:1991–2008

Fassbender B (2012a) Article 2(1). In: Simma B, Khan D, Nolte G, Paulus A (eds) The Charter of the United Nations—commentary, 3rd edn. Oxford University Press, Oxford, pp 133–165

Fassbender B (2012b) Westphalia, peace of (1648). In: Wolfrum R (ed) The Max Planck encyclopedia of public international law. Oxford University Press, Oxford, http://opil.ouplaw.com/home/EPIL. Accessed 10 June 2014

Fisch J (1979) Krieg und Frieden im Friedensvertrag eine universalgeschichtliche Studie über Grundlagen und Formelemente des Friedensschlusses. Kett-Cotta, Stuttgart

Fitzmaurice M (2008) Dynamic (evolutive) interpretation of treaties, part I. Hague Yearb Int Law 21:101–156

Fitzmaurice M (2010) Dynamic (evolutive) interpretation of treaties and the European Court of Human Rights. In: Orakhelashvili A, Williams S (eds) 40 years of the Vienna Convention on the Law of Treaties. British Institute of International and Comparative Law, London, pp 55–95

Fraser JT (1987) Time, the familiar stranger. University of Massachusetts Press, Amherst

Geiss I (ed) (1979) Der Berliner Kongress 1878. Protokolle und Materialien. Boldt, Boppard am Rhein

Grewe WG (ed) (1988) Fontes historiae iuris gentium Quellen zur Geschichte des Völkerrechts. de Gruyter, Berlin
Grewe WG (ed) (1992) Fontes historiae iuris gentium Quellen zur Geschichte des Völkerrechts. Walter de Gruyter, Berlin
Grewe WG (ed) (1995) Fontes historiae iuris gentium Quellen zur Geschichte des Völkerrechts. Walter de Gruyter, Berlin
Grewe WG (2000) The epochs of international law (translated and revised by Mihael Byers M). Walter de Gruyter, Berlin
Grotius H (1925) On the law of war and peace (De jure belli ac pacis libri tres) (translation of the 1646 edition by Kelsey FW). Clarendon Press, Oxford
Higgins R (1968) Policy considerations and the international judicial process. Int Comp Law Q 17:58–84
Higgins R (1994) Problems and process: international law and how we use it. Oxford University Press, Oxford
Kant I (1796) Festschrift zum Ewigen Frieden Ein philosophischer Entwurf
Kaser M (1993) Ius gentium. Böhlau, Köln
Kinnebrock W (2014) Was macht die Zeit wenn sie vergeht? CH Beck, München
Koh HH (1997) Why do nations obey international law? Yale Journal of International Law 106:2599–2659
Koselleck R (1997) The temporalisation of concepts. Finish Yearb Polit Thought 1:16–24
Kuhn TS (1996) The structure of scientific revolution, 3rd edn. University of Chicago Press, Chicago
Le Poidevin R, MacBeath M (1993) Introduction. In: Le Poidevin R, MacBeath M (eds) The philosophy of time. Oxford University Press, Oxford, pp 1–12
Lepard BD (2010) Customary international law: a new theory with practical applications. Cambridge University Press, Cambridge
Letsas G (2004) The truth in autonomous concepts: how to interpret the ECHR. Eur J Int Law 15:279–305
Linderfalk U (2011) The application of international legal norms over time: the second branch of interpretemporal law. Neth Int Law Rev 58:147–172
McDonald A, Brollowski H (2012) Security. In: Wolfrum R (ed) The Max Planck encyclopedia of public international law. Oxford University Press, Oxford, http://opil.ouplaw.com/home/EPIL. Accessed 10 June 2014
McDougal MS (1956) Law as a process of decision: a policy-oriented approach to legal study. Natl Law Forum 1:53–72
McMillan R (2015) The leap second is about to rattle the internet. But there's a plot to kill it. http://www.wired.com/2015/01/leap-second-rattle-internet-theres-plot-kill. Accessed 10 June 2014
Neff SC (2005) War and the law of nations: a general history. Cambridge University Press, Cambridge
Nolte G (2012) Between contemporaneous and evolutive interpretation: the use of 'subsequent practice' in the judgment of the International Court of Justice concerning the case of *Costa Rica v. Nicaragua* (2009). In: Hestermeyer HP, König D, Matz-Lück N, Röben V, Seibert-Fohr A, Stoll P, Vöneky S (eds) Coexistence, cooperation and solidarity, Martinus Nijhoff Publishers, Leiden, Boston, pp 1675–1684
Nolte G (ed) (2013) Treaties and subsequent practice. Oxford University Press, Oxford
Nussbaum A (1958) A concise history of the law of nations, 2nd edn. Macmillan, New York
O'Connell ME (1999) New international legal process. Am J Int Law 93:334–351
Plucknett TFT (2001 [1956]) A concise history of the common law. 5th edn. Lawbook Exchange, Union
Raimondo F (2008) General principles of law in the decisions of international criminal courts and tribunals. Martinus Nijhoff Publishers, Leiden
Roberts A (2011) Comparative international law? The role of national courts in creating and enforcing international law. Int Comp Law Q 60:57–92

Rosa H (2003) Social acceleration: ethical and political consequences of a desynchronized high–speed society. Constellations 10:3–33
Russel B (1926) Relativity: philosophical consequences. Encyclopedia Britannica. http://www.britannica.com/EBchecked/topic/1988269/Bertrand-Russell-on-relativity#toc323194. Accessed 10 June 2014
Sands P (1995) International law in the field of sustainable development. Br Yearb Int Law 65:303–381
Schilling O (1919) Das Völkerrecht nach Thomas von Aquin. Herdersche Verlagsbuchhandlung, Freiburg
Schlüter B (2010) Developments in customary international law. Brill, Leiden
Schrijver N (2008) The evolution of sustainable development in international law: inception, meaning and status. Recueil des Cours de l'Académie de Droit International 329:217–412
Simma B, Alston P (1988–1989) The sources of human rights law: custom, jus cogens, and general principles. Aust Yearb Int Law 12:82–108
Smith JE (1969) Time, times, and the 'right time': Chronos and Kairos. Monist 53:1–13
Sorokin PA, Merton RK (1937) Social time: a methodological and functional analysis. Am J Sociol 42:615–629
Steiger H (1992) Völkerrecht. In: Brunner O, Conze W, Koselleck R (eds) Geschichtliche Grundbegriffe Historisches Lexikon zur politisch-sozialen Sprache in Deutschland, Verw-Z. Klett-Cotta, Stuttgart
Steiger H (2004) Peace treaties from Paris to Versailles. In: Lesaffer R (ed) Peace treaties and international law in European history. From the late middle ages to world war one. Cambridge University Press, Cambridge, pp 59–99
Suárez F (1944) [1612]) Treatise on laws and God the lawgiver [*De Legibus, ac Deo Legislature*] Humphrey Milford. Clarendon Press, Oxford
Textor J (1916 [1680]) Synopsis of the law of nations (Synopsis juris gentium) (translation of the edition of 1680 by Bate JP). Carnegie Institution of Washington, Washington
Venzke I (2012) How interpretation makes international law: on semantic change and normative twists. Oxford University Press, Oxford
Verdross A, Simma B (1984) Universelles Völkerrecht. Theorie und Praxis. Duncker & Humblot, Berlin
Villiger ME (1997) Customary international law and treaties, 2nd edn. Kluwer, The Hague
von Clausewitz C (1832–1834) Vom Kriege. Berlin
Watts A (ed) (1999) Final draft articles not yet having resulted in the conclusion of a treaty and reports other than final draft articles. Oxford University Press, Oxford
Winkler G (1995) Zeit und Recht. Springer, Wien
Wolff C (1934) Law of nations treated according to a scientific method (Jus Gentium Methodo Scientifica Pertractatum) (translation of the edition of 1764 by Drake JH). Clarendon Press, Oxford
Zouche R (1916 [1650]) Exposition of fecial law and procedure, or of law between nations, and questions concerning the same (*Iuris et Iudicii Fecialis, Sive, Iuris Inter Gentes, et Quaestionum de Eodem Explicatio*) (translation of the edition of 1650 by Brierly JL). Carnegie Institution of Washington, Washington

Chapter 6
(Inter)Temporal Considerations in the Interpretative Process of the VCLT: Do Treaties Endure, Perdure or Exdure?

Panos Merkouris

δὶς ἐς τὸν αὐτὸν ποταμὸν οὐκ ἂν ἐμβαίης.
You cannot enter the same river twice.
(Heraclitus)

Abstract When interpreted, sometimes treaties have to go through a trial by fire and are found either to be 'living instruments' evolving alongside the relevant changes both in law and in facts or to have a 'fixed' meaning. The aim of the present article is to examine how intertemporal considerations find their way into the interpretative process and what the effects are on the treaties being interpreted. Do these changes in law and fact actually change the treaty itself, or do they merely trigger a latent quality already existing in the treaty itself? Does time change the treaty, or does it merely 'unfold' it? This question will be examined through the lens of the main philosophical theories on identity, persistence, time and change (endurantism, perdurantism and exdurantism), and by focusing on the 'direct' (principle of contemporaneity and evolutive interpretation) and 'indirect' (Article 31(3)(c) and the intertemporal application of the rules of interpretation) points of entry of intertemporal considerations in the interpretative process. Through this examination the elements that weigh upon the judicial interpretative process and tip the scales either in favour of an evolutive interpretation or in favour of the principle of contemporaneity, will be identified, as well as the limits of any such interpretation. In this manner, an answer will be arrived at as to whether, from an interpretative perspective, treaties endure, perdure or exdure.

Keywords Interpretation · Evolutive interpretation · Dynamic interpretation · Intertemporal law · Contemporaneity · Law of treaties · Vienna Convention on the Law of Treaties · Endurantism · Perdurantism · Exdurantism

P. Merkouris (✉)
Lecturer on International Law, University of Groningen, The Netherlands
e-mail: p.merkouris@rug.nl

M. Ambrus and R.A. Wessel (eds.), *Netherlands Yearbook of International Law 2014*,
Netherlands Yearbook of International Law 45, DOI 10.1007/978-94-6265-060-2_6

Contents

6.1 Introduction 122
6.2 Definitional Issues 125
 6.2.1 Endurantism, Perdurantism, and Exdurantism 125
 6.2.2 Intertemporal Law 128
 6.2.3 Principle of Contemporaneity and Evolutive/Dynamic Interpretation 129
6.3 Silence Can Speak Volumes: The Lack of Explicit References to Intertemporal Considerations in the VCLT 134
 6.3.1 Pre-VCLT Considerations on the Topic 134
 6.3.2 Rejection of Explicit Incorporation of the Doctrine of Intertemporal Law in the VCLT: Draft Article 56 135
 6.3.3 Rejection of Explicit Solutions to Intertemporal Considerations Through the Backdoor of Article 31 137
6.4 Points of Entry of Intertemporal Considerations in Article 31 VCLT 139
 6.4.1 Direct Point of Entry 139
 6.4.2 Indirect Point of Entry 144
6.5 Limits 150
6.6 Conclusion 151
References 152

6.1 Introduction

In the philosophy of Heraclitus of Ephesus, change was of central importance. In the quote cited above, Heraclitus touches upon the paradox of change and of identity. If you enter a river at one point in time the river will consist of a certain amount of water and of certain droplets. If you enter at a later time what you would perceive as the 'same' river, so Heraclitus posits, you will actually be entering a different river. The body of water that surrounded you during your first immersion has now moved on. It has meandered its way towards the delta of the river. The second time around you are entering a qualitatively and quantitatively different river. Various solutions have been offered to reconcile this paradox with our common understanding of time, change and identity, ranging from, on the one hand, it being a false paradox due to the use of 'same' as meaning two different things simultaneously to, on the other hand, theories of persistence and viewing words as 'time-worms'.[1]

An in-depth analysis of this discourse would fall outside the scope of the present chapter, it helps, however, in highlighting the fact that the passage of time and change go hand in hand, in all manifestations of the cosmos. Law could not be an exception and is subject to the altering effects of time. This topic has been the focal point of seminal academic works.[2] In the context of international law one

[1] *Infra* Sect. 6.2.1.

[2] Sorensen 1973, at 35–36; Sorensen 1975, at 339–374; Rosenne 1960, at 11–75; Cançado Trindade 1978, at 232–257; McWhinney 1984, at 179–199; Tavernier 1979; Greig 2001; d'Amato 1992, at 1234; de Visscher 1963, at 66–69; Sur 1974, at 207–210; Greig 2007, at 163 *et seq.*; de Aréchaga 1978, at 48–50.

such manifestation can be found in the interpretation of treaties. When interpreted, sometimes treaties have to go through a trial by fire and are found either to be 'living instruments' evolving alongside the relevant changes both in law and in facts or to have a 'fixed' meaning.

The aim of the present article is to examine how temporal considerations find their way into the interpretative process and what are the effects on the treaties being interpreted. Do these changes in law and fact actually change the treaty, or are they merely a latent quality already existing in the treaty itself? Does time change the treaty, or does it merely 'unfold' it as Max Frisch would put it?[3] All of these ideas, and the philosophical theories on identity, persistence, time and change connected to them, which explain the terms employed in the *sous-titre* of this chapter ('Do Treaties Endure, Perdure or Exdure?'), will be addressed in Sect. 6.2.

The necessity of adopting this analytical viewpoint is two-fold. Firstly, the entire system of international law has always been a compromise between two key-functions; providing long-term stability and legal certainty, on the one hand, and ensuring the viability, adaptability and relevance of the system by allowing change, growth and evolution of the relevant legal rules on the other. Second, the overarching theme of the present Volume is that of 'Temporariness in International Law'. Consequently, it is essential that we first determine the main concepts of identity, persistence and change. If we do not know, what identity, persistence and change are, how could we possible offer any meaningful answer as to whether treaties change in time or remain the same, and what the elements and limits are that affect any such determination.

The theme of the Volume also colours the particular elements of the interpretative process that will be the focus of the analysis. Temporal considerations are almost ubiquitous in Articles 31 and 32 of the 1969 Vienna Convention on the Law of Treaties (VCLT).[4] To name but a few instances where temporal considerations play a role in the interpretative process: subsequent practice,[5] subsequent agreements and 'relevant rules' of Article 31(3)(c).[6] As a detailed exposition of all these elements would be impossible within the confines of a single chapter, the analysis will focus mainly on the 'points of entry' of temporal considerations, and in particular those which are connected to the notion of inter-temporality.[7]

---

[3] The actual quote is: 'Time does not change us. It merely unfolds us' (original text: 'Die Zeit verwandelt uns nicht, sie entfaltet uns nur'); Frisch 1950, at 21.

[4] 1969 Vienna Convention on the Law of Treaties, 1155 UNTS 331.

[5] This is a topic of analysis by the ILC, with Nolte as *Special Rapporteur*. This project is very aptly named 'Treaties over Time/Subsequent Agreements and Subsequent Practice in Relation to Interpretation of Treaties'. All the relevant documents and discussions can be found at http://legal.un.org/ilc/guide/1_11.htm. Accessed 18 May 2014.

[6] I.e. which rules are relevant, those at the time of the conclusion of the treaty, or those at the time of the interpretation of the treaty.

[7] Hence the selection of the word '(inter)temporal' in the title of the chapter.

There are two main points of entry of (inter)temporal considerations in the interpretative process:

(1) *Direct point of entry: Contemporaneity or Dynamic Interpretation.* According to Fitzmaurice one of the main principles of interpretation is the principle of contemporaneity, i.e. that '[t]he terms of a treaty must be interpreted according to the meaning which they possessed … at the time when the treaty was originally concluded'.[8] There is, however, one important caveat: '[unless] it was the intention of the parties that the meaning or scope of a term or expression used in the treaty should follow the development of the law.'[9]

What we will examine is whether international jurisprudence has a tendency to give weight to particular elements in order for it to conclude that a treaty is to follow the principle of contemporaneity or should be interpreted dynamically. Such elements are, indicatively, the intention of the parties, the object and purpose of a treaty and the nature of the words employed in the treaty being interpreted.

(2) *Indirect point of entry: Intertemporal Considerations within Article 31(3)(c) and in the Application of the Rules of Interpretation.* Article 31(3)(c) of the VCLT states that during the interpretative process account shall be taken of 'all relevant rules of international law applicable in the relations between the parties'. Although the text itself does not make any explicit reference to temporal considerations, its silence speaks volumes. An analysis of the preparatory work of the VCLT will show that one major point of consideration was again a temporal one. Which rules could be considered as relevant, *the rules at the time of the conclusion of the treaty or the rules at the time of the interpretation of the treaty*? This connection could also be transposed to the rules of interpretation themselves. When a court interprets a treaty, which rules of interpretation should it apply. The rules of interpretation contemporaneous to the treaty or the rules of interpretation at the time of the interpretation of the treaty?

In order to highlight the ties and overlaps between these two points of entry the present chapter in Sect. 6.2 will clarify certain concepts central to the following analysis. Section 6.3 will provide an overview of the preparatory work of the VCLT on intertemporal law. In Sect. 6.4 the analysis will move on to an examination of both the direct and indirect points of entry of intertemporal considerations in the interpretative process of the VCLT and the elements that factor in opting either in favour of a dynamic/evolutive interpretation or in favour of the principle of contemporaneity. Finally, in Sect. 6.5, we will attempt to map the limits, if any, to which the judges are restricted when engaging in dynamic/evolutive interpretation.

---

[8] Fitzmaurice 1957, at 212.

[9] Thirlway called this an '*intertemporal renvoi*'. Thirlway 1991, at 57.

6.2 Definitional Issues

Before embarking on an examination of the manner in which intertemporal considerations infiltrate the interpretative process it is appropriate to first clarify the meaning and content of several of the concepts that will be the crux of the analysis.

6.2.1 Endurantism, Perdurantism, and Exdurantism

The first thing we need to address is the terms used in the *sous-titre* of the article. The ideas of time, change, identity and persistence have 'persisted' from ancient Greek philosophy to modern times. The first systematic attempts to tackle these concepts from a logical and philosophical point of view were connected to paradoxes. Paradoxes were a favourite tool of ancient Greek and Roman philosophers in order to highlight either the pitfalls of our own preconceptions or the limits of our quest for true knowledge.[10] There is a wide number of paradoxes that relate to the aforementioned concepts. For instance: (i) *Heraclitus' river paradox*, according to which one is never able to enter the same river twice; (ii) *Theseus' ship paradox*, according to which the question is at which point (if any) the ship stopped being his ship and became a new one due to the replacement of rotten planks to the extent that the entire ship ended up being comprised of newer pieces of wood[11]; and (iii) *Chrysippus' paradox*. Chrysippus, a 3rd century BC Stoic philosopher, posited the following. There is a man called Dion. There is also Theon, who consists of Dion minus his left foot. If Dion's left foot is amputated then what happens to the relationship between Dion and Theon, are they still two different things that simply occupy the same space, has Dion ceased to exist and been subsumed by Theon, or has the reverse taken place, i.e. Theon being subsumed by the now-amputee Dion?[12]

An analysis of these paradoxes falls outside the scope of this chapter, nonetheless, all have as a common denominator the aforementioned concepts of time, change, identity and persistence. Consequently, a brief examination of the main

[10] For instance, Agrippa posited that true knowledge is impossible to achieve, as any logical argument would eventually lead to one of the following three scenarios: (i) *argumentum ad absurdum*, an argument leading to a paradox/absurd (ii) *argumentum ad infinitum*, an argument leading to a self-referential, circular argument (iii) an axiomatic argument, an argument accepting a supposition that cannot be proven or disproven. This is known as *Agrippa's trilemma*. For an analysis of the problems and modern responses to this trilemma, see Klein 2008.

[11] Plutarch 1914, Chapter 23.1. A more modern variant of this paradox was posited by Hobbes. If the planks that were replaced were gathered and gradually a new ship was built in a different location, which of the two ships would be the true *Theseus' ship*, or alternatively do we at any point have a situation where instead of one *Theseus ship* we end up with two *Theseus' ships* existing at the same time? Hobbes 1656, at Chapter XI, Sect. 7, at 100. See also Deutsch 2007.

[12] Philonis 1891, c. 9, at 15–16. For analysis of this paradox, see Burke 1994; Carter 1997.

philosophical approaches to these concepts will allow us to better understand their function within the sphere of treaty interpretation and also demonstrate firstly what the subtitle selected for this chapter means, and, second, why it was considered to be reflective of the interpretative approaches to the (un)changing nature of treaties.

Various philosophical theories have been proposed throughout history to account for change in time. The two most prominent schools of thought are known as *endurantism* (endurance theory) and *perdurantism* (perdurance theory). The main difference between endurantism and perdurantism is the manner in which things persist and how change is accounted for.[13] Endurantists hold that things have only spatial elements/parts and are 'wholly present whenever they exist'.[14] This creates some difficulties as to accounting for how things can change.[15] Sorensen, gives a great account of the problems that one may face in applying strictly endurantism in conjunction with *Leibniz's Law of Identity*.[16]

> The Heracliteans did have a logical argument for the universality of change. If *x* is identical to *y* and *x* has property *F*, then *y* has property *F* [indiscernibility of identicals] ... If Socrates when ill is identical to the man who recovered, then every property possessed by the ill Socrates is possessed by the recovered Socrates. But then the healthy Socrates would still be ill. What appears to be a single individual, Socrates enduring through time is actually a succession of individuals. The Heracliteans conclude that our ordinary use of *identical* is loose talk founded on mere resemblance. Socrates before and after his illness are only identical in the way that distinct grains of salt are identical.[17]

In order to account for change through time, and avoid the above paradoxes, endurantists have proposed various theories such as presentism,[18] temporal-relationism[19] and adverbialism,[20] none of which however is without its difficulties.

On the other end of the spectrum is perdurantism. Unlike endurantists, perdurantists posit that things not only have spatial parts but temporal parts as well.[21]

---

[13] Haslanger 2005, at 315–354.

[14] Hawley 2010.

[15] Known also as problem of 'temporary intrinsics'. Gallois 2011, para 2.3.

[16] Leibniz's Law of Identity is an ontological principle according to which if two objects are one and the same they have the exact same properties (also known as the 'indiscernibility of identicals'). The converse is also referred to as Leibniz's law, i.e. that if two objects have all the same properties they are one and the same thing (also known as the 'identity of indescernibles'). Gallois 2011, para 1; Forrest 2010. Here, we concern ourselves with the first version of Leibniz's law of identity.

[17] Sorensen 2003, at 77.

[18] The view that only objects in the present exist. Everything in the past and the future does not exist. Hawley 2010, para 3.

[19] The view that 'objects change by standing in different relations to different times'. Hawley 2010, para 3.

[20] The view that time and change is simply a way of expressing the manner in which an object possesses a particular property. For instance, in the aforementioned ill vs. healthy Socrates example: If Socrates is ill in the morning and healthy in the afternoon, then Socrates possesses the ill-property in a morning way, and the healthy-property in an afternoon way. Hawley 2010, para 3.

[21] Ibid., para 2.

According to them an object at any given moment is never wholly present, as its persistence has to be looked also from the perspective of the fourth dimension, that of time. Hence, an object at a specific 'time-slice'[22] is only partially present. From the perdurantist point of view objects are seen and referred to as 'space-time worms'.[23] As a worm wriggles along the earth, 'space-time worms' wriggle along a four-dimensional plane, along both space and time. Similar to a worm that does not exist wholly at a particular point or two-dimensional plane, but exists in space, objects are only partially present at any particular point in time. Their whole presence can be identified only by looking at the span of their existence along the fourth-dimension axis, thus giving the impression of a worm.

Because time and temporal parts are such an important factor in distinguishing between endurantism and perdurantism, the former and its associated theories are referred to as three-dimensionalism (3D-ism), whereas the latter where time considerations are predominant is referred to as four-dimensionalism (4D-ism).

Finally, there are other theories which try to combine elements of both endurantism and perdurantism. The most notable of these is *exdurantism*, known also as 'stage theory'. According to exdurantism, objects have temporal parts,[24] which are referred to as stages. However, unlike perdurantism, exdurantism argues that an object is wholly present 'at momentary regions that lack temporal extension'.[25] The question then that arises is if an object is wholly present at different 'time-slices', how is this different from endurantism and how can this be the same object? With respect to the first question, endurantism does not accept the existence of temporal parts, whereas 'stage theory' is actually based on their existence. As to the second question, the key idea is that objects persist through time by exduring, i.e. 'by standing in temporal *counterpart* relations to later and earlier object stages'.[26] The difference between perdurantism and exdurantism is that whereas the former views an object as a continuity, as a 'space-time worm', exdurantism views the object as a compilation of the sum of 'time-slices' or 'stages', where the object exists wholly in each and every one of them. How does this translate in an example taken from everyday life? Take, for instance, movies. Movies take advantage of the persistence of vision.[27] Due to the speed with which the film roll is played we seem to perceive one continuous image, e.g. a train moving. However, if one slows down the film roll, one will easily see that the image previously perceived as 'moving' is nothing more than the sum of still images. In the same manner exdurantism posits that objects are the

[22] I.e. at a particular temporal point or period.

[23] Not to be confused with physics and 'wormholes'. Hawley 2010, para 2; Sorensen 2003, at 77 and 143.

[24] And in this sense it is closer to perdurantism, and falls under the general rubric of 4D-ism.

[25] Balashov 2011, at 14.

[26] Ibid.

[27] The fact that the human eye retains an image for a small fraction of a second. Consequently, if a second image is played within that time frame one will be superimposed on the other giving the illusion of movement.

sum of an infinite amount of stages, the 'still images' from our previous example, where the object is wholly present at each and every one of them.

In summation:

- endurantism holds that an object does not have temporal parts and that it exists wholly at every instant;
- perdurantism holds that an object is a 'space-time worm'. It has both spatial and temporal parts, and it exists only partially at any given moment; and finally,
- exdurantism holds that an object has both spatial and temporal parts, but because it is the sum of its various 'object-stages' it exists wholly within any given moment.

6.2.2 Intertemporal Law

Connected to these theories of identity and change within the context of international law is the notion of intertemporal law. The most oft-cited quote on intertemporal law is that of Judge Huber in the *Island of Palmas case*:

> a juridical fact must be appreciated in the light of the law contemporary with it ... The same principle which subjects the act creative of a right to the law in force at the time the right arises, demands that the *existence of the right, in other words its continued manifestation, shall follow the conditions required by the evolution of law.*[28]

However, pinpointing the exact content of intertemporal law has been somewhat more elusive, so much so in fact that Higgins argued that the quote has been read 'in the most remarkably extensive fashion, as providing obligatory rules in circumstances that it never addressed, with consequences that it never intended'.[29] This uneasiness as to the precise nature, scope and content of intertemporal law is equally reflected in the variety of terms in which it has been employed: 'international intertemporal law',[30] 'doctrine of intertemporal law',[31] 'rule of intertemporal law',[32] 'intertemporal principle',[33] 'principle of the inter-temporal law',[34] 'principle of the intertemporality of law'[35] to name but a few.

---

[28] *The Island of Palmas case (or Miangas) (Netherlands v USA)*, PCA, Award of 4 April 1928, RIAA Vol. 2 (1949), at 845 (emphasis added).

[29] Higgins 1997, at 516.

[30] Schwarzenberger 1952, at 559.

[31] Elias 1980, at 285 *et seq.*

[32] *Jan de Nul NV and Dredging International NV v Egypt*, Award, ICSID Case No. ARB/04/13, 24 October 2008, para 132.

[33] *ATA Construction, Industrial and Trading Company v Jordan*, Award, ICSID Case No. ARB/08/2, 12 May 2010, para 109; *Mondev International Limited v USA*, Award, ICSID Case No. ARB(AF)/99/2, 11 October 2002, para 70 (hereinafter *Mondev*).

[34] *MCI Power Group LC and New Turbine Incorporated v Ecuador*, Award, ICSID Case No. ARB/03/6, 26 July 2007, para 133.

[35] Ibid., para 89.

Due to this uncertainty, it is necessary to determine whether intertemporal law has any connection to the process of interpretation or if it functions on a completely different sphere and thus is irrelevant to the interpretative process. Huber's *dictum* consists of two legs, the first relating to the creation of a right, and the second to its continued manifestation. Both legs of Huber's *dictum* concern the determination of the existence or non-existence of rights, not the determination of its content. It for this reason that one could get the impression that intertemporal law *stricto sensu* and interpretation have two very distinct functions and should not be conflated with one another.[36]

However, the contrary view that accepts some form of linkage between intertemporal law and the process of interpretation is not without its merit. Both doctrine[37] and judicial practice[38] seem to have no problem in accepting the possibility of transposition of the rationale behind intertemporal law to the interpretative process. Characteristically, Fitzmaurice argued that the principle of contemporaneity,[39] can be understood as a 'particular application of the doctrine of inter-temporal law [within the context of treaty interpretation]'.[40]

Based on the above, the doctrine of intertemporal law can be transposed to the interpretative process. Nonetheless and in order to avoid the doctrinal uncertainties surrounding intertemporal law, the term that was selected in the title was not 'intertemporal law' or 'doctrine of intertemporal law' but instead '(inter)temporal considerations in the interpretative process of the VCLT'. An additional reason was also that the term 'considerations', as well as the inclusion of the prefix 'inter' between brackets, was felt to better reflect the dual nature of the evolution of a particular term. Specifically, the meaning of a particular term can change due to the evolution not only of law but of facts as well, whereas intertemporal law as such and based on Huber's *dictum* seems to focus only on the evolution of the law.

6.2.3 *Principle of Contemporaneity and Evolutive/ Dynamic Interpretation*

The response to which legal system prevalent at subsequent time-periods should be the one decisive for interpretative purposes is not an easy one and definitely not

[36] Linderfalk 2008, at 117–118.

[37] Kotzur 2008, paras 11–12; Elias 1980, at 301. Fitzmaurice 1953, 5–8; Fitzmaurice 1957, 225–227; Fitzmaurice 2008a, at 113; McLachlan 2005, at 316.

[38] *Arbitration Regarding the Iron Rhine ('Izjeren Rijn') Railway (Belgium v Netherlands)*, PCA, Award of 24 May 2005, para 79 (hereinafter *Iron Rhine Arbitration*); *The Right to Information on Consular Assistance in the Framework of the Guarantees of the Due Process of Law (Mexico v USA)*, IACtHR, Advisory Opinion, 1 October 1999, Concurring Opinion of Judge Cançado Trindade, para 9 (hereinafter *Right to Information on Consular Assistance*); *Caesar v Trinidad and Tobago*, IACtHR, Judgment of 11 March 2005, Separate Opinion of Judge Cançado Trindade, para 10.

[39] And by implication evolutive interpretation.

[40] Fitzmaurice 1957, at 225.

one to which a clear-cut answer can be given. Prior to the conclusion of the VCLT, Fitzmaurice took it upon himself to try and distill from the jurisprudence of the ICJ the principles of treaty interpretation. In his series of articles in the *BYIL* he identified several principles of interpretation, one of which was the *principle of contemporaneity*,[41] According to this principle

> [t]he terms of a treaty must be interpreted according to the meaning which they possessed, or which would have been attributed to them, and in the light of current linguistic usage, at the time when the treaty was originally concluded.[42]

Several years later and in the same series of articles, Thirlway reaffirmed this principle but added one requirement:

> Provided that, where it can be established that it was the intention of the parties that the meaning or scope of a term or expression used in the treaty should follow the development of the law, *the treaty must be interpreted so as to give effect to that intention*.[43]

International jurisprudence has evolved along those lines, with some tribunals recognizing the principle of contemporaneity,[44] while others opting for a more 'evolutive/dynamic' interpretation.[45]

---

[41] Also known as '*contemporanea expositio*'; Kotzur 2009, para 11.

[42] Fitzmaurice 1957, at 212; generally on the principle of contemporaneity: Fitzmaurice 1953, at 5–8; Thirlway 2006, at 65 *et seq.*

[43] Thirlway 2006, at 57 (emphasis added). In this context, Thirlway in his earlier writings used the term '*intertemporal renvoi*' to describe situations in which the intention of the parties is deemed to have been 'to subject the legal relations created to such law as might from time to time thereafter become effective'; Thirlway 1989, at 135.

[44] *Minquiers and Ecrehos (France v UK)*, ICJ, Judgment of 17 November 1953, at 56; *Case Concerning Rights of Nationals of the United States of America in Morocco, (France v USA)*, ICJ, Judgment of 27 August 1952, at 189 (hereinafter *US Nationals in Morocco*); *Aegean Sea Continental Shelf (Greece v Turkey)*, ICJ, Judgment of 19 December 1978, Dissenting Opinion of Judge de Castro, at 63, para 4 (hereinafter *Aegean Sea Continental Shelf*); *Case Concerning Right of Passage over Indian Territory (Portugal v India)*, ICJ, Merits, Judgment of 12 April 1960, at 37; *Case Concerning a Boundary Dispute between Argentina and Chile Concerning the Frontier Line between Boundary Post 62 and Mount Fitzroy (Argentina v Chile)*, Award of 21 October 1994, para 130 (hereinafter *Laguna del Desierto*); *Kasikili/Sedudu Island (Botswana v Namibia)*, ICJ, Judgment of 13 December 1999, para 25 (hereinafter *Kasikili/Sedudu Island*); *The Grisbådarna Case (Norway v Sweden)*, PCA, Award of 23 October 1909, RIAA Vol. 11 (1961), at 159 (hereinafter *Grisbådarna* case); *North Atlantic Coast Fisheries Case (Great Britain v USA)*, PCA, Award of 7 September 1910, RIAA Vol. 11 (1961), at 196 (hereinafter *North Atlantic Coast Fisheries*); *Western Sahara*, ICJ, Advisory Opinion, 16 October 1975, para 126; *Temple of Preah Vihear (Cambodia v Thailand)*, ICJ, Judgment of 15 June 1962, Dissenting Opinion of Judge Spender, at 128; *Dispute Regarding Navigational and Related Rights (Costa Rica v Nicaragua)*, ICJ, Judgment of 13 July 2009, Separate Opinion of Judge Skotnikov, para 5 (hereinafter *Dispute Regarding Navigational Rights*).

[45] *Legal Consequences for States of the Continued Presence of South Africa in Namibia (South West Africa) notwithstanding Security Council Resolution 276*, ICJ, Advisory Opinion, 21 June 1971, para 53 (hereinafter *Namibia Advisory Opinion*); *Aegean Sea Continental Shelf*, para 77; *Case Concerning the Gabčíkovo-Nagymaros Project (Hungary v Slovakia)*, ICJ, Judgment of 25 September 1997, para 112 (hereinafter *Gabčíkovo-Nagymaros Project)*; *Case Concerning the Delimitation of Maritime Boundary between Guinea-Bissau and Senegal (Guinea Bissau*

Evolutive/dynamic interpretation reveals the present content of a particular term, its 'current frontier'.[46] Various terms have been used to describe this interpretative approach such as 'evolutionary interpretation'[47] 'evolutive interpretation'[48] or 'dynamic interpretation'.[49] Whether these terms differ from one another or whether they can be used interchangeably is a matter of academic debate. International jurisprudence similarly does not offer much assistance in resolving this issue. The terms 'dynamic' and 'evolutive' have been used in all possible variations. Within one and the same sentence or paragraph one can find reference to these terms: (i) expressed in the alternative, i.e. 'dynamic or evolutive'[50] (ii) cumulatively, i.e. 'evolutive and dynamic',[51] and (iii) both cumulatively and in the alternative in the same judgment.[52] Helgesen, attempts a distinction by using the term '"evolutive" as covering the situation where the Court gives answers to new facts, societal changes, an issue which has never been before the Court. While "dynamic" interpretation [on the other hand] … refers primarily to the situation where the Court gives new answers to old facts.'[53] Irrespective of whether this distinction is actually reflected in international judicial practice and for reasons of simplicity of this chapter the term that will be used from this point onwards will be 'evolutive interpretation' as being more closely linked linguistically to the idea of 'living instruments' that need to evolve in order to survive.

The connection of evolutive interpretation with intertemporal law is not only demonstrated by its ties with the principle of contemporaneity but is further

---

Footnote 45 (continued)
v Senegal), Arbitral Award of 31 July 1989, RIAA Vol. 20. (1993), paras 80–85; *Iron Rhine Arbitration*, paras 79–81; *Dispute Regarding Navigational Rights*, Declaration of Judge Guillaume, paras 9–16; *Tyrer v UK*, ECtHR, No. 5856/72, 25 April 1978, para 31; *Matthews v UK*, ECtHR, No. 24833/94, 18 February 1999, para 39. On evolutive/dynamic interpretation, see Fitzmaurice 2008a, at 101–153; Fitzmaurice 2008b, at 125–170; Fitzmaurice 2009, at 1–31; Bernhardt 2000, at 11 *et seq*; Letsas 2007, at 58–79; Brölmann 2005, at 34–36; Bjorge 2014; Dawidowicz 2011.

46 *Right to Information on Consular Assistance*, Concurring Opinion of Judge Ramirez.

47 *Mayagna (Sumo) Awas Tingni Community v Nicaragua*, IACtHR Judgment of 31 August 2001, para 148; *Gabčíkovo-Nagymaros Project*, Separate Opinion of Judge Bedjaoui, para 5; *RosInvest Company UK Limited v Russian Federation*, Award on Jurisdiction, SCC Case No. V079/2005, 1 October 2007, paras 39–40 (hereinafter *RosInvest v Russia*).

48 *Daimler Financial Services AG v Argentina*, Award, ICSID Case No. ARB/05/1, 22 August 2012, para 267; *Mondev*, para 123; *Bámaca Velásquez v Guatemala*, IACtHR, Judgment of 25 November 2000, Separate Opinion of Judge Cançado Trindade, para 37.

49 Fitzmaurice 2008a, Fitzmaurice 2009.

50 *Caesar v Trinidad and Tobago*, Separate Opinion of Judge Cançado Trindade, para 10; *Right to Information on Consular Assistance*, Concurring Opinion of Judge Cançado Trindade, para 3.

51 *Meftah v France*, ECctHR, No. 32911/96, 26 July 2002; Concurring Opinion of Judge Lorenzen joined by Hedigan.

52 *Hirst v UK*, EctHR, No. 74025/01, 6 October 2005, Joint Dissenting Opinion of Judges Wildhaber, Costa, Lorenzen, Kovler and Jebens.

53 Helgesen 2011, at 276.

substantiated by the fact that it has been referred to as the 'intertemporal dimension'[54] and the 'temporal issue'[55] in treaty interpretation.[56]

There is an extensive jurisprudence on evolutive interpretation, which is not restricted simply to human rights courts judgments,[57] but covers those of other international judicial or quasi-judicial bodies.[58]

Evolutive interpretation can occur along two main tracks: (i) evolution of fact and (ii) evolution of law.[59] Along similar lines, Georgopoulos although analyzing mainly 'generic terms'[60] adopts the terms '*renvoi mobile*' and '*ouverture du texte*'.[61] In the latter case ('*ouverture du texte*'), the openness of the terms used in the treaty text allows for the content of the norm to change alongside the factual situation contemplated. This would be a case of 'evolution of fact'. On the other hand, in the case of '*renvoi mobile*' the norm reflects at each time it is being

---

54 *Caesar v Trinidad and Tobago*, Separate Opinion of Judge Cançado Trindade, para 10.

55 Higgins 1994, at 797.

56 These two descriptions of evolutive interpretation also were one of the bases for selecting '(inter)temporal' as the most accurate term for the title of this article.

57 Indicatively: *Goodwin v UK*, ECtHR, No. 28957/95, 11 July 2002; *Schalk and Kopf v Austria*, ECtHR, No. 30141/04, 24 June 2010; *Vo v France*, ECtHR, No. 53924/00, 8 July 2004, para 82; *Tyrer v UK*, para 31; *Loizidou v Turkey*, ECtHR, No. 15318/89, 23 March 1995, para 71.

58 Indicatively: *Merrill & Ring Forestry LP v Canada*, Award, UNCITRAL, 31 March 2010, para 190 *Mondev*, paras 116–125; *ADF Inc. v USA*, Award, ICSID Case No. ARB(AF)/00/1, 9 January 2003, paras 181–184, 190; *Waste Management Inc. v Mexico*, Award, ICSID Case No. ARB(AF)/00/3, 30 April 004, para 93; *GAMI Investment, Inc. v Mexico*, Award, UNCITRAL, 15 November 2004, para 95; *Namibia Advisory Opinion*, para 53; *Aegean Sea Continental Shelf*, para 77; *Gabčíkovo-Nagymaros Project*, para 112; *Iron Rhine Arbitration*, paras 79–81; *Dispute Regarding Navigational Rights*, Declaration of Judge Guillaume, paras 9–16; *USA—Import Prohibition of Certain Shrimp and Shrimp Products*, WTO Appellate Body, WT/DS58/AB/R, 6 November 1998, para 130 and footnotes 110–113 (hereinafter *US-Shrimp (AB)*).

However, it has to be recognised that evolutive interpretation is often associated almost in a Pavlovian way with human rights instruments. This is a point to which we shall return in Sect. 6.4.1.1. At this point, suffice it to say that in human rights jurisprudence there is a tendency to refer to the nature of the instruments being interpreted as, indicatively, (i) 'living instruments'; *Judge v Canada*, HRC, Communication No. 829/1998, 5 August 2002, para 10.3; *R.R. v Poland*, ECtHR, No. 27617/04, 26 May 2011, para 186; *E.B. v France*, ECtHR, No. 43546/02, 22 January 2008, para 92; *Hatton and others v UK*, ECtHR, No. 36022/97, 8 July 2003, Joint Dissenting Opinion of Judges Costa, Ress, Türmen, Zupančič and Steiner, para 2; (ii) 'live instruments'; *Yakye Axa Indigenous Community v Paraguay*, IACtHR, Judgment of 17 June 2005, para 125; *Case of the Mapiripán Massacre v Colombia*, IACtHR, Judgment of 15 September 2005, para 106; (iii) instruments of the 'always speaking type'; *M, Re, King v Bristow Helicopters Limited*, House of Lords, Appeal Judgment, 28 February 2002, [2002] UKHL 7.

59 It has been argued that evolutive interpretation is linguistic in nature, that it is 'based on the linguistic usage of the term at the time of interpretation'. Ress 2002, at 23. However, as Helmersen rightly points out this is only fitting for terms that actually have the capacity to evolve linguistically, not for the rest. Helmersen 2013, at 129.

60 On 'generic terms', see *infra* Sect. 6.4.1.2.

61 Georgopoulos 2004, at 132–134.

interpreted the evolution of the law to which it is connected. As the law changes so does the content of that norm.[62] This situation would be one of 'evolution of law'.

Examples of what international courts and tribunals have considered as evolution of fact are medical and scientific advancements,[63] societal and cultural changes,[64] moral developments,[65] and the socio-economic situation of a State (including current living conditions).[66] On the other hand, customary international law,[67] international treaties,[68] and even domestic law[69] have all been considered when determining the content of a term that follows the 'evolution of law'.

As a final note, it has to be stressed that this tug-of-war between the principle of contemporaneity and evolutive interpretation guided the focus of the title on the three main approaches to explaining persistence and change through time, i.e. endurantism, perdurantism and exdurantism. These philosophical schools of thought were selected as they seem to reflect the same challenges that the different approaches to intertemporal considerations in the interpretative process face. On the one hand, we have the principle of contemporaneity, which argues that the terms of a treaty should be understood as they stood at the time of the conclusion of a treaty, which seems to correspond to endurantism. A treaty is to be understood as being completely there.[70] On the other hand, we have evolutive interpretation, which seems to reflect on the

---

[62] See *Aegean Sea Continental Shelf*, analysed in more detail in Sect. 6.4.1.2.

[63] *Gabčíkovo-Nagymaros Project*, paras 104 and 107; *Vo v France*, Dissenting Opinion of Judge Ress, para 5.

[64] *Right to Information on Consular Assistance*, Concurring Opinion of Judge Cançado Trindade, para 4; *Öztürk v Germany*, ECtHR, No. 8544/79, 21 February 1984, Dissenting Opinion of Judge Bernhardt.

[65] *Cossey v UK*, ECtHR, No. 10843/84, 27 September 1990, Joint Dissenting Opinion of Judges Palm, Foighel and Pekkanen, para 5.

[66] *Yakye Axa Indigenous Community v Paraguay*, para 125; *Gómez Paquiyauri and others (on behalf of Gómez Paquiyauri and Gómez Paquiyauri) v Peru*, IACtHR, Judgment of 8 July 2004, para 165; ibid., Partly Concurring and Partly Dissenting Opinion of Judge Fogel, para 33; *Mayagna (Sumo) Awas Tingni Community v Nicaragua*, para 146; *Case of the 'Street Children' (Villagrán Morales et al.) v Guatemala*, IACtHR, Judgment of 19 November 1999, para 193; *Right to Information on Consular Assistance*, para 114; *Tyrer v UK*, para 31.

[67] *Merrill & Ring Forestry LP v Canada*, para 190; *Mondev*, paras 116–25; *ADF Inc. v USA*, paras 181–184, 190; *Waste Management Inc. v Mexico*, para 93; *GAMI Investment, Inc. v Mexico*, para 95.

[68] *Sawhoyamaxa Indigenous Community of the Enxet-Lengua People v Paraguay*, IACtHR, Judgment of 29 March 2006, para 117; *Yakye Axa Indigenous Community v Paraguay*, paras 124–131; *Mayagna (Sumo) Awas Tingni Community v Nicaragua*, paras 148 and 149; *Gómez Paquiyauri and others v Peru*, paras 165–166; *Right to Information on Consular Assistance*, para 114; *Case of the 'Street Children' v Guatemala*, paras 193–194; *Juridical Status and Human Rights of the Child*, IACtHR, Advisory Opinion, 28 August 2002, para 24.

[69] *Öcalan v Turkey*, ECtHR, No. 46221/99, 12 May 2005, paras 162–164; *Right to Information on Consular Assistance*, Concurring Opinion of Judge Cançado Trindade, para 7; *Marckx v Belgium*, ECtHR, No. 6833/74, 13 June 1979; *Dudgeon v UK*, ECtHR, No. 7525/76, 22 October 1981, para 60.

[70] At least *ratione materiae*. *Ratione personae* might be somewhat more problematic, as the parties to a treaty may change through time, but as was shown in Sect. 6.2.1 endurantism has some ways to circumvent issues of change.

interpretative plane either the perdurantist or the exdurantist school of thought, depending on whether one sees the treaty as continuous instrument a 'space-time worm' or simply as a collection of interpretative 'still images' that are taken each and every time a judicial body is called to interpret the treaty in question.

But before making any premature claims regarding the nature of treaties, let us first examine whether during the preparation of the VCLT the ILC members were aware of the connection of Article 31 with intertemporality, and whether the existing direct and indirect 'points of entry' of intertemporal considerations were a conscious choice, with an intended specific content and range of function.

6.3 Silence Can Speak Volumes: The Lack of Explicit References to Intertemporal Considerations in the VCLT

6.3.1 Pre-VCLT Considerations on the Topic

It would be wrong to assume that the *Island of Palmas* case, that was the first instance where the issue of intertemporal law grabbed the attention of international law practitioners and scholars.

The two patriarchs of international law had already taken position on the issue of time and change on the interpretation of treaties. Both Vattel and Grotius unequivocally came down on the side of the principle of contemporaneity arguing that '[l]anguages vary incessantly and the signification and force of words change with time. When an ancient act is to be interpreted, we should then know the common use of the terms at the time when it was written.'[71]

Originally, the concept of intertemporal considerations within the interpretative process had failed to register a significant impact on the deliberations of the *Institut de Droit International* (IDI). Only Lauterpacht during the Sienna Session (1952) made passing references to the issue.[72] Almost two decades later the IDI returned to the subject of intertemporal law with a vengeance, devoting the Wiesbaden Session on the matter culminating in a Resolution.[73] It has to be noted that the discussions attempted to address all aspects of intertemporal law, not just the interpretative ones, yet, the solution at which the members of IDI arrived was almost a *verbatim* reproduction of Huber's dictum.[74]

---

71 De Vattel 1793, Book II, Chapter XVII, para 272.

72 Lauterpacht, in: IDI 1952, at 405.

73 IDI 1975, at 536–541.

74 Ibid., paras 1, 3 and 4.

So what had transpired during these two IDI Sessions that could explain such a shift in focus? The answer can be found in the *travaux préparatoires*[75] of the VCLT and it is exactly to those that we shall now turn our attention.

6.3.2 Rejection of Explicit Incorporation of the Doctrine of Intertemporal Law in the VCLT: Draft Article 56

In his Third Report on the Law of Treaties *Special Rapporteur* Waldock proposed an article entitled 'Inter-temporal Law'. In this he essentially adopted Judge Huber's structure in his famous *Island of Palmas dictum*, substituting the terms of 'appreciation' and 'manifestation' with the terms 'interpretation' and 'application'.[76] Paragraph 1 of Draft Article 56 is a statement of the principle of contemporaneity, a principle which, according to *Special Rapporteur* Waldock, was supported by the international jurisprudence of the time.[77] Of import is the fact that Waldock felt the need to elaborate further on the driving force behind this jurisprudence. According to him, the reason why international courts and tribunals in that jurisprudence opted for the principle of contemporaneity was that it was closest to the *will of the parties*, especially considering that most of these disputes related to boundary treaties and related issues. It is only logical to assume that the parties would have wanted in such instances to resolve the matter once and for all and not for the boundaries to ebb and flow in tandem with the tidal forces of evolving delimitation principles of international law.[78]

This Draft Article sparked a fiery debate amongst the ILC members on several levels. Some objected to the apparent contradistinction between interpretation and

[75] *Lato* sensu, or *travaux préparatoires* of the second order. The debate on whether ILC discussions can be considered as preparatory work can be seen in the comments made by the Chairman, Tunkin, and El-Erian in: ILC, Summary record of the 873rd meeting, UN Doc. A/CN.4/SR.873, 20 June 1966, paras 25, 27, and 34, respectively. Rosenne was originally opposed to this idea. ILC, Summary record of the 872nd meeting, UN Doc. A/CN.4/SR.872, 17 June 1966, para 35. However, he was later persuaded by the arguments put forward by Tunkin. ILC, Summary record of the 873rd meeting, UN Doc. A/CN.4/SR.873, 20 June 1966, para 28.

[76] The text of the proposed Draft Article 56 went as follows: 'Article 56 – Inter-temporal law, 1. A Treaty is to be interpreted in the light of law in force at the time when the treaty was drawn up, [but] 2. Subject to paragraph 1, the *application* of a treaty shall be governed by the rules of international law in force at the time *when the treaty is applied.*' (emphasis added). Sir Humphrey Waldock, Special Rapporteur, Third report on the law of treaties, UN Doc. A/CN.4/167 and Add.1-3, 3 March–7 July 1964, at 8–9.

[77] *Grisbådarna* case at 159–160; *North Atlantic Coast Fisheries*, at 196; *US Nationals in Morocco*, at 189.

[78] Sir Humphrey Waldock, Special Rapporteur, Third report on the law of treaties, UN Doc. A/CN.4/167 and Add.1-3, 3 March–7 July 1964, at 10.

application,[79] others that the issue tackled topics that were addressed by or at least co-dependent on other areas of treaty law,[80] while others argued whether there was a hierarchical relationship between the two paragraphs.[81] Irrespective of this, the common denominator on which all ILC members seemed to agree was that the will of the parties was the decisive criterion for establishing which rules applied to a particular treaty *medio tempore*.[82] This fragmentation of approaches on Draft Article 56 was equally reflected in the comments made by the Governments, with some arguing in favour of a strict adherence to the principle of contemporaneity,[83] while others in favour of evolutive interpretation.[84] As to what should be the decisive criterion there were two main attractors: intention of the parties[85] and good faith.[86]

Following this, *Special Rapporteur* Waldock decided to omit Draft Article 56 from his Sixth Report. A critical factor in this decision was probably the fact that

[79] Paredes, in: ILC, Summary record of the 728th meeting, UN Doc. A/CN.4/SR.728, 21 May 1964, para 12. The debate on the exact content of these terms and whether they can be clearly distinguished from one another continues even today: McNair 1961, at 365; de Visscher 1963, at 27–28; Coing 1970, at 540–542; Sur 1974, at 193; Yasseen 1976, at 9–10; Bos 1984, at 112; Kolb 2006; Klabbers 2007, at 144; Gardiner 2008, at 27; Gourgourinis 2011, at 31–57; *Applicability of the Obligation to Arbitrate under Section 21 of the United Nations Headquarters Agreement of 26 June 1947*, ICJ, Advisory Opinion, 26 April 1988, Separate Opinion of Judge Shahabuddeen, at 59.

[80] Verdross, in: ILC, Summary record of the 728th meeting, UN Doc. A/CN.4/SR.728, 21 May 1964, para 6; Elias, Luna, Tunkin, El-Erian and Lachs, in: ILC, Summary record of the 729th meeting, UN Doc. A/CN.4/SR.729, 22 May 1964, paras 18–19, 30–32, 41–44, 49, and 53–55, respectively.

[81] Three main approaches were expressed as to this point: (i) that the principle of contemporaneity was the rule and evolutive interpretation the exception; Paredes (ILC, Summary record of the 728th meeting, UN Doc. A/CN.4/SR.728, 21 May 1964, paras 12–13) and Luna (ILC, Summary record of the 729th meeting, UN Doc. A/CN.4/SR.729, 22 May 1964, paras 31–37); (ii) that evolutive interpretation was the rule and the principle of contemporaneity was the exception; Castrén (ILC, Summary record of the 729th meeting, UN Doc. A/CN.4/SR.729, 22 May 1964 , para 3); and (iii) that the two paragraphs of Article 56 were not in conflict and not in a hierarchical relationship with respect to one another but that they should be applied in a complementary fashion; Rosenne, Briggs and Lachs (ILC, Summary record of the 729th meeting, UN Doc. A/CN.4/SR.729, 22 May 1964, paras 14–15, 38–40 and 54 respectively).

[82] Luna (ILC, Summary record of the 729th meeting, UN Doc. A/CN.4/SR.729, 22 May 1964, para 30); similarly de Aréchaga, Paredes (ILC, Summary record of the 728th meeting, UN Doc. A/CN.4/SR.728, 21 May 1964, paras 10–11, and 12–14 respectively) and Tsuruoka (ILC, Summary record of the 729th meeting, UN Doc. A/CN.4/SR.729, 22 May 1964, paras 24–26).

[83] UK, in: Sixth Committee, 20th Session, 843rd Meeting, 7 October 1965, UN Doc. A/C.6/20/SR.843, para 25.

[84] Greece: Sixth Committee, 20th Session, 845th Meeting, 11 October 1965, UN Doc. A/C.6/SR.845, paras 41–42.

[85] Kenya, in: Sixth Committee, 20th Session, 850th Meeting, 13 October 1965, UN Doc. A/C.6/SR.850, para 40; Syria, in: Sixth Committee, 20th Session, 845th Meeting, 11 October 1965, UN Doc. A/C.6/SR.845, para 9.

[86] The Netherlands in: ILC, Report of the International Law Commission on the work of its 18th Session—ANNEX, 4 May–19 July 1966, UN Doc. A/6309/Rev.l, reproduced in: YILC [1966] Vol. II, at 322–323, para 29.

the two legs of Draft Article 56 were being dealt with in other parts of the Draft Articles. In more detail, the first paragraph of Draft Article 56, '[a] treaty is to be interpreted in the light of law in force at the time when the treaty was drawn up', was supposed to be reflected in the Draft Articles on interpretation under discussion,[87] while the second paragraph, '[s]ubject to paragraph 1, the application of a treaty shall be governed by the rules of international law in force at the time when the treaty is applied', was considered to be regulated by Draft Article 68, which tackled the issue of modification of treaties.

It is perhaps ironic that references to intertemporal considerations in both of these Articles did not survive the scrutiny of future discussions and none of them found their way into the VCLT.[88] Nonetheless, during the Vienna Conferences on the Law of Treaties, Waldock reiterated that intertemporal law was fraught with difficulties and that the ILC had made the conscious and tactical choice of abandoning making explicit references to it, since otherwise its members would have gotten bogged down in addressing the highly mercurial relationship between customary law and treaty law.[89] The fact that the deletion of Draft Article 56 did not stir up too much controversy among the delegations of the Governments during the Vienna Conference on the Law of Treaties, seems to be a pretty good indication that these concerns also reverberated with the States.

6.3.3 Rejection of Explicit Solutions to Intertemporal Considerations Through the Backdoor of Article 31

Apart from Draft Article 56, intertemporal considerations found their way also into the debates on the rules of treaty interpretation and in particular what would eventually become Article 31(3)(c) VCLT. As with Draft Article 56 the main question was which rules were the ones pertinent for the interpretation of the treaty. Should a treaty be interpreted in the light of the rules in force at the time of the conclusion of the treaty or in force at the time of the interpretation of a treaty? Strong views were expressed in support of both approaches.[90] In an attempt to try and find a common ground for negotiation Special Rapporteur Waldock redrafted the text of then Draft Article 70 (later to become Article 31(3)(c) VCLT) to read:

---

[87] See Sect. 6.3.3.

[88] Any reference to intertemporal law was omitted from the relevant articles on interpretation, while Draft Article 68 was cannibalized and traces of it can be found in Articles 30 and 39–41 VCLT.

[89] Waldock, in: United Nations 1969, at 184, para 74.

[90] In favour of interpretation taking into account the rules at the time of the conclusion of the treaty were Yasseen, Pal and the Chairman; ILC, Summary record of the 765th meeting, UN Doc. A/CN.4/SR.765, 14 July 1964, paras 56–59, 75–76 and 80, respectively. In favour of interpretation taking into account the rules at the time of the interpretation of the treaty were Tunkin, Verdross and Bartos. Ibid., paras 48–49, 62 and 63–66, respectively.

'1.(b) in the light of the rules of international law [in force at the time of its conclusion]',[91] but the debate continued with even greater fervor.[92]

For this reason, in his Sixth Report on the Law of Treaties Waldock decided to remove the part that was within brackets. The Draft Article now read: '1. A treaty shall be interpreted … in the light of … (b) the rules of international law'.[93] This idea of wording the rule of interpretation in a manner that maximized its potential for flexibility,[94] seemed to have gained traction. Whereas the ILC members were previously polarized between adopting a solution that would take into account rules either at the time of the conclusion or at the time of the interpretation of a treaty, now they seemed to be rallying around the idea of ensuring a certain flexibility of the rule that would collapse into the proper solution on an ad hoc basis, guided by the intention of the parties.[95] It was this approach that was reflected in the final version of Article 31(3)(c) VCLT that was the basis of the discussions of the 1969 Vienna Conference on the Law of Treaties. As with the deletion of Draft Article 56, the delegations of the participating States were in agreement as to the solution adopted by the ILC, i.e. that of opting for a flexible approach rather than a rigid rule. As the delegation of the Netherlands very succinctly put it, since both the doctrine of intertemporal law and the rules on interpretation were essentially manifestations of the principle of good faith, there was no need for an explicit rule. It was the latter's application that would give the solution in each scenario as to whether the principle of contemporaneity or the evolutive interpretation was the most apposite response.[96]

[91] Waldock, in: ILC, Summary record of the 769th meeting, UN Doc. A/CN.4/SR.769, 17 July 1964, para 3.

[92] Rosenne, Briggs, Tunkin, Waldock, the Chairman, Yasseen, Amado and Verdross, in: ibid., paras 16, 21, 24, 25, 27, 28, 30, 32 respectively.

[93] Waldock, in: ILC, Summary record of the 869th meeting, UN Doc. A/CN.4/SR.869, 14 June 1966, para 59.

[94] Waldock and de Luna, in: ILC, Summary record of the 770th meeting, UN Doc. A/CN.4/SR.770, 20 July 1964, paras 33 and 34, respectively.

[95] (i) in favour of deletion: Verdross and Rosenne, in: ILC, Summary record of the 870th meeting, UN Doc. A/CN.4/SR.870, 15 June 1966, paras 13 and 21, respectively; Tsuruoka, in: ILC, Summary record of the 871st meeting, UN Doc. A/CN.4/SR.871, 16 June 1966, para 38; (ii) in favour of the intention of the parties being the decisive criterion: Comments by de Luna and de Aréchaga in: ILC, Summary record of the 870th meeting, UN Doc. A/CN.4/SR.870, 15 June 1966, paras 10–11 and 72–73, respectively; El-Erian, in: ILC, Summary record of the 871st meeting, UN Doc. A/CN.4/SR.871, 16 June 1966, para 31; Waldock, in: ILC, Summary record of the 872nd meeting, UN Doc. A/CN.4/SR.872, 17 June 1966, paras 9–10; (iii) in favour of retention of some reference to intertemporal law: Ago and Bartos, ILC, Summary record of the 870th meeting, UN Doc. A/CN.4/SR.870, 15 June 1966, paras 58 and 89–92, respectively; the Chairman, in: ILC, Summary record of the 871st meeting, UN Doc. A/CN.4/SR.871, 16 June 1966, paras 52–53.

[96] The Netherlands, in: Sixth Committee, 21st Session, 903rd Meeting, 4 October 1966, UN Doc. A/C.6/SR.903, para 15.

6.4 Points of Entry of Intertemporal Considerations in Article 31 VCLT

6.4.1 Direct Point of Entry

The examination of the discussion leading up to the VCLT revealed that although intertemporal considerations and their direct and indirect 'points of entry' within Article 31 VCLT, had been spotted by the ILC members, nonetheless the position that prevailed was that the less said the better. Flexibility though silence was considered to best serve the purpose of Article 31 VCLT, rather than explicit solutions incorporated within the text of that Article.

Similarly to the ILC, international jurisprudence seems also to favour a 'flexible approach'.[97] According to this

> approach using conventional language, or the "relevant rules of international law", the interpreter of a treaty will sometimes have to draw upon the language and rules that were in existence when the interpreted treaty was concluded, and sometimes upon the language and rules existing at the time of interpretation.[98]

The manner in which the interpreter will select one way or the other is reflective of the three mains schools of interpretation. Some argue that this decision is based on the object and purpose of the treaty,[99] while others posit that the nature of the terms[100] is the critical element. Finally there is another group, which holds that the intention of the parties is not only the critical element,[101] but ubiquitous in any kind of justification one might put forward with respect to adopting an evolutive interpretation.

6.4.1.1 Object and Purpose of the Treaty

The object and purpose of a treaty is sometimes used as a building block in order to establish the validity of evolutive interpretation. In the *Gabčíkovo-Nagymaros Project* case, for instance, the ICJ's analysis seems to be teetering between the intention of the parties, on the one hand, and the nature of the obligations contained in the treaty and its object and purpose, on the other.[102] This reflects a growing trend in international jurisprudence to justify recourse to evolutive interpretation based on the nature of the text being interpreted, i.e. its object and purpose. There are two groups of treaties where this trend is most pronounced:

---

[97] Linderfalk, identifies three approaches to solving intertemporal issues: (i) the categorically static approach (ii) the categorically dynamic approach and (iii) the flexible approach. Linderfalk 2008, at 113.

[98] Ibid.

[99] Bernhardt 2000, at 16–17; Jennings and Watts 1992, at 1282.

[100] Engelen 2004, at 285–286.

[101] de Aréchaga 1978, at 49; Sinclair 1984, at 140.

[102] *Gabčíkovo-Nagymaros Project*, paras 111–112, and 140.

(i) human rights treaties (and to a lesser degree environmental treaties) and (ii) constituent instruments of international organisations.

With respect to human rights (and environmental) treaties, the idea is that because of the uniqueness and importance of the rights protected by these instruments, their existence and continued relevance must be secured in the face of challenges posed by a constantly changing legal and societal environment.[103] The extensive jurisprudence, especially of the European Court of Human Rights (ECtHR) and the Inter-American Court of Human Rights (IACtHR), on the matter seems to *prima facie* support this point.[104] However, that is not to say that human rights treaties are an automatic exception to the principle of contemporaneity, and that to them only evolutive interpretation should be applied. If one scrutinizes the relevant cases it becomes readily apparent that the argument based on the object and purpose of the human rights treaties, is not a self-standing one. On the contrary, it is predicated on the intention of the parties. Since '[human rights treaties] represent the very archetype of treaty instruments in which the Contracting Parties *must have intended* that the principles and concepts which they employed should be understood and applied in the light of developing social attitudes'.[105] More than a decade earlier, Higgins had arrived at the same conclusion. '"[G]eneric clauses" and *human rights provisions* are not really random exceptions to a general rule … [but] an application of a wider principle – *intention of the parties, reflected by reference to the object and purpose* – that guides the law of treaties'.[106] Consequently, the reason why evolutive interpretation may seem to be more tailored to the needs and particularities of human rights (and environmental) treaty provisions is not simply and solely because of their object and purpose, but because this very object and purpose r*eflects the intention (explicit or presumed) of the parties*. The object and purpose argument in favour of evolutive interpretation is simply a variant of the 'time-will' (intention) of the parties.

The same arguments hold true for the second group of treaties for which evolutive interpretation has been argued to be better tailored *in lieu* of the principle of contemporaneity, i.e. constituent instruments of international organizations. Sands and Klein have argued that '[t]here is some authority for the proposition that a treaty of constitutional character should be subject to different rules of interpretation to allow for the "intrinsically evolutionary nature of a constitution"'.[107] Based on that it is no big leap to conclude that 'given the changing nature of the problems and circumstances international organizations have to confront, *a degree*

---

[103] *Caesar v Trinidad and Tobago*, Separate Opinion of Judge Cançado Trindade, para 11, citing *Loizidou v Turkey*, para 75; *'Other Treaties' Subject to the Advisory Jurisdiction of the Court*, IACtHR, Advisory Opinion, 24 September 1982; *Restrictions to the Death Penalty*, IACtHR, Advisory Opinion, 8 September 1983; *The Effect of Reservations on the Entry Into Force of the American Convention on Human Rights*, IACtHR, Advisory Opinion, 24 September 1982.

[104] Generally see Bjorge 2014; Letsas 2007.

[105] *RosInvest v Russia*, para 39 (emphasis added).

[106] Higgins 1996, at 181 (emphasis added).

[107] Sands and Klein 2009, at 454, citing Jennings and Watts 2008, at 1268; *US Nationals in Morocco*, at 211.

of evolutionary adaptation is the only realistic approach to realizing the underlying purposes of the organization as laid down in its constituent instrument.'[108]

However, looking closely at the arguments in support of evolutive interpretation of these instruments by virtue of their 'intrinsically evolutionary nature' it is notable that not a single author argues either that constituent instruments of international organisations are an automatic exception to the principle of contemporaneity or that object and purpose is the basic reason for recourse to evolutive interpretation. All of the relevant analysis in doctrine sooner or later comes back to the acknowledgement that for the purposes of evolutive interpretation the nature of the treaty is a reflection of the intention of the parties.[109] Of note is Brölmann's excellent analysis on the topic, who draws attention to the fact that teleological interpretation and evolutive interpretation should not be conflated with one another, and that it is actually teleological rather than evolutive interpretation that features more prominently in the interpretation of these treaties.[110]

Consequently, object and purpose of a treaty may assist international judges in determining whether a particular provision should be interpreted evolutively or not, but it can never be the sole basis of this determination. Recourse to evolutive interpretation will unerringly be based on the expressed or presumed intention of the parties. By the same token, no automatic exceptions (either of human rights treaties or of constituent instruments of international organisations) to the principle of contemporaneity can be deduced from international jurisprudence. Any exception will, once again, be based on the intention of the parties.

6.4.1.2 'Generic Terms'

The text itself and, in particular, the linguistic characteristics of the terms being interpreted may also have a bearing on the intertemporal dimension in the interpretation of treaties. A term, which is 'generic' may push an international court or tribunal in the direction of opting for an evolutive interpretation.[111] Various attempts have been to define what exactly a 'generic term' is. It has been described as a 'variable concept',[112] a term with 'evolutionary potential',[113] 'whose content

[108] *RosInvest v Russia*, para 39 (emphasis added).

[109] Schermers and Blokker 2011, paras 1155–1156 and 1347; Sands and Klein 2009, at 454; Blokker 2013; Sato 1996, at 150–160.

[110] Brölmann 2012, at 512–514.

[111] *Iron Rhine Arbitration*, paras 79–80; *Nationality Decrees Issued in Tunis and Morocco*, PCIJ, Advisory Opinion, 7 February 1923, at 24; *Aegean Sea Continental Shelf*, paras 74–7; *Gabčíkovo-Nagymaros Project*, para 112; *US-Shrimp (AB)*, para 130; *Dispute Regarding Navigational Rights*, paras 65–67.

[112] Reuter, in: ILC, Summary record of the 871st meeting, UN Doc. A/CN.4/SR.871, 16 June 1966, para 23.

[113] *Mondev*, para 119.

the parties expected would change through time',[114] and whose 'meaning was intended to follow the evolution of the law'.[115] Despite the fact that a generally accepted definition of 'generic term' continues to elude us, an *ex ante* determination of the 'generic' or not nature of a term could prove useful as it may be quite a forceful argument in favour of evolutive interpretation.

Drawing inspiration from linguistics Linderalk and Helmersen attempt such an *ex ante* determination. The former, identifies three groups of 'referring expressions'[116]: (i) 'definite referring expressions', which refer to one or more specific phenomena (ii) 'indefinite referring expressions', which refer to one or more non-specific phenomena and (iii) 'generic referring expressions', which refer to one or more phenomena as they change in time.[117] Out of these groups only the 'generic referring expressions' are not time-bound since 'no relationship is established between the time of the utterance and the time when the referent was assumed to exist'.[118] Consequently, such expressions by their nature offer 'stronger reasons for *the assumption* that the parties expressed their agreement in such a way that (a) the treaty agrees with the conventional language that exists at the moment of interpretation, and that (b) the treaty will have effects consistent with the international law then in force'.[119]

Helmersen suggests a different taxonomy. According to him, 'generic terms' can be characterised as either (i) 'value driven' or (ii) 'non-value driven' and linguistically as either (i) 'evolving' or (ii) 'non-evolving'.[120] Combining these two taxonomies creates a set of four different groups of 'generic terms: (i) 'value-driven non-evolving', (ii) 'value driven evolving', (iii) 'non-value driven non-evolving' and (iv) 'non-value driven evolving'. 'Non evolving terms', irrespective of whether they are 'value driven' or not, are open to evolutive interpretation only on the basis of the terms being given a 'special meaning', as per under Article 31(4) VCLT. 'Value driven evolving' terms by definition would be assumed to have 'evolutionary potential' as that is the presumed intention of the parties for selecting these terms. Finally, for 'non-value driven evolving' terms the *in casu* tribunal would not be able to rest on the previous assumptions but would have to go into a detailed analysis in order to determine the 'time-will' of the parties.[121] Furthermore, according to Helmersen, in the jurisprudence of the ICJ a presumption seems to be

---

[114] *Kasikili/Sedudu Island*, Declaration of Judge Higgins, para 2.

[115] *Aegean Sea Continental Shelf*, para 77.

[116] 'Referring expression' is an expression used by an 'utterer' for the purpose of 'reference'. In turn 'reference' refers to the relationship between an expression and what the expression stands for in the world at the time that it is uttered; Linderfalk 2008, at 129.

[117] Ibid., at 130–131. An example of 'generic referring expression' is the term 'territorial status of Greece'. See *Aegean Continental Shelf*.

[118] Ibid., at 132.

[119] Ibid., at 135.

[120] Helmersen 2013, at 139.

[121] Ibid., at 139.

emerging in favour of evolutive interpretation when two conditions are met: (i) when the term is 'generic' and (ii) when the treaty is of unlimited duration.[122]

All the above attempts to linguistically pre-determine whether a term should be interpreted evolutively or not raise many interesting points. However, as in the previous section on 'Object and Purpose', the text of the treaty and the 'generic' nature of terms cannot and are not the sole basis for opting for evolutive interpretation. First of all, in very few cases are there any indications given as to why some terms are characterized as 'generic'[123] and in no case has this been done on a strictly linguistic basis. Unfortunately, in most cases the judges simply say they are so and therefore they are; *post hoc ergo propter hoc*. Furthermore, even in the cases where 'generic terms' are used to allow recourse to evolutive interpretation, it is not the text which is the sole basis for justifying such recourse, but what is actually hidden behind the text, the 'time-will' of the parties, i.e. their intention to allow certain terms to evolve or to force them to remain static in time.[124] Judge Higgins, once again, draws our attention that neither the text, nor the object and purpose of a treaty can be the sole basis for evolutive interpretation. These are mere reflections of the true basis. It is always the intention of the parties (specifically, their 'time-will') that should be the international judge's Northern star when examining whether an evolutive interpretation should be opted for.

> [The aim] is *not to discover a mythical 'ordinary meaning'* … we must never lose sight of the fact that *we are seeking to give flesh to the intention of the parties*, expressed in generalized terms in 1890. We must trace a thread back to this point of departure. *We should not*, as the Court appears at times to be doing, decide what *in abstracto* the term 'the main channel' might today mean, *by a mechanistic appreciation of relevant indicia*. Rather, our task is to decide what general idea the parties had in mind, and then make reality of that general idea through the use of contemporary knowledge.[125]

6.4.1.3 Intention of the Parties

The principle of contemporaneity as identified by Fitzmaurice and elaborated on in the writings of Thirlway, provides that the intention of the parties determines whether the terms of the treaty being interpreted should retain the meaning they

---

[122] Helmersen 2013, at 135–138; *Dispute Regarding Navigational Rights*, paras 65–67; *Aegean Sea Continental Shelf*, para 77.

[123] *Ambiente Ufficio SpA and others v Argentina*, ICSID Case No. ARB/08/9, Decision of 8 February 2013, para 492; *Siemens AG v Argentina*, ICSID Case No. ARB/02/8, Decision of 3 August 2014, para 114 (Respondent's claim).

[124] *Namibia Advisory Opinion*, para 53; *Aegean Sea Continental Shelf*, para 77; *Dispute Regarding Navigational Rights*, para 66; ibid., Separate Opinion of Judge Skotnikov, para 6; *Siemens AG v Argentina*, para 114 (Respondent's claim). In all of these cases, the relevant judicial body although making use of 'generic terms', always comes back to the fact that the selection of such terms reflects the intention of the parties to allow these terms to evolve (i.e. is a reflection of the 'time-will of the parties').

[125] *Kasikili/Sedudu Island*, Declaration of Judge Higgins, paras 3–4.

had at the conclusion of the treaty or whether they should follow the evolution of fact or law. It is this intention that is the critical element to be considered. Since so far we have talked about 'time-slices', and 'space-time worms', it is only appropriate to refer to this intention of the parties that determines the temporal destiny of a particular term as the 'time-will' of the parties. This 'time-will' may be identified by reference to the text of the treaty, the drafting history, the object and purpose of the treaty, state practice, as well as other relevant treaties.[126]

As was demonstrated above both the ideas of the principle of contemporaneity and evolutive interpretation are premised on the intention of the parties, their 'time-will'. This preliminary observation was reaffirmed as we went through the *travaux préparatoires* of Article 31 VCLT. The same conclusion was reached in Sects. 6.4.1.1 and 6.4.1.2 by examination of the relevant international jurisprudence. It would be unnecessary to reproduce all the relevant passages. However, one additional point needs to be made here. The *Namibia Advisory Opinion* is sometimes used as one of the first examples where the Court resorted to evolutive interpretation based on the 'generic' nature of the terms.[127] However, as we already saw the selection of these terms leads to a presumption regarding the 'time-will' of the parties.[128] Hence, we come back to the intention of the parties as the critical element. To strengthen this point, it is noteworthy that both Fitzmaurice in his Dissenting Opinion[129] and Thirlway in his writings[130] criticised the Court because they could find no evidence of this evolutive 'time-will' of the parties and the Court had failed to provide any evidence of such intent.

Consequently, irrespective of which school of interpretation one takes as a starting point, and irrespective of which presumptions may apply, in all situations the deciding factor either directly or indirectly was and still is the 'time-will' of the parties.

6.4.2 *Indirect Point of Entry*

Apart from the aforeanalysed 'direct points of entry' intertemporal considerations also find their way in the interpretative process indirectly. Below two 'indirect points of entry' have been identified: (i) the 'relevant rules' of Article 31(3)(c)

---

126 These could be either 'relevant rules' under Article 31(3)(c), or *in pari materia* treaties; *Daimler Financial Services AG v Argentina*, paras 220 *et seq.* Article 31(3)(c) and *in pari materia* treaties have been termed in the alternative, because the issue of whether *in pari materia* treaties fall under Article 31(3)(c) is still a matter of academic debate. See also Engelen 2004, at 291; Higgins 1996, at 180–181; Fitzmaurice 2008b; Yasseen 1976, at 66–67.

127 The exact wording of the ICJ was 'by definition evolutionary'. *Namibia Advisory Opinion*, para 53.

128 'The Parties to the Covenant [by selecting these generic terms] *must consequently be deemed to have accepted them as such* [i.e. non-static and evolutive]'. *Namibia Advisory Opinion*, para 53 (emphasis added).

129 Ibid., Dissenting Opinion of Judge Fitzmaurice, para 85.

130 Thirlway 1989, at 137; Fitzmaurice 2008b.

and (ii) the question of which rules of interpretation, and specifically which 'time-slice' or 'stage' the international courts and tribunals should apply when interpreting a treaty. Through both of these points of entry the normative content of a rule may be determined by means of taking into account other rules or principles, and thus be affected indirectly by those norms.

6.4.2.1 'Relevant Rules' at the Time of the Conclusion of the Treaty or at the Time of the Interpretation of the Treaty?

As shown above in Sect. 6.3.3, one of the main problems with respect to the doctrine of intertemporal law finding its expression in the text of Article 31, was whether Article 31(3)(c) VCLT should at the end be complemented by the expression 'at the time of the conclusion of the treaty'. Eventually the ILC opted for the deletion of that particular wording.

The non-inclusion of 'at the time of the conclusion of the treaty' in the final text has been interpreted in a variety of ways. Jacobs argues that the abandonment of that particular sentence implies that Article 31(3)(c) VCLT includes 'subsequent developments not initially envisaged by the parties'.[131] Greig, on the other hand, adopts a more contextual approach to the interpretation of that intentional omission. Since Article 31(3)(a) and (b) VCLT refer to future events, this should also colour our understanding of Article 31(3)(c) VCLT. Hence it covers both rules of international law at the time of the conclusion of a treaty and rules of international law at the time of the interpretation of the treaty.[132]

From the discussion within the ILC one can come to the conclusion that the understanding was that a flexible approach was necessary. Including a rigid solution, in the form of a sentence like 'at the time of the conclusion of the treaty', would fail to take into account the most decisive criterion in deciding intertemporal issues within the interpretative process, the 'time-will' of the parties. Consequently, any reference to 'relevant rules' would be decided on the basis of this 'time-will' as is the case for all other intertemporal-related interpretative issues, as shown from the analysis in Sects. 6.4.1.1–6.4.1.3. In fact, even though there is no explicit reference to this 'time-will'-based approach in the text of Article 31 VCLT, it is included in the term 'relevant'. Any international court or tribunal in order to determine the 'relevance' of a rule would have amongst others to examine the 'temporal relevance' of the treaty being considered for the purposes of Article 31(3)(c) VCLT.[133]

In the case of the human rights courts, the practice seems to reflect this. Although regrettably there is no discussion as to the 'time-will' of the parties in the context of Article 31(3)(c) VCLT, nonetheless there is always reference to the

---

[131] Jacobs 1969, at 331.

[132] Greig 2001, at 46.

[133] Merkouris 2015, Chapters 1 and 2.

'living instrument' nature of the treaty as a whole, which as mentioned above implies that the 'time-will' of the parties was for the treaty to evolve. This is also reaffirmed in the cases where the courts have referred to an evolution not of fact, but of law.[134] In any event, both the IACtHR[135] and the ECtHR[136] have referred without hesitation to posterior treaties in order to interpret the American Convention on Human Rights (ACHR)[137] and the European Convention on Human Rights (ECHR)[138] respectively. Interesting is also the fact that the IACtHR tends to refer to 'the *corpus juris* of international human rights',[139] which again would seem to be an indirect reflection of the 'time-will' of the parties for the treaty to follow the evolution of this *corpus juris*.[140]

The jurisprudence of the other international courts and tribunals is a little bit more problematic. Despite the fact that they also refer both to anterior and posterior treaties they do so without any examination regarding the 'time-will' of the parties.[141] It can only be presumed that such considerations may have entered the judicial mind during the examination of whether a particular treaty was 'relevant' for the interpretative purposes of Article 31(3)(c) VCLT, however, unless this is put down in writing it can only remain a tentative presumption. This presumption becomes even more difficult to establish with certainty because international judicial bodies also offer only indirect *indicia* as to what they take into account for

---

[134] See Sect. 6.2.3.

[135] *Villa García and others v Colombia*, IACtHR, Judgment of 1 July 2006, para 157; *Juridical Status and Human Rights of Undocumented Migrants*, IACtHR, Advisory Opinion, 17 September 2003, para 120; *Right to Information on Consular Assistance*, paras 112–115; *Gómez Paquiyauri and others v Peru*, paras 165–166; *Case of the 'Street Children' v Guatemala*, paras 193–194; *Juridical Status and Human Rights of the Child*, para 24; *Serrano Cruz and Serrano Cruz v El Salvador*, IACtHR, Preliminary Objections, Judgment of 23 November 2004, para 119.

[136] ECtHR Research Division 2011, at 1–41; Merkouris 2015, Chapters 1 and 2; Pitea 2013, at 545–559.

[137] 1969 American Convention on Human Rights, 1144 UNTS 123.

[138] 1950 European Convention for the Protection of Human Rights and Fundamental Freedoms, 213 UNTS 221.

[139] See *Villa García and others v Colombia*, para 157; *Juridical Status and Human Rights of Undocumented Migrants*, para 120; *Right to Information on Consular Assistance*, paras 112–115; *Gómez Paquiyauri and others v Peru*, paras 165–166; *Case of the 'Street Children' v Guatemala*, paras 193–194; *Juridical Status and Human Rights of the Child*, para 24; *Serrano Cruz and Serrano Cruz v El Salvador (Preliminary Objections)*, para 119.

[140] Interesting also, is the fact that the IACtHR in its jurisprudence makes no reference whatsoever to whether these other treaties to which it can refer have to be applicable in the relations between the parties to the treaty or between the parties to the dispute. In fact its practice seems to suggest that it opts for the latter solution as long as the treaty is deemed to be 'relevant'; *Serrano Cruz and Serrano Cruz v El Salvador (Preliminary Objections)*, para 119; see also *Yakye Axa Indigenous Community v Paraguay*, para 125; *Tibi v Ecuador*, IACtHR, Judgment of 7 September 2004, para 144; *Gómez Paquiyauri and others v Peru*, para 164; *Case of the 'Street Children' v Guatemala*, paras 192–193; *Right to Information on Consular Assistance*, para 113.

[141] For a detailed analysis of the relevant jurisprudence see Merkouris 2015, Chapters 1 and 2.

purposes of determining relevance.[142] Despite this, a proper application of Article 31(3)(c) VCLT requires a flexible approach, where a treaty's relevance will be deemed ad hoc on the basis of, amongst others, the 'time-will' of the parties.

6.4.2.2 The Intertemporal Application of the Rules of Interpretation

Another interesting manifestation of an 'indirect point of entry' stems from the interplay between the intertemporal law doctrine and the principle of non-retroactivity. The latter is a recognised principle of international law,[143] and has been incorporated in Article 4 of the VCLT.

The logical implication of this provision is that the VCLT does not apply either to itself or to any treaty that was concluded prior to its entry into force (27 January 1980). Consequently, if a treaty was concluded prior to 1980 then the rules of interpretation that should be applied are not the VCLT rules of interpretation, but their customary law counterparts.

So far so good, but it is at this point where things start to become somewhat tricky. Let us say, for instance, that we have a treaty concluded in 1890 and being interpreted in 2015. The VCLT clearly does not apply. What would apply would be the customary rules on interpretation. The ICJ is very fond of saying that the VCLT rules on interpretation reflect customary international law[144] but customary law of which point in time? To argue that the content of the customary rules on interpretation has remained unchanged throughout the ages seems somewhat counterintuitive.[145] Yet, this is what the ICJ did in the *Kasikili/Sedudu Island* case, which revolved around the interpretation of an 1890 treaty between Britain and Germany, that later determined the boundary between Botswana and Namibia. The ICJ argued that despite the fact that neither Botswana nor Namibia was a party to the VCLT, Article 31 was applicable 'inasmuch as it reflects

---

[142] Ibid.; Merkouris considers that the term 'relevant' is the least analysed but perhaps the most important term of Article 31(3)(c) VCLT. From the jurisprudence he concludes that the term 'relevant' is nothing more than the application of the 'proximity criterion', which consists of: (i) party proximity (ii) linguistic proximity (iii) subject-matter proximity and (iv) temporal proximity. Recently, the WTO AB affirmed Merkouris' conclusions on the importance of relevance in: *EC–Large Civil Aircraft*, WTO Appellate Body, WT/DS316/AB/R, 18 May 2011, para 845.

[143] *The Chamizal case (Mexico v. USA)*, Award of 15 June 1911, RIAA Vol. 11 (1961), at 343; *Clipperton Island Arbitration (Mexico v. France)*, Award of 28 January 1931, RIAA Vol. 2 (1949), at 1105–1111; *Ambatielos case (Greece v. UK)*, ICJ, Preliminary Objections, Judgment of 1 July 1952, at 40; Cheng 1987; McNair 1957, at 1–19; von Verdross 1935, at 195–251; Reuter 1964, at 263–283; Tavernier 1979, at 116–117.

[144] *Kasikili/Sedudu Island*, para 18; citing *Case Concerning the Territorial Dispute (Libyan Arab Jamahariya/Chad)*, ICJ, Judgment of 3 February 1994, para 41 (hereinafter *Libya/Chad Territorial Dispute*); *Case Concerning Oil Platforms (Iran v USA)*, ICJ, Merits, Judgment of 6 November 2003, para 23.

[145] For an example of gradual changes in the understanding and possibly customary content of the use of preparatory work in the interpretative process, see Merkouris 2010, at 75–98.

customary international law'.[146] Judges Oda[147] and Higgins[148] expressed some thoughts and concerns on the intertemporal issues raised by this practice, but did this only *in passim* and in the end seemed to accept the Court's application of Article 31 *qua* customary international law. What is worrying is that this was neither the first nor the last time that international courts and tribunals used the argument that Articles 31 and 32 VCLT reflect customary international law to interpret treaties, going as far back as the 19th century,[149] to which the VCLT clearly did not apply and in respect of which it would have been at least logical to inquire whether the content of the customary rules of interpretation of the time was identical.[150] So what could be the possible results of such an enquiry?

Scenario 1: The rules of interpretation have remained unchanged during the last two centuries. Although this scenario seems to be the one suggested by the practice of the international courts and tribunals it seems somewhat counterintuitive compared to the radical changes seen in the international community as a whole. It is true that jurisprudence of that time seems to indicate that no earth-shattering changes have taken place, with respect to the content of the rules of interpretation,[151] but from there to argue that no change at all has taken place is quite a leap,[152] and one that cannot and should not be taken by international courts and tribunals without at least some sort of research and judicial analysis.

Scenario 2: The rules of interpretation are an exception to the principle of contemporaneity. Any treaty must be interpreted in accordance with the rules of interpretation at the time of the interpretation of the treaty. Although this scenario would also resolve any difficulties with the existing practice of international courts and tribunals, nonetheless it would fly in the face of everything we have seen so far with respect to the principle of contemporaneity and evolutive interpretation. In all cases, the decisive criterion is the 'time-will' of the parties. Automatic and mechanical applications of such exceptions, as has been seen *supra*, are to be avoided unless they are accompanied by strong *indicia* that such is the intention of the parties.

---

[146] *Kasikili/Sedudu Island*, para 18.

[147] Ibid., Separate Opinion of Judge Oda, para 4.

[148] Ibid., Declaration of Judge Higgins, para 4.

[149] Some cases are: *Libya/Chad Territorial Dispute*; *Case Concerning Oil Platforms*; *Case Concerning Sovereignty over Pulau Ligitan and Pulau Sipadan (Indonesia/Malaysia)*, ICJ, Judgment of 17 December 2002; *Case Concerning Avena and Other Mexican Nationals (Mexico v USA)*, ICJ, Judgment of 31 March 2004. Linderfalk offers a long list of cases where international courts and tribunals have simply used the 'jail-free' card of Article 31 as reflecting customary international law to indirectly apply the VCLT rules on interpretation to much earlier treaties. Linderfalk 2011, at 163–165.

[150] These concerns are also raised by Greig 2001, at 113–114; Fox 2010, at 64–65, Linderfalk 2011, at 163–165; Shaw 2000, at 968.

[151] *Charles van Bokkelen case (USA v Haiti)*, Award of 24 May 1888, Moore International Arbitrations Vol. 2 (1898), at 1849; *Samoan Claims (Germany, Great Britain and USA)*, Award of 14 October 1902, RIAA Vol. 9 (1959), at 25; the *Chamizal case*.

[152] And one not reflecting the actual changes in the rules of interpretation. See Merkouris 2010.

Scenario 3: The rule of interpretation to be applied is the rule at the time of the conclusion of the treaty (in the case of our example, 1890), unless the 'time-will' of the parties was for the treaty to evolve and be interpreted by reference to the relevant rules at the time of the interpretation of the treaty. This scenario seems to come closer to the paradigms we have examined above and the relationship between the principle of contemporaneity and evolutive interpretation. The principle of contemporaneity is the rule and evolutive interpretation can be resorted to *only if the parties so intended.* Similarly, the rules of interpretation to be applied should be the ones contemporaneous to the conclusion of the treaty (principle of contemporaneity), unless the parties intended for the treaty to evolve and for it to be interpreted by the interpretative rules as they also evolved. However, this scenario would require international courts and tribunals to engage in a serious analysis of: (i) what the 'time-will' of the parties was and (ii) what the content of the contemporaneous customary rule of interpretation was. If the 'time-will' was for the treaty to evolve then a similar 'time-will' could be presumed for the rules of interpretation. But what happens if the 'time-will' of the parties was for the treaty to remain static? A question which brings us to the next scenario.

Scenario 4: The rule of interpretation to be applied is the rule at the time of the conclusion of the treaty and the 'time-will' of the parties was for the treaty to remain static. In this situation the rule of interpretation to be applied would be the one contemporaneous to the 1890 treaty. The only possible avenue to apply the modern rules of interpretation would be if one could prove that the Article 31(3)(c) VCLT customary law equivalent in 1890 had a content to the effect of '*all relevant rules of international law at the time of the interpretation of the treaty*'. In such a case the 2015 rules on interpretation would be taken into account by virtue of them being relevant. Furthermore, this would not conflict with the principle of non-retroactivity, because (i) they would not be applied, but 'taken into account and (ii) the 2015 rules of interpretation *would not apply retroactively.* On the contrary the 1890 rules of interpretation would *take the 2015 rules into account prospectively.*

However, this construction would be extremely implausible on several grounds: (i) the analysis of the VCLT *travaux préparatoires* clearly demonstrated that the customary equivalent of Article 31(3)(c) VCLT did not have such a content and the situation would probably be no different at all at earlier times and (ii) it would seem to conflict with the idea that the 'time-will' of the parties is the decisive factor. How could the parties want a treaty to be static on the one hand, but interpreted by modern (evolved) rules on interpretation, on the other?

The above scenarios were used to highlight that the issue of which rule of interpretation applies in the interpretation of a treaty, contrary to what seems to be suggested by jurisprudence, is fraught with difficulties and extremely complex. It simply cannot be pushed aside by repeating the mantra that the VCLT rules on treaty interpretation are a 'reflection of customary international law'. It is an issue intrinsically connected to intertemporality and must receive equal attention and analysis not just by academics but by jurisprudence alike.

6.5 Limits

Evolutive interpretation allows a treaty, like a 'living tree', to expand and grow to adapt to modern challenges and tackle problems that the drafters had and could not foresee. However, such growth and expansion of the treaty is not unrestricted, otherwise this would be the equivalent of giving the judges a *pouvoir de légiférer*. Consequenlty, evolutive interpretation has limits.[153]

The first of these is *jus cogens*. By the very definition of *jus cogens* as norms from which no derogation is possible, one can logically conclude that the interpretative process could never allow for an interpretation that would result in such a derogation. Consequently, no evolutive interpretation is allowed to go against *jus cogens* norms.[154]

Another limit is the principle of non-retroactivity. In Sect. 6.4.2.2 the interplay between intertemporal law and the principle of non-retroactivty was touched upon. The principle of non-retroactivity does not conflict *ipso facto* with intertemporal law, it however provides the outer limit beyond which no evolutive interpretation can be permitted.[155]

The most important however, limit is that evolutive interpretation should always observe the general rule laid down in Article 31 VCLT,[156] and in particular the text of the provision being interpreted,[157] its context,[158] and the intention of the parties.[159]

---

153 Or precautions as Judge Bedjaoui characterized them. *Gabčíkovo-Nagymaros Project*, Separate Opinion of Judge Bedjaoui, para 5.

154 *Application of the Convention on the Prevention and Punishment of the Crime of Genocide (Bosnia and Herzegovina v Serbia and Montenegro)*, ICJ, Judgment of 26 February 2007, Joint Declaration of Judges Shi and Koroma, para 2; *South-West Africa(Second Phase) (Liberia and Ethiopia v South Africa)*, ICJ, Judgment of 18 July 1966, Dissenting Opinion of Judge Tanaka, at 293–295; IDI 1975, at 536; Kotzur 2009, para 13; McWhinney 1984, at 183; Georgopoulos 2004, at 146.

155 *ATA Construction, Industrial and Trading Company v Jordan*, para 109; *Mondev*, para 70.

156 *Gabčíkovo-Nagymaros Project*, Separate Opinion of Judge Bedjaoui, para 5.

157 *Al-Saadoon and Mufdhi v UK*, ECtHR, No. 61498/08, para 119; *Feldbrugge v Netherlands*, ECtHR, No. 8562/79, 29 May 1986, Joint Dissenting Opinion of Judges Ryssdal, Bindschedler-Robert, Lagergren, Matscher, Sir Evans, Bernhardt and Gersing, para 24; *Albert and Le Compte v Belgium*, ECtHR, No. 7299/75, 10 February 1983, Partly Dissenting Opinion of Judge Matscher, para 3.

158 *Soering v UK*, ECtHR, No. 14038/88, A/161, 7 July 1989, para 103.

159 *Gabčíkovo-Nagymaros Project*, Separate Opinion of Judge Bedjaoui, para 7.

Finally, another limit, and the common denominator of the ones previously mentioned, is that evolutive interpretation may never amount to a revision of the treaty.[160] Treaty revision is within the purview of its parties, not of the judges. Any evolutive interpretation that leads to a *de facto* revision of the treaty, essentially amounts to an exercise of a of *pouvoir de légiférer* by the judges, which has always been held both by jurisprudence and doctrine to be forbidden territory.[161] As Dupuy very eloquently put it: '[m]emory must remain loyal and not serve to rewrite history; a treaty belongs to its authors and not to the judge'.[162]

6.6 Conclusion

This chapter started with a question: 'Do treaties endure, perdure or exdure'? These three verbs represent three philosophical schools on identity, time and change. Endurantism holds that an object does not have temporal parts and that it exists wholly at every instance. Perdurantism, on the other hand, views objects as 'space-time worms', consisting of both spatial and temporal parts, and only a fraction of it existing at any given moment. Exdurantism, tries to bridge the above two schools. In it objects have both spatial and temporal parts. An object, according to exdurantism is simply the sum of its various 'object-stages', each of which exists autonomously in a counterpart relationship to the others, consequently the object exists wholly within any given moment.

The question then was whether these considerations could be transposed to treaties as well, particularly with respect to how time affects them. The prism selected to test this hypothesis was 'the intertemporal considerations in the interpretative process'. How does time affect the rules being interpreted? There were two main points of entry through which intertemporal considerations influenced interpretative outcomes, 'the direct point of entry', where time affected the content of a norm as such, and the 'indirect point of entry' where it was not the norm itself that changed through time, but its normative context, i.e. the rules surrounding it, the system in which it functions, the 'relevant rules' of Article 31(3)(c) VCLT.

---

160 Ibid., para 5; *Kasikili/Sedudu Island*, Declaration of Judge Higgins, para 2; *Laguna del Desierto*, para 157; *Claude Reyes and others v Chile*, IACtHR, Judgment of 19 September 2006, Separate Opinion of Judge Ramírez, paras 1 and 3.

161 *Bayatyan v Armenia*, ECtHR, No. 23459/03, 7 July 2011, Dissenting Opinion of Judge Gyulumyan, para 2; *Meftah v France*, Concurring Opinion of Judge Lorenzen joined by Hedigan; Helmersen 2013, at 137; Thirlway 1989, at 142; French 2006, 296–297.

162 Dupuy 2011, at 129. Although, citing Chief Justice Holmes, he acknowledges that when international judges seek the presumed intention of the parties 'evolutionary interpretation is not simply an exercise of memory; it tends towards prophecy'. In this case, it will be difficult to determine when the judge is still within the prescribed limits of evolutive interpretation or when s/he has crossed the line of *pouvoir de légiférer*. Ibid., at 126–127, citing Holmes 1897, at 458.

By examining the preparatory work of the ILC and the relevant jurisprudence we concluded that this was a constant battle between the principle of contemporaneity, on the one hand, and the evolutive interpretation, on the other. The former requires terms to be understood as frozen in time. A treaty at every single 'time-slice' is completely there and unchanged. So according to the principle of contemporaneity a treaty endures. Evolutive interpretation, on the other hand, is based on the premise that the evolution of fact and law affects the content of a treaty. Consequently, depending on one's ontological point of view, either the treaty at any given 'time-slice' is never wholly there, *ergo* it perdures, or if one is of the view that a treaty is relevant only at the point when it is being interpreted, then it would seem that the treaty is nothing more than a series of changing 'judicial snap-shots'. In this sense, the treaty exdures.

So which of the two (the principle of contemporaneity or evolutive interpretation) is the optimal solution? As was revealed by the VCLT *travaux prératoires* and international case-law, this depends on a number of factors. Presumptions in favour of the one or the other have been submitted on the basis of the object and purpose of the treaty, the nature of the obligation, and the nature of the terms employed. However, all seem to share a common denominator: the 'time-will' of the parties, i.e. what was the intention of the parties with respect to the effect that time would have on the content of the rules of the treaty.

Returning to the original question; what do treaties do? Do they endure, perdure or exdure? No *ex ante* 'catch-all' response is possible, or for that matter desirable. Each treaty has to be examined ad hoc and the 'time-will' (the intention) of the parties will be the deciding element, no matter what shape and form that takes.[163] But since change, identity, persistence and most importantly time were the underlying motifs of this article, if one were to press for an answer to the question how do treaties respond to change through time, by enduring, perduring or exduring, the most appropriate response would be[164]: 'only the "time-will" will tell'!

References

Balashov Y (2011) Persistence. In: Callender E (ed) The Oxford handbook of philosophy of time. Oxford University Press, Oxford, pp 13–40

Bernhardt R (2000) Evolutive treaty interpretation, especially of the European Convention on Human Rights. German Yearb Int Law 42:11–25

Bjorge E (2014) The evolutionary interpretation of treaties. Oxford University Press, Oxford

Blokker N (2013) Constituent instruments: creating a genie that may escape from the bottle? In: Cogan JK, Hurd I, Johnstone I (eds) (forthcoming) The Oxford handbook of international organizations.

---

[163] Text, context, practice, preparatory work, presumption due to the nature of the obligations, due to the object and purpose of the treaty, or due to the nature of the terms and the unlimited duration of the treaty etc.

[164] And if the present author is allowed to coin a phrase and simultaneously indulge in a bit of consonance.

Oxford University Press, Oxford. http://papers.ssrn.com/sol3/papers.cfm?abstract_id=2448190. Accessed 18 May 2014
Bos M (1984) A methodology of international law. North-Holland, Netherlands
Brölmann C (2005) Limits of the treaty paradigm. In: Fitzmaurice M, Craven M (eds) Interrogating the treaty: essays in the contemporary law of treaties. Wolf Legal Publishers, Nijmegen, pp 29–39
Brölmann C (2012) Specialized rules of treaty interpretation: international organizations. In: Hollis DB (ed) The Oxford guide to treaties. Oxford University Press, Oxford, pp 507–524
Burke MB (1994) Dion and Theon: an essentialist solution to an ancient puzzle. J Philos 91:129–139
Cançado Trindade AA (1978) The time factor in the application of the rule of exhaustion of local remedies in international law. Rivista di Diritto Internazionale 61:232–257
Carter WR (1997) Dion's left foot (and the price of Burkean economy). Philos Phenomenol Res 57:371–379
Cheng B (1987) General principles of law as applied by international courts and tribunals. Grotius, Cambridge
Coing H (1970) Trois formes historiques d'interprétation du droit glossateurs, pandectistes, école de l'exégèse. Revue Historique de Droit Français et Etranger 48:531–543
d'Amato (1992) International law, intertemporal problems. In: Bernhardt R, Bindschedler RL (eds) Encyclopedia of Public International Law, vol II. North-Holland, Amsterdam, pp 1234–1236
Dawidowicz M (2011) The effect of the passage of time on the interpretation of treaties: some reflections on *Costa Rica v. Nicaragua*. Leiden J Int Law 24:201–222
de Aréchaga EJ (1978) International law in the past third of a century. Recueil des Cours de l'Academie de Droit International 159:1–344
De Vattel (1793) The law of nations or principles on the law of nature applied to the conduct and affairs of nations and sovereigns. GGJ & J Robinson, London
de Visscher Ch (1963) Problémes d' interprétation judiciaire en droit international public. Pedone, Paris
Deutsch H (2007) Relative identity. http://plato.stanford.edu/entries/identity-relative/. Accessed 18 May 2014
Dupuy P-M (2011) Evolutionary interpretation of treaties: between memory and prophecy. In: Cannizzaro E (ed) The law of treaties beyond the Vienna Convention. Oxford University Press, Oxford, pp 123–137
ECtHR Research Division (2011) The use of Council of Europe treaties in the case-law of the European Court of Human Rights. http://www.echr.coe.int/Documents/Research_report_treaties_CoE_ENG.pdf. Accessed 18 May 2014
Elias TO (1980) The doctrine of intertemporal law. Am J Int Law 74:285–307
Engelen FA (2004) Interpretation of tax treaties under international law: a study of articles 31, 32 and 33 of Vienna Convention on the Law of Treaties and their application to tax treaties. International Bureau of Fiscal Documentation, Amsterdam
Fitzmaurice G (1953) The law and procedure of the International Court of Justice 1951-54: general principles and sources of law. Br Yearb Int Law 30:1–70
Fitzmaurice G (1957) The law and procedure of the International Court of Justice 1951-54: treaty interpretation and other points. Br Yearb Int Law 33:203–293
Fitzmaurice M (2008a) Dynamic (evolutive) interpretation of treaties—part I. Hague Yearb Int Law 21:101–153
Fitzmaurice M (2008b) The tale of two judges: Sir Hersch Lauterpacht and Sir Gerald Fitzmaurice—human rights and the interpretation of treaties. Revue Hellénique de Droit International 61:125–170
Fitzmaurice M (2009) Dynamic (evolutive) interpretation of treaties—part II. Hague Yearb Int Law 22:1–31

Forrest P (2010) The identity of indiscernibles. http://plato.stanford.edu/entries/identity-indiscernible/. Accessed 18 May 2014

Fox H (2010) Article 31(3)(a) and (b) of the Vienna Convention and the *Kasikili/Sedudu Island* case. In: Fitzmaurice M, Elias O, Merkouris P (eds) Treaty interpretation and the Vienna Convention on the Law of Treaties: 30 years on. Martinus Nijhoff, Leiden, pp 59–74

French D (2006) Treaty interpretation and the incorporation of extraneous legal rules. Int Comp Law Q 55:281–314

Frisch M (1950) Tagebuch 1946–1949. Suhrkamp, Frankfurt

Gallois A (2011) Identity over time. http://plato.stanford.edu/entries/identity-time/. Accessed 18 May 2014

Gardiner R (2008) Treaty interpretation. Oxford University Press, Oxford

Georgopoulos Th (2004) Le droit intertemporel et les dispositions conventionelles evolutives—quelle thérapie contre la vieillesse des traités? Revue Génerale de Droit International Public 108:123–148

Gourgourinis A (2011) The distinction between interpretation and application of norms in international adjudication. Journal of International Dispute Settlement 2:31–57

Greig D (2001) Intertemporality and the law of treaties. Br Inst Int Comp Law, London

Greig D (2007) The time of conclusion and the time of application of treaties as points of reference in the interpretative process. In: Fitzmaurice M, Craven M, Vogiatzi M (eds) Time, history and international law. Martinus Nijhoff, Leiden, pp 163–217

Haslanger S (2005) Persistence through time. In: Loux MJ, Zimmerman DW (eds) The Oxford handbook of metaphysics. Oxford University Press, Oxford, pp 315–354

Hawley K (2010) Temporal parts. http://plato.stanford.edu/entries/temporal-parts/. Accessed 18 May 2014

Helgesen JE (2011) What are the limits to the evolutive interpretation of the European Convention on Human Rights? Hum Rights Law J 31:275–281

Helmersen ST (2013) Evolutive treaty interpretation: legality, semantics and distinctions. Eur J Legal Stud 6:127–148

Higgins R (1994) Problems and process: international law and how we use it. Oxford University Press, Oxford

Higgins R (1996) Some observations on the inter-temporal rule in international law. In: Makarczyk J (ed) Theory of international law at the threshold of the 21st century. Kluwer Law International, The Hague, pp 173–181

Higgins R (1997) Time and the law: international perspectives on an old problem. Int Comp Law Q 46:501–520

Hobbes (1656) Elements of philosophy the first section, concerning body. R & W Leybourn, London

Holmes OW (1897) The path of the law. Harv Law Rev 10:457–478

IDI (Institut de Droit International) (1952) De l' interprétation des traités. Annuaire de l' Institut de Droit International 44:359–406

IDI (Institut de Droit International) (1975) The intertemporal problem in public international law. Annuaire de l'Institut de Droit International 56:536–541

Jacobs FG (1969) Varieties of approach to treaty interpretation: with special reference to the Draft Convention on the Law of Treaties before the Vienna diplomatic conference. Int Comp Law Q 18:318–346

Jennings RY, Watts AD (eds) (1992) Oppenheim's international law—Volume 1: Peace, Parts 2 to 4. Longman, London

Jennings RY, Watts AD (eds) (2008) Oppenheim's international law, 9th edn. Oxford University Press, Oxford

Klabbers J (2007) Reluctant Grundnormen: Articles 31(3)(C) and 42 of the Vienna Convention on the Law of Treaties and the fragmentation of international law. In: Fitzmaurice M, Craven M, Vogiatzi M (eds) Time, history and international law. Martinus Nijhoff, Leiden, pp. 149–161

Klein PD (2008) Contemporary responses to Agrippa's trilemma. In: Greco J (ed) The Oxford handbook of skepticism. Oxford University Press, Oxford, pp 484–503
Kolb R (2006) Interprétation et création du droit international: Esquisses d'une herméneutique juridique moderne pour le droit international public. Bruylant, Bruxelles
Kotzur M (2008) Intertemporal law. Max Planck Encyclopedia of Public International Law. http://opil.ouplaw.com/view/10.1093/law:epil/9780199231690/law-9780199231690-e1433?rskey=Ebz4oV&result=4&prd=EPIL. Accessed 18 May 2014
Letsas G (2007) A theory of interpretation of the European Convention on Human Rights. Oxford University Press, Oxford
Linderfalk U (2008) Doing the right thing for the right reason—why dynamic or static approaches should be taken in the interpretation of treaties. Int Community Law Rev 10:109–141
Linderfalk U (2011) The application of international legal norms over time: the second branch of intertemporal law. Neth Int Law Rev 58:147–172
McLachlan C (2005) The principle of systemic integration and article 31(3)(c) of the Vienna Convention. Int Comp Law Q 54:279–320
McNair AD (1957) The general principles of law recognised by civilised nations. Br Yearb Int Law 33:1–19
McNair AD (1961) The law of treaties. Clarendon Press, Oxford
McWhinney E (1984) The time dimension in international law, historical relativism and intertemporal law. In: Makarczyk J (ed) Essays in international law in honour of Judge Manfred Lachs. Martinus Nijhoff, The Hague, pp 179–200
Merkouris P (2010) 'Third party' considerations and 'corrective interpretation' in the interpretative use of *travaux préparatoires*: is it Fahrenheit 451 for preparatory work? In: Fitzmaurice M, Elias O, Merkouris P (eds) Treaty interpretation and the Vienna Convention on the Law of Treaties: 30 years on. Martinus Nijhoff, Leiden, pp 75–98
Merkouris P (2015) Article 31(3)(c) VCLT and the principle of systemic integration: normative shadows in Plato's cave. Martinus Nijhoff, Leiden
Philonis (Philo of Alexandria) De aeternitate mundi. Reproduced in: Cumont F (ed) (1891) De aeternitate mundi. George Reimeri, Berlin
Pitea C (2013) Interpreting the ECHR in the light of 'other' international instruments: systemic integration or fragmentation of rules on treaty interpretation? In: Boschiero N, Scovazzi T, Pitea C, Ragni C (eds) International courts and the development of international law: essays in honour of Professor Tullio Treves. TMC Asser Press, The Hague, pp 545–559
Plutarch (1914) Theseus. Reproduced in: Perrin B (ed) Plutarch's lives, Harvard University Press, Cambridge
Ress G (2002) The interpretation of the Charter. In: Br Simma (ed) The Charter of the United Nations: a commentary, 2nd edn. Oxford University Press, Oxford, pp 13–32
Reuter P (1964) Le recours de la Cour de Justice des Communautés Européennes à des principes généraux de droit. In: Rolin H, Salmon JA (eds) Mélanges offerts à Henri Rolin: Problèmes de droit des gens. Pedone, Paris, pp 263–283
Rosenne S (1960) The time factor in the jurisdiction of the International Court of Justice. Sythoff, Leyden
Sands Ph, Klein P (2009) Bowett's law of international institutions, 6th edn. Sweet & Maxwell, London
Sato T (1996) Evolving constitutions of international organizations: a critical analysis of the interpretative framework of the constituent instruments of international organizations. Kluwer Law International, The Hague
Schermers HG, Blokker NM (2011) International institutional law: unity with diversity, 5th, rev edn. Martinus Nijhoff, Leiden
Schwarzenberger G (1952) A manual of international law, 3rd edn. Stevens, London
Shaw MN (2000) Case concerning Kasikili/Sedudu Island (Botswana/Namibia). Int Comp Law Q 49:964–978

Sinclair I (1984) The Vienna Convention on the Law of Treaties, 2nd edn. Manchester University Press, Manchester
Sorensen M (1973) Le problème dit du droit intertemporel dans l'ordre international – Rapport provisoire. Annuaire de l'Institut de Droit International 55:1–116
Sorensen M (1975) Le problème dit du droit intertemporel dans l'ordre international. Annuaire de l'Institut de Droit International 56:339–374
Sorensen R (2003) A brief history of the paradox: philosophy and the labyrinths of the mind. Oxford University Press, Oxford
Sur S (1974) L' interprétation en droit international public. Librairie Générale de Droit et de Jurisprudence, Paris
Tavernier P (1979) Recherches sur l' application dans le temps des actes et des règles en droit international public: problèmes de droit intertemporel ou de droit transitoire. Librairie Générale de Droit et de Jurisprudence, Paris
Thirlway H (1989) The law and procedure of the International Court of Justice 1960–1989: part one. Br Yearb Int Law 60:1–157
Thirlway H (1991) The law and procedure of the International Court of Justice 1960–1989: part two. Br Yearb Int Law 62:1–75
Thirlway H (2006) The law and procedure of the International Court of Justice 1960–1989: supplement 2006: part three. Br Yearb Int Law 77:1–82
United Nations (1969) United Nations Vienna Conference on the Law of Treaties, first session. United Nations, New York
von Verdross A (1935) Les principes généraux du droit dans la jurisprudence internationale. Recueil des Cours de l'Academie de Droit International 52:191–251
Yasseen MK (1976) L' interprétation des traités d'après la Convention de Vienne sur le Droit des Traités. Recueil des Cours de l'Academie de Droit International 151:1–114

Chapter 7
Shifting Demands in International Institutional Law: Securing the United Nations' Accountability for the Haitian Cholera Outbreak

Kate Nancy Taylor

Abstract The permanent legal framework governing international organisations vests organisations with a substantial degree of autonomy in determining their own liability with respect to private law claims. This level of autonomy is particularly pronounced in the case of the United Nations. Since 1946, the United Nations has enjoyed a standard of absolute immunity from the jurisdiction of domestic courts in order to protect the organisation's proper functioning. Thus, when individuals have private law claims against the organisation, the UN is obliged to settle claims privately, and individuals have no further recourse to courts. This regime creates a startling accountability gap, most recently highlighted by the UN's handling of 5000 private law claims which emerged in response to the allegedly negligent importation of cholera into Haiti by UN peacekeepers. To date, the UN has refused to settle these claims amicably. The UN's jurisdictional immunity now operates as a critical barrier to redress for the cholera claimants. This remedial deficit represents a structural gap which is indefensible in light of a shifting paradigm in international law, which increasingly favours human rights and respect for the rule of law over the autonomy of international organisations. This article examines both permanent and temporary solutions to closing this accountability gap, which could potentially alleviate the intractable position faced by the cholera claimants and similar victims in the future.

Keywords Accountability · International organisations · Human rights · Jurisdictional immunity · Mothers of Srebrenica · Remedies · United Nations

---

Kate Nancy Taylor is a legal researcher at the Monash University, Department of Business Law and Taxation. The author would like to thank Professor Sarah Joseph, for her kind supervision during the preparation of this paper.

K.N. Taylor (✉)
Faculty of Law, Monash University, Melbourne, Australia
e-mail: kate.taylor2@monash.edu

M. Ambrus and R.A. Wessel (eds.), *Netherlands Yearbook of International Law 2014*,
Netherlands Yearbook of International Law 45, DOI 10.1007/978-94-6265-060-2_7

Contents

7.1 Introduction 158
7.2 The Responsibility of the UN for the Cholera Outbreak 159
7.3 The UN's Jurisdictional Immunity 161
7.4 Alternative Modes of Dispute Settlement 164
7.4.1 The UN's Obligation to Settle Private Law Disputes 164
7.4.2 Would the Cholera Claims Fall Within the Scope of the UN's Liability? 165
7.4.3 Dispute Settlement Mechanisms in UN Peacekeeping Operations 169
7.5 Shifting Demands in the Law of International Organisations 172
7.5.1 Would a Domestic Court Be Willing to Adjudicate the Cholera Claims? 172
7.5.2 Elevating the Cholera Claims to an International Level 176
7.5.3 The Rule of Law in the UN and the Handling of the Cholera Claims 178
7.5.4 The Human Rights Imperative 180
7.5.5 Demands for the Enhanced Accountability of the UN 183
7.6 Permanent Versus *Ad Hoc* Solutions 187
7.6.1 Theorising Permanent Solutions 187
7.6.2 *Ad Hoc* Solutions: A Revised Role for Domestic Courts? 189
7.7 Conclusion 191
References 192

7.1 Introduction

In 2010, a Nepalese contingency of United Nations (UN) peacekeepers brought cholera to Haiti, a country recently devastated by an earthquake. The UN's haphazard disposal of human waste at its peacekeeping base allowed raw sewage to flow directly into one of Haiti's main sources of drinking water. The sanitation conditions at the UN base were contrary to well-established standards on the treatment of wastewater in humanitarian missions. The introduction of the cholera bacteria into Haiti's water supply triggered an epidemic, causing the death of more than 8,000 people, and the illness of 700,000 more.[1]

The *prima facie* negligent circumstances surrounding the cholera outbreak have given rise to thousands of claims in tort for compensation against the UN. The UN has intimated that it will not address these claims, and as such, the victims of the cholera outbreak have not been afforded any redress for their personal injury and death arising from acts attributable to the UN.

The legal accountability of the UN is governed by a unique regime that treats private claims against the organisation differently from private claims against other legal entities. Namely, the UN has jurisdictional immunity before domestic courts. In the case of private law disputes, the UN has an obligation to make provisions for alternative modes of dispute settlement. The UN is vested with this

[1] Pan American Health Organization and World Health Organization, Epidemiological update: cholera, 2014, http://reliefweb.int/sites/reliefweb.int/files/resources/2014-jun-27-cha-cholera-epi-update.pdf. Accessed 5 September 2014.

jurisdictional immunity based on the organisation's need to conduct its operations free from interference by domestic courts.

The cholera claims raise serious, and arguably novel questions about the legal accountability of the UN and other international organisations (IOs)[2] with similar immunity standards. Presently, there is no independent court with jurisdiction to review the UN's decisions regarding its own liability. Although the UN has a duty to settle private law disputes amicably, the organisation has sole discretion over when and with whom it does so. As the UN has decided not to settle the cholera claims, the claimants appear to have no other mode of recourse to obtain redress for their harm.

The central thesis of this paper is that the remedial deficit faced by the cholera claimants is indefensible in light of a shifting paradigm in international law, which increasingly favours human rights and respect for the rule of law over the autonomy of IOs. Arguably, the cholera claims are the first claims against the UN, which truly expose the extent of the structural gap in the present accountability regime. As the UN ordinarily settles its private law claims amicably, questions about the role of the rule of law and human rights in the UN's treatment of private law claims have not been extensively examined by the academic community. The UN's unsatisfactory treatment of the cholera claims now demands that these issues be examined more thoroughly. It is imperative that the present institutional framework, first conceived of in 1946, adapts to new demands of human rights and the rule of law.

7.2 The Responsibility of the UN for the Cholera Outbreak

It has now been credibly established that the UN's peacekeeping mission in Haiti, MINUSTAH,[3] was the source of the importation of cholera into Haiti.[4] The Nepalese contingent of UN peacekeepers, comprised of 1280 personnel, was exposed to a cholera epidemic in Nepal immediately prior to their deployment to Haiti in October 2010. The contingent was not screened for cholera before arriving in Haiti. The Nepalese peacekeepers were then stationed at the MINUSTAH camp

[2] IOs are organisations created by states (or other IOs) usually on the basis of a treaty, endowed with a minimum of permanent organs, for the purpose of fulfilling certain common tasks. Amerasinghe 1996, at 8.

[3] The United Nations Stabilisation Mission in Haiti ('MINUSTAH') was originally established pursuant by the UN Security Council on 30 April 2004 to support the transitional government in Haiti. Following the earthquake of 12 January 2010, the Security Council increased the overall force levels of MINUSTAH to support immediate recovery, reconstruction and stability efforts. UNSC Res. 1542, 30 April 2004; UNSC Res. 1908, 19 January 2012; UNSC Res. 1927, 4 June 2010.

[4] Frerichs et al. 2012; Piarroux et al. 2011.

in Mirebalais, established above the Meille Tributary, which flows into the Artibonite River, Haiti's largest river. The Artibonite River is a critical source of water in central Haiti.[5] Shortly after the peacekeepers arrived, the first cases of cholera appeared in a village downstream from the MINUSTAH camp[6] Epidemiologists observed sanitary deficiencies, including a pipe discharging sewage from the camp directly into the Meille Tributary.[7] According to the UN's Independent Panel of Experts investigating the outbreak, the sanitation conditions at the MINUSTAH camp were not sufficient to prevent fecal contamination of the Meille Tributary.[8] DNA fingerprinting of the *vibrio cholera* isolates from Haiti and Nepal collected during 2010 was a 'perfect match'.[9]

While it is accepted from an epidemiological and microbiological perspective that MINUSTAH peacekeepers imported cholera into Haiti, the more controversial aspect of the case relates to the legal accountability of the UN for its role in causing the outbreak. The UN, as a legal entity, is responsible for the wrongful acts committed by personnel under its effective control and command.[10] Thus, claims relating to damage caused by UN peacekeepers under the organisation's control are properly addressed to the UN, rather than to the host state receiving the peacekeeping contingent (Haiti) or the state deploying the troops (Nepal).[11] In November 2011, 5000 victims of cholera submitted a Petition of Relief to the UN claiming compensation for wrongful death and personal injury.[12] The claimants alleged that the cholera outbreak was directly attributable to the negligence, gross negligence and/or recklessness of the UN and its subsidiary, MINUSTAH.

Without attempting to examine the merits of these allegations, this chapter examines the remedial mechanisms available to private law claimants once a *prima facie* case in tort against the UN has arisen. The UN has a clear obligation to settle private law claims under Section 29 of the Convention on the Privileges and Immunities of the United Nations (hereinafter General Convention).[13] The Secretary–General has confirmed that 'claims for compensation submitted by third parties for personal injury or death … incurred as a result of acts

[5] Concannon and Lindstrom 2011, at 1167.

[6] Frerichs et al. 2012.

[7] Piarroux et al. 2011, at 1162.

[8] Cravioto et al. 2010, at 3.

[9] Ibid., at 27.

[10] Wellens 2002, at 100.

[11] United Nations Secretariat, Responsibility of international organisations: comments and observations received from international organisations, UN Doc A/CN.4/545, 25 June 2004, at 28.

[12] The claimants are individuals seeking compensation for their own injuries from cholera, or as relatives on behalf of family members who contracted or died from cholera.

[13] 1946 Convention on the Privileges and Immunities of the United Nations, 1 UNTS 15 (hereinafter General Convention).

committed by members of a UN peacekeeping operation' are claims 'of a private law character'.[14]

To date, the UN has maintained that the cholera claims are not a private law dispute which would require settlement according to the UN's own procedures.[15] The organisation has stated:

> With respect to the claims submitted, consideration of these claims would necessarily include a review of political and policy matters. Accordingly, these claims are not receivable pursuant to Section 29 of the [General Convention].[16]

Owing to the UN's jurisdictional immunity, the cholera claimants are unable to seek review of the UN's decision before a domestic court. Despite this, three separate class action suits against the UN have been filed in courts in New York in respect of the cholera outbreak since October 2013.[17] The claimants argue that US courts should deny the UN's jurisdictional immunity in light of the organisation's failure to settle the claims according to its own procedures. The US courts have not yet decided whether the UN's immunity would apply in these circumstances.

7.3 The UN's Jurisdictional Immunity

It is unlikely, despite the New York filings, that the cholera claims will be heard before a domestic court. In its member states, the UN enjoys sweeping exemptions from legal process, which includes jurisdictional immunity barring any domestic suits against the UN, and immunity from execution or enforcement measure.[18] The legal basis for the UN's legal immunity with respect to the cholera claims is contained within the UN Charter,[19] the General Convention,[20] and the Status of Forces Agreement concluded between the UN and the Government of Haiti

---

[14] Report of the Secretary-General, Procedures in place for implementation of Article VIII, Section 29, of the Convention on the Privileges and Immunities of the United Nations, UN Doc A/C.5/49/65, 24 April 1995; Report of the Secretary-General, Administrative and budgetary aspects of the financing of United Nations peacekeeping operations, UN Doc. A/51/389, 20 September 1996, paras 6–8 (hereinafter Secretary-General's Peacekeeping Liability Report).

[15] United Nations Department of Public Information, Haiti cholera victims' compensation claims 'not receivable' under Immunities and Privileges Convention, United Nations tells their representatives, UN Doc. SG/SM/14828, 21 February 2013.

[16] Letter from Patricia O'Brien, Under Secretary-General for Legal Affairs to Brian Concannon Jr, 21 February 2013, at 2.

[17] *Georges et al. v United Nations* et al., SD NY Civ No 1:13-cv-07146-JPO, filed 9 October 2013; *LaVenture v United Nations et al.*, ED NY Civ No 1:2014-cv-01611, filed 11 March 2014; *Petit Homme Jean-Robert et al. v United Nations,* SD NY, Civ No 1:2014-cv-01545, filed 6 May 2014.

[18] Reinisch 2011, at 133.

[19] Article 105 of the 1945 Charter of the United Nations, 1 UNTS VXI (hereinafter UN Charter).

[20] Section 2 General Convention.

('UN-Haiti SOFA').[21] Since the earliest days of the UN's existence, its jurisdictional immunity has been a stalwart feature of the international institutional legal order. Deeply ingrained in the Charter, General Convention and UN peacekeeping practice, it does not look set to change.

The UN Charter specifies that the UN possesses juridical personality in its member states.[22] By virtue of this juridical personality, the UN can be the subject of legal duties and legal rights, of performing legal transactions and of suing and being sued.[23] However, this juridical personality under Article 104 is immediately coupled with broad legal immunity. Article 105(1) of the Charter provides that the UN 'shall enjoy in the territory of each of its Members such privileges and immunities as are necessary for the fulfillment of its purpose.'[24]

The General Convention further defines the scope of the immunity granted by the Charter. Section 2 of the General Convention specifies that the UN shall enjoy immunity 'from every form of legal process' unless the UN 'has expressly waived its immunity.'[25] Thus, the General Conventions extends the 'functional' scope of the immunity under the Charter, and vests the organisation with a standard of absolute immunity.[26] The UN's power to waive its immunity under Section 2 of the General Convention is discretionary, and the UN is under no legal obligation to do so.[27] The Secretary–General has not shown any willingness to waive the organisation's immunity with respect to the cholera claims.

The UN-Haiti SOFA affirms that MINUSTAH, as a subsidiary organ of the UN, enjoys the status, privileges and immunities of the UN in accordance with the General Convention.[28] Thus, by virtue of the SOFA, MINUSTAH enjoys absolute immunity from every form of legal process. This operates as a contractual form of legal immunity, existing between the Haitian government and the UN. The legal immunity granted to MINUSTAH peacekeeping forces is not peculiar to the Haiti mission. The UN-Haiti SOFA is a replica of the 'Model SOFA' promulgated by the

---

[21] Agreement between the United Nations and the Government of Haiti Concerning the Status of the United Nations Operation in Haiti, signed 9 July 2004, 2271 UNTS 235 (hereinafter UN-Haiti SOFA).

[22] Article 104 UN Charter.

[23] Kelsen 1950, at 329.

[24] Artice 105(1) UN Charter.

[25] Section 2 General Convention.

[26] The UN has interpreted the phrase 'every form of legal process' to include all forms of process before national authorities, whether judicial, administrative or executive, and has consistently refused to receive legal service on its premises. Reinisch 2009.

[27] The Secretary-General is under a specified 'duty' to waive the immunity of an official or expert in any case where, in the Secretary-General's opinion, the immunity would impede the course of justice and can be waived without prejudice to the interests of the UN. See Sections 21 and 23 General Convention. This waiver provision only applies to waive by the Secretary-General of the immunity of a UN official or expert, not the organisation itself. See Rawski 2002, at 111.

[28] Article 15 UN-Haiti SOFA.

Secretary–General in 1999,[29] the terms of which have formed the legal basis of all UN peacekeeping operations since its introduction.

As expressed in the UN Charter,[30] the organisation's jurisdictional immunity is based on the notion of functional necessity. By providing for absolute immunity under the terms of the General Convention, member states were in agreement that individual states should not be able to hinder the effective working of the UN through their domestic courts.[31] Thus, the grant of jurisdictional immunity operates to secure the organisation's independence and attempts to guarantee its functioning. McKinnon Wood also stressed that the organisation must be protected against baseless actions 'brought by the numerous cranks, fanatics or cantankerous people who may believe that … they have suffered wrongs' at the hands of the UN.[32] However, the effect of absolute immunity also leaves individuals with credible claims without the protection of domestic courts.

Domestic courts have always upheld the absolute character of the UN's jurisdictional immunity. The UN's immunity was most recently cast into light by the *Mothers of Srebrenica* litigation, which came before the Supreme Court of the Netherlands in 2012.[33] The plaintiffs alleged that the UN was liable for the failure of Dutch peacekeepers operating under a UN mandate to prevent the genocide against Bosnian Muslims at Srebrenica in 1995.[34] The Supreme Court of the Netherlands confirmed that Dutch courts were not competent to hear the action directed against the UN. Even though the prohibition on genocide was a particularly grave matter of international law and a rule of *jus cogens,* the seriousness of the subject matter was thought not to have been capable of overriding the organisation's immunity.[35] The Court found that the only possible interpretation of the immunity defined in the General Convention is that the UN is entitled to the most far-reaching immunity, 'in the sense that the UN cannot be summoned to appear before any domestic court in the [160] countries that are parties to the [General Convention].'[36]

---

[29] Report of the Secretary-General, Model status-of-forces agreement for peace-keeping operations, UN Doc. A/45/295, 9 October 2009 (hereinafter Model SOFA).

[30] Article 105 UN Charter.

[31] Memorandum of Law of Amici Curiae International Law Scholars and Practitioners In Support of Plaintiffs' Opposition to the Government's Statement of Interest in *Georges et al. v UN et al.*, SD NY Civ No 1:13-cv-07146-JPO, 15 May 2014 (hereinafter Amici Curiae in *Georges et al. v UN et al.*).

[32] McKinnon Wood 1944, at 143–144, quoted in Schemers and Blokker 2001, at 1612. McKinnon Wood was originally referring to the League of Nations, but the rationale applies in kind to the UN.

[33] *Mothers of Srebrenica v The Netherlands and the United Nations,* ILDC 1760, 13 April 2012 (Supreme Court of the Netherlands) (hereinafter *Mothers of Srebrenica*).

[34] See Brockman-Hawe 2011.

[35] Faith 2013, at 360. This principle was reiterated with respect to sovereign jurisdiction in *Jurisdictional Immunities of the State (Germany v Italy; Greece Intervening)* ICJ, Judgment of 3 February 2013.

[36] *Mothers of Srebrenica*, para 4.1.1.

In light of the absolute character of the UN's jurisdictional immunity, it is unlikely that a domestic court would be willing to hear a substantive review of the cholera claims in tort. Any reading of the Srebrenica judgments lead inexorably to the conclusion that the UN's jurisdictional immunity has always been, and it will ever be thus. The remote possibility of a domestic court adopting a different approach to the UN's immunity, based on the claimants' right of access to a court, will be discussed further in Sect. 7.5.

7.4 Alternative Modes of Dispute Settlement

7.4.1 The UN's Obligation to Settle Private Law Disputes

Crucially, the jurisdictional immunity enjoyed by the UN is a purely procedural barrier to domestic courts; it is not intended to diminish the organisation's substantive liability. The International Court of Justice (ICJ) has confirmed that the question of jurisdictional immunity is distinct from the issue of compensation for any damages incurred as a result of acts of the UN.[37]

However, the UN's jurisdictional immunity substantially changes the mode of adjudication of claims against the UN, which would apply if the same acts were attributable to a private party or a state. It falls upon the UN to establish alternative mechanisms for the settlement of private law disputes. These mechanisms are intended to fill the accountability gap that otherwise faces individuals with private law claims against the UN. Noting that 'procedural justice is an essential precondition for substantive justice',[38] it becomes clear that the existence and effective functioning of an alternative mode of dispute settlement is central to the realisation of substantive justice for the cholera claimants. The following section will examine the present accountability structures which are in place, in theory, to address questions of liability of the UN's wrongful acts.

The UN's obligation to make provision for alternative settlement modalities exists under Section 29 of the General Convention, which reads as follows:

> The United Nations shall make provisions for appropriate modes of settlement of:
>
> (a) Disputes arising out of contracts or other disputes of a private law character to which the UN is a party.

As the UN is placed outside the jurisdictional reach of domestic courts, and as yet, there is no international court with authority to bind the UN, adherence to the legal obligation under Section 29 of the General Convention rests on the political

[37] See *Difference Relating to Immunity from Legal Process of a Special Rapporteur of the Commission on Human Rights,* ICJ, Advisory Opinion, 29 April 1998, para 69.

[38] Wellens 2002, at 97.

goodwill of the UN. The imperative to do so has, in the past, attracted fairly strong attention as a matter of UN policy. In 1965, the Secretary–General stated:

> It has always been the policy of the UN, acting through the Secretary-General, to compensate individuals who have suffered damages for which the Organisation was legally liable. This policy is in keeping with generally recognised legal principles and with the [General Convention].[39]

7.4.2 Would the Cholera Claims Fall Within the Scope of the UN's Liability?

It is necessary to establish whether the cholera claims constitute a 'private law dispute', which must be settled by the UN. The UN has argued that the claims 'are not receivable' pursuant to Section 29 of the General Convention. In opposition to the UN's stance, the following section will illustrate that, having regard to the nature of the cholera claims, the UN has an obligation to hear the claims under the terms of its own liability regime.

In 1996, the Secretary–General published a report which addresses the scope of the UN's liability for the activities of UN peacekeeping forces, as well as procedures for the handling of third-party claims and the limitations to its liability.[40] The parameters set out in that report do not appear to preclude the UN's liability with respect to the cholera claims. There are three key issues which must be addressed to illustrate that point. Firstly, it must be shown that the cholera claims constitute a *prima facie* private law dispute in tort. Secondly, it must be shown that the damage suffered by the claimants did not arise out of 'operational necessity', an accepted exemption from liability under the Secretary–General's report. Thirdly, it is necessary to show that the UN's stated response that the claims are not receivable—because they entail a 'review of policy and political matters'—is not an exception to liability under the UN's established regime.

7.4.2.1 A 'Private Law Dispute'

Both the General Convention and the UN-Haiti SOFA clearly indicate that the UN will make provisions for the settlement of 'private law disputes' only. The UN has stated that personal injury arising from the ordinary operation of the UN forces is one of the most commonly encountered private law claims.[41] Affirming the cholera claims' private law character, the UN's maintenance of the sewage systems at

---

[39] Letter dated 6 August 1965 from the Secretary-General addressed to the acting permanent representative of the Union of Soviet Socialist Republics, UN Doc. S/6595, UN Juridical Yearbook 1965, 6 August 1965, at 41.

[40] Secretary-General's Peacekeeping Liability Report. See also Third-party liability: temporal and financial limitations, UNGA Res 52/247, UN Doc A/Res/52/247, 17 July 1998.

[41] Secretary-General's Peacekeeping Liability Report, para 3.

the peacekeeping base can be considered a *prima facie* tort claim, which could have been brought before any domestic court in the world as a civil claim but for the organisation's jurisdictional immunity.[42] Tort claims brought by private parties 'fit squarely within the definition of private law claims'.[43]

However, not all claims brought by private parties can be characterised as private law claims. Here, a distinction can be drawn between the private law character of the cholera claims, and a claim brought by private citizens against the UN asserting that peacekeepers wrongly exercised their strategic or policy-making discretion that led to individuals suffering harm.[44] The latter type of claim was argued in the *Mothers of Srebrenica* case. In that case, the UN refused to settle the dispute concerning its alleged failure to prevent genocide on the basis that it was not a private law dispute. In the cholera case, the acts and omissions causing the harm were not done pursuant to any strategic function of the UN. The liability question, arising from damage caused by the sanitation conditions at the MINUSTAH camp, does not touch upon UN policy decisions. Rather, the conduct that caused harm relate to the failure of the UN to abide by numerous codes in place for humanitarian assistance regarding the treatment of wastewater.[45] Rather than being 'policy decisions', the UN's maintenance of the sanitation facilities at its peacekeeping base appears to have occurred *contrary* to the UN's policy.

7.4.2.2 Matters of Operational Necessity

The UN's obligation to settle third-party claims in Haiti extends to claims for personal injury, illness and death, *except for those arising out of operational necessity*.[46] This exception applies where the UN causes damage arising out of the necessary actions of a peacekeeping force in the course of carrying out its operations in pursuance of its mandate.[47] The rationale for this exemption from liability is that by inviting a peacekeeping force into its territory, the host state has consented to damage arising from the ordinary operations of the peacekeeping force.[48] For an action (and liability for its consequent damage) to fall within this

---

[42] International Commission of Jurists 2008, at 3. The Commission notes, '[i]n every jurisdiction, despite differences in terminology and approach, an actor can be held liable under the law of civil remedies if through negligent or intentional conduct it causes harm to someone else.'

[43] Amici Curiae in *Georges et al. v UN et al.*, 2014, at 9.

[44] Ibid.

[45] Alvarez 2014; The Sphere Project 2010; United Nations High Commissioner for Refugees 2007; World Health Organization 2011.

[46] UN-Haiti SOFA, Article 54.

[47] Secretary-General's Peacekeeping Liability Report, para 14.

[48] In such circumstances, it falls upon the host state to compensate any individuals who suffer damage: Prescott 2001, at 173. See also Secretary-General's Peacekeeping Liability Report, para 9. The Secretary-General has set out the formula for determining whether damage occurred as a result of operational necessity. Ibid., para 14.

exception, 'the action must be strictly necessary and not a matter of mere convenience or expediency'.[49] In the present case, the matter of operational necessity as an exception to liability does not seem to be at issue,[50] and the UN has not sought to invoke the exception.

7.4.2.3 Refuting the UN's 'Policy and Political Matters' Response

The UN has communicated that the cholera claims are not the sort of dispute of a private law character envisioned by Section 29 of the Convention. The only elaboration provided by the UN is that, 'with respect to the claims submitted, considerations of these claims would necessarily include a review of political and policy matters'.[51] Some critics of this stance have argued that 'such a bald statement is baffling on its face, because no such exception to section 29 exists'.[52] There appear to be two potential interpretations of the UN's statement, both of which can be refuted.

Firstly, the UN could be arguing that because the claims 'necessarily include a review of political and policy matters', the claims are not of a private law character. There is no doubt that the cholera outbreak in Haiti has implications for the policy and practice of UN peacekeeping operations. For example, the UN's Independent Panel of Experts on the Cholera Outbreak in Haiti gave seven key policy recommendations based on the findings of the report.[53] However, those implications are conceptually distinct from the matter of compensation for personal injury and death arising from the UN's activities.

The claim that the UN's liability in the present case would necessarily entail a 'policy review' is a truism that does not exempt the organisation from liability. A policy review by the UN in the present case would necessarily flow from liability in the same way that a civil suit ordinarily prompts a party to review its offending behaviour. If conduct gives rise to liability, it is prudent for a party to try to prevent that conduct from reoccurring, so as to avoid future liability. Alvarez notes that 'virtually all tort claims … raise questions about the day to day policies of the entity being sued'.[54] It is not tenable to conclude that such a review reduces the liability of any party for its tortious conduct. It has never been mentioned by the UN as an exemption from liability that would render claims 'not receivable'.

---

[49] Secretary-General's Peacekeeping Liability Report, para 14.

[50] Letter from Mario Joseph, Brian Concannon Jr and Ira Kurzban to Patricia O'Brien, Under Secretary-General for Legal Affairs, 7 May 2013, at 5.

[51] Letter from Patricia O'Brien, Under Secretary-General for Legal Affairs to Brian Concannon Jr, 21 February 2013, at 2.

[52] Kurzban et al. 2013.

[53] Cravioto et al. 2010, at 30.

[54] Alvarez 2014.

A second interpretation of the UN's statement could relate to the fact that answering the dispute would entail questions about the adequacy of the UN's practices. Presumably, such questions could constitute interference with UN policy decisions. This argument draws upon one of the primary rationales of jurisdictional immunity—namely that the functioning of international organisations would be seriously hampered if national courts could make pronouncements over the UN's policy decisions.[55] That argument could be plausible in relation to claims that a duty of care was breached by failing to require the UN peacekeepers to be tested for cholera prior to deployment. But the argument would not be tenable in relation to claims that the sanitation conditions at the peacekeeping base did not meet applicable standards. In the first case, the question would address the adequacy of UN standards—namely the fact that the UN does not currently require asymptomatic peacekeepers to be tested for cholera prior to deployment.[56] In the second case, the question would go towards whether the UN's practices were in conformity with standards that were already in place regulating the treatment of wastewater in humanitarian missions. To deny review in the second case would be tantamount to the UN refusing to compensate an individual injured by a negligently driven peacekeeping vehicle, because answering the dispute would involve a review into the conduct of the driver. This second interpretation of the UN's argument would problematically entail that it was pursuant to UN *policy* that the sanitation conditions at the peacekeeping base were insufficient to prevent fecal contamination into the Artibonite River.

It is particularly problematic for the UN to assert that a private law dispute, which would necessarily entail review of political or policy matters, cannot be settled under Section 29 of the General Convention. The flagrancy of that argument is illustrated by recalling the primary rationale behind Sections 2 and 29 of the General Convention (granting absolute immunity and the obligation to provide alternative modes of dispute settlement respectively). Specifically, the UN is granted jurisdictional immunity in domestic courts based on the need to preclude judgments from being made about UN policy by domestic courts. Thus, the grant of immunity was coupled with an obligation to establish alternative modes of disputes settlement, which would be competent to settle private law disputes, which might entail questions about UN policy. Such claims are deliberately placed outside the purview of domestic courts and precisely into the jurisdiction of the UN's own settlement mechanisms.

[55] Muller 1995, at 151.

[56] The UN Guidelines for Medical Screening of Peacekeepers recommends microbiological testing of stools for cholera only when clinically indicated. See United Nations Department of Peacekeeping Operations 1999. See also Cravioto et al. 2010, at 12. They note that once medical examinations were completed, soldiers were given a 10 day free period to visit their families in Nepal before deployment to Haiti.

7.4.3 Dispute Settlement Mechanisms in UN Peacekeeping Operations

If it is accepted that the cholera claims constitute a private law dispute which must be settled by the UN, there remains the question of what form of dispute settlement mechanism should be utilised by the UN in this case.[57] There are two alternative modes of dispute settlement, which are relevant for individuals who suffer damage as a result of the tortious actions of UN peacekeeping operations: standing claims commissions—originally envisaged by the UN-Haiti SOFA—and the local claims review board process—constituting current UN practice for the settlement of private law disputes. These mechanisms will be examined in turn.

7.4.3.1 The UN's Standing Claims Commissions

The UN has an obligation under para 55 of the UN-Haiti SOFA to establish a standing claims commission in Haiti. The claims commission is intended to have 'compulsory jurisdiction to settle third-party claims' brought against MINUSTAH.[58] This contractual obligation under the UN-Haiti SOFA is similarly incumbent on the UN in all its peacekeeping missions.[59] In practice, however, the standing claims commissions envisioned under the UN SOFAs have never been established. In November 2011, the cholera claimants tried without success to submit their claims to the UN to be heard before a claims commission.[60] The UN has expressly refused to establish a standing claims commission in Haiti.[61]

In theory, claims commissions are supposed to be a proportionate counterweight to the UN's jurisdictional immunity, and the effect that immunity has on claimants who would have otherwise been eligible to have their claims heard in a domestic court. The UN SOFAs are drafted 'in conformity' with Section 29 of the

[57] The method of dispute settlement which is employed by the UN in any private law dispute depends on the identity of the claimant and the precise nature of the claim. For disputes between the UN and its employees and agents, such means involve recourse to internal organs of the UN. Contractual parties in private disputes with the UN are generally resolved by recourse to arbitration, pursuant to a standard arbitration clause contained in contracts to which the UN is a party. See Wellens 2002.

[58] Article 54 UN-Haiti SOFA. The term 'third party' used in the SOFA is a references to individuals, as opposed to the UN itself (or its employees) or the state receiving peacekeeping troops.

[59] Paragraph 51 Model SOFA.

[60] The Petition for Relief sent to the UN on behalf of the cholera victims in November 2011 specifically mentioned the UN's failure to establish a standing claims commission as required by the UN-Haiti SOFA. Petition for relief from Mario Joseph, Brian Concannon Jr and Ira Kurzban to MINUSTAH Claims Unit, 3 November 2011.

[61] Letter from Patricia O'Brien, Under Secretary-General for Legal Affairs to Brian Concannon Jr, 5 July 2013.

General Convention,[62] as the claims commissions are to provide the specific mode of dispute settlement for claims arising from peacekeeping operations.

The claims commissions were envisioned by the UN to afford claimants certain safeguards of adjudicative independence and impartiality. If it existed, a claims commission in Haiti would be comprised of three members—one appointed by the UN Secretary-General, another appointed by the Haitian government, and a chairman jointly appointed by the Secretary-General and the government.[63] The Secretary-General has proffered that the claims commissions would thus provide a model under which the organisation and host state are 'on equal footing'.[64] However, Wellens rightly notes that the Secretary-General's claim is unsubstantiated, as there is no acquired operational experience against which the effectiveness of such a procedure can be judged.[65]

The cholera case illustrates that the most glaring deficiency in the claims commission regime is that there is no legal recourse available to individuals in circumstances where the UN has unilaterally refused to establish the commission. The obligation to establish a claims commission in accordance with the SOFA exists as a contractual obligation as between the UN and Haiti. Under the terms of the SOFA, there is a mechanism available to the Haitian government to trigger the establishment of the claims commission with the intervention of the President of the ICJ.[66]

However, the institutional strength of the Haitian government, its close dependence on the UN for its security, and international donors for its economy,[67] renders this an unlikely outcome in the cholera case. These power differentials severely compromise the capacity of the Haitian government to protect its citizens from the wrongful conduct of the UN. For instance, at the time of the outbreak in 2010, the MINUSTAH budget was equivalent to approximately one-third of the Haitian government's total annual budget for all government services.[68] The Haitian government is also heavily dependent on foreign aid, much of which is channeled through the UN. Haiti's dependency on aid 'has contributed to the government's reluctance to assert the rights of its people vis-à-vis the UN.'[69]

---

[62] Secretary-General's Peacekeeping Liability Report, para 7.

[63] Article 55 UN-Haiti SOFA.

[64] Secretary-General's Peacekeeping Liability Report, para 20.

[65] Wellens 2002, at 103.

[66] Article 55 UN-Haiti SOFA provides that if, within 30 days of the appointment of the first member of the commission (which could be appointed by the government), no agreement as to the chairman is reached by the two parties, the President of the ICJ may, at the request of either party, appoint the chairman. Once a chairman is appointed, the two-member quorum would be satisfied. The Secretary-General would then be bound to use his best endeavours to ensure compliance with any awards made by the commission.

[67] See Heine and Thompson 2001.

[68] Institute for Justice and Democracy in Haiti and The John Marshall Law School, Cholera as a grave violation of the right to water in Haiti, Submission to Catarina de Albuquerque, Special Rapporteur on the human right to safe drinking water and sanitation, 2014, at 5.

[69] Ibid.

It is therefore unlikely that the Haitian government will take action to counter the UN's refusal to establish a claims commission. To date, it has shown no willingness to intervene on the cholera claimants' behalf. Problematically, it appears that the strength of the claims commission mechanism presupposes a functioning and efficient government with political capital to spend against the world's largest IO. In practice, states that require peacekeeping operations are unlikely to have the political power to engage in such a procedure. It does not appear likely that the UN will establish a standing claims commission according to its SOFA obligations. The fact that the current accountability regime does not provide an additional safeguard to apply in such circumstances is a substantial accountability gap in the current framework.

7.4.3.2 Local Claims Review Boards

In practice, private law disputes arising out of UN peacekeeping operations are settled through internal 'local claims review boards' ('LCRBs').[70] UN practice has favoured the use of these *ad hoc* boards over the more formal standing claims commissions. LCRBs are routinely created *in situ* by peacekeeping missions to settle third-party claims 'when the need arises'.[71] The settlements and *ex gratia* payments made by a LCRBs are never publicly disclosed.

As the UN has deemed the cholera claims to be 'not receivable', the settlement of the claims through an LCRB is unlikely. Nevertheless, it is worth examining the ways in which an LCRB would work *if* the UN attempted to provide such recourse to the cholera claimants.

As an internal body of the UN, an LCRB is composed exclusively of UN staff members. The composition of the board in this way inevitably 'leaves the investigation, processing and final adjudication of the claims entirely in the hands of the Organisation'.[72] This has prompted the International Law Association (ILA) to raise serious concerns about the independence of the boards and the objectivity of their rules. The ILA has argued that the procedure is not an adequate alternative to domestic courts to ensure the protection of private individuals' interests and rights.[73]

It can be argued that an LCRB is not an appropriate forum to hear cholera claims, which involves thousands of claimants and could involve complex issues such as causation and remoteness in tort. Significantly, a typical LCRB consists of staff members 'performing administrative functions', and will include a Legal Adviser, or a staff member with legal training 'where possible'.[74] Thus, there are

---

[70] LCRBs are established within a peacekeeping mission, on the basis of authority delegated by the Controller: Secretary-General's Peacekeeping Liability Report, para 22.

[71] Ibid., para 25; See also Shraga 2000, at 409; Verdirame 2011, at 225.

[72] Secretary-General's Peacekeeping Liability Report, para 20.

[73] International Law Association 2014, at 39.

[74] Secretary-General's Peacekeeping Liability Report, para 20, fn 6.

serious questions to be asked about its competency in general to settle private law disputes. In 1996, the Secretary-General noted that the increasing number and complexity of claims that had arisen from UN operations had taxed the ability of the organisation to deal with claims efficiently and promptly, leading to unfair delays to claimants.[75] Alvarez has noted that the UN is 'better at accepting its legal responsibilities' when the responsibility involves 'small-scale' breaches of tort law, such as car accidents involving UN peacekeepers.[76] An internal administrative procedure could be appropriate in those cases. However, it cannot be realistically suggested that an LCRB, constituted in its ordinary form, would be competent to decide the organisation's liability and compensation orders regarding the cholera claims. The limitations of the LCRB process expose the enormous remedial deficit faced by individuals injured by UN peacekeepers.

7.5 Shifting Demands in the Law of International Organisations

7.5.1 Would a Domestic Court Be Willing to Adjudicate the Cholera Claims?

In the absence of a claims commission, the cholera claimants are in the intractable position whereby there is no forum to which their private law claims may be brought without the consent of the UN. This dilemma is a classic illustration of what has been referred to as the 'accountability gap'[77] in the law of IOs. It should be asked whether a domestic court would be willing to lift the UN's jurisdictional immunity and allow the cholera case to come before a domestic court. An examination of this question may help to reveal the extent to which domestic courts are able to react and adapt to the permanent accountability structures which exist in international institutional law. It is contented that the capacity of a domestic court to react flexibly is a new and much-needed solution to the shifting demands that the human rights of victims be prioritised over the autonomy of IOs.

It is most commonly argued that domestic courts should refuse to uphold the jurisdictional immunity of IOs in circumstances where the organisation has failed to make an alternative dispute mechanism available to individuals with private law claims.[78] In the UN context, such an argument rests on the proposition that the oper-

[75] Ibid., para 26.

[76] Do international organisations really advance the rule of law—a dialogue with Professor Jose Enrique Alvarez and Dr. David Malone, 10 September 2013, United Nations University, at 3 (hereinafter Do International Organisations Advance the Rule of Law).

[77] Reinisch 2013, at 572.

[78] See, e.g., Ryngaert 2010.

ation of Section 29 of the General Convention is a condition precedent to the UN's enjoyment of jurisdictional immunity under Section 2 of the General Convention.

To date, domestic courts have always upheld the absolute character of the UN's immunity, and have been unwilling to accept such a reading of the two relevant provisions in the General Convention. The 'traditional approach' to the relationship between the UN's jurisdictional immunity and Section 29 of the General Convention was illustrated first in the *Manderlier* case before the Belgian Court of Appeal in 1969.[79] In that instance, the Belgian Court found that the Convention establishes no link between the two provisions. In its advisory opinion in the *Cumaraswamy* case in 1999, the ICJ confirmed this traditional approach to the UN's immunity.[80] Undoubtedly, the UN's absolute legal immunity before domestic courts still represents the black letter of the General Convention.

However, it must be noted that occasionally, European jurisprudence tends to be more sympathetic to the 'human rights approach' to the jurisdictional immunities of IOs. This view pays deference to an individual's right of access to a court. The human rights approach typically entails a domestic court inquiring into whether an aggrieved individual can have their private law claims heard by an IO's internal redress mechanisms. This represents a departure from the traditional approach to immunities, which focuses primarily on the relationship between the domestic court's obligation, as an apparatus of the state, to uphold an IO's immunity. That obligation is owed to IOs in international law, for instance, under the terms of the General Convention in the case of the UN. On the other hand, the human rights approach focuses more sharply on the relationship between the forum state and its human rights obligation to provide individuals with meaningful access to a court. That right entails that in the determination of his or her legal rights and obligations, everyone is entitled to a fair and public hearing by a competent, independent and impartial tribunal established by law.[81] Therefore, the human rights approach recognises that by upholding the jurisdictional immunity of an IO, the forum state may be violating its obligations to individuals under international human rights law.

Within Europe, the human rights approach was first evoked in the seminal case of *Waite and Kennedy* before the European Court of Human Rights (ECtHR) in 1999.[82] In that case, the ECtHR addressed the compatibility of the jurisdictional

[79] *Manderlier v United Nations and Belgium,* Court of Appeals of Brussels, 69 ILR 139, 15 September 1969.

[80] *Difference Relating to Immunity from Legal Process of a Special Rapporteur of the Commission on Human Rights,* ICJ, Advisory Opinion, 29 April 1998.

[81] Article 6(1) of the 1950 Convention for the Protection of Human Rights and Fundamental Freedoms, 213 UNTS 222 (hereinafter ECHR); Article 14(1) of the 1966 International Covenant on Civil and Political Rights, 999 UNTS 171 (hereinafter ICCPR); Article 10 of the Universal Declaration of Human Rights, UN Doc A/810, 10 December 1948.

[82] *Waite and Kennedy v Germany*, ECtHR, No. 26083/94, 18 February 1999; *Beer and Reagan v Germany*, ECtHR, No. 28934/95, 18 February 1999.

immunity granted to IOs with the plaintiffs' right of access to a court.[83] The ECtHR found that it was not a violation of the plaintiffs' right under the European Convention on Human Rights (ECHR) for German courts to recognise the jurisdictional immunity of the European Space Agency. In determining whether this was a proportionate restriction on the right of access to a court, the Court reasoned that a 'material factor' to be taken into account was whether the applicants had available to them 'reasonable alternative means to protect effectively their rights' under the ECHR.[84] Thus, a state might be in violation of its obligation to provide access to a court if it grants immunity in circumstances where the IO does not provide an alternative method of dispute settlement. It must be noted that while the Court found the existence of an alternative settlement mechanism to be a 'material factor' to be considered, the ECtHR's judgment falls short of stating that such a mechanism would be an essential precondition to the granting of immunity.

Since the *Waite and Kennedy* decision, domestic courts in states bound by the ECHR are increasingly cognisant of the inherent conflict between the immunity of IOs and the human right of access to a court. There is growing recognition that if access to justice is not possible within an IO, domestic courts may be under an obligation to lift immunity in order to meet their human rights obligations *vis-à-vis* the claimant.[85] Notably, in a small number of cases before domestic courts, jurisdictional immunity has been denied to IOs where the IO has failed to provide an alternative dispute mechanism.[86] However, the different approaches taken by these national courts may be related to the applicable national legal order and the specific text of the applicable immunity provisions.[87] Currently, no uniform approach has emerged from European domestic courts.

Domestic courts have never adopted the human rights approach to cases concerning the jurisdictional immunity of the UN. The traditional approach was recently affirmed with respect to the UN in the *Mothers of Srebrenica* case. When the *Stichting Mothers of Srebrenica* case came before the ECtHR in 2013, the Strasbourg Court confirmed that the Netherlands' approach did not violate the claimants' right of access to a court under the ECHR.[88] The ECtHR found that to rule otherwise entailed

---

[83] Article 6(1) ECHR.

[84] *Waite and Kennedy v Germany,* para 68.

[85] Ryngaert 2010, at 144. Typically, the issue is brought before domestic courts in claims relating to employment disputes between IOs and their employees.

[86] Reinisch 2013, at 574. See, e.g., *Siedler v Western European Union*, Court of Appeals of Brussels, 617 ILDC 53, 17 September 2003. Not only did the Court in *Siedler* assess the availability of internal mechanisms, it engaged in a full-scale determination of the adequacy of the procedures. The Court found that the Western European Union did not comport with the guarantees necessary for a fair trial.

[87] For instance, in Italy, the relationship between immunity and the right of access to court is a 'purely domestic issue' as it concerns the relationship between two provisions in the Italian Constitution. Bonafé 2013, 529.

[88] *Stichting Mothers of Srebrenica and Others v The Netherlands,* ECtHR, No, 65542/12, 11 June 2013 (hereinafter *Stichting Mothers of Srebrenica*).

the risk of allowing individual states to interfere with matters which are 'fundamental to the mission of the United Nations to secure international peace and security'.[89]

Thus, both the Dutch Supreme Court and the ECtHR were aware that any domestic adjudication of the *Mothers of Srebrenica* claims would involve an evaluation of the UN Security Council's Resolutions and its failure to use military force, and would therefore constitute domestic interference with the UN's maintenance of international peace and security. The same policy rationale for judicial abstention in suits against the UN is not directly applicable in relation to the cholera claims. For instance, Rashkow highlights that the failure to use military force in the Srebrenica case is a 'very different thing' from the claims of negligence in the cholera case—alluding to the fact that the Srebrenica claims may constitute a public, rather than private, law dispute—as they involve questions about the UN's failure to use military force to prevent genocide.

The cholera claims are of a different character to the Srebrenica claims. Undeniably, the genocide at Srebrenica constituted a failure of the UN to live up to the terms of the UN Protection Force mandate. This abject and unintended failure was strictly related to that mandate, and the Security Council's performance in maintaining international peace and security.[90] It is within that context that the Srebrenica claims arose. The damage caused by the cholera outbreak, on the other hand, did not arise as a consequence of the UN's failure to fulfil its mandate. The cholera outbreak arose as an unintended consequence of the peacekeeping operation that lies, in a sense, entirely *outside* the UN's mandate.[91] Any judicial review of the cholera claims would not entail the same public law considerations that are inherent in the Srebrenica claims. This distinction between the claims fortifies Rashkow's argument that cholera claims are more likely to constitute a 'classically' private law dispute than the Srebrenica claims.[92]

Notwithstanding the private law character of the cholera claims, the 'special position' of the UN still operates as a critical barrier to the legal accountability of the organisation before domestic courts. It was noted by the Dutch Court of Appeal in *Mothers of Srebrenica* that the UN has a 'special position' in the international community to maintain and restore international peace and security—a responsibility not shared by any other IO.[93] The Court reasoned that the immunity granted to the UN is therefore 'closely connected to the public interest pertaining to keeping peace and safety in the world.'[94] Domestic courts have thus differentiated the

---

[89] Ibid., para 154.

[90] Mégret 2007, at 250–251.

[91] For the distinction between the *Mothers of Srebrenica* claims and other 'unintended consequences' of a peacekeeping mission, see Mégret 2007, at 250–251.

[92] Rashkow 2013, at 343.

[93] *Mothers of Srebrenica v The Netherlands and the United Nations*, The Hague Court of Appeal, 200.022.151/01, 20 March 2010, para 5.7.

[94] Ibid.

UN from other IOs, claiming that though there are circumstances where immunity may not lie for a smaller IOs, the UN has unquestionable and absolute immunity.[95] This 'special position' limits the extent to which one may hope that the *Waite and Kennedy* jurisprudence will influence future decisions regarding the UN's jurisdictional immunity.

The present state of affairs suggests that the human rights approach to jurisdictional immunities is unlikely to be adopted in a domestic court outside of Europe, or in relation to the UN. Therefore, domestic courts are not well positioned to rectify the remedial deficit currently faced by the cholera claimants. This limits the extent to which it might be thought that domestic courts could respond pragmatically to the strict orthodoxy that defines the UN's jurisdictional immunity. However, the burgeoning emphasis on the individual's right of access to court does place increased pressure on the UN to make adequate provisions for the settlement of private law disputes.

7.5.2 Elevating the Cholera Claims to an International Level

The current remedial deficit facing the cholera claimants is attributable to the fact that accountability structures for the UN are still largely based on a 'traditional state-centered understanding of international law and diplomacy'.[96] These structures have not yet responded reactively to the increasing emphasis on an *individual's* right to a remedy. In line with this approach, individuals cannot assert their rights *vis-à-vis* an IO without the intervention of their state. Typically, purely political accountability regimes for IOs were regarded as sufficient means to control organisations. The state-centered approach to the accountability of IOs allows member states to assert their interests through the organisation's formal governance structures.[97]

As the UN's current accountability regime is still predominantly governed by the traditional state-centered approach, the only remedial options, which appear to be available to the Haitian cholera claimants involve the elevation of the claims to an international level. Necessarily, this would require the intervention of the Haitian government. This could take a number of forms. As described above, the Haitian government does have the power, under the terms of the SOFA, to trigger the establishment of a claims commission. Haiti could also have recourse to Section 30 of the General Convention, which provides that if a difference arising out of the interpretation or application of the Convention occurs between the UN

[95] In *Brzak v United Nations*, the Court stated 'whatever immunities are possessed by other IOs, the General Convention 'unequivocally grants the UN absolute immunity without exception.' *Brzak v United Nations*, 2nd Cir, 597 F.3d 107, 2010, para 112.

[96] Herz 2008, at 472.

[97] Ibid.

and a member state, a request shall be made for an advisory opinion from the ICJ which 'shall be accepted as decisive by the parties'.

Additionally, Haiti could attempt to exercise diplomatic protection against the UN. This entails the right of a state to bring an action on behalf of its nationals whose rights and interests have been injured by another subject of international law.[98] Under this procedure, the state espouses the victims' claims, aggregates and submits them to the UN, and negotiates a lump-sum settlement on the injured parties' behalf. However, there is very little evidence of the exercise of diplomatic protection in the context of UN peacekeeping operations. This is because the UN typically settles its private law disputes with injured third parties in accordance with the UN's LCRB procedure. The negotiation of lump sums between a number of European states and the UN as compensation for damage caused by UN Operation in the Congo in the 1960s appears to be the only case made public.[99]

The exercise of diplomatic protection is of limited value in the cholera case, because it strictly entails the responsibility of the UN to states. As the Secretary-General has acknowledged, 'the choice of a lump-sum settlement as a mode of handling third-party claims is largely dependent on the state's willingness to espouse the claims of its nationals.'[100] The international responsibility of the UN is therefore meaningless to individuals who are seeking redress for injury against the UN without the support of their state. States have ultimate discretion as to whether they espouse a diplomatic claim.[101] In the present case, the Haitian government does not appear to have the institutional strength to do so. International diplomatic power is 'not a characteristic typical of states hosting peacekeepers'.[102] It is not surprising, therefore, that commentators have noted that individuals with claims against IOs are 'likely to prefer remedies which they are entitled to pursue in their own name'.[103] It appears that elevating the cholera claims to an international plane does not give rise to any practically available remedial mechanisms for the claimants.

The traditional state-centered approach to the accountability of the UN is unsatisfactory. It presupposes that states have the capacity to intervene on behalf of individuals harmed by the UN's activities. This has two unacceptable consequences. Firstly, if the UN refuses to settle private law claims and the member state of the affected parties does not attempt to implement accountability measures against the UN, then the individuals are left entirely without redress for the wrongful actions of the organisation. Secondly, the current regime is inconsistent with the rule of law, which requires that when public powers contravene their legal

[98] States may only take up the claims of their nationals and exercise diplomatic protection vis-à-vis an IO if all internal remedies have been exhausted, unless there are no appropriate and effective mechanisms available. International Law Association 2014, at 37.

[99] Zwanenburg 2008, at 44.

[100] Secretary-General's Peacekeeping Liability Report, para 37.

[101] Wickremasinghe and Guglielmo 2001, at 473.

[102] Dannenbaum 2010, at 126.

[103] Wickremasinghe and Guglielmo 2001, at 475.

obligations, whether international or national, they are accountable on the basis of the law.[104] In domestic legal orders, the exercise of governmental powers is subject to adjudication by independent courts. As the UN is not amenable to the jurisdiction of any domestic or international court, there is no commensurable way of ensuring that the UN is accountable on the basis of the law.

7.5.3 The Rule of Law in the UN and the Handling of the Cholera Claims

The UN's handling of the cholera claims illustrates that 'too much autonomy might in fact be threatening to the rule of law in international relations.'[105] The rule of law plays a prominent role in the UN's discourse on governance at both the national and international levels,[106] and the UN General Assembly has recognised that the rule of law applies to IOs, including the UN and its principal organs.[107] However, as a concept which has traditionally developed according to the relationship between a national government and individuals under its jurisdiction,[108] its role within the UN's own system of governance is not immediately clear. The rule of law, as it is conceptualised at the domestic level, cannot be simply transposed to the governance of IOs.[109] For example, the existence of an independent judicial system, which is seen as an essential prerequisite for upholding the rule of law,[110] is inapplicable at the UN level. Alvarez highlights that even though the UN frequently asserts that it applies the rule of law to its own activities, 'there are few concrete examples of how this works'.[111]

That said, certain elements of the rule of law which afford fairness to individuals in their dealings with public institutions can be applied, and indeed are expected to apply, to the UN. The Secretary-General's own conception of the rule

[104] Nollkaemper 2011, at 4.

[105] Collins and White 2010, at 3.

[106] See Farrall 2007, at 32–35. Farrall identifies five difference separate meanings of 'rule of law' in Security Council practice.

[107] Declaration of the High-level Meeting of the General Assembly on the rule of law at the national and international levels, UN Doc. A/Res/67/1, 30 November 2012, para 2 (hereinafter The Rule of Law at National and International Levels).

[108] The classical conception of the rule of law at the national level, propounded by A.V. Dicey, involves three central tenets: (1) absolute supremacy of the regular law, as opposed to the influence of arbitrary power; (2) equality before the law or the equal subjection of all classes to the ordinary law; (3) the law of the constitution is not a source of human rights, but the consequence of inherent human rights and these are upheld by the common law as defined by the courts. Dicey 1959, at 110–112.

[109] See generally Beaulac 2007; Chesterman 2008.

[110] The Rule of Law at National and International Levels, para 14.

[111] Do International Organisations Advance the Rule of Law.

of law has as its core a system of governance in which public power is accountable to laws that are legitimately created, and which ensure the protection and promotion of human rights.[112] The Secretary-General also noted that adherence to the rule of law requires, *inter alia*, fairness in the application of law, the avoidance of arbitrariness, and procedural and legal transparency.[113]

Even if it is conceded that the cholera claims do not fall within the scope of the harm compensable under the UN's liability regime, the UN's handling of the cholera claims has given rise to serious questions about the rule of law in the UN's procedures. The principle of transparency, regarded as central to the operation of the rule of law, requires that decision-making concerning the exercise of power should be as clear and transparent as possible.[114] Transparency ensures that powers are not exercised arbitrarily. The reasoning leading to a particular decision should be clear to those affected by the ultimate decision, as well as to the broader public.[115]

The UN's response to the cholera claims is in evident breach of any standards of transparency which would reasonably be expected of the organisation. The need for transparency in the cholera case is particularly pronounced, as the UN has unilateral discretion as to whether Section 29 of the General Convention applies, and there is no scope for external review of that decision. In this sense, the organisation gets the 'final word' about the applicability of Section 29 in relation to the claims. That decision should therefore be adequately explained, in order to show the decision was not made arbitrarily. However, the UN's decision to summarily reject the claims was only explained by the organisation through a terse statement that the claims would 'necessarily include a review of political or policy matters'.[116] No further explanation was provided by the UN to support that contention. As argued above, the UN's response is particularly inexplicable, as a 'review of political or policy matters' has never constituted a reason to exempt the organisation from liability in the past.

It is important to note that Section 29 of the General Convention does not entail that the UN is under an unconditional obligation to submit all claims to settlement modalities. Like all legal entities, the UN must be effectively 'protected against malicious or frivolous claims'.[117] If the cholera claims were indeed malicious or frivolous, then presumably the UN would be able to dispose of the claims as unmeritorious on the basis of the absence of a *prima facie* case. However, the

[112] Report of the Secretary-General, Delivering justice: programme of action to strengthen the rule of law at the national and international levels, UN DOC A/66/749, 16 March 2012.

[113] Ibid.

[114] Farrall 2007, at 185.

[115] Ibid.

[116] Letter from Patricia O'Brien, Under Secretary-General for Legal Affairs to Brian Concannon Jr, 21 February 2013, at 2.

[117] Harpignies 1971, at 453.

UN's decision that a claimant does or does not have a *prima facie* case cannot be made arbitrarily. While the UN has never explicitly stated what its decision entails, a former UN Legal Officer has suggested that the determination would normally require (1) the existence of a relationship between the UN and the claimant, whether based on contract or tortious liability; and (2) the existence of damage allegedly suffered by the claimant, during the course of that relationship.[118] If the UN had indeed made such a determination with respect to the cholera claims, it is unclear on what basis the UN's findings should be withheld from the claimants. Recalling that the UN is vested with a substantial amount of autonomy on the basis of functional necessity, it is difficult to see why the functioning of the UN demands that those reasons be kept secret. In the absence of adequate reasons, it is impossible to know whether or not the UN exercised its power to settle the claims arbitrarily.

At the very least, the UN should have gone to greater lengths to explain why the cholera claims have been regarded as a separate category of damage to that ordinarily compensated by the organisation. This is tied to an important principle of the rule of law, namely the principle of consistency in the treatment of like cases.[119] This principle requires that power should be exercised in a consistent and predictable manner.[120] If like cases should generally be treated alike, the UN should explain why the cholera claims require a departure from the general statement that 'it has always been the policy of the UN … to compensate individuals who have suffered damages for which the Organisation was legally liable'.[121] It is suggested that if the UN wishes to continue to propagate and advance the rule of law in a legitimate manner, the organization will need to work towards more effective incorporation of the rule of law into its own practice.

7.5.4 The Human Rights Imperative

Part of the need to respond to the cholera claims adequately is based on the growing expectation that the UN, rather than merely 'promoting' respect for human rights, should adhere to the norms of international human rights law itself. It may be said that the cholera claims also entail the responsibility of the UN for human rights violations. The 'human rights imperative' refers to the idea that the UN's accountability regime must take, as one of its primary objectives, the protection of individual human rights. As has been argued, the characterisation of the cholera claims as a

[118] Ibid., at 454.

[119] International Law Association 2014, at 12.

[120] Farrall 2007, at 205.

[121] Letter dated 6 August 1965 from the Secretary-General addressed to the acting permanent representative of the Union of Soviet Socialist Republics, UN Doc. S/6595, 6 August 1965, UN Juridical Yearbook 1965, at 41.

private law dispute in tort entails questions about the human right of access to a court, although this has been assessed as an obligation owed by a state to individuals. However, the human rights imperative in the cholera case also extends to the substantive compliance by the UN with international human rights norms.[122]

It is well settled that the UN possesses international legal personality and is a subject of international law, capable of possessing international rights and duties.[123] Although IOs have generally shown a reluctance to acknowledge in explicit terms a legal obligation to comply with human rights,[124] 'the underlying tenor of recent developments' is that IOs are bound by general international law, including any human rights norms that can be viewed as customary law or general principles of law.[125] In light of this shift, the UN is increasingly expected not only to promote human rights compliance by states, but also to abide by the same rules itself.[126]

The UN's responsibility for the cholera outbreak seems to entail four key human rights violations. Firstly, in the case of over 8,000 deceased victims of the cholera outbreak, the UN may have violated the right to life and the right against arbitrary deprivation of life.[127] The right to life constitutes a norm of customary international law,[128] and therefore it is a right which the UN has a legally binding obligation to respect by virtue of its international legal personality.

Secondly, in the case of individuals who suffered from cholera and survived, the UN may have violated the victim's human right to health.[129] The International Covenant on Economic, Social and Cultural Rights (ICESCR) acknowledges the right of everyone to the enjoyment of the highest attainable standard of physical and mental health.[130] This right has been specifically regarded as entailing the prevention, treatment and control of epidemic diseases.[131]

Thirdly, the UN's introduction of sewage containing the cholera bacteria into the Artibonite River may constitute a breach of the right to water.[132] The right to water exists as a necessary condition to the operation of the right to adequate

[122] Wellens 2002, at 215.

[123] *Reparations for Injuries Suffered in the Service of the United Nations,* ICJ, Advisory Opinion, 11 April 1949; Shaw 2008, at 190.

[124] Wellens 2002, at 15.

[125] Reinisch 2009, at 420; Mégret and Hoffmann 2003, at 314.

[126] Reinisch 2009, at 420.

[127] Article 6 ICCPR; Article 8 UDHR.

[128] Ramcharan 1985, at 3.

[129] Article 25(1) UDHR; Article 12 of 1966 International Covenant on Economic, Social and Cultural Rights, 993 UNTS 3 (ICESCR).

[130] Article 12 ICESCR.

[131] Article 12(2)(c) ICESCR.

[132] See Institute for Justice and Democracy in Haiti and The John Marshall Law School, Cholera as a grave violation of the right to water in Haiti, Submission to Catarina de Albuquerque, Special Rapporteur on the human right to safe drinking water and sanitation, 2014.

standard of living,[133] and the right to health.[134] The right to water has been recognised as 'indispensible for leading a life in human dignity' and 'a prerequisite to the realisation of all other human rights'.[135]

However, as the UN is not a signatory to the ICESCR guaranteeing the right to health and the right to water, it is incorrect to say the UN is legally bound to respect the second and third rights mentioned above. While it has been argued that the minimum core obligations in relation to the right to health and water are binding under customary international law,[136] the lack of uniform state practice casts that assertion into doubt.[137] Despite this technicality, the UN's role in the cholera outbreak was specifically mentioned by the Special Rapporteur on the Human Right to Safe Drinking Water and Sanitation,[138] who emphasised the UN's obligation to 'investigate the allegations in order to establish responsibility for any violations, and to ensure the alleged victims' right to a remedy, including compensation, if warranted'.[139]

The fourth violation of human rights is attached to the UN's failure to settle the cholera claims, and appears to be a violation of the claimants' right to a remedy. The right to a remedy may be seen as a norm of customary international law,[140] and includes the procedural right of effective access to a fair hearing and the substantive right to a remedy.[141] By failing to settle the cholera claims, the UN has failed at both of these limbs to protect the claimant's right to a remedy.

The characterisation of the cholera outbreak as a series of human rights violations also raises interesting questions about the type of forum that would be the most appropriate to hear the claims. Under the SOFA regime, it is presumed that a claims commission is the most appropriate forum for hearing claims of personal injury and death arising out of the acts and omissions of peacekeeping troops. This may be true

---

[133] Article 11 ICESCR.

[134] Article 12 ICESCR.

[135] Committee on Economic, Social and Cultural Rights, General Comment No 15: The Right to Water, UN Doc. E/C.12/2002/11, 20 January 2003.

[136] Concannon and Lindstrom 2011, at 1167.

[137] On the customary status of the right to health, see Kinney 2001, at 1464. On the customary status of the right to water, see Scanlon et al. 2004, at 9. The authors there note that while over 60 domestic constitutions refer to environmental obligations, less than one-half expressly refer to the right of its citizens to a healthy environment. Only the South African Bill of Rights enshrines an explicit right of access to sufficient water.

[138] Catarina de Albuquerque, Special Rapporteur, Report of the Special Rapporteur on the human right to safe drinking water and sanitation, UN Doc. A/HRC/27/55, 30 June 2014, para 34.

[139] Ibid.

[140] Shelton 2005, at 182. See also Basic principles and guidelines on the right to a remedy and reparation for victims of violations of international human rights and humanitarian law, UN Doc. A/RES/60/147, 21 March 2006.

[141] Wellens 2003, at 1162.

of straightforward disputes, such as car accidents, in which case the UN's current procedures could be a suitable forum to deal with claims. However, the 'mechanisms for determining the UN liability in peace operations were not set up with violations of international human rights law in mind'.[142] The current procedural regime may not be appropriate to deal with cases in which serious violations of human rights are in issue, even though the conduct may simultaneously be categorised as a private law dispute in tort.[143] This is true of the claims commissions process, and *a fortiori* with respect to the less formal LCRB process. This raises the question of whether IOs should be amenable to the jurisdiction of international human rights tribunals—which could be the most appropriate forum to hear such claims involving human rights violations. While not a remedial option for the cholera claimants, subjecting the UN to the jurisdiction of human rights tribunals may be contemplated as a more permanent solution to the accountability gap in the future.

As the law currently stands, the human rights characterisation of the cholera claims does not increase the availability of remedial mechanisms for the claimants, as there is no international human rights court competent to adjudicate human rights claims against the UN. Although a violation of human rights by an IO engages the international responsibility of the organisation,[144] the present legal framework governing the international responsibility of IOs largely 'leaves individuals out in the cold'.[145] The Articles on the Responsibility of International Organizations (ARIO), adopted by the International Law Commission (ILC) in 2011,[146] for instance, is strictly drafted in terms of the duty of reparations for injury as one owed by IOs directly to other subjects of international law, namely states or other IOs. Furthermore, an organisation's responsibility under the ARIO can only be invoked by a state or another IO.[147] However, the fact that the cholera claims can be 're-clothed'[148] as a series of human rights violations reaffirms the gaping accountability deficit, which effectively vests the UN with impunity for its violations of human rights abuses.

7.5.5 Demands for the Enhanced Accountability of the UN

As has been shown, individuals do not have the ability to bring private law claims against the UN without the consent of the organisation, or without the intervention of their state. Until recently, this was not a significant cause for concern from the

---

142 Mégret 2007, at 265.

143 Wickremasinghe and Guglielmo 2001, at 483.

144 International Law Association 2014, at 5.

145 See Von Bogdandy and Steinbruck Platise 2012, at 67.

146 Responsibility of International Organizations.

147 Ibid. See also Von Bogdandy and Steinbruck Platise 2012, at 73.

148 Wickremasinghe and Guglielmo 2001, at 480. See Virgo 2001, at 325.

perspective of individuals who were harmed by the UN's activities. Ordinarily, the UN settles private law disputes amicably in accordance with various modalities prompted by Section 29 of the General Convention, thus avoiding the need to assert immunity before national courts.[149] Accordingly, the unique regime governing private law claims against the UN did not evoke widespread criticism that the UN was using its jurisdictional immunity to evade or minimise its liability for damage it had caused. Seemingly, there was no pressing reason why the current accountability framework required significant revision.

Recently, both the Haitian cholera claims and the *Mothers of Srebrenica* claims have provided large-scale illustrations of the remedial deficit facing individuals harmed by the allegedly tortious acts of the UN. Undeniably, this gap has exposed the extent to which the international rules currently in force are capable of changing according to modern ideals about the place of the individual in international law.

The accountability gap in the present case may be defined in the following way—if the UN refuses to settle disputes amicably, individuals have no further means of recourse against the organisation. The UN's legal obligation to settle disputes according to Section 29 of the General Convention therefore rests on the political goodwill of the UN. There is no court available to individuals, which is competent to rule on whether the organisation's decision to do so, or refusal to do so, has been exercised properly or improperly.

The traditional approach to the accountability of IOs must now be eschewed in favour of new forms of legal accountability, consistent with the rule of law, which are capable of being enforced at the request of individual claimants. This entails a shift away from the narrowly circumscribed political accountability of the UN to its member states, in favour of an approach which pays greater deference to the rule of law and rights of individuals.

Alvarez highlights that the cholera case 'straddles two distinct cultures'.[150] On the one hand, there is the culture of the General Convention, which allows the UN to have unilateral discretion as to when, where and to whom it will be legally accountable. According to this culture, the acts and omissions of the 'venerable' UN 'receive the benefit of the doubt'.[151] Further, the UN's exercise of its powers lacks transparency unless the organisation itself lifts the veil.[152] On the other hand, there is a culture strongly influenced by the human rights imperative, in which both states and IOs alike are increasingly expected to provide remedies for the injuries they cause. This culture demands that individuals should be entitled to enforce their rights in their own name.

The practice of IOs and domestic courts is still overwhelmingly in favour of the traditional approach, prioritising the legal autonomy of the UN. This level of autonomy is predicated on the idea that the functions of the UN are of such

149 Rashkow 2013, at 341.

150 Alvarez 2014.

151 Ibid.

152 Ibid.

fundamental importance that the organisation should be 'given the space and means to do whatever it can to achieve them'.[153] Thus, the UN's expansive privileges and immunities are justified on the basis that autonomy would guarantee the independence and functional effectiveness of the organisation. Autonomy in these circumstances generally refers to self-government, and the authority asserted by an entity to regulate itself.[154] The logical corollary is, however, that the more autonomy an organisation is vested with, the harder it is to control. With regard to the jurisdictional immunity granted to IOs, this creates a 'tremendous turf war' between the two competing values of autonomy and control,[155] pursuant to which the injurious acts of an IO are not open to judicial scrutiny.

There is now an increasing awareness, at least within academic scholarship, that the UN is unjustifiably placed outside the broader accountability regime, under which large 'global actors' (such as states, multinational corporations and non-governmental organisations) are legally accountable for the injuries they cause.[156]

It is not the case that immunity rules are not capable of adapting to changing standards and the needs of the international community. Historically, at a state level, the sovereign immunity granted to foreign governments before domestic courts was of an absolute standard comparable to that now enjoyed by the UN. However, the doctrine of state immunity has over time become increasingly limited, and now draws a distinction between acts *jure imperii* (acts of state) and *jure gestionis* (private acts),[157] the latter of which can be heard in the courts of foreign states. The distinction at state level was born out of a growing discomfort with exempting foreign governments from the rule of law, and serves to provide fairness to private litigants.[158] The erosion of absolute sovereign immunity illustrates that 'immunity is not a static institution but adapts as the world changes around it'.[159]

If the UN continues to rely on the orthodoxy of jurisdictional immunity, while simultaneously denying mechanisms for redress to victims, the organisation faces losing its legitimacy in the eyes of the public at large, who are the subject of its

[153] Klabbers 2001, at 123.

[154] Sari 2011, at 258.

[155] Klabbers 2001, at 122.

[156] See Reinisch 2009.

[157] This distinction cannot be drawn with respect to the jurisdictional immunity of IOs. The restrictive state immunity doctrine governing the sovereign immunity of States are not relevant to the differently based immunity of IOs, which are purely functional and designed to protect their ability to function independent from governments. Suy 1980, at 227–228.

[158] Herz 2008, at 481. Further, state immunity does not place states entirely out of reach of judicial review, as states are not exempted from the jurisdiction of their domestic courts—the legal accountability of states is therefore well secured in comparison to that of IOs.

[159] Faith 2013, at 372.

functions.[160] The ICJ has stated in the *Effect of Awards* case that 'it would hardly be consistent with the expressed aim of the Charter to promote freedom and justice for individuals … that [the UN] should afford no judicial or arbitral remedy to its staff for the settlement of any disputes which may arise between it and them.'[161] Given the ICJ's reference to 'justice for individuals', it is difficult to see why that same proposition would not apply to disputes between the UN and individuals injured by its activities.

One commentator has noted that it would be 'quite ironic to negate the rights of individuals on the assumption that they might be incompatible with the functions of IOs.'[162] Nowhere is that more true than within the realm of peacekeeping operations,[163] where the UN frequently attempts to export human rights and the rule of law to states through 'good governance' activities. In Haiti, the UN Security Council's mandate explicitly charges the MINUSTAH peacekeepers with duties regarding the restoration and maintenance of the rule of law.[164] The mandate also includes an undertaking to support the government of Haiti in its efforts to promote and protect human rights, and ensure accountability for human rights abuses and redress for victims.[165] It would thus be expected that the organisation adhere to those principles itself. It has been noted that the UN's attempts to build national accountability mechanisms in Haiti, including courts and national human rights institutions, has created a 'curious paradox' whereby the UN itself falls largely outside of any accountability framework.[166] If the UN itself is entitled to undermine the rule of law and violate human rights with impunity, it is difficult to see how their overall mandate could be meaningfully fulfilled.

The need for the UN to be a model for human rights and the rule of law is particularly pronounced in Haiti, where the MINUSTAH mission is frequently criticised for human rights violations and resulting organisational impunity.[167] Animosity towards the UN in Haiti is palpable. In the days after it was first rumoured that the UN had imported cholera into Haiti, hundreds of Haitians marched on the MINUSTAH base in Meille, with demonstrations spreading to

---

[160] The question of the legitimacy of IOs is complicated by the fact that IOs deal with a 'multi-level audience'—at a domestic level, legitimacy signifies the acceptance of government by the majority of its citizens. If that concept is transposed to IOs, that are created by member states, legitimacy also depends on how they perform in the eyes of the governments of their member states. Junne 2001, at 191.

[161] *Effect of Awards of Compensation Made by the United Nations Administrative Tribunal*, ICJ, Advisory Opinion, 13 July 1954.

[162] Arsanjani 1981, at 175.

[163] The UN's Brahimi Report championed the use of rule of law elements and human rights in its comprehensive recommendations for peace operations in 2000. Brahimi et al., Report of the Panel on the United Nations Peace Operations, UN Doc. A/55/305–S/2000/809, 21 August 2000.

[164] UNSC Res. 1542, 30 April 2004.

[165] Ibid.

[166] Concannon and Lindstrom 2011, at 1185.

[167] See Halling and Bookey 2008.

Port-au-Prince and riots in Cap Haitien.[168] Reportedly, distrust of the UN's cholera eradication programs lingers, and the issue has strained the peacekeepers' relationship with the population.[169] The UN's lack of accountability for the outbreak has exacerbated tensions spurred by numerous allegations that peacekeepers frequently engage in criminal behaviour in Haiti with impunity,[170] including acts of sexual violence and the excessive use of force.[171]

In this way, the UN's enjoyment of jurisdictional immunity may actually be impeding the organisation's ability to fulfil its mandate in Haiti, as it is no longer seen as a credible organisation within the country.[172] That point undermines the 'functional necessity' basis on which the UN is granted immunity in the first place—jurisdictional immunity may be making it harder, not easier, for the UN to fulfil its peacekeeping mandates.

7.6 Permanent Versus *Ad Hoc* Solutions

7.6.1 Theorising Permanent Solutions

In the preceding chapters, this paper has set out the vast accountability gap in the law of international institutions. It has been argued that in light of the shifting demands of human rights law and the contemporary emphasis on the international rule of law, this accountability gap must be closed. The challenge ahead lies in striking a delicate balance between preserving the necessary degree of functional autonomy for IOs while simultaneously ensuring the availability of redress mechanisms to victims. Thus, an essential question is whether the present accountability regime requires a permanent structural change to address the concerns highlighted in this paper.

At least two potential permanent structures can be envisioned, which could offer a more stable and predictable legal order for individuals with private claims against UN peacekeeping operations. Firstly, Schrijver conceives of a 'Central Claims Commission', constituted similarly to the mission-specific standing claims commissions discussed in Sect. 7.4 of this paper) which could offer a permanent forum for aggrieved individuals for all peacekeeping missions.[173] Schrijver argues that the UN Dispute Tribunal and Appeals Tribunal for internal employment and personnel disputes would be instructive in the establishment of such a commission.[174]

[168] D. Sontag, In Haiti, global failures on a cholera epidemic, *The New York Times*, 2013, www.nytimes.com/2012/04/01/world/americas/haitis-cholera-outraced-the-experts-and-tainted-the-un.html?pagewanted=all&_r=0. Accessed 5 September 2014.

[169] Ibid.

[170] Ibid.

[171] Kurzban et al. 2013.

[172] See Halling and Bookey 2008; Concannon and Lindstrom 2011; Faucher and Piarroux 2011.

[173] Schrijver 2013, at 596.

[174] Ibid.

The establishment of a Central Claims Commission would carry the benefit of reflecting precisely the type of claims-settling mechanism envisioned by the UN for peacekeeping missions. In theory, its constitution and procedures would already be well equipped to handle private law claims arising out of peacekeeping operations. As a mission-specific claims commission has never been established, it is impossible to speak from any empirical standpoint about the efficacy of this proposed solution.

A second option is the establishment of an ombudsperson as a permanently available internal redress mechanism for peacekeeping operations.[175] The ombudsperson model has been adopted at an international level on a number of occasions and within a number of institutions.[176] It is suggested that an ombudsperson would be capable of exercising independent and impartial oversight over the activities of an IO.[177] Verdirame highlights that an Ombudsperson's semi-judicial nature also gives them power to indicate remedies for individuals, and can promote a rights-based approach to accountability questions rather than one restricted to financial accountability.[178] This approach may therefore be preferable in circumstances where the IO's wrongful conduct is more aptly characterised as a human rights violation, rather than a private law matter.[179]

The two options canvassed here indicate that more permanent changes to the accountability regime of the UN are feasible and certainly require further evaluation. The establishment of a permanent and globally available mechanism would ensure that the UN could never be in a position to refuse to establish a forum to which claims against the organisation could be brought. The primary benefit of such a mechanism is that a permanently available forum would always be open to hear petitions from claimants. Aggrieved individuals would have recourse to a guaranteed and predictable legal forum, the availability of which is not dependent on the consent of the UN or host state.

It is also suggested that such a forum would also need to comply with basic features of the rule of law, which could better ensure procedural fairness and transparency to claimants. The forum would need to openly provide reasons as to why a particular private law claim can or cannot be settled by the organisation. It is worth recalling that the Secretary-General's own conception of the rule of law that requires, *inter alia*, fairness in the application of law, the avoidance of arbitrariness,

---

[175] Verdirame highlights that a suggestion to establish a universal Ombudsperson in the area of peacekeeping was made in the aftermath of the intervention in Somalia. Verdirame 2011, at 333 fn 62.

[176] Ombudspersons have been created within the European Union as well as the World Bank, through the creation of the Compliance Advisor Ombudsman. A mission-specific ombudsperson was established by the United Nations Mission in Kosovo, and by the Security Council in 2009 to hear complaints from individuals placed on the sanctions lists of certain anti-terrorism committees of the Security Council. See Schrijver 2013, at 597.

[177] Verdirame 2011, at 332.

[178] Ibid.

[179] See Sect.7.5.4.

and procedural and legal transparency.[180] The establishment of a permanently available mechanism which made its determinations in a transparent manner could help to bring UN practice in line with these central tenets of the rule of law.

7.6.2 Ad Hoc Solutions: A Revised Role for Domestic Courts?

While it seems that a permanent and transparent forum could alleviate the current accountability gap, there has been no indication from the UN that it considers such a change to be necessary or desirable. In the absence of any permanent, universally available mechanism, which is capable of binding the UN, there is a clear need for such pragmatic and flexible solutions to close the accountability gap. In circumstances where the UN is unwilling to respond to the claims according to its obligation under the General Convention, it is worth considering whether there may be a revised role for domestic courts in closing the accountability gap.

Any approach entailing a revised role for domestic courts would need to account for the UN's role in the maintenance of international peace and security, and the fact that domestic courts are understandably reticent to make the organisation subject to the full gamut of a state's domestic laws, lest the proper functioning of the organisation be impeded.

A sensible compromise could be for domestic courts to provide declaratory judgments in disputes between individuals and the UN. A domestic court could provide a judgment stating whether or not a *prima facie* case exists between the parties. Without going to the merits of the case, a host state's court could therefore provide a ruling as to whether an IO has breached its obligation to provide alternative dispute settlement mechanisms.[181] The benefit of a declaratory judgment is that it would leave the UN free to choose how to remedy the situation. From the UN's perspective, a declaratory judgment is the least intrusive remedy that a court could afford a claimant.[182]

If domestic courts were to make a declaratory judgment about the applicability of Section 29 of the General Convention, this would not mean that the UN would be subject to all the national laws of the domestic state. This allays a well founded fear that IOs would be seriously hampered if organisations were expected to adhere to the varying domestic laws of every state in which they conduct operations.[183]

---

[180] Report of the Secretary-General, Delivering justice: programme of action to strengthen the rule of law at the national and international levels, UN DOC A/66/749, 16 March 2012.

[181] Gaillard and Pingel-Lenuzza 2002, at 4.

[182] See Shelton 2005, at 255.

[183] The Court in *Marvin R Broadbent et al. v Organization of American States et al.* noted that 'denial of immunity opens the door to divided decisions of the courts of different member states passing judgment on the rules, regulations, and decisions of the international bodies. Undercutting uniformity in the application of staff rules or regulations would undermine the ability of the organization to function effectively.' *Marvin R Broadbent et al. v Organization of American States et al.*, DC Cir, 628 F.2d 27, 1980.

Thus, a declaratory judgment preserves the functional independence of an IO, while still providing an additional mechanism to better ensure the legal accountability of the UN and compliance with its legal obligations.

A declaratory judgment from a domestic court could have a similar effect to the operation of Section 30 of the General Convention, under which member states may seek an advisory opinion on legal disputes arising out of the operation of the Convention. The crucial distinction between a domestic court and the ICJ in these circumstances is that recourse to a domestic court would be accessible to individuals. For the reason discussed in Sect. 7.5.2, settlement mechanisms which rely on the intervention of the state to initiate proceedings are of no value in cases where individuals do not have the support of their state.

It must be noted that the argument in favour of declaratory relief issued by domestic courts does carry some serious flaws which render the solution less desirable than the permanent mechanisms discussed above. Firstly, the solution presupposes an independent judiciary which would be willing to adjudicate a *prima facie* case notwithstanding the unwillingness of the state's governments to espouse the claims at an international level. For example, Halling and Bookey remark that the instability of the Haitian legal system makes a suit against the UN in Haiti 'practically impossible'.[184] Potential claimants would therefore have to initiate civil proceedings for a declaratory judgment in a domestic court that would be willing and able to offer such relief. Nollkaemper highlights that a domestic court's willingness to settle international claims would depend on a variety of factors—these include the legal culture, domestic courts and individual judges in varying degrees are open to consider and give effect to international law.[185] The availability of this relief may therefore depend on the claimant's ability to establish a nexus to the jurisdiction of an independent domestic court willing to respond effectively to the claim.

Secondly, as discussed in Sect. 7.5.1, domestic courts have always upheld the absolute character of the UN's immunity. The efficacy of this solution would therefore depend on domestic courts in the future taking a stronger human rights approach to jurisdictional immunities, as enunciated by the ECtHR in *Waite and Kennedy*.[186] Whether or not a domestic court would be willing to offer declaratory relief in these circumstances is uncertain. While the possibility of a revised approach to the jurisdictional immunity of IOs is uncertain, it is not impossible. The gradual erosion of absolute sovereign immunity provides an apt illustration that 'immunity is not a static institution, but adapts as the world changes around it'.[187] Nevertheless, the reliance on domestic courts in this way may undermine predictability and equality in the availability of a forum for individuals harmed by IOs.[188]

---

[184] Halling and Bookey 2008, at 476–477.

[185] Nollkaemper 2011, at 10–11.

[186] See *Waite and Kennedy v Germany*, ECtHR, No. 26083/94, 18 February 1999; *Beer and Reagan v Germany* ECtHR, No. 28934/95, 18 February 1999.

[187] Faith 2013, at 372.

[188] For a discussion on the adjudication of international rule of law before domestic courts, see Nollkaemper 2011.

Thirdly, the proposed solution regarding declaratory relief does not actually guarantee that the UN would respond appropriately if a domestic court provided a ruling that a *prima facie* case existed between the parties. While it is hoped that declaratory relief issued by a domestic court would provide an impetus for the UN to settle the dispute, there is the possibility that the UN could simply ignore such a judgment.

Thus, while a revised role for domestic courts could offer a pragmatic ad hoc solution to the present accountability gap, there is certainly no guarantee that this solution will provide a more stable and predictable legal order for claimants. In the absence of a permanently available mechanism for claimants, this ad hoc solution at least attempts to provide an additional layer of legal accountability to the UN's unilateral discretion to determine its own liability. By revising the role of domestic courts, we avoid succumbing to the 'skeptical realist position' described by Nollkaemper, which holds that 'because the major players do not wish to subject themselves in international courts, there is no point in pursuing an international rule of law.'[189] Refuting the skeptical realist position, Nollkaemper contends that the international rule of law does require accountability mechanisms, and suggests that we should adopt a more flexible understanding of the nature and form of such mechanisms.[190] Thus, while the solution does not offer the same guarantees of predictability and equality which would be ensured by a permanent mechanism, a new role for domestic courts could help to fill the accountability gap while more permanent solutions are explored and established in the future.

7.7 Conclusion

The emergence of the Haitian cholera claims has exposed an unacceptable lacuna in the present international legal order which must be addressed. The UN's treatment of the claims signifies a worrying departure from the ordinary practice of the organisation in dealing with private law claims, which has, in the past, possibly been 'overly generous in an effort to avoid the filing of claims in national courts or, possibly, further controversy and adverse publicity'.[191]

The cholera claims have exposed the limited extent to which the present accountability regime governing UN peacekeeping operations is able to meet current demands about human rights law and the rule of law. It has also revealed the need for international immunity rules to be dynamic, rather than static, in their application. Static immunity rules will continue, unacceptably, to leave individuals out in the cold.

---

[189] Nollkaemper 2011, at 5–6.

[190] Ibid.

[191] Rashkow 2013, at 342.

The accountability deficit cannot persist for two primary reasons. Firstly, from an institutional perspective, jurisdictional immunity should never allow IOs to deviate from the general principle that legal entities are responsible for the injuries they cause. To allow otherwise is to allow IOs to operate above the law. Secondly, from a human rights perspective, individuals whose rights are adversely affected by the acts of an IO should never be left without adequate procedural and substantive remedial protection.

It is impossible for the UN to fulfil its mandate to establish the rule of law and respect for human rights in Haiti if the organisation itself operates outside the law. The UN should not be entitled to 'treat Haiti as a charity case rather than a space where legal obligations exist.'[192] Not only will the UN have failed to live up to its mandate, but the future stability of Haiti's legal order will invariably be influenced by the fact that an enormous organisation was able to enter the country, violate otherwise applicable laws and human rights standards, and ultimately leave with impunity.

While there is hope that 'an international environment which emphasises the rule of law will continue to put pressure on IOs to close accountability gaps',[193] to date, political pressure and pleas about the moral legitimacy of the UN have not been successful in influencing the organisation's behaviour with respect to the cholera claims. Pressure from outside the organisation has seemingly had no effect on the impenetrable wall created by the UN's jurisdictional immunity and its unilateral discretion to settle claims.

While it does not appear that the immunity rules under the General Convention are set to change in the near future, it is certainly worth exploring the establishment of a permanent and universally available settlement mechanism to deal with such claims. A properly established permanent mechanism could provide the requisite degree of transparency and consistency so as to satisfy the demands that the UN's practices conform to the rule of law.

In the absence of a permanent mechanism, there may also be a role for domestic courts in providing declaratory relief, which could potentially alleviate the accountability deficit. The additional level of legal accountability offered by national courts could compel the UN to ensure that its alternative dispute settlement mechanisms are functioning effectively.

References

Alvarez J (2014) The United Nations in the time of cholera. Am J Int Law Unbound. www.asil.org/blogs/united-nations-time-cholera. Accessed 5 Sept 2014

Amerasinghe CF (1996) Principles of institutional law of international organizations. Cambridge University Press, Cambridge

[192] Concannon and Lindstrom 2011, at 1147.

[193] Reinisch 2013, at 581.

Arsanjani MH (1981) Claims against international organizations: quis custodiet ipsos custodes. Yale J World Public Order 7:131–176
Beaulac S (2007) An inquiry into the international rule of law. Working Paper No 24, European University Institute
Bonafé BI (2013) Italian courts and the immunity of international organizations. Int Organ Law Rev 10:505–537
Brockman-Hawe BE (2011) Questioning the UN's immunity in the Dutch courts: unresolved issues in the Mothers of Srebrenica litigation. Wash Univ Glob Stud Law Rev 10:727–748
Chesterman S (2008) An international rule of law? Am J Comp Law 56:331–362
Collins R, White ND (2010) Moving beyond the autonomy-accountability dichotomy: reflections on institutional independence in the international legal order. Int Organ Law Rev 7:1–8
Concannon B Jr, Lindstrom B (2011) Cheaper, better, longer-lasting: a rights-based approach to disaster response in Haiti. Emory Int Law Rev 25:1145–1191
Cravioto A et al (2010) Final report of the independent panel of experts on the cholera outbreak in Haiti. www.un.org/News/dh/infocus/haiti/UN-cholera-report-final.pdf. Accessed 5 Sept 2014
Dannenbaum T (2010) Translating the standard of effective control into a system of effective accountability: how liability should be apportioned for violations of human rights by member state troop contingents serving as United Nations peacekeepers. Harv Int Law J 51:113–192
Dicey AV (1959) Introduction to the study of the law of the constitution. Macmillan, London
Faith K (2013) *Stichting Mothers of Srebrenica v Netherlands*: does U.N. immunity trump the right of access to a court? Tulane J Int Comp Law 22:359–376
Farrall JM (2007) United Nations sanctions and the rule of law. Cambridge University Press, Cambridge
Faucher B, Piarroux R (2011) The Haitian cholera epidemic: is searching for its origin only a matter of scientific curiosity? Clin Microbiol Infect 17:479–480
Frerichs RR, Keim PS, Barrais R, Piarroux R (2012) Nepalese origin of cholera epidemic in Haiti. Clin Microbiol Infect 18:158–163
Gaillard E, Pingel-Lenuzza I (2002) International organisations and immunity from jurisdiction: to restrict or bypass. Int Comp Law Q 51:1–15
Halling M, Bookey B (2008) Peacekeeping in name alone: accountability for the United Nations in Haiti. Hastings Int Comp Law Rev 31:461–486
Harpignies RH (1971) Settlements of disputes of a private law character to which the Untied Nations is a party: a case in point: the arbitral award of 24 September 1969 in *Re Starways Ltd v. United Nations*. Revue Belge de Droit Int 7:451–468
Heine J, Thompson S (2001) Fixing Haiti: MINUSTAH and beyond. United Nations University Press, New York
Herz S (2008) International organizations in the U.S. courts: reconsidering the anachronism of absolute immunity. Suffolk Transnatl Law Rev 31:471–532
International Commission of Jurists (2008) Report of the International Commission of Jurists expert legal panel on corporate complicity in international crimes: volume III civil remedies. www.icjcanada.org/ICJfre/fr/document/doc_2008-10_vol3.pdf. Accessed 5 Sept 2014
International Law Association (2014) Accountability of international organisations. In: Report of the Seventy-first Conference, Berlin
Junne GCA (2001) International organizations in a period of globalization: new (problems of) legitimacy. In: Coicaud JM, Heiskanen V (eds) The legitimacy of international organizations. United Nations University, New York, pp 189–220
Kelsen H (1950) The law of the United Nations: a critical analysis of its fundamental problems. London Institute of World Affairs, London
Kinney ED (2001) The international human right to health: what does this mean for our nation and world? Indiana Law Rev 34:1457–1475
Klabbers J (2001) Autonomy, constitutionalism and virtue in international institutional law. In: Collins R, White ND (eds) International organizations and the idea of autonomy. Routledge, London, pp 120–140

Kurzban I et al (2013) UN Accountability for Haiti's cholera epidemic. Am J Int Law Unbound. http://www.asil.org/blogs/un-accountability-haiti%E2%80%99s-cholera-epidemic. Accessed 5 Sept 2014
Mégret F (2007) The vicarious responsibility of the United Nation. In: Aoi C, de Coning C, Thakur R (eds) Unintended consequences of peacekeeping operation. United Nations University Press, New York, pp 250–267
Mégret F, Hoffmann F (2003) The UN as a human rights violator? Some reflections on the United Nations' changing human rights responsibilities. Human Rights Q 25:314–342
Muller AS (1995) International organisations and their host states: aspects of their legal relationship. Kluwer Law International, London
Nollkaemper A (2011) National courts and the international rule of law. Oxford Scholarship Online, Oxford
Piarroux R et al (2011) Understanding the cholera epidemic, Haiti. Emerg Infect Dis 17:1161–1167
Prescott JM (2001) Claims. In: Fleck D (ed) The handbook of the law of visiting forces. Oxford University Press, Oxford, pp 159–186
Ramcharan B (1985) The concept and dimensions of the right to life. In: Ramcharan B (ed) The right to life in international law. Martinus Nijhoff Publishers, Leiden, pp 1–32
Rashkow B (2013) Immunity of the United Nations. Int Organ Law Rev 10:332–348
Rawski F (2002) To waive or not to waive: immunity and accountability in U.N. peacekeeping operations. Conn J Int Law 18:103–131
Reinisch A (2009) Convention on privileges and immunities of the United Nations. UN Audiov Libr Int Law. http://legal.un.org/avl/pdf/ha/cpiun-cpisa/cpiun-cpisa_e.pdf. Accessed 5 Sept 2014
Reinisch A (2011) Privileges and immunities. In: Klabbers J, Wallendahl A (eds) Research handbook on the law of international organizations. Edward Elgar, Cheltenham, pp 132–155
Reinisch A (2013) To what extent can and should national courts fill the accountability gap. Int Organ Law Rev 10:572–587
Ryngaert C (2010) The immunity of international organizations before domestic courts: recent trends. Int Organ Law Rev 7:121–148
Sari A (2011) Autonomy, attribution and accountability: reflections on the *Behrami* case. In: Collins R, White ND (eds) International organizations and the idea of autonomy. Routledge, London, pp 257–277
Scanlon J, Cassar A, Nemes N (2004) Water as a human right. IUCN environmental law and policy paper no. 51
Schermers H, Blokker N (2001) International institutional law: unity within diversity. Martinus Nijhoff Publishers, Leiden
Schrijver N (2013) Beyond Srebrenica and Haiti. Int Organ Law Rev 10:588–600
Shaw M (2008) International law, 6th edn. Cambridge University Press, Cambridge
Shelton D (2005) Remedies in international human rights law, 2nd edn. Oxford University Press, Oxford
Shraga D (2000) UN peacekeeping operations: applicability of international humanitarian law and responsibility for operations-related damage. Am J Int Law 94:406–412
The Sphere Project (2010) Humanitarian charter and minimum standards in humanitarian response: minimum standards in water supply, sanitation and hygiene promotion. www.ifrc.org/PageFiles/9530/The-Sphere-Project-Handbook-20111.pdf
Suy E (1980) Brief for the United Nations as amicus curiae: *Marvin R. Broadbent et al v Organization of American States*: decision of 8 January 1980. United Nations Juridical Yearbook, pp 227–238
United Nations Department of Peacekeeping Operations (1999) Medical support manual for United Nations peacekeeping operations, 2nd edn. http://physiciansforhaiti.org/wp-content/uploads/2013/04/DPKO-MSM.pdf
United Nations High Commissioner for Refugees (2007) Handbook for emergencies www.refworld.org/pdfid/46a9e29a2.pdf

Verdirame G (2011) The UN and human rights: who guards the guardians?. Cambridge University Press, Cambridge

Virgo G (2001) Characterization, choice of law and human rights. In: Scott C (ed) Torture as tort: comparative perspectives on the development of transnational human rights litigation. Hart Publishing, Oxford, pp 325–342

Von Bogdandy A, Steinbruck Platise M (2012) ARIO and human rights protection: leaving individuals in the cold. Int Organ Law Rev 9:67–76

Wellens K (2002) Remedies against international organisations. Cambridge University Press, Cambridge

Wellens K (2003) Fragmentation of international law and establishing an accountability regime for international organizations: the role of the judiciary in closing the gap. Mich J Int Law 25:1159–1181

Wickremasinghe C, Guglielmo V (2001) Responsibility and liability for violations of human rights in the course of UN field operations. In: Scott C (ed) Torture as tort: comparative perspectives on the development of transnational human rights litigation. Hart Publishing, Oxford, pp 465–489

World Health Organization (2011) Technical notes on drinking water, sanitation and hygiene in emergencies. www.who.int/water_sanitation_health/publications/2011/tn13_excreta_disposal_en.pdf?ua=1. Accessed 5 Sept 2014

Zwanenburg M (2008) UN peace operations: between independence and accountability. Int Organ Law Rev 5:23–74

Chapter 8
Protecting Human Rights During Emergencies: Delegation, Derogation, and Deference

Evan J. Criddle

Abstract Leading human rights treaties permit states as a temporary measure to suspend a variety of human rights guarantees during national crises. This chapter argues that human rights derogation is best justified as a temporary mechanism for empowering states to protect human rights, rather than as a device for enabling national authorities to advance their own interests in a manner that compromises human rights protection. Human rights treaties use broad legal standards to entrust states with responsibility for deciding what measures are best calculated to maximise human right protection during emergencies. For this delegation of authority to operate effectively, international tribunals must accord a healthy measure of deference to state derogations. Deference to state derogations is not warranted, however, if circumstances suggest that national authorities are not prepared to serve as impartial, rights-optimising trustees for their people.

Keywords Human rights · Emergencies · Temporariness · Delegation · Derogation · Deference · Margin of appreciation · Rules · Standards · Individualism · Altruism

---

Professor of Law and Tazewell Taylor Research Professor, William & Mary Law School. The author wishes to express his appreciation to Monika Ambrus and Ramses Wessel for their invitation to participate in this symposium on 'Temporariness in International Law'. Special thanks also to Angela Banks, Trey Childress, Diane Desierto, John Linarelli, Gerald Neuman, Fionnuala Ní Aolaín, James Nickel, Thomas Poole, William Scheuerman, Scott Sheeran, and several anonymous reviewers for helpful comments at various stages of this project.

E.J. Criddle (✉)
William & Mary Law School, Williamsburg, VA, USA
e-mail: ejcriddle@wm.edu

M. Ambrus and R.A. Wessel (eds.), *Netherlands Yearbook of International Law 2014*, Netherlands Yearbook of International Law 45, DOI 10.1007/978-94-6265-060-2_8

Contents

8.1 Introduction 198
8.2 The Resilience of Derogation Standards 201
8.3 Derogation Standards as Delegations 206
8.4 Deference for an Altruistic Regime 212
8.5 Conclusion 218
References 219

8.1 Introduction

International human rights law (HRL) obligates states to respect, protect, and fulfill basic norms of humane treatment, but few of these requirements are set in stone. Many human rights treaties contain limitation clauses, which permit states to restrict the protection afforded by various human rights in deference to important values such as public health and safety.[1] Derogation clauses likewise permit states to suspend various civil and political rights during public emergencies.[2] Most economic and social rights are framed as aspirational standards that states agree to pursue without committing to any singular pathway for the 'progressive realization' of these rights.[3] Indeed, only a handful of human rights such as the prohibitions against slavery, genocide, and torture are widely accepted as peremptory norms that bind all states at all times and in all circumstances.[4] As a result, most human rights norms are subject to dynamic application over time, allowing states to adapt human rights protection to changing circumstances.

How HRL responds to public emergencies, in particular, challenges the idea that human rights are timeless and unchanging entitlements that human beings may claim at all times and in all circumstances. By authorising states to derogate from certain human rights commitments during public emergencies, leading human rights agreements such as the International Covenant on Civil and Political Rights (ICCPR),[5] the American Convention on Human Rights (American Convention),[6] the Arab Charter of Human Rights (Arab Charter),[7] and the European Convention on Human Rights

[1] See, e.g., Articles 14(1), 19, 21, 22 of the 1966 International Covenant on Civil and Political Rights, 999 UNTS 171 (hereinafter ICCPR); Article 4 of the 1966 International Covenant on Economic, Social and Cultural Rights, 993 UNTS 3 (hereinafter ICESCR).

[2] See, e.g., Article 4(1) ICCPR.

[3] See, e.g., Article 2 ICESCR.

[4] See, e.g., Article 4(2) ICCPR.

[5] See Article 4(1) ICCPR.

[6] See Article 27(1) of the 1969 American Convention on Human Rights, 1144 UNTS 123 (hereinafter American Convention).

[7] See Article 4(1) of the 2004 Revised Arab Charter on Human Rights, reprinted in 12 International Human Rights Report 893 (2005) (hereinafter Arab Charter).

and Fundamental Freedoms (European Convention)[8] effectively allow states to design their own temporary, ad hoc human rights regimes.

How should the international community ensure that states do not abuse this authority to suspend human rights norms? In his classic monograph, *The Concept of Law*, H.L.A. Hart outlines three techniques that a legal system might employ to regulate injurious conduct.[9] First, a legal system could establish bright-line rules to identify and prohibit specific harmful activities in advance. Second, a legal system could establish broad standards and delegate 'to an administrative, rule-making body… the task of fashioning rules adapted to their special needs.'[10] Third, where 'it is impossible to identify a class of specific actions to be uniformly done or forborne', a legal system could establish a broad standard of 'reasonable' conduct and require regulated parties to satisfy this standard '*before* it has been' fully specified by a lawmaking or adjudicatory body.[11] The delegation of rule-specifying authority to administrators and courts enables a legal system to tailor the application of open-textured legal standards to specific factual contexts in a more nuanced manner.[12]

Human rights regimes employ a mix of rules and standards to regulate derogation during public emergencies. Some derogation norms are plainly rule-like, including the requirements that states issue an official notice of derogation, refrain from invidious discrimination, and satisfy their other international obligations.[13] These rules, which limit the choices available to national authorities *ex ante*, advance rule of law values by providing 'the advantages of predictability, stability, and constraint'.[14] Nonetheless, the heart of human rights derogation regimes consists of open-textured standards that require further specification. When national crises prompt states to consider human rights derogation, the states must decide whether suspending ordinary human rights safeguards is 'strictly required by the exigencies of the situation.'[15] This strict-necessity standard demands case-specific analysis. In Hart's typology of regulatory regimes, it raises the question whether national authorities or international treaty bodies should be understood to bear primary responsibility for translating the standard into rules tailored to a particular crisis. Should derogation provisions be understood primarily as delegations of lawmaking authority to states to decide when, and to what extent, derogation is 'strictly necessary'? Or should these provisions be viewed primarily as delegations to international human courts and commissions, the institutions that are responsible for supervising state human rights compliance?

---

[8] See Article 15(1) of the 1950 Convention for the Protection of Human Rights and Fundamental Freedoms, 213 UNTS 221 (hereinafter European Convention).

[9] See generally Hart 2012, Chap. VII.

[10] Ibid., at 131.

[11] Ibid., at 132.

[12] See Kaplow 1992, at 559 (distinguishing rules from standards based on 'whether the law is given content ex ante or ex post').

[13] See, e.g., Article 4 ICCPR.

[14] Schauer 2013, at 1191.

[15] Article 4(1) ICCPR.

International opinion on this question remains divided. Some subscribe to the view that HRL entrusts international treaty bodies with ultimate responsibility for determining how derogation standards apply to particular emergencies. According to this model, human rights derogation reflects a limited concession to 'reason of state' (*raison d'etat*)—a safety valve that a state may use when its existential interest in self-preservation clashes with its positive human rights commitments to its people.[16] If a state's survival as a political community is in jeopardy, the state may derogate from its human rights commitments temporarily to the extent strictly necessary to ensure its own survival. Robust scrutiny by international treaty bodies is necessary, under this account, to mitigate the conflicts of interest arise between public institutions and political elites, whose survival is preserved, and their people, whose derogable human rights are sacrificed, during national crises. By asserting the ultimate prerogative to decide how general derogation standards apply to particular emergencies, international treaty bodies intercede as neutral arbiters between a state and its people to protect the integrity of HRL against erosion in state practice.

A second tradition, realised most fully in the jurisprudence of the European Court of Human Rights (ECtHR), offers a markedly different account of human rights derogation. The second tradition suggests that the purpose of derogation provisions is to empower national authorities to protect human rights *more* effectively, not less. During a genuine public emergency, circumstances may arise where a state's strict fidelity to some derogable human commitments (e.g., freedom of assembly) might hamper its efforts to protect nonderogable rights (e.g., the right to life). Far from representing a cynical concession to the practical limits of law as a constraint on state power, this second tradition views derogation as a mechanism for optimising human rights protection overall in times where human rights norms temporarily conflict with one another. By entrusting national authorities with responsibility to recalibrate human rights protections for particular public emergencies, this tradition acknowledges the international community's reliance on national authorities to fully realise HRL's overarching aspirations. The ECtHR's controversial 'margin of appreciation' doctrine resonates with this account insofar as it invites international treaty bodies to respect national authorities as the primary trustees for humanity.

This chapter explores these two traditions in human rights theory and practice. Section 8.2 considers how the legal standards in human rights derogation provisions might function alternatively as delegations of rulemaking authority to states, on the one hand, or to international treaty bodies, on the other. Section 8.3 defends the view that human rights derogation is best justified as a temporary mechanism for empowering states to protect human rights, rather than as a device for enabling national authorities to advance their interests in a manner that compromises human rights protection. Section 8.4 considers how this rights-optimising conception of human rights derogation should inform the approach that international treaty bodies such as the ECtHR, the Inter-American Court of Human Rights (IACtHR), and the UN Human Rights

[16] See, e.g., The Siracusa Principles on the Limitation and Derogation Provisions in the International Covenant on Civil and Political Rights, reprinted in 7 Human Rights Quarterly 3 1985 (hereinafter Siracusa Principles).

Committee (UNHRC) take in reviewing human rights derogations. Although this article defends the margin of appreciation doctrine, it argues that deference to national authorities should be tempered, if not abandoned altogether, in contexts such as domestic counterinsurgency where conflicts of interest disqualify national authorities from serving as neutral, rights-optimizing trustees for their people. A somewhat counterintuitive lesson of this approach is that the margin of appreciation doctrine may be least justified in national crises where the life of the state itself is most acutely threatened.

8.2 The Resilience of Derogation Standards

Human rights treaties such as the ICCPR, the American Convention, the Arab Charter, and the European Convention are widely understood to employ a multi-step inquiry to determine whether states may derogate from their human rights obligations. The first step is to consider whether the applicable convention designates a particular human rights norm as being subject to derogation.[17] Second, assuming the human rights norm in question is derogable, states are required under each agreement to provide notice concerning the scope of their derogation.[18] Third, each of these agreements contemplates that states may suspend ordinary human rights protections only temporarily during 'public emergencies'.[19] Fourth, each agreement restricts human rights derogation to circumstances where this extraordinary measure is 'strictly required' by the exigencies of the crisis,[20] are consistent with their other international obligations, and do not reflect invidious discrimination.[21]

Legal standards comprise the heart of human rights derogation regimes. In determining whether a genuine 'public emergency' exists at step three, the ICCPR, the Arab Charter, and the European Convention each permit derogation only when exigent circumstances pose a demonstrable threat to 'the life of the nation'.[22] The American Convention uses a slightly different, but similarly broad formulation, requiring states to show that a 'war, public danger, or other emergency' threatens the 'independence or security of a State Party'.[23] Because these instruments do not define key terms such as 'life of the nation', 'public danger', or 'independence and security', they

[17] See Article 4(1)–(2) Arab Charter; Article 27(1)–(2) American Convention; Article 15(1)–(2) European Convention; Article 4(1)-(2) ICCPR.

[18] See Article 4(3) Arab Charter; Article 27(3) American Convention; Article 15(3) European Convention; Article 4(3) ICCPR.

[19] See Article 4 Arab Charter; Article 27 American Convention; Article 15(1) European Convention; Article 4(1) ICCPR.

[20] See Article 4(1) Arab Charter; Article 27(1) American Convention; Article 15(1) European Convention; Article 4(1) ICCPR.

[21] See, e.g., Article 4(1) Arab Charter; Article 27(1) American Convention; Article 15(1) European Convention; Article 4(1) ICCPR.

[22] See Article 4(1) ICCPR; Article 15(1) European Convention; Article 4(1) Arab Charter.

[23] Article 27(1) American Convention.

force national authorities and international tribunals to exercise judgment in deciding whether a particular national crisis qualifies as a full-fledged 'public emergency'.

Step four follows a similar pattern. The ICCPR, Arab Charter, and European Convention state simply that the extent of a state's derogation must be 'strictly required by the exigencies of the situation'.[24] The American Convention also provides that derogation must be 'strictly required' to preserve the 'independence or security of a State Party'.[25] These standards do not pre-commit states to any particular responsive measures *ex ante*; they simply invite states to tailor their derogation from human rights norms in response to the unique demands of particular emergencies. Thus, in several crucial respects, the ICCPR, American Convention, Arab Charter, and European Convention all rely on open-textured legal standards to regulate states' recourse to derogation during public emergencies.[26]

To be ripe for enforcement, the legal standards that govern human rights derogation require translation into more specific rules. As Hart recognised, this process can proceed along one of two tracks.[27] First, derogation standards could function as delegations of rule-making authority to administrative bodies, which would then bear the responsibility to determine how the standards will apply to particular public emergencies. In the context of human rights derogation, this rule-making function could be carried out by international treaty bodies before a crisis arises, or it could be accomplished by national authorities issuing a notice of derogation at the time they confront an emerging crisis. Such measures have the advantage of providing specific guidance to rights-holders before emergency measures are deployed. The obvious disadvantage is that rules established *ex ante* may prove insufficiently supple to adapt to the complex and dynamic challenges that arise during a rapidly evolving crisis. As an alternative to rule-making, derogation standards could be understood as *de facto* delegations to international treaty bodies for post hoc review. This approach may offer less specific direction to national actors and human rights-holders *ex ante*, but it would enable HRL to tailor its rules more closely to the precise contours of a particular problem *ex post*.[28]

Each of these approaches finds support in the practice of international treaty bodies. Human rights derogation standards have been treated at times as delegations of rule-making authority to international commissions,[29] as delegations of

[24] Article 4(1) ICCPR.

[25] Article 27(1) American Convention.

[26] Of course, there are also significant differences between these instruments, including their descriptions of the types of emergencies that support derogation, the information that must be conveyed in a notice of derogation, and the specific human rights norms that they identify as derogable or nonderogable. Other human rights instruments such as the African Charter on Human and Peoples Rights do not contain derogation clauses.

[27] See Hart 2012, Chap. VII.

[28] Legal standards that resist specification both *ex ante* (through rulemaking) and *ex post* (through adjudication) effectively become non-justiciable political questions.

[29] See, e.g., Human Rights Committee, General Comment No. 5: Derogations (Article 4), U.N. Doc. HRI/GEN/1/Rev. 9, May 27, 2008 (hereinafter General Comment 5); Human Rights Committee, General Comment No. 29: States of Emergency (Article 4), U.N. Doc. CCPR/C/21/Rev.1/Add.11, 31 August 2001 (hereinafter General Comment 29).

rule-making authority to states,[30] and as delegations of adjudicatory authority to international human rights tribunals.[31]

Consider first the option of treating derogation standards as delegations for rule-making. None of the major human rights treaties expressly authorises an administrative body to promulgate rules to implement broadly formulated derogation standards. The closest any of these instruments comes to delegating rule-making power is Article 40(4) ICCPR, which authorises the U.N. Human Rights Committee (HRC) to provide 'general comments' when states report on their human rights practices.[32] The HRC has used its general comment authority on two occasions to clarify the ICCPR's derogation standards.[33] While not technically an exercise of administrative rule-making, these general comments serve in practice as guidance documents that clarify the HRC's views regarding the general application of ICCPR standards. For the most part, however, these general comments have preserved the context-sensitive, standard-based structure of Article 4 ICCPR. For example, while the HRC has characterized derogation as an 'exceptional and temporary' measure that can be taken only in response to a 'threat to the life of the nation',[34] it has not defined precisely how a state should ascertain whether a particular disturbance constitutes a 'threat to the life of the nation'. Nor has the HRC developed bright-line rules for evaluating what measures a state may employ in derogation of its human rights commitments. Instead, the HRC has stated simply that emergency measures must be necessary and proportionate to restore a 'state of normalcy where full respect for the Covenant can again be secured.'[35] These guidelines are quintessential standards that defer the task of context-sensitive rule-specification for downstream actors.[36]

---

[30] See, e.g., *Murray v. United Kingdom*, No. 14310/88, 28 October 1994, para 90; *Ireland v. the United Kingdom*, ECtHR, No. 5310/71, 18 January 1978, para 207.

[31] See, e.g., Habeas Corpus in Emergency Situations (Articles 27(2) and 7(6) American Convention), IACtHR, Advisory Opinion OC-8/87, 30 January 1987.

[32] Article 40(4) ICCPR.

[33] See General Comment 5; General Comment 29.

[34] General Comment 5, para 3; General Comment 29, para 2.

[35] General Comment 29, paras 1, 3.

[36] To the extent that the HRC has introduced bright-line rules for human rights derogation, these rules can be divided into two relatively narrow categories. First, the Committee has endeavored to clarify how nonderogable human rights norms apply to emergencies, affirming, *inter alia*, that the prohibition against 'unacknowledged detention' and 'fundamental requirements of a fair trial' such as the presumption of innocence 'must be respected during a state of emergency'. Ibid., paras 13(b) and 16. Second, the HRC has introduced a number of bright-line rules for derogation procedures. According to the HRC, this notice 'should include full information about the measures taken and a clear explanation of the reasons for them, with full documentation attached regarding their law.' Ibid., para 17. See also General Comment 29, para 2 (emphasising that a 'State party must have officially proclaimed a state of emergency' to honor 'principles of legality and rule of law at times when they are most needed').

Legal experts have proposed additional norms, principles, and procedures to guide future human rights derogation. See, e.g., Siracusa Principles, at 7, paras 23–30 (proposing, *inter alia*, that a crisis must affect the whole population in all or part of a state's territory, not 'merely local or relatively isolated threats,' and threaten a state's physical integrity or political independence to qualify as a genuine 'public emergency').

On several occasions, human rights courts have used case-by-case adjudication to generate rules for prospective application in future cases. For example, in the *Greek Case (Denmark, Norway, Sweden and the Netherlands v. Greece)*,[37] the ECtHR held that a national crisis must satisfy four criteria to qualify as a genuine 'public emergency': (1) the threat must be actual or imminent; (2) its effects must involve the whole nation; (3) the continuance of the organised life of the community must be threatened; and (4) the crisis or danger must be exceptional, in the sense that normal limitations on human rights are inadequate.[38] Although announced in the course of an adjudicatory proceeding, and formally lacking precedential authority, these criteria were widely perceived to give the European Convention's derogation regime a harder rule-like edge, providing guidance to states in anticipation of future crises. Subsequent years have witnessed a softening of these rule-like criteria, however, as the ECtHR has reformulated the criteria to maintain a more standard-based derogation regime.

Illustrative of these trends is the ECtHR's 2009 decision in *A and Others v. United Kingdom*.[39] In the wake of the 9/11 terrorist attacks in New York City and Washington, D.C., the United Kingdom declared a public emergency and enacted new legislation, the Anti-terrorism, Crime and Security Act 2001. The purpose of the Act was to address the 'continuing' threat that international terrorism posed for residents of the United Kingdom.[40] To this end, the Act authorised the arrest and prolonged detention of foreign nationals who might pose security threats but who, for one reason or another, could not be removed or deported from the country. Recognising that this measure may be inconsistent with the human 'right to liberty and security' as defined in the European Convention, the United Kingdom submitted notice that it 'had decided to avail itself of the right of derogation.'[41]

Eleven individuals later challenged their detention before the ECtHR, arguing that the United Kingdom's derogation did not satisfy the European Convention because, *inter alia*, the emergency 'was not of a temporary nature'.[42] Although neither the European Convention nor the ICCPR expressly requires that public emergencies be 'temporary', the ECtHR acknowledged the HRC's assertion in General Comment No. 29 that measures derogating from the ICCPR 'must be of an exceptional and temporary nature.'[43] Consistent with its prior decisions, however, the Court rejected the petitioners' assertion that states bear a burden to establish that the exigent circumstances necessitating human rights derogation are temporary. The Court acknowledged that 'the duration of [an] emergency' may be

---

[37] *Greek Case*, ECtHR, Nos. 3321/67, 3322/67, 3323/67 and 3344/67, 5 November 1969, para 113.

[38] *Greek Case*, ECtHR, Nos. 3321/67, 3322/67, 3323/67 and 3344/67, 5 November 1969.

[39] *A & Others v. United Kingdom*, ECtHR, No. 3455/05, 19 February 2009.

[40] Ibid., para 11.

[41] Ibid.

[42] Ibid., para 175.

[43] Ibid., paras 110, 178. See generally General Comment No 29, para 2.

relevant when evaluating the 'proportionality of [a state's] response', but it stressed that even entrenched national crises such as the United Kingdom's decades-long counter-terrorism campaign in Northern Ireland and Turkey's longstanding counterinsurgency operations against Kurdish separatists could support derogation if responsive measures were strictly necessary and proportional to the threat.[44] According to the Court, states do not bear a burden to establish that their emergency measures will be of a fixed duration; they need only commit to lift the emergency measures whenever the threat to 'the life of the nation' disappears or the measures taken are no longer strictly necessary and proportional to address the threat. Thus, rather than impose a bright-line temporariness rule that would unduly inhibit states' capacity to fulfill their responsibility to protect, the Court in *A and Others* wisely focused instead on the principles of necessity and proportionality—context-sensitive legal standards that are more finely attuned to the altruistic legal relationship that HRL ordains.

The Court's rule-skepticism in *A and Others* was not limited to whether emergency measures must be 'temporary'. In the course of its decision, the Court also called into question several rule-like features of the European Commission's four-factor test from the *Greek Case*. For example, the Court offered a flexible interpretation of the requirement that terrorist attacks must be 'imminent' to support human rights derogation. Although the United Kingdom made the case that a terrorist attack 'might be committed without warning at any time', it did not establish that any particular attack was actually imminent.[45] Nor could it reasonably do so, given the uncertain nature of the threat. In recognition of this fact, the Court softened the imminence criterion's edges—giving it a more standard-like character—to permit derogation in response to attacks of an indeterminate, but reasonably foreseeable, character. The Court also rejected the European Commission's suggestion that exigent circumstances must threaten 'institutions of government' or a state's 'existence as a political community' to qualify for human rights derogation. According to the Court, the prospect of significant civilian casualties alone within a single zone of a single city would suffice to demonstrate a threat to 'the life of the nation' justifying emergency measures.[46] In each of these respects, the Court systematically dismantled rules

[44] *A and Others v. United Kingdom*, ECtHR, No. 3455/05, 19 February 2009, para 178 (citing *Ireland v. United Kingdom*, *Brannigan v. McBride*, and *Marshall v. United Kingdom)*.

[45] Ibid., para 177. For an argument that no threat to the life of the nation was 'imminent', see also Hughes 2007, at 54.

[46] *A and Others v. United Kingdom*, ECtHR, No. 3455/05, 19 February 2009, para 179 (citing the July 2005 suicide bombings in central London). See also Macdonald 1997. 'The Convention should not be interpreted in a way that prevents states from taking action to avert the aggravation of localized emergencies.' Macdonald 1997, at 240.

from the *Greek Case,* affirming the need to preserve a more flexible, standard-based approach.[47]

International tribunals have been even less willing to impose fixed rules for determining which particular measures are 'strictly necessary' to resolve an emergency. Generally speaking, courts and commissions appear to accept that the 'strict necessity' requirement, which constrains state responses to emergencies, is not well-suited to a priori evaluation outside the context of particular emergencies. Thus, despite the international community's episodic efforts to fashion more determinate rules for human rights derogation, the emergency regimes of the ICCPR, American Convention, Arab Charter, and European Convention remain persistently standard-based at their core.

8.3 Derogation Standards as Delegations

The resiliency of HRL's derogation standards means that evaluating whether, or to what extent, human rights may be suspended during emergencies continues to be a case-specific inquiry. Rather than develop an exhaustive code of rules to regulate emergencies *ex ante*, HRL allows states to formulate emergency measures in response to the unique circumstances of particular national crises, and it authorises human rights tribunals to review these measures for compliance with the applicable standards. What remains unclear, and deeply controversial, is whether the broad standards in human rights derogation provisions should be understood primarily as delegations of rule-specifying authority to national authorities, the first-responders during times of national crisis, or to international treaty bodies, the institutions charged with supervising state performance. Before answering this question, however, it may be helpful to lay the groundwork by offering some general observations about how HRL uses legal standards to structure the juridical relationship between states and their people.

Legal theorists have long recognised that a legal system's choice between rules and standards is not merely a technical question of efficient regulatory design, but may also reflect a normative vision for the parties' legal relationship. For example, Duncan Kennedy has argued that the distinction between rules and standards

---

[47] One plausible reading of *A and Others* is that the decision collapses steps three and four of the Court's traditional analysis for evaluating human rights derogation into a single inquiry: states may derogate from their human rights commitments whenever such measures are 'strictly required' to guarantee basic security under the rule of law for their people. On this reading, whether a 'public emergency' exists is no longer an independent legal requirement but a legal conclusion that follows from the application of HRL's strict-necessity standard. Under the logic of *A and Others*, therefore, a crisis constitutes a genuine 'public emergency' if derogation is strictly necessary to satisfy the state's sovereign responsibility to protect its people. Cf. Sheeran 2013, at 553 (proposing that courts treat the existence of a 'public emergency' as a political question).

reflects a jurisprudential divide between legal regimes that are based on a spirit of 'individualism' versus those that are based on a spirit of 'altruism'.[48] In regimes based on individualism, regulated parties are free to pursue their own ends, subject only to constraints that they or their sovereign affirmatively impose *ex ante*. Generally speaking, the common law of contract is an individualistic regime. Contracting parties are presumed to engage in 'arms-length' negotiation, each pursuing their own interests, and each bound to pursue their counterparty's interest only to the extent that discrete duties have been specified by agreement in advance. Beyond these contractual duties, contracting parties are free to pursue their own self-interest; they bear no obligation to make further accommodations for the changing interests of their counterparty.

A jurisprudence of altruism, in contrast, views regulated parties as bearing relational obligations of affirmative devotion to use entrusted authority to pursue others' ends, not merely their own. The paradigmatic private-law example of a jurisprudence of altruism is the law of fiduciaries, which requires regulated parties to use their discretionary power over the legal or practical interests of their beneficiaries for the exclusive benefit of their beneficiaries.[49] As Daniel Markovits has explained, fiduciaries are retained to take *initiative* on behalf of their beneficiaries, not merely to comply with rules fixed *ex ante*. Hence,

> [f]iduciary duties of loyalty and care … reflect a natural response to the structural problems out of which fiduciary relations generally arise. A fiduciary relation becomes appealing partly because a principal requires her agent to act in ways that she cannot substantially specify *ex ante* and cannot directly evaluate *ex post*. In such cases, fiduciary obligation substitutes for the specification of contract duties and the verification of performance.[50]

Because fiduciary relationships are dynamic, and because the temptations for opportunism and shirking that arise in such relationships cannot be fully specified in advance, the law relies on standards to fill in the details *ex post*. On this view, standards are the tools that legal systems employ to encode a jurisprudence of altruism.

Of course, identifying rules with individualism and standards with altruism is too tidy, and Kennedy's thesis has been justly criticised for over-simplifying the rule/standard dynamic. As critics have noted, individualist regimes commonly deploy standards in contexts where the complexity or uncertainty of a particular environment would prevent rules from safeguarding the parties' respective interests. Conversely, altruist regimes often use rules to underscore parties' other-regarding obligations and enhance coordination.[51] Indeed, arguably the defining feature of fiduciary relationships is a bright-line rule: the 'duty of loyalty', which prohibits fiduciaries from engaging in self-interested transactions without their

---

[48] See Kennedy 1976, at 1714–1724.

[49] Markovits 2014.

[50] Ibid.

[51] Schlag 1985, at 420.

beneficiaries' consent.[52] Like individualistic regimes, altruistic regimes also commonly employ rules to set technical or procedural baselines that facilitate external monitoring and judicial review.[53] Thus, the mere fact that a particular legal regime employs rules or standards does not, in and of itself, establish that it has an individualistic or altruistic character.

Although Kennedy's claim about the relationship between legal standards and altruism is problematic, it does offer an important insight: when individualistic and altruistic regimes deploy legal standards, they take very different approaches to downstream rule-production. In individualistic regimes, neither party authorises the other to define how open-ended legal standards apply in particular circumstances; rather, legal standards serve as delegations of authority exclusively to courts to resolve any disputes between the parties about the interpretation or application of law. In contrast, legal standards operate very differently in altruistic regimes, which entrust one party with discretionary power to take initiative for the benefit of another. In altruistic regimes, parties and courts serve as co-delegates of rule-making power: the entrusted party (e.g., corporate officer, administrative agency) bears primary responsibility for translating broad legal standards into administrable rules, but courts supervise to address abuses of this discretion. Courts routinely accord a measure of deference, therefore, when they review the entrusted party's actions. For example, U.S. courts review corporate officers' compliance with the 'duty of care' very deferentially, thereby affirming that corporate officers—not courts—are primarily responsible for determining what measures are best calculated to advance the interests of their shareholders.[54] Similarly, in administrative law, national courts tend to pay considerable deference to administrative agencies, treating ambiguous standards in legislation as delegations of authority to agencies to decide what measures are best suited to advance public interests.[55] Individualistic and altruistic legal regimes thus reflect different assumptions about whether standards reflect delegations of authority to the parties, to courts, or both.

Does HRL reflect a jurisprudence of individualism or altruism? Human rights obligations are often characterised as individualistic constraints on states' sovereign independence. When states covenant to refrain from outrages against human dignity such as arbitrary detention, forced disappearance, and torture, they purportedly assume obligations that have an objective character. HRL does not confer discretion on national authorities to decide once and for all what these obligations entail; although states will necessarily take the first cut at these questions, HRL

[52] See Restatement (Second) of Agency, 1958, § 387 (describing fiduciaries' obligation to beneficiaries primarily as a duty 'to act solely for the benefit of the principal in all matters connected with his agency').

[53] See Kaplow 1992, at 563–564.

[54] For discussing the business-judgment rule in corporate law, see *Aronson v. Lewis*, 473 A.2d 805, 1 March 1984, at 812.

[55] See, e.g., *Chevron U.S.A., Inc. v. National Res. Defense Council, Inc.*, 467 U.S. 837, 1984, at 843–844.

commits the ultimate responsibility for defining the content and application of HRL norms to international courts and commissions.

This account of HRL as an individualistic regime is plausible in some respects, but it is difficult to square with some core features of HRL. While it is certainly true that states bear negative duties under HRL to respect various human rights prohibitions, and these duties are facially compatible with a jurisprudence of individualism, these duties are equally compatible with a jurisprudence of altruism.[56] Moreover, HRL also places states under affirmative duties to protect and fulfill human rights—duties that require national authorities to set aside their own self-interest to pursue the interests of their people. This is most obviously true for economic, social, and cultural rights, which commit states to use the resources at their disposal to develop and implement a coordinated plan for advancing the economic, social, and cultural well-being of their people.[57] But it is equally true of civil and political rights. Under the ICCPR, for example, it is not enough for states to refrain from imposing slavery upon their people; they must also 'ensure' respect for the prohibition by adopting laws that prohibit slavery and by prosecuting violations of these laws within their jurisdictions.[58] States are expected to take initiative to develop institutions, policies, and procedures in order to satisfy the ICCPR's directive that '[n]o one shall be held in slavery', 'servitude', or 'forced or compulsory labor'.[59] The case law developed by the ECtHR supports this altruistic vision by requiring states to take action so that the beneficiaries of the rights and freedoms enshrined in the Convention are able to enjoy these legal protections effectively.[60] In practice, of course, eradicating slavery and other forms of human trafficking has proven to be a thorny challenge for even the most affluent and conscientious states. Nonetheless, like agents or trustees in private fiduciary law, states under HRL bear broad obligations of affirmative devotion to use their powers and resources altruistically to protect and fulfill human rights to achieve the progressive realisation of these objectives for their people. Thus, the positive, programmatic character of states' obligations to respect, protect, and fulfill human rights undercuts the idea that HRL can be captured fully by a jurisprudence of individualism.

Despite these features of HRL, some human rights lawyers have characterised derogation provisions in individualistic terms.[61] The purpose of derogation clauses, under this account, is to address the conflicts of interest that arise when national

[56] See Fox-Decent and Criddle 2009 explaining how nonderogable human rights norms are consistent with a fiduciary conception of state authority under HRL.

[57] Article 2(1) ICESCR.

[58] Article 2 ICCPR.

[59] Article 8 ICCPR.

[60] See, e.g., *Marckx v. Belgium*, ECtHR, 6833/74, 13 June 1979, para 31 (explaining that the European Convention 'does not merely compel the State to abstain from … interference [with family life]' but also imposes 'positive obligations inherent in an effective "respect" for family life').

[61] See, e.g., Chowdhury 1989, at 58–59 (observing that the International Commission of Jurists considered it 'axiomatic that, for the protection of human rights, the greatest possible degree of judicial control should be striven for').

crises jeopardise states' existential interest in self-preservation. By permitting national authorities to invoke 'the life of the nation'[62] or the 'independence or security of a State Party'[63] as a trump card against certain human rights claims during public emergencies, HRL enables them to modify their legal obligations in settings where the conflict between their own (individualistic) interests and their (altruistic) legal obligations to their people are in greatest tension. Approached from this perspective, treating derogation standards as delegations to national authorities would make little sense, because it would invite national authorities to serve as judges and parties to the same cause. Instead, there would be a particularly strong case for international tribunals to conduct searching, independent review of human rights derogations to decide for themselves whether state derogations are strictly necessary to preserve the 'life', 'independence', or 'security' of the state.

This understanding of human rights derogation as a concession to *raison d'état*, while superficially plausible, has failed to attract much support among international lawyers. Few subscribe to the idea that national authorities may use derogation as a device *solely* for self-preservation, deliberately disregarding their general obligations to respect, protect, and fulfill human rights for the benefit of their people. Instead, the dominant view has been that derogation standards such as 'the life of the nation' must be defined according to *human* interests, not the interests of national authorities *per se*.[64] Far from releasing states to pursue their own independent objectives, international human rights treaties contemplate that states will use derogation solely for other-regarding purposes, suspending human rights protections only to the extent strictly necessary to re-establish their capacity to protect and fulfill human rights for their people. During a time of war, for example, a state may find it necessary to impose curfews or deny access to public roads temporarily in a departure from the human 'right to liberty of movement' to ensure that military personnel and supplies can travel swiftly to respond to attacks and deliver assistance to those in need.[65] When states take initiative in this manner to protect their people, their temporary derogation from other human rights commitments such as freedom of movement or expression may fit commodiously within a jurisprudence of altruism. Human rights derogation provisions and limitation provisions thus share a common structure, entrusting states with responsibility to narrow the scope of protection temporarily for some of their people where such measures are strictly necessary to 'secur[e] due recognition and respect for the rights and freedoms of others.'[66] By committing responsibility to states in this

[62] See Article 4(1) ICCPR; Article 15(1) European Convention; Article 4(1) Arab Charter.

[63] Article 27(1) American Convention.

[64] See, e.g., Siracusa Principles, para 39. These Principles suggest that human rights derogation is permissible only to safeguard 'the physical integrity of the population, the political independence or the territorial integrity of the State or the existence or basic functioning of institutions indispensable to ensure and project the rights recognized in the Covenant'.

[65] See Article 12(1) ICCPR.

[66] Article 29(2) of the 1948 Universal Declaration of Human Rights, UNGA Res. 217 A(III), 10 December 1948.

fashion, HRL situates states not only as subjects of HRL, but also, as temporary co-authors of HRL during public emergencies.

In light of these features, HRL standards have often been understood as delegating discretionary power primarily to national authorities, with international treaty bodies occupying a secondary and subsidiary position.[67] By entrusting states with responsibility to take initiative for protecting and fulfilling the human rights of their people, HRL frames the relationship between states and their people in altruistic terms that are inconsistent with a rule-based legal framework. While some hard rules such as the prohibition against torture may be consistent with a jurisprudence of altruism,[68] the whole point of human rights derogation is to enable states to protect their people in contexts where HRL's reliance on rules (e.g., negative duties to respect human rights) could prevent states from maintaining the conditions necessary for the protection and fulfilment of human rights for all. A derogation regime that relied upon rules to define when a 'public emergency' existed would simply replicate the rule-rigidity problem that the derogation regime itself was designed to solve. Moreover, as a practical matter, any effort to devise comprehensive rules for human rights derogation must come to grips with the fact that, in Alexander Hamilton's words, 'it is impossible to foresee or to define the extent and variety of national emergencies, and the correspondent extent and variety of the means which may be necessary to satisfy them. The circumstances that endanger the safety of nations are infinite.'[69] The error costs associated with a rule-bound regime are therefore likely to be unacceptably high 'relative to the performance of a fully informed and fully competent decisionmaker using a standard.'[70] If derogation is strictly necessary to maximise human rights protection during an emergency, shackling states to legal rules established *ex ante* has the potential to unduly compromise their ability to protect their people. To the extent, therefore, that HRL entrusts states with responsibility to act altruistically for the benefit of their people, it also demands a derogation regime with the flexibility and dynamism that only standards can supply.

---

[67] See Shany 2005, at 915, arguing that the choice of standards 'marks a preference for pluralism and diversity over uniformity in law-application, and the empowerment of decentralized national decision-makers at the expense of their international counterparts').

[68] Evan Fox-Decent and I have argued elsewhere that the nonderogable character of the prohibition against torture is consistent with a spirit of altruism because a state that violated this norm could not plausibly claim to treat its people as equal beneficiaries under the rule of law. See Criddle and Fox-Decent 2012, at 55–56. Even the prohibition against torture cannot be reduced entirely to bright-line rules, however, because it is difficult to specify ex ante precisely how states should allocate their resources to enforce the prohibition within their jurisdictions.

[69] Hamilton 1787; cf. Kaplow 1992, at 564 (observing that standards are better suited than rules to govern 'heterogeneous behavior, in which each type of relevant activity may be rare').

[70] Vermeule 2000, at 92.

8.4 Deference for an Altruistic Regime

If legal standards are indispensable tools for regulating human rights derogation, how should international law translate these standards into rules? Should derogation standards be understood primarily as delegations of rule-making authority to international courts and commissions? Or should they be construed as delegations to states to develop 'rules adapted to their special needs'?[71]

How a particular legal regime translates legal standards into rules reveals much about its jurisprudential commitments. Individualistic regimes tend to reject the idea that standards authorise a regulated party to fashion rules of its own design. In relationships governed by ordinary contractual principles, for example, the exercise of unilateral rule-making power by either party would undermine the regime's underlying premise of normative individualism. Responsibility therefore falls to the courts to translate the legal standards enshrined in contracts into discrete rules that would govern the respective rights and liabilities of the parties.

The same cannot be said of legal regimes that are premised on a jurisprudence of altruism. Because altruistic regimes entrust a party with discretionary power for the purpose of enabling the entrusted party to take initiative affirmatively for the benefit of another, the entrusted party serves as the primary delegate for realising the aspirations that are encoded in legal standards.[72] In altruistic regimes, legal standards carve out a space within which the entrusted party may exercise discretionary power for the benefit of others.[73] Courts, in contrast, play a comparatively modest, subsidiary role in altruistic regimes. Courts are not responsible for translating legal standards into specific rules, thereby directing precisely how an entrusted party should exercise discretionary power; rather, courts are tasked with merely policing the outer limits of an entrusted party's rule-making power. Judicial intervention becomes necessary where there has been a manifest abuse of discretion—for example, where an entrusted party has ignored or unreasonably applied relevant standards, has engaged in self-interested behaviour, has declined to treat their beneficiaries even-handedly, or has employed a patently inadequate decision-making process.

Taken at face value, some pronouncements from international human rights courts appear to reject the altruistic approach in favour of judicial administration of derogation standards. In *Brannigan and McBride v. United Kingdom*, for example, the ECtHR explained that 'judicial control of interference by the executive with the individual's right to liberty … is implied by one of the fundamental principles of a democratic society, namely the rule of law.'[74] Hence, 'it is ultimately

---

[71] Hart 2012, at 131.

[72] In U.S. law, these principles are evident in fields as diverse as the law of fiduciaries and administrative law. See Criddle 2006.

[73] Cf. Smith and Lee 2014 (characterising fiduciary discretion as a decision-making space); Strauss 2012 (defining the Chevron doctrine in U.S. administrative law in these terms).

[74] *Brannigan and McBride v. United Kingdom*, ECtHR, Nos. 14553/89, 14554/89, 25 May 1993, para 48.

for the Court to rule whether the measures were "strictly required"', including (1) whether a derogating measure 'was a genuine response to the emergency situation', (2) whether 'it was fully justified by the special circumstances of the emergency', and (3) whether 'adequate safeguards were provided against abuse'.[75] Taken out of context, statements such as these may convey the (false) impression that the ECtHR views itself as the sole delegate for translating the European Convention's general standards into rules applicable to specific contexts.

The better view, however, is that the ECtHR's 'margin of appreciation' jurisprudence reflects a jurisprudence of altruism. Under the margin of appreciation doctrine, human rights bodies supervise state responses to public emergencies, but states take the lead in modifying the European Convention's general regime to address grave threats to the human rights of their people.[76] In *Brannigan and McBride*, for example, the Court emphasised that 'it falls to each Contracting State, with its responsibility for "the life of [its] nation," to determine whether that life is threatened by a "public emergency" and, if so, how far it is necessary to go in attempting to overcome the emergency.'[77] The Court recognised, in short, that international law charges states with primary responsibility for determining how HRL's general safeguards should be modified in contexts where unwavering adherence to these safeguards would prevent the state from protecting its people from grave threats. Hence,

> [i]t is not the Court's role to substitute its view as to what measures were most appropriate or expedient at the relevant time in dealing with an emergency situation for that of the Government which have direct responsibility for establishing the balance between the taking of effective measures to [preserve the life of the nation] on the one hand, and respecting individual rights on the other.[78]

Under the margin of appreciation doctrine, it is national authorities, not the ECtHR, that are entrusted with primary responsibility for designing temporary

[75] *A and Others v. United Kingdom*, ECtHR, No. 3455/05, 19 February 2009, para 184.

[76] See *Case 'Relating To Certain Aspects Of The Laws On The Use Of Languages In Education In Belgium' v. Belgium*, ECtHR, Nos. 1474/62, 1677/62, 1691/62, 1769/63, 1994/63, 2126/64, 23 July 1968, paras 33–34 (emphasising the subsidiary character of the Court's oversight function).

[77] *Brannigan and McBride v. United Kingdom*, ECtHR, Nos. 14553/89, 14554/89, 25 May 1993, para 43. See also *A and Others v. United Kingdom*, ECtHR, No. 3455/05, 19 February 2009, para 174 ('The object and purpose underlying the [European] Convention, as set out in Article 1, is that the rights and freedoms should be secured by the Contracting State within its jurisdiction.').

[78] *Brannigan and McBride v. United Kingdom*, ECtHR, Nos. 14553/89, 14554/89, 25 May 1993, para 59 (citing *Ireland v. United Kingdom* and *Klass and Others v. Germany*); cf. *Handyside v. United Kingdom*, ECtHR, No. 5493/72, 7 December 1976, at 22 (noting that the ECtHR cannot assume the role of national courts and legislatures when balancing conflicting interests); *Case 'Relating To Certain Aspects Of The Laws On The Use Of Languages In Education In Belgium' v. Belgium*, ECtHR, Nos. 1474/62, 1677/62, 1691/62, 1769/63, 1994/63, 2126/64, 23 July 1968, paras 34–35 (stating that the court cannot assume the role of national authorities). Commentators have observed that the margin of appreciation doctrine has its genesis in continental administrative law—another area where discretionary power is entrusted to institutions for altruistic purposes subject to obligations of reasoned justification. See, e.g., Gross and Ní Aoláin 2001, at 626.

human rights regimes that are adapted to the demands of particular public emergencies.

This conception of the margin of appreciation doctrine marks a significant departure from other leading accounts of the doctrine. Some legal scholars have argued that the primary purpose of the margin of appreciation doctrine is to accommodate moral pluralism through democratic policy-making.[79] Others have argued that the Court employs the margin of appreciation as an accommodation to principles of comity, reflecting the Court's felt need 'to avoid damaging confrontations between the Court and Contracting States over their respective spheres of authority.'[80] Yet, another strain of legal scholarship suggests that deference is warranted because national authorities, '[b]y reason of their direct and continuous contact with the pressing needs of the moment, … are in principle in a better position than the international judge to decide both on the presence of such an emergency and on the nature and scope of derogations necessary to avert it.'[81] While these considerations all support deference, none is sufficient to justify the margin of appreciation doctrine. Concerns about democratic legitimacy, comity, and comparative institutional competence are plainly inadequate to support deference to national authorities if HRL entrusts international treaty bodies alone with authority to determine whether human rights derogation satisfies the applicable legal standards. Deference to national authorities is justified only to the extent that HRL entrusts national authorities as the primary agents for deciding what measures are necessary to protect and fulfill human rights during emergencies.

If HRL's derogation standards commit rule-making power to states in the first instance, should human rights bodies abstain from reviewing state emergency measures?[82] International courts have wisely resisted this option. Human rights treaties contemplate that international courts and commissions will play a key role in supervising public emergencies to ensure that national authorities do not flagrantly abuse their derogation authority.[83] Deference under the margin of appreciation does not necessarily mean wholesale abdication to national authorities. As the ECtHR explained in *Handyside v. United Kingdom*, '[t]he domestic margin of appreciation … goes hand in hand with a European supervision.'[84] This principle finds expression, as well, in Protocol 15 amending the European Convention.[85]

---

[79] See, e.g., Benvenisti 1999, at 844; Mahoney 1998.

[80] MacDonald 1993, at 123. See also Shany 2005, at 918.

[81] *Brannigan and McBride v. United Kingdom*, ECtHR, Nos. 14553/89, 14554/89, 25 May 1993, para 59. Orin Gross and Fionnuala Nì Aolàin have challenged the view that during emergencies national authorities are better positioned than international tribunals to evaluate the need for emergency measures; see Gross and Nì Aolàin 2001, at 638.

[82] See Sheeran 2013, at 495.

[83] See *Brogan and Others v. United Kingdom*, ECtHR, Nos. 11209/84, 11234/84, 11266/84, 11386/85, 29 November 1988, para 58.

[84] *Handyside v. United Kingdom*, ECtHR, No. 5493/72, 7 December 1976, paras 47–48.

[85] Protocol No. 15 Amending the Convention for the Protection of Human Rights and Fundamental Freedoms, 24 April 2013.

Protocol 15 '[a]ffirm[s] that the High Contracting Parties, in accordance with the principle of subsidiarity, have the primary responsibility to secure the rights and freedoms defined in this Convention and the Protocols thereto, and that in doing so they enjoy a margin of appreciation'. At the same time, however, Protocol 15 also stresses that states-parties remain 'subject to the supervisory jurisdiction of the [ECtHR]'.[86] Even under the margin of appreciation's deferential standard, the 'burden lies on [states] to justify their acts' during judicial review.[87]

The absence of such a reasoned justification is a sufficient ground for finding a violation of the Convention. For example, in *Brannigan & McBride v. United Kingdom*, the Court held that the United Kingdom had abused its emergency powers by prolonging the detention and interrogation of two residents of Northern Ireland without an adequate justification.[88] Likewise, in *Aksoy v. Turkey*, the Court reasoned that a two-week delay in presenting a citizen-detainee before a judge 'exceeded the Government's margin of appreciation' because it 'could not be said to be strictly required by the exigencies of the situation.'[89] In each of these settings, the Court recognised the legitimacy of states' primary role in fashioning temporary emergency measures from the European Convention's raw standards, but it also underscored that states must be prepared to offer reasonable justifications that are worthy of respect.[90] These decisions underscore the principle that states ultimately bear the burden to establish a plausible factual predicate for any purported 'threat to the life of the nation' and to explain why the measures they have taken to deal with the crisis are reasonable applications of relevant derogation standards.

A corollary of this duty of reasoned justification is that the *degree* of deference accorded to national authorities under the margin of appreciation doctrine may depend upon the rationality and thoroughness of a state's legal rationale. An explanation that does not take into account all of the relevant legal standards, ignores key facts, or reaches a conclusion inconsistent with established law will qualify for judicial censure.[91] A state that fails to provide a rational justification for human rights derogation would fail to meet its obligations as neutral arbiter between the conflicting human rights claims of its people.[92]

---

[86] Ibid. Article 1.

[87] *Murray v. United Kingdom*, ECtHR, 14310/88, 28 October 1994, para 38.

[88] *Brannigan and McBride v. United Kingdom*, ECtHR, Nos. 14553/89, 14554/89, 25 May 1993, para 48.

[89] *Aksoy v. Turkey*, ECtHR, No. 21987/93, 18 December 1996.

[90] Cf. Gross 1998, at 498 (expressing concern about 'the pernicious use of the [margin of appreciation] doctrine to avoid conducting an independent examination of the evidence').

[91] See Shany 2005, at 927 (suggesting other factors).

[92] See *Landinelli Silva v. Uruguay*, HRC, Comm. No. 34/1978, 8 April 1981 para 8.3 (emphasising that states are 'duty-bound to give a sufficiently detailed account of the relevant facts' to facilitate review, and that '[i]f the respondent Government does not furnish the required Justification itself, … the Human Rights Committee cannot conclude that valid reasons exist to legitimate a departure from the normal legal regime prescribed by the Covenant').

Another limitation on the margin of appreciation doctrine follows from the idea that HRL enlists national authorities to author temporary regimes for the protection of human rights during public emergencies: international courts and commissions should withhold deference to state derogation decisions where there are compelling reasons to believe that national authorities did not qualify as neutral arbiters. A common feature of altruistic regimes is that judicial deference is predicated on a presumption that parties have acted impartially, according due regard to the interests of all of their beneficiaries without regard to their own self-interest. Where a party has discriminated arbitrarily against some of its beneficiaries or has engaged in self-interested transactions, courts will set aside the party's decision or require disgorgement of any ill-gotten gains.[93] In a similar spirit, HRL prohibits states from derogating from their human rights commitments in a manner that reflects discrimination against a protected group. When states suspend derogable human rights such as freedom of expression, movement, or association, such action must be facially neutral and reflect due regard for the potential disparate impact that it may have against vulnerable groups or individuals.[94] If emergency measures transgress these principles, the margin of appreciation doctrine simply does not apply.

Application of the margin of appreciation may also be inappropriate if national authorities have demonstrated a consistent disregard in the past for their basic human rights commitments. Although derogation provisions may empower altruistic governments to protect human rights more effectively during public emergencies, they may also furnish a pretext for tyrannical governments to limit human rights protections without good cause. In deciding whether to defer to state derogations, international courts need not cast a blind eye on clear evidence that national authorities have demonstrated a flagrant and systematic disregard for the human rights of their people in other contexts.

Similarly, international courts and commissions should temper the margin of appreciation doctrine's application in contexts where there are good reasons to believe that national authorities' concerns about self-preservation are likely to render them unreliable agents for protecting the human rights of their people. To determine how much deference national authorities should receive under this standard, international tribunals should consider the extent to which emergency conditions generate conflicts between the interests of national authorities and their people. In a national crisis involving a threat of future terrorist attacks against civilian targets such as universities, power plants, or sports stadiums, international tribunals may have relatively little cause for concern about national authorities' ability to serve as impartial arbiters in designing temporary human rights regimes. Absent evidence of discrimination, international tribunals may reasonably

---

[93] See, e.g., *Snepp v. United States*, 444 U.S. 507, 19 February 1980, at 515.

[94] See Hennebel 2011, at 60 (observing that in the jurisprudence of the Inter-American Court of Human Rights, vulnerable groups that historically have been the subject of discrimination such as children, women, indigenous groups, and disabled persons receive 'stronger protection').

presume that when states derogate from their human rights commitments, their overarching purpose is to protect and fulfill human rights for their people. Conversely, when the threat to 'the life of the nation' comes from a domestic insurgency that seeks to overthrow the government itself, national institutions may experience greater temptation to pursue their own self-preservation in a manner that is not 'strictly necessary'. While some deference to national authorities might still be warranted based on their greater familiarity with facts on the ground, international tribunals should review the state's responsive measures closely to ensure that national authorities do not become effectively judge and party to the same cause. Whether international tribunals should pay deference to national authorities thus depends on the character of the public emergency. The greater the peril that a crisis poses to a government's self-preservation, the greater may be the justification for declaring a public emergency to maintain public order. On the other hand, the more a crisis threatens a government's survival, the greater the threat that a government's choice of responsive measures may be infected by institutional self-interest, and thus the weaker the case may be for international tribunals to defer to the government's choice of responsive measures.

These dynamics may help to explain and justify differences in the application of the margin of appreciation doctrine between the European and inter-American human rights systems. Unlike the ECtHR, the Inter-American Commission on Human Rights (Inter-American Commission) and the Inter-American Court on Human Rights (IACtHR) have not applied the margin of appreciation doctrine consistently in their jurisprudence.[95] The IACtHR's unwillingness to apply a deferential standard of review arguably reflects the fact that the IACtHR began its work at a time when much of Latin America was ruled by unelected military dictators and the Court's docket was flooded with cases of states using torture, forced disappearances, and extrajudicial killing to suppress political dissent.[96] Indeed, the IACtHR has frankly acknowledged that it views human rights derogation with a jaundiced eye:

> It cannot be denied that under certain circumstances the suspension of guarantees may be the only way to deal with emergency situations and, thereby, to preserve the highest values of a democratic society. The Court cannot, however, ignore the fact that abuses may result from the application of emergency measures not objectively justified in the light of the requirements prescribed in Article 27 [of the American Convention] and the principles contained in other relevant international instruments. This has, in fact, been the experience of our hemisphere.[97]

Given this sobering experience, it should come as no surprise that the IACtHR has been reluctant to treat national authorities as altruistic agents for their people during times of crisis. If national authorities are perceived to use human rights

---

[95] See Legg 2012, at 31 (observing that the IACtHR lacks 'a well-established doctrine of deference" and that "a number of cases seem to imply that there will be no deference to states').

[96] See, e.g., Candia 2014; Contreras 2012, at 28.

[97] Habeas Corpus in Emergency Situations (Articles 27(2) and 7(6) of the American Convention on Human Rights), IACtHR, Advisory Opinion OC-8/87, 30 January 1987, para 20.

derogation for self-interested purposes—to enhance their own leverage against domestic insurgents or political opponents, often during national crises of their own creation—the trust necessary to sustain a margin of appreciation cannot reasonably be sustained. A jurisprudence of individualism focused on rules, rather than a standard-based jurisprudence of altruism, naturally becomes the operative regulatory paradigm.[98]

The experience of the IACtHR illustrates why the margin of appreciation doctrine should not be treated as all-or-nothing proposition. While human rights derogation may be designed to empower states to protect human rights more effectively overall during public emergencies, international tribunals need not turn a blind eye when states are manifestly unprepared to perform this role. There is little reason for international tribunals to apply a margin of appreciation, for example, if national authorities within a particular state have manifested clear disregard for the interests of their people by engaging in a consistent pattern of grave human rights abuse. Similarly, the presumption that states derogate for altruistic purposes should be set aside in settings such as domestic counterinsurgency operations where national authorities' emergency measures are susceptible to concerns for self-preservation. Although the altruistic character of HRL often means granting a healthy margin of appreciation to national authorities, it may require international tribunals to withhold deference where past oppression or conflicts of interest disqualify national authorities from presenting themselves as neutral, rights-optimising trustees for their people. In these settings, international tribunals will be best positioned to determine whether the measures a state has taken in response to a public emergency are 'strictly required by the exigencies of the situation.'[99]

8.5 Conclusion

The idea that international law needs to develop more concrete rules for human rights derogation has become a common refrain in legal scholarship. Given the frequency with which states abuse their emergency powers during national crises, the yearning for more determinate rules to constrain state discretion is understandable. There are good reasons, however, why the international community continues to employ open-textured standards to regulate human rights derogation.

[98] This may help to explain why the IACtHR has developed a more rule-focused jurisprudence than its European counterpart, including recognition of a greater number of human rights norms as 'regional jus cogens.' See, e.g., *Roach and Pinkerton*, Case 9647, IACHR, Resolution No 3/87, OEA/ser.L./V./II.71, doc. 9 rev. 1, 22 September 1987, at 168–170 (characterising 'execution of children' as a jus cogens norm); cf. Schauer 2013, at 1191–1193 (noting that 'rules can empower criticism in ways that standards do not').

Similarly, it has been suggested that the absence of a derogation provision in the African Charter on Human and Peoples Rights reflects a 'historical legacy both in colonial and postcolonial societies' in which emergency powers were abused. See Cowell 2013, at 153.

[99] Article 4(1) ICCPR.

By authorising states to decide when and how to derogate from their international obligations, HRL entrusts states with primary responsibility to determine what measures are necessary to protect and fulfill human rights for their people during national crises. Broad derogation standards are the mechanism HRL employs to structure its jurisprudence of altruism, empowering states to design temporary human rights regimes that are tailored to the specific exigencies of particular national crises. The role of human rights tribunals, in contrast, is more limited: to ensure that states do not abuse their discretionary power by imposing self-serving, discriminatory, or arbitrary and capricious limitations on human rights. The controversial margin of appreciation doctrine honors this entrustment of authority, ensuring that international tribunals give a healthy measure of deference to the context-sensitive judgments of national decision-makers during temporary crises. Judicial deference to national authorities should not, however, be applied indiscriminately. If national authorities fail to support their human rights derogations with reasoned deliberation, if their behavior reflects a pattern of abusive conduct, or if their altruistic mission has been compromised by conflicts of interest, international tribunals should not hesitate to withhold deference. Thus, a state's authority to derogate from human rights guarantees during public emergencies is conditioned upon the state serving as a faithful trustee for its people.

References

Benvenisti E (1999) Margin of appreciation, consensus, and universal standards. N Y Univ J Int Law Politics 31:843–855

Candia G (2014) Comparing diverse approaches to the margin of appreciation: the case of the European and the Inter-American Court of Human Rights. Pontificia Universidad Católica de Chile Law School, Working Paper No. 1

Chowdhury SR (1989) Rule of law in a state of emergency: the Paris minimum standards of human rights norms in a state of emergency. Pinter Publishers, London

Contreras P (2012) National discretion and international deference in the restriction of human rights: a comparison between the jurisprudence of the European and the Inter-American Court of Human Rights. Northwest J Int Hum Rights 11:28–82

Cowell F (2013) Sovereignty and the question of derogation: an analysis of Article 15 of the ECHR and the absence of a derogation clause in the ACHPR. Birbeck Law Rev 1:135–162

Criddle EJ (2006) Fiduciary foundations of administrative law. UCLA Law Rev 54:117–183

Criddle EJ, Fox-Decent E (2012) Human rights, emergencies and the rule of law. Hum Rights Q 34:39–87

Fox-Decent E, Criddle EJ (2009) The fiduciary constitution of human rights. Leg Theory 15:301–336

Gross O (1998) Once more into the breach: the systematic failure of applying the European Convention on Human Rights to entrenched emergencies. Yale J Int Law 23:437–501

Gross O, Nì Aolàin F (2001) From discretion to scrutiny: revisiting the application of the margin of appreciation doctrine in the context of Article 14 of the European Convention on Human Rights. Hum Rights Q 23:625–649

Hamilton A (1787) The federalist No. 23. Reprinted in: Rossiter C (ed) (1961) The federalist papers. The Penguin Group, New York

Hart HLA (2012) The concept of law, 3rd edn. Oxford University Press, Oxford

Hennebel L (2011) The Inter-American Court of Human Rights: the ambassador of universalism. Quebec J Int Law Special edition:57–97
Hughes E (2007) Entrenched emergencies and the 'war on terror': time to reform the derogation procedure in international law? N Y Int Law Rev 20:1–65
Kaplow L (1992) Rules versus standards: an economic analysis. Duke Law J 42:557–629
Kennedy D (1976) Form and substance in private law adjudication. Harv Law Rev 89:1685–1778
Legg A (2012) The margin of appreciation doctrine in international human rights law. Oxford University Press, Oxford
Macdonald RSJ (1993) The margin of appreciation. In: Macdonald RSJ, Matscher F, Petzold H (eds) The European system for the protection of human rights. Martinus Nijhoff Publishers, Dordrecht, pp 83–124
Macdonald RSJ (1997) Derogations under Article 15 of the European Convention on Human Rights. Columbia J Transnatl Law 36:225–267
Mahoney P (1998) Marvelous richness of diversity or invidious cultural relativism? Hum Rights Law J 19:1–6
Markovits D (2014) Sharing ex ante and ex post. In: Gold A, Miller PB (eds) Philosophical foundations of fiduciary law. Oxford University Press, Oxford
Schauer F (2013) Official obedience and the politics of defining 'law'. South Calif Law Rev 86:1165–1194
Schlag P (1985) Rules and standards. UCLA Law Rev 33:379–430
Shany Y (2005) Toward a general margin of appreciation doctrine in international law? Eur J Int Law 16:907–940
Sheeran SP (2013) Reconceptualizing states of emergency under international human rights law: theory, legal doctrine, and politics. Mich J Int Law 34:491–557
Smith GD, Lee JC (2014) Fiduciary discretion. Ohio State Law J 75:609 et seq
Strauss P (2012) Deference is too confusing—let's just call them 'Chevron space' and 'Skidmore weight'. Columbia Law Rev 112:1143–1173
Vermeule A (2000) Interpretive choice. N Y Univ Law Rev 75:74–149

Chapter 9
Temporary Protection: Hovering at the Edges of Refugee Law

Jean-François Durieux

Abstract As a subject of international law, the refugee is inherently temporary: refugee status exists in order to fill the gap caused by a breakdown of the normal bond between citizen and state with 'international protection', until this bond can be restored, either with the original state of nationality, or with another state. While this ambition is clear, the practice of refugee protection under the current, post-1951 regime has exposed the serious problem international refugee law (IRL) faces with regard to the tail-end of protection, also known as 'durable solutions'. This chapter studies the most prominent attempt made by UNHCR and states within the refugee regime at re-invigorating the temporary character of international protection—namely the mechanism known as 'temporary protection'. While the concept can be traced to formulations of 'temporary refuge' in the 1980s, temporary protection (TP) truly emerged as a term of art in the 1990s, as Western Europe was faced with a large-scale influx of forced migrants from the former Yugoslavia. In 2001, TP was the subject of an EU directive, which partly clarified the relationship of TP to mainstream IRL—notably whether TP should be seen as a substitute for, or a prelude to, the operation of the 1951 Refugee Convention. Ambiguity has remained the hallmark of the TP concept, however, not least in UNHCR's attempts at formalising a TP regime outside the European ambit. After examining the main features of these attempts, the chapter concludes that, while the EU directive should be taken seriously, a continuing doctrine of temporary protection outside established IRL is both legally unsound and politically unconvincing.

Keywords Refugee · International protection · Temporary protection · 1951 Convention · Cessation · Repatriation · Derogation · Emergency

---

Programme Director, International Institute of Humanitarian Law, San Remo, Italy; Research Associate, Refugee Studies Centre, University of Oxford, UK.

J.-F. Durieux (✉)
International Institute of Humanitarian Law, San Remo, Italy
e-mail: alibabadurieux@gmail.com

M. Ambrus and R.A. Wessel (eds.), *Netherlands Yearbook of International Law 2014*,
Netherlands Yearbook of International Law 45, DOI 10.1007/978-94-6265-060-2_9

Contents

9.1 Introduction 222
9.2 Time in the International Legal Regime 226
9.2.1 Time as 'Attachment' 226
9.2.2 Time as Deadline 227
9.2.3 A Clash of Times 230
9.3 Temporary Protection in Europe, 1992–2001 232
9.3.1 A Time of Crisis 233
9.3.2 After the Crisis 240
9.4 Hovering on 244
9.5 Conclusion: Time for a Showdown 249
References 252

9.1 Introduction

In the words of two leading scholars in the discipline, international refugee law is 'an incomplete legal regime of protection, imperfectly covering what ought to be a situation of exception'.[1] This finding is doubly relevant to the overarching theme of this volume of the *Netherlands Yearbook of International Law*. Indeed, as this chapter will show, the *time* dimension of refugee status at international law is the source of both its acceptability as a regime of exception, and of some of the most glaring gaps in that regime. As a subject of international law, the refugee is inherently temporary: refugee status exists in order to fill the gap caused by a breakdown of the normal bond between citizen and state with 'international protection', until this bond can be restored, either with the original state of nationality, or with another state. 'The claim for inclusion in a host community is ... a consequence of exclusion by the host community'.[2] The international protection of refugees has therefore been described as surrogate protection, a 'back-up to the protection one expects from the state of which an individual is a national ... meant to come into play only in situations when that protection is unavailable'.[3]

It is fairly obvious that, within the Westphalian social order that underpins modern public international law, surrogate protection is meant to be exceptional. This exception tends to be recurrent, however, and its regulation is as old as that of the 'normal' condition—the protection exercised by the state of nationality—from which it derogates. Asylum has a long and distinguished history indeed, both in

---

[1] Goodwin-Gill and McAdam 2007, at 1.

[2] Noll 2000, at 75.

[3] *Attorney General v. Ward,* Supreme Court of Canada [1993] 2 SCR 689. In a similar vein, in the UK House of Lords, Lord Clyde ruled that '[w]hat [the Convention] seeks to achieve is the preservation of those rights and freedoms for individuals where they are denied them in their own state. Another state is to provide a surrogate protection where protection is not available in the home state'. *Horvath v. Secretary of State for the Home Department* [2001] 1 AC 489, at 16.

practice and in doctrine.[4] Contemporary international refugee law (IRL), however, is a rather under-developed segment of the vast body of post-WWII, UN Charter-based human rights and humanitarian law. Its customary basis is thin, consisting mainly of the rule known as *non-refoulement,* which 'prescribes, broadly, that no refugee should be returned to any country where he or she is likely to face persecution, other ill-treatment, or torture'.[5] Whether *non-refoulement,* in either this or another formulation, has attained the status of a principle of customary international law is actually debated among scholars.[6] Treaty law of universal vocation, which at this time binds over 140 states, is limited to one Convention and one Protocol, supplemented by one refugee-specific instrument at the regional (namely, African) level.[7] The 1951 Convention has definitely proved its resilience, having survived countless political crises, and offered relief to millions of refugees, since its adoption. It must be noted, however, that the bulk of its provisions regulate the status of refugees once admitted, and need to be transposed into the Parties' domestic legal order in order to be effective. International cooperation, while crucial to the functioning of the international refugee regime, is referred in non-binding terms only in the Convention's Preamble.[8] An international organisation—the Office of the United Nations High Commissioner for Refugees (UNHCR)—was established in 1950 and vested with supervisory powers over the implementation of the Convention. It was also given a broad mandate to 'provid[e] international protection, under the auspices of the United Nations, to refugees' and to seek 'permanent solutions for the problem of refugees'.[9] The personnel of UNHCR, as well as the agency's Executive Committee, have been instrumental in developing, over the years, a considerable amount of soft law in the form of

---

[4] For one of the most complete recent analyses of the historical roots and evolution of international refugee law and its relationship to the theory and practice of asylum, see Chetail 2011. See also Goodwin-Gill and McAdam 2007, Chap. 7 on the modern concept of asylum.

[5] Goodwin-Gill and McAdam 2007, at 201. The principle is reflected in Article 33 of the 1951 Convention relating to the Status of Refugees, 189 UNTS 150 (hereinafter: the 1951 Convention, or the Convention).

[6] See, among others, Goodwin-Gill and McAdam 2007, at 345–354; Lauterpacht and Bethlehem 2003. Contra: Martin 1989; Hathaway 2005, at 366, 2010. Goodwin-Gill posits the existence of a customary norm of 'refuge' distinct from *non-refoulement.* Goodwin-Gill 2014.

[7] 1951 Convention; 1967 Protocol relating to the Status of Refugees, 606 UNTS 267 (hereinafter the Protocol); 1969 Convention on the Specific Aspects of Refugee Problems in Africa, 1000 UNTS 46.

[8] '[A] satisfactory solution of a problem of which the United Nations has recognized the international scope and nature cannot … be achieved without international co-operation'. See also Recommendation IV D of the Conference of Plenipotentiaries on the Status of Refugees and Stateless Persons, which stipulates the following: '*Recommends* that Governments continue to receive refugees in their territories and that they act in concert in a true spirit of international co-operation in order that these refugees may find asylum and the possibility of resettlement.' 1951 Convention relating to the Status of Refugees and Stateless Persons, 189 UNTS 150.

[9] 1950 Statute of the Office of the United Nations High Commissioner for Refugees, Annex, UNGA Res. 428(V), 14 December 1950, para 1 (hereinafter Statute).

conclusions, declarations and guidelines on a wide range of issues, including those on which treaty law is silent.[10]

It is interesting to note that UNHCR was set up for an initial period of three years.[11] This is symptomatic of a cautious mood, which can be traced back to the League of Nations' origins of the modern refugee regime. In the inter-war period, refugee problems tended to be defined and addressed one at a time.[12] The Convention itself, with its time limitation and optional geographic reservation, does not represent a major departure from past approaches: it looks mainly towards the past.[13] On the other hand, it contains an objective, non-situational definition of 'refugee', which clearly allowed the instrument to deal with a new refugee problem arising in the early 1950s—namely, fugitives from the Soviet bloc. Still, it is only through the adoption of the 1967 Protocol[14] that the Convention became truly forward-looking, so that the legal regime instituted in 1951 could apply to (potentially) every new refugee situation. The ambition of the post-Protocol regime is huge: for every refugee in the world, at any time, there must be a state providing asylum. What is surprising is that this open-ended commitment was made without the backing of any fresh legal tools: no formula was proposed to determine how states should share responsibilities and otherwise co-operate, not only with regard to asylum, but also with a view to finding 'permanent solutions for the problem of refugees'.[15] This lacuna proved to be particularly problematic as, during the same years, many states in the developing world—starting with newly independent African states—acceded to the Convention and Protocol. With the multiplication of refugee crises in the global South, the modalities of responsibility—and burden-sharing in the international regime—changed radically: 'physical' burden-sharing, i.e. the distribution of refugee caseloads through relocation and resettlement, became the exception, while fiscal or financial burden-sharing

---

[10] On the role of the Executive Committee and the contribution of its Conclusions to international refugee law, see Goodwin-Gill and McAdam 2007, at 47–49 and 215–217.

[11] Statute, para 5. UNHCR's mandate was renewed by the General Assembly every five years until 2004, at which time it became open-ended. UNGA Res. 58/153, 24 February 2004.

[12] For a good account of pre-UN international arrangements for the protection of refugees, see Hathaway 1984.

[13] Article 1A(2) of the 1951 Convention: 'For the purposes of the present Convention, the tem 'refugee' shall apply to any person who: (1) *Has been considered a refugee* under [previous arrangements and conventions]; (2) *As a result of events occurring before 1 January 1951* and owing to a well-founded fear of being persecuted for reasons of race, religion, nationality, membership of a particular social group or political opinion, is outside the country of his nationality and is unable or, owing to such fear, is unwilling to avail himself of the protection of that country...' (emphasis added). Article 1B allows Contracting States to declare that they understand 'events occurring before 1 January 1951' to mean 'events occurring *in Europe*' before that date.

[14] The purpose of the Protocol was to remove the time limitation from the 1951 Convention's definition of 'refugee', so that 'equal status [could] be enjoyed by all refugees', including those in new situations that 'have arisen since the Convention was adopted'. Preamble of the 1967 Protocol.

[15] See Bem 2004; Davies 2007.

became the rule, largely governed by donor states in the exercise of their discretion. In the absence of parameters to define what a 'fair share' may be, complaints of being short-changed are likely to be heard each time a new refugee situation appears on the map—especially where large numbers are involved.[16]

How to organise international cooperation and to assign protection responsibilities is even more problematic where frontline states are not party to the Convention. Conclusion No. 22 of UNHCR's Executive Committee, adopted in 1981, purports to 'reaffirm the basic minimum standards for [the] treatment' of 'asylum seekers forming part of large-scale influxes'. These standards are ostensibly less generous than the provisions of the 1951 Convention.[17] However, this Conclusion must be read in context, namely the continuing outflow of refugees from Vietnam, whose rickety boats reached—if they were lucky—the shores of non-party states.[18] The exodus of 'boat people' also provided the background for the emergence of a new concept in refugee doctrine, namely: 'temporary refuge'. In the mid-1980s, Perluss and Fitzpatrick Hartman, subsequently supported by Goodwin-Gill, argued that a customary norm of temporary refuge existed, which prohibited the forcible repatriation of 'refugees' in a broader category than as defined by the 1951 Convention. Their argument was based in part on a general duty to rescue people in distress, and in part on an enlarged concept of *non-refoulement.*[19] This doctrine, which some commentators regard as a precursor to 'temporary protection',[20] is better seen as an attempt at establishing, *even for non-party states*, a duty to admit refugees on their territories until a solution can be found *elsewhere*. Recourse to customary norms was a response tailored to a crisis affecting a region that was (and still is) by and large outside the universal legal regime. The refuge expected from Southeast Asian states for the Vietnamese refugees was temporary 'not because the causes of flight were thought to be of short duration', but because it included, on the part of Western states, 'the promise of resettlement'.[21]

This chapter will primarily deal with the responsibilities of States that *are* party to the 1951 Convention (as amended by the 1967 Protocol) towards refugees in, or seeking entry into, their territories. Though international cooperation—or rather the lack thereof—looms large over this discussion, the focus of

---

[16] On the effects of unfair burden-sharing on the faithful application of 1951 Convention standards, see Goodwin-Gill and McAdam 2007, at 340–345; and generally Durieux and McAdam 2004; Durieux and Hurwitz 2004.

[17] Executive Committee of the High Commissioner's Programme, Conclusion No. 22 (XXXII) Protection of asylum-seekers in situations of large-scale influx, 21 October 1981.

[18] In the sub-region, only The Philippines was party to the Convention. Though further removed from the source country, Australia—another State Party—did receive 'boat people', too, and played a major role in shaping the doctrine of 'temporary refuge'.

[19] Goodwin-Gill 1986; Perluss and Fitzpatrick Hartman 1986.

[20] These include Fitzpatrick 2000; and Goodwin-Gill and McAdam 2007.

[21] Fitzpatrick 1994, at 462.

analysis will remain on what the Convention dictates, rather than on what it omits. The question we intend to address can be formulated as follows: how does international refugee law manage 'refuge time'? In other words, borrowing from the dual mandate of UNHCR, how does it regulate the transition from 'protection' to 'solutions'? After setting the general parameters of this discussion in the next section, we shall focus on the most prominent attempt made by UNHCR and states within the refugee regime at re-invigorating the temporary character of international protection—namely the mechanism known as 'temporary protection' (TP) as it emerged in Europe in the 1990s. The title of this chapter is a tribute to the late Joan Fitzpatrick, a leading thinker on both temporary refuge and TP, whose work will be amply cited herein.[22] Her suggestion that TP continues to 'hover ... at the edges of refugee law'[23] will lead us to clarify the relationship of TP to the 1951 Convention, then, in the final sections of this chapter, to put into question the continuing relevance of a doctrine of temporary protection outside the Convention-based regime.

9.2 Time in the International Legal Regime

The 1951 Convention manages 'refuge time' in two ways. On the one hand, it establishes a gradation of rights, the accrual of which is contingent upon, *inter alia*, the length of stay on territory. On the other hand, the Convention makes it clear that refugee status is not meant to last forever, and it provides for the circumstances in which it shall terminate. In the following we deal briefly with each of these aspects in turn, before exposing areas of tension between the two.

9.2.1 Time as 'Attachment'

The content of refugee status under the Convention is determined by the superposition of 'two cumulative conditions governing, first the criteria of entitlement (the applicability of the norm) and, second, the standard of treatment'.[24] Entitlement criteria distinguish three levels of applicability: a core set of basic guarantees apply to 'refugees'

[22] The reader who is familiar with Joan Fitzpatrick's opus, or simply with US immigration law, may wonder why this chapter does not make any reference to 'temporary protected status' (TPS), which is indeed a term of art in the law of the United States. The reason for this deliberate omission is that TPS, unlike TP, does not operate as an admission mechanism. It operates as a defence against deportation, and therefore 'encompasses only those beneficiaries who somehow manage to penetrate the territory'. Fitzpatrick 1994, at 48.

[23] Fitzpatrick 2000, at 305.

[24] Chetail 2014, at 45–46.

without any further qualification[25]; those who are present within the territory benefit from additional rights, especially if they are lawfully present[26]; finally, residence entitles refugees to such rights and benefits as administrative assistance, access to wage-earning employment or liberal professions (where the residence is lawful) or the protection of intellectual property (where the residence is both lawful and habitual).[27] Once these criteria are fulfilled, the precise content of the norm is determined by reference to the corresponding entitlements of ordinary aliens, most-favoured foreigners, or nationals of the country of asylum, as the case may be. One can agree with Chetail that 'the legal regime deriving from the superposition of various entitlement criteria with different standards of treatment remains extremely complex', and that the task of 'finding a cogent rationale in such byzantine gradation' is not an easy one.[28] A rationale can be found, however, once this complex architecture is recognised as an 'incremental protection regime' following the 'intensity of the territorial bond' between the refugee and her State of asylum. 'In sum, the longer the refugee remains in the territory of the State Party, the broader the range of entitlements.'[29] In the same vein, Hathaway refers to 'levels of attachment' and equates refugee status under the Convention with an 'assimilative path'.[30] In sum, the logic of the Convention is to provide refugees with rights and obligations that over time get gradually closer to those of citizens of the host state, with naturalisation as the recommended outcome.[31]

9.2.2 *Time as Deadline*

Until the refugee is naturalised (which is neither mandatory nor extremely common in state practice worldwide),[32] she remains protected by her special status.

[25] These are the prohibition of discrimination, the acquisition of movable and immovable property, free access to domestic courts, rationing, primary education, fiscal equality, transfer of assets, and the protection against *refoulement.*

[26] Presence triggers the benefit of freedom of religion, the issuance of identity papers, and the guarantee of non-penalisation for illegal entry. Lawful presence is further required for engaging in self-employment, freely moving within the territory, and being protected against expulsion.

[27] Lawful residence also entails the right of association, access to housing and public relief, labour rights protection, social security, and the issuance of travel documents.

[28] Chetail 2014, at 42.

[29] Ibid., at 43.

[30] Hathaway 2005, at 369 and 156.

[31] Article 34 of the Convention. 'The Contracting States shall as far as possible facilitate the assimilation and naturalization of refugees. They shall in particular make every effort to expedite naturalization proceedings and to reduce as far as possible the charges and costs of such proceedings.'.

[32] In States that consider themselves as 'countries of immigration', such as Canada and the US, naturalisation may intervene after a few years of the refugee obtaining permanent resident status. In most States Parties to the Convention, though, the transition from permanent or long-term residence to citizenship is far from automatic or simple. In the global South, naturalisation of refugees remains exceptional.

However, to suggest that this status might last longer than necessary would run counter to the other objective of refugee law, which is to resolve the 'anomaly' represented by refugeehood and surrogate protection in the international social order. The Convention provides, therefore, for a number of circumstances under which its special protection 'shall cease to apply'.[33] To start with, an individual refugee may at any time, through her own actions, indicate that international protection is no longer required because she no longer experiences a fear of persecution. Cessation of refugee status thus flows from circumstances such as voluntary repatriation and re-establishment in the country of origin, or the acquisition of a new nationality and the protection which derives therefrom.[34] These cessation clauses based on voluntariness will be discussed in this chapter only in relation to the doctrine of voluntary repatriation. It is rather the cessation clause in Article 1C(5) of the Convention that will be focused on because, under this provision, the will of the refugee yields to objective circumstances, and the protection of refugee law comes to an end if the refugee 'can no longer, because the circumstances in connexion with which [s]he has been recognized as a refugee have ceased to exist, continue to refuse to avail [her]self of the protection of the country of [her] nationality'.[35]

Even though this cessation clause responds to a legitimate state concern about migration control, including the prerogative of deporting aliens whose stay is no longer justified,[36] states Parties rarely invoke it. There are, according to Fitzpatrick, three main reasons for this. The first has to do with administrative convenience, namely '[t]he factual predicates for cessation may be too resource-intensive to satisfy', requiring lengthy procedures for the (re-)examination of individual cases. So '[w]hy divert scarce resources to remove persons who do not pose a threat and who may be productive members of the community?'[37] This question already points to the second reason, which is that 'many asylees obtain a more enduring immigration status prior to the occurrence of major political changes in their state of origin.'[38] As time goes by, the development of ties with or within the country of asylum tends to become more relevant to the

[33] Article 1C of the 1951 Convention.

[34] Article 1C(1)–(4) of the 1951 Convention.

[35] The second paragraph of Article 1C(5) of the 1951 Convention exempts from cessation a refugee 'falling under section A(1) of this Article who is able to invoke compelling reasons arising out of previous persecution for refusing to avail himself of the protection of the country of nationality.'.

[36] It must be understood that return to the country of origin is not the inevitable consequence of cessation of refugee status under Article 1C(5) of the 1951 Convention. States of asylum may, upon cessation of refugee status, grant another type of lawful residence to the refugee(s) concerned. At the same time, the emphasis in this particular clause on conditions in the State of origin makes it especially appealing to asylum States that contemplate repatriation as the best—possibly the only—solution to the refugee problem at hand.

[37] Fitzpatrick 1999, at 353.

[38] Ibid., at 352.

refugee's right to remain than the changing conditions in the country of origin.[39] Finally, it is evident that 'the circumstances in connexion with which' a refugee has been recognised are seldom purely 'individual'. The same set of circumstances (say, persecutory practices against a particular ethnic or religious group) force large numbers of potential victims out of their countries in search of asylum, and where many refugees of the same nationality find themselves in a same asylum state, cessation under Article 1C(5) of the Convention may entail the repatriation of a substantial number of aliens—something which states are 'often reluctant for political reasons to force',[40] let alone the administrative and logistical difficulties involved.[41]

Whether the initiative stems from the state of origin or from asylum states stricken with compassion fatigue, the fact is, with regard to the application of Article 1C(5) of the Convention, that states prefer to act collectively in declaring an entire refugee situation terminated. To this end, they tend to either seek, or follow, the advice of UNHCR.[42] In practice, such instances of 'group' cessation are infrequent, and they invariably occur many years, at times decades, after the emergence of a refugee situation.[43] UNHCR explains that a 'premature or insufficiently grounded application of the ceased circumstances clause can have serious consequences', including the severing of ties to family, social networks and employment in the host country, as well as 'persons being compelled to return to a volatile situation'.[44] It recommends, therefore, that (i) cessation be applied only once it has been ascertained that 'conditions within the country of origin have changed in a profound and enduring manner'[45]; and (ii) procedures for determining general

[39] The passing of time and the establishment of ties with the host country can also, under human rights law, limit the removal powers of the State. As Costello shows, in cases concerning the legality of deportation of settled migrants, the European Court of Human Rights has on several occasions found an interference with the right to respect for private and family life. Costello 2015. See, e.g., *Üner v The Netherlands*, ECtHR, No. 46410/99, 18 October 2006.

[40] Fitzpatrick 1999, at 352, citing the US examples of Nicaragua and Haiti. Obviously, mass expulsion also faces legal obstacles under human rights law.

[41] The recent examples of Rwanda and Angola, as well as the precedents of former Socialist States in Eastern Europe, highlight another political dimension of cessation on account of changed circumstances, namely its attractiveness not only to States of asylum, but also and perhaps more importantly to States of origin, especially where these have undergone substantial regime changes. The interest of the 'changed' State may not necessarily or primarily be to facilitate the return of its exiled citizens, but rather to 'turn the page' on a dark chapter of its history and to project to the world the image of a responsible, peace-loving and functioning democracy.

[42] UNHCR has this competence under Article 6A 1950 Statute.

[43] For a recapitulation of cessation declarations by UNHCR, see Long 2013. In April 2014, UNHCR recommended invoking cessation in respect of refugees from Croatia displaced by the 1991-5 conflict. See http://www.refworld.org/docid/533d813f4.html. Accessed 10 July 2014.

[44] UNHCR, Guidelines on international protection: cessation of refugee status under Article 1C(5) and (6) of the Convention relating to the Status of Refugees (the «Ceased Circumstances» Clauses), Doc. HCR/GIP/03/03, 10 February 2003, paras 6 and 7.

[45] Ibid.

cessation be 'fair, clear and transparent'.[46] Furthermore, UNHCR's Executive Committee has declared it to be a 'general principle that all refugees affected by general cessation must have a possibility, upon their request, to have such application in their cases reconsidered on international protection grounds relevant to their individual case'.[47] Durieux and Hurwitz have argued that these strict requirements 'are a source of frustration for States', especially for states in the global South that are faced with large refugee populations whom they are unable and/or unwilling to integrate. As a result, states 'tend to take the legal and policy battle to a seemingly more open field, namely the doctrine of voluntary repatriation', which is discussed in the next section.[48]

9.2.3 A Clash of Times

The management of 'refuge time' is the source of an obvious tension within the 1951 Convention regime. Premature return to a continuing situation of persecution or violence is clearly prohibited by the *non-refoulement* principle. Changes in the country of origin are usually slow to come about, and take much longer to stabilise. Meanwhile, attachment leads to integration, which becomes the default solution. In the words of Coles, refugee law has 'tended to be biased in favour of local integration rather than repatriation'.[49] Of course, it can be argued that the *practice* of Western states in implementing the Convention during the Cold War willingly aggravated such a bias, as it was then politically convenient to welcome and integrate the 'champions of freedom' who had run away from Communist rule—and the Iron Curtain made sure that the numbers would remain manageable. Yet, it is true that the letter of the Convention, coupled with UNHCR's cautious approach to 'changed circumstances', creates an imbalance in respect of how cessation intervenes. Individual cessation of refugee status through voluntary repatriation is foreseen, but the Convention is silent about the *transition* from refugee status to reinstatement of the protection of the state of origin—i.e., about how to prepare (refugees, as well as the state of origin) for voluntary repatriation. Historically, this gap has been filled on a situation-by-situation basis, through the adoption of so-called 'tripartite agreements' expressing the commitments of one or several states of asylum, the state of origin/return, and UNHCR. Besides guaranteeing

46 Ibid., paras 6–8. See also (b) of the Executive Committee Conclusion on the 'Cessation of Status', which refers in (b) to the 'fundamental, stable and durable character of the changes'. Executive Committee Conclusion No. 69(XLIII) 'Cessation of Status', 9 October 1992, para B (hereinafter Conclusion No. 69).

47 Conclusion No. 69, para d. On this basis, all refugees are allowed to seek the exemption 'for compelling reasons arising out of previous persecution', which Article 1C(5) of the 1951 Convention foresaw for refugees recognised before 1951. See note 34.

48 Durieux and Hurwitz 2004, at 114.

49 Coles famously referred to the 'exilic bias' of the Convention. Coles 1989, at 373.

the voluntary character of repatriation, these agreements usually provide for conditions of safety upon return, non-penalisation for having sought and enjoyed asylum abroad, amnesties and the like.[50] They also guarantee UNHCR's right of access to returnees in order to monitor the consequences of repatriation. While such tripartite agreements have been instrumental—especially in Africa—in the affirmation of binding principles in the repatriation context, their limitations are equally evident: they are restricted to a particular movement of return and usually time-bounded; they tend to intervene late in the 'life' of a refugee situation—albeit usually well before cessation under 1C(5) of the Convention;[51] and they rely heavily on the will (or at least the willingness) of refugees to return.

When refugees do not feel inclined to return, how far can the host state (or UNHCR, for that matter) go in order to change their minds—i.e., in UNHCR jargon, to 'promote voluntary repatriation'? The 1951 Convention does not address this question.[52] Its terms suggest that (i) fully voluntary, i.e. spontaneous and uncoerced repatriation is the best way of effecting return; and (ii) return to the country of origin regardless of the refugees' will—or squarely against it—is only possible after invocation of the cessation clause in Article 1C(5) of the Convention. However, as noted by Durieux and Hurwitz, state practice paints 'various shades of voluntariness (or, conversely, of coercion) … [b]etween these two clear-cut scenarios'.[53] 'Increasingly, "safe return" has become part of the policy thinking of governments', occupying an 'interim position' between the refugee deciding to go back home on her own free will and the host state exercising its deportation prerogatives against overstaying migrants.[54] The literature on the tension between 'safe' and 'voluntary' return—short of cessation—is too vast to be aptly summarised here.[55] Suffice to note, for our purposes, that the parameters of the debate have shifted over time. As early as in the 1980s in Africa, the 'safe return' discourse aimed at dealing with 'unreasonable' objections to return, arising either within a scenario of promotion of voluntary repatriation, or among a 'residual' caseload hanging on after the majority of the refugees had returned. With the Cold War, however, the West discovered the appeal of repatriation as the 'ideal' solution to refugee problems. To take the state of origin to task and to engage its protection responsibilities *vis-à-vis* its exiled citizens became an objective in itself, alongside reducing the burden on asylum states. In a dramatic reversal of the former 'exilic bias' of the international regime, international protection could be

[50] See Zieck 1997, in particular Chapter V.

[51] Durieux and Hurwitz 2004, at 129–131.

[52] Note that the 1969 (African) Convention refers to the 'essentially voluntary character' of repatriation. Article 5 of the 1969 African Convention governing the Specific Aspects of Refugee Problems in Africa, 1001 UNTS 45 (hereinafter 1969 African Convention). For a critique, see Barutciski 1998.

[53] Durieux and Hurwitz 2004, at 133.

[54] Goodwin-Gill and McAdam 2007, at 496.

[55] The main ingredients of the debate can be found in Zieck 1997; Barutciski 1998; Bagshaw 1997; Takahashi 1997; Vedsted-Hansen 1997; Long 2013.

thought of as a simple way-station on a course that had started in state X and would inevitably end up there, too. The irruption of TP into the policy discourse of European states and UNHCR in the early 1990s made it urgent to address the question as to whether this conception of international protection could be accommodated within the Convention-based regime, or could only be designed outside it. It is to this question that we now turn.

9.3 Temporary Protection in Europe, 1992–2001

Soon after the end of the Cold War, the violent break-up of Yugoslavia and the attendant egregious violations of human rights and humanitarian law constituted 'a watershed in the formalization of temporary protection'.[56] As massive flows of refugees, including many victims of 'ethnic cleansing' policies, started pouring into Central and Western Europe, the interest of scholars and policy-makers in temporary refuge and other 'flexible' and 'pragmatic' protection mechanisms, which had flagged in the 1980s, rose again with a vengeance. Precisely what kind of mechanism TP was, and what needs it was meant to meet, was far from clear at the outset—and a fair amount of confusion prevailed over both doctrine and practice throughout the decade.[57] What matters the most, though, is that—unlike temporary refuge in Southeast Asia—TP was conceived by and for States that were all bound by the 1951 Convention, and it directly challenged either the Convention's letter, or its spirit, or both. This challenge was directed very specifically to the time dimensions of the Convention, which we have outlined in the previous section. In essence, TP was conceived as a *return-oriented protection mechanism*, within which 'the focus on return as the most appropriate solution' provided the rationale for 'standards of treatment which emphasize the provisional aspect of the refugees' stay … and *minimize*, at least in the initial stages, *efforts to promote integration*'.[58]

[56] Durieux and Hurwitz 2004, at 138.

[57] The literature on TP in the 1990s is vast. In addition to the authors cited in this section, see Van Selm Thorburn 1998; Kälin 2001; Kerber 1999, and references therein. See also UNHCR, Note on international protection, UN Doc. A/AC.96/830, 7 September 1994. Chapter IV C of the Note refers to 'a broad consensus on the need to provide protection, including asylum on at least a temporary basis, to refugees forced to flee war or serious civil disorders as well as to those fleeing persecution', and suggests to this end 'the adoption of guiding principles embodied in a global or regional declaration'. This language is symptomatic of the ambiguity, which endured throughout the decade, regarding the personal scope of TP. That UNHCR would recommend a non-binding declaration to address the needs of refugees fleeing persecution is, to say the least, odd—given that these refugees fall within the scope of the 1951 Convention.

[58] UNHCR, Note on international protection, UN Doc. A/AC.96/830, 7 September 1994, para 50.

9.3.1 A Time of Crisis

Writing in 2000, Fitzpatrick aptly noted that '[r]ecent European practice has emphasized circumstances of arrival in designating the beneficiaries of temporary protection, rather than the causes of flight'.[59] The most relevant of such circumstances are definitely the size and suddenness of the influx. This is an important observation, echoed by Durieux and Hurwitz who ascertain that 'two distinct issues, the size of the influx and the personal scope of protection, were merged into one'.[60] As is often the case in mass influx situations finding their origin in generalised armed conflict, European states receiving asylum seekers from the former Yugoslavia could not be sure that every individual in the group was a *bona fide* refugee as defined in the 1951 Convention. Nonetheless, the predominantly refugee character of the flow could not be denied. When the High Commissioner for Refugees for the first time called for 'a flexible system of temporary protection' on behalf of 'persons fleeing former Yugoslavia', she was explicitly referring to people fleeing '[s]ystematic expulsions, forcible relocation, assassinations and other forms of persecution … for no other reason but their national, ethnic or religious origin'.[61] Those were, simply put, Convention refugees. The challenge, faced by UNHCR and prospective asylum states, did not, therefore, reside in the causes of flight, but rather in the size of the (actual and potential) refugee caseload, and in the nature of the conflict. As regards the former, Kjaerum aptly observed that '[i]n Western Europe today … the major reason for the introduction of temporary protection is the inability of the European countries to co-ordinate their efforts sufficiently to allow for equal burden-sharing'.[62] Lack of solidarity was indeed what made this refugee situation an emergency—i.e., a situation overwhelming the resources normally assigned to refugee status determination and refugee protection. Regardless of the numbers involved, a large-scale influx of refugees into several wealthy European states need not create an emergency, so long as responsibilities are shared among those states. Sadly, 'burden-sharing was a dismal failure during

[59] Fitzpatrick 2000, at 305.

[60] Durieux and Hurwitz 2004, at 136.

[61] Statement of Mrs. Sadako Ogata, United Nations High Commissioner for Refugees, to the International Meeting on Humanitarian Aid for Victims of the Conflict in the former Yugoslavia, Geneva, 29 July 1992, www.unhcr.org/3ae68fac1a.html. Accessed 10 July 2014.

[62] Kjaerum 1994, at 447.

the Yugoslav crisis',[63] which allowed those states that were most exposed, such as Germany, to seek the same kind of justification as states in the developing world for a less than welcoming attitude towards new and prospective asylum seekers.

As regards the latter issue—the specificity of the conflict in the former Yugoslavia—, High Commissioner Ogata's words deserve close scrutiny: 'I believe the nature of the conflict is such that a flexible system of temporary protection would respond adequately to the emergency situation and encourage return as the most desirable and feasible solution.'[64] There seem to be two interwoven rationales in this sentence. In one sense, the nature of the conflict refers to the 'new – horrifying – twist' of the conflict in the former Yugoslavia, where '[d]isplacement seems to be the goal, not just the result of the war, with the motive clearly being ethnic relocation'.[65] This characteristic made it morally compelling to reverse ethnic cleansing, which can only be achieved through 'return home'. However, there is also a hint in the High Commissioner's statement that this result can be achieved promptly—that the nature of the conflict is such that return following temporary refuge, that is, *early* return, looks like a 'feasible solution'.[66] Thus, Ogata's move

[63] Fitzpatrick 1999, at 372. See also Noll 1997. Quoting UN figures, International Crisis Group 1997 reported that close to one half of the pre-war population of Bosnia and Herzegovina (4.3 million) were displaced during the 43 months of war. One million of the displaced remained within the country, and over 1.2 million refugees were dispersed throughout 25 host states. By early 1996, Germany was host to 345,000 Bosnians under TP, Austria to 80,000 and Sweden to 61,500, while other EU Member States were hosting only a few thousand. Outside the EU, Croatia was host to 288,000 refugees from Bosnia, and the Federal Republic of Yugoslavia to 253,000. In her July 1992 statement, the HC could have been stronger on the burden-sharing responsibilities of states. True, she stated that 'all States, within or outside the region, should provide temporary protection', but in the next sentence she almost discouraged offers of resettlement places as a measure of solidarity. Contra: the note on international protection prepared by the UNHCR argued that TP 'also implies burden sharing and international solidarity, including assistance, where required, to the countries most directly affected' as well as 'reception of refugees, particularly the most vulnerable, outside the immediately affected region.' UNHCR, Note on international protection, UN Doc. A/AC.96/830, 7 September 1994, para 22.

[64] Statement of Mrs. Sadako Ogata, United Nations High Commissioner for Refugees, to the International Meeting on Humanitarian Aid for Victims of the Conflict in the former Yugoslavia, Geneva, 29 July 1992, www.unhcr.org/3ae68fac1a.html. Accessed 10 July 2014.

[65] Ibid.

[66] As for the adjective 'flexible', which Ogata used to qualify the desired TP regime, it can only be understood as inviting States not to be too preoccupied with the letter of the 1951 Convention, or at least to depart from their own past practice under the Convention, which favoured long-term stay and integration. Clearly, the High Commissioner's analysis of the conflict and its implications for refugee protection must be read in context—i.e., bearing in mind the tremendous pressure put by Western European States on both the Convention and UNHCR itself. In a less tense environment, the High Commissioner could have said—more in keeping with established refugee law—that (i) in a post- cold war era it was all right to apply the Convention with the flexibility built into it, notably through recognition of refugee status without delay and cessation as soon as possible; and (ii) the Convention allowed group determination of refugee status, and the former Yugoslavia was a good case in point given what she herself described as the causes of the exodus.

to encourage return as 'the most desirable and feasible solution' was based on a mix of moral argument and wishful thinking. On the side of moral argument,

> [r]eturn … fundamentally … will require the reaffirmation of the basic human right to return home in safety and dignity and for an end to all practices and actions which force people out of their homes and block the prospects of return. I consider this point to be of crucial importance. Otherwise, measures to protect and assist refugees will amount to complicity in the policy of 'ethnic cleansing'.[67]

The moral duty not only to end but indeed to 'reverse' ethnic cleansing came to justify and deepen European States' reluctance to allow refugees to integrate. As for the wishful thinking part, it was captured well by Fitzpatrick: 'Duration figures largely in the conceptualization of TP, though it is often impossible to predict the time frame of refugee crises'[68]—not least the crisis that was then unfolding in the midst of Europe. There was an unspoken assumption in the promotion of TP for former Yugoslavia refugees, that because they had fled precipitously they would be able to return promptly. As UNHCR noted in 1994,

> [o]ne of the principal reasons for applying the term 'temporary' to protection given to persons fleeing conflicts or acute crises in their country of origin is the expectation – or at least the hope – that international efforts to resolve the crisis will, within a fairly short period, produce results that will enable the refugees to exercise their right to return home in safety.[69]

The UNHCR note candidly acknowledged that '[a]s the situation in Bosnia and Herzegovina shows, hopes for an early safe return are not always realized.' It insisted, nonetheless, that the provision of TP had to be seen 'as part of a comprehensive programme of concerted international action that includes prevention and solutions'—echoing the High Commissioner's 1992 tabling of a 'comprehensive humanitarian initiative in former Yugoslavia' consisting of seven elements.[70] The implicit (political) message to states reads: if you work harder on solutions (as well as prevention), you may be justified in offering a lesser quality of protection.

---

67 Statement of Mrs. Sadako Ogata, United Nations High Commissioner for Refugees, to the International Meeting on Humanitarian Aid for Victims of the Conflict in the former Yugoslavia, Geneva, 29 July 1992, www.unhcr.org/3ae68fac1a.html. Accessed 10 July 2014. She referred in her statement to SC Resolution 752 of 15 May 1992, which called 'upon all parties and others concerned to ensure that forcible expulsions of persons from the areas where they live and any attempts to change the ethnic composition of the population, anywhere in the former Socialist Federal Republic of Yugoslavia, cease immediately; and [e]mphasize[d] the urgent need for humanitarian assistance, material and financial, taking into account the large number of refugees and displaced persons and fully supports the current efforts to deliver humanitarian aid to all the victims of the conflict and to assist in the voluntary return of displaced persons to their homes'. Ibid., paras 6 and 7.

68 Fitzpatrick 2000, at 299.

69 UNHCR, Note on international protection, UN Doc. A/AC.96/830, 7 September 1994, paras 50 and 51.

70 Ibid.; Statement of Mrs. Sadako Ogata, United Nations High Commissioner for Refugees, to the International Meeting on Humanitarian Aid for Victims of the Conflict in the former Yugoslavia, Geneva, 29 July 1992, www.unhcr.org/3ae68fac1a.html. Accessed 10 July 2014.

Indeed, *quality* and *duration* of protection are intimately inter-connected in the conceptualisation of TP. Precisely, TP involves putting brakes on the 'integrating machinery' of the Convention because of an expectation that refugees will return home within a near future: duration of sojourn is 'linked to standards of treatment' where 'social and economic benefits facilitate local integration and deter repatriation'.[71] With the withholding of such benefits, Kjaerum has argued, 'a signal is sent to the refugee that his or her stay in the specific country is only temporary.'[72] This echoes Fitzpatrick's observation that TP regimes 'may be consciously structured to cultivate [the refugees'] natural desire for repatriation and to encourage the recipients to conceive of exile as limited in time.'[73] In sum, what European states expected from TP was a protection regime that, instead of facilitating local integration and deterring repatriation (which 'normal' application of the Convention was deemed to involve), would in fact deter local integration and facilitate repatriation.

9.3.1.1 The Quality of Protection

European states' approaches to the contents of temporary protection—i.e., basically, what rights and benefits should be withheld—varied significantly, and there is no room in this chapter for a detailed comparison of national practices.[74] It appears, however, that restrictions were mainly introduced in three areas—not surprisingly, those with the highest integration potential. First, the ability of new arrivals to lodge an asylum claim was severely curtailed in many states, and purely and simply excluded in a few. In terms of status, this had the effect of creating a category of protection-seekers below that of formal asylum seekers, i.e. those persons whose claims are being processed. From an international law point of view, the practice of denying access to an asylum procedure raised an even more serious problem, since states Parties to the 1951 Convention owe to each other, as well as to refugees, a duty to assess, whenever a person seeks the protection of the Convention, whether this request is well founded or not. The right to seek asylum is proclaimed in the Universal Declaration of Human Rights,[75] and UNHCR warned—both during and after the crisis—that TP 'should not become a substitute for the right of refugees to seek and enjoy asylum in accordance with internationally agreed standards.'[76] On the whole, though, restrictions of this fundamental right were tolerated, to wit a

[71] Fitzpatrick 2000, at 299.

[72] Kjaerum 1994, at 450.

[73] Fitzpatrick 2000, at 299.

[74] But see Kerber 1999; Kjaerum 1994, and references therein.

[75] Article 14(1) of the 1948 Universal Declaration of Human Rights, UNGA Res. 217 A(III), 10 December 1948. 'Everyone has the right to seek and to enjoy in other countries asylum from persecution.'.

[76] UNHCR, Note on international protection, UN Doc. A/AC.96/898, 3 July 1998, para 18.

document emanating from UNHCR's Standing Committee in 1997, which, among several 'procedural models', envisaged an acceptable situation in which 'States deny or suspend access to individual status determination during the stay in the country of refuge.'[77] Whether or not they were allowed to lodge an asylum claim, 'beneficiaries' of TP were often denied the right to work—even in those countries that allowed asylum seekers to engage in wage-earning or self-employment pending a decision on their claims. The objective was clearly to avoid economic and social integration by cutting the refugee from the labour market, even though—in some states at least—the numbers were so high that they could not, in the short term, be absorbed by that market anyhow. Furthermore, the 'return orientation' of TP was manifested through an array of restrictions and adjustments to the right to education (notably by obliging refugee children to follow classes in their own native language); and to family reunification.[78]

9.3.1.2 The Duration of Protection

Cessation of TP, as Fitzpatrick astutely observed,

> has a dual aspect. First, TP *may* be terminated, and its beneficiaries repatriated, when conditions in the state of origin permit return in safety and with dignity. Second, TP *should* be terminated, and a solution not involving involuntary repatriation provided, when danger persists in the state of origin and TP beneficiaries can no longer tolerably be maintained in uncertainty or under standards of treatment that fall substantially short of the 1951 Convention.[79]

In this sub-section we discuss these two distinct 'cessation' issues in turn.

For those States—most prominently Germany and Austria—that attached particular importance to TP as a prelude to repatriation, the defining factor triggering return had to be the end of armed conflict in the Western Balkans. In several jurisdictions, TP for Bosnians was extended from year to year, or for six months at a time, and was meant to terminate around six months after the end of hostilities. UNHCR chose to maintain some ambiguity over the issue, suggesting in 1994 that

> if conditions in the country of origin change sufficiently for the better to make possible the refugees' return in safety and dignity, arrangements can be made, in consultation with UNHCR, for [TP] to be phased out, ideally through voluntary repatriation.[80]

Then peace broke out in Bosnia—through the signing of the Dayton Peace Agreement (DPA) in November/December 1995—, forcing all stakeholders to show their cards and, if possible, to agree on criteria for refugee return. Germany, fixated

---

[77] UNHCR Standing Committee, Progress report on informal consultations on the provision of international protection to all who need it, UN Doc. EC/47/SC/CRP.27, 30 May 1997, para 4(h).

[78] Kjaerum discusses these restrictions in the light of human rights and refugee law. Kjaerum 1994, at 450–455.

[79] Fitzpatrick 2000, at 302–304.

[80] UNHCR, Note on international protection, UN Doc. A/AC.96/830, 7 September 1994, para 50.

on the end of hostilities and nothing else, refused to extend its deadline for TP expiry beyond August/September 1996, with plans to return 200,000 Bosnians by July 1997.[81] However, UNHCR was able to convince all other refugee-hosting states that deadlines had better be accompanied, if not replaced, by safety benchmarks. Pursuant to the DPA, UNHCR was to develop a plan allowing for an 'early, peaceful, orderly and phased' return of refugees and displaced persons.[82] By linking the phasing of return to implementation of the commitments assumed by the DPA Parties, UNHCR cleverly construed 'peaceful and phased' to actually mean 'safe', and to qualify the adjective 'early'. Although the Repatriation Plan's three phases were dated,[83] the deadlines could only be indicative since repatriation could only occur once TP was lifted, and TP should be maintained until (i) full implementation of the military aspects of DPA; (ii) proclamation of the required amnesty; and (iii) the establishment and functioning of mechanisms for the protection of human rights—all of these being Dayton commitments. Furthermore, UNHCR recommended that TP should not be lifted until the OSCE had certified that conditions were satisfactory for elections.[84] It also urged that persons unable or unwilling to return to their place of previous residence due to changes in territorial control and in the ethnic composition of the region concerned should be the final category considered for return, owing to their special vulnerability—clearly, another mechanism of protection through phasing. Last but not least, UNHCR warned that some refugees would be in need of continuing protection—without, however, explaining how this need could be allowed to surface, or be assessed.

The 'elephant in the room' within the Repatriation Plan was, of course, the existing legal framework based on the 1951 Convention, which the peace accords could not possibly displace. True to its promise of a 'flexible' protection system, UNHCR went out of its way to address all protection issues involved in the lifting of TP and 'early' return without referring to the Convention. This conscious effort notwithstanding, what shows through clearly in UNHCR's Plan is the 'spirit' of the Convention, as well as UNHCR's reluctance to abandon the relatively safe legal grounds on which it had, over the years, developed its doctrine and built its credibility. The rather ambiguous debate over 'safe return' that followed the signing of

[81] Durieux and Hurwitz 2004; Bagshaw 1997, note 157; Andersen 1996, at 203. Bagshaw points out the inflexibility of Germany, which was hosting over forty percent of the Bosnian refugees based outside the immediate region, forced UNHCR into a compromise at variance with what it had recommended generally, and had been followed by other European States.

[82] Article I(5) of the 1995 General Framework Agreement for Peace in Bosnia and Herzegovina, Annex 7, 14 December 1995.

[83] UNHCR announced it would initially concentrate on a million people displaced within Bosnia itself, followed by about 670,000 in neighbouring ex-Yugoslav republics. The largest part of those and an additional 200,000 refugees from other third countries were expected to return home between April and November 1996. Large-scale return from EU States was not foreseen until mid-1997.

[84] All references to the UNHCR Repatriation Plan are taken from Bagshaw 1997 and/or Andersen 1996. See also Van Selm Thorburn 1998, at 152.

the DPA confirmed Fitzpatrick's intuition that TP termination as a prelude to repatriation 'involves issues analogous to those that arise under Article 1C(5) for Convention refugees'. She saw this as rather problematic, since '[w]ithout a promise that termination of TP will be simpler and more automatic than cessation of Convention refugee status ... the incentives for states to adopt binding legal standards on temporary protection are diminished substantially'.[85] UNHCR was clearly not prepared to concede any *automatic* cessation, because it knew that in the minds of states termination of TP was synonymous with (almost) immediate return, and the safety of repatriation could not be assessed on the basis of a single 'event'—not even the signing of a peace agreement. Could the agency offer a *simpler* process of cessation—albeit without the name? Actually, the only important difference between the safety benchmarks in the Repatriation Plan and those generally read into Article 1C(5) of the Convention is that the latter can be assessed with relative calm, years after the end of the crisis, and often with the results of a 'live test' in hand—namely, the level of reintegration of spontaneous and other voluntary returnees. In contrast, where return is contemplated soon after the brokering of a fragile peace, basic conditions of safety must be not only assessed, but often actually engineered, so to speak, 'on the run'. Beyond basic safety, the 'profound' and 'enduring' nature of the changes in the country of return cannot be objectively assessed—it becomes a matter of faith, hope, or mere speculation. Time spent waiting for durable, stable change is a luxury, which many states having espoused TP thought they could not afford. This may have made 'termination of TP' a simpler decision to make, but definitely not a simpler process overall. The risks involved in a premature or ill-conceived decision—that repatriation might not take hold, that minority returns might re-ignite conflict, etc.—were not eliminated by the decision to effect 'early return'. Those risks were simply 'repatriated' along with the refugees, and they had to be managed post-return, inside Bosnia, by a host of political, human rights and humanitarian actors whose reports had to be analysed and acted upon on a regular basis.[86] The jury is still out on the question whether, on the whole, termination of TP for Bosnians resulted in a lesser financial or political burden on European states, as compared to what would have happened if 'normal' cessation rules had been followed.

We now turn to the second 'cessation' issue identified by Fitzpatrick, namely: for how long may Convention rights be suspended? When should TP as a special regime expire? The practice of European states in the 1990s does not provide a straightforward answer to this question, not only because practices varied considerably from one state to another, but also because, in some states at least, 'beneficiaries of TP' were treated according to the same standards as Convention refugees. The difference, which is far from insignificant, was that such generous treatment was ostensibly presented as a gracious, humanitarian gesture, rather than

[85] Fitzpatrick 1999, at 372.

[86] The Humanitarian Issues Working Group, established by UNHCR in 1992, was subsumed under the Dayton Peace Implementation Council in 1996. It continued to meet on a regular basis until 2000—although by that time its attention had largely shifted to Kosovo.

a matter of international obligation. By 1997, a prudent consensus emerged to the effect that TP should be replaced by a more secure form of protection after a lapse of five years.[87] It was probably not a coincidence that this standard surfaced precisely five years after the beginning of the crisis, and at a time when repatriation was already underway. Some host states, such as The Netherlands, had actually started converting the TP status of Bosnians to permanent residence at the end of their third year of stay.[88]

9.3.2 After the Crisis

Repatriation issues—most notably, the challenge of 'minority returns'[89]—occupied central stage during the years immediately following the signing of the DPA. This and other DPA implementation challenges obscured the fact that most Bosnians who had originally received some modality of TP were able, during the same period, to regularise their status in almost half of EU member states.[90] National TP regimes were phased out very much in the way they had been introduced, i.e., in a cacophony. In 1997, therefore, interest in the formalisation of TP would have waned, had it not been for the activism of the European Commission, which under the Maastricht Treaty had assumed a new role, albeit still modest, in the harmonisation of migration and asylum policies of EU member states.[91] One year later, the Amsterdam Treaty elevated the harmonisation of those policies to the supranational level, and the Tampere Council of October 1999 laid out the agenda, which included the 'step[ing] up … [of] efforts to reach agreement on the issue of temporary protection for displaced persons on the basis of solidarity between Member States'.[92] Most significantly, though, it was a fresh conflict in the Balkans that made TP a popular concept again: the 1999 NATO campaign in

---

87 Fitzpatrick 2000, at 302 and note 190.

88 Van Selm Thorburn 1998, at 224.

89 See Bagshaw 1997; International Crisis Group 1997. In the case of Bosnia, 'minority return' meant the return of an individual to an entity not under her own ethnic group's control. The original ethical justification for TP, namely the condemnation of ethnic cleansing, was reflected in Annex 7 to the Dayton Peace Accords, which affirmed the right of all refugees and displaced persons 'freely to return to their *homes*'. The reversal of ethnic cleansing, i.e. the 're-mixing' of diverse ethnic groups within Bosnia, thus became the preferred durable solution, and whether it could be achieved or not became the key criterion for assessing whether return to (particular areas of) Bosnia could be considered 'safe'.

90 Durieux and Hurwitz 2004, at 162.

91 See EU Commission, Proposal to the Council for a joint action based on Article K3 para 2 lit.b of the Treaty on European Union, concerning temporary protection of displaced persons, COM(1997) 93 final, 5 March 1997. Remarkably, the Commission's proposal kept the burden-sharing dimension of TP alive.

92 Presidency Conclusions, Tampere European Council, 15 and 16 October 1999, para 16, www.europarl.europa.eu/summits/tam_en.htm. Accessed 10 July 2014.

Serbia and Kosovo entailed an unprecedented movement of Kosovar refugees—around 900,000—across the borders to the Former Yugoslav Republic of Macedonia (FYROM), Albania and Montenegro. The massive outflow to FYROM, in particular, led the authorities to close the border to would-be refugees, which increased the pressure to undertake evacuations out of the sub-region.[93] In contrast to the ad hoc approach to TP in the Bosnian crisis, this time UNHCR was able to rapidly establish precise refugee rights and obligations in the countries of destination of the evacuees.[94] Fitzpatrick echoed the enthusiastic mood: 'The unprecedented Humanitarian Evacuation Programme to airlift Kosovar refugees to temporary safety in European and more distant States exemplifies TP's appeal and adaptability.'[95] It must be stressed, however, that in the eyes of asylum states the success of that programme did not reside so much in the evacuation per se as it did in its happy ending, whereby the vast majority of the evacuated refugees were both willing and able to return to (the UN-administered) Kosovo within a matter of months. At last, the temporary character of TP had been vindicated.

The European Commission explicitly acknowledged that the experience—and no doubt the confidence—gained during the Kosovo crisis had influenced the Proposal it put forward in October 2000 for a Council Directive on TP, which was eventually adopted in July 2001.[96] The TP Directive attempts to meet two goals, namely: solidarity and consistency. The first objective is to ensure that, in future refugee emergencies, member states will act in concert and in a 'spirit of solidarity'—something which, as seen above, was in very short supply at the outset of the former Yugoslavia crisis. On this front, the outcome of EU negotiations is disappointing: 'solidarity' is clearly short-changed in the Directive, its prominence in the title of the instrument notwithstanding. The only 'measures promoting a balance of efforts between Member States' mentioned in the text are of procedural nature, or rely on a pre-existing common 'pot of gold' in the form of the European Refugee Fund.[97] It appears that no member state was more willing in 2001 than in 1992 to commit to a predictable formula for the distribution of responsibilities and costs. Furthermore, the potential of the Directive as the driver of a truly collective response is also weakened by the mechanism it provides for the activation of TP Union-wide. This involves a proposal by the Commission (which itself may be seized of a request by a member state) and a Council decision adopted by a qualified majority.[98] While this procedure is far from odd within the EU context, in view

[93] Suhrke et al. 2000, at 6, para 31.

[94] Ibid., at 93, para 462.

[95] Fitzpatrick 2000, at 279.

[96] EU Council Directive 2001/55/EC on minimum standards for giving temporary protection in the event of a mass influx of displaced persons and on measures promoting a balance of efforts between Member States in receiving such persons and bearing the consequences thereof, 20 July 2001 (hereinafter TP Directive).

[97] Chapter VI TP Directive.

[98] Article 5 TP Directive.

of its complexity it does not seem well suited to emergency situations that require quick action and justify resort to a mechanism 'of exceptional character'.[99] In view of these two shortcomings, the risk of the Directive remaining dead letter is real.

The second objective of the Directive, meanwhile, is to harmonise the practice of all member states faced with the same emergency, as regards the contents and duration of the temporary protection granted to the incoming 'displaced persons' (the Directive carefully avoids calling them 'refugees'). On this front, the Directive is far from disappointing. Indeed, it resolves a fair number—though not all—of the ambiguities that had marred the doctrine, and above all the practice, of TP in the preceding decade. Welcome clarifications are found in five main areas:

(1) TP is affirmed as a '*procedure* of exceptional character' to be applied 'in the event of a mass influx or imminent mass influx'.[100] Emphasis on the procedural character of TP is essential, as it discards the notion that TP might constitute an alternative or additional *status*. While affixing a TP 'label' on an instance of mass displacement does not prejudge recognition of the displaced as Convention refugees (Article 3), it does not rule it out either: among the displaced persons, there may be some who 'fall within the scope of Article 1A of the 1951 Refugee Convention'.[101] As a procedural tool, TP comes close to—but deliberately stops short of—*prima facie* recognition of the refugee character of all members of a group, which is practised in other parts of the world.[102]

(2) The Directive clarifies another key point: the operation of the Convention cannot be suspended, regardless of the size or suddenness of the influx. The principle that '[p]ersons enjoying temporary protection must be able to lodge an application for asylum at any time'[103] is an important and necessary re-affirmation of the universal right to seek asylum, which implies the right to seek the specific protection of the 1951 Convention in States that are bound by it. The 'twist' introduced by the Directive is in its Article 17(2): while claims must be registered 'at any time', as long as TP applies decisions on these claims may be delayed. Tricky as this caveat may look, it is not likely to shock seasoned refugee lawyers, for (reasonable) delays in the adjudication of asylum claims are not a new phenomenon in state practice. In the spirit of the Directive, the delaying of decisions responds both to the anticipated inability of asylum systems to cope with large numbers of applications, and to the volatility or fluidity of outflow-causing situations in countries of origin. Even in non-emergency contexts, however, backlogs of asylum applications are a

[99] Article 1 TP Directive.

[100] Article 2(a) TP Directive.

[101] Article 2(c) TP Directive.

[102] *Prima facie* determination of refugee status consists in designating an entire class of asylum-seekers, usually identified solely by their nationality and date of arrival, as refugees without resorting to a case-by-case examination of their claims under the Convention. See Durieux and Hurwitz 2004, at 117–122.

[103] Article 17(1) TP Directive.

common, if deplorable, phenomenon in most European states—to the effect that a waiting period of two years for a first instance decision can hardly be perceived as extraordinary or unacceptable.[104]

(3) EU law clearly portrays TP as a prelude to the 'normal' operation of the 1951 Convention. This prelude is filled with protection contents that compare well with what the Convention mandates on behalf of refugees: the issuance of personal documentation, the right to work, to housing, to social welfare, to education and to family reunification are all guaranteed by the Directive. Adherence to high standards in times of crisis may be difficult to obtain, even in wealthy European states. Still, member states can hardly object, since their domestic legislations are, as a rule, well ahead of Convention standards as regards the rights of lawful foreign residents in general; and human rights law forbids them to discriminate against a class of aliens on the basis of nationality.[105]

(4) The 'return orientation' of TP is represented in the Directive in two ways. First, pursuant to its Article 6, the Council may at any time decide (by a qualified majority) that TP shall come to an end because the situation in the country of origin is 'such as to permit the safe and durable return of those granted [TP]'. The meaning of 'safe and durable' is briefly explicated by reference to 'respect for human rights and fundamental freedoms and Member States' obligations regarding *non-refoulement*'. Of course, given point 2) above, the ending of TP by Council decision does not, in and by itself, cause the 'safe and durable return' to happen. Hence, the importance of Article 21 of the TP Directive, which requires member states to 'take the measures necessary to make possible the voluntary return' of displaced persons, and additionally encourages the provision of 'exploratory visits' so that decisions to return are well informed. As the 1951 Convention is silent on the facilitation of voluntary repatriation, this is a welcome provision. Upon the insistence of some member states, Article 22 was added that provides for 'enforced return' upon expiry of TP. This reference is, however, more symbolic than practical, given the obligation made on states to hear asylum claims and to adjudicate them, latest once TP has expired. It is only upon final denial of those claims that a state would be in a position to deport the unsuccessful applicants. In that case Article 22 of the Directive recommends that states consider 'any compelling reasons which may make return impossible or unreasonable in specific cases'.

---

[104] Still hoping that they could dispense with a procedure altogether, some Member States wished to discourage asylum seekers from formally lodging a claim. Article 19 provides, therefore, that the 'status' of TP beneficiary and that of asylum seeker cannot be enjoyed concurrently: if one lodges an asylum claim during TP, one falls back into the asylum seeker category. The sunny side of this provision is that it supposes TP standards of treatment better than those available to asylum-seekers.

[105] See, in particular, Article 14 of the 1950 Convention for the Protection of Human Rights and Fundamental Freedoms, 213 UNTS 222; and Article 21 of the 2012 Charter of Fundamental Rights of the European Union, 2012/C 326/02, 26 October 2012.

(5) Whether or not a movement of return is initiated, the exceptional mechanism of TP cannot be maintained for more than two years—unless a fresh decision is made by the Council, extending the duration of TP by up to one year.[106] These are short deadlines, when compared with earlier proposals that regarded a maximum duration of five years as reasonable.

9.4 Hovering on …

As the EU Directive was nearing finalisation, Fitzpatrick noted with some assurance that '[t]he EU framework will undoubtedly influence discussions on formalized TP within the United Nations, and is likely to exert a significant shaping influence on future international agreements concerning TP.'[107] With hindsight, one cannot but conclude that this forecast was overly optimistic. Thus far, the TP Directive does not seem to have influenced any agreement at international or even regional level. One important reason for this is that the Directive is not taken seriously by the very states that adopted it in the Council, which is bound to considerably reduce its attractiveness to non-EU member states. Most recently, UNHCR has suggested that activation of TP may be the appropriate response to the growing influx of Syrian asylum seekers into the EU, which has put unbearable pressure on the reception and processing resources of member states on the southern and eastern borders of the Union, Bulgaria in particular.[108] Sadly, this call has remained unheeded. Clearly, the potential for replication or adaptation of the EU framework outside Europe is not boosted by member states' own apathy.

It does not help either that the key features of the Directive are misrepresented in scholarly literature. On the critical issue of termination of TP, Edwards writes that the TP Directive 'was set up … to suspend – and in some instances to not apply – not only procedures for the determination of refugee status but also Convention obligations to refugees, including the cessation clauses'.[109] In support of this last point, she claims that '*[i]nstead of* the cessation clauses, the termination of [TP] status … occurs, under Article 6(1): (a) when the maximum duration has been reached …; or (b) at any time, by Council's decision'.[110] This interpretation is clearly incorrect: as seen in the previous section, TP under the EU Directive is nothing more than a prelude to full application of the 1951 Convention, at least for those beneficiaries of TP who, considering themselves refugees, have—at any time

---

106 Article 6 TP Directive.

107 Fitzpatrick 2000, at 305.

108 'UNHCR Head of Policy calls for more solidarity for Syrians among EU States', www.icmc.net/article/unhcr-head-policy-calls-more-solidarity-syrians-among-eu-states. Accessed 10 July 2014.

109 Edwards 2012, at 602.

110 Ibid., note 35 (emphasis added).

during TP, or upon termination of the same—made a formal asylum claim. Those who are recognised as refugees will benefit from the protection of the Convention until such protection is no longer required—i.e., the Convention's cessation clauses *will* apply to them. TP does not displace, much less replace, the cessation clauses. If any municipal law (in a state party to the Convention) allows for 'cessation clauses [to be] considered not to be applicable, and instead persons are and can be returned as soon as the triggering event has been resolved',[111] that law is at variance with both EU and international refugee law—Edwards could have made this point more forcefully. Where she writes that 'formalised cessation rules are not always available or expected under temporary protection schemes, with a focus on speedy return … at times regulated merely by administrative discretion',[112] one hopes that she is describing bad practice, and not attempting to set a new standard.

Misperceptions of what is, after all, the only extant 'temporary protection scheme' binding more than one State, do not augur well for 'discussions on formalized TP within the United Nations'. As a matter of fact, discussions have been far from intense or sustained, except possibly within UNHCR itself. The organisation has referred to TP, in rather loose terms, to describe '[h]ospitality in the Middle East', but it has acknowledged that the phrase (and perhaps the concept) has not taken root in that region, whether in respect of refugees from Iraq in 2003 or, more recently, refugees from Syria.[113] Since no refugee-hosting State in the Middle East is party to the Convention (and Turkey has maintained the geographical limitation it entered at the time of accession), the standards of protection advocated by UNHCR have been more akin to 'temporary refuge' and the stipulations of Executive Committee Conclusion No. 22, discussed in the first section of this chapter. There is no sign of a 'formalisation of TP' through a regional agreement in the Middle East, nor for that matter in any other region.

On the doctrinal side, however, UNHCR has attempted to develop the TP concept further, regularly re-introducing it in both internal and external documents. On the whole, these efforts have failed to clarify the grey areas that were so hotly debated in the 1990s, and which constitute the 'red threads' of this chapter. Let us consider, first, the difficult question of the relationship of 'termination of TP' to cessation on account of changed circumstances under the 1951 Convention. In 2003 UNHCR issued, as part of its regular guidelines on international protection, a document explicating 'Cessation of refugee status under Article 1C(5) and (6) of the 1951 Convention'.[114] These guidelines refer briefly to 'temporary protection schemes' (though the only example cited is the EU Directive), stating that 'even though the cessation doctrine does not formally come into play, this form of

---

[111] Ibid.

[112] Ibid., at 612.

[113] UNHCR, Discussion Paper, Roundtable on temporary protection, 19–20 July 2012, para 5, www.unhcr.org/506d85849.html. Accessed 10 July 2014.

[114] See Article 6A of the 1950 Statute.

protection is built upon the 1951 Convention framework and members of the group may well be or include refugees under the Convention'. Consequently,

> [d]ecisions by States to withdraw [TP] should ...be preceded by a thorough evaluation of the changes in the country of origin. Such decisions should also be accompanied by an opportunity for those unwilling to return and requesting international protection to have access to an asylum procedure.[115]

It is hard to detect in these recommendations a clarification of the specificity of TP *vis-à-vis* the 1951 Convention, or, for that matter, to understand what aspects of the 'cessation doctrine' are absent from 'temporary protection schemes'. To be sure, when (several years later) the Assistant High Commissioner called for 'an internationally agreed doctrine of temporary protection, which would ensure the availability of interim protection to people in temporary need',[116] she acknowledged the persistent dearth of standards on the subject: '[t]he indicators of safety have to be made more precise' (than what?) and 'the role of voluntariness as an aspect of return in temporary protection situations needs to be better defined'. With regard to the former (indicators of safety), a 2012 Discussion Paper[117] observes that a 'maximalist' approach, adopting 'the same standards as those envisaged' in Article 1C(5) of the Convention, would 'undermin[e] one of [TP's] main advantages'.[118] In contrast, a '"minimalist" approach may only require a change in conditions allowing for a return in dignity and safety'.[119] However, the document does not specify the criteria to be used in order to assess the 'safety and dignity' of return, referring only to the very general definitions of the UNHCR Handbook on Voluntary Repatriation.[120] It must be borne in mind that, in the said Handbook, safety and dignity of return are *additional* conditions to be met *over and above*, not in lieu of, voluntariness.[121] This reference is hard to reconcile, therefore, with the 'minimalist approach' it claims to support: what is left, in the final analysis, of TP's 'main advantage'?

---

[115] Ibid., para 24.

[116] Feller 2011, at 9. Note, however, that the example given is 'seriously at-risk persons fleeing devastation and disaster'—i.e., persons unlikely to require the protection of refugee law.

[117] UNHCR, Discussion Paper, Roundtable on temporary protection, 19–20 July 2012, www.unhcr.org/506d85849.html. Accessed 10 July 2014. This was the first of two meetings of experts convened by UNHCR in San Remo, Italy, evidently in response to the Assistant High Commissioner's call.

[118] Ibid., at 8.

[119] Ibid.

[120] Ibid., 9. See also UNHCR, Handbook—Voluntary repatriation: international protection, 1 January 1996, www.unhcr.org/3bfe68d32.html. Accessed 10 July 2014.

[121] This is acknowledged in the latest UNHCR guidelines, which posit that '[t]emporary protection/stay ends when … [i]t is determined – on the basis of an objective assessment based on clear indicators – that the situation causing the displacement has ended, and *voluntary* [our emphasis] return is reasonable and can be carried out in safety and dignity'. UNHCR, Guidelines on temporary protection or stay arrangements, February 2014, www.refworld.org/docid/52fba2404.html. Accessed 10 July 2014.

If we turn to what Fitzpatrick called the other 'cessation aspect' of TP, we find a similar degree of confusion in UNHCR's evolving doctrine. This aspect, the reader will recall, concerns the permissibility and, if permitted, the scope and duration of a suspension or 'freezing' of Convention rights in States that are party to the 1951 Convention. On this fundamental question, the latest UNHCR guidelines are totally silent. Commentators have rightly been alarmed by the lack of any reference to a maximum duration of TP in this document—not least because they have read it in the light of prior UNHCR documents.[122] These include the 2012 Discussion Paper,[123] which suggests that suspension of rights in the 1951 Convention may be justified on a number of grounds. While the current status of this Discussion Paper is unclear, what it says on this subject is relevant to our discussion, and deserves therefore a brief analysis. First comes a reminder that 'any suspension of rights in the 1951 Convention as they apply to refugees needs to be justified',[124] which is definitely correct though perhaps insufficient: should it not have added that such justifications must also be provided by law? Be that as it may, the document proceeds to identify four 'possible explanations to reconcile the co-existence' of TP and the Convention. While all four merit critical scrutiny, for the sake of conciseness we will limit our review to one only, as being directly relevant to the question at hand.[125] According to UNHCR, what may justify a suspension of Convention rights is the 'impact of the [influx] on the stability and security of the receiving State, at least in its initial stages'.[126] Recourse to TP on this ground is deemed 'particularly relevant in mass influx and other emergency situations'—which is indeed consistent with the history of temporary protection, as we have seen above. What is definitely more surprising, not to say worrying, is the assertion that within this context 'temporary suspension *or derogation* of [sic] the Convention' *is permitted.*[127] This is, to our knowledge, the first time that the concept of derogation is used by UNHCR in relation to TP. On the one hand, this innovation makes sense, since derogation regimes in human rights law acknowledge and address the difficulties that states face in guaranteeing rights in exceptional circumstances—something which TP also purports to do. On the other hand, the reference to derogation within the 1951 Convention-based regime looks rather odd, since the Convention does not allow for derogation in mass influx

---

[122] Kagan 2014.

[123] See UNHCR, Discussion Paper, Roundtable on temporary protection, 19–20 July 2012, www.unhcr.org/506d85849.html. Accessed 10 July 2014.

[124] Ibid., para 26.

[125] The other three justifications are (i) that the persons concerned are not refugees within the 1951 Convention's definition; (ii) that the situation is fluid and requires a 'wait and see' attitude on the part of receiving States; and (iii) that a group protection response is deemed most appropriate because individual status determination would be impracticable or overly burdensome.

[126] Ibid.

[127] Ibid. (emphasis added).

situations.[128] The Discussion Paper circumvents this rather serious problem by referring, in a footnote, to Article 9 of the Convention, according to which nothing shall prevent a contracting state,

> in time of war or other grave and exceptional circumstances, from taking provisionally measures which it considers to be essential to the national security in the case of a particular person, pending a determination by the Contracting State that that person is in fact a refugee and that the continuance of such measures is necessary in his case in the interest of national security.[129]

That this odd reference was confined to a footnote is probably revealing of some unease on the part of the drafters of the Discussion Paper.[130] To suggest that, despite its reiterated focus on 'a particular person', Article 9 of the Convention could find an application in situations of mass influx, strikes us as a dangerous extrapolation. And, one feels compelled to add, extrapolation has no place in a regime of derogation, which—on the contrary—needs to be explicit and circumscribed by very precise limits, lest it be abused.[131] Derogation clauses, as is well known, are subject to five principles, one of which is the requirement of notification and proclamation, with the accompanying guarantees of monitoring and supervision.[132] None of this is present in the 1951 Convention. It can be argued, *de lege ferenda,* that the addition of a derogation clause to existing Convention provisions would be a useful move; and that whatever problems it might raise would be 'less severe than those which occur on a daily basis when the Convention is set aside in favour of ad hoc mechanisms'.[133] Indeed, those states parties that are interested in a 'formalisation of TP', as well as UNHCR, might usefully direct their efforts away from more ad hoc formulas and toward the definition of a lawful derogation clause in situations of emergency. Until such time, however, there will be no basis for derogation, properly-so-called, in treaty-based refugee law.

---

[128] Regarding the drafting history of the Convention on the issue of derogation and the (defeated) UK proposal to insert a clause permitting the same 'at times of national crisis', see Hathaway 2005, at 261; Durieux and McAdam 2004, note 66; Edwards 2012, at 618–620.

[129] Article 9 of the 1951 Convention.

[130] Edwards, on the other hand, develops the same argument at length. See Edwards 2012, at 620–624.

[131] On the principles of exceptional threat, non-derogability of fundamental rights, proportionality (including temporariness), non-discrimination, and proclamation and notification, see Durieux and McAdam 2004; and Edwards 2012. The purpose of derogation regimes in human rights law is 'to *prevent* States from curtailing individual freedoms for reasons of national interest, as opposed to motives for the common good'. MacDonald 1997, at 226 (emphasis added). On the dubious concept of implied or informal derogations which in any event would be subject to 'the same limitations [as] express derogation', see Edwards 2012, at 625.

[132] Human Rights Committee, General Comment No. 29: States of Emergency (Article 4), UN Doc CCPR/C/21/Rev.1/Add.11, 31 August 2001. See also Criddle 2015

[133] Durieux and McAdam 2004, at 23.

9.5 Conclusion: Time for a Showdown

The question asked at the outset of our discussion was: how does international refugee law manage 'refuge time'? In the course of the analysis, it became apparent that a tension exists between two dimensions of time management in the 1951 Convention, namely: the incremental acquisition of 'assimilative' rights in the country of asylum, on the one hand; and, on the other, the imperative of 'ceasing' refugee status on account of changed circumstances in the state of origin. This tension is particularly manifest in mass influx situations, not least because of the heavy burden such influxes impose upon receiving states—a burden which is not shared according to binding standards. Large-scale influxes, it is well worth recalling, have been the rule, rather than the exception, in the history of refugee movements; and no part of the world has been spared, as evidenced by the crisis, to which European TP was a response. Our next finding has been that the 'clash of times' inherent in the regime has not been resolved satisfactorily in law, despite (or perhaps because of) the agitation that prevailed in Western Europe in the 1990s. Once the crisis had subsided, the EU harmonisation process allowed a number of important clarifications to surface, which were translated into a binding Directive. Sadly, this development does not seem to have aroused much interest outside the EU—a state of affairs, for which EU member states' lack of enthusiasm (and political commitment) is in good part responsible.

This rather sober assessment inevitably begs the question: is TP, after all, a useful vehicle for advancing refugee law? Is it the tool states need in order to resolve contradictions, fill gaps, and correct weaknesses in extant international law? Can it be the basis for a supplement, or (in a more daring spirit) a contemporary alternative, to the 1951 Convention?

We strongly believe the answer to this question must be: no—for two main reasons. The first is that TP is still, twenty years down the line (thirty, if one traces it back to 'temporary refuge'), far too amorphous a concept. Early on, Fitzpatrick and others made significant efforts to break the TP discourse down into issues that could be assessed and addressed within a rigorous framework of international law—including customary international law and general principles of international law in addition to identifiable treaty law in the human rights and humanitarian fields. Today, building for example on the EU Directive, a similar effort could arguably smoothen some of the rough edges of TP through a fresh display of imagination and legal skills. But who will rise to this task? For good or bad reasons, UNHCR has been left to its own devices in this field, and—as shown in the previous section—it has not been able to articulate a convincing 'doctrine of temporary protection'. Far from dispelling prior ambiguities, its latest guidelines introduce yet another 'tool'—'temporary stay arrangements'—and make it look as though UNHCR is trying to evade the tough legal questions raised by its earlier pronouncements.[134] The very notion of 'arrangement' is hard to grasp in legal terms.

This brings us to the second cause for scepticism. What was, in the early 1990s, touted as a major attraction of TP—namely, its flexibility—turned out to be a weakness. Upon perusing the extensive literature on TP, including many UNHCR documents, one is never sure whether TP operates within, or outside, the established legal framework based on the 1951 Convention. TP seems to constantly hover *at the edges* of refugee law—without ever landing either this side, or that side, of the line. Ambiguity over this fundamental point may well have been 'constructive' during the former Yugoslavia crisis—it is definitely not appropriate at this time, when what is needed is legal explanation and consolidation.

Let us, therefore, put TP down to rest. Let us accept it as a term of art in EU law, and keep insisting—as UNHCR has done—on the implementation of the Directive whenever needed, and for further refinement of its provisions through practice. Beyond this ambit, it is preferable to acknowledge that a once useful concept has run its course, and to deal with the questions it raised within known legal frameworks. We should, in other words, *re-frame* TP issues into the Convention-based regime. As early as 1997, a group of government officials convened to a round of UNHCR consultations signalled that 'the risks in the formalization of the concept of temporary protection lie in the potential for it to dilute the protection of the 1951 Convention and reduce the incentive of States to accede to the Convention.'[135] We have submitted that these risks would indeed be mitigated if we abandoned the TP concept. But what can be offered in its stead that would strengthen the protection of the Convention and enhance its attractiveness to non-party states? Here are a few pointers.

Many states parties are clearly struggling—and not only in mass influx situations—with the difficult transition from admission and protection to durable solutions. The Convention should not, however, be accused of bias in this regard. To the contrary, the tension we have described in the foregoing sections suggests that, in fact, the Convention is biased *neither* in favour of integration, *nor* in favour of repatriation. In reality, all refugee situations, large or small, have always been resolved through a mix of these two 'happy ends'. A faithful implementation of the Convention involves reconciling these seemingly contradictory objectives. Reflecting on the lessons of TP in Europe, Kjaerum identified the challenge with great precision: it is 'to create a policy which allows the refugee to live a fruitful life … without being

---

[134] It can only add to the confusion that UNHCR should expand the personal scope of TP arrangements to cover 'mixed population movements, including boat arrivals' and victims of 'other humanitarian crises'. UNHCR, Guidelines on temporary protection or stay arrangements, February 2014, para 9, www.refworld.org/docid/52fba2404.html. Accessed 10 July 2014. See also Article 6A of the 1950 Statute.

[135] Standing Committee, Progress report on informal consultations on the provision of international protection to all who need it, Doc. EC/47/SC/CRP.27, 30 May 1997, para 5.

marginalised from the rest of the community, on the one hand, and which, on the other hand, keeps his or her mind open to the possibility of returning home'.[136]

The TP rhetoric has also distracted the attention of states parties away from Convention standards on cessation. The prospect of cessation is important because it forces states to 'think solutions', and allows them to do so in concert—including, as early as possible, the state of origin in this concert. The firm legal parameters of the debate, namely the prohibition of *refoulement* and the termination of refugee status under 1C(5) of the Convention, make no room for a 'safe return' that depends on neither the refugees' will, nor on significant changes in the country of origin/return. On the other hand, it may in the light of current practice be excessive to require that conditions in the country of origin should change 'in a profound and enduring manner' before cessation can be envisaged and discussed. The plain language of Article 1C(5) of the Convention does not require as much. In the final analysis, the dynamic process whereby conditions conducive to return are assessed, discussed and—wherever possible—created is more important and productive than any 'authoritative' declaration of cessation. This process should start much earlier in the life of a refugee situation than has been the case in the past. It could usefully borrow some modalities and techniques from the tripartite or multipartite discussions that in current practice revolve around the conditions for voluntary repatriation.

When faced with a large-scale influx of refugees, states need time to adjust their procedures and re-direct their resources (and/or seek additional resources). It is not in their interest to deny or minimise the refugee character of the flow, for this would cut them off from the resources of other states in the regime and UNHCR. But to allow reluctant host states to violate the Convention by maintaining the refugees in a state of limbo does not do any service to the international legal framework. International law should, therefore, acknowledge that refugee influxes may create an emergency situation; and regulate such a state of emergency by allowing a lawful 'breathing space'—i.e., derogation within specified, verifiable limits. Now that UNHCR has uttered the word 'derogation', albeit in rather unsatisfactory terms, it should seriously adopt the negotiation of a limited derogation clause to the Convention as an urgent challenge.

Even assuming that a derogation regime may function well throughout a time-bound emergency, the post-emergency will still need to be dealt with. 'If derogation time is to be used constructively, it must open up real opportunities for international solidarity and burden-sharing in the pursuit of durable solutions.'[137] Solidarity remains, unfortunately, the Achilles' heel of the international refugee regime. There is little hope that binding norms of universal application can be adopted in this domain, and firmer rules for burden-sharing are likely to be easier to negotiate on a 'situational' basis, i.e., with regard to a specific refugee problem. At the same time, it would be sensible to make measures of solidarity available in priority to states that are party to the Convention: in addition to creating an

[136] Kjaerum 1994, at 447.

[137] Durieux and McAdam 2004, at 24.

incentive for non-party states to accede, this priority would highlight the significance of the Convention as a 'coalition'[138] of the willing—and collectively able—to rise to the challenges of international protection in today's world.

References

Andersen E (1996) The role of asylum states in promoting safe and peaceful repatriation under the Dayton agreements. Eur J Int Law 7:193–206

Bagshaw S (1997) Benchmarks or Deutschmarks? Determining the criteria for the repatriation of refugees to Bosnia and Herzegovina. Int J Refug Law 9:556–592

Barutciski M (1998) Involuntary repatriation when refugee protection is no longer necessary: moving forwards after the 48th session of the Executive Committee. Int J Refug Law 10:236–255

Bem K (2004) The coming of a 'blank cheque': Europe, the 1951 Convention, and the 1967 Protocol. Int J Refug Law 16:609–627

Chetail V (2011) Théorie et pratique de l'asile en droit international classique: etude sur les origins conceptuelles et normatives du droit international des réfugiés. Revue de Droit International Public CXV:625–651

Chetail V (2014) Are refugee rights human rights? An unorthodox questioning of the relations between refugee law and human rights law. In: Rubio-Marin R (ed) Human rights and immigration. Oxford University Press, Oxford, pp 19–72

Coles G (1989) Approaching the refugee problem today. In: Loescher G, Monahan L (eds) Refugees in international relations. Oxford University Press, Oxford, pp 373–410

Costello C (2015) The human rights of migrants and refugees in European law. Oxford University Press, Oxford forthcoming

Criddle EJ (2015) Protecting human rights during emergencies: delegation, derogation and deference. Netherlands Yearbook of International Law 45:197–220

Davies SE (2007) Redundant or essential? How politics shaped the outcome of the 1967 protocol. Int J Refug Law 19:703–728

Durieux JF, Hurwitz A (2004) How many is too many? African and European legal responses to mass influxes of refugees. Ger Yearb Int Law 47:105–159

Durieux JF, McAdam J (2004) *Non-refoulement* through time: the case for a derogation clause to the Refugee Convention in mass influx emergencies. Int J Refug Law 16:4–24

Edwards A (2012) Temporary protection, derogation and the *1951 Refugee Convention*. Melb J Int Law 13:595–635

Feller E (2011) The Refugee Convention at 60: still fit for its purpose? www.unhcr.org/4ddb679b9.html. Accessed 5 Aug 2014

Fitzpatrick J (1994) Flight from asylum: trends toward temporary 'refuge' and local responses to forced migrations. Va J Int Law 35:13–70

Fitzpatrick J (1999) The end of protection: legal standards for cessation of refugee status and withdrawal of temporary protection. Georget Immigr Law J 13:343–381

Fitzpatrick J (2000) Temporary protection of refugees: elements of a formalized regime. Am J Int Law 94:279–306

Goodwin-Gill GS (1986) Non-refoulement and the new asylum seekers. Va J Int Law 26:897–920

Goodwin-Gill GS (2014) Non-refoulement and temporary refuge. In: Cantor DJ, Durieux JF (eds) Refuge from inhumanity? War refugees and international humanitarian law. Brill Nijhoff, Leiden, pp 433–459

Goodwin-Gill GS, McAdam J (2007) The refugee in international law, 3rd edn. Oxford University Press, Oxford

[138] See Noll 2003.

Hathaway JC (1984) The evolution of refugee status in international law: 1920-1950. Int Comp Law Q 33:348–380
Hathaway JC (2005) The rights of refugees under international law. Cambridge University Press, Cambridge
Hathaway JC (2010) Leveraging asylum. Tex Int Law J 45:503–536
International Crisis Group (1997) Refugees and internally displaced persons in B-H. www.refworld.ord/docid/3ae6a6d20.html. Accessed 5 Aug 2014
Kagan M (2014) UNHCR issues new guidelines on temporary protection. They need a rewrite. http://rsdwatch.wordpress.com/2014/03/20/unhcr-issues-new-guidelines-on-temporary-protection-they-need-a-rewrite/. Accessed 5 Aug 2014
Kälin W (2001) Temporary protection in the EC: refugee law, human rights and the temptation of pragmatism. Ger Yearb Int Law 44:202–236
Kerber C (1999) Temporary protection in the European Union: a chronology. Georget Immigr Law J 14:35–50
Kjaerum M (1994) Temporary protection in Europe in the 1990s. Int J Refug Law 6:444–456
Lauterpacht E, Bethlehem D (2003) The scope and content of the principle of non-refoulement. In: Feller E, Türk V, Nicholson F (eds) Refugee protection in international law: UNHCR's global consultations on international protection. Cambridge University Press, Cambridge, pp 78–177
Long K (2013) Back to where you once belonged: a historical review of UNHCR policy and practice on refugee repatriation. UNHCR Policy Development and Evaluation Service, Geneva, PDES/2013/14
MacDonald RSJ (1997) Derogations under Article 15 of the European Convention on Human Rights. Columbia J Transnatl Law 36:225–268
Martin DA (1989) Effects of international law on migration policy and practice. Int Migrat Rev 23:547–578
Noll G (1997) Prisoners' dilemma in fortress Europe: on the prospects for equitable burden-sharing in the European Union. Ger Yearb Int Law 40:405–437
Noll G (2000) Negotiating asylum: the EU acquis, extraterritorial protection and the common market of deflection. Kluwer Law International, The Hague
Noll G (2003) Risky games? A theoretical approach to burden-sharing in the asylum field. J Refug Stud 16:236–252
Perluss D, Fitzpatrick Hartman J (1986) Temporary refuge: emergence of a customary norm. Va J Int Law 26:551–626
Suhrke A, Barutciski M, Sandison P, Garlock R (2000) The Kosovo refugee crisis. An independent evaluation of UNHCR's emergency preparedness and response. UNHCR Evaluation and Policy Analysis Unit, Geneva
Takahashi S (1997) The UNHCR handbook on voluntary repatriation: the emphasis of return over protection. Int J Refug Law 9:593–612
van Selm Thorburn J (1998) Refugee protection in Europe: lessons of the Yugoslav crisis. Kluwer Law International, The Hague
Vedsted-Hansen J (1997) An analysis of the requirements for voluntary repatriation. Int J Refug Law 9:559–565
Zieck M (1997) UNHCR and voluntary repatriation of refugees: a legal analysis. Kluwer Law International, The Hague

Chapter 10
Between the Devil and the Deep Blue Sea: Enhancing Flexibility in International Climate Change Law

Harro van Asselt

Abstract The evolving nature of the climate change problem makes it challenging to govern it through a single set of rules fixed in time. Scientific insights into the causes and impacts of climate change are subject to constant changes. Further, the socio-economic and political conditions prevailing in different countries continue to alter over time. This chapter first assesses how the primary international legal response, the regime established by the United Nations Framework Convention on Climate Change, has sought to cope with these temporal challenges, and suggests that while various flexibility mechanisms are in place, the climate regime often finds it hard to adapt to changing conditions. In a second step, the chapter examines an alternative in the form of proposals that aim to make international climate change law more adaptive through a pluralist approach. The chapter critically reviews these proposals, and suggests that while the rigidities of the existing climate regime certainly need to be addressed, considerations of predictability and stability should not be sacrificed at the altar of flexibility. To conclude, therefore, the chapter explores the options for enhancing flexibility within the current architecture for international climate change law.

Keywords Climate change · Compliance · Differentiation · Flexibility · Kyoto Protocol · Pluralism · Polycentric governance · UNFCCC

This chapter was written in the context of the Sida-funded project 'Orchestrating International Climate Policy' and the Swedish Research Council (Formas) project 'Navigating Institutional Complexity: Causes, Consequences and Policy Responses'. The author thanks Kati Kulovesi, Fariborz Zelli, an anonymous reviewer, and the editors of the *Yearbook* for their valuable comments. The usual caveat applies.

H. van Asselt (✉)
Stockholm Environment Institute, Oxford, UK
e-mail: harro.vanasselt@sei-international.org

M. Ambrus and R.A. Wessel (eds.), *Netherlands Yearbook of International Law 2014*,
Netherlands Yearbook of International Law 45, DOI 10.1007/978-94-6265-060-2_10

Contents

10.1 Introduction 256
10.2 Flexibility in the United Nations Climate Change Regime 258
10.2.1 Delegated Law-Making 259
10.2.2 Scientific Input 260
10.2.3 Review and Amendment 262
10.2.4 Entry into Force, Reservations and Withdrawal 265
10.2.5 Differentiation 266
10.2.6 Implementation 268
10.2.7 Compliance 269
10.2.8 Flexibility in the Climate Change Regime: Advances and Limitations 271
10.3 A Pluralist Approach to International Climate Change Law as an Alternative Model 272
10.3.1 The Virtues of a Pluralist Approach 273
10.3.2 The Baby and the Bathwater 276
10.4 Enhancing Flexibility in International Climate Change Law 278
10.5 Conclusions 281
References 282

10.1 Introduction

International environmental law in general, and international law on climate change in particular, has become fertile ground for contemporary debates in international law. International law on climate change is inevitably fragmented, and insights from the issue area are of immediate relevance for the debate on the causes and consequences of the fragmentation of international law.[1] International law on climate change is further characterized by informal international law-making, meaning that it holds lessons for studying the emergence and effectiveness of law-making in which the notion of state consent no longer plays the same role as in traditional international law.[2] International climate change law also involves a variety of non-state actors in its creation and implementation, thereby informing discussions on the respective roles of state and non-state entities in international law.[3]

This chapter shows that, as in these other debates, international climate change law offers valuable insights for studying temporariness and temporality in international law. The nature of climate *change*—implied by the very term—is variable across time and space.[4] Scientific insights into the causes and impacts of climate change are subject to constant changes. Several decades of climate research have shown a clear evolution in scientific insights. The First Assessment Report of the Intergovernmental Panel on Climate Change (IPCC), published in 1990, was still somewhat cautious, indicating that '[e]missions resulting from human activities

[1] Young 2011; Van Asselt 2014.

[2] Van Asselt et al. 2014; see also Krisch 2014.

[3] Giorgetti 1999; Dannenmaier 2011.

[4] See also Briner et al. 2014, at 8–9.

are substantially increasing the atmospheric concentrations of the greenhouse gases' and that '[t]hese increases will enhance the greenhouse effect, resulting on average in an additional warming of the Earth's surface'.[5] Twenty-three years and several assessment reports later, the IPCC concluded with much more confidence that it is over 95 percent certain that human activities contribute to an increase in the global average temperature.[6] However, uncertainties will inevitably remain, and scientific insights into the causes and effects of climate change will continue to change over time. Another aspect subject to change is technology. Although technological advances (e.g., lower-cost renewable energy technologies) may inform the possible legal responses, they may also exacerbate the problem (e.g., technologies to extract fossil fuels at lower costs). Further, the socio-economic conditions prevailing in different countries continue to alter over time. In 1992, the largest carbon dioxide emitter was the United States; in 2013, it is China, whose emissions are still rapidly growing. Also in terms of economic development, the situation is no longer the same. Countries like Singapore and South Korea have reached levels of economic development that now surpass some European countries like the Czech Republic.[7] Finally, demographic developments—population growth in some countries, decline in others—also hold implications for the scale of the problem, as well as its resolution.

These changing circumstances make it challenging to govern the problem of climate change through a single set of rules fixed in time, and therefore point to the need for a flexible, dynamic and adaptive legal system. At the same time, the flexibility necessary to address the temporary nature of the subject matter may well challenge one of the core rationales of legal norms: to provide legal certainty and predictability and, more broadly, to uphold the rule of law.[8]

Drawing on scholarship on flexibility mechanisms in international law, this chapter therefore first examines how adaptive the primary international legal response, the regime established by the 1992 United Nations Framework Convention on Climate Change (UNFCCC), has been. This is important as '[i]nstitutions must be designed to allow for adaptation because some current understanding is likely to be wrong, the required scale of organization can shift, and biophysical and social systems change'.[9] To this end, the contribution examines how the drafters of the UNFCCC and the 1997 Kyoto Protocol have sought to cope with temporal challenges, and suggests that while various flexibility

---

[5] IPCC, Policy summary. Prepared by IPCC Working Group I, 1990, at 52, https://www.ipcc.ch/ipccreports/far/wg_I/ipcc_far_wg_I_spm.pdf. Accessed 20 August 2014.

[6] IPCC, Climate change 2013: the physical science basis. Working Group I contribution to the Fifth assessment report of the Intergovernmental Panel on Climate Change. Summary for policymakers, 2013, at 15.

[7] World Bank, World development indicators 2013, http://wdi.worldbank.org/. Accessed 20 August 2014. The Republic of Korea's per capita gross national income in 2012 was US$ 20,870; that of the Czech Republic was US$ 18,720.

[8] On this tension in international environmental law generally, see Ebbesson 2010.

[9] Dietz et al. 2003, at 1909.

mechanisms are in place, the climate regime often finds it hard to adapt (Sect. 10.2). In a second step, the chapter examines a possible alternative in the form of proposals aimed at making international climate change law more adaptive and flexible through a pluralist approach. The chapter critically reviews these proposals, and suggests that while the rigidities of the existing climate regime certainly need addressing, considerations of predictability and stability need not be sacrificed at the altar of flexibility (Sect. 10.3). In other words, the temporary nature of the climate challenge should not undermine the rule of law governing this issue area. The chapter therefore explores the middle ground for enhancing flexibility within the current architecture for international climate change law (Sect. 10.4), before ending with some concluding thoughts (Sect. 10.5).

10.2 Flexibility in the United Nations Climate Change Regime

From a rational choice perspective, flexibility mechanisms in international law can be an important means for parties to manage the risks of joining an agreement by determining the terms of cooperation.[10] Such mechanisms offer a way to manage uncertainty in the evolution of an international legal regime and respond to changes over time.[11] A wide variety of flexibility mechanisms exist, with Laurence Helfer distinguishing between unilateral mechanisms, invoked by one state only, and collective ones, which are available to all parties to va treaty.[12] In addition, one can discern 'adaptive flexibility' (i.e., flexibility offered to one Party), 'transformative flexibility' (i.e., flexibility affecting the entire regime),[13] as well as 'means flexibility' (i.e., flexibility with regard to the means of implementation).[14] This section presents a non-exhaustive overview of elements of the UN climate change regime that enhance its flexibility, and discusses the advances made, as well as remaining limitations. It argues that while the climate regime is flexible by design, its adaptability in practice is limited, particularly when it comes to taking into account changing national circumstances and responding to new scientific insights.

[10] Helfer 2013, at 175.

[11] Thompson 2010.

[12] Helfer 2013, at 179.

[13] Koremenos et al. 2001, at 773. 'Adaptive' and 'transformative' flexibility overlap to a large extent with Helfer's 'unilateral' and 'collective' flexibility mechanisms.

[14] Thompson 2010, at 271.

10.2.1 Delegated Law-Making

The ‘second wave’ of international environmental law[15] showed awareness of the temporal nature of its subject matter. This awareness was evidenced by the emergence of the ‘framework-protocol’ approach, under which a general framework treaty outlines overarching objectives, guiding principles and puts in place institutional structures for further negotiations, and more specific commitments are included in a subsequent protocol to the framework treaty. The approach was also employed in the context of climate change, where the Kyoto Protocol adds flesh to the UNFCCC by establishing legally binding emission quantitative emission reduction and limitation obligations. The framework-protocol approach facilitates regime-building even in the absence of a complete picture of the problem or consensus on the appropriate response.[16] Moreover, the approach allows nation states to respond to changing circumstances and scientific insights while cooperating under a common framework. As the UNFCCC does not specify the decision-making process for adopting a protocol,[17] it has been approached as an amendment in practice (see Sect. 10.2.3).

Perhaps more important for the climate regime’s flexibility has been the possibility to refine and elaborate treaty provisions through decision-making by the Conferences of the Parties (COPs). COP decisions do not constitute treaty changes, but they can add substance to often vaguely formulated provisions in a way that does not differ much from formally amending a treaty.[18] Following the adoption of the Kyoto Protocol in 1997, the COP (serving as Meeting of the Parties to the Protocol) has put in place institutional arrangements for, and developed detailed rules on, for instance, the Protocol’s market-based mechanisms and compliance procedures.[19] Such decisions are not devoid of normative substance, and in practice may have a significant impact on the behaviour of state and non-state actors. For instance, the decision to make certain project types (in)eligible for crediting under the Kyoto Protocol’s Clean Development Mechanism (CDM) may have a very real impact on investment decisions on the carbon market.[20]

---

[15] Francioni 2012, at 445.

[16] Bodansky 1993, at 494.

[17] Article 17 of the 1992 United Nations Framework Convention on Climate Change, 1771 UNTS 163 (hereinafter UNFCCC).

[18] Churchill and Ulfstein 2000; Brunnée 2002.

[19] French and Rajamani 2013, at 443–448.

[20] Various types of projects have been excluded, notably nuclear energy projects (UNFCCC, Decision 17/CP.7, Modalities and procedures for a clean development mechanism, as defined in Article 12 of the Kyoto Protocol, UN Doc. FCCC/CP/2001/13/Add.2, 21 January 2002, at preamble) and avoided deforestation (Kyoto Protocol, Decision 16/CMP.1, Land use, land-use change and forestry, UN Doc. FCCC/KP/CMP/2005/8/Add.3, 30 March 2006, Annex, para 13), whereas other project types have been included, such as carbon capture and storage (Kyoto Protocol, Decision 10/CMP.7, Modalities and procedures for carbon dioxide capture and storage in geological formations as clean development mechanism project activities, UN Doc. FCCC/KP/CMP/2011/10/Add.2, 15 March 2012).

Whether COP decisions amount to *law*-making remains an open question, however, and needs to be examined on a case-by-case basis.[21]

A limitation to the flexibility offered by delegated law-making through COP decisions is that, in the absence of agreement on decision-making rules, they in practice require consensus among Parties.[22] As a consequence, it was possible that resistance from a few vocal countries prevented the adoption of the Copenhagen Accord in 2009.[23] Subsequent practice has shown, however, that individual countries have been over-ruled.[24] In 2011, Mexico and Papua New Guinea tabled an amendment,[25] seeking to introduce majority voting to the UNFCCC—and thereby enable Parties to respond more rapidly to changing circumstances—but such proposals to reform decision-making procedures remain heavily contested.[26]

10.2.2 Scientific Input

To reflect the evolution of scientific insights in a legal regime, it is of paramount importance that decision-makers have access to the best available and most up-to-date scientific information. The UNFCCC established the Subsidiary Body for Scientific and Technological Advice (SBSTA) to provide the COP with 'timely information and advice on scientific and technological matters relating to the Convention' and to provide 'assessments of the state of scientific knowledge relating to climate change and its effects'.[27] The SBSTA itself is a political body, and does not generate scientific knowledge. Instead, it communicates advice based on the latest scientific information to the COP. Therefore, the role of international bodies that conduct scientific assessments is an essential complement to the role of SBSTA.

The most well-known scientific assessment body in the area of climate change is the IPCC, established in 1988. The IPCC itself does not carry out scientific research,

---

[21] Brunnée points out that, from a formal point of view, lawmaking by treaty bodies might be considered to be based on a form of implied state consent. (Brunnée 2002, at 23–31.) However, Wiersema concludes that 'consensus-based COP activity … cannot be seen as giving rise to stand-alone legal or even political obligations' and that COP decisions 'hold little meaning but for their connection to the treaty'. (Wiersema 2009, at 245.) In other words, the legal force of COP decisions depends on the connection to the treaty obligation, and the type of obligation set forth in the treaty. See also Brunnée 2002, at 24.

[22] The Rules of Procedures of the COP were never adopted. The Rules of Procedure of the COP, UN Doc. FCCC/CP/1996/2., 22 May 1996. Disagreement hinges on the issue of majority voting (as laid out in several alternatives under Rule 42). See Yamin and Depledge 2004, at 442–443.

[23] The Accord was instead merely 'taken note of'. See UNFCCC, Decision 2/CP.15, Copenhagen Accord, UN Doc. FCCC/CP/2009/11/Add.1, 30 March 2010.

[24] On the evolving meaning of 'consensus' in international climate change law, see Rajamani 2011, at 515–518; and French and Rajamani 2013, at 448–451.

[25] Revised proposal from Papua New Guinea and Mexico to amend Articles 7 and 18 of the Convention, UN Doc. FCCC/CP/2011/4/Rev.1, 9 December 2011.

[26] Vihma and Kulovesi 2013, at 251.

[27] Article 9 UNFCCC.

Table 10.1 Scientific input in the climate regime: the role of different bodies

COP	SBSTA	IPCC
• Periodic assessment of treaty obligations	• Advice to COP on basis of scientific assessments	• Production of regular scientific assessments
• Guidance for SBSTA	• Identification of research priorities	• Production of specific assessment at the request of SBSTA (and self-initiated)
• Advice requests to SBSTA	• Formulate requests to scientific bodies	• Identification of research priorities
• Consideration of SBSTA advice	• Cooperation with other organizations	• Cooperation with other organizations
• Cooperation with other organizations		

Adapted from Lohan 2006

but assesses the existing scientific information through a thorough review process. It generates regular scientific assessment reports on the causes, consequences and responses to climate change. In addition, the IPCC also publishes shorter Special Reports and Technical Papers at the request of SBSTA. Table 10.1 offers an overview of the different roles of the COP, SBSTA and the IPCC with respect to scientific input in the climate change regime.

A positive perspective on this science-policy interface would suggest that 'the institutional structure drawn upon by the UNFCCC optimizes the input of scientific information into the decision making process, as long as the IPCC works according to its current procedures'.[28] Viewed more critically, however, it can be pointed out that this structure does not guarantee that the scientific information will actually be incorporated in decisions. The process of drafting the Summary for Policymakers accompanying each IPCC report has become heavily politicised, with governments seeking to reflect their political positions in the document.[29] Peter Haas therefore concludes that the way in which the IPCC provides scientific information to the UNFCCC does not result in usable knowledge for the Parties and is not reflected in the climate agreements.[30] This is visible, in particular, with respect to aggregate mitigation efforts, with the gap between pledged emission reductions and the internationally agreed goal[31] to keep temperature increases below 2 °C relative to pre-industrial times still widening.[32] Moreover, the mere observation that scientific information is taken up properly in the policy process does not say anything about the speediness with

28 Ibid., at 307.

29 For a discussion, see Dubash et al. 2014.

30 Haas 2004, at 583.

31 UNFCCC, Decision 1/CP.16, The Cancun agreements: outcome of the work of the ad hoc working group on long-term cooperative action under the Convention, UN Doc. FCCC/CP/2010/7/Add.1, 15 March 2011, para 4.

32 Rogelj et al. 2010.

which this occurs. This is important especially in the case of the climate regime, as some changing insights into mitigation options as well as climate impacts call for swift policy responses.

10.2.3 Review and Amendment

An important way to adjust a treaty regime to exogenous developments over time is by providing for the review of the original treaties and including possibilities for amending them when deemed necessary.

Both climate treaties include various provisions for review. In a general review clause, the UNFCCC instructs the COP to '[p]eriodically examine the obligations of the Parties and the institutional arrangements under the Convention, in the light of the objective of the Convention, the experience gained in its implementation and the evolution of scientific and technological knowledge'.[33] It further provides for a review of the adequacy of some of its core commitments by its first session, drawing on 'best available scientific information and assessment of climate change and its impacts, as well as relevant technical, social and economic information'.[34] This review led to the 'Berlin Mandate' at the first COP in 1995, which in turn launched the negotiations for the Kyoto Protocol.[35] While the provision could thus be said to underscore the dynamic character of the climate regime, a second review never followed. Finally, the Convention provides for a review of its Annexes by the end of 1998.[36] While this provision was hardly used,[37] its framing offers a potential avenue to reflect changes in socio-economic conditions over time.[38]

---

[33] Article 7(2)(a) UNFCCC.

[34] Article 4(2)(d) UNFCCC. A second review had to take place by the end of 1998.

[35] UNFCCC, Decision1/CP.1, The Berlin mandate: review of the adequacy of Article 4, para 2(a) and (b), of the Convention, including proposals related to a protocol and decisions on follow-up, UN Doc. FCCC/CP/1995/7/Add.1, 6 June 1995.

[36] Article 4(2)(f) UNFCCC.

[37] In 1997, Croatia, the Czech Republic, Liechtenstein, Monaco, Slovakia and Slovenia were added to Annex I. See UNFCCC, Decision 4/CP.3, Amendments to the list in Annex I to the Convention under Article 4.2(f) of the Convention, UN Doc. FCCC/CP/1997/7/Add.1, 25 March 1998. Malta joined in 2009, and Cyprus followed in 2011. See UNFCCC, Decision 3/CP.15, Amendment to Annex I to the Convention, UN Doc. FCCC/CP/2009/11/Add.1, 30 March 2010; and UNFCCC, Decision 10/CP.17, Amendment to Annex I to the Convention, UN Doc. FCCC/CP/2011/9/Add.2, 15 March 2012. Although Turkey and Kazakhstan were also interested in making use of the review with a view to respectively being removed from and added to Annex I, Parties could not reach consensus. See Yamin and Depledge 2004, at 106.

[38] As further discussed below, it remains to be seen whether this potential can be reaped. A proposal by the Russian Federation to amend Article 4(2)(f) UNFCCC to provide for a periodical review (rather than the single review mentioned in the provision) met with significant resistance from developing countries. The Russian proposal can be found at: https://unfccc.int/files/parties_and_observers/notifications/application/pdf/msg_parties_proposal_amendart4.pdf. Accessed 20 August 2014.

The Kyoto Protocol also offers several opportunities for reviewing the adequacy of its commitments. It contains a general clause providing for a periodical review by the COP similar to that of the UNFCCC.[39] More specifically, for Annex B Parties (i.e., the developed countries that have signed up to specific emission limitation or reduction targets) Article 3(9) Kyoto Protocol suggests that the consideration of future commitments needs to start seven years before the end of the first commitment period (2008–2012).[40] The Protocol also provides for a separate periodical review in light of the latest scientific information. Unlike the one-off Article 3(9) Kyoto Protocol review, however, this review covers the commitments of all Parties (including developing countries), and is not limited to the mitigation-oriented commitments.[41] Although two reviews were held in this context, these reviews were not to 'lead to new commitments for any Party'.[42] Moreover, the second review ended without a clear outcome or a plan for follow-up in 2008.[43]

Amendments to the climate treaties may be adopted without any limitations as to their substance.[44] Both the UNFCCC and Kyoto Protocol indicate that amendments should be agreed upon by consensus or, if this turns out to be infeasible, a three-fourth majority.[45] While the majority voting procedure in theory enhances flexibility, as it could allow for overruling obstructionist states, in practice 'international regimes are heavily dependent on voluntary action on the part of member states when it comes to matters of implementation', meaning that 'it is important to avoid alienating key members via the use of decision-making procedures that seem coercive'.[46] Nevertheless, as Farhana Yamin and Joanna Depledge point out, '[a]lthough voting rarely takes place in [multilateral environmental agreements], the *possibility* of voting ensures that no Party, or small group of Parties can veto evolution of the regime in the face of widespread agreement'.[47] Should amendments be adopted, they are binding only to those parties that have accepted them, creating a potentially complex network of legal relations between Parties.[48]

Another way to adapt is to make changes in the Annexes to the climate agreements, and hence change the commitments only for certain Parties. For the UNFCCC, the adoption of changes to the Annexes follows the same procedure as

[39] Article 13(4)(b) of the 1997 Kyoto Protocol to the United Nations Framework Convention on Climate Change, 2303 UNTS 148 (hereinafter Kyoto Protocol).

[40] Article 3(9) Kyoto Protocol.

[41] Article 9 Kyoto Protocol.

[42] UNFCCC, Decision 4/CMP.3, Scope and content of the second review of the Kyoto Protocol pursuant to its Article 9, UN Doc. FCCC/KP/CMP/2007/9/Add.1, 14 March 2008, para 3.

[43] Akanle et al. 2008, at 10.

[44] Bodansky 2009, at 3.

[45] Article 15 UNFCCC; Article 20 Kyoto Protocol.

[46] Young 2010, at 93.

[47] Yamin and Depledge 2004, at 547.

[48] Bodansky 2009, at 3.

an amendment.[49] However, as the entry into force requirements for changing the Annexes are more relaxed, such changes are 'a more expedient way of incorporating material of an essentially factual nature into the regime than is possible through the use of amendments'.[50] Changing the Annexes to the Kyoto Protocol is more difficult, given the fact that they comprise the core commitments of individual Parties, and define the scope of the agreement by listing the greenhouse gases covered. More specifically, the Protocol states that 'any amendment to Annex B shall be adopted only with the written consent of the Party concerned'.[51]

Up to 2009, proposed amendments to the climate treaties were few and far between. Proposed amendments by Turkey and Kazakhstan to change the Annexes to the UNFCCC met with resistance.[52] Belarus' proposal to amend Annex B of the Kyoto Protocol to allow it to assume emission reduction obligations was adopted in 2006, but is unlikely to enter into force due to a lack of ratifications.[53] The number of proposals increased sharply in 2009. The reasons for this related to the heightened expectations that at the Copenhagen climate summit at the end of 2009 a new international agreement would be adopted, combined with the provision in the climate treaties that an amendment needs to be sent to Parties at least six months in advance of a meeting before it can be adopted.[54] Whereas several developing countries sought to act upon the mandate under Article 3(9) Kyoto Protocol by proposing amendments including specific new commitments for Annex B Parties,[55] some developed countries instead tabled amendments putting forward an entirely different legal architecture from that of the Protocol.[56] Parties in Copenhagen, as has been extensively discussed elsewhere,[57] did neither adopt any of these amendments nor any other legally binding agreement. Three years later, however, Parties in Doha ultimately adopted an amendment—yet to enter into force—in response to Article 3(9) Kyoto Protocol, inscribing new targets for a second commitment period (from 2013 to 2020) for the European Union, its Member States and a few other countries.[58] The long and winded inception

[49] Article 16(2) UNFCCC.

[50] Yamin and Depledge 2004, at 549.

[51] Article 21(7) Kyoto Protocol.

[52] See note 27 above. An amendment allowing Turkey to be removed from Annex II was adopted in 2002, however. See UNFCCC, Decision 26/CP.7, Amendment to the list in Annex II to the Convention, UN Doc. FCCC/CP/2001/13/Add.4, 21 January 2002.

[53] Kyoto Protocol, Decision 10/CMP.2, Proposal from Belarus to amend Annex B to the Kyoto Protocol, UN Doc. FCCC/KP/CMP/2006/10/Add.1, 2 March 2007.

[54] Article 15(2) UNFCCC; Article 20(2) Kyoto Protocol.

[55] See, e.g., http://unfccc.int/resource/docs/2009/cmp5/eng/07.pdf. Accessed 20 August 2014.

[56] See, e.g., Australia's 'national schedules' approach: http://unfccc.int/resource/docs/2009/cmp5/eng/10.pdf. Accessed 20 August 2014.

[57] See, e.g., Bodansky 2010; Rajamani 2010.

[58] Kyoto Protocol, Decision 1/CMP.8, Amendment to the Kyoto Protocol pursuant to its Article 3, para 9 (the Doha Amendment), UN Doc. FCCC/KP/CMP/2012/13/Add.1, 28 February 2013. Japan, Russia and New Zealand did not inscribe any new targets, whereas Canada had, by that time, withdrawn from the Protocol.

period of this amendment can be considered a reflection of the challenges faced when Parties to the climate treaties need to make substantive changes that touch the core of the climate regime—i.e., who needs to do what by when.

10.2.4 Entry into Force, Reservations and Withdrawal

Provisions on entry into force (of both treaties and amendments), as well as reservations and withdrawals by individual Parties offer another opportunity to enhance flexibility in the design of a legal regime. Such provisions set important parameters for Parties' legal obligations by specifying when such obligations begin to apply, whether any unilateral opt-outs are allowed and whether and how a Party can cease to be bound.

The entry into force requirements of the UNFCCC were rather lenient,[59] ensuring a rapid entry into force of the framework treaty less than two years after its adoption. The Kyoto Protocol introduced more challenging hurdles. Not only did it require at least 55 Parties to ratify, it also stipulated that these Parties should include Annex I Parties responsible for at least 55 percent of the total carbon dioxide emissions in 1990. In terms of flexibility, this provision created a 'handicap'.[60] While the provision sought to avoid a situation where the fate of the Protocol's entry into force depended entirely on the United States,[61] it led to several compromises on the part of the European Union to ensure the participation of other Annex I Parties such as Japan, Canada and, notably, the Russian Federation. These compromises are primarily reflected in rules on the use of carbon sinks (see further Sect. 10.2.6), and while they arguably enhanced the regime's flexibility (in terms of methods for accounting for emissions as well as implementing commitments), they also jeopardized the environmental integrity of the Kyoto targets by creating new loopholes.[62]

Like most other multilateral environmental agreements, the climate treaties state clearly that no reservations are allowed.[63] While this arguably limits the flexibility of the treaties, it also prevents the emergence of a complex web of bilateral legal relationships, and ensures that the fragile compromises reached in the treaties are not unravelled at a later stage.[64] Flexibility, in short, has to be built into the treaty itself.

---

[59] Article 23 UNFCCC.

[60] Young 2010, at 93.

[61] Yamin and Depledge 2004, at 552.

[62] See generally Boyd et al. 2008.

[63] Article 24 UNFCCC; Article 26 Kyoto Protocol.

[64] Sands and Peel 2012, at 103–104.

The provisions on withdrawal in both climate treaties arguably enhance flexibility, as they allow for a Party to withdraw provided a prior notification has been submitted.[65] Withdrawal clauses can be seen as a form of 'insurance', where Parties seek to minimise the risks of potentially high compliance costs of a treaty by allowing for unilateral treaty exit.[66] Yet, the consequence of having a withdrawal provision (specifically, one that does not pose any high barriers) is that it may in fact be used, with potentially detrimental consequences for future international cooperation. While it was perhaps expected that the need to keep up a good international reputation would deter countries from exiting, Canada notoriously made use of the provision in 2011, when it submitted its notification of withdrawal.[67] Canada was well off track to meet its Kyoto targets, but rather than being found to be in non-compliance, it chose to exit. The risks of such a precedent are highlighted by Helfer, who points out 'that states will invoke exit clauses opportunistically (or credibly threaten to do so) whenever economic, political, or other pressures make compliance costly or inconvenient' and that 'states that would prefer to cooperate but fear that their treaty partners may quit the agreement have less incentive to invest in treaty compliance'.[68] Although neither scenario described by Helfer has materialized yet in the climate regime, there is a possibility that they will in the future, particularly if states cannot avail of other flexibility mechanisms.

10.2.5 Differentiation

As an elaboration of the principle of 'common but differentiated responsibilities and respective capabilities',[69] the UNFCCC divides its Parties into two major blocks, emerging from the initial classification of Parties into Annex I (including a richer Annex II) and the default category of non-Annex I countries. The same approach is reinforced in the Kyoto Protocol, which focuses on Annex B and non-Annex B countries. Both treaties contain commitments applying to all countries, but add specific commitments for Annex I/B countries. Notably, non-Annex B countries do not have any emission reduction commitments under the Kyoto Protocol.

While the division into two Annexes arguably simplifies the negotiation process, it can be criticized for not taking into account changing circumstances in countries. Developed countries, in particular, have argued for abandoning the distinctions introduced by the Annexes. Such calls have met with fierce resistance from several developing countries, particularly large emerging economies such as China and India,

---

[65] Article 25 UNFCCC; Article 27 Kyoto Protocol.

[66] Helfer 2005, at 1591; Meyer 2010, at 389.

[67] Canada to withdraw from Kyoto Protocol, *BBC News*, 13 December 2011, http://www.bbc.co.uk/news/world-us-canada-16151310. Accessed 20 August 2014.

[68] Helfer 2013, at 181.

[69] Article 3(1) UNFCCC.

which have insisted that the 'firewall' of the Annexes needs to be maintained. Therefore, since 'the addition and deletion of names of countries from Annex I is closely related to the broader issues raised by the evolution of mitigation commitments of non-Annex I Parties',[70] any proposed change to the Annexes has been a sensitive issue.

The diverging views between developed and developing countries came sharply into focus during the negotiations on a follow-up agreement to the Kyoto Protocol in the mid-2000s. A first departure from the 'firewall' approach to differentiation was agreed in the 2007 Bali Action Plan, which called for 'nationally appropriate mitigation commitments or actions' by developed country Parties (rather than referring to Annex I/B countries) and 'nationally appropriate mitigation actions' for developing country Parties (rather than referring to non-Annex I/B countries).[71] This trend continued in subsequent COPs in Copenhagen, Cancún and Durban. Notably, the decision launching the Durban Platform on a future climate agreement specifies that such an agreement will be 'applicable to all Parties'.[72]

More importantly, however, further differentiation is already quite common in the climate regime.[73] The UNFCCC refers, for instance, to the 'special situations of the least developed countries';[74] to 'economies that are vulnerable to the adverse effects of the implementation of measures to respond to climate change';[75] to countries 'undergoing the process of transition to a market economy';[76] and to the special needs and circumstances of a range of different countries, including 'small island countries', 'countries with low-lying coastal areas', fossil-fuel producing countries, etc.[77] Differentiation can also be observed in specific issue areas. With respect to the CDM, initiatives have sought to promote the 'equitable distribution' of CDM projects, for instance through capacity-building initiatives in sub-Saharan Africa[78] and a loan scheme for countries with less than 10 projects.[79] Likewise, over the years a differentiated approach to climate change finance has been followed. The Cancún

[70] Yamin and Depledge 2004, at 106.

[71] UNFCCC, Decision 1/CP.13, Bali action plan, UN Doc. FCCC/CP/2007/6/Add.1, 14 March 2008, para 1(b)(i) and (ii).

[72] UNFCCC, Decision 1/CP.17, Establishment of an ad hoc working group on the Durban platform for enhanced action, UN Doc. FCCC/CP/2011/9/Add.1, 15 March 2012, para 2. According to the so-called 'Like-minded Developing Countries' group (which includes China and India), 'applicable to all' does not mean that there should be uniformity in application. This group of countries still very much resists moving away from the Annex I/non-Annex I distinction. See, e.g., UNFCCC, Submissions from the like-minded developing countries, UN Doc. FCCC/ADP/2013/CRP.1, 19 November 2013, paras 7 and 13.

[73] Brunnée and Streck 2013; Pauwelyn 2013.

[74] Article 4(9) UNFCCC.

[75] Article 4(10) UNFCCC.

[76] Article 4(6) UNFCCC.

[77] Article 4(8)(i) UNFCCC.

[78] See http://cdm.unfccc.int/Nairobi_Framework/index.html. Accessed 20 August 2014.

[79] Kyoto Protocol, Decision 3/CMP.6, Further guidance relating to the clean development mechanism, UN Doc. FCCC/KP/CMP/2010/12/Add.2, 15 March 2011.

Agreements, for example, stipulate that 'funding for adaptation will be prioritized for the most vulnerable developing countries, such as the least developed countries, small island developing States and Africa.'[80]

The principle of common but differentiated responsibilities and respective capabilities provides a legal argument in favour of differentiation between Parties with different contributions to the climate problem and different capacities to reduce emissions. Essentially, the principle offers a basis for treating countries differently if national circumstances vary, and thereby allows for enhancing flexibility in the climate regime.

10.2.6 Implementation

The extent to which a treaty prescribes a certain conduct is another important determinant for its flexibility. Given its nature as a framework treaty, it is unsurprising that the conduct prescribed in the UNFCCC is rather broadly formulated, with the important exception of provisions on monitoring and reporting. For instance, the most concrete elaboration of an emissions goal is for all Parties, individually and/or jointly, to return to their 1990 emissions level.[81] Moreover, the treaty stipulates that Annex I Parties are to 'adopt national policies and take corresponding measures on the mitigation of climate change',[82] without specifying what types of policies and measures would be desirable.

The Kyoto Protocol is more concrete when it comes to emission reduction targets, which are specified for all Annex B Parties. It also adds detail on the means of implementation by including a list of possible policies and measures, but the text of the provision—'such as'—makes clear that the list is meant to be non-exhaustive.[83] The non-mandatory and non-exhaustive nature of the list of policies and measures means that states are in principle free to decide how to reduce their greenhouse gas emissions, leaving them with much discretion in achieving their targets. For instance, countries can opt to reduce emissions by putting in place renewable energy or energy efficiency policies or by adopting policies to enhance the carbon uptake of sinks (e.g., by increasing forested land). Moreover, Parties are given 'what' flexibility with respect to the sources of emissions: the Protocol covers a 'basket' of greenhouse gases,[84] with Parties free to choose which emissions to reduce. This is of significance, as it allows Parties to target emission sources that are not deeply entangled with their economies. The flipside of this approach is

---

80 Decision 1/CP.16, para 95.

81 Article 4(2)(b) UNFCCC.

82 Article 4(2)(a) UNFCCC.

83 Kyoto Protocol, Article 2(a). In the negotiations leading up to the Kyoto Protocol, the European Union sought to include a mandatory list of policies and measures in the treaty, but this met with resistance from developed and developing countries alike. See Depledge 2000, at 19–21.

84 Kyoto Protocol, Annex A.

that it will inevitably pose challenges in measuring progress, as the equivalence of different types of emission reductions will need to be established before they can be aggregated.

Flexibility in the implementation stage is further enhanced by the introduction of three market-based mechanisms in the Kyoto Protocol. Although some form of flexibility mechanism was already included in the UNFCCC—in the guise of Activities Implemented Jointly[85]—the idea of market mechanisms in international climate policy was only fully embraced through the Kyoto Protocol. Importantly, the Kyoto mechanisms offer 'where' flexibility to achieve cost-effective emission reductions by allowing Parties to reduce emissions outside of their jurisdiction.[86] First, through international emissions trading, Annex I Parties can buy or sell emission units representing 1 metric tonne carbon dioxide equivalent from or to other Annex I Parties.[87] Second, through the CDM, Annex I Parties may invest in emission reduction projects in non-Annex I countries. The emission reduction credits subsequently generated can be used up to a certain extent to meet the Kyoto targets.[88] The third flexibility mechanism, Joint Implementation, follows a similar logic, but is aimed specifically at countries undergoing the transition to a market-based economy (i.e., countries in Central and Eastern Europe).[89] The only limitation to this 'where' flexibility comes in the form of a vaguely formulated recital that the use of the Kyoto mechanisms 'shall be supplemental to domestic action and that domestic action shall thus constitute a significant element of the effort made by each Party'.[90]

Following Kyoto, and with a view to ensuring sufficient participation to allow the Protocol to enter into force (see Sect. 10.2.4), new rules were agreed by Kyoto Parties that provided for even more flexibility, particularly by relaxing rules in the area of carbon sinks.[91] In short, it should be clear that the climate treaties leave Parties considerable flexibility regarding the means of implementation.

10.2.7 Compliance

The design of a compliance mechanism can directly affect a Party's costs of compliance, and therefore provides another avenue for either enhancing or limiting flexibility. Moreover, non-compliance itself can be seen as the ultimate unilateral

[85] Article 4(2)(a) UNFCCC.

[86] The Protocol, however, does not offer 'when' flexibility (i.e., reducing emissions at the point in time when costs are lowest).

[87] Article 17 Kyoto Protocol.

[88] Article 12 Kyoto Protocol.

[89] Article 6 Kyoto Protocol.

[90] UNFCCC, Decision 15/CP.7, Principles, nature and scope of the mechanisms pursuant to Articles 6, 12 and 17 Kyoto Protocol, UN Doc. FCCC/CP/2001/13/Add.2, 21 January 2002, at recital. For a critique, see van Asselt and Gupta 2009, at 338–339.

[91] Thompson 2010, at 284–286.

flexibility mechanism:[92] a Party can allow itself room for manoeuvring by not complying with its commitments (although such a strategy may backfire in cases where non-compliance involves sanctions).

Although Parties to the UNFCCC were invited to consider a 'multilateral consultative process',[93] no compliance mechanism has been established under the Convention. By contrast, the Kyoto Protocol put in place a compliance mechanism that combined the virtues of the two main schools of thought in compliance theory: through the Enforcement Branch of its Compliance Committee, it allows for penalties in case Kyoto Parties do not meet key obligations (reflecting the 'enforcement' school in compliance theory); and through its Facilitative Branch, it assists countries to return to compliance (corresponding to the 'managerial' school).[94] The managerial school, in particular, emphasises how compliance should be viewed as a continuous process requiring 'compliance management' rather than one-off findings of non-compliance combined with sanctions,[95] highlighting the role of compliance mechanisms in promoting flexibility.

Although the flexibility built into the functioning of the Enforcement Branch is rather limited (it is to 'determine' non-compliance and 'apply' consequences, such as penalties[96]), the room for manoeuvring for the Facilitative Branch is greater.[97] The mandate of the latter includes

> providing *advice and facilitation* to Parties …, promoting compliance by Parties with their commitments under the Protocol, *taking into account the principle of common but differentiated responsibilities and respective capabilities* …. It shall also take into account the *circumstances pertaining to the questions before it.*[98]

In line with the notion of compliance management, the Facilitative Branch can enter into a dialogue with Parties that are at risk of non-compliance. However, mainly due to the later-than-expected entry into force of the Protocol, the facilitative function of the Compliance Committee has been under-utilized.[99] Nevertheless, this facilitative role has in part been assumed by the expert review teams, which were established by the Kyoto Protocol to review Parties' reports and submit 'questions of implementation'.[100] Evaluations of the functioning of the

---

92 Alter 2005, at 141, cited by Helfer 2013, at 177.

93 Article 13 UNFCCC.

94 A prime example of the 'enforcement' school is Downs et al. 1996. A key contribution to the 'managerial' school is Chayes and Chayes 1995.

95 Chayes et al. 1995.

96 Kyoto Protocol, Decision 27/CMP.1, Procedures and mechanisms relating to compliance under the Kyoto Protocol, UN Doc. FCCC/KP/CMP/2005/8/Add.3, 30 March 2006, Annex, section V, paras 4–5.

97 On the compliance mechanism in the climate regime generally, see Brunnée 2003; and Oberthür and Lefeber 2010.

98 Decision 27/CMP.1, Annex, section IV, para 4 (emphases added).

99 Doelle 2013, at 170–172.

100 Article 8 Kyoto Protocol.

compliance system underline that Parties' national circumstances have been taken into account, but point out that this has been done in an inconsistent fashion.[101]

10.2.8 Flexibility in the Climate Change Regime: Advances and Limitations

The previous sub-sections have shown that flexibility has been the rule rather than the exception in the *design* of the United Nations climate change regime. The types of flexibility comprise 'adaptive', 'transformative' as well as 'means' flexibility.

Adaptive flexibility can be observed, for instance, in the withdrawal provision that allowed Canada to exit from Kyoto in 2011, or in the Protocol's compliance mechanism which allows for a measured response to different cases of non-compliance. Transformative flexibility is clear from the provisions on review and amendment, as well as the system of delegated law-making through the COP, which allows for a response to changing insights and circumstances without seeking recourse to formal re-negotiation processes. Means flexibility is present in the climate treaties through the provisions allowing significant discretion with respect to mitigation policies and measures, as well as through the Kyoto Protocol's flexibility mechanisms.

These examples show that the designers of the Convention were well aware of the temporal nature of the subject matter. While the UNFCCC establishes an overarching objective and guiding principles for the climate regime, and the Kyoto Protocol sets clear rules for developed countries to reduce their emissions (thus enhancing legal certainty and predictability), the flexibility mechanisms offer Parties (individually and collectively) significant leeway.

Yet notwithstanding the flexibility built into the design of both climate treaties, the discussion has also clearly shown that there are problems with the existing regime when it comes to adapting to changing circumstances *in practice*. Despite institutional arrangements for the provision of scientific input into the policy-making process and a reference to precaution in the UNFCCC,[102] it remains unclear whether the UNFCCC process is able to properly reflect changing scientific insights that stress the importance of rapid and deep emission cuts. An interesting test case in the immediate future in this regard will be to examine whether Parties will acknowledge and embrace scientific findings that to stay below 2 °C with over 75 % certainty, it is necessary to limit cumulative carbon dioxide emissions between 2000 and 2050 to 1000 gigatonnes.[103] Although Parties have established a review process from 2013 to 2015 'to periodically review the adequacy of the long-term global goal ..., in the light of the ultimate objective of the Convention, and overall progress towards achieving it',[104]

---

[101] Doelle 2013.

[102] Aticle 3(3) UNFCCC.

[103] Meinshausen et al. 2009, at 1158.

[104] Decision 1/CP.16, para 138.

it remains to be seen whether the longer-term objectives will influence short- to mid-term goals and actions. The experience of the climate regime in terms of setting ambitious and concrete goals does not bode well, and it is perhaps too much to expect a translation of scientific insights into specific emission reduction commitments. As a consequence, it will remain difficult to measure progress toward any long-term objective.

Related to this, the current climate regime is arguably not well-aligned with the structure of the climate change problem. As Oran Young explains,

> [t]his misfit is, first and foremost, a function of the fact that the relevant biophysical systems are dynamic and prone to changes that are nonlinear, irreversible, and surprising, whereas the regime is sluggish and unable to respond in a nimble fashion to such changes in the climate system.[105]

The climate regime is marked by an incremental approach, with each COP making only minimal progress. Variations of the criticism 'the process has been saved, but not the climate' underline this incremental approach.[106] This step-by-step approach is related to the challenge of achieving consensus between more than 190 countries,[107] which forms a significant limitation to the flexibility with which the UNFCCC's decision-making bodies can respond to changing circumstances.

Another limitation to the flexibility of the climate regime is its lack of a dynamic system of commitments. In the face of continuing resistance to change the current system of Annexes (i.e., the 'firewall'), it will be difficult to adapt the regime to changing circumstances (e.g., a change in greenhouse gas emissions; economic growth or stagnation; increased vulnerability; etc.) in different countries. Although further differentiation among countries is slowly creeping into the regime (as discussed in Sect. 10.2.5), it remains doubtful that abandoning the Annexes system entirely will be possible—at least in the short term.

10.3 A Pluralist Approach to International Climate Change Law as an Alternative Model

The discussion so far has highlighted that the adaptability of the climate regime is limited in at least two important respects: the evolution of commitments in accordance with changing national circumstances; and changing the overall ambition in light of new scientific evidence. Critics of the regime have not only pointed to these weaknesses but, in response, have also proposed alternative models that

105 Young 2010, at 116.

106 See, e.g., http://www.sei-international.org/op-ed/1929-qcancun-may-have-saved-the-un-process-but-not-the-climateq. Accessed 20 August 2014.

107 Vihma and Kulovesi 2013.

could fare better in terms of flexibility and adaptability. This section will examine one such model in particular, namely a pluralist approach to international climate change law and governance.

10.3.1 The Virtues of a Pluralist Approach

In recent years, an extensive body of literature on legal pluralism at the global level has emerged.[108] Krisch distinguishes between 'institutional' and 'systemic' pluralism. The former relies on overarching norms to resolve interactions between different legal systems (e.g., the subsidiarity principle), whereas the latter, is rather characterized by 'decentred management of diversity',[109] meaning that it is up to individual legal systems to determine their relationships *vis-à-vis* each other. Although legal pluralism has been discussed in the context of domestic law, the focus here is on *global* legal pluralism.[110] This concept generally refers to the simultaneous governance of a specific issue area by a variety of international, transnational and national legal regimes.

Perhaps surprisingly, insights from the study of global legal pluralism have rarely been applied to the case of climate change.[111] This is surprising given that scholars coming from a range of different backgrounds have highlighted the potential advantages of a multi-pronged, decentralized approach to global climate change governance as compared to the 'single regime' approach of the UNFCCC.[112] Notably, the late Elinor Ostrom advocated a 'polycentric' approach to tackling climate change.[113] Others, in turn, have favoured a 'bottom-up approach',[114] 'experimentation',[115] 'adaptive management'[116] or even 'clumsy solutions' to the climate problem.[117] It is well beyond the scope of this chapter to discuss these various contributions in detail. Yet, one thing they have in common is that the models they present purportedly offer greater flexibility through

[108] See, e.g., Fischer-Lescano and Teubner 2004; Krisch 2010; Berman 2012.

[109] Krisch 2010, at 77.

[110] Cf. Koskenniemi 2007, at 20.

[111] Notable exceptions include Osofsky 2007; Kulovesi 2013.

[112] Pluralism as a description of the legal landscape applicable to a certain issue area should be distinguished from pluralism as a normative goal. From a descriptive point of view, the response to climate change *is* already pluralist, with the UNFCCC being flanked by a wide range of public, private and public-private initiatives at multiple levels of governance. See Biermann et al. 2009; Keohane and Victor 2011; Zelli 2011; Moncel and Van Asselt 2012.

[113] Ostrom 2010.

[114] Rayner 2010.

[115] Hoffmann 2011. On experimentalist governance at the global level generally, see de Búrca et al. 2014.

[116] Thompson 2006.

[117] Verweij et al. 2006.

institutional diversity and decentralisation. A similar virtue is generally ascribed to legal pluralism.[118] It is therefore helpful to first outline the basic reasoning: how could a pluralist approach enhance flexibility?

The virtues of a pluralist approach to international climate change law primarily stem from the fact that it 'accounts better for divergences in community values, priorities, and perspectives in light of the distributive consequences at stake in the production of global public goods.'[119] By doing so, a pluralist approach is more likely to be implemented, as it better reflects the views and interests of those (state and non-state) actors responsible for emission reductions and adapting to the impacts of climate change. A decentralized approach in which states take measures that they deem appropriate—in contrast to an approach where overall and individual targets are established in hierarchical fashion—allows for the consideration of both the costs and benefits of taking action,[120] allowing for better alignment with states' economic interests. Given that such interests and preferences are likely to change over time, a pluralist approach can thus be said to better respond to changing national circumstances, facilitating the contestation over norms that may be perceived excessively static.

The potential inclusiveness of a wide range of actors—in contrast to the mainly intergovernmental climate change negotiations—further strengthens the pluralist argument. Climate governance is increasingly shaped by, and affects, a multitude of actors beyond the nation state. Such actors not only include the usual suspects such as environmental nongovernmental organizations and energy suppliers, but also participants in carbon markets,[121] sub-national governments seeking to reduce emissions or build climate resilience locally,[122] insurance industries concerned about the impacts of climate change[123] and so on. A pluralist approach embraces this diversity and acknowledges that international climate change law and governance necessarily involves this diversity of actors. By doing so, it arguably allows for a more flexible, comprehensive and deeper response to the climate problem.

A third advantage of a pluralist approach is that it implicitly encourages experimentation. A variety of national, regional and international policy or governance approaches opens up significant potential for 'learning by doing', where successful experiments can share experiences and be transferred across jurisdictions. An example often referred to in this context are the 'laboratories' conducting experiments

[118] Krisch 2010, at 78–81.

[119] Shaffer 2012, at 686. Global public goods have been defined 'as outcomes (or intermediate products) that tend towards universality in the sense that they benefit all countries, population groups and generations. At a minimum, a global public good would meet the following criteria: its benefits extend to more than one group of countries and do not discriminate against any population group or any set of generations, present or future.' Kaul et al. 1999, at 16. Climate change mitigation meets this definition.

[120] Barrett 2007, at 245.

[121] Bernstein et al. 2010.

[122] Bulkeley 2010.

[123] Jagers and Stripple 2003.

with greenhouse gas emissions trading at the subnational level in the United States, with each of these systems drawing on different design elements, allowing for possible lessons learnt.[124] By learning lessons from past experiences it is possible to adapt the legal system to changing insights and circumstances over time. Whether this potential is realized, however, depends on various factors, including agreement on broad goals, reporting mechanisms facilitating learning and the ability to regularly change goals, policies and procedures.[125] Of course, some experiments—by definition—are doomed to fail. The appeal of a pluralist approach, however, is that with the existence of a variety of initiatives there will be other fall-back options.[126]

Related to this, a pluralist approach also draws attention to the multi-level nature of climate change law and governance.[127] Acknowledging the co-existence and interaction of multiple legal systems at different levels is an important step towards a more integrated response to climate change. Moreover, cross-fertilization can facilitate learning across different levels of governance. To stick with the example of emissions trading systems mentioned in the preceding paragraph, trading schemes developed at national or subnational levels could learn from the rules and methods designed at the global level (e.g., in the context of the CDM) and vice versa.[128]

Lastly, pluralist approaches have been defended through systemic arguments: the complex or 'wicked' nature of the climate problem[129] requires an equally complex response, meaning that any centralized, 'top-down' approach is bound to fail.[130] Such an approach would further account for the contested nature of both the problem and its solutions.[131] In other words, a pluralist response to climate change shows a better 'fit' with the underlying socio-economic and environmental problem(s),[132] and therefore is arguably better able to respond to changes related to the problem.

Taken together, the arguments in favour of a pluralist approach to international climate change law in terms of enhancing flexibility are certainly compelling. At this point, however, it should be remembered that flexibility or even adaptability in itself are not necessarily the main objectives of international climate change law, but rather a means to an end—the latter being defined in the UNFCCC as the 'stabilization of greenhouse gas concentrations in the atmosphere at a level that would prevent dangerous anthropogenic interference with the climate system',[133] and

---

124 Victor et al. 2006, at 1820; Ostrom 2010, at 553–554.

125 For an overview of the conditions of 'experimentalist governance', see Sabel and Zeitlin 2012.

126 Cf Haas 2004, at 3.

127 See also Scott 2011; Peel et al. 2012.

128 Cole 2011, at 409–411.

129 On wicked problems, see Rittel and Weber 1973; in the context of climate change, see Lazarus 2009 and Levin et al. 2012.

130 Boyd 2011.

131 See generally Hulme. On legal pluralism and contestation, see Krisch 2010, at 81–85.

132 Cf Young 2002.

133 Article 2 UNFCCC.

translated by the international community as the objective to keep global temperature increases below 2 °C above pre-industrial levels.[134] The specific risks of blindly accepting the virtues of a pluralist approach for the sake of expedience and flexibility are discussed next.

10.3.2 The Baby and the Bathwater

Martti Koskenniemi succinctly phrased his criticism of legal pluralism as follows: 'The problem with legal pluralism lies in the way it ceases to pose demands on the world.'[135] This critique resonates also in the case of climate change. While the appeal of a pluralist approach to address a complex and contested problem is undeniable, the politics of climate change will affect both centralized and decentralized approaches to international climate change law and governance. This becomes clear, in particular, when critically examining proposed alternatives that suggest moving away from the UNFCCC in more detail.

Lamenting the 'excessive multilateralism'[136] of the UNFCCC/Kyoto Protocol, various scholars advocating a pluralist approach have proposed to focus any governance effort only on the major emitters, at times referred to as 'minilateralism'.[137] Yet, while this may make intuitive sense—at least from the perspective of flexibility and adaptability—it also misses one of the points of why the UNFCCC was created in the first place. For developing countries, which are disproportionately affected by climate change, the UNFCCC offers the key avenue to draw attention to their plight. Although it is unlikely that the UNFCCC will provide a forum for imposing some form of liability on large emitters, it still provides a crucial link between the causes of climate change (i.e., greenhouse gas emissions) and its impacts. Breaking this link by solely focusing on large emitters would mean that support to developing countries vulnerable to climate impacts would morph into some form of charity.

Another element of several proposals advocating a pluralist approach is their focus on international technology cooperation.[138] Criticizing the climate regime's limited advances in terms of clean technology development and transfer, the benefits of technology-oriented agreements outside the UNFCCC involving non-state actors have been suggested as a useful way forward.[139] This enhances flexibility by not only seeking to reduce emissions through specific targets—the approach of the Kyoto Protocol—but also by incentivizing action by the private sector.

---

[134] See, e.g., Decision 1/CP.16, para 4.

[135] Koskenniemi 2007, at 23.

[136] Hulme 2009, at 313.

[137] See, e.g., Victor 2007; Naím 2009.

[138] Barrett 2007.

[139] De Coninck et al. 2008; Galiana and Green 2009.

Again, there is some validity to this criticism, and technology-oriented agreements outside the UNFCCC could indeed be more effective in reducing emissions in the long run—the jury is still out. Yet, a simple change of venue (or a multiplication thereof) to discuss and implement technology development and transfer does not alter the highly politicized nature of the issue at hand. The reasons for the slow progress in the UNFCCC are largely related to questions of whether developed countries need to transfer clean technologies to developing countries on a concessional basis, and whether intellectual property rights help or hinder technology transfer.[140] Such questions will emerge both within and outside the UNFCCC, even if it may be possible that—given the involvement of key actors such as the private sector holding the intellectual property rights—initiatives outside the UNFCCC will be more effective in addressing these issues. In any case, what the advocates of technology-oriented approaches rarely clarify is how the proposed alternatives build on the progress, however limited, made within the UNFCCC.[141]

A diversity of policy instruments and experimentation with such instruments is another common thread in proposals emphasizing a pluralist approach. However, it has been observed that 'incremental policies can create a path dependence that prevents or inhibits the development of better alternatives',[142] meaning that learning can be stymied by the creation of vested interests in a certain policy approach. To some extent, this is evident in the European Union, where decision-makers have been reluctant to give up on its flagship instrument, an EU-wide emissions trading system, in spite of continued problems with its implementation.[143]

More generally, one of the key lines of reasoning underlying a pluralist approach is the need to ensure that climate action is in line with the interests and perspectives of different state and non-state actors. This reasoning can be criticized for its lack of a common vision to protect global public goods (in this case the aggregate-effort good of climate stabilization). While changes in national circumstances may be important, it is difficult to distinguish between changes in environmental and socio-economic circumstances over time that may form a valid reason for adapting international norms, and mere changes in political preferences. It is for this reason that Gregory Shaffer argues that in some cases a more centralized legal architecture is warranted.[144] Indeed, unguided by a common vision, it is unclear how the sum of what is 'appropriate' for certain states or non-state actors will add up to emission reductions that are sufficient to prevent climate change impacts perceived as

[140] See, e.g., Singh Ghaleigh 2011. In recent years, more progress has been booked with the establishment of the Technology Mechanism in the Cancún Agreements. Decision 1/CP.16, paras 117 ff.

[141] See van Asselt 2014, at 83–118.

[142] Coglianese and d'Ambrosio 2008, at 1423.

[143] Van Asselt 2015.

[144] Shaffer 2012, at 685 and 689. Shaffer does not mention leakage', where mitigation action in one jurisdiction may lead to displacement of emissions to another jurisdiction. This provides another argument against a decentralized approach to the collective action problem of climate change. See Coglianese and d'Ambrosio 2008, at 1419–120.

dangerous by at least some states. Although such a positive outcome cannot be excluded per se, pledges made by UNFCCC Parties so far do not suggest this is likely.[145] Moreover, it remains unclear how action beyond the state can be aggregated with a view to assessing how all the different pieces of the puzzle add up.[146] Hence, a pluralist approach may actually *increase* uncertainty rather than manage it.

The point of this section is not to discard pluralist approaches as such. However, one emerging message is that a pluralist approach, notwithstanding its multiple advantages, does not necessarily deliver stable and predictable outcomes. To enhance flexibility in international climate change law the baby should therefore not be thrown out with the bathwater. Instead, a more cautious and nuanced approach would be to examine (i) how flexibility could conceivably be enhanced within the climate regime; and (ii) how the virtues of a pluralist approach could be exploited through the already existing diversity of approaches in international climate change law and governance. The penultimate section will explore these two options, although both merit further analysis.

10.4 Enhancing Flexibility in International Climate Change Law

Several of the mechanisms discussed in Sect. 10.2 can potentially be improved to make the climate regime more adaptive and flexible. First, there is space to better utilise the system of delegated law-making through COP decisions. Over time, this system has been able to take into account changing scientific insights (as highlighted by the Cancún Agreements' embrace of the 2 °C target[147]), changing technical insights (as evidenced by the gradually expanded rulebook for the CDM), changing national circumstances (as suggested by the Bali Action Plan's inclusion of 'nationally appropriate mitigation actions' for developing countries[148]) and changing political priorities (as indicated by the increasing attention paid to adaptation and finance in COP decisions[149]). At the same time, the consensus rule places limits on what COP decisions can achieve, particularly when it comes to more controversial questions. While it is unlikely—and also not necessarily desirable[150]—that this rule can be changed,

[145] Rogelj et al. 2010.

[146] This important question is receiving mounting attention in policy circles. For a discussion of the contribution of so-called 'international cooperative initiatives' to climate change mitigation, see, e.g., UNEP 2013, at 29–32.

[147] Decision 1/CP.16, para 4. The speed at which UNFCCC Parties this happened is questionable, however. The European Council already agreed on the target in 1996. See Council of Ministers, Council conclusions of the 1939st Meeting, 25 June 1996, http://europa.eu/rapid/press-release_PRES-96-188_en.htm?locale=en. Accessed 20 August 2014.

[148] Decision 1/CP.13, at para 1(b)(ii).

[149] See, e.g., Decision 1/CP.16.

[150] Particularly from the perspective of smaller, less politically powerful Parties.

turning attention to procedural issues in the run-up to a new agreement for the post-2020 period (to be adopted in Paris in December 2015) could prove to be useful. In particular, it could be examined whether it is possible to introduce majority voting for some of the less contested agenda items (i.e., issues that are perceived to be less intrusive of national sovereignty) to facilitate speedier decision-making for at least some of the issues being negotiated.[151] Such proposals are already on the negotiation agenda, and may be taken up in the lead-up to the Paris summit.[152] A different proposal has been to make better use of the various limited membership bodies within the UNFCCC (rather than establish them outside of it).[153] While it remains to be seen whether any of these suggestions will gain traction, a window of opportunity exists in the current negotiations. Such procedural changes could help the COP better fulfil the delegated law-making function envisaged in the Convention, and improve the transformative flexibility of the regime, while the objective and principles of the treaty offer the necessary safeguards that such flexibility does not undermine the rule of law.

Second, it is possible to continue the trend of further differentiation while maintaining the current system of Annexes. In addition to the examples listed in Sect. 10.2.5, a promising suggestion would be to differentiate between Parties by type of commitment. Whereas the Kyoto Protocol is framed with reference to economy-wide quantified emission reduction or limitation targets, a range of other types of commitments are conceivable (energy efficiency targets; targets for shares of renewable energy; sector-specific targets; commitments to invest in technology development; etc.).[154] Other methods of differentiation could draw on the experience of other multilateral environmental agreements (such as the Montreal Protocol on ozone-depleting substances), and include grace periods for specific groups of countries and the use of different base years for emissions accounting.[155] More importantly, however, from the perspective of flexibility and adaptability, would be to establish a dynamic system of 'graduation', where countries gradually take on (more stringent) commitments.[156] A system allowing for the incremental move from one type of commitments to another could be based on ad hoc criteria or on pre-defined rules, with the latter adding an element of stability to a flexible system.[157]

A third option is directly related to the design of a post-2020 climate agreement, particularly its possible inclusion of new review processes. At the nineteenth COP in Warsaw in December 2013, Parties decided to launch a process 'to initiate

---

[151] A distinction between agenda items is foreseen also in Rule 42 of the Rules of Procedures; see note 22.

[152] Vihma 2015.

[153] Vihma and Kulovesi 2013.

[154] Bodansky 2003, at 50–55.

[155] Honkonen 2009, at 259 and 261.

[156] Michaelowa et al. 2005; Gupta 1998.

[157] Berk and den Elzen 2001.

or intensify domestic preparations for their intended nationally determined contributions' on the road to the Paris agreement.[158] These 'contributions'—no agreement could be reached on the word 'commitments'—are expected at least by some Parties to be reviewed through a multilateral process.[159] Similarly, the implementation of the emission reduction commitments laid down in a post-2020 agreement can be subjected to further review.[160] Given the lessons learned from the review provisions of the UNFCCC and the Kyoto Protocol, the question becomes how to design such a review process in such a way that it takes into account changing national circumstances and changing scientific insights. The former could be done by basing any review on equity-related criteria (historical contribution to the climate problem; share of overall greenhouse gas emissions; emissions per capita; etc.). The latter could be achieved by linking any review to overall, long-term climate stabilization goals.[161]

Other options to strengthen the flexibility of the climate regime from within are conceivable, and should be further explored. The main point here is that the possibilities to strengthen the flexibility of international climate change law through the UNFCCC have not yet been exhausted.

The second proposal is to make better use of the existing plurality of approaches, including the UNFCCC. This requires moving away from abstract arguments on whether a centralized or pluralist architecture is 'better' or 'more effective' towards questions of interactions and possible coordination between different (legal and non-legal) systems.[162] As William Boyd puts it:

> Plural, polycentric, nested forms of new governance hold considerable appeal in the abstract, but we need much more experience, more thick description, of how these forms of governance are taking shape in various environmental domains, and how enabling environments that allow for coordination and translation across the diversity of normative orders can be constructed in a manner that builds upon the informal processes and institutions that all formal order depends upon.[163]

In a similar vein, in his defence for legal pluralism in a 'postnational' world, Nico Krisch suggests it is important to devise 'interface norms' to coordinate different legal systems.[164] The UNFCCC ought to be well placed to help construct these

---

[158] UNFCCC, Decision 1/CP.19, Further advancing the Durban platform, UN Doc. FCCC/CP/2013/10/Add.1, 31 January 2014, para 2(b).

[159] See Submission by Greece and the European Commission on Behalf of the European Union and Its Member States, http://unfccc.int/files/bodies/application/pdf/el-02-28-eu_adp_ws1_submission.pdf. Accessed 20 August 2014.

[160] See U.S. Submission on Elements of the 2015 Agreement, http://unfccc.int/files/documentation/submissions_from_parties/adp/application/pdf/u.s._submission_on_elements_of_the_2105_agreement.pdf. Accessed 20 August 2014.

[161] For a specific proposal, see Morgan et al. 2013.

[162] Van Asselt and Zelli 2014.

[163] Boyd 2011, at 516.

[164] Krisch 2010, at 285 ff.

'enabling environments' or 'interface norms'. In recent years, intergovernmental cooperation outside of the UNFCCC has come to the fore in the climate negotiations under the guise of 'international cooperative initiatives', which could contribute to the overall mitigation ambition.[165] The increasing acknowledgment of this potential contribution has led to calls for 'tracking' and 'recognition' of the contribution of such initiatives.[166] The rationale behind such calls is obvious: it would help assess to what extent initiatives outside the UNFCCC help contribute to climate change mitigation objectives and ensure that basic principles of the climate treaties—notably that of common but differentiated responsibilities—would be respected. Such proposals offer one way to draw on the virtues of the existing institutional diversity, while at the same time still linking this diversity to overall objectives and principles. An outstanding question is to what extent the UNFCCC could or should be the proverbial spider in the web, or whether it would simply be one of many legal systems.

10.5 Conclusions

The international legal regime for climate change finds itself between the devil and the deep blue sea: it needs to be flexible enough to adapt to deal with a problem characterised by rapidly changing scientific insights and political and socio-economic circumstances, while at the same time maintaining the stability and predictability that form the basis of ongoing international cooperation.

This chapter has first analyzed how the existing regime has sought to walk this tightrope. It has suggested that in spite of a range of flexibility mechanisms built into the design of the regime, there are certain aspects limiting the regime's ability to adapt in practice. Notably, Parties have been unable to respond to ever-increasing calls for more rapid and deeper emission cuts. Furthermore, the broad classification into two Annexes that continues to be part and parcel of both climate treaties is hard to change, even though the 'firewall' between the two groups of countries seems to be slowly crumbling.

The rigidities of the climate change regime—both perceived and real—have led to calls for radically different architectures for international climate change law and governance. The chapter offered a brief discussion of one such model: a pluralist approach emphasising decentralized action and building on the wide range of initiatives in the area of climate change launched around the world. The merits of a pluralist approach should be duly acknowledged: it is better in line with national and local realities; it promotes participation of a wide range of actors beyond the state; it allows for experimentation; and it offers a better 'fit' with the wicked problem of climate change. However, the flexibility offered by a pluralist approach

---

[165] See http://unfccc.int/focus/mitigation/items/7907.php. Accessed on 20 August 2014.

[166] Hale 2013.

is not an objective in itself. The chapter has shown that several features of pluralist approaches could be criticized from the viewpoint of overall ambitions to achieve climate stabilization or their effects on smaller, less powerful countries.

The chapter has not sought to develop conclusions on which is the 'better' legal architecture. Instead, it has raised two questions that deserve further scrutiny. First, to what extent can we improve the balance between flexibility and stability in the design of the climate change regime itself? And second, how can we make use of the pluralism that already exists in international climate change law? With respect to the first question, the chapter has suggested that there still is ample scope for better utilizing the climate regime's flexibility mechanisms, for instance, making changes to procedural rules or by creating a more fine-grained and dynamic system of differentiation, or creating new review processes that link to changing conditions. Acknowledging the political limitations to some of these suggestions, the chapter has suggested that, in any event, there are benefits to enhancing coordination between the UNFCCC and the multitude of initiatives in the area of climate change.

On a concluding note, it should be evident that the issue area of climate change holds lessons for the study of temporality in international law. It can serve as a case study for studying the effectiveness of specific flexibility mechanisms (including those outlined in Sect. 10.2) in dealing with a problem that is in constant flux. Moreover, it offers insights into the advantages and drawbacks of legal architectures, and the tensions between ensuring flexibility and stability in international cooperation, particularly in the context of global public goods. Such insights could be linked to ongoing debates on the respective merits of constitutionalism versus legal pluralism,[167] although ideally they would need to be corroborated through complementary studies in other issue areas.

References

Akanle T et al. (2008) Summary of the fourteenth conference of parties to the UN Framework Convention on Climate Change and fourth meeting of parties to the Kyoto Protocol, 1–12 December 2008. Earth Negotiations Bulletin, vol 12

Alter K (2005) International courts are not agents! The perils of the principal-agent approach to thinking about the independence of international courts. Am Soc Int Law Proc 99:138–141

Barrett S (2007) A multitrack treaty system. In: Stavins RN, Aldy JE (eds) Architecture for agreement: addressing global climate change in the post-Kyoto world. Cambridge University Press, Cambridge, pp 237–259

Berk MM, den Elzen MGJ (2001) Options for differentiation of future commitments in climate policy: how to realise timely participation to meet stringent climate goals? Clim Policy 1:465–480

Berman PS (2012) Global legal pluralism: a jurisprudence of law beyond borders. Cambridge University Press, Cambridge

Bernstein S et al (2010) A tale of two Copenhagens: carbon markets and climate governance. Millennium 39:161–173

[167] See, e.g., Krisch 2010.

Biermann F et al (2009) The fragmentation of global governance architectures: a framework for analysis. Glob Environ Politics 9:14–40
Bodansky D (1993) The United Nations Framework Convention on Climate Change: a commentary. Yale J Int Law 18:451–558
Bodansky D (2003) Climate commitments: assessing the options. In: Diringer E (ed) Beyond Kyoto: advancing the international effort against climate change. Pew Center on Global Climate Change, Washington DC, pp 37–60
Bodansky D (2009) Legal form of a new climate agreement: avenues and options. Pew Center on Global Climate Change, Washington DC
Bodansky D (2010) The Copenhagen climate change conference: a postmortem. Am J Int Law 104:230–240
Boyd E et al (2008) UNFCCC negotiations (pre-Kyoto to COP-9): what the process says about the politics of CDM-sinks. Int Environ Agreem Politics, Law Econ 8:95–112
Boyd W (2011) Climate change, fragmentation, and the challenges of global environmental law: elements of a post-Copenhagen assemblage. Univ Pa J Int Law 32:457–550
Briner G et al (2014) Built to last: designing a flexible and durable 2015 climate change agreement. OECD, Paris
Brunnée J (2002) COPing with consent: law-making under multilateral environmental agreements. Leiden J Int Law 15:1–52
Brunnée J (2003) The Kyoto Protocol: testing ground for compliance theories? ZaöRV 63:255–280
Brunnée J, Streck C (2013) The UNFCCC as a negotiating forum: towards common but more differentiated responsibilities. Clim Policy 13:589–607
Bulkeley H (2010) Cities and the governing of climate change. Annu Rev Environ Resour 35:229–253
Chayes A, Chayes AH (1995) The new sovereignty: compliance with international regulatory agreements. Harvard University Press, Cambridge
Chayes A et al (1995) Active compliance management in environmental treaties. In: Lang W (ed) Sustainable development and international law. Graham and Trotman Ltd, London, pp 75–89
Churchill RR, Ulfstein G (2000) Autonomous institutional arrangements in multilateral environmental agreements: a little-noticed phenomenon in international law. Am J Int Law 94:623–659
Coglianese C, d'Ambrosio J (2008) Policymaking under pressure: the perils of incremental responses to climate change. Conn Law Rev 40:1413–1429
Cole DH (2011) From global to polycentric climate governance. Clim Law 2:395–413
Dannenmaier E (2011) The role of non-state actors in climate compliance. In: Brunnée J et al (eds) (2012) Promoting compliance in an evolving climate regime. Cambridge University Press, Cambridge, pp 149–176
De Búrca G et al (2014) Global experimentalist governance. Br J Polit Sci 44:477–486
de Coninck H et al (2008) International technology-oriented agreements to address climate change. Energy Policy 36:335–356
Depledge J (2000) Tracing the origins of the Kyoto Protocol: an article-by-article textual history, FCCC/TP/2000/2
Dietz T et al (2003) The struggle to govern the commons. Science 302:1907–1912
Doelle M (2013) Compliance and enforcement in the climate change regime. In: Hollo EJ et al (eds) Climate change and the law. Springer, Berlin, pp 165–188
Downs G et al (1996) Is the good news about compliance good news about cooperation? Int Organ 50:379–406
Dubash NK et al (2014) Political implications of data presentation. Science 345:36–37
Ebbesson J (2010) The rule of law in governance of complex socio-ecological changes. Glob Environ Change 20:414–422
Fischer-Lescano A, Teubner G (2004) Regime-collisions: the vain search for legal unity in the fragmentation of global law. Mich J Int Law 25:999–1046

Francioni F (2012) Realism, utopia and the future of international environmental law. EUI working papers law 2012/11
French D, Rajamani L (2013) Climate change and international environmental law: musings on a journey to somewhere. J Environ Law 25:437–461
Galiana I, Green C (2009) Let the global technology race begin. Nature 462:570–571
Giorgetti C (1999) From Rio to Kyoto: a study of the involvement of non-governmental organizations in the negotiations on climate change. NYU Environ Law J 7:201–245
Gupta J (1998) Leadership in the climate regime: inspiring the commitment of developing countries in the post-Kyoto phase. RECIEL 7:178–188
Haas PM (2004) Addressing the global governance deficit. Glob Environ Politics 4:1–15
Hale T (2013) How the UNFCCC can drive climate ambition in advance of a treaty: record, review, reinforce, recruit. Blavatnik School of Government, Oxford
Helfer L (2005) Exiting treaties. Va Law Rev 9:1579–1648
Helfer LR (2013) Flexibility in international agreements. In: Dunoff JL, Pollack MA (eds) Interdisciplinary perspective on international law and international relations: the state of the art. Cambridge University Press, Cambridge, pp 175–196
Hoffman MJ (2011) Climate governance at the crossroads: experimenting with a global response after Kyoto. Oxford University Press, New York
Honkonen T (2009) The principle of common but differentiated responsibility in post-2012 climate negotiations. RECIEL 18:257–267
Hulme M (2009) Why we disagree about climate change: understanding controversy, inaction and opportunity. Cambridge University Press, Cambridge
Jagers S, Stripple J (2003) Climate governance beyond the state. Glob Gov 9:385–399
Kaul I et al (1999) Global public goods: international cooperation in the 21st century. Oxford University Press, Oxford
Keohane RO, Victor DG (2011) The regime complex for climate change. Perspect Politics 9:7–23
Koremenos B et al (2001) The rational design of international institutions. Int Organ 55:761–799
Koskenniemi M (2007) The fate of public international law: between technique and politics. Mod Law Rev 70:1–30
Krisch N (2010) Beyond constitutionalism: the pluralist structure of postnational law. Oxford University Press, Oxford
Krisch N (2014) The decay of consent: international law in an age of global public goods. Am J Int Law 108:1–40
Kulovesi K (2013) Exploring the landscape of climate law and scholarship: two emerging trends. In: Hollo EJ et al (eds) Climate change and the law. Springer, Berlin, pp 31–62
Lazarus RJ (2009) Super wicked problems and climate change: restraining the present to liberate the future. Cornell Law Rev 94:1153–1233
Levin K et al (2012) Overcoming the tragedy of super wicked problems: constraining our future selves to ameliorate global climate change. Policy Sci 45:123–152
Lohan D (2006) Assessing the mechanisms for the input of scientific information into the UNFCCC. Colo J Int Environ Law Policy 17:249–308
Meinshausen M et al (2009) Greenhouse-gas emission targets for limiting global warming to 2 °C. Nature 458:1158–1162
Meyer T (2010) Power, exit costs, and renegotiation in international law. Harv Int Law J 51:379–425
Michaelowa A et al (2005) Graduation and deepening: an ambitious post-2012 climate policy scenario. Int Environ Agreem Politics, Law Econ 5:25–46
Moncel R, van Asselt H (2012) All hands on deck! Mobilizing climate change action beyond the UNFCCC. RECIEL 21:163–176
Morgan J et al (2013) A pathway to a climate change agreement in 2015: options for setting and reviewing GHG emission reduction offers. World Resources Institute, Washington DC
Naím M (2009) Minilateralism: the magic number to get real international action. Foreign Policy, July/August, pp 5–8

Oberthür S, Lefeber R (2010) Holding countries to account: the Kyoto Protocol's compliance system revisited after four years of experience. Clim Law 1:133–158
Osofsky H (2007) Climate change litigation as pluralist legal dialogue? Stanf Environ Law J 26:181–238
Ostrom E (2010) Polycentric systems for coping with collective action and global environmental change. Glob Environ Change 20:550–557
Pauwelyn J (2013) The end of differential treatment for developing countries? Lessons from the trade and climate change regimes. RECIEL 22:29–41
Peel J et al (2012) Climate change law in an era of multi-level governance. Transnatl Environ Law 1:245–280
Rajamani L (2010) The making and unmaking of the Copenhagen Accord. Int Comp Law Q 59:824–843
Rajamani L (2011) The Cancun climate change agreements: reading the text, subtext and tea leaves. Int Comp Law Q 60:499–519
Rayner S (2010) How to eat an elephant: a bottom-up approach to climate policy. Clim Policy 10:615–621
Rittel HWJ, Webber MM (1973) Dilemmas in a general theory of planning. Policy Sci 4:155–169
Rogelj J et al (2010) Copenhagen pledges are paltry. Nature 464:1126–1128
Sabel CF, Zeitlin J (2012) Experimentalist governance. In: Levi-Faur D (ed) The Oxford handbook of governance. Oxford University Press, Oxford, pp 169–183
Sands P, Peel J (2012) Principles of international environmental law. Cambridge University Press, Cambridge
Scott J (2011) The multi-level governance of climate change. Carbon Clim Law Rev 4:25–33
Shaffer G (2012) International law and global public goods in a legal pluralist world. Eur J Int Law 23:669–693
Singh Ghaleigh N (2011) Barriers to climate technology transfer—the chimera of intellectual property rights. Carbon Clim Law Rev 4:220–235
Thompson A (2006) Management under anarchy: the international politics of climate change. Clim Change 78:7–29
Thompson A (2010) Rational design in motion: uncertainty and flexibility in the global climate regime. Eur J Int Relat 16:269–296
van Asselt H (2014) The fragmentation of global climate governance: consequences and management of regime interactions. Edward Elgar, Cheltenham
van Asselt H (2015, forthcoming) The design and implementation of greenhouse gas emissions trading systems. In: Carlarne C et al (eds) The Oxford handbook of international climate change law. Oxford University Press, Oxford
van Asselt H, Gupta J (2009) Stretching too far: developing countries and the role of flexibility mechanisms beyond Kyoto. Stanf Environ Law J 28:311–378
van Asselt H, Zelli F (2014) Connect the dots: managing the fragmentation of global climate governance. Environ Econ Policy Stud 16:137–155
van Asselt H et al (2014) The changing architecture of international climate change law. In: van Calster G, Vandenberghe W (eds) Research handbook on climate change mitigation law. Edward Elgar, Cheltenham
Victor DG (2007) Fragmented carbon markets and reluctant nations: implications for the design of effective architectures. In: Stavins RN, Aldy JE (eds) Architecture for agreement: addressing global climate change in the post-Kyoto world. Cambridge University Press, Cambridge, pp 133–160
Victor DG et al (2006) A Madisonian approach to climate policy. Science 309:1820–1821
Verweij M et al (2006) Clumsy solutions for a complex world: the case of climate change. Public Admin 84:817–843
Vihma A (2015, forthcoming) Climate of consensus: managing the decision making in the UN climate change negotiations. RECIEL 24

Vihma A, Kulovesi K (2013) Can attention to the process improve the efficiency of the UNFCCC negotiations? Carbon Clim Law Rev 6:242–251

Wiersema A (2009) The new international law-makers? Conferences of the parties to multilateral environmental agreements. Mich J Int Law 31:231–287

Yamin F, Depledge J (2004) The international climate change regime: a guide to rules, institutions and procedures. Cambridge University Press, Cambridge

Young MA (2011) Climate change law and regime interaction. Carbon Clim Law Rev 4:147–157

Young OR (2002) The institutional dimensions of environmental change: fit, interplay, and scale. MIT Press, Cambridge

Young OR (2010) Institutional dynamics: emergent patterns in international environmental governance. MIT Press, Cambridge

Zelli F (2011) The fragmentation of the global climate governance architecture. WIREs Clim Change 2:255–270

Chapter 11
Commissions of Inquiry: Flexible Temporariness or Permanent Predictability?

Christian Henderson

Abstract Temporary commissions of inquiry have become more prominent over the past decade, with their establishment particularly noticeable in the context of the Arab Spring. Along with their increased prominence they have also displayed certain features of an adjudicative nature. Although primarily established as fact-finding bodies, their mandates now regularly include making assessments as to potential violations by particular entities of international human rights law and international humanitarian law. This chapter examines the impact that commissions of inquiry as temporary creations have had upon international law and, more specifically, upon international legal adjudication, in particular the traditional formality of international legal adjudication, the principle prohibiting intervention in the internal affairs of states, and procedural fairness. While the temporariness of commissions of inquiry is in many ways unproblematic, this chapter identifies certain problems and examines the possibilities for the establishment of a permanent commission as a means to rectify some of the issues associated with their current temporary nature.

Keywords Fact-finding commissions of inquiry · Adjudication · Non-intervention · Procedural fairness · Arab Spring

---

Senior Lecturer in Law and Director of the Human Rights and International Law Unit at the University of Liverpool.

C. Henderson (✉)
University of Liverpool, Merseyside, UK
e-mail: christian.henderson@liverpool.ac.uk

M. Ambrus and R.A. Wessel (eds.), *Netherlands Yearbook of International Law 2014*, Netherlands Yearbook of International Law 45, DOI 10.1007/978-94-6265-060-2_11

Contents

11.1 Introduction ... 288
11.2 Commissions of Inquiry as Temporary Adjudicative Bodies of International Law ... 289
11.3 The Impact of Temporary Commissions of Inquiry Upon International Legal Adjudication ... 295
11.3.1 The Formality of International Legal Adjudication ... 295
11.3.2 The Principle of Non-intervention ... 300
11.3.3 Procedural Fairness ... 303
11.4 Concluding Remarks: A Permanent Commission of Inquiry? ... 307
References ... 310

11.1 Introduction

Commissions of inquiry (CoIs) are bodies established on a temporary basis to undertake fact-finding missions in order to offer some form of judgment or conclusion upon particular incidents of the use of force, armed conflict, or alleged human rights violations. As a concept they are not a new phenomenon and can be traced back to the *Maine* inquiries of 1898, which were established by both the US and Spain following an explosion on a US battleship.[1] Since that time they have taken on various incarnations from pure fact-finding bodies to providing a form of legally binding arbitration.[2] However, there has recently been a discernible rise in their utilisation, in particular in the context of the Arab Spring.[3] These contemporary CoIs, while not producing legally binding outcomes, nonetheless carry out various adjudicative functions, from determining applicable legal frameworks and the scope of the legal rules and norms in question to determining whether particular acts amount to violations of these rules and norms.

Given the incident-specific context in which they operate, the temporariness of CoIs seems at first glance to be an inherent and necessary feature. Yet, in certain other institutional legal contexts there has been a move—and some might say a natural and logical one—away from temporary institutions to those of a permanent nature. The establishment of the permanent International Criminal Court (ICC), which followed the temporary context-specific precedents of the International Criminal Tribunal for the former Yugoslavia (ICTY) and International Criminal Tribunal for Rwanda (ICTR), is an obvious example of this. However, CoIs have, in many respects, demonstrated a shift away from an under-utilised permanent body—the International Humanitarian Fact Finding Commission (IHFFC) that was established in 1977 but which has rarely been utilised since[4]—to the increasingly

---

[1] Merrills 2011, at 41–42.

[2] See Sect. 11.2 for more on the different forms that CoIs have taken.

[3] CoIs have been established in the context of the uprisings in Bahrain, Libya, and Syria.

[4] The IHFFC was established in Article 90 of 1977 Additional Protocol I to the 1949 Geneva Conventions, 1125 UNTS 3.

frequent establishment of those of a temporary nature, such as in Darfur,[5] Libya,[6] Syria,[7] and North Korea.[8] Today, CoIs, whether established by states, regional organisations, or by the various organs of the United Nations,[9] offer what may be the only, or at least most formal, treatment of the legal issues raised in the context of a particular conflict or crisis, and perhaps represent an important shift in the *modus operandi* of the international community in seeking at least some accountability for violations of international law.

The central purpose of this chapter is to examine the impact that CoIs as temporary creations have had upon international law and, more specifically, upon international legal adjudication. After setting out their contemporary function as temporary adjudicative bodies of international law, it identifies and examines three areas of international legal adjudication which are perhaps most sensitive to impact through the emergence and utilisation of CoIs. These are the traditional formality of international legal adjudication, the principle prohibiting intervention in the internal affairs of states, including the consensual basis for international adjudication, and finally, procedural fairness. While the temporariness of the commissions is unproblematic from many perspectives, certain identifiable problems nonetheless arise. This chapter lastly examines the possibilities for the establishment of a permanent CoI as a means to rectify some of the issues associated with their current temporary nature.

11.2 Commissions of Inquiry as Temporary Adjudicative Bodies of International Law

It is hard to find elements of a legally adjudicative nature within the *Maine* inquiries of 1898, which are regarded as the first CoIs, whether in their mandates, personnel, or outcomes.[10] However, they 'sufficiently impressed the delegates to the Hague Peace Conference of 1899 for them to give serious attention to the issue of fact-finding in international disputes.'[11] Indeed, following on from these formative CoIs of a purely fact-finding nature, and in an initial attempt to provide some form of regulation to them, the 1899 Hague Convention for the Peaceful Settlement of

[5] UNSC Res. 1564, 18 September 2004, para 12.

[6] Situation of Human Rights in the Libyan Arab Jamahiriya, UN Doc. A/HRC-S/15/1, 25 February 2011, para 11.

[7] Situation of Human Rights in the Syrian Arab Republic, UN Doc. A/HRC-S/17/1, 22 August, 2011, para 13.

[8] Situation of Human Rights in the Democratic People's Republic of Korea, UN Doc. A/HRC/RES/22/13, 21 March 2013, para 4.

[9] This article consciously excludes reports issued by non-governmental organisations, such as Human Rights Watch, as its focus will be upon CoIs in which states have been involved in their creation.

[10] Merrills 2011, at 41–42. They were, by contrast, focused almost exclusively on the disagreement over the interpretation of evidence.

[11] Ibid., at 42.

Disputes envisaged such inquires to be used for disputes of fact and not questions of law and that their findings should not be obligatory.[12] However, CoIs have nonetheless generally shifted from pure fact-finding bodies to providing at least some form of legal adjudication, even if not often of a legally binding nature. This shift did not take long to manifest itself as in the *Dogger Bank* inquiry of 1904, which involved a naval dispute between England and Russia,

> [T]he duty to apportion 'blame' appeared to assign the Commission an arbitral as well as a fact-finding function. The admirals who made up the Commission, no doubt wisely, sought to underplay this aspect of their work and in a decision of somewhat ambiguous legal import, demonstrated what later experience was to confirm, that in the interests of dispute settlement, legal and factual issues need not always be sharply distinguished.[13]

While for many years these CoIs were, as in the *Dogger Bank* inquiry, composed almost exclusively of naval officers, the *Tubantia* inquiry 1921 between Germany and the Netherlands was the 'first case in which a commission of inquiry had included a lawyer among its members'[14] and, despite the parties not accepting the commission's report as binding, was 'also notable for the extent to which the proceedings resembled arbitration'.[15] The *Tiger* inquiry of 1917, between Germany and Norway, was the first CoI in which the report was accepted as binding upon the parties.[16] Things developed further with the *Red Crusader* inquiry of 1961 involving Denmark and Great Britain as

> in respect of its composition, its procedure and its findings the … Commission was a fundamentally judicial operation. A majority of the Commission were jurists and had the tribunal been a court of arbitration its blend of legal and non-legal expertise would have been in no way unusual.[17]

As in the *Red Crusader*, the task given to the *Letelier and Moffitt* CoI of 1988 between the US and Chile 'was essentially judicial and this was reflected in all stages of its work.'[18] For example, 'it is notable that the *Compromis* specifically required the Commission to give its decision "in accordance with applicable principles of international law"' and that '[t]he Commission's decision, like the report in the *Red Crusader*, included several important legal rulings, as well as numerous findings of fact.'[19] Indeed, 'the Commission which was eventually set up functioned less as an inquiry commission'—of the traditional type and like that that are

[12] The 1899 Convention for the Pacific Settlement of Disputes, 1 Bevans 230, at 230. See also ibid. While this article will generally employ the term 'commissions of inquiry' there does not appear to be any generally distinguishing features of these bodies from 'fact-finding' missions.

[13] Merrils 2011, at 44.

[14] Ibid., at 47.

[15] Ibid.

[16] Ibid., at 46.

[17] Ibid., at 50.

[18] Ibid., at 52.

[19] Ibid., at 53.

in existence today[20]—and 'more like a court of arbitration, producing a binding decision and deciding issues of law as well as fact.'[21] It was, in essence, a notable departure from the concept and function of the CoI as envisaged in the 1899 Hague Convention, manifesting a discernable shift in their nature from being non-legal and non-binding bodies towards operating increasingly like courts of law, albeit of a temporary nature, arbitrating disputes between two states.

Contemporary CoIs, however, and particularly those of the past 10 years, have led to another reshaping of our understanding of the nature and function of CoIs. Objections might immediately be raised to describing these CoIs, as with those described above, as 'adjudicative' bodies or mechanisms on the basis that they are not formally established judicial bodies. Yet, while the commissioners of some contemporary CoIs have included judges,[22] to claim that CoIs cannot represent a new form of legal adjudication upon this basis would seem unduly restrictive. The Oxford English Dictionary, for example, imposes no such boundaries, stating only that adjudication is 'an act of determining, settling, or awarding something *judicially, or by a similar legal or official process*'.[23] In this respect it is significant that CoIs have been described as 'quasi-judicial bodies' in the context of international adjudication,[24] with Alvarez drawing little distinction between 'judicial' and 'quasi-judicial' bodies.[25] The CoI on Darfur itself stated that 'in classifying the facts according to international criminal law, the Commission adopted an approach proper to a judicial body.'[26]

It is also perhaps important to address the *function* and process of CoIs, as opposed to their *personnel*. It was on this basis that Merrills described many of the earlier CoIs above as 'judicial'. In this respect, however, modern CoIs rarely offer a dispute settlement function between states, as did the earlier CoIs above, and certainly not of an arbitral nature. Yet, this again is not decisive as to their adjudicative nature. For example, in the chapter of the *Oxford Handbook of International Adjudication* which examines 'the main functions of international adjudication', it is acknowledged that international adjudication is often portrayed as 'interstate dispute settlers engaged in avoiding or deterring threats to the peace'.[27] However, it is also acknowledged that this 'does not really describe, for example, the functions of international criminal courts (which pits a prosecutor, who might be seen as a representative of the international community, against an individual), [or] regional human rights courts (which consider whether states have abused individual rights)'.[28]

---

[20] For more on contemporary CoIs see further in this section.

[21] Merrills 2011, at 53.

[22] See Sect. 11.3.1.

[23] Oxford English Dictionary, http://www.oed.com (emphasis added). Accessed 15 July 2014.

[24] See Buchan 2014.

[25] Alvarez 2005, at 516.

[26] See Report of the International Commission of Inquiry on Darfur to the United Nations Secretary-General, UN Doc. S/2005/60, 1 February 2005, at para 14.

[27] Alvarez 2014, at 159.

[28] Ibid., at 169.

Indeed, '[i]nternational adjudication, as much else in international law, no longer involves states as the only litigants.'[29] Thus while CoIs are very often not of an inter-state nature, and following the general shift from *inter*-state to *intra*-state conflicts,[30] they can arguably be encompassed into the modern definition of adjudication.

An additional objection to viewing contemporary CoIs in the context of more formal adjudicative mechanisms might be raised in respect to the non-binding nature of their findings. Yet, there is nothing to suggest that the reports of adjudicative bodies must be binding. Furthermore, '[a]lthough these bodies are not fully judicial and therefore the contents of the reports that they produce are not legally binding, this certainly does not mean that they are without significance.'[31] On the contrary, while often still described as 'fact-finding' missions, they nonetheless also—and importantly—provide more general determinations as to whether violations of international law have taken place. A good example of this is provided in the mandate for the CoI in Darfur which was set up

> to investigate reports of violations of international humanitarian law and human rights law in Darfur by all parties – to determine whether or not acts of genocide have occurred – to identify the perpetrators of such violations with a view to ensuring that those responsible are held accountable.[32]

This is a significant shift from the arbitral nature that CoIs formerly occasionally possessed, as identified above. The shift from offering a dispute settlement function between states to providing a more general form of legal accountability perhaps could be attributed, along with the shift from inter-state to intra-state conflicts, to the emergence of the recognition of the *erga omnes* nature of the laws and obligations under focus.[33] The relatively recent emergence of the Responsibility to

[29] Ibid.

[30] During this period not a single CoI has been established to provide a medium for dispute settlement between states. Even the CoI on Israel's forcible intervention in Lebanon in 2006 examined only the actions of Israel and their impact upon civilians. See Report of the Commission of Inquiry on Lebanon pursuant to Human Rights Council resolution S-2/1, UN Doc. A/HRC/3/2, 23 November 2006. See also, generally, Stewart 2007. Perhaps the closest one might come to finding such an inter-state dispute settlement function in a contemporary CoI, particularly given the fact that the CoI itself determined the conflict to be of an international nature, is the CoI on the Gaza conflict of 2008/09 in which the commission was mandated to investigate *all* violations of international humanitarian law and international human rights law during this conflict. See Report of the United Nations Fact-Finding Mission on the Gaza Conflict, UN Doc. A/HRC/12/48, 25 September 2009. See also, generally, Yihdego 2012.

[31] Buchan 2014, at 496.

[32] UNSC Res. 1564, 18 September 2004, at para 12. Frulli notes that this a good example of an 'accountability driven mandate'. Frulli 2012, at 1329. See also the mandate for the CoI on the Gaza conflict: Report of the United Nations Fact-Finding Mission on the Gaza Conflict, UN Doc. A/HRC/12/48, 25 September 2009.

[33] In the *Barcelona Traction* case the protection of human rights was characterised by the ICJ as an obligation *erga omnes*, thus making their protection a concern of all states. See *Case concerning Barcelona Traction, Light and Power Company Ltd (Belgium v. Spain)*, ICJ, Merits, Judgment of 5 February 1970, at 32.

Protect concept (R2P), which highlighted the primary responsibility of states to protect those within their borders along with the secondary responsibility of the international community in this respect, may have furthered this shift,[34] in addition to the fact that, unlike many of the earlier CoIs, the UN has taken a leading role in their establishment.[35]

Furthermore, contemporary CoIs often go beyond 'merely' identifying violations of international human rights law, international humanitarian law, and international criminal law to making in fact quite detailed determinations on points of international law, a function traditionally associated with more formal and permanent legal adjudicative bodies. For example, CoIs have often made determinations as to the applicable legal framework in regards to the factual situations they have been called upon to investigate. A manifestation of this assumed role can be found in the classification of armed conflicts as either international or non-international, an exercise that determines the applicable branch of international humanitarian law. This was something that the CoI in Darfur, for example, engaged in.[36] The CoI on Darfur also set out in some detail the relevant international obligations binding upon both the government and the rebels.[37] In doing so the CoI was building upon the case law of the ad hoc international criminal tribunals for the former Yugoslavia and Rwanda and upon the rules as set out in the ICC statute.[38]

CoIs have also made determinations as to the scope of the legal norms at issue and, in some cases, have provided significant developments in the law. The CoI on Syria, for example, engaged in detailed discussions on whether particular acts amounted to violations of international humanitarian law or human rights law.[39] Furthermore, the CoI on Darfur pronounced upon what amounts to a protected group for the purposes of the Genocide Convention,[40] while one may contend that the report of the CoI on Yugoslavia was 'a first step towards the gradual recognition of sexual crimes not only as war crimes but also as a method or means of

34 The concept was first introduced in Report of the International Commission on Intervention and State Sovereignty, *The Responsibility to Protect*, December 2001, http://responsibilitytoprotect.org/ICISS%20Report.pdf. Accessed 15 July 2014. For a comprehensive examination of its contours, see, generally, Knight and Egerton 2012.

35 In this respect, '[t]he UN, moving beyond traditional fact-finding, has begun to entrust commissions of inquiry with the search for evidence of IHL violations and with a prima facie evaluation of the facts based on international legal parameters, so as to ensure accountability for serious IHL violations and other international crimes.' Frulli 2012, at 1328–1329.

36 See Report of the International Commission of Inquiry on Darfur to the United Nations Secretary-General, UN Doc. S/2005/60, 1 February 2005, paras 74–76.

37 Ibid., paras 142–174.

38 As pointed out by Akande and Tonkin 2012.

39 See, for example, Report of the Independent Commission of Inquiry on the Syrian Arab Republic, UN Doc. A/HRC/S-17/2/Add.1, 23 November 2011, paras 84–100.

40 Report of the International Commission of Inquiry on Darfur to the United Nations Secretary-General, UN Doc. S/2005/60, 1 February 2005, section 2.

warfare, when perpetrated in a systematic way and used as a strategy to weaken the enemy.'[41]

In the absence of an alternative international adjudicative mechanism, or at least one in a position to exercise its jurisdiction, CoIs do seem to be an additional form of not only resolving contested facts but also obtaining authoritative determinations as to whether violations of international law have taken place and, if so, who is responsible, as well as the making of important pronouncements upon international law. Their interventions may not only embolden one of the parties to the conflict in its particular claims but also influence public perceptions as to the legality of the actions of those involved. Indeed, the reports of these commissions and the decisions reached, though not formally binding, may end up being just as authoritative, whether in the public, political or legal realm, as more formal permanent judicial processes as well as often establishing facts that then become difficult to dispute.[42] As a consequence, the treatment of legal issues in a CoI is of some significance, as it provides what may be the only, or at least most formal, treatment of them in the context of a particular situation or conflict.

The four functions of international adjudication, not necessarily equally discernable in each adjudicative body, have been identified as dispute settlement, fact-finding, law making, and governance.[43] Given the fact that on the basis of the above it can be said that most contemporary CoIs have performed these functions, and thus have arguably assumed an important role in international legal adjudication, it becomes questionable whether they have replaced or, at least, are beginning to replace, more formal modes of adjudication. In any case, they may nonetheless enhance adjudicative mechanisms where those exist, either by providing the impetus for calls of referral to the ICC,[44] as we have witnessed, for example, in the context of the CoIs on Darfur,[45] Libya, and Syria but also very recently with the publication of the CoI on North Korea, through to the findings of CoIs being drawn upon by other adjudicative mechanisms, something that was witnessed, for example, in the use of report of the Porter Commission by the International Court

[41] Frulli 2012, at 1327.

[42] Akande and Tonkin 2012.

[43] Alvarez 2014. In respect to the final of these functions, governance, Alvarez has stated that '[w]hether or not adjudicators resort to normative policy judgments, their clarifications of law and fact serve a governance function by reducing uncertainty within distinct regimes as well as within states.' Ibid., at 176. As the above description of some of the work of contemporary CoIs demonstrates, this is a function which they have also arguably performed.

[44] Frulli describes this as 'prosecution oriented fact-finding'. Frulli 2012, at 1330.

[45] The CoI on Dafur stated that 'it would make an assessment of possible suspects that would pave the way for future investigations, and possible indictments, by a prosecutor.' See Report of the International Commission of Inquiry on Darfur to the United Nations Secretary-General, UN Doc. S/2005/60, 1 February 2005, para 15. This resulted in 'the issuance of an authoritative determination of serious IHL violations that prompted the Security Council to refer the situation to the ICC.' Frulli 2012, at 1329.

of Justice (ICJ) in the *DRC v Uganda* case.[46] The CoIs in Yugoslavia and Rwanda are also, of course, demonstrative of how CoIs may lead to the establishment of further ad hoc bodies in the form of international criminal tribunals.[47]

11.3 The Impact of Temporary Commissions of Inquiry Upon International Legal Adjudication

The previous section demonstrated that in their contemporary form CoIs provide a significant additional, albeit temporary, form of accountability. Their underlying fact-finding nature means that they do so firstly by exposing, documenting, and clarifying events that have taken place within certain states or during the course of a conflict. Secondly, as highlighted above, they have also had an impact upon particular branches of international law and their substantive individual rules and norms through determining specific violations, pronouncing upon the scope of these rules and norms, as well as in some cases developing them.[48] However, there are three specific aspects of international legal adjudication which are, due to the temporariness of CoIs, particularly sensitive to their emergence and increasingly frequent utilisation: the traditional formality of international legal adjudication, the principle prohibiting intervention in the internal affairs of states, and procedural fairness. This section will briefly set out if, and if so how, these aspects have been impacted upon by contemporary CoIs before going on to examine whether a need exists to replace these temporary bodies with a permanent creation.

11.3.1 The Formality of International Legal Adjudication

Given the adjudicative function that contemporary CoIs appear to possess, the informality by which they are established is, in many respects, surprising. Judicial institutions or accountability mechanisms are most often formally established through a statute, treaty, or a charter, whereas CoIs, on the other hand, are not. Yet, this may not be a feature of their temporariness as the temporary International Criminal Tribunals (ICTs) were also established under a statute annexed to a

[46] The Porter Commission, chaired by Justice David Porter, was a CoI established by the Ugandan government in 2001 and issued its findings in May 2003. The ICJ found the CoI's factual findings particularly reliable due to the standards employed by the CoI and the testimony of Ugandan officials. *Case Concerning Armed Activities on the Territory of the Congo (Democratic Republic of the Congo v Uganda)*, ICJ, Judgment of 19 December 2005.

[47] These CoIs were established by the UNSC pursuant to UNSC Res. 780, 6 October 1992 and UNSC Res. 935, 1 July 1994, respectively.

[48] See, for example, Yihdego 2012; Stewart 2007; and Heller 2014.

resolution of the UNSC.[49] The formality regarding the establishment of adjudicative mechanisms might as such not be dependent upon whether they are temporary or permanent, but instead upon the concrete and direct consequences attached to the findings of the body, in particular whether or not they are legally binding and the consequences flowing from this.

However, even if we are to explain the informality behind the establishment of CoIs by the absence of powers to produce legally binding outcomes, they will nonetheless often have a broader impact than some of the more formally established mechanisms for accountability, such as the ICJ. For example, the findings and reports of CoIs might lead to the establishment of ad hoc ICTs, domestic investigation and prosecution, or referral to the ICC. They might also make other recommendations such as ratifying the Rome Statute of the ICC, releasing persons who are arbitrarily detained, or allowing full media access. Finally, they may provide the only, or at least most formal, treatment of the legal issues. It might as such be argued that the non-binding nature of the outcomes of CoIs makes such formal establishment unnecessary, while the flexibility in the outcomes they may ultimately provide makes it unattractive.

While CoIs may be established by a broader range of actors than more traditional formal modes of legal adjudication, which in itself is indicative of their informality, the authority, significance and impact that a particular CoI will ultimately possess will be dependent to a large extent upon the identity and authority of the actor behind its establishment. For example, CoIs established by states investigating actions that they themselves have been involved in will always have problems with presenting themselves and their findings as impartial. Such an accusation might be targeted towards the Turkel Commission which was established by the Israeli government to investigate the Gaza flotilla raid and the blockade of Gaza and which ultimately cleared the government and the military of any wrongdoing and of any violation of international law.[50] This perception in regards to a lack of impartiality was not, however, a problem in connection with the CoI on Bahrain, which 'was established and funded by the King of Bahrain, but the commission conducted investigations and administered its budget independently, and ultimately delivered a report that was highly critical of the ruling regime.'[51]

Individuals and organs of the UN have not escaped criticism in this respect. The UN Human Rights Council (UNHRC), in its now embedded role of establishing

---

[49] See UNSC Res. 827, 25 May 1993; and UNSC Res. 955, 8 November 1994, and associated annexes.

[50] See the Public Commission to Examine the Maritime Incident of 31st May 2010, January 2011, http://www.turkel-committee.com/index.html. Accessed 15 July 2014. There was widespread criticism of the Turkel Commission as a tool to justify the raid and the blockade of Gaza. See The public has a right to know: The government's efforts to avoid a thorough and credible investigation of the flotilla affair seem more and more like a farce, *Haaretz*, 13 June 2010, http://www.haaretz.com/print-edition/opinion/the-public-has-a-right-to-know-1.295797. Accessed 15 July 2014.

[51] Akande and Tonkin 2012. See, in general, Bahrain Independent Commission of Inquiry, 23 November 2011, http://www.bici.org.bh/. Accessed 15 July 2014.

CoIs, has been accused of establishing those with certain predispositions, one sided mandates, and ultimately possessing no powers of enforcement.[52] This may mean in many cases that they have lacked impact, for example, in the subsequent criminal prosecution of alleged offenders.[53] Question marks have also been placed over the authority of the UN Secretary-General to establish CoIs.[54] Those established by the UN Security Council (UNSC), on the other hand, arguably possess a greater level of authority in that they have required the support of the permanent members of the Council. The flip side to this, of course, is that CoIs established by this organ have proved rare for this very reason.[55] They are, however, potentially supported by powers of enforcement immediately at the UNSC's disposal, of both a non-forcible and forcible nature, which other organs of the UN, such as the UNHRC, UN Secretariat, or UN General Assembly, lack.

Furthermore, it would appear that in addition to the general informality of the establishment of CoIs they are also free to define the breadth and contours of their mandate. This means that what they ultimately do does not necessarily mirror what they were established to do. For example, they may not have been mandated to address violations of international law at all but go on to subsequently place a substantial focus upon them, as demonstrated by the UK's Chilcot Inquiry on its involvement in the conflict in Iraq between 2001 and 2009. This particular CoI was expressly established by Gordon Brown, the UK's Prime Minister, with the intention of 'learn[ing] the lessons from the events surrounding the conflict' so as to 'strengthen the health of our democracy, our diplomacy and our military',[56] with no mention of international law. The Chilcot Inquiry subsequently expressly interpreted its mandate so as to address international legal issues arising from the conflict. At the launch of the inquiry on 30 July 2009, for example, its Chair, Sir John Chilcot, provided it with a mandate to 'judge[…] … the arguments about the legality of the conflict.'[57] While at first this may be taken to be in regards to the issues surrounding the legality of the invasion of Iraq in March 2003, the Inquiry also addressed legal issues that arose throughout the period under focus, that is, between the summer of 2001 to the end of July in 2009.[58]

Alternatively, CoIs may not have been asked to address violations of a particular branch of international law, yet, they nonetheless proceed to do so. For example, the

[52] Frulli 2012, at 1332–1337.

[53] Ibid., at 1335–1336.

[54] Akande and Tonkin 2012. The UN Secretary-General established the Palmer Committee on the Israeli blockade on Gaza and the Sri Lanka Panel of Experts, among others.

[55] In particular, CoIs in Rwanda, Yugoslavia, and Darfur.

[56] See http://www.publications.parliament.uk/pa/cm200809/cmhansrd/cm090615/debtext/90615-0004.htm. Accessed 15 July 2014.

[57] See Statement of Sir John Chilcot, Chairman of the Iraq Inquiry, at a news conference on Thursday, 30 July 2009, http://www.iraqinquiry.org.uk/about/statement.aspx. Accessed 15 July 2014.

[58] However, given that its report is only expected in 2014 the extent of its ultimate focus upon the legal issues awaits to be seen.

CoI in Syria was established by the UNHRC in resolution S-17/1 on 23 August 2011 'to investigate all alleged violations of *international human rights law* since March 2011 in the Syrian Arab Republic'.[59] Yet, even in its first report in November 2011 when there was no discernable armed conflict within Syria, the CoI provided itself with a mandate that went beyond that provided to it so as to address possible violations of international humanitarian law and international criminal law.[60] Of course, while there are issues of procedural fairness arising from this aspect of its informality,[61] the flexibility provided by the underlying informality of this particular form of international legal adjudication may ultimately ensure greater accountability as CoIs are able to pursue different avenues of inquiry depending upon the changing circumstances presented by the investigation and the facts found.

Lastly, in connection with their mandates, CoIs may be asked to address suspected breaches of the law by one of the parties to a conflict, yet, go on to also determine those of other parties. An example of this practice can be found in the CoI established by the UNHRC to investigate Israel's *Operation Cast Lead* in Gaza in 2008–2009. UNHRC resolution S-9/1 of 12 January 2009 mandated the UN Fact-Finding Mission on the Gaza Conflict to investigate 'all violations of international human rights law and international humanitarian law *by the occupying Power, Israel, against the Palestinian people* throughout the Occupied Palestinian Territory, particularly in the occupied Gaza Strip, due to the current aggression.'[62] The chief of the mission, Richard Goldstone, accepted to chair the Commission only after rebalancing the mandate.[63] Subsequently, in the final report of the Commission, the mandate was stated as being to investigate

> *all violations of international human rights law and international humanitarian law that might have been committed at any time* in the context of the military operations that were conducted in Gaza during the period from 27 December 2008 and 18 January 2009, whether before, during, or after.[64]

While the report of the Goldstone Commission came in for much criticism,[65] this correction to the *ratione personae* scope of its mandate is one aspect that is to be applauded.[66] Such one-sided mandates put the credibility and impartiality of the

---

[59] UNHRC Res. S-17/1, 23 August 2011, para 13 (emphasis added).

[60] See 1st report of the Commission of Inquiry on the Syrian Arab Republic, UNHRC Res. S-17/2/Add.1, 23 November 2011.

[61] See Sect. 11.3.3.

[62] The grave violations of human rights in the Occupied Palestinian Territory, particularly due to the recent Israeli military attacks against the occupied Gaza Strip, UNHCR Res. S-9/1, 12 January 2009, para 14 (emphases added).

[63] Frulli 2012, at 1334, note 37.

[64] See Report of the United Nations Fact-Finding Mission on the Gaza Conflict, UN Doc. A/HRC/12/48, 25 September 2009 (emphasis added). For a comprehensive analysis, see, in general, Yihdego 2012.

[65] See, in general, Yihdego 2012.

[66] Although as the CoI on Lebanon demonstrates, a power to rebalance the mandate is one that is not always exercised.

CoI in jeopardy, two elements which have been widely recognised as essential for successful investigations.[67] In addition, there are several rules of international humanitarian law in which it is normally essential to examine the actions of both the attacker *and* the defender, for example, in determining whether a civilian object was a lawful target.[68] While this rebalancing of the mandate was as such undoubtedly the correct thing to do in terms of protecting the authority of the CoI, the informality surrounding this delegation of powers from the formal establishing authority to the commission itself is surprising on the one hand, given the adjudicative functions that CoIs today possess, yet understandable on the other given the flexibility that states have seemingly entrusted CoIs with.

As a final point, the informality that CoIs have introduced into international legal adjudication is also reflected in the fact that even in those CoIs in which determining violations of the law is given prominence, the members are very often not judges, or even lawyers of any description. While the CoIs on Darfur and Gaza, for example, had judges or those with judicial experience involved,[69] the CoI on Syria has never had any judges as members and was not originally established with any international lawyers among its membership, although this changed with the departure of Yakin Ertürk from the Commission in March 2012 and the subsequent appointment of Carla del Ponte and Professor Vitit Muntarbhorn in September 2012.[70] The Commission does have a secretariat that is possessed of a broad range of expertise in the field of human rights investigations and international law. This is not exactly an unusual arrangement for a CoI. As a slight variation on this model, the UK's Chilcot Inquiry on the Iraq conflict does not have a lawyer, let alone an international lawyer among its members, but instead an external adviser on international law in the form of Dame Rosalyn Higgins. Nonetheless, while, as noted above, the Chilcot Inquiry addressed legal issues, they are not its main focus, unlike with the CoI on Syria, where they are. In this respect, while the initial panel of the CoI on Syria had notable experience in the field of human rights, given that the key mandate of the Commission was in connection with international human rights *law*, the appointment of at least one expert with a specific legal background from the beginning might have been a sensible move, as has been the case with other CoIs. The broader significance of this, perhaps, is that there is apparently no longer a need for judges, or even the involvement of lawyers, or lawyers with specific expertise in the field in question, in making potentially significant determinations of international law. Ultimately, along with the other elements identified above, such flexibility is both a cause and a product of their informality as an adjudicative mechanism.

---

[67] See, for example, Boutruche 2011; Frulli 2012.

[68] Stewart 2007, at 1041; Frulli 2012, at 1335; Boutruche 2011, at 22–26.

[69] For example, Antonio Cassese was a part of the CoI on Darfur while Richard Goldstone chaired the CoI on the Gaza conflict.

[70] Carla del Ponte was former Chief Prosecutor of two United Nations international criminal tribunals while Vitit Muntarbhorn is an international law professor.

11.3.2 The Principle of Non-intervention

The principle of non-intervention 'involves the right of every sovereign State to conduct its affairs without outside interference.'[71] While the exact contours of this principle are not clearly defined, Article 2(7) of the Charter of the United Nations (UN Charter) provides that '[n]othing contained in the present Charter shall authorize the United Nations to intervene in matters which are essentially within the domestic jurisdiction of any state' and states have repeatedly reaffirmed that '[n]o State has the right to intervene, directly or indirectly, for any reason whatever, in the internal or external affairs of any other State.'[72] An important element in the way that the ICJ in the *Nicaragua* case of 1986 defined unlawful intervention was that a transgression of the principle occurs only once the act of intervention takes on a form of 'coercion'.[73] In particular, any intervention must not dictate 'matters in which each State is permitted, by the principle of State sovereignty, to decide freely', for example, a state's political, economic, social and cultural choices.[74] Thus, while comment is regularly made regarding situations that are occurring in another state, the principle of non-intervention only becomes engaged once the intervening state or organisation seeks to coerce that state into making certain choices or taking—or being subjected to—certain actions.[75]

This raises the question as to how CoIs might potentially pose a challenge to the principle of non-intervention. Traditionally, and as a result of their sovereignty and independence and as a manifestation of the principle of non-intervention, states were not subject to the external authority or scrutiny of other states, or institutions created by other states, without their consent. Similarly, before an international court or tribunal has jurisdiction over a dispute involving a particular state, that state must accept the authority of the court or tribunal to rule upon it.

[71] *Military and Paramilitary Activities in and Against Nicaragua (Nicaragua v United States)*, ICJ, Jurisdiction and Admissibility, Judgment of 26 November 1984, para 202.

[72] See, for example, Declaration on the Inadmissibility of Intervention in the Domestic Affairs of States and the Protection of Their Independence and Sovereignty, UNGA Res. 2131 (XX), 21 December 1965, para 1; Declaration on Principles of International Law Concerning Friendly Relations and Co-operation among States in Accordance with the Charter of the United Nations, UNGA Res. 2625 (XXV), 24 October 1970, annex; Article 19 of the 1948 Charter of the Organization of American States, 119 UNTS 3.

[73] *Military and Paramilitary Activities in and Against Nicaragua (Nicaragua v United States)*, ICJ, Jurisdiction and Admissibility, Judgment of 26 November 1984, at para 205; Declaration on the Inadmissibility of Intervention in the Domestic Affairs of States and the Protection of Their Independence and Sovereignty, UNGA Res. 2131 (XX), 21 December 1965, paras 1–2, 5; Declaration on Principles of International Law Concerning Friendly Relations and Co-operation among States in Accordance with the Charter of the United Nations, UNGA Res. 2625 (XXV), 24 October 1970, annex, para 1, principle 3.

[74] *Military and Paramilitary Activities in and Against Nicaragua (Nicaragua v United States)*, ICJ, Jurisdiction and Admissibility, Judgment of 26 November 1984.

[75] Henderson 2013, at 647.

Consent for more formal, and permanent, mechanisms of adjudication, such as the ICC and the ICJ, is normally provided through the signing and ratification of a treaty or, in the case of the ICC in certain circumstances or in the case of the ICTs, through the UNSC's enforcement mandate.[76] In the domestic context, state authorities are often subject to judicial review by a higher court within the state, while the actions of individuals and other actors are subject to civil and criminal proceedings, through the constitutional apparatus of that particular state, thereby negating the need for consent by the authorities or individuals concerned.

In this respect, and in light of the fact that they have, arguably, come to represent a new form of international legal adjudication, '[t]he establishment of these commissions appears to depart from the principle of consent which applies to international adjudication.'[77] Indeed, '[f]ar from having the consent of the State under investigation, international commissions of inquiry often operate against the will of that State.'[78] For example, while not having the consent of either the Assad government or the opposition forces under investigation, the CoI in Syria has operated against the will of both, or at least without their consent. In the absence of a consensual basis or a Chapter VII mandate CoIs may consequently represent an unlawful intervention into the affairs of the state concerned, with their rise to prominence thus posing a more general challenge to the principle of non-intervention as demonstrated through their general departure from the traditionally accepted principle of consent.

However, to determine whether this is the case one first needs to be clear as to the activities that CoIs actually engage in. As noted above, for an infringement of this rule the intervention must represent a form of coercion so that a state's political, economic, social, and cultural choices are no longer freely made. Of course, CoIs do more than just discuss issues and the actions of states and those present within its borders, in that they expose situations in and involving other states and pass judgment, albeit of a non-binding nature, on the actions of these actors, including often making recommendations.[79] This in itself imposes a certain pressure upon the state to take, or refrain from taking, certain actions. It may also

---

[76] In the case of these tribunals the UNSC in the respective establishing Chapter VII resolutions had 'decided' that all states shall cooperate fully with the tribunal. See UNSC Res. 827. 25 May 1993, at para 4; and UNSC Res. 955, 8 November 1994, para 2, respectively. Article 13(b) of the 1998 Rome Statute of the International Criminal Court, 2187 UNTS 90, also makes clear that the ICC may exercise its jurisdiction if '[a] situation in which one or more of such crimes appears to have been committed is referred to the Prosecutor by the Security Council acting under Chapter VII of the Charter of the United Nations'. The principle of non-intervention found in Article 2(7) UN Charter 'shall not prejudice the application of enforcement measures under Chapter Vll.'

[77] Akande and Tonkin 2012.

[78] Ibid.

[79] The CoI in Syria, for example, made several recommendations, including putting an end to gross human rights violations, initiating prompt independent and impartial investigations, and allowing access by the Commission and outside observers. See Report of the Independent Commission of Inquiry on the Syrian Arab Republic, UN Doc. A/HRC/S-17/2/Add.1, 23 November 2011, Section 6.

lead to domestic prosecutions.[80] Furthermore, as was witnessed recently with the CoIs on Syria and North Korea, they will often lead to calls for a referral of the situation to the ICC. Such a referral, however, could only take place under a Chapter VII resolution of the UNSC, thus *prima facie* ruling out unlawful intervention. Similarly, the CoIs on Yugoslavia and Rwanda led to the establishment of ad hoc ICTs, both of which were again established through the UNSC invoking its Chapter VII powers.[81] In this respect it might be tentatively concluded that CoIs have not impacted upon, much less pose a threat to, the principle of non-intervention.

Yet, while much of the work of CoIs is carried out outside of the territory of the state concerned, to ensure that their mandate is credibly achieved CoIs will often need to enter the territory of the state concerned to undertake various interviews and investigations. It is perhaps only in this context in which the principle of non-intervention becomes engaged, as any entry onto the territory of a state by a CoI established by another state or organisation without the consent of the state concerned would represent a clear breach of the principle.

In the context of those established within the UN system, it might conceivably be argued that states have implicitly agreed through their membership of the UN Charter to the creation of this form adjudication.[82] However, any organ establishing a CoI would only be able to grant it powers to enter the territory of another state to the extent that it is within its competence to do so. In this respect, it is not always clear that the UN organs that establish CoIs have the necessary competence. In particular, given that it is the UNHRC that has become the primary organ in establishing CoIs, if a CoI established by this organ were to enter the territory of a state without its consent, or even if the UNHRC were to provide such a mandate to a CoI in the first place, this would constitute an unlawful form of intervention in the affairs of the state concerned. Being a UN organ it is, under Article 2(7) UN Charter, prohibited from intervening in matters which are essentially within the domestic jurisdiction of any state. Of course, it might be argued in the context of a situation such as Syria, for example, that the flow of refugees on such a scale means that the conflict is by no means an entirely internal matter for the state. While even if the situation had become so internationalised this would still not provide the legal authority for a CoI established by a state, the UN Secretary General, the UNHRC, or a regional organisation to intervene in this way; the principle of non-intervention does not prejudice the application of enforcement measures by the UNSC under Chapter VII of the UN Charter. Yet, the CoIs established by the UNHCR have not received an express authorisation by the UNSC under Chapter VII to fulfil their mandate. The UNSC could, in theory at least, issue a binding order to the government concerned to cooperate, a precedent for which can be found in October 2005 when the Council demanded that Syria cooperate

[80] Although as the CoI on the Gaza conflict demonstrated, this is not often the case.

[81] See UNSC Res. 827, 25 May 1993; and UNSC Res. 955, 8 November 1994.

[82] Akande and Tonkin 2012.

fully with the Lebanon inquiry and detain any identified suspects.[83] Yet, in the absence of a Chapter VII order or mandate the fulfilment of this part of their work legally requires the cooperation and consent of the government concerned. In practical terms, however, even if the Council provided such a mandate, an intervention of this nature would be most unlikely to take place without prior consent and cooperation of the state concerned.

11.3.3 Procedural Fairness

There are no standardized guidelines or practices regarding the way in which CoIs conduct themselves, arguably stemming from a perception that their temporary informal nature renders them unnecessary. As Bassouini has noted, 'there is nothing to guide, instruct, or assist the heads and appointees to these missions of how to better carry out their mandates.'[84] The ICJ and ICC act under their respective statutes that set out procedural matters,[85] and the ad hoc ICTs also operate under a statute and separately adopted rules of procedure and evidence.[86] Yet, while there have been various informal drafts of guidelines for fact-finding missions and various suggestions that a formal set of guidelines might be needed,[87] none have ultimately been adopted.

This is especially surprising in the context of the UN where the UNHCR has, in particular, developed a practice in establishing CoIs over the past 10 years. As Bassouni critically observes, even though CoIs, as an institutional mechanism of the UN, have been in existence for decades,

> every new Commission, fact-finding body, or mandate for individual fact-finding is ad hoc. There is no institutional memory, and there is no system by which the experiences of the past can be used to benefit the future. It is beyond logical explanation to find that the UN has established no model or standard database and that no model or standard process for field investigations exist, including no protocols for mass grave exhumations or reconstruction of events, and no large-scale interviews of victims and witnesses.[88]

---

[83] See UNSC Res. 1636, 31 October 2005, para 11.

[84] Bassiouni 2001, at 40.

[85] Articles 39–64 of the 1945 Statute of the International Court of Justice, 1 UNTS 993; Articles 53–61 of the 1998 Rome Statute of the International Criminal Court, 2187 UNTS 90.

[86] Updated Statute of the International Criminal Tribunal for the former Yugoslavia, as last amended by UNSC Res. 1877, 7 July 2009; Updated Rules of Procedure and Evidence, IT/32/ Rev. 44, 10 December 2009; Statute of the International Criminal Tribunal for Rwanda, UNSC Res. 955, 8 November 1994; and Rules of Procedure and Evidence, MICT/1, 8 June 2012 .

[87] See, for example, Kaufman 1969; Guidelines on international human rights fact-finding visits and reports, 1 June 2009, http://www.unhcr.org/refworld/docid/4a39f2fa2.html. Accessed 15 July 2014.

[88] Bassiouni 2001, at 48.

What is perhaps equally troubling from the perspective of procedural fairness is that '[i]n addition, there is no universally accepted standard of proof to which commissions of inquiry must conform.'[89] For example, in both establishing facts and attributing responsibility for violations of the law, the standard of proof used in the CoI on Syria was 'reasonable suspicion'.[90] The CoI on Syria's website, by contrast, uses 'reasonable grounds to believe'[91] leading one to question whether, and if so how, these two are different. In either case, the standard adopted appears to be along the lines of the civil standard of 'balance of probabilities' which was to be met when the Commission obtained a 'reliable body of evidence, consistent with other information indicating the occurrence of a particular incident or event'.[92] It is one that the Commission itself acknowledged as being 'a lower standard of proof than that applied in criminal proceedings.'[93]

However, the CoI on Syria was not necessarily acting out of line with other CoIs in adopting this standard. The CoI on Darfur, for example, and being conscious of the 'limitations inherent in its powers',[94] was clear that it would 'obviously not make final judgments as to criminal guilt; rather it would make an assessment of possible suspects that would pave the way for future investigations, and possible indictments by a prosecutor'.[95] In this light it went on to decide that 'it could not comply with the standards normally adopted by criminal courts (proof beyond reasonable doubt) or with that used by international prosecutors and judges for the purposes of confirming indictments (that there must be a prima facie case).'[96] Instead, it concluded—and in strikingly similar terms to the Syrian CoI—that 'the most appropriate standard was that requiring a reliable body of material consistent with other verified circumstances, which tends to show that a person may reasonably be suspected of being involved in the commission of a crime.'[97]

The adoption of such a low standard can be questioned on a number of levels. First, given that it was consciously paving the way for future prosecutions it is not clear why it refrained from using the '*prima facie*' standard, which appears to exist precisely for this purpose. Secondly, and alternatively, given the obvious

[89] Frulli 2012, at 1326. See, in general, Wilkinson 2011.

[90] Report of the Independent Commission of Inquiry on the Syrian Arab Republic, UN Doc. A/HRC/S-17/2/Add.1, 23 November 2011, para 5.

[91] See http://www.ohchr.org/EN/HRBodies/HRC/IICISyria/Pages/AboutCoI.aspx. Accessed 15 July 2014.

[92] Report of the Independent Commission of Inquiry on the Syrian Arab Republic, UN Doc. A/HRC/S-17/2/Add.1, 23 November 2011, para 5.

[93] Ibid.

[94] Report of the International Commission of Inquiry on Darfur to the United Nations Secretary-General, UN Doc. S/2005/60, 1 February 2005, para 15.

[95] Ibid., para 15.

[96] Ibid.

[97] Ibid.

difficulties in apprehending President al-Bashir for the purposes of prosecution in the ICC, the CoI may provide *the* final judgment on the legal issues involved thus placing question marks over the rationale behind the adoption of such a low standard of proof. Thirdly, and linking in with what was said above regarding the impact that CoIs have had upon the formality of international legal adjudication, the chosen standard of proof was adopted by the CoIs themselves, rather than by their creators, the UNHRC in the case of the CoI on Syria or the UNSC in the case of the CoI on Darfur. Lastly, the fact that the CoIs adopted such a low standard yet stressed that it would make its findings upon a 'reliable body' of evidence also raises further questions. How, for example, was the reliability of the evidence to be determined? In gathering its evidence the CoI on Syria relied heavily on the testimony of defectors from the Syrian regime.[98] Yet, their reliability was not seemingly questioned by the CoI despite it not being beyond the realms of possibility that such individuals might have a certain axe to grind against the Assad regime.

Notwithstanding the reliance upon such evidence, and the use on occasion of extensive powers in obtaining it, there has been little systematic consideration of the notion of procedural fairness for those who might be found responsible by CoIs, in particular those on the lists of perpetrators of crimes that various CoIs have drawn up, as well as for witnesses, victims and their next-of-kin.[99] As such, the use of a transparent, consistent, justified and justifiable standard of proof and methodology amongst CoIs in obtaining evidence is needed.

Perhaps one explanation for the adoption of a lower standard of proof is the lower level of resources that CoIs have access to compared to their more formal and permanent counterparts.[100] These are, of course, of a financial nature.[101] Yet, the ad hoc nature of CoIs also means that there is inconsistency in the expertise and experience of Members of the various commissions, as noted above. Furthermore, there is a distinct lack of a division of labour within CoIs, with

[98] See, for example and in general, Report of the Independent Commission of Inquiry on the Syrian Arab Republic, UN Doc. A/HRC/S-17/2/Add.1, 23 November 2011.

[99] Akande and Tonkin 2012. As Akande and Tonkin further note, this consideration is perhaps necessary as CoIs 'often take statements from a large number of complainants and witnesses, some use subpoena powers and powers of search and seizure, and they may have privileged access to relevant sources and the ability to speak freely as a result of the immunity conferred upon them.' Ibid.

[100] Bassiouni notes that '[t]hese missions seldom have the resources or the ability to do effective field work or empirical research. Consequently, they rely heavily on the NGOs, government reports, and the media. Many rapporteurs, or whatever their actual designation may be, produce reports even though they never set foot in the territory where their investigation takes place.' Bassiouni 2001, at 42. Boutruche has noted that '[p]hysical, financial and human resources are … a prerequisite for a fact-finding body to carry out its work in optimal conditions.' Boutruche 2011, at 118.

[101] This is not to say, however, that other mechanisms of adjudication are necessarily well funded.

experts on human rights addressing issues involving international humanitarian law. In this respect,

> [t]he focus on human rights violations and the involvement of human rights law experts in fact-finding missions investigating violations committed in the context of an armed conflict may lead to distortion with respect to the evaluation of the lawfulness of the conduct of military operations.[102]

This is not to say that this will necessarily always be the case. But the mere prospect of it poses problems in connection with credibility and procedural fairness.

A major complaint with many forms of international adjudication is the appearance of selectivity in the instances that receive treatment. Indeed, this is not a complaint specific to CoIs and can be seen in the establishment of ad hoc ICTs, or if and when referrals are made to the ICC. Similarly, there is little predictability as to the situations that are deemed to warrant a CoI, with decisions essentially contingent upon political and extraneous circumstances. Indeed, whether in the context of domestic CoIs, or those established by the UN, widespread political support is required for the establishment and functioning of the CoI. Parallels can also be made with the UNSC in its role in more generally maintaining international peace and security, in particular when it might be willing to act under the R2P doctrine.[103] The selectivity element in this context was made explicit in para 139 of the World Summit Outcome document when states openly stated that they were only prepared to take action in the context of R2P crises on a 'case-by-case' basis.[104] We witness a similar mentality in regards to the creation of CoIs. Indeed, states are wary of creating permanent obligations or institutions for the fear of being bound in the future, thus militating against the prospect for any support for a permanent CoI.[105]

Finally, it is arguably the case that the main reason for the establishment of permanent courts and tribunals of law, aside from the frequency and relative ease with which they are able to be accessed, is to enable a generally consistent interpretation and application of the law, one of the central hallmarks of procedural fairness. CoIs essentially apply the same branches of international law, yet, primarily due to the various factors outlined above there is the possibility for different, perhaps inconsistent, applications of the law. While this aspect is not necessarily absent in the context of permanent legal institutions, their permanence, along with the associated features this provides, does, nonetheless, generally ensure a more consistent approach to the law, with the ICJ being a relatively good example. This does, however, raise the prospect of the establishment of a permanent CoI.

---

102 Frulli 2012, at 1332. See also Boutruche 2011, at 108.

103 For more on R2P, see Knight and Egerton 2012.

104 2005 World Summit Outcome Document, UNGA Res. A/60/L.1, 15 September 2005, para 139.

105 See Sect. 11.4.

11.4 Concluding Remarks: A Permanent Commission of Inquiry?

Some of the elements of concern identified in this paper, which can be attributed, at least in part, to the temporary nature of CoIs, raises the question as to whether the creation of a permanent CoI would be a progressive step in the evolution of this mechanism of legal adjudication. The *temporary* CoIs on Yugoslavia, Rwanda and Cambodia led to the establishment of *temporary* international criminal tribunals. Now that we have a *permanent* international criminal court, thus eradicating the need for the establishment of many tribunals in the future, might it also be sensible to establish a *permanent* CoI, thus eradicating the need for those of a temporary nature?

The concept of a permanent CoI is not new with the idea originally floated as far back as 1967.[106] With the relatively recent practice of temporary CoIs being established by the UNHCR fresh impetus might now exist for the establishment of one. The idea is, in many respects, an attractive one. A permanent CoI could be petitioned by UN organs, regional organisations and individual states. Such a body would potentially possess greater authority and transparency, as well as having a qualified, independent and semi-permanent membership on hand and possibly more efficient and effective means of inquiry. Furthermore, the potential for consistency that a permanent body might provide would not only be beneficial for the branches of international law concerned, in that they could be interpreted and applied in a more consistent fashion, but the resulting increased predictability would also be of benefit to the states and non-state actors involved in having a clearer perception as to how their actions are likely to be judged. Ultimately, however, while such a body may lose the flexibility that contemporary examples of CoIs exhibit, it may increase the chances for justice, fairness, and accountability. However, we might use the IHFFC as a test case in reflecting upon the possibility of the establishment of such a permanent body. While the IHFFC might be considered a 'sleeping beauty' ready to be awoken,[107] there are issues with its utilisation and states have, in any case, simply not wished to resort to it.[108] The prospects for a successful permanent CoI on this basis are not good.

In any case, even if a permanent CoI were to be established, it would still not prevent states and other actors from establishing them on an ad hoc basis. The fact that they can be established by different actors for different purposes and, perhaps

---

[106] Cassese 2012, at 297.

[107] See, in general, Kalshoven 2002.

[108] Furthermore, in the contemporary context the revitalisation of the IHFFC would not provide a comprehensive solution to situations as we have witnessed in the Arab Spring, given its sole focus on issues of IHL but with the blurring that has occurred in these uprisings between civil disturbances and civil wars.

cynically, with underlying predispositions as to the outcomes of the issues under focus, means that they are an attractive option. They in this sense provide these different actors with a flexible means of providing at least the appearance of accountability. Furthermore, as we have witnessed in other recent developments, such as with the R2P concept, states do not wish to restrict or bind themselves but instead wish to proceed upon a 'case-by-case' basis.[109]

Temporary CoIs do, however, also provide many benefits of a more objective kind. For example, many can be deployed at the same time, whereas a permanent body may well be limited to only one or perhaps a handful of cases. While CoIs may provide what may be the only, or at least most formal, treatment of the legal issues involved in a particular context, they may also be rapidly deployed to build a criminal case for the purposes of future prosecution before evidence is lost or destroyed. More broadly, they may lead the UNSC to determine the existence of a threat to the peace and to adopt enforcement measures against states or other actors causing the threat. In this sense, and not being bound by formalised procedures and guidelines that would ultimately be produced in connection with the establishment of a permanent CoI, they may be flexible and adapted to different situations. While these practical benefits of temporary CoIs are undeniable they also, as discussed above, pose significant challenges from the perspective of international law. As such, arguably there is a need to reconcile the flexibility of temporary CoIs with the increased formality and procedural fairness that would be potentially offered by one of a permanent nature. Consequently, the best solution appears to be to provide more regulation to the 'ad hoc-ery' that has become a trait of CoIs,[110] with the overriding objective of increasing credibility, impartiality, and authority.

While the flexibility attached to the informality of their establishment can be maintained as this appears to be associated with the direct consequences attached to the findings of the particular adjudicative body as opposed to whether it is temporary or permanent, the rationale for the establishment of the CoI must nonetheless be clear. Particularly in the UN context, the reasons for the establishment of a CoI by a particular organ of the UN should be spelt out, along with the actual and potential consequences of this. In this sense, there needs to be more transparency in the trigger mechanisms for the establishment of a CoI with a clearly stated purpose, that is, whether it is prosecution or, more generally, accountability driven.

Although the establishing actor will have a guiding motivation in mind in establishing the CoI, it will also most likely be unaware of the details of the legal issues that the conflict or situation gives rise to, thus leaving the specific details of the mandates to be determined by the members of the CoI. However, there needs to be more of a discernable dialogue between the establishing actor and the members of the CoI resulting in clearer and more elaborately expressed mandates that are formally approved by the establishing actor. These can, and should, be flexible enough to take into account any subsequent changes to the mandate that are made

---

[109] See 2005 World Summit Outcome Document, UNGA Res. 60/1, 24 October 2005, paras 138–139.

[110] Franck and Fairley 1980, at 312.

necessary either by changing circumstances on the ground or the subsequent findings of the CoI. But if, and when, broader changes become necessary, they should also be formally approved by the establishing actor.

In adding a degree of permanence into temporary CoIs, a roster of commissioners and support staff that can be called upon by any actor could be drawn up, and perhaps formally approved by the UNGA. While the Dutch presented a proposal to the UN General Assembly in 1967 to establish a permanent CoI, this was rejected, but it did lead to the adoption of GA Resolution 2329 (XXII) on 18 December 1967 which requested the UN Secretary-General to establish a roster of experts for future CoIs,[111] something which has yet to materialise. A wide variety of expertise could be included to take into account the different situations that might arise that require investigation. It is perhaps also the case that simply the existence of such a roster would call into question the motives of those who decided to establish a CoI outside of it, and thus require them to justify their actions.

Lastly, and perhaps most fundamentally, consistency and procedural fairness, including the perceptions of it, need to be improved. While a permanent CoI might have obvious advantages in this respect, the adoption of procedural and evidential guidelines, including coverage of relevant standards of proof, which provide a form of regulation, at the very least to UN CoIs, could be drafted and adopted as a UNGA resolution. These could be wide-ranging to take into account aspects of witness protection and the use of interpreters.[112] In addition, a way in which temporary, albeit regular, bodies might establish not only consistency in procedure but also precedent regarding the interpretation and application of the law, is through the establishment of a database of CoIs or, as Bassouini calls it in the UN context, an 'institutional memory'.[113] Having such a database would minimise the potential for contradictions in the conclusions of different commissions regarding the meaning and applicability of different legal rules and norms, but would also provide a basis to test the validity of the research in order to assess the plausibility of the conclusions thus possibly minimising the occasions where different situations receive a different standard of legal adjudication.[114] With things the way that they are, 'it is safe to say that no scientific research methodology would consider the above-described approach as anything but selective, insufficient, unreliable and, at best, anecdotal.'[115] Ultimately, it appears that while no fixed permanent physical institution has been formed, as a temporary form of legal adjudication the CoI is here to stay, and the above measures would in this respect provide a greater form of credibility that too many CoIs have been found lacking.

---

111 Cassese 2012, at 297.

112 See Boutruche 2011, at 117–120.

113 Bassiouni 2001, at 48.

114 As Bassiouni states, 'there is no way of comparing the results of different, though substantively similar, missions. This principle applies equally well to ongoing missions that produce multiple reports, where it is at times difficult to compare working methods pursued during the mission and the results they produce.' Ibid., at 41.

115 Ibid.

References

Akande D, Tonkin H (2012, April 6) International commissions of inquiry: a new form of adjudication? EJIL Talk! www.ejiltalk.org/international-commissions-of-inquiry-a-new-form-of-adjudication/. Accessed 10 July 2014

Alvarez A (2005) International organizations as law-makers. Oxford University Press, Oxford

Alvarez A (2014) What are international judges for? The main functions of international adjudication. In: Romano C, Alter K, Shany Y (eds) The Oxford handbook of international adjudication. Oxford University Press, Oxford, pp 158–178

Bassiouni MC (2001) Appraising UN Justice-related fact-finding missions. J Law Policy 5:35–49

Boutruche T (2011) Credible fact-finding and allegations of international humanitarian law violations: challenges in theory and practice. J Confl Secur Law 16:105–140

Buchan R (2014) The *Mavi Marmara* incident and the application of international humanitarian law by quasi-judicial bodies. In: Jinks D, Maogoto J, Solomon S (eds) Applying international humanitarian law in judicial and quasi-judicial bodies: international and domestic aspects. TMC Asser Press, The Hague, pp 479–503

Cassese A (2012) Fostering increased conformity with international standards: monitoring and institutional fact-finding. In: Cassese A (ed) Realizing utopia: the future of international law. Oxford University Press, Oxford, pp 295–303

Franck TM, Fairley HS (1980) Procedural due process in human rights fact-finding by international agencies. Am J Int Law 74:308–345

Frulli M (2012) Fact-finding or paving the road to criminal justice: some reflections on United Nations commissions of inquiry. J Int Crim Justice 10:1323–1338

Heller KJ (2014, forthcoming) The International Commission of Inquiry on Libya: a critical analysis. In: Meierhenrich J (ed) International commissions: the role of commissions of inquiry in the investigation of international crimes. Oxford University Press, Oxford

Henderson C (2013) The provision of arms and 'non-lethal' assistance to governmental and opposition forces. Univ NSW Law J 36:642–681

Kalshoven F (2002) The International Humanitarian Fact-Finding Commission: a sleeping beauty. HV 4:213–216

Kaufman B (1969) The necessity for rules of procedure in *ad hoc* United Nations investigations. Am Univ Law Rev 18:739–768

Knight WA, Egerton F (eds) (2012) The Routledge handbook of the responsibility to protect. Routledge, Abingdon

Merrills JG (2011) International dispute settlement, 5th edn. Cambridge University Press, Cambridge

Stewart JG (2007) The UN Commission of Inquiry on Lebanon: a legal appraisal. J Int Crim Justice 5:1039–1059

Wilkinson S (29 April 2011) Standards of proof in international humanitarian and human rights fact-finding and inquiry missions. Geneva Academy of International Humanitarian Law and Human Rights in close cooperation with Geneva call. http://www.geneva-academy.ch/docs/reports/Standards%20of%20proo%20report.pdf. Accessed 10 July 2014

Yihdego Z (2012) The Gaza mission: implications for international humanitarian law and UN fact-finding. Melb J Int Law 13:1–59

Chapter 12
Special Temporary Measures and the Norm of Equality

Adeno Addis

Abstract Temporary laws or measures arise in different circumstances to deal with a wide array of perceived problems or concerns. This essay deals with one specific kind of temporary measures, which are provided for in international human rights treaties: 'preferential treatments' or 'positive measures', as they are called. The essay examines whether these measures undermine the predictability and stability of the norm of equality on which behalf they are said to have been adopted. The essay argues that these measures will be inconsistent with and destablise equality only if equality is understood narrowly as a principle that only requires sameness of treatment rather than the more substantive notion of equality (equality of opportunity) that this essay endorses and advances.

Keywords Equality · Equal opportunity · Exceptions · Temporariness · Temporary measures

Contents

12.1 Introduction 312
12.2 The Nature of Special Temporary Measures 317
  12.2.1 Special Rights and Special Measures 317
  12.2.2 The Nature of Special Measures 318
12.3 Equality and Special Measures 321
  12.3.1 Equality as Non-discrimination (Equality of Treatment) 321
  12.3.2 Equality as Equality of Opportunity 322
12.4 Temporariness and Predictability: The Issue of Durational Limit 325
12.5 Temporariness and Predictability: The Virtue of Candor 327
12.6 Conclusion 329
References 330

W. Ray Forrester Professor of Public and Constitutional Law, Tulane University School of Law, New Orleans, U.S.A.

A. Addis (✉)
Tulane University School of Law, New Orleans, USA
e-mail: aaddis@tulane.edu

M. Ambrus and R.A. Wessel (eds.), *Netherlands Yearbook of International Law 2014*,
Netherlands Yearbook of International Law 45, DOI 10.1007/978-94-6265-060-2_12

12.1 Introduction

Equality is a fundamental political and legal norm. Ronald Dworkin, who invested his considerable intellectual energy to understanding the nature of equality, once observed that no government 'is legitimate that does not show equal concern for the fate of all those citizens over whom it claims dominion and from whom it claims allegiance.'[1] Equality as a norm is, therefore, important in two senses. First, and most importantly, it demands that individuals be treated as having equal worth. Second, a government that does not comply with the demands of this norm is one that does not deserve to be treated as legitimate.

The norm is enshrined in both domestic and international law. The constitutions of almost all countries give prominent position to the ideal of equality.[2] And many international documents announce the fundamental nature of the norm. The preamble of the United Nations Charter, the founding document of the United Nations, 'reaffirms faith … in the equal rights of men and women.' Article 1 of the Charter is more expansive when it declares that one of the purposes of the United Nations is to promote and encourage 'respect for human rights and for fundamental freedoms for all without distinction as to race, sex, language, or religion.'[3] Equal concern for and equal treatment of every individual is affirmed as one of the purposes that the United Nations was established to pursue.

The ideal of equality is also central in core international human rights documents. Those documents declare, even more explicitly and in a more extended way, that equality is a basic norm, which signatory States are required to provide, protect, and promote.[4] The United Nations Human Rights Committee in its General Comment 18 declared that 'non-discrimination, together with equality before the law and equal protection of the law without any discrimination, constitute a basic and general principle relating to the protection of human rights.'[5] There is unanimity among international human rights documents that equality is a cornerstone concept in international human rights law and every state is required to show 'equal concern'[6] for the fate of those over whom it has jurisdiction and

[1] Dworkin 2002, at 1.

[2] See, for example, Articles 14–18 Indian Constitution; Article 8(1) Malaysian Constitution; Article 19(1) Russian Constitution; Section I(a) South African Constitution; Amendment XIV U.S. Constitution.

[3] Article 55(c) of the 1945 Charter of the United Nations, 1 UNTS XVI.

[4] Universal Declaration of Human Rights, UNGA Res. 217A, 10 December 1948. Article 1 reads: 'All human beings are born free and equal in dignity and rights.' See also Article 2(1) of the 1966 International Covenant on Civil and Political Rights, 999 UNTS 171.

[5] See Human Rights Committee, General Comment 18: Non-discrimination, U.N. Doc. HRI/GEN/1/Rev. 1 at 28, 10 November 1989, para 1 (hereinafter General Comment 18).

[6] The phrase 'equal concern' is that of Dworkin's. See Dworkin 1977, at 180; Dworkin 2002, at 1.

from whom it expects allegiance. And some have declared the norm to be a rule of customary international law as well.[7]

Yet, international human rights documents and some national laws[8] provide for what they call special temporary measures (sometimes referred to as 'affirmative action', 'preferential treatment' and 'positive measures'),[9] which on the face of it appear to be inconsistent with this general and fundamental norm. Some human rights conventions provide in the text itself for those special and temporary measures while at the same time affirming the centrality of equality in the state's treatment of people under its jurisdiction. The International Convention on the Elimination of All Forms of Racial Discrimination (CERD) and the Convention on the Elimination of All Forms of Discrimination against Women (CEDAW) are the two core human

---

[7] See *South West Africa Cases* (*Ethiopia v. South Africa*; *Liberia v. South Arica*), ICJ, Second Phase, Judgment of 18 July 1966, Dissenting Opinion of Judge Tanaka, at 291. Judge Tanaka concluded that 'the norm of non-discrimination ..., has become a rule of customary international law.' See also *Legal Consequences for States of the Continued Presence of South Africa in Namibia (South-West Africa) Notwithstanding Security Council Resolution 276* (1970), ICJ, Advisory Opinion of 21 June 171, Separate Opinion of Judge Ammoun, at 64. In his separate opinion Judge Ammoun declared that '[o]ne right which must certainly be considered a pre-existing binding customary norm, which the Universal Declaration on Human Rights codified is the right to equality.' See also Article 9 of the UNESCO Declaration on Race and Racial Prejudice, E/CN.4/Sub.2/1982/2/Add.1, annex V, 1982. '[T]he principle of equality ... and rights of all beings and all people ... is generally accepted and recognized principle of international law.'

[8] A number of countries have adopted a version of affirmative action (positive action, preferential treatment, etc.). Those include Australia, Brazil, Canada, India, Malaysia, South Africa and the United States. In some countries, the special measures are provided for through executive action (e.g. U.S.A.) while in others the measures are explicitly allowed by the constitution. For example, the Article 14 of the Indian Constitution provides that '[n]othing ... shall prevent the State from making any special provision for the advancement of any socially and educationally backward classes of citizens or for the Scheduled Castes and the Scheduled Tribes.' See also Indian Constitution Chapter 2, Section 9(2). And still in others, special measures are provided for by statutes. Australia provides for special measures in the Racial Discrimination Act 1975. The statute is meant to implement Australia's obligations under the 1966 International Convention on the Elimination of All Forms of Racial Discrimination, 660 UNTS 195 (hereinafter CERD).

[9] The Human Rights Committee has referred to these measures as 'positive measures' and 'affirmative action'. See Human Rights Committee, General Comment 28: Equality of Rights between Men and Women, U.N. Doc. CCPR/C/21/Rev.1/Add.10, 29 March 2000, para 3; Human Rights Committee, General Comment 23: The Rights of Minorities, CCPR/C/21/Rev.1/Add.5, 26 April 1994, para 6.2; General Comment 18, para 10. See also CEDAW Committee, General Recommendation 25: Temporary Special Measures, para 17 (hereinafter General Recommendation 25). Some refer to the programs as 'positive discrimination'. But I think Marc Bossuyt is right in his observation that the phrase 'positive discrimination' unwisely couples two terms that appear to be contradictory to the extent that discrimination is not seen as a positive thing. Marc Bossuyt, Preventing discrimination: the concept and practice of affirmative action, E/CN.4/sub.2/2007/21, 17 June 2002.

rights treaties that explicitly authorise the adoption of temporary measures.[10] Other core human rights conventions have been read (by the relevant monitoring committees) as authorising special measures.[11] The general principle of equality is said to coexist happily with those measures that have been referred to as special and temporary.

In this essay I shall explore whether these 'special temporary measures' are, by their very nature, *exceptions* to the norm of equality, temporary interruptions to the ideal of equality, and if so what the long-term impact of these measures is on the very idea of equality (its predictability and stability).

The notion of 'exception' suggests a limit on a general rule to fulfill its mandate. For those who think that these special measures are temporary exceptions to the ideal of equality, the worry is that the norm of equality may be seriously undermined by the adoption of such temporary measures. The analogy here is the effect that emergency measures often have on constitutional and legal sovereignty.[12] Under this account, exceptions to the application of a norm, however temporary and however intended to be in pursuit of the general norm in the long run, undermine the coherence and predictability of the norm itself.

While I agree that special temporary measures do raise important questions about their relationship to the norm of equality, I argue that the analogy with emergency exceptions is misplaced and the worry that these measures will undercut the very coherence of the norm of equality is unwarranted. I argue that unlike

---

[10] See Article 1(4) CERD. 'Special measures taken for the sole purpose of securing adequate advancement of certain racial or ethnic groups or individuals requiring such protection as may be necessary in order to ensure such groups or individuals equal enjoyment or exercise of human rights and fundamental freedoms shall not be deemed racial discrimination.' See also Article 4 of the 1979 Convention on the Elimination of All Forms of Discrimination Against Women, 1249 UNTS 13 (hereinafter CEDAW). 'Adoption by States parties of temporary special measures aimed at accelerating de facto equality between men and women shall not be considered discrimination.'

[11] See, e.g., *Franz Nahlik v. Austria*, Communications No. 608/1995, U.N. Doc. CCPR/C/57/D/608/1995, 22 July 1996, para 8.2. The Human Rights Committee observed that the International Covenant on Civil and Political Rights allows states to take 'affirmative measures ... in appropriate cases to ensure that there is equal access to public service for all citizens.' In numerous comments on country reports the Committee has also recommended that certain states adopt special measures while also praising those who have adopted such measures. General Comment 5 of the of the Committee of the International Covenant on Economic, Social, and Cultural Rights also shows that the Committee supports 'special measures intended to bring about de facto equality for men and women and for disadvantaged groups is not a violation of the non-discrimination [principle].' Committee on Economic, Social and Cultural Rights, General Comment 5: Persons with Disabilities, U.N. Doc E/1995/22 at 19, 25 November 1994.

[12] The idea of exception was prominently introduced by the German political theorist Carl Schmitt in the context of emergency powers. Schmitt 1985, at 13. 'For a legal order to make sense, a normal situation must exist, and he is the sovereign who definitely decides whether this normal situation actually exists.' But the complicated relationship between the norm and its exceptions is also applicable in other areas. For a modern and more extended treatment of the notion of exception, see Agamben 2005.

emergency measures, which suspend constitutional sovereignty, these special and temporary measures do not leave the general norm of equality in suspension for a temporary period. Rather, they assume and prepare the ground for a more defensible *conception* of equality.[13] In this sense, special temporary measures are simultaneously inside and outside the norm of equality. They suspend non-discrimination in its narrow and formal sense while preparing the ground for a broader and more robust notion of equality. By 'non-discrimination' I mean to refer to what in the United States is called the 'anti-discrimination' principle, the idea that the state is only required to provide sameness of treatment. 'Similar things should be treated similarly'.[14] Thus, according to this principle distinguishing on the bases of, e.g., race or gender and distributing parcels of goods and activities on these bases is not providing equal treatment.[15]

The conception of equality that these temporary measures assume and are in furtherance of is what I shall refer to as *equality of opportunity*. Equalising opportunities involves a good deal more than well-policed laws enforcing non-discrimination. Opportunities are never really equal unless societies have dealt with, in some way, the inequitable effects of past unequal access to advantages and resources.[16] Justice Ruth Ginsburg of the United States Supreme Court emphasised this point in a recent dissenting opinion.[17]

The notion of equality of opportunity has four especially compelling attractions to international legal theorists. First, unlike non-discrimination (in the way I have described it above), equality of opportunity allows us to take into account the effects of unfair and unequal distributions of goods and advantages in the past in how we conceptualise equality in the present. Second, unlike equality of welfare (equality of outcome), equality of opportunity recognises that different people value different things and hence societies cannot meet the mandate of equality by handing out identical parcels of goods and activities.[18] Indeed, the object of equal opportunity is to

---

[13] For a distinction between concepts and conceptions see Dworkin 1977, at 134–36.

[14] Fiss 1976, at 108. See also *Aderand Construction, Inc. v. Pena*, 515 US. 189, 12 June 1995 (Justice Thomas, concurring), at 240.

[15] I realize that the word 'non-discrimination' has been interpreted in Europe and in the human rights field as being synonymous with equality, but it has never been clear to me how the link or the relationship between the two concepts is worked out. One author working in the area of European Community Law notes that 'the non-discrimination principle is essentially the non-dynamic part of the equality package.' Ellis 1997, at 180. The question is what does the dynamic part look like and how should we clarify the link between robust and narrow notion of equality. That is what this essay will attempt to do.

[16] This unequal access is often cumulative and multigenerational. But the fact that it is such does not diminish the reality that it is the cause of the present vulnerability of the relevant minority groups.

[17] *Fischer v. University Texas at Austin, et al.* 570 U.S., 24 June 2013. 'I have several times explained why government actors including state universities, need not be blind to the lingering effects of an "overtly discriminatory past", the legacy of "centuries of law-sanctioned inequality".' Ibid., slip opinion, at 3.

[18] Phillips 2006, at 18–32.

work towards an "'optimal" equilibrium that reflects the actual distribution of talent in society.'[19] Third, again unlike equality of welfare, equality of opportunity acknowledges people as responsible agents accountable for the choices they make and the actions they take. Equality of opportunity is superior to equality of welfare to the extent that it takes seriously and is committed to the idea of personal responsibility and individual agency. Fourth, equality of opportunity better reconciles the special temporary measures that human rights documents and committees have adopted and the general norm of equality that is declared to be a fundamental international legal principle. In sum, if equality is understood as equality of opportunity, then special temporary measures do not undermine the long-term stability or certainty of the ideal of equality, but rather they focus us on a coherent and defensible notion of equality.

Of course, durational limit is essential if special temporary measures are not to transform equality of opportunity into equality of welfare (result), which I argue is not consistent with the idea of individuals as responsible agents accountable for the actions that they take and for the choices that they make. The essay will indicate what factors should inform the appropriate durational limit. At bottom, the argument of this essay is that whether in the realm of domestic or international law, temporary special measures are (or should be) in the service of equality of opportunity and would need to be terminated when that objective has been achieved. Determining whether or not that objective has been achieved in a given circumstance will often not be easy. As I shall explain later, this is why there is a need for institutional setups that require adopters and implementers of such policies to engage in periodic reviews and justification of the continuing need for such policies both (and especially) domestically and before international tribunals. One thing, however, must be clear: an arbitrary expiration date is as illogical as an indefinite pursuit of preferential policies.

The essay is organised in a manner that is intended to facilitate an orderly examination of the issue. Section 12.2 describes the nature of special temporary measures and distinguishes them from special rights although admittedly there are some overlaps between the two. Section 12.3 explores the relationship between special measures and the norm of equality and argues that these measures cannot be viewed as exceptions to the norm of equality if equality is understood as equality of opportunity. In Sects. 12.4 and 12.5 the article signals the importance of durational limits and political and legal candor to ensure that special temporary measures are not transformed into a process of undermining the very notion of equality as equality of opportunity. The conclusion is meant to raise two issues. First, it points out that special temporary measures are not unique in that temporary laws and measures are common phenomena adopted to deal with a wide array of perceived problems and concerns. Second, the conclusion introduces the notion of critical mass that I have utilised and developed in considerable detail in an earlier article to suggest that the concept perhaps help us to determine when it is time to end the temporary measures.

[19] Ginsburg 2014, at 349.

12.2 The Nature of Special Temporary Measures

12.2.1 Special Rights and Special Measures

Before I describe the nature of special measures, let me draw an important distinction, lest there be a misunderstanding. The special measures that are the concern of this essay are very different from the special rights that are granted to certain minorities as a group. Examples of the latter are rights given to certain minorities such as the right of minorities to enjoy their own culture, profess and practice their own religion and use their own language[20] as well as the special rights (e.g. the right to land) recognized for indigenous peoples.[21] These are *rights* and they are *permanent*. They are special rights, because the rights are provided to the individual within a particular group and the exercise of the right is premised on the protection and flourishing of the group. For example, an individual's right to speak a minority language would be meaningless unless the linguistic minority of which the individual is a member is recognized as possessing a right as a group and as a result is able to survive and even flourish.[22]

The special measures that are the focus of this essay, on the other hand, are not rights but policies in pursuit of a general and non-group specific individual right. Special measures here are not meant to confer special rights. Indeed, to the contrary, many treaty bodies have on many occasions declared that the maintenance of these measures indefinitely would constitute a violation of the right of others (a violation of the non-discrimination principle). In the American context, Justice Sandra Day O'Connor of the United States Supreme Court and the author of the majority opinion of a major affirmative action case, made a statement in the closing lines of the opinion which attracted a great deal of attention and some confusion. '[A]ll government use of race must have a logical end point', she wrote.[23] That is fair enough and consistent with what international human rights committees have been saying, but then she added the following: 'We expect that 25 years from now, the use of racial preferences will no longer be necessary to further the interest approved today.'[24] Justice O'Connor not only signaled that these are temporary measures and must have a logical end but she apparently was confident enough to suggest a time frame as well.[25] Justice O'Connor's worry, of course, is that temporary measures that do not have (or assume) an end point will destabilise

---

[20] Article 27 of the 1966 International Covenant on Civil and Political Rights, 999 UNTS 171 (hereinafter ICCPR).

[21] Committee on the Elimination of Racial Discrimination, General Recommendation 32: The Meaning and Scope of Special measures in the International Convention on the Elimination of All Forms of Racial Discrimination, CERD/C/GC/32, 24 September 2009, para 15.

[22] Addis 2001, at 719–789; Addis 1992, at 648–674.

[23] *Grutter v. Bollinger*, 539 U.S. 306, 23 June 2003, at 342.

[24] '[A]ll government use of race must have a logical end point.' Ibid., at 343.

[25] Ibid.

our notion of equality—the idea that equality is individual (not group) specific and that it is about individuals having equal opportunity not equal welfare. I shall say something about durational limit and its effect on the norm of equality in a later part of this chapter, but for the moment what is important is to realise that the special temporary measures that are the concern here are very different from the special rights of minorities.

12.2.2 The Nature of Special Measures

Some international human rights documents or the committees that were set up to monitor the rights in those documents refer to these programs as 'special measures'.[26] Other human rights documents refer to them as 'temporary special measures'.[27] What makes them 'temporary' appears to be clear. They are meant to end when the purposes for which they were adopted has been achieved. As CEDAW's Committee in its General Comment 25 put it, '[s]uch measures should … not be deemed necessary forever.'[28] The purposes might be to accelerate '*de facto* equality' between certain groups.[29] Or it might be to ensure 'groups or individuals equal enjoyment or exercise of human rights and fundamental freedoms'.[30] Or, as CEDAW put it, the objective may be to ensure 'equality of opportunity'.[31] It is, of course, never easy to determine as to whether and when those goals are met, but for the moment it is sufficient to note that these measures are considered to be temporary and taken for the 'sole'[32] purpose of achieving those specific goals.

In what sense are they 'special'? One straightforward reading, adopted by some, is that they are special because they are meant to achieve specific goals.[33] The specificity of the goals determines their specialness. However, that reading does not seem to me plausible to distinguish these measures from other measures, for every measure in that sense is special for it is adopted to achieve certain specific goals.

[26] Article 1(4) CERD.

[27] Article 4 CEDAW.

[28] The CEDAW Committee, however, has a very permissive notion of 'temporary'. '[T]he meaning of "temporary" may, in fact, result in the application of such measures for a long period of time.' The Committee continues: 'The duration of a temporary special measure should be determined by its functional result in response to a concrete problem and not by a predetermined passage of time.' General Recommendation 25, para 20.

[29] Ibid., para 6.

[30] Article 1(4) CERD.

[31] Article 4 CEDAW.

[32] Article 1(4) CERD.

[33] '[T]he real meaning of "special" in the formulation of Article 4, paragraph 1, is that the measures are designed to serve specific goal.' General Recommendation 25, para 21.

Perhaps the notion of special measure could reasonably be read to imply that there is a departure from a normal or ordinary process. So, perhaps one way to understand the notion of 'special' in this case is to say that the measures are a departure from the application of the general and abstract norm of equality. Under this reading, the relationship between these special measures and equality could be analogised to the relationship between emergency measures and ordinary juridical sovereignty.[34] Each of the former is viewed as an exception to (or as a suspension of) the latter (the general norm). The special measures are outside the norm of equality in the same way that emergency powers (rules) might be said to be outside the law itself. In both of these cases, so the argument goes, the particular special act is an *exception* to the general norm.[35] But quite often, even in relation to emergency measures it is not clear that those who adopt those measures view them as either inside or outside the norm of juridical sovereignty itself. In a speech he delivered to Congress when it finally convened, President Abraham Lincoln of the United States justified some of his actions (such as the suspension of *habeas corpus*) during the American Civil War, which many considered as unconstitutional, by claiming that 'whether strictly legal or not' the measures he took were born out of 'public necessity'. He asked: 'Are all the laws but one to go unexecuted and the Government itself go to pieces lest the one be violated?'[36] The first part of Lincoln's statement seems to suggest that 'necessity' is an exception to (outside of) the law itself. That is, necessity has no law (*necessitate legem non habet*). But the second part seems to suggest that the exception is in fact implied in the very notion of juridical sovereignty, for he claims that the suspension of the laws was done in the service of sovereignty itself. So, even in relation to emergency exceptions the view of some seems to be that exceptions are both internal and external to the juridical order.

But if you view these special measures as operating in a universe where the general norm (equality) is suspended, then you might be tempted to conclude that temporary measures do not have a lasting effect on the general norm. They operate on a different plane in the same way that a state of emergency, or the 'state of exception', as some refer to it,[37] operates outside the ordinary rule of law. When the emergency is over we are back to constitutional government and when the special measures have achieved their goal we are back to a stable and predictable notion of equality with which we started. This argument seems to me to be erroneous in relation to both special temporary measures and state of emergencies. Each, in fact, has a lasting effect on the general norm or what is considered to be normal,

---

[34] See Schmitt 1985; Agamben 2005.

[35] In fact, state of emergencies is referred to as a 'state of exceptions'.

[36] Message to a special session of Congress, July 4, 1861. See also Agamben 2005, at 15. 'The state of exception in which Germany found itself during the Hindenburg presidency was justified by [Carl] Schmitt on a constitutional level by the idea that the president acted as the 'guardian of the constitution'.

[37] See Agamben 2005; Schmitt 1985.

but in different ways. In relation to state of emergencies, even if the threat that induced the state of emergency (the state of exception) is gone and normal structures of the state are restored, the notion of what is normal is often perceptibly altered. The impact of the terrorist attack of September 11, 2001 and the American government response to it have had long-lasting effects on the American body politic, by blurring the distinction between normalcy and emergency, war and peace, as two different states of affairs.[38]

In relation to special temporary measures, the long term impact is of a different kind. Special measures do not simply suspend non-discrimination (formal equality) for a period, but they require us to think of equality very differently. That is, special temporary measures are not exceptions to the general norm of equality but an aspect of a way of understanding the norm of equality itself.[39] Under this reading and as I shall show later, the exception is both outside and inside the norm itself.[40] By that I mean to suggest that the special measures require us to suspend the norm of non-discrimination (formal equality) but the suspension of the non-discrimination is done so as to reflect on a broader and more defensible notion of equality than the notion of non-discrimination, as defined above, recommends. When both CEDAW and CERD declare that these temporary special measures 'shall not be considered discrimination',[41] they cannot be saying that the norm of equality is suspended in relation to this specific circumstance, but rather that the measures are consistent with (or even required by) the norm itself. Indeed, each of them indicates in the same article that the maintenance of 'separate rights for different racial groups' or 'unequal and or separate standards' between men and women would be considered inconsistent with the norms of equality or non-discrimination.

---

[38] Addis 2007a.

[39] Indeed, human rights treaties provide specifically for circumstances when the application of a norm is to be suspended. They include 'derogation' provisions that allow the suspension temporarily of most rights in the covenants in times of public emergency threatening the life of the nation. See, e.g., Article 4 ICCPR; Article 15 of the 1950 European Convention for the Protection of Human Rights and Fundamental Freedoms, 213 UNTS 221 (hereinafter ECHR); Article 27 of the 1969 American Convention on Human Rights, 1144 UNTS 123 (hereinafter ACHR). But even under these circumstances discrimination solely on the ground of race, colour, sex, language, religion and social origin is prohibited. That is, even in times of public emergency the principle of non-discrimination cannot be suspended.

[40] Agamben 2005, at 23. 'In truth, the state of exception is neither external nor internal to the juridical order, and the problem of defining it concerns precisely a threshold, or a zone of indifference, where inside and outside do not exclude each other but rather blur with each other.'

[41] See Article 4(1) CEDAW (adopting such measures 'shall not be considered discrimination as defined in the present Convention."); Article 1(4) CERD ('[s]pecial Measures … shall not be deemed racial discrimination'); General Recommendation 25, para 18 ('[t]he Committee considers that States parties that adopt and implement such measures under the Convention do not discriminate against men.').

12.3 Equality and Special Measures

12.3.1 Equality as Non-discrimination (Equality of Treatment)

Non-discrimination is a prohibition on the state from making any distinction and/or preference among people within its territory and subject to its jurisdiction in the provision of the rights provided for by the various human rights conventions.[42] When it acts in a non-discriminatory way (taking a seemingly neutral stance), the state is of course acting in the context of private and public acts and practices that have shaped the individuals and their circumstances before it. And yet non-discrimination would suggest that the state be agnostic about those circumstances. So, if non-discrimination is the only conception of equality that is in play, then special temporary measures seem to be inconsistent with it.

Now, human rights treaties themselves or the committees that monitor those rights have specifically and often declared that temporary measures 'shall not be considered discrimination as defined' in the particular convention.[43] To be sure, those conventions and committees indicate that there are circumstances where special measures cross from being consistent with to being contrary to the norm of non-discrimination. This happens when those measures lead to 'the maintenance of unequal or separate standards'[44] for different groups and when they are continued 'after the objectives for which they were taken have been achieved.'[45] The Special Rapporteur on affirmative action, Marc Bossuyt, was more general in his report about the relationship between non-discrimination and special measures. He observed that '[n]on-discrimination and affirmative action if not carefully framed may clash with each other.'[46] The Special Rapporteur is right about that but what is the proper frame that would allow coexistence?

I do not believe that the attempts to reconcile non-discrimination and affirmative action by international conventions and committees have been successful. First, the idea that you can avoid contradiction by simply deeming them to be consistent as a matter of treaty declaration is rather unhelpful. Consistency by declaratory fiat is no consistency at all. If they are consistent it has to be because they are

[42] See Articles 2 and 26 ICCPR; Article 2 of the 1966 International Covenant on Economic, Social and Cultural Rights, 993 UNTS 3 (hereinafter ICESCR); Article 1 CERD; Article 1 CEDAW; Article 2 of the 1981 African Charter on Human and Peoples' Rights, 21 ILM 59; Article 1 ACHR; Article 1 ECHR.

[43] Article 4 CEDAW; Article 1(4) CERD; General Recommendation 25, para 18; Committee on the Elimination of Discrimination against Women, General Recommendation 13: Equal Remuneration for Work of Equal Value, 1989, paras 32–33.

[44] Article 4(1) CEDAW.

[45] Article 1(4) CERD.

[46] Marc Bossuyt, Preventing Discrimination: The Concept and Practice of Affirmative Action, E/CN.4/Sub.2/2002/21, 17 June 2002, para 83.

conceptually so not because a particular body simply declared them to be so. Second, even when the conventions and committees indicate that there could be inconsistency between the norm of non-discrimination and the special measures that are allowed, their description of the circumstances under which such inconsistency occurs is not very helpful. So, for example, both CEDAW and CERD declare that the maintenance of 'separate or unequal standards' is contrary to the norm of non-discrimination. But that way of putting it seems to me to assume the very issues that have to be resolved. When exactly do policies cross from being acceptable special measures to being 'separate' or 'unequal' standards? After all, special measures are so because they make a distinction between the members of the majority and members of the relevant minority along some measures and to one degree or another they apply separate or unequal standards at that particular moment.[47]

12.3.2 Equality as Equality of Opportunity

The inconsistency between equality and the special measures occurs if and only if equality is defined narrowly as non-discrimination. But as I have argued earlier, non-discrimination is not a sufficient understanding of equality, because when the state takes the seemingly neutral stance of non-discrimination at a given moment of time it freezes in place the unequal arrangements that have led to the particular circumstance whether those circumstances are the result of past *de jure* discriminatory practices or private orderings that systematically disadvantaged or excluded members of a particular group. Non-discrimination under these circumstances is no friend of equality.

For non-discrimination to be consistent with the notion of equal treatment or equality, the condition that needs to exist is that of fair equal opportunity.[48] By fair equality of opportunity, I mean to refer to the circumstances captured by John Rawls who used the phrase in his book *A Theory of Justice*.[49] It requires that we should arrange institutions in such a way that persons with the same native talent and the same ambition should have the same prospect of success in the competition for social and economic advantages.

But the notion of fair equal opportunity in the way that Rawls defined it is part of an ideal theory. Rawls famously made a distinction between ideal and non-ideal

---

[47] The doctrinal response that that occurs when there is 'no objective and reasonable justification and when there is proportionality between the aim sought and the means employed' does not deal with the conceptual issue. It merely shifts the problem to a case by case seemingly objective process that raises the conceptual issue at every decisional point.

[48] Rawls 1971.

[49] Ibid., at 9 and 244–248. As he put it, '[v]iewed the theory of justice as a whole, the ideal part presents a conception of a just society that we are to achieve if we can.' Ibid., at 246.

theories. An ideal theory is one on which Rawls's work, especially his *A Theory of Justice*,[50] concentrates. By an ideal theory Rawls meant to refer to a theory that would tell one how and why a truly just society is constituted and consequently when a society is unjust (when it falls short of the ideal).[51] An ideal theory gives one the outline of the principles by which a human society is structured so as to make it the fairest given 'men as they are and laws as they might be', as Rawls put it citing Rousseau.[52] However, an ideal theory does not tell you what to do when, as it is often the case, you find yourself in an unjust society and you wish to correct the injustice. Rawls calls this the province of non-ideal theory.[53] Non-ideal theory is concerned with the processes by which real existing and often unjust societies might be brought into compliance with the conditions of ideal theory. Non-ideal theory must, therefore, 'necessarily have a strong transitional structure.'[54] Temporary special measures are policies intended to deal with the unjust consequences of an unjust history, a way to combat a special form of the failure of fair equality of opportunity.[55] Viewed this way, special measures are pragmatic, transitional steps that focus us on a coherent and defensible notion of equality rather than suspending or undermining the ideal of equality.

When members of a group—such as racial minorities and women—have been systematically subjected to inequalities of advantages (either *de jure* or *de facto*) the only way to provide equality of opportunity would be to distribute resources in a way that would open up genuinely equal opportunity for participants. To think of the principle of equality as being synonymous with the principle of non-discrimination in a society which has been stratified on the basis of group membership where the stratification was systematically shaped by both public and private institutions, is to simply reinforce the inequities of advantages. For opportunities

---

[50] Ibid., at 244–48.

[51] Ibid.

[52] Rawls 1999, at 7. Rawls interprets the phrase 'men at they are' as referring to 'persons' moral and psychological natures and how that nature works within a framework of political and social institutions.' Ibid.

[53] Rawls 1971, at 244–248. For a recent clarification and extension of the distinction between ideal and non-ideal theories, see Simmons 2010, at 5–36. Hendrix 2013, at 116–143. Rawls idea of an ideal theory has been challenged by various authors from various angels. See, for example, Sen 2006, at 215–238; Mills 2005, at 165–184; Farrelly 2007, at 844–864; Valentini 2009, at 332–355; Goodin 1995, at 37–56.

[54] Hendrix 2013, at 120.

[55] John Simmons has recently argued that there are two major roadblocks to compliance with an ideal theory. The first involves natural or historical contingencies. An example of this is the existence of severe poverty and the lack of resources to overcome it. Even if every member of the political community is motivated to pursue justice and to achieve the fairest society (to comply with an ideal theory), the lack of resources may make it hard to achieve such a society. The second roadblock involves individuals and groups deliberately choosing to diverge from the appropriate standards that define the ideal society even when they know that the standards are morally proper. This essay is mainly concerned about this latter roadblock. See Simmons 2010, at 5–36.

to be equal under these circumstances, there needs to be social intervention to neutralise the inequitable effects of past arrangements and social backgrounds. Equal opportunity requires that opportunities must be equalised by social intervention. That entails distribution of advantages and resources that would open up a genuine process of equal opportunity. By 'resources' I mean to refer to not just material resources but cultural and other resources as well.

But let me emphasise here that what is inconsistent with the norm of equality is not the mere unequal distribution of resources but unequal distribution that is not the result of the choices that people have made or on circumstances over which people have no control. While the non-discrimination principle simply ignores the inequitable effects of social and historical backgrounds in its application of the principle of equality, those who view equality in terms of equality of welfare (equality of outcome) seem to disregard the agency of individuals and the responsibility that should attach to individual choices. Under equality of welfare, people's individual responsibility for their own lives is not given due consideration.

By equality of welfare I mean to refer to what Ronald Dworkin meant when he used the phrase: 'a person's welfare is a matter of his success in fulfilling his preferences, goals and ambitions, and so equality of success as a conception of equality of welfare, recommends distribution and transfer of resources until no further transfer can decrease the extent to which people differ in such success.'[56] When people talk about the relationship between the norm of equality and preferential treatments they often use the de facto *versus de jure*[57] or substantive versus formal label. The argument often is that the former of the pair is much more compatible with the norm of equality than the latter. Preferential treatments are seen to bring about substantive rather than formal or de facto rather than mere *de jure* equality.[58] Often, it is not quite clear what the terms 'substantive' and '*de facto*' actually mean. De facto equality presumably refers to factual equality,[59] but what metric of equality would be taken to be sufficient factual equality is never clear. It appears that both substantive and factual equalities could reasonably be understood as supporting the idea of equality as equality of welfare such that they will require us to adjust the distribution of power and resources whenever there is inequality

---

[56] Dworkin 2002, at 17.

[57] Article 4 CEDAW expresses this understanding.

[58] CEDAW Committee views de facto and substantive equality as interchangeable. See General Comment 25, para 8. 'In the Committee's view, a purely formal legal or programmatic approach is not sufficient to achieve women's de facto equality with men, which the Committee interprets as substantive equality.'

[59] Francesco Capotorti, Study on the Rights of Persons Belonging to Ethnic, Religious and Linguistic Minorities, Special Rapporteur of the Sub-Commission on Prevention of Discrimination and Protection of Minorities, UN Doc. No. E/CN.4/Sub.2/384/Rev.1., 1979, at 41. '[T]he concept of protection of minorities implies special measures in favour of a minority group .... The purpose of the measure is to institute factual equality between the members of the Minority groups and other individuals.'

regardless of whether the inequality is the result of choices people have made. One could interpret some statements of CEDAW's Committee as endorsing this position.[60]

I argue that equality of opportunity is a better conception of equality than equality of welfare, for at least two reasons. First, it recognises that different people value different things and hence equalising by simply handing out identical parcels of goods or activities does not capture the essence of what it means to be equal. Equality of opportunity teaches that citizens should be equal not in the welfare they achieve but in the opportunities they have for achieving welfare. Second, unlike equality of welfare, equality of opportunity acknowledges and factors in the idea of people as responsible and accountable for the choices they make and the things they do.

To treat people as being of equal worth is partly to treat their choices as choices of responsible agents when those choices are not impermissibly constrained by a history of systematic private and public exclusions of individuals with certain physical, cultural or social traits. Equality of opportunity demands that no one should be worse off than others because of circumstances over which he/she has no control (such as race and gender). Temporary special measures, I have argued, are compatible with equality only if we adopt equality of opportunity as the appropriate conception of equality, because it demands equalising those things for which people cannot be fairly held responsible but it continues to hold individuals accountable for what they do or do not do with those opportunities. It is attentive to historical and current exclusions and deprivations but it is also sensitive to, and values, human agency.[61]

12.4 Temporariness and Predictability: The Issue of Durational Limit

The purpose of this essay has been to explore the question as to whether what appear to be exceptional pragmatic temporary measures (affirmative action policies) undermine the viability and predictability of the general norm of equality on which behalf they were adopted by states either voluntarily or with a strong nudge from international human rights tribunals and committees. I have argued that preferential policies in the way they have been conceived do not undermine the general norm of equality, but rather they orient us towards a broader and more defensible and sustainable conception of equality.[62] As I have argued earlier,

[60] See General Recommendation 25, para 9. 'Equality of results is the logical corollary of de facto or substantive equality.'

[61] I am not unaware that every individual choice is socialized and to that extent there are no purely autonomous choices. Socialisation constrains our choices. See Mason 2000. But that is not the sort of constraint that special measures and this essay are concerned with.

[62] For a distinction between concepts and conceptions see Dworkin 1977, at 134–36.

equalising opportunities requires a great deal more than enforcing non-discrimination. Opportunities are never really equal unless societies have dealt with, in some way, the inequitable effects of past unequal access to advantages and resources. Just like any transitional structure of non-ideal theory, affirmative action measures must comply with two conditions. First, they are temporary and transitional in nature. Second, they must not just be about 'the elimination of particular or salient injustices',[63] but be oriented toward the overall goal of achieving equality of opportunity. But how does one deal with the question of duration?

Every international human rights document or the committees that monitor the rights in those documents declare that these special measures are temporary and must have a logical end period.[64] They cannot be necessary for ever, as one human rights committee put it.[65] But who sets the time limit and what are the conditions under which those policies should be discontinued? Given the fact that I have argued that equality is achieved when there is genuine equal opportunity for members of the relevant groups, one straightforward answer would be that they should be discontinued when there is equality of opportunity. But how do we ensure that those policies are not entrenched as a permanent means of pursuing equality of welfare (outcome) or even worse as political strategies for a segmented and ethnicised politics in which case the very idea of equality would be permanently undermined?

As I noted earlier, one unusual answer has been the answer Justice O'Connor of the United States Supreme Court gave in her majority opinion in a major affirmative action case. She gave a time limit within which the special policies would be expected to have achieved their goals. She notes, '[w]e expect that 25 years from now, the use of racial preferences will no longer be necessary to further the interest approved today.'[66] Although Justice O'Connor clearly did not mean to suggest that affirmative action is to be discontinued in twenty five years (she merely expressed hope), she certainly seems to be anxious to signal that a workable durational limit is in order if a strategy adopted in support of a viable conception of equality does not turn into a means of entrenching inequality or become a source of severe ethnic and racial fracture and conflict.

However, an arbitrary expiration date is as illogical as an indefinite pursuit of preferential policies. The duration of special (transitional) measures may be significant in some circumstances but relatively short in others. Different spheres (say education) may require different durational consideration. But the idea of a thorough and comprehensive review of these policies periodically

---

[63] Simmons 2010, at 21–22.

[64] *Grutter v. Bollinger*, 539 U.S. 306, 23 June 2003, at 342.

[65] General Recommendation 25, para 20. 'Article 4, paragraph 1, explicitly states the 'temporary' nature of such special measures. Such measures should therefore not be deemed to be necessary forever, even though the meaning of 'temporary' may, in fact, result in the application of such measures for a long period of time.'

[66] *Grutter v. Bollinger*, 539 U.S. 306, 23 June 2003, at 343.

where the designers and implementers of such policies are called to justify (in certain circumstances to an independent or third party) the need for the continued existence of these policies (in the particular form) is in order. There are a number of factors that need to be weighed in the reviewing process. These include: the positive contribution these policies have made towards entrenching equality of opportunity for members of historically excluded or disadvantage groups (the 'sole' purpose of the programs); the costs that these programs have imposed on third parties' right to equal opportunity; the unavailability of other ways (with less impact on third parties) to provide equality of opportunity; and how well the cost of these programs has been distributed among segments of the society. The last factor is worth emphasising. Not infrequently, the measures adopted to enhance equal opportunity for members of disadvantaged groups have had less than incidental impact on a segment of the majority population, which itself has been on the losing end of the distribution of goods and advantages. Special temporary measures should be designed in such a way that the cost of ushering in the conditions of equal opportunity is spread out among many segments of the society. Although directed at the issue of durational limit, it is, of course, inevitable that the application of these factors will also affect the type of measures that are available or could be adopted. The requirement of temporariness will exclude certain actions as unavailable, for it is in the nature of things that effective temporary measures will have to be crafted very differently from measures that are intended to last long and to be effective in the long run.

Let me finally make a more general point about the factors that I have listed in the preceding paragraph. If one were to take them together the conclusion at which one would arrive is that since non-ideal theory is concerned with 'a range of second-best options'[67] as a way of getting us to the ideal (fair equal opportunity in our case), what strategy is employed (both in terms of the nature of the program and the durational limit) should be informed by how the strategy will contribute to the achievement of the ultimate goal.

12.5 Temporariness and Predictability: The Virtue of Candor

In a dissent she wrote in a high profile affirmative action case that was decided in 2003,[68] Justice Ruth Ginsburg of the United States Supreme Court made this observation in a footnote: 'Among constitutionally permissible options, those that candidly disclose their consideration of race seems to me preferable to those that

[67] Hendrix 2013, at 121.

[68] *Gratz v. Bollinger*, 539 U.S. 244, 23 June 2003.

conceal it.'[69] Justice Ginsburg repeated this observation in a recent affirmative action case (again in a dissent).[70]

What constitutes candor and why is it important in this circumstance? By candor, Justice Ginsburg seems to suggest that decision-makers must be both honest and transparent about the objectives they seek to achieve and the means by which they seek to achieve it. Ginsburg's observation about candor was made in a recent high profile affirmative action case.[71] In that case, the plaintiff challenged the program adopted by the University of Texas that considered race as 'one of many "plus factors" in an admission program that considered the overall individual contribution of each candidate'[72] as race-based and thus subject to the strictest of scrutiny while viewing Texas' Top Ten Law as permissibly race neutral.[73]

Why is candor important in relation to temporary measures such as affirmative action policies? First, honest and transparent decision-making will force decision-makers to clearly articulate the purpose and defend the means forthrightly rather than dealing with subterfuge and obfuscation which is likely to lead to public cynicism and loss of institutional legitimacy. Second, a candid presentation of a policy is likely to lead to a more robust and periodic review of the necessity of that policy and less likely for the policy to be entrenched as a permanent feature of the political landscape. When policies are not clearly and candidly articulated, then the possibility of those policies working themselves into the political process as permanent features, delinked from the initial purpose (equal opportunity) for which they were adopted, is high. Third, the requirement of candor will constrain the exercise of impermissible and destructive ethnic politics through the use of such measures.

Put simply, the argument is that the requirement of candor has the potential to lead to the adoption of better considered and justified policies as well as ensuring that the policies will continually be evaluated as temporary policies. One could add to these prudential arguments the normative concern that public decision-makers should not mislead the public on whose behalf they make those decisions.

---

[69] Ibid., n. 11, at 305.

[70] *Fischer v. University Texas at Austin, et al.* 570 U.S., 24 June 2013, at 3. 'Among constitutionally permissible options, I remain convinced, "those that candidly disclose their consideration of race [are] preferable to those that conceal it."'.

[71] Ibid.

[72] Ibid. (Justice Kennedy writing for the majority).

[73] The Top Ten Law 'grants automatic admission to any public college, including the University, to all students in the top 10 % of their class at high schools in Texas.' Ibid. (Justice Kennedy), at 3. But to the extent that this program diversifies the student body, as the plaintiff argues, it is so because most public schools are highly segregated by race and/or ethnicity. This is as much about race (perhaps even more so) than the 'plus' factor.

12.6 Conclusion

Temporary laws or measures are common. They arise in different circumstances to deal with a wide array of perceived problems or concerns. Some might have been adopted to cover the period during which the permanent regulatory structure is fully developed and adopted. Interim constitutions are a good example of that.[74] Other temporary measures might have been adopted for the purpose of discovering more information to determine as to what would be or should be the most optimal regulatory regime to deal with the specific problem. Once the relevant information is available through the workings of temporary measures (and after the law has elapsed), then permanent schemes will be put in place.[75] At other times, temporary measures are put in place as means for accommodating competing claims which may not have been reconcilable if permanent measures or rules were attempted thereby creating new policy space for further political bargains.[76]

The temporary measures that I have explored here are different from the above in three ways. They are not adopted to gather more information for a permanent regulatory scheme based on race or gender. Indeed, the whole idea of special temporary measures is ultimately to make those characteristics largely irrelevant for regulatory purposes. Second, there is actually a consensus on the general principle toward which these policies are meant to nudge us (the norm of equality) even though there is still controversy as to what conception of equality is the most appropriate or defensible. I have argued that equality of opportunity should be the standard of appraisal. Third, the measures are (and are considered to be) inherently temporary, for their continuation as a permanent feature of a regulatory scheme or regime will undermine (at least will be inconsistent with) a central principle of both human dignity and democratic governance—individuals be treated as having equal worth—the very thing on which behalf these policies are adopted.

When do these policies then cross from being acceptable temporary measures in the service of equality to undermining the coherence and predictability of the norm of equality? I have argued that the conception of equality for which these measures are or should be adopted and by which they should be evaluated is equality of opportunity. And when do we know whether equality of opportunity has been achieved? This is, of course, fact-dependent and would vary from case to case, jurisdiction to jurisdiction, etc. But if one were to make a general

74 See Varol 2014.

75 Ginsburg 2014, at 327. 'What is unique about temporary law, however, is the information revealed not (or not only) by the law's enactment – its consequences when the law is in effect—but after the law lapses.'

76 Ginsburg 2014, at 326. '[T]emporary regulation creates new policy space for political bargains.' Ginsburg 2014, at 337.

observation it would be that the time to end the temporary measures is when there is a critical mass of members of the relevant group in the relevant field such that the change towards equal opportunity will be self-sustaining.[77]

References

Addis A (1992) Individualism, communitarianism, and the rights of ethnic minorities. Notre Dame Law Rev 67:615–676

Addis A (2001) Cultural integrity and political unity: the politics of language in multilingual states. Ariz State Law J 33:719–789

Addis A (2007a) 'Informal' suspension of normal processes: the 'war on terror' as an autoimmunity crisis. Boston Univ Law Rev 87:323–346

Addis A (2007b) The concept of critical mass in legal discourse. Cardozo Law Rev 29:97–148

Agamben A (2005) State of exceptions. University of Chicago Press, Chicago

Dworkin R (1977) Taking rights seriously. Harvard University Press, Cambridge

Dworkin R (2002) Sovereign virtue: the theory and practice of equality. Harvard University Press, Cambridge

Ellis E (1997) The principle of equality of opportunity irrespective of sex: some reflections on the present state of European Community law and its future development. In: Dashwood A, O'Leary S (eds) The principle of equal treatment in EC law. Sweet and Maxwell, London, pp 172–188

Farrelly C (2007) Justice in ideal theory: a refutation. Polit Stud 55:844–864

Fiss O (1976) Groups and the equal protection clause. Philos Public Aff 5:107–177

Ginsburg et al (2014) Libertarian paternalism, path dependence, and temporary law. Univ Chic Law Rev 81:291–359

Goodin R (1995) Political ideals and political practices. Br J Polit Sci 25:37–56

Hendrix BA (2013) Where should we expect social change in non-ideal theory? Polit Theory 41:116–143

Mason A (2000) Equality, personal responsibility and gender socialization. Proc Aristot Soc 100:227–246

Mills C (2005) Ideal Theory as Ideology. Hypotia 20:165–184

Phillips A (2006) 'Really' equal: opportunities and autonomy. J Polit Philos 14:18–32

Rawls J (1971) A theory of justice. Harvard University Press, Cambridge

Rawls J (1999) The law of peoples. Harvard University Press, Cambridge

Schmitt C (1985) Political theology: four chapters on the concept of sovereignty. University of Chicago Press, Chicago

Sen A (2006) What do we want from a theory of justice? J Polit Philos 103:215–238

Simmons AJ (2010) Ideal and nonideal theory. Philos Public Aff 38:5–36

Valentini L (2009) On the apparent paradox of ideal theory. J Polit Philos 17:332–355

Varol O (2014) Temporary constitutions. Calif Law Rev 102:409–464

[77] Although it is now commonly invoked in the social, political and legal domains, the notion of critical mass has scientific origin. In the scientific world, the phrase is used to refer to the precise minimum level of fissionable plutonium or uranium required to start and sustain a chain reaction of nuclear fission which in turn will lead to explosion. In the social sciences critical mass is used to indicate a threshold of participants (tipping point) necessary to bring about and sustain the desired outcome. In an earlier work I have explored how the notion of critical mass can be applied in relation to special temporary measures. See Addis 2007b.

Chapter 13
Paradise Postponed? For a Judge-Led Generic Model of International Criminal Procedure and an End to 'Draft-as-You-Go'

Michael Bohlander

Abstract Since 1945, international criminal justice has been one continuous construction site, an expression of the attitude of international stakeholders and policy-makers that favours temporary solutions to contemporary problems. Even with the creation of the ICC that has not really changed. This chapter will set out a few fundamental and rather radical ideas that aim at initiating a thorough rethinking of the way criminal proceedings at the international level are regulated and run today. It sees itself very much as a call for a principled re-evaluation and for a move away from the attempts of the last two decades of arriving at a genuine amalgam of diverse systems by the method of judicial trial and error. The existing model(s) is/are an exemplary expression of the temporariness of international law, because it/they proceed(s) from a refusal by international law-makers to engage in drafting a permanent model that retains fairness standards while striving for maximum efficiency and that is meant to be applied across the board to any (new) tribunal—an approach that would lead to much greater certainty of law than is currently the case because of an increase in cross-institutional comparability. The chapter contends that while both adversarial and judge-led systems in their own national settings can achieve comparable levels of fairness, they differ in efficiency and that a judge-led model is better suited for the international arena and should be made the foundation for any future permanent procedural framework. However, the temporary nature of the present system which mainly uses adversarial models is based to a large extent on an unprincipled reliance on supposedly 'ready-made' and 'tried and tested' solutions from as well as the experience of staff employed at previous tribunals.

Chair in Comparative and International Criminal Law, Durham Law School, UK. With apologies to John Mortimer. The author would like to thank Mohamed Badar, Caroline Fournet, Berend Keulen, Stefan Kirsch, Simon Minks, Wolfgang Schomburg, Peter Wilkitzki and the Yearbook's editors and anonymous reviewers for helpful comments on an earlier draft. The usual disclaimers apply.

M. Bohlander (✉)
Durham Law School, Durham, UK
e-mail: michael.bohlander@dur.ac.uk

M. Ambrus and R.A. Wessel (eds.), *Netherlands Yearbook of International Law 2014*,
Netherlands Yearbook of International Law 45, DOI 10.1007/978-94-6265-060-2_13

The use of the adversarial model is thus not based on a principled evaluation of its usefulness and effectiveness in the international context but on a default attitude of the lawyers creating and populating international tribunals, and possibly the diplomatic community in the wider sense.

Keywords International criminal proceedings · Fairness · Efficiency · Judge-led model · Adversarial model · Ad hoc law-making · Judicial law-making · Sources of international criminal law · Control over the prosecution

Contents

13.1 Introduction 332
13.2 A Case in Point: The STL 337
13.3 The Conceptual Framework: Purpose, Fairness and Efficiency 341
13.3.1 Characteristics of Domestic Procedures 341
13.3.2 Problems of International Procedure: Geo-Politics, Mass Atrocities and Creation of a Historical Record 342
13.3.3 Sources of International Criminal Procedure: The Limited Role of Human Rights Law 343
13.3.4 International Criminal Procedure and General Sources of International Law 344
13.3.5 Efficiency in Fairness: The Path Forward 345
13.4 Preferring the Judge-Led Model: Reasons and Parameters 346
13.4.1 Romantic Views of the Role of the Judge in the Adversarial Trial 346
13.4.2 Absence of the Dichotomy Between Spheres of Professional and Lay Adjudication 347
13.4.3 Efficiency Aspects: Adversarial Versus Judge-Led Model 348
13.5 Conclusion 354
References 355

13.1 Introduction

Since 1945, international criminal justice has been one continuous construction site, an expression of the attitude of international stakeholders and policy-makers that favours temporary solutions to contemporary problems. Even with the creation of the International Criminal Court (ICC) that has not really changed. This chapter will try to set out a few fundamental and rather radical ideas that aim at initiating a thorough rethinking of the way criminal proceedings at the international level are regulated and run today. The author, prior to his 10 years as an academic in a common law university in England, served in the German judiciary for 13 years, in an international tribunal for two, and has had first-hand experience of the English criminal justice system as a barrister's pupil; he thus hopes to have gained a deeper insight into the practical as well as theoretical framework of both civil and common law procedural models. The chapter does not make any claim about being able to address all of the basic issues of all stages of the proceedings and will focus mainly on the trial phase in the wider sense, i.e. from the preparation of the indictment onwards, as the centrepiece of criminal proceedings; it sees itself very much as a call for a principled re-evaluation and for a move away from the attempts of the last two decades of arriving at a genuine amalgam of diverse systems by the method of judicial trial and error.[1] The history of international criminal procedure until the advent of the ICC has substantially been one of cobbling together building blocks from different traditions in order to create a new *sui generis* system based on extrapolations from Article 38(1) of the Statute of the International Court of Justice (ICJ) and the history of Nuremberg, Tokyo and the other post-war military tribunals. This eclectic approach has unfortunately been combined with a plethora of regulatory lacunae left to the judges of the tribunals by the international (for want of a better word:) law-making bodies, a criticism that applies to the ICC as well, albeit clearly to a lesser degree. Yet, the recent spate of cases over the accused's duty to be present at the hearings in the context of the Kenyatta Proceedings and the clear political overtones in the decisions, including the fact that the Assembly of States Parties (ASP) later caved into the pressure from the African Union, should be sufficient evidence that even fairly basic and otherwise settled procedural concepts can acquire allergenic qualities in the system of international criminal law when they come into contact with the catalyst of international comity of states.[2] The 'sui generis' system seems nonetheless to have had mainly adversarial overtones.[3] Even in cases where the statute of a tribunal, such as the Special Tribunal for Lebanon (STL),[4] provides for the adaptation of a civil law model,[5] the court's judges in their rule-making power have, as will be shown below, blindsided the drafters of the Statute and introduced a way for the Court to revert to what is in essence an adversarial model. The adversarial procedure is then infused with token civil law content, which creates unnecessary friction. For example, the introduction of the use of written statements as evidence at the International Criminal Tribunal for former Yugoslavia (ICTY) in the wake of its completion strategy was meant solely to speed up the trials, but it also had ramifications into the legitimacy of the rules of

[1] On the issues of 'legacy' and the different 'goals' of international criminal justice, see the wide-ranging chapter by Eser 2011 at 108 ff. Eser already identified many of the same issues referred to in this paper. Yet, he appeared to refrain from making similarly drastic demands.

[2] Only recently was this made plain again at the national level in *R (on the application of Khan) v. Secretary of State for Foreign and Commonwealth Affairs*, when the Court of Appeal stated that in the context of a murder trial against a British national who had provided intelligence to US forces who then used it for a deadly drone attack, a finding that the operator of the drone was guilty of murder would 'inevitably be understood by the US as a condemnation of them'. *R (on the application of Khan) v. Secretary of State for Foreign and Commonwealth Affairs* [2014] All ER (D) 112 (Jan), paras 34–37, 44, 55, 56.

[3] See, for example, the admission by Judge O-Gon Kwon of the ICTY in a speech in 2011, in Sluiter et al. 2013, at 1417.

[4] UNSC Res. 1757, 30 May 2007, Annex: Agreement between the United Nations and the Lebanese Republic on the establishment of a Special Tribunal for Lebanon (hereinafter STL Statute).

[5] The Cambodian Court, the ECCC, has a judge-led trial model as far as questioning of witnesses is concerned that is similar to that of the Lebanese law. See Sluiter et al. 2013, at 703 and the text below.

evidence and the fairness to the accused, as well as their right to confront witnesses in an otherwise adversarial setting, leading Judge David Hunt to remark famously in the *Milosevic* case that the interpretation of Rule 92*bis* by the Appeals Chamber majority left a 'spreading stain' on the reputation of the ICTY.[6] Interesting as the

---

[6] *Prosecutor v. Slobodan Milosevic*, Appeals Chamber, Admissibility of Evidence in Chief in the Form of Written Statement, Case No. IT-02-54-AR73.4, Dissenting Opinion of Judge David Hunt (Majority Decision given 30 September 2003), 21 October 2003, paras 19–22 (footnotes omitted). Judge Hunt was quite vociferous in his criticism and some excerpts from the dissent are warranted. He said, citing an English judge, Lord Atkin: 'I know of only one authority which might justify the suggested method of construction: "When I use a word", Humpty Dumpty said in rather a scornful tone, "it means just what I choose it to mean, neither more nor less." "The question is", said Alice, "whether you can make words mean so many different things." "The question is", said Humpty Dumpty, "which is to be master – that's all". Judge Hunt then went on: 'The Appeals Chamber [...] has no power to alter the ordinary meaning of words used in the Rules. The tender of the written statement of a witness to take the place of his oral testimony on the matters with which that statement deals, and notwithstanding that the witness has attested to its truth orally, necessarily falls within the phrase "the evidence of a witness in the form of a written statement in lieu of oral testimony" in Rule *92bis*(A). Accordingly, it is admissible only insofar as it goes to proof of a matter other than the acts and conduct of the accused or (as a matter of discretion) the acts and conduct of those in close proximity to the accused. The Majority Appeals Chamber Decision drives a horse and cart through the previous interpretation of Rule *92bis*, and it seriously prejudices the accused [...]. I recently stated, in an appeal from the Rwanda Tribunal, that the very proper endorsement by the Security Council "in the strongest terms " of the Completion Strategy of the Yugoslav Tribunal should not be interpreted as an encouragement by the Security Council to the Tribunal to conduct its trials so that they would be other than fair trials. It is necessary to repeat that statement in the present case in order to apply it directly to the Majority Appeals Chamber Decision. That Decision unfortunately follows the trend of other recent decisions of the Appeals Chamber which reverse or ignore its previously carefully considered interpretations of the law or of the procedural rules, with a consequential destruction of the rights of the accused enshrined in the Tribunal's Statute and in customary international law. The only reasonable explanation for these decisions appears to be a desire to assist the prosecution to bring the Completion Strategy to a speedy conclusion. I have been unable to agree with those decisions because I do not believe that, in doing so, I would be performing my duties "honourably, faithfully, impartially and conscientiously" as the solemn declaration which I took when I became a judge of the Tribunal requires me to do. The international community has entrusted the Tribunal with the task of trying persons charged with serious violations of international humanitarian law. It expects the Tribunal to do so in accordance with those rights of the accused to which reference is made in the previous paragraph. If the Tribunal is not given sufficient time and money to do so by the international community, then it should not attempt to try those persons in a way which does not accord with those rights. In my opinion, it is improper to take the Completion Strategy into account in departing from interpretations which had earlier been accepted by the Appeals Chamber where this is at the expense of those rights. This Tribunal will not be judged by the number of convictions which it enters, or by the speed with which it concludes the Completion Strategy which the Security Council has endorsed, but by the fairness of its trials. The Majority Appeals Chamber Decision and others in which the Completion Strategy has been given priority over the rights of the accused will leave a spreading stain on this Tribunal's reputation.'

developments in international criminal law may appear if viewed as a 'legal laboratory', the fact remains that courts, which deal with putting people away for many years for horrendous crimes, must first of all strive for legal certainty. This chapter will argue that the current unprincipled state of affairs is unsatisfactory, that mostly adversarially-based mixed systems make little sense in the international forum,[7] are responsible for delays and disadvantaging the defence, and that a move to a judge-led system is necessary, which protects the defence and keeps the prosecution in check by, among other things, ensuring sanctions for premature assurances[8] of trial-readiness—an issue brought into sharp relief again at the STL in the controversy about joining the case of a fifth accused at the eleventh hour to that of the four first accused when the trial was weeks away, when their case had been developing for far over a year and the identity of the fifth accused had been known all along as well.

With the rise of the major role for victims' groups in pre-trial and trial proceedings, the defence in a party-driven model is now facing a second adversary who is a purely interest-driven player in the game, one whom the judges will be reluctant to control because of the rising global criminal justice policy emphasis on victims' rights—an emphasis that tends to forget asking itself the question *whose* victims they are before a final conviction is entered. In the case of mass atrocities based on factually complex and drawn-out armed conflicts with a vast number of affected people, linking the fate of any *one* of the victims to the person in the dock is highly problematic and runs the risk of politicising the trial as well as demonising the defence. A model based in principle on judicial non-interference in the process may not be fit for purpose to counter these concerns, which have been recognised even by seasoned common law lawyers.[9]

The existing model(s) is/are an exemplary expression of the temporariness of international law, because it/they proceed(s) from a refusal by international law-makers to engage in drafting a model that retains fairness standards while striving for maximum efficiency and that is applied across the board to any (new) tribunal—an approach that would lead to much greater certainty of law than is currently the

[7] The author is aware that this attitude is bucking the current trend in international criminal law, which still attempts to arrive at a proper and reliable amalgamation or even celebrates diversity. For reference only, see the recent special section of the 2013 volume of the *Leiden Journal of International Law*: Nerlich 2013, at 777; Doherty 2013, at 937; Jackson and M'Boge 2013, at 947; and Byrne 2013, at 991.

[8] There may, however, also be different understandings of what the function of an indictment is. In the ICTY it seemed that it had almost the effect that an authorisation by the ICC Pre-Trial Chamber for the initiation of an investigation has; in civil law countries such as Germany, for example, the indictment is the final product of the investigations.

[9] Simons 2006. 'Steven Kay, a British court-appointed lawyer for Mr. Milosevic, said the adversarial system "utterly fails to deal with trials of the Milosevic type".'

case because of an increase in cross-institutional comparability.[10] The chapter contends that while both adversarial and judge-led[11] systems[12] in their own national settings can achieve comparable levels of fairness, they differ in efficiency and that a judge-led model is better suited for the international arena. It is useful to provide the conceptual setting against the background of which all the following arguments should be read, and these words could be repeated as an introduction under each and every subheading. The temporary nature of the present system which mainly uses adversarial models is based to a large extent on an unprincipled reliance on supposedly 'ready-made' and 'tried and tested' solutions from, as well as the experience of staff employed at previous tribunals. The use of the adversarial model is thus not based on a principled evaluation of its usefulness and effectiveness in the international context but on a default attitude of the lawyers creating and populating international tribunals, and possibly the diplomatic community in the wider sense. In other words, the chapter argues that the current approach is *de facto* using the adversarial model as a drafting template for almost any new tribunal without engaging in a thorough and needs-based investigation of the demands of efficiency underlying international criminal justice. As will be shown at the example of the Lebanon Tribunal, sometimes the opposing intentions of the drafters of a Statute are undermined by adversarially-minded judges. The author does not advance the suggestion that the adversarial model as such lacks capacity for permanence, and if the international justice system had used the inquisitorial approach in the same manner as it has the adversarial one, the same comments would apply *mutatis mutandis*. Yet, as things stand at the moment, the temporary quality is *factually* tied to the adversarial model. If we want to advance to a permanent and coherent procedural paradigm,

[10] One must praise the Herculean effort of the contributors to the immensely useful book edited by Sluiter, at a synthesis of the existing law and practice of international criminal procedure, and the recommendations offered for future policy directions. Proceeding in their research and recommendations as they did from the existing and historical international tribunals and courts as a basis for their extrapolations, a really drastic departure from the current framework did not, indeed could not emerge, especially in an environment where the judges are in possession of the case file in advance of the trial. In the loose context of the trial stage this reluctance can be seen at the examples of an aversion to legal re-characterisation of facts based on the defining function of the indictment (Sluiter et al. 2013, at 487 f.), separate sentencing hearings (ibid., at 543), the order of the presentation of evidence and the role of the judges—where express reference is made to the 'common law concern about excessive judicial interference in the examination by counsel' (ibid., at 654), judicial powers to question, subpoena and control the examination of witnesses and control over the sequence of case presentation—recommendations: none (ibid., at 706, 720, 733, 743).

[11] This expression seems preferrable to the historically charged 'inquisitorial', although the latter is still the more common usage.

[12] Although the author has previously bemoaned the fact that other procedural traditions originating outside the common law-civil law dichotomy have been persistently kept out of the picture in international criminal law, one must realise the practical necessities and accept that for the purposes of advancing towards an international unified model, the discussion will mainly take place between the adversarial and the judge-led paradigms as spawned by the common and civil law traditions. It is also unclear from the existing published materials to which extent other systems are willing or able to contribute meaningfully to the debate.

we must now undertake such a principled study and a needs-based analysis. This chapter will argue that the outcome of such an examination should lead to the adoption of a judge-led procedure.

This new paradigm will also require a new kind of international judge, namely persons with massive trial experience and the capacity to run a trial pro-actively—a radical departure from the (alleged) ideal of the impartial and more or less passive umpire that still pervades much of the thinking in international criminal justice and allows for the recruitment of candidates who do not have that experience—although gratifyingly this particular concern seems to be on the decline.

The author is under no illusion that anything like this will happen anytime soon, yet the debate should be had and the aim should be to arrive at a coherent and monolithic concept of international criminal procedure that rises above the petty and often still preciously guarded idiosyncracies of each system, as well as the lack of trans-systemic understanding among the judges and practitioners. It is no secret that the legitimacy of international criminal courts, and of international criminal law in general, is still hotly contested in many parts of the world for political and legal reasons, and the ad hoc manner of establishing them with the often ensuing non-chalant disregard exhibited by the international players for the legal system of the respective target country serves as an additional irritant. If there was a permanent system that applied to all international trials and which everyone was apprised of in advance, no-one could legitimately complain about—at least—this facet of the picture anymore.

13.2 A Case in Point: The STL

To clarify the point made about the STL and temporariness, it bears remembering that this tribunal was not meant to address international offences such as war crimes, crimes against humanity or genocide, but a simple if major terrorist attack in Lebanon and that it should apply substantive Lebanese law. The international involvement was merely due to the inability of the Lebanese judicial system to deal with this kind of violence itself. That did not stop the STL Appeals Chamber with its former President Cassese as reporting judge from trying to internationalise the domestic law on terrorism in its (in)famous Rule 176*bis* decision[13] and from muddying the waters by introducing international concepts of participation and multiple charging when the need for that was not entirely clear from looking at the

[13] *Prosecutor v. Ayyash et al.* Appeals Chamber, Interlocutory Decision on the Applicable Law: Terrorism. Conspiracy, Homicide, Perpetration, Cumulative Charging, Case No. STL-11-01/I, 16 February 2011. But see the decision on the reconsideration of this decision, where the Appeals Chamber—this time without Judge Cassese—already adopted a more flexible approach. *Prosecutor v. Ayyash et al.*, Appeals Chamber, Decision on Defence Requests for Reconsideration of the Appeals Chamber's Decision of 16 February 2011, Case No. STL-ll-01IPT/ACIR176bis, 18 July 2012, para 37.

domestic law. The procedural part was left in a mixed state but especially on the conduct of the trial proceedings there was an interesting reference in the STL Statute, namely Article 20(2):

> Unless otherwise decided by the Trial Chamber *in the interests of justice*, examination of witnesses shall commence with questions posed by the presiding judge, followed by questions posed by other members of the Trial Chamber, the Prosecutor and the Defence.[14]

This mode of questioning is clearly reminiscent of the judge-driven civil law model which applies in Lebanese law, unless the interests of justice require something else. The Rules of Procedure and Evidence (RPE) drafted by the judges provide for a means of avoiding the statutory approach, and it is the reasoning that is interesting.

> Rule 145 Questioning of Witnesses
>
> (A) Where the Trial Chamber *considers that the file submitted by the Pre-Trial Judge enables it to adopt the mode of proceeding outlined in Article 20(2) of the Statute*, after the opening statements of the Parties and of any victim participating in the proceedings, each witness shall first be questioned by the Presiding Judge and any other member of the Chamber, then by the Party that has called the witness, and subsequently cross-examined by the other Party, if the other Party elects to exercise its right of cross-examination. The witness may also subsequently be re-examined by the calling Party.
>
> (B) Where the Trial Chamber considers that the file submitted by the Pre-Trial Judge *is not such as to enable it to adopt the mode of proceeding envisaged in Article 20(2) of the Statute*, after the opening statements of the Parties and of any victim participating in the proceedings, the witnesses called before the Trial Chamber shall first be examined by the Party that called them, then cross-examined by the other Party, if the other Party elects to exercise its right of cross-examination. The witness may also subsequently be re- examined by the calling Party. The Presiding Judge and other members of the Trial Chamber may at any time ask questions.
>
> (C) The Trial Chamber may decide to depart from the modes of proceeding provided for in paras (A) and (B) wherever it considers that this is required by the interests of justice.[15]

Note that Article 20(2) STL Statute talks about the interests of justice as the only criterion for deviating from the normal order of things. Rule 145(A) introduces a new concept, namely the question whether in effect the prosecution dossier submitted by the pre-trial judge as the 'case file' is sufficient for the trial chamber judges to run the trial themselves. It already deviates without any apparent justification from the clear order established in Article 20(2) STL Statute: Court—prosecution—defence; the Statute does not refer to who called the party. It is in substance identical with the rules under Lebanese criminal procedure, namely Articles 180 and 181 of the 2001 Code of Criminal Procedure (CCP) for proceedings before the single judge and Articles 255–260

[14] Article 20(2) STL Statute (emphases added).

[15] Rules of Procedure and Evidence, ICC-ASP/1/3 (Part.II-A), 9 September 2002 (hereinafter RPE) (emphases added).

CPP for trial before the full criminal court; Article 260 CPP even restricts the right of the parties to ask questions of witnesses in that they have to be made through the presiding judge. The CPP is available on the STL's website and, indeed, one of the Lebanese appellate judges was responsible for its publication at the time the CPP was passed.

Rule 145(B) then takes the bold step to say that if the case file is not sufficient for the judges to proceed as under Article 20(2), the chamber may revert to adversarial mode. In other words, if the file does not provide a sound basis to the standard required to follow the procedure as foreseen in the hierarchically superior Statute, another procedure can be followed which divests the trial chamber of the control of the presentation of the evidence and shifts control to the prosecution. This is in substance nothing else but allowing the prosecution—via the pre-trial judge—to declare trial readiness when it is in fact not ready, because if it were, then the file would contain all the material the trial chamber would need to proceed as ordered by Article 20(2) STL Statute. How this can be in the interests of justice is unclear, to say the least. It might in extreme cases also mean that even though the case file was as complete as possible at the time, the judges could revert to adversarial mode if none of them was comfortable with or experienced in running a pro-actively judge-led trial.[16] Given the systemic or professional provenance of many international judges in general that would not seem to be an unreasonable inference.

In the context of the STL there would have been enough experienced Lebanese judges who could have used the Lebanese system effortlessly. The presiding judge did not have to be an international one. No-one suggests that the Lebanese judges would be biased merely *qua* being Lebanese—otherwise they should not be on the bench under the criteria of Article 9(1) STL Statute. Yet, the Lebanese judges would have been uncomfortable with and lacked experience in the largely adversarial

[16] In this context, it is not uncommon to hear the question 'how does this affect justice?'. This question seems to proceed from an undefined and almost nebulously philosophical idea of justice that is distinct and uncoupled from any of its real-world incarnations within a particular procedural framework and is akin to asking whether the trial would not be 'fair' otherwise. The answer to that is, firstly, that, as we have accepted, both adversarial and inquisitorial models can achieve comparable levels of fairness but as we shall argue, they do not reach the same degree of efficiency. Secondly, and more to the theoretical point, it is the procedural model as set out in a statute etc. that defines the ambit of the powers of the prosecution and the judges, as well as the rights of the defence and the victims. It is dangerous to tamper with a balanced system based on whims arising from perceived individual injustices, as this tends to upset the balance and lead to inroads into a party's legal positions, and more often than not those of the defence. Finally, although positivism does no longer have a very favourable press these days when the famous Radbruch formula about unjust law is trotted out regularly, it bears reminding oneself that to rely on a notion as abstract as that of 'natural justice' for use—in an individual case—as a substantive corrective criterion to procedural rules laid down by (a written) law is at the end of the day nothing short of allowing judges to discard such laws if they deem them unfair or unwieldy, beyond the reach of the method of accepted teleological interpretation. Substance without form is arbitrariness.

set-up brought about by the RPE. Why this was done when Article 28(2) STL Statute states that in drafting the RPE

> the judges shall be guided, as appropriate, by the Lebanese Code of Criminal Procedure, as well as by other reference materials reflecting the highest standards of international criminal procedure, with a view to ensuring a fair and expeditious trial

remains open to question. Why not simply adopt the relevant sections of the CPP and make sure they comply with the afore-mentioned standards? Maybe because that would have made the ubiquitous 'tribunal-hopping' of staff and prosecutors from other tribunals more difficult? Maybe because the first President in charge of the STL had already had the experience of drafting a set of RPE at another international tribunal and it seemed less burdensome to adapt these to the STL's environment—with the innovation of a separate pre-trial (but not investigating) judge already having been secured in the Statute? But then the one major controversial item in the STL and CPP arsenal of procedural tools from a human rights standards point of view, namely the trial *in absentia*, had also already been anchored in Article 22 STL Statute—for obvious reasons, because no-one at the time really anticipated that any of the suspects would ever attend trial, not least since Hezbollah had always made that clear. The Statute itself is thus somewhat contradictory with respect to what it regards as the 'highest standards of international criminal procedure', when all other international courts and tribunals, including the European Court of Human Rights, have always shied away from the procedure *in absentia* like, as it were, the Devil from holy water. Finally, what the exact content of Rule 145(C) RPE is, remains equally uncertain: neither judge-led nor adversarial but …? The judges of the STL's Trial Chamber in the case of *Ayyash* et al. predictably reverted to the adversarial mode when the trial began on 16 January 2014.[17]

This brief excursion into the law of just one tribunal has hopefully shown what effects the 'draft-as-you-go' approach as an expression of temporariness can entail. It opens the building of the administration of justice up to intruders with separate agendas and to political negotiations that would appear to fit and fix the temporary emergency and to fill the temporary gaps in the law needed for the fixing. A proper and detailed Code of International Criminal Procedure applicable to any and all international criminal courts and tribunals—and this chapter in the final analysis argues for nothing less—would mean a big step away from these constant uncertainties. After all, no-one would want to be faced with a justice system as it currently exists on the international level, were they to face trial at home even on lesser charges than genocide. In this context, the highest international justice standards must not fall below their highest national counterparts—and legal certainty is a fundamental one among their number.

[17] See *Prosecutor v. Ayyash* et al., Trial Chamber, Directions on the Conduct of the Proceedings, Case No. STL-11-01/T/TC, 16 January 2014.

13.3 The Conceptual Framework: Purpose, Fairness and Efficiency

13.3.1 Characteristics of Domestic Procedures

Before a decision about the proper shape of what one might call a Code of International Criminal Procedure can be made, we need to examine the conceptual framework of international criminal proceedings. What are international trials meant to achieve? What can they achieve? One should guard against exaggerated expectations. It is helpful to start with the national framework and function of a trial. A trial at domestic level is meant to establish the criminal guilt of an individual accused. The offences are in most cases clearly circumscribed by the domestic laws on criminal offences. The general part on modes of liability, attempts, participation, *mens rea* etc. is also normally fairly settled. There is usually a long history of case law, which may be either legally binding if a system subscribes to *stare decisis*, or factually binding because no judge risks being overturned by going against the settled jurisprudence of the appellate courts. Depending on the procedural system, the court or the parties will be in charge of adducing the evidence and structuring the trial; in the first case, the parties often have a corresponding right to ask the court to hear additional evidence, in the latter it is mostly their own responsibility. Each system will be embedded in a wider cultural context, which will in turn decide whether a mode of trial is seen as fair or not. Some societies put a great emphasis on lay participation as a damper on state intrusion, and accept the attendant occasional incoherence in the system based on laymen's inclination to favour justice in the individual case over enforcing rules consistenly. Others prefer to make an effort for a principled approach, and thus value the role of professionally trained judges more. Some systems see their judges as neutral umpires, others ask them to descend into the arena. Some restrict the fact-finding to lay-persons and questions of law to professional judges, others allow a mixture or even do without any lay element at all. Mirjan Damaška set this basic picture out many years ago and his analysis is still worth reading.[18] However, especially in adversarial settings such as, for example, the United Kingdom, the rise of managerial judging[19] raises the question of whether the traditional picture of the disinterested umpire can still be upheld.[20] What can be said, however, is that each of the two systems in its own cultural environment is capable of achieving adequate levels of fairness accepted as sufficient by the host society, even though a different society might disagree.

[18] Damaška 1986.

[19] Critically McEwan 2011.

[20] On managerial judging in international criminal courts, see Langer 2005.

13.3.2 Problems of International Procedure: Geo-Politics, Mass Atrocities and Creation of a Historical Record[21]

When we shift to the international level we find, firstly, that (geo-)political factors enter into the picture, which do not tend to feature prominently in the everyday domestic trial environment. An international tribunal is always caught between the political interests of states and/or international organisations which often already surface in the negotiations about their establishment, their jurisdiction and their financing, staffing etc. Secondly, atrocities of a scale common to most international tribunals do not normally occur in domestic settings and thus have a greater impact on human emotions and the need for understanding their origins as a first step in preventing their repetition. Thirdly, and most of all, however, we find that there is no common cultural milieu and agreement about what determines a fair trial, absent certain insular, but in nature generic, findings by human rights courts etc., the applicability of which to the international courts is, however, sometimes contested by reference to their unique nature or the complexity of the proceedings before them, most prominently in the context of remand in custody, as recently highlighted in the *Seselj* trial at the ICTY.[22]

The first two factors, namely geo-politics and the scale of the atrocities, have led some[23] to argue that an international trial is not merely meant to establish individual guilt, but also to create a historical record for the victimised region on which possibly reconciliation efforts at national level could be based. It is here that the difference between the adversarial and—to use the traditional expression—'inquisitorial' system comes to light. An essentially party-driven system, as currently used in the international courts, cannot perform this function because apart from any information necessary for establishing the core offence elements and the so-called *chapeau elements*, such as 'armed conflict', 'widespread or systematic' etc., the party leading the evidence will not be interested in presenting any evidence that might confute its claim. The disclosure regime that is meant to remedy this imbalance is imperfect to say the least, because although the prosecution is under an obligation to disclose exculpatory material, no-one knows whether they actually are in possession of such material and the necessarily helpless blanket requests often made by the defence to disclose material are routinely turned down by the prosecution for lack of specificity, and that attitude is sanctioned by the judges who term such defence applications as impermissible 'fishing expeditions'. Similarly, the prosecution in most tribunals has taken to literally burying defence teams under millions of pages of documents 'disclosed' on CD-ROMs or by other electronic means, and the practice continues almost unchecked. This despite the

[21] See also Eser 2011.

[22] See *Prosecutor v. Vojislav Seselj*, Trial Chamber, Decision on continuation of proceedings, Case No. IT-03-67-T, 13 December 2013, paras 18–24.

[23] See, for example, the references and discussion in Sluiter et al. 2013, at 60, 62–63.

fact that the defence is at a material disadvantage in all international criminal trials when it comes to accessing raw evidence, because of a lack of equality of arms based not infrequently on a refusal of the countries concerned to cooperate with the defence teams. An inquisitorial approach could alleviate such ambush or non-cooperation tactics to some extent, yet we must face up to the reality that even proactive judges must at the end of the day work with the material the prosecution says it has unearthed and diclosed in the investigative and pre-trial phase of the proceedings—unless a real investigating judge was used, as, for example, in the Extraordinary Chambers in the Courts of Cambodia (ECCC), albeit there in a purely national context. After that the court has no real chance of doing its own digging on anything approaching a major and thorough scale. Lastly, in both systems judicial economy and scarcity of resources militate against any attempt at a thorough historical *Aufarbeitung* of the events. Thus even in a judge-led environment the control over the incriminating—and, absent an active pre-trial defence, also over much of the exculpatory—evidence ultimately rests with the prosecution.

Against such a background, it is futile to speak of record creation as an aim of international trials and it should consequently be ruled out from our considerations as to what constitutes legitimate purposes of international criminal proceedings. The purpose of an international trial, like its domestic counterpart, can and should only be the decision on the individual guilt of the accused. From what we have said above, it is also evident that while there may be an incremental advantage of the judge-led approach of making sure that all relevant evidence is presented, this advantage may be seen as negligible if the prosecution is determined not to 'play ball', as it were. This particular aspect of fairness cannot be solved satisfactorily by either system. We must thus look for other mechanisms, which will be described below.

13.3.3 Sources of International Criminal Procedure: The Limited Role of Human Rights Law

Some have argued that an amalgamated international procedure could be based to a large extent on distilling human rights standards. While national proceedings are run by actors on often minutely choreographed tracks set out by detailed procedural codes and case law embedded in and originating from a more or less monolithic and homogenous legal and moral culture of the host society, the picture on the international level is entirely different. There is no homogenous attitude as to which *kind* of procedure is fair and just, if we leave a few of the fundamental truths from provisions such as, for example, Article 6 of the European Convention on Human Rights (ECHR), aside. The role of human rights regulation is restricting the reach of the state *vis-à-vis* the citizens' private sphere, and even without Strasbourg's time-honoured margin-of-appreciation doctrine the human rights framework is much too crude a tool to be useful in shaping the nuts-and-bolts functions of a country's or of an international criminal procedure. Human rights law tells us nothing about whether we should have an adversarial or judge-led procedure, lay judges, a jury (and if so what kind of jury), a single judge or a panel of judges and for which offences, a *juge d'instruction* or an independent prosecutor, a *chambre d'accusation*, a grand jury or admission of the indictment to trial by the trial court or the investigating judge, whether and to what extent cross-examination and re-examination of witnesses should take place etc. All human rights law tells us is that if we use a certain model, it must in its operation comply with the basic rules of fairness emanating from the *generic* human rights standards, and as we said above each of these models can achieve human rights compliance within their own frameworks—yet problems may arise when we mix them. One should also be on guard against perhaps unwittingly transposing certain domestic ideosyncracies about fairness into the interpretation of international-level human rights from one's own domestic background, i.e. reading something into them which one then 'reads out' again in the process of analysis.

While human rights law has a relatively straightforward ambit of application since its main purpose is to be used to regulate behaviour of states with respect to individuals affected by their actions, this becomes much more difficult in an environment consisting of international criminal courts tasked with adjudicating upon ill-defined crimes using even less well-defined general principles committed in a target country whose legal order may be entirely different from the prevailing views of the international community. International comity of states can then also create massive problems in finding common ground.[24] In principle, international criminal courts are not addressees of existing human rights instruments but have bound themselves either via their case law or have been bound by references to human rights law in their constituent documents. Yet, even human rights standards can vary from region to region. Would an Arab be able to rely on the specificities of the 2004 Arab Charter on Human Rights or a Muslim to rely on the 1990 Cairo Declaration of Human Rights in Islam, if and to the extent that they might diverge from the Universal Declaration of Human Rights or the ICCPR, and where such a diversion could have an impact on that person's case before an international criminal court? These are but a few points but it seems questionable that the answer to the appropriate model for international criminal proceedings can be gleaned from human rights law alone.

13.3.4 International Criminal Procedure and General Sources of International Law

Article 38 Statute of the ICJ contains for all practical purposes a (possibly non-exhaustive) list of the sources of international law. As far as international criminal procedure is concerned, most of the work has to be done under the headings of

[24] A good example would be the question of wheter the national criminalisation of LGBT persons can be a crime against humanity, namely persecution, and the less than progressive response of the drafters of the ICC Statute to the concerns of a number of conservative states, both from Islamic and Christian backgrounds, about acknowledging 'sexual orientation' as a category of the term 'gender' in its Article 7(3). See Bohlander 2014b.

customary law and general principles of law recognised by all nations. Customary law in this context takes us back mainly to the field of human rights standards and the reference to general principles take us back to square one: what to do when you have massively conflicting approaches to procedural models arising out of centuries of geo-political influence of a few colonising cultural systems across the globe? As we saw earlier, even in a *prima facie* closed system, such as the ICC, there will be lacunae and need for interpretation because the law is anything but settled, Elements of Crimes, RPE and Regulations of the Court notwithstanding. This frustration may have led to a de facto uncoupling of the method of argument on the international level from its domestic roots in that the system has by now become self-referencing, i.e. using its own precedents beginning with Nuremberg, Tokyo and the post-war military tribunals and stretching to the ICTY, ICTR as well as the tribunals and courts for Sierra Leone, Cambodia, Lebanon, Bosnia etc. as a basis for future extrapolations rather than returning to the coalface of national principles. If this trend to self-referencing could be verified, it would in the present context mean a perpetuation of mostly adversarial and in essence common law approaches. And yet, there would still remain a variety of interpretations denying an adequate level of certainty and homogeneity. However, even if the courts were to go back to the national principles proper and engaged in grass-roots research, the picture would not look much better, because as the author has shown elsewhere[25] the research exercise is always massively selective and depending on the linguistic commands of the people doing the research. The creation of a separate and dedicated legal research advisory section staffed by people from a wide range of legal systems and with a broad spectrum of language command has apparently not been considered worth following up. In sum, the diagnosis must be that reliance on the usual process of finding international law is not fit for purpose if we want to reach a stage of necessary certainty of law.

13.3.5 Efficiency in Fairness: The Path Forward

If we accept that both the adversarial and judge-led systems can achieve the required level of procedural fairness if they are applied in their pure form, then efficiency becomes the deciding factor. International criminal courts are enormously expensive affairs and making sure that their budgets are guaranteed year on year is one of the major concerns of their operation. The same applies to the accused's right to a speedy trial. While this principle has actually been used in various instances to justify the *restriction* of defence rights, the international tribunals have from the beginning struggled with maintaining an acceptable length of detention before a decision at trial level is made and have constantly referred to the 'unique' circumstances in and the massive difficulties under which they have to

[25] Bohlander 2011, with references to previous studies.

operate as justification, especially as far as collecting evidence[26] in situ is concerned. Yet, this argument, if it is sound at all, would be acceptable only to the extent that the system does all it can to make sure delays are not caused by avoidable organisational slack. There is cause to doubt that this is currently happening.

If we stop arguing about alleged model-inherent deficiencies in fairness, then the financial and operational strictures of international criminal justice and the right to a speedy trial demand that we choose the most efficient model of the two, all things being equal with regard to fairness, and stick to that. In the event of unforeseeable and unavoidable gaps in the law, a modified application of the principles of Article 38 ICJ Statute should ensue in that only jurisdictions that use a system of sufficient similarity should be used to provide comparative material, obviating the deleterious effects of trans-systemic transplants. The use of only one model that would apply across the board to all international criminal tribunals and courts would also ensure that the potential for continuos professional education for practitioners and judges would be massively enhanced and that the training of new candidates for a pool of international practitioners could be better organised and streamlined. The reasons why and how a judge-led model appears better suited for international criminal proceedings will be set out in the next section.

13.4 Preferring the Judge-Led Model: Reasons and Parameters

13.4.1 Romantic Views of the Role of the Judge in the Adversarial Trial

For many people, the adversarial model has an aura of perfect fairness,[27] because its paradigm is the disinterested judge who makes sure the parties play by the rules but does not become entangled in the actual sparring between them herself. However, every seasoned adversarial practitioner knows that the judge

[26] There may (still) be an unspoken consensus among those populating the international criminal institutions, the 'no-impunity'-driven NGOs, parts of academia and, of course, the politicians that the prosecution should always be given more time to look for evidence to ensure a conviction of those one already knows are guilty and to ensure satisfaction for 'the victims'—with the latter's increasing procedural visibility and participation in international proceedings before conviction contributing a particularly destabilising element; yet, to say so is profoundly politically incorrect these days. Needless to say that this attitude may have a lot to do with the one displayed by the proponents of the record-creating function addressed above, and that it has no place in a balanced view of the administration of criminal justice.

[27] Sluiter even goes as far as saying that 'international human rights are based on an underlying assumption that criminal proceedings shall be of an adversarial character'. In the context of the citation of bringing charges what is meant there is probably that they shall follow an *accusatory* model and not the historical 'inquisitorial' model where prosecutor, judge and enforcer were the same person. Sluiter et al. 2013, at 480.

has a huge potential for influencing the outcome of the case by her decisions on which evidence to admit and other incidental orders, but most seriously through her summing-up to the jury. There are prosecution-minded and defence-minded judges, and probably more of the former, not least because of the selection process in some common law tradition countries which still would seem to put a lot of weight on matters such as whether the candidate has in the past represented government branches or the prosecution service in court. It needs to be borne in mind that in those jurisdictions where the jury do not give reasons for their verdict, the attack on the safety of the verdict is based on the summing-up of the judge and any other decisions that may have crucially impacted on the course of the trial—but not on the jury's verdict. The romantic view of the adversarial approach has also begun to suffer severe corrosion from the managerial judging campaign—while managerialism is an irritant artefact in an adversarial setting, it causes much less friction in a judge-led one. The adversarial judge has the case file but he is at the same time not allowed to structure the trial himself merely because he knows at least the prosecution's case and under modern managerial rules also quite a lot of the defence case in advance. Since he is part of the state he cannot be allowed to 'present the state's case against the accused'—a choice of words that does not properly translate into the judge-led model where 'finding the material truth' about a certain chain of events is the paramount goal, not 'proving a case'. Judge-led systems, to be fair, face similar concerns about judges who tend to favour the prosecution's side of the case, not least in those countries such as Germany, where in some of the states a career shift between bench and prosecution service and back to the bench is anything but unusual and, as some say, indeed required in order to move up the ranks. However, at least in cases of serious crime, the system has provided for its own checks on that particular problem, among others by using collegiate panels and by requiring the panel to give reasons for conviction/acquittal and sentence, which are subject to full appellate scrutiny.

13.4.2 Absence of the Dichotomy Between Spheres of Professional and Lay Adjudication

Another reason that speaks against the adversarial model in an international setting is that the trials are without exception professional-judge-only affairs. There is no jury, there are no lay judges. The adversarial paradigm is in part historically and traditionally—if not necessarily conceptually—connected to the distinction between finding facts and law in a judge-and-jury system. The jury is not meant to know anything of the dossier or case file and to base its findings solely on what they are presented with at trial. Contamination of the jury by material extrinsic to the trial is to be avoided. Similarly, even in cases of lay judges sitting with the professionals in a judge-led scenario and where the lay assessors have almost full judicial stature, human rights law imposes restrictions on what material they can have access to and how, as explained for the German context by the Strasbourg Court in *Elezi*.[28] This concern about lay contamination is conceptually[29] invalid in a system that allows the professional judges to have the case file in advance and to engage in structuring the ambit and progress of the case from an early stage through pre-trial conferences and decisions.

Nor should one argue for the inclusion of a lay element in international courts. The domestic problems of lay involvement increase exponentially on the international level, both conceptually and logistically. The horrific nature of the events and most importantly the graphic nature of some of the evidence in international trials routinely transcend even the worst cases on a domestic level and are sufficient to try the resilience of any hardened professional, much more so that of a lay person. On the practical side, lay participants usually have a job and their employers will be very reluctant to let them go for the periods normally envisaged for these trials, not to speak of possible sequestration necessary to avoid media contamination etc. Finally, as far as infusing and tempering the professional process with a lay person's unspoilt common sense and experience is concerned, in the context of international trials that would also mean ensuring cultural understanding of the target country—yet, lay assessors or jurors from the conflict regions would almost by definition have to be excluded for obvious fear of bias. For good reason therefore, international courts use only professionals, which means that the typical mechanisms for avoiding lay bias are irrelevant and prior knowledge of the case file has to be checked by other controls. If one gives the judges advance knowledge of the prosecution case file, they should be allowed to use it. Equally, once the case file goes to the court, full procedural control should shift to the judges and the prosecution in particular would have to be held to have produced all the material it needs to prove its case, with attendant sanctions for late or additional evidence.

13.4.3 Efficiency Aspects: Adversarial Versus Judge-Led Model

In the following section we shall look at a number of pressure points in practice—some of them will be of a rather nuts-and-bolts character, but looking at practice without looking into the moving parts of the engine, as it were, will ultimately be of little help.

---

[28] *Elezi v. Germany*, ECtHR, No. 26771/03, 12 June 2008.

[29] Naturally, the sociological question of whether professional judges can be contaminated by prior knowledge of the case file—they can, of course—is an entirely different matter and must be countered by other mechanisms, as explained above.

13.4.3.1 Preparedness for Trial and Controlling the Prosecution

A judge-led model based on possession of the case file by the trial court with the ensuing control over the structuring of the proceedings by the panel would appear to have distinct advantages over a party-driven adversarial model, even if one takes into account efforts at managerial judging and restricting adversarial excesses in the international context, especially when one looks at the practical side and less at the theoretical underpinnings. The efficiency of the adversarial setting depends very much on the preparedness of the parties for trial and as almost all cases in the adversarial procedures of the international criminal courts have shown and as was already mentioned above, the major issue is the de facto control by the prosecution over the evidence and its monopoly of access to domestic state cooperation, its not infrequent reticence to full and manageable disclosure to the defence and the reluctance or inability of the judges to interfere with the prosecution's conduct of a case. One particular example of this was the practice of the prosecution exhibited in some cases to use one set of materials to gain the confirmation of an indictment *ex parte* while dropping those materials, either in whole or in part, from the evidence they will use at trial—if they do not intend to use them at trial the defence may face difficulties in making submissions arising from the confirmation materials. Even though the judges may have the case file, as at the STL, for example, they may still leave control of the presentation of the evidence to the parties and in that context that means mainly the prosecution since more often than not the bulk of the evidence will come from their side. The judges thus have no proper control over the case flow and the time needed, which creates knock-on effects on case allocation and planning for other proceedings. The parties present their respective evidence in turn, not structured along evidential issues with direct confrontation of prosecution and defence evidence over identical issues. Thus, given the ususal timelines along which international trials develop, it may happen that the defence evidence[30] on a particular fact will be heard many months after that of the prosecution, a fact that will hardly serve to focus the court's deliberations on the probative value of the evidence or the credibility of witnesses. The prosecution will be exposed to the constant temptation to go to trial with less than a fully prepared case, especially if it can hope that the court will take a lenient view on amendments of the indictment and additional evidence, a hope that is not necessarily diminished by the current practice of more or less passive judicial attitude.

---

[30] Simon Minks, who prosecuted the Somali piracy case of *Dhow* in the Netherlands, informed the author of an interesting twist in the Dutch proceedings, where defence counsel asked the court for an advance payment on costs of over € 16,000 in order to travel to Somalia and conduct their own investigations. The advance was granted, yet at the time of writing the parties were arguing whether and to what extent the evidence produced by that visit was admissible at trial. Email from Simon Minks of 18 February 2014 (on file with the author).

13.4.3.2 Control Over the Presentation of Evidence and Exclusion Rules

The adversarial approach also means that, leaving aside some prior disclosure obligations, the defence will not need to show its hand until the prosecution has rested. The latter is in principle, to be fair, also the case in the judge-led model, yet if the court is using an event-structured trial schedule, a defence that wishes to engage rather than torpedo the trial will have every incentive to cooperate by naming its evidence in time so that the schedule can accommodate it—a non-cooperative defence naturally raises different questions of trial control which we cannot delve into here.[31] A lot will in this context also depend on involving the defence in a meaningful manner at as early a stage as possible, something which can admittedly be difficult given the often real concerns over witness intimidation and evidence tampering. At the end of the day, the procedure must also provide for sanctions against frivolous delaying tactics by both sides, and exclusion of late evidence the admission of which would lead to inexcusable and unacceptable delays may be one—although obviously ultimate—possibility. The courts and tribunals have mostly shied away so far from invoking the exclusionary rule for late additional evidence at trial; the appellate stage presents a slightly different picture, however. It may be questionable whether this leniency has always been a wise choice, especially insofar as creating a proper international trial culture is concerned and ensuring that the general suspicion under which the defence is often held is acknowledged and abolished. In particular, once the dossier is made the basis for structuring and organising the trial, the prosecution should move into the same position as the defence and have to show cause for any additional evidence not contained in the dossier. It bears reminding that the effect of not employing an exclusionary rule of some sort[32] more often than not disadvantages the defence and this is again in part the impact of an attitude mentioned above that allows a measure of latitude to the prosecution partly because of the seriousness of the charges involved and the still prevailing[33] 'no-impunity' attitude in much of the international community.

[31] Suffice it to say that in the complex environment of international proceedings, even under a judge-led model an early defence disclosure could be required with attendant sanctions for vexatious and frivolous violations as long as this does not lead to a model where the defence would be forced to assist towards a conviction—different models exist, such as the drawing of adverse inferences or the exclusion of late evidence etc., yet, it needs to be remembered that they all carry a great potential for causing miscarriages of justice. If the defence has reliable evidence that is exculpatory, one would, however, assume that it is normally in the interests of the accused that this is presented at as early a stage as possible.

[32] On exclusion of evidence as a sanction see Sluiter et al. 2013, at 812.

[33] See Bohlander 2014a.

13.4.3.3 Admission of the Indictment by the Trial Court

Inquisitorial or judge-led features that might help streamline the proceedings can begin at the stage of admitting an indictment when an indictment is understood as the *final result* of previous exhaustive investigations—as it should be—and not in the sense of an authorisation to investigate in the first place. Do we really need to separate the decision-making on admission of the indictment and at trial level? Would it not be in the best interests of the parties if they knew the views of the judges who are actually going to try the case about whether there is a *prima facie* case or whether the evidence might be insufficient and in need of supplementary investigations?[34] It is accepted at the international level that having been involved in confirming an indictment does not preclude a judge from sitting on the trial afterwards.[35] Indeed, some civil law systems, such as Germany, operate that model—with the particular emphasis on the defence normally being given full access to the dossier at that time and being able to make preliminary observations on fact and law before a decision on admission is taken. The author as a former criminal judge in the German courts has extensive experience with this kind of procedure and in the very few cases where the prosecution file did give rise to further questions, these could be addressed before the trial got under way and before delays could lead to disruptions and potential adjournments with prejudice, i.e. when after the lapse of certain time limits the trial would have to start afresh. This experience and that of other colleagues would also seem to militate against the general concern that knowledge of the case file and involvement in admitting an indictment per se causes bias and pre-established views of the case with the trial judges. It is a question of training and awareness and last, but not least, trial experience. A decision made on the basis of a dossier is based on one side of the story and not infrequently quite different things can happen at trial. This should also serve as a caution against the excessive use of written material, the one aspect that is so often (mis-)characterised as a 'typical' civil law input.

13.4.3.4 No Pre-trial Briefs or Opening Statements

Since the proceedings are held before professional judges who ideally have the full case file, there is reason to question the need for lenghty pre-trial briefs and opening statements. A seasoned judge can match the material from the case file to the indictment, and in any event, an indictment can be drafted in such a way as to include exact references to the evidence in the file in relation to the individual facts pleaded in the indictment.[36] It might have been the case that in the

[34] This concern is recognised, for example, in Sluiter et al. 2013, at 486 f.

[35] Sluiter et al. 2013, at 816.

[36] For an example, see a specimen indictment from German procedure in Bohlander 2012, at 282.

early days the judges were not used to such criminal trial work and needed an executive summary in the form of a pre-trial brief, as it were, to know what the case was going to be about. In a model where it is the judges who decide the flow of the case, the need for such a stage becomes questionable. Opening statements make even less sense in a judge-only model. They are useful for jury trials to give the jurors a sense of the case of the prosecution. In a fully informed judge-driven environment the only purpose opening statements can have is either playing to the (global) gallery in the wider sense, or giving the media a run-down of the case for their easy consumption. Both would not be legitimate reasons for wasting court time and resources. The trial is run in open court and media can attend, but the trial is not run *for* the media. That kind of concern can be addressed by the public outreach unit of the prosecution.

13.4.3.5 Judgments, Decisions and Orders: Timing and Styling of Drafting

Another area in dire need of improvement is that of the delivery and drafting of judgments and substantial decisions,[37] an issue where a tighter judicial control and a changed judicial attitude could also deliver huge efficiency savings. As far as the timing is concerned, Mirjan Damaška has rightly criticised[38] the practice that in many cases the accused remain in custody during the invariably long periods between closing speeches and delivery of the judgment even if they are ultimately acquitted and the judges already have made up their mind to that effect long before the written judgment is delivered. Damaska correctly demands a move to delivery of the verdict in an oral summary judgment as soon as possible after the deliberations and the presentation of the written reasons after that—again something that is common, for example, in German procedure. Given that the time limits for justifying an appeal run from the date the accused or the prosecution obtain a copy of the written reasons, there must, however, be a corrective to the effect that this drafting period cannot last ad libitum. More decisions and orders on incidental matters should be made from the bench, giving succinct reasons, without any follow-up written versions.

That takes us to another major factor causing delay: the style of the judgments. Even given the complexity of the cases before international courts, it is hard to see why a judgment needs to run to thousands of pages and footnotes in four volumes. The judgment style in the courts and tribunals, no doubt due to a lack of training and criminal judicial experience with quite a number of the

[37] Another issue that cannot be addressed here at length is the need for a repression of interlocutory appeals on issues that logically precede the final judgment. See for the German model Bohlander 2012, at 252 ff.

[38] Sluiter et al. 2013, at 1421.

judges[39] and the record-creating attitude of some, has so far been overly verbose and aimed at an almost complete reproduction of the evidence and the legal and factual arguments of the parties, despite the fact that unlike many civil law traditions, the international courts have verbatim transcripts on which any appeals argument relating to factual inaccuracy can be easily based. At trial level that is in the final analysis irrelevant, it makes more sense at the appellate level where the appellant normally has to attack a judgment with specific arguments, although again there are systems that do not require a fully-fledged argument as far as the application of the substantive law to otherwise undisputed facts is concerned. Judgments are often drafted—by inexperienced legal officers more than the judges[40]—as the case develops, especially the factual findings and the evidence, a practice which through human inertia inevitably leads to retention of much more information than is necessary in the final document, because it is already there and it would otherwise seem a wasted effort, or to massive duplication of work if a judge changes his mind after drafting has already gone on, as the author himself could experience at the ICTY. Drafting proper—as opposed to updating a skeleton judgment—should thus not start before the judges have made up their mind on the law and the facts, and it should strive at condensing the facts considered proven by the court and not reproducing the evidence and the legal arguments of the parties *in extenso*. Each party will find out from the court's own exposition of the law whether their legal opinion carried any weight with the judges.

[39] One should not overlook the fact that in many common law systems with a judge-and-jury model the trial judge will not write a reasoned judgment related to the verdict, since that is the jury's domain. He may express the reasons for sentencing into the record. Proper judgment drafting often begins only at the appellate level, and even then there are marked differences in style between the free-flowing judicial narratives of common law judges and the highly structured and formalised approaches of, for example, the German, Spanish and French judiciaries who on top of that often sit without juries and/or whose relationship to the jury is different from the common law environment. Many common law judges will thus not have had much experience in drafting judgments, let alone in complex cases.

[40] See the revealing Concurring Opinion of 13 November 2013 by Judge Antonetti in the *Seselj* case, where he said: 'The Trial Chamber was confronted with the successive departure of the Chamber's legal officers for personal reasons linked to the Tribunal's Completion Strategy which led them to opt for other jobs. Consequently, every departure of a person in charge entailed the induction of a new person in charge, which was one of the reasons for extending deadlines. During deliberations, three legal officers successively left the Chamber to take up other jobs. I believe that, had there been better management and recruitment that took into consideration the exigencies of this case, we could have had a person in charge of the legal team on a permanent basis until the reading of the judgement so that we would not be faced with this kind of difficulty. In my opinion, there has been a serious breakdown in management since, unfortunately, I do not have the legal power to recruit such a person myself and to issue him orders and directions in the exercise of his function. In a sense, the Judges are prisoners of a system where their only role is to wait for drafts from legal officers who fall under the Registrar's, not the Judges', administrative authority. If the current staff is not retained, there may be consequences for the work of the future Chamber.' The idea that the judges might want to do their own drafting did not seem to have occurred to him. *Prosecutor v. Seselj*, Trial Chamber, Judge Antonetti's Concurring Opinion on Decision Inviting the Parties to Make Submissions on Continuation of Proceedings, Case No. IT-03-67-T, 13 November 2013, at 2.

13.5 Conclusion

This contribution could only address some of the problem areas caused by the temporariness of international criminal justice, yet, it is hoped that it has impressed the need for more attention to be given to what can be realistically expected from a criminal trial, also and not least on the technical levels, to ensure compliance with one major aspect of the rule of law—certainty of law. Certainty of law as a pivotal facet of the idea of justice requires a sustained, coherent and principled engagement by the relevant stakeholders in the international community with the aim of reducing any margins of judicial appreciation that can impact on a defendant's rights, and in a criminal justice context almost any judicial action can. One cannot arrive at certainty of law by merely discussing different traditions and leaving it to judicial trial and error through trial and appellate judgments of any number of courts, which is regrettably the practice followed by today's international criminal courts and tribunals. It is also not acceptable merely to copycat existing procedural templates simply because they are considered 'ready-made' or to have been 'tried and tested' in previous international courts and tribunals. Much of that has to do with a protectionist attitude regarding one's own domestic legal system and a critical view of 'how the others do it'. One needs to realise—or from time to time remind oneself—that while in each domestic setting a homogenous legal culture has over time shaped society's views of what is a 'just' procedural model, and that indeed each of those is perfectly capable of achieving an adequate standard of fairness, no such joint legal culture and hence no joint view of fairness exist on the international level. We cannot leave it to the laborious process of case-by-case development to arrive at a common mould, because all the time we are putting people away and imposing the ultimate moral sanction—and it would seem on a very shaky foundation indeed. This process, which is hard enough in any national environment, is made much more difficult at the international level where the deleterious impact of (geo-)politics is felt with much greater immediacy, as the recent affair at the ICC and ASP over the duty of the accused to attend trial has shown. It is not good enough to say that this is how international law works—we have to try harder. After Nuremberg and Tokyo until 1993, the prospect of an international court for mass atrocities was seen by many as an illusion. The ICTY's substantive law was based on customary international law, its procedural law was not since it followed mainly one legal tradition. Only 5 years later, the Rome Statute was adopted which gave birth to the first properly treaty-based court, which, however, still had and has many areas of uncertainty that might benefit from a more systematic and analytical revision of its law and potentially even an amendment of its Statute and Rules, although that is admittedly not a very realistic option. Yet, as long as new international(ised) courts such as, for example, the planned Kosovo Tribunal,[41] keep popping up from

[41] See, for example, http://jurist.org/paperchase/2014/04/kosovo-lawmakers-vote-to-create-war-crimes-court.php or www.dw.de/neues-kriegsverbrechertribunal-im-kosovo/a-17590527. Accessed 3 August 2014. At the time of writing, no official information about the shape of the tribunal was available.

the ground, there is a need for such an endeavour. Imagine what an honest, radical and concerted international effort aimed at drafting a detailed procedural law for all international courts and tribunals could yield in the next five years.

References

Bohlander M (2011) Radbruch redux: the need for revisiting the conversation between common and civil law at root level at the example of international criminal justice. Leiden J Int Law 24:393–410

Bohlander M (2012) Principles of German criminal procedure. Hart Publishing, Oxford

Bohlander M (2014a) Nullum crimen sine poena—Zur Unberechenbarkeit völkerstrafrechtlicher Lehrenbildung. In: Alwart H et al (eds) Freiheit und Freiheitsverluste in Rechtsregime, Gesellschaft und Wissenschaft. Mohr/Siebeck Verlag, Tübingen, pp 45–63

Bohlander M (2014b) Criminalising LGBT persons under national criminal law and article 7(1)(h) and (3) of the ICC Statue. Global Policy 5(4):401–414

Byrne R (2013) Drawing the missing map: what socio-legal research can offer to international criminal trial practice. Leiden J Int Law 26:991–1007

Damaška M (1986) The faces of justice and state authority. Yale University Press, New Haven

Doherty TA (2013) Evidence in international criminal tribunals: contrast between domestic and international trials. Leiden J Int Law 26:937–945

Eser A (2011) Procedural structures and features of international criminal justice: lessons from the ICTY. In: Swart B et al (eds) The legacy of the International Criminal Tribunal for the former Yugoslavia. Oxford University Press, Oxford, pp 108–148

Jackson J, M'Boge Y (2013) The effect of legal culture on the development of international evidentiary practice: from the 'robing room' to the 'melting pot'. Leiden J Int Law 26:947–970

Langer M (2005) The rise of managerial judging in international criminal law. Am J Comp Law 53:835–909

McEwan J (2011) From adversarialism to managerialism: criminal justice in transition. Legal Stud 31:519–546

Nerlich V (2013) Daring diversity. Why there is nothing wrong with 'fragmentation' in international criminal procedures. Leiden J Int Law 26:777–781

Sluiter G et al (eds) (2013) International criminal procedure. Principles and rules. Oxford University Press, Oxford

Part II
Dutch Practice in International Law

Chapter 14
Platforms, Protestors and Provisional Measures: The *Arctic Sunrise* Dispute and Environmental Activism at Sea

Richard Caddell

Abstract On 18 September 2013, a team of Greenpeace activists attempted to board the *Prirazlomnaya* oil platform, situated within the Russian exclusive economic zone, intending to disrupt drilling activities and raise awareness of Arctic environmental issues. This action resulted in the subsequent arrest of 30 individuals associated with the protest, as well as that of the *Arctic Sunrise*, a Greenpeace support vessel sailing under the Dutch flag. The plight of the so-called 'Arctic 30' dominated global headlines until their release under a general amnesty by Russia in December 2013. Meanwhile, the arrest of the vessel prompted the commencement of arbitral proceedings by the Netherlands against Russia, a process that had yet to be concluded at the time of writing. In November 2013, however, the International Tribunal for the Law of the Sea upheld a Dutch petition for provisional measures, including the release of the vessel and its crew subject to the payment of a bond. In so doing, the Tribunal faced the issue of non-participation by a respondent state for the first time, while also developing arguably a 'back-door' position on prompt release. In the meantime, aspects of the legality of environmental activism at sea remain somewhat uncertain which, given that a considerable number of protest vessels are registered to the Netherlands, may engage the litigative attention of the Dutch authorities in future incidents.

Keywords Provisional measures · UN convention on the law of the sea 1982 · Non-appearance of respondent state · Prompt release · Freedom of speech · Oil platforms

---

Senior Research Associate and Nippon Foundation Senior Nereus Fellow, Netherlands Institute for the Law of the Sea, Utrecht University.

R. Caddell (✉)
Netherlands Institute for the Law of the Sea, Utrecht University, Utrecht, The Netherlands
e-mail: j.r.caddell@uu.nl

M. Ambrus and R.A. Wessel (eds.), *Netherlands Yearbook of International Law 2014*,
Netherlands Yearbook of International Law 45, DOI 10.1007/978-94-6265-060-2_14

Contents

14.1 Introduction 360
14.2 The *Arctic Sunrise* Dispute 362
14.2.1 Jurisdiction of the Tribunal 365
14.2.2 Non-participation of the Respondent State 368
14.2.3 Prompt Release and Provisional Measures 370
14.3 Platforms and Protest Activism 374
14.3.1 Offshore Installations and the Law of the Sea 374
14.3.2 Freedom of Speech at Sea 378
14.4 Concluding Remarks 382
References 383

14.1 Introduction

In recent years, the legal position of protest actions at sea has become a matter of increasing significance. Marine protests have proved to be a particularly attractive tactic for many campaign groups, since the dramatic media coverage that invariably accompanies such activities commands considerable public attention, often helping to generate additional support for the cause in question. Protest activism at sea is by no means a recent phenomenon[1]; the localised blockading of ports has long been an effective weapon for disgruntled coastal interests, although nautical campaigning has steadily expanded to become more pelagic in scope since the late 1960s. Many modern exponents now spend extended periods at sea in pursuit of their targets, traversing a variety of zones of maritime jurisdiction in the process and engaging in activities that operate at the limits of—and sometimes beyond—the current legal parameters of entitlements to free speech and assembly.

Maritime protest also varies significantly in format and conduct. This may entail essentially passive activism, in which campaigners merely observe and document the activities in question and express their dissent in a non-obstructive manner,[2] a practice dubbed 'bearing witness' by Greenpeace.[3] Alternatively, many campaign groups have considered that such tactics are unlikely to provoke

[1] On earlier questions raised by the legality of such approaches see Plant 1983, at 146–162 (examining activities dating back to 1971). See also Plant 2002.

[2] The 'mere shadowing' of a vessel appears to be a universally accepted application of the principle of freedom of navigation: Plant 1983, at 153.

[3] See further Teulings 2011, at 223–225. As General Counsel for Greenpeace, Teulings is keen to draw a clear distinction between this approach and the tactics of more militant activists. In the interests of proper balance, however, it should be observed that in the context of Arctic oil platforms Greenpeace has engaged in more disruptive manifestations of direct action protest that clearly extend beyond mere observation and placarding.

the desired changes in policy and behaviour. Accordingly, more interventionist forms of direct action have been deployed to physically impede the activity in question, which has increasingly led to violent clashes at sea. This approach has been perhaps most vividly illustrated by the regular campaigns waged by the Sea Shepherd Conservation Society against the Japanese Antarctic whaling fleet, a decade-long saga that has degenerated from a series of entertaining Corinthian escapades into a significant nautical hazard, culminating in dangerous collisions between vessels in remote Polar waters, the sinking of a yacht and, ultimately, the spectre of piracy proceedings in at least one jurisdiction.[4] As is the case with land-based protests,[5] the legal response to activism at sea involves a fine balancing act between the competing imperatives of protected and socially-valuable rights to protest and the need to ensure wider issues of public safety. Marine campaigning also carries an inherent risk of civil and criminal penalties, as well as the possibility of serious physical injury[6]—a prospect for which states seemingly carry at least a moral obligation to ensure that their nationals exhibit an appreciation.[7]

The legal position concerning activism at sea has a particular resonance for the Netherlands, since a number of campaign groups have found an accommodating home for many of their key protest vessels within the Dutch shipping registry. This has created occasional diplomatic and legal difficulties for the national authorities. As the flag state of vessels operated by Sea Shepherd, the Dutch authorities, together with Australia, New Zealand and the US, have been moved to issue regular quadripartite statements upholding broad support for freedom of speech at sea, yet condemning certain actions of its nationally-registered vessels and urging respect for

[4] *Institute of Cetacean Research and Others* v. *Sea Shepherd Conservation Society and Watson*, 9th Cir., 725 F.3d 940, 2013, overturning an earlier decision of the US District Court in *Institute of Cetacean Research et al.* v. *Sea Shepherd Conservation Society et al,* W. D. Wash, 860 F. Supp 2d 1216, 2012 that had been distinctly more favourable to the activists. On the legal issues raised by these campaigns, see Mossop 2012; Doby 2013. Notwithstanding the US position, a successful piracy action is considered unlikely to be forthcoming against Sea Shepherd under the current Japanese provisions, even though new legislation was adopted in 2009 which, in principle, considered such harassment to potentially lie within the scope of the law. Kanehara 2011, at 206.

[5] On the challenges inherent in balancing competing considerations raised by protest activism see Mead 2010, at 57–117.

[6] A vivid example being the distinctly ill-advised attempt by the pro-Palestinian activist crew of the *Mavi Marmara* in 2010 to navigate through an Israeli blockade, duly sustaining six fatalities and a host of serious injuries.

[7] Sir Geoffrey Palmer, Report of the Secretary-General's Panel of Inquiry on the 31 May 2010 flotilla incident, September 2011, para 159, http://www.un.org/News/dh/infocus/middle_east/Gaza_Flotilla_Panel_Report.pdf. Accessed 9 January 2015.

navigational safety.[8] Such concerns have also led to calls for the Netherlands to review the grant of flag privileges and to reinforce procedures to facilitate the expulsion of delinquent vessels, although wholesale amendments to national laws on vessel registration have thus far been resisted.[9] The Netherlands also remains the flag state of a considerable number of vessels operated by Greenpeace, notably the *Arctic Sunrise*. The arrest of this veteran protest ship in September 2013, following the attempted boarding of the controversial *Prirazlomnaya* oil platform by activists in the Russian exclusive economic zone (EEZ), subsequently prompted arbitration proceedings between the Netherlands and the Russian Federation. These proceedings remain in progress and are likely to formally conclude in 2015. In November 2013, however, the International Tribunal for the Law of the Sea (ITLOS) considered a request by the Netherlands for the grant of provisional measures to release the vessel and its crew. This action, the twenty-second case submitted to the Tribunal thus far, resulted in an order delivered in favour of the petition by the Netherlands. Moreover, the position taken by ITLOS may have intriguing implications for future detention actions heard by this forum, in addressing the issue of non-engagement by the respondent state and, arguably, pioneering a basis for the prompt release of vessels that may exceed the intentions prescribed by the 1982 UN Convention on the Law of the Sea.[10] This chapter, accordingly, examines the issues raised in the dispute and the reasoning of the Tribunal in granting the release of the *Arctic Sunrise*, before addressing a wider series of emerging questions pertaining to the legality of oil platform protests.

14.2 The *Arctic Sunrise* Dispute

The *Arctic Sunrise* incident is illustrative of long-standing environmental concerns over the prospective expansion of industrial activities within the Arctic region. In recent years, the Arctic has been transformed from a comparative legal and political backwater into an arena of global strategic interest. The projected reduction of

---

[8] See, most recently, Joint statement on whaling and safety at sea, 20 December 2013, http://www.rijksoverheid.nl/ministeries/bz/documenten-en-publicaties/vergaderstukken/2013/12/20/joint-statement-on-whaling-and-safety-at-sea-2013.html. Accessed 9 January 2015. No such statement was issued in 2014, largely due to the limited whaling activities undertaken by Japan that year following the ruling by the International Court of Justice in March 2014 that these activities had failed to qualify as 'scientific research': *Case Concerning Whaling in the Antarctic (Australia* v. *Japan*: *New Zealand Intervening)*, ICJ, Judgment of 31 March 2014. Prior to the ICJ judgment, however, there were a series of conflicts at sea between protest vessels and Japanese whaling ships. On 19 December 2014, Sea Shepherd was ruled to have been in contempt of an injunction issued in 2013 by the US courts, restraining the organisation from navigating within 500 metres of the Japanese fleet. *Institute of Cetacean Research and Others* v. *Sea Shepherd Conservation Society and Paul Watson*, On a Motion for Contempt, 9th Cir., No. 12-35266, 2014.

[9] This has led to some friction with Japan, which in September 2014 criticised the response of the Netherlands as the flag state of at least one Sea Shepherd vessel to be insufficient. Chair's Report of the 65th Meeting of the International Whaling Commission, 2014, para 272.

[10] 1982 United Nations Convention on the Law of the Sea, 1883 UNTS 396 (hereinafter LOSC).

Polar ice coverage has raised the tantalising economic prospect of a dramatic increase in industrial and shipping possibilities in these waters, prompting considerable interest in securing access to the natural resources of the region on the part of both Arctic and non-Arctic States.[11] Nevertheless, strong concerns have been voiced as to the potential environmental ramifications of the wholesale economic development of the Arctic, with calls to preserve the region as an unsullied wilderness area of global significance.[12] Particular reservations have been expressed over the poorly regulated pursuit of hydrocarbons in these waters, with the damage wrought by the *Exxon Valdez* tanker disaster in Alaska in 1989 serving as a stark reminder of the dangers posed by oil to the highly sensitive marine environment of the Arctic. Indeed, the apocalyptic ecological prospect of a *Deepwater Horizon*-style calamity in this region has prompted the European Parliament to adopt a Resolution calling for 'a ban on oil drilling in the icy Arctic waters of the EU and the EEA'.[13]

In 2010 Greenpeace launched its 'Save the Arctic' campaign, a suite of activities that has included information gathering, environmental education and outreach, advocacy at pertinent regional and international fora and a series of direct action campaigns against offshore oil and gas installations in a variety of jurisdictions. Particular ire has been reserved for the *Prirazlomnaya* oil platform, operated by the Russian energy giant Gazprom and situated in the Pechora Sea in northern Arctic waters. Strong concerns have been expressed, both by NGOs and the European Parliament, over the relatively lax approach to the regulation of Arctic

[11] A number of claims to extended continental shelves in the Arctic have been submitted to the Commission on the Limits of the Continental Shelf, most recently as announced by the Danish Ministry of Foreign Affairs on 15 December 2014 in respect of Greenland. Denmark and Greenland will today file a submission regarding the continental shelf north of Greenland, 15 December 2015, http://um.dk/en/news/newsdisplaypage/?newsID=71574E42-6115-4D16-9C8A-4C056F8603F3. Accessed 9 January 2015. Meanwhile, numerous non-Arctic States have developed national strategies to frame their strategic objectives and interactions with the region, including many jurisdictions far removed from Arctic waters. In November 2014 the IMO adopted a mandatory International Code for Ships Operating in Polar Waters, which is expected to enter into effect in 2017. Although applicable to both Polar regions, this instrument was primarily developed with increased Arctic navigation in mind.

[12] Bastmeijer 2009.

[13] European Parliament Resolution on the EU Strategy for the Arctic, 2013/2595(RSP), 12 March 2014, para 33. Oil and gas legislation adopted by the EU prior to the *Arctic Sunrise* dispute also considered the potential problems raised by Arctic expansion—notwithstanding the relatively limited ability of its institutions to secure additional regulatory standards in this region—noting, *inter alia*, that '[t]he serious environmental concerns relating to the Arctic waters require special attention to ensure the environmental protection of the Arctic in relation to any offshore oil and gas operation, including exploration, taking into account the risk of major accidents and the need for effective response.' Directive 2013/30/EU of the European Parliament and of the Council of 12 June 2013 on safety of offshore oil and gas operations and amending Directive 2004/35/EC, 52nd Recital.

hydrocarbon operations assumed by the Russian authorities.[14] In August 2012 the *Arctic Sunrise* was used as a base to launch a first high-profile protest against the *Prirazlomnaya* rig on account of its oil spill response plan having expired, thereby rendering Gazprom's continued operations technically illegal under Russian law. Six activists briefly scaled the platform, while another group chained themselves to the anchor of its primary support vessel, the *Anna Akhmatova*, disrupting drilling activities for five days.

On 18 September 2013, Greenpeace activists attempted to board the platform again. Four inflatable boats were launched from the *Arctic Sunrise* which, at the material time, was apparently situated at a nearby point within the Russian EEZ, yet outside the three-mile exclusion zone established by the national authorities around the *Prirazlomnaya*.[15] The activists were swiftly apprehended at the base of the platform. Later that day, the Russian authorities directed a diplomatic note to their Dutch counterparts announcing their intention to arrest the *Arctic Sunrise*. The vessel was duly boarded in the Russian EEZ on 19 September, an operation that involved firing eleven warning shots, and subsequently sailed under arrest to Murmansk.

The criminal charges against the arrested activists and the legal basis for their detention would oscillate considerably over the course of the following weeks. Between 26 September and 3 October 2013 the various members of the 'Arctic 30'—as they were swiftly dubbed by the global media—were each individually charged with piracy, despite a categorical public assertion by President Vladimir Putin that the activists were 'obviously' not pirates.[16] On 4 October, in response to the piracy charges, the Netherlands formally commenced arbitral proceedings pursuant to Annex VII of the LOSC. In the meantime, a combination of official communications between Russia and the Netherlands, as well as municipal legal proceedings against the *Arctic Sunrise* itself, demonstrated a litany of inconsistencies concerning the basis for the arrest and ongoing detention of the vessel. Concurrent with the initial attempt to board the *Prirazlomnaya*, the Russian authorities informed the Netherlands by a diplomatic note on 18 September that the *Arctic Sunrise* was to be seized due to alleged terrorism offences. On 1 October a further diplomatic note

[14] Indeed, in arguably the most prominent example of diplomatic concern over the regulatory regime adopted by Russia for offshore installations in these waters, the European Parliament expressed 'its strong concern regarding the rush for oil exploration and drilling in the Arctic without adequate standards being enforced, such as on the Gazprom *Prirazlomnaya* platform in the Russian EEZ.' European Parliament Resolution on the EU Strategy for the Arctic, 2013/2595(RSP), 12 March 2014, at para 32.

[15] This version of events is based on evidence provided by Greenpeace and incorporated in the Dutch submission to ITLOS. There has been no credible suggestion that the *Arctic Sunrise* at any time transgressed into the exclusion zone surrounding the rig—a distinction of significance, as discussed below—since Russia declined to submit any contrary evidence to ITLOS, and thus far the subsequent arbitral panel, to dispute this assertion.

[16] Putin: Greenpeace Activists Not Pirates but They Violated International Law, *RT*, 27 September 2013, http://rt.com/news/putin-greenpeace-pirates-arctic-323/. Accessed 9 January 2015.

asserted that the vessel had been visited by Russian law enforcement officials pursuant to powers under Articles 56, 60 and 80 LOSC and Article 36(1)(1) of the domestic Federal Law 'On the Exclusive Economic Zone of the Russian Federation'. By 7 October, however, a national court order for the seizure of the *Arctic Sunrise* revealed that this position had subsequently shifted back to a foundation of piracy, while on 18 October an administrative judgment found the master of the vessel guilty of 'erratic navigation'.[17] On 23 October the initial piracy charges brought against the arrested activists were downgraded to those of 'hooliganism' and resisting arrest, following widespread political and legal condemnation of the original indictment.[18]

14.2.1 Jurisdiction of the Tribunal

In accordance with Article 287 LOSC, arbitral proceedings under Annex VII of the LOSC were instituted by the Netherlands against Russia, alleging that the boarding, arrest and detention of the *Arctic Sunrise* in the Russian EEZ without the prior consent of the flag state contravened Articles 58(1) and 87(1)(a) LOSC, in addition to the rights to liberty and security and to leave a state's territory on the part of the vessel's crew founded under Articles 9 and 12(2) of the International Covenant on Civil and Political Rights 1966.[19] The Netherlands accordingly sought a declaration from the tribunal that these actions were internationally wrongful acts and that Russia should thereby cease and desist such violations, provide appropriate assurances and guarantees of non-repetition and facilitate full reparation for the injury caused thereby.

Under Article 290(1) LOSC, provisional measures may be prescribed by a court or tribunal if it considers that it *prima facie* has jurisdiction over the dispute and if such measures are 'appropriate under the circumstances to preserve the respective rights of the parties to the dispute or to prevent serious harm to

[17] Full details of these bases are cited in Annexes 1, 3 and 6 of the Dutch request for Provisional Measures. *The 'Arctic Sunrise' Case (Kingdom of the Netherlands* v. *Russian Federation)*, ITLOS, Request for the Prescription of Provisional Measures under Article 290, para 5, of the United Nations Convention on the Law of the Sea, 21 October 2013, http://www.itlos.org/fileadmin/itlos/documents/cases/case_no.22/Request_provisional_measures_en_withtranslations.pdf. Accessed 9 January 2015.

[18] The potential applicability of the offence of piracy to protests conducted against oil platforms is considered below in Sect. 14.3.1.

[19] International Covenant on Civil and Political Rights, 999 UNTS 171 (hereinafter ICCPR). It has been observed that the dual nature of these claims, based as they are on both navigational matters and human rights considerations, might present jurisdictional complications for the arbitral tribunal in due course. Oude Elferink 2014, at 279. As noted below, however, the refusal by the tribunal of an *amicus curiae* petition by Greenpeace specifically engaging the human rights elements of the protest may suggest that the panel is minded to pay closer attention to the specific law of the sea aspects of the dispute.

the marine environment, pending the final decision'. In view of the urgency of many marine-related disputes and the time-frame necessary to convene an Annex VII tribunal, Article 290(5) LOSC permits ITLOS to facilitate consideration of provisional measures in its stead if, absent agreement to the contrary between the parties, a period of two weeks has elapsed from the time of the initial request for interim relief and 'if it considers that *prima facie* the tribunal which is to be constituted would have jurisdiction and that the urgency of the situation so requires.' Receiving no satisfactory response from the Russian authorities, the Netherlands accordingly filed a request for provisional measures before ITLOS on 21 October 2013. The following day, Russia stated that it neither accepted the Annex VII process in this context nor did it intend to participate at the ITLOS proceedings.[20] With the exception of a polite statement declining its involvement within the Annex VII arbitration,[21] the Russian Federation has remained steadfastly aloof to the ongoing judicial machinations of the dispute.

Russia's objection to the arbitration process has been founded on the basis of a Declaration made upon ratifying the LOSC on 12 March 1997, in which

> [t]he Russian Federation declares that, in accordance with article 298 of the United Nations Convention on the Law of the Sea, it does not accept the procedures, provided for in section 2 of Part XV of the Convention, entailing binding decisions with respect to disputes concerning the interpretation or application of articles 15, 74 and 83 of the Convention, relating to sea boundary delimitations, or those involving historic bays or titles; disputes concerning military activities, including military activities by government vessels and aircraft, *and disputes concerning law-enforcement activities in regard to the exercise of sovereign rights or jurisdiction*; and disputes in respect of which the Security Council of the United Nations is exercising the functions assigned to it by the Charter of the United Nations.
>
> The Russian Federation, bearing in mind articles 309 and 310 of the Convention, declares that it objects to any declarations and statements made in the past or which may be made in future when signing, ratifying or acceding to the Convention, or made for any other reason in connection with the Convention, that are not in keeping with the provisions of article 310 of the Convention. The Russian Federation believes that such declarations and statements, however phrased or named, cannot exclude or modify the legal effect of the provisions of the Convention in their application to the party to the Convention that made such declarations or statements, and for this reason they shall not be taken into account by the Russian Federation in its relations with that party to the Convention.[22]

---

[20] *Note verbale* of the Embassy of the Russian Federation in Berlin, 22 October 2013, https://www.itlos.org/fileadmin/itlos/documents/cases/case_no.22/Note_verbale_Russian_Federation_eng.pdf. Accessed 9 January 2015.

[21] *Note verbale* from the Russian Federation to the Permanent Court of Arbitration, 27 February 2014 http://www.pca-cpa.org/showfile.asp?fil_id=2532. Accessed 9 January 2015.

[22] Declaration of the Russian Federation upon the ratification of the Law of the Sea Convention, 12 March 1997, http://www.un.org/depts/los/convention_agreements/convention_declarations.htm. Accessed 9 January 2015 (emphasis added).

Nevertheless, while apparently prescribing a basis to avoid the compulsory settlement mechanisms of the LOSC, the Declaration may be considered to have been founded upon a circular and ultimately flawed position. While Article 298 LOSC does allow for the elaboration of optional exceptions on the basis of law enforcement activities, the provision clearly provides that such exemptions apply only to the specific disputes addressed under Article 297(2) and (3) LOSC.[23] These issues are confined to marine scientific research and fisheries matters respectively. In contrast, the present dispute engaged—in the clear view of the Applicant, at least[24]—an alleged breach by the coastal state of the freedom of navigation enjoyed by foreign vessels within the national EEZ, as prescribed under Article 58 LOSC. The position concerning this potential cause for international litigation is instead addressed under Article 297(1) LOSC. It therefore lies outside the scope of national discretion to exclude particular matters from the compulsory jurisdiction of the court, as contemplated under Article 298 LOSC. The distinction is significant given the explicit reference to Articles 309 and 310 LOSC within the Russian Declaration, since these provisions preclude further reservations or statements on the part of the ratifying state that are not expressly permitted by the LOSC, or that purport to exclude or modify the effect of its terms. Read cumulatively, the practical effect of the Declaration rather undermines the Russian assertion that disputes engaging law enforcement activities concerning the exercise of national rights or jurisdiction are excluded from the jurisdiction of an international tribunal. Indeed, the Declaration essentially serves to emphasise that the ability of a contracting party to exclude from the jurisdiction of a tribunal incidents arising from law enforcement operations should be strictly limited to the specific contexts of marine scientific research and fisheries infractions, while simultaneously reinforcing the principle that attempts to undermine this clear position through contrary national declarations should be strongly deterred in order to facilitate the consistent interpretation and operation of the Convention.

As Churchill observes, ‘the reasoning in the provisional measures orders of the ITLOS is not always entirely adequate or convincing’.[25] This is especially true of the Tribunal in this context, which confined its rejection of the Russian position to a mere sentence,[26] an exercise in brevity that may be considered counter-productive. This was rectified to a considerable degree on 26 November 2014, when the Annex VII Tribunal delivered a unanimous award on jurisdiction that comprehensively

[23] Article 298(1)(b) LOSC.

[24] Request for the Prescription of Provisional Measures under Article 290, para 5, of the United Nations Convention on the Law of the Sea, 21 October 2013, paras 19–22 and 25, http://www.itlos.org/fileadmin/itlos/documents/cases/case_no.22/Request_provisional_measures_en_withtranslations.pdf. Accessed 9 January 2015.

[25] Churchill 2015, at 22.

[26] *The ‘Arctic Sunrise’ Case (Kingdom of the Netherlands* v. *Russian Federation)*, ITLOS, Request for the Prescription of Provisional Measures, Order, 22 November 2013, para 45 (hereinafter *The ‘Arctic Sunrise’ Case*).

addressed the Russian Declaration and declared categorically that the effect of this statement did not preclude law enforcement activities pursuant to Article 297(1) LOSC from the jurisdiction of the dispute resolution mechanisms of the 1982 Convention.[27] Meanwhile, and within the context of the ITLOS decision, the sparse exploration of this issue generated a degree of consternation among individual members of the Tribunal, with Judges Wolfrum and Kelly of the view that '[a] convincing reasoning is missing but is called for'.[28] Moreover, Judge Jesus considered the concise treatment of this issue to be especially troublesome, since this was ultimately the only legal point that Russia had sought to make in response to the Dutch petition.[29] These concerns notwithstanding, there was seemingly strong endorsement for the Tribunal's decision on the practical effect of the Russian Declaration,[30] which accordingly raised practical and legal questions concerning the intended non-engagement of the respondent in the subsequent proceedings.

14.2.2 Non-participation of the Respondent State

The effect of the Russian position, even if the national Declaration *strictu senso* provided no legitimate basis to avoid the jurisdiction of the Tribunal in the present case, meant that ITLOS was confronted by an instance of non-appearance for the first time in its tenure. Non-appearance before international courts and tribunals is an infrequent, although regrettable, eventuality and one that has been within the contemplation of the constituent statutes of various judicial bodies. Annex VI of the LOSC, through which the Statute of the International Tribunal for the Law of the Sea is articulated, is no different in this regard and, by virtue of Article 28 of Annex VI, prescribes a basis for proceeding in a case of default:

> When one of the parties does not appear before the Tribunal or fails to defend its case, the other party may request the Tribunal to continue the proceedings and make its decision. Absence of a party or failure of a party to defend its case shall not constitute a bar to the proceedings. Before making its decision, the Tribunal must satisfy itself not only that it has jurisdiction over the dispute, but also that the claim is well founded in fact and law.

[27] *Arctic Sunrise Arbitration (Kingdom of the Netherlands* v. *Russian Federation),* Arbitral Tribunal, Award on Jurisdiction, 26 November 2014, paras 70–78, http://www.pca-cpa.org/showpage.asp?pag_id=1556. Accessed 9 January 2015.

[28] *The 'Arctic Sunrise' Case*, Joint Separate Opinion of Judge Wolfrum and Judge Kelly, para 9.

[29] *The 'Arctic Sunrise' Case*, Separate Opinion of Judge Jesus, para 5.

[30] Judge Golitsyn considered the application for provisional measures to be 'inadmissible' but did not address the nuances of the Russian Declaration, basing this view instead on the convoluted timeline of the incident and concluding that the prior obligation to exchange views pursuant to Article 283 of the LOSC had not been met. *The 'Arctic Sunrise' Case*, Dissenting Opinion of Judge Golitsyn, paras 1–14. In this respect, he disagreed with the general finding of the Tribunal that the Netherlands had been able to consider attempts to reach an alternative resolution with the Russian authorities to have been exhausted. *The 'Arctic Sunrise' Case*, paras 72–78. Judge Kulyk, the only other dissenting voice, objected to the Order ultimately granted by the Tribunal but not, seemingly, its jurisdictional entitlement to make it. *The 'Arctic Sunrise' Case*, Dissenting Opinion of Judge Kulyk.

Notwithstanding this clear position—and, moreover, the explicit references within the Dutch submission to this provision—consideration of Article 28 of Annex VI within the Order of the Tribunal is distinctly conspicuous by its absence. Instead, the Tribunal based the decision to continue its deliberations upon a review of the relevant provisions of the Statute of the International Court of Justice (ICJ Statute) and the jurisprudence of that Court. In this respect, Article 53 ICJ Statute provides that the appearing party may request a ruling in favour of its claim, subject to the proviso that the ICJ has jurisdiction over the dispute and that the action is well founded in fact and law. Article 28 of Annex VI was modelled upon this provision, albeit with the distinction that a state may only request a continuation of the proceedings before ITLOS, rather than an explicit ruling in its favour. In reality, there is little practical distinction since Article 53(2) ICJ Statute clarifies that a claim must still be adjudged to be well founded: it does not prescribe a walkover mechanism for undefended, yet spurious, actions. The regime of non-appearance before the ICJ is buttressed by an obligation that the defaulting party be given an opportunity to present its observations.[31] Finding that Russia had been accorded ample occasion to do so, the Tribunal considered that the Netherlands should not be disadvantaged by its subsequent non-appearance[32] and the status of the respondent as a party to the proceedings accordingly remained unchanged.[33]

While the practical distinction between the respective Statutes may be considered essentially minimal, the failure to undertake a reasoned evaluation of the scope of Article 28 of Annex VI nonetheless sat uneasily with individual members of the Tribunal. Judges Wolfrum and Kelly attributed this oversight to a purported inconsistency with Article 290 LOSC: Article 28 of Annex VI refers to the 'jurisdiction' of the Tribunal, yet the process for the grant of provisional measures envisaged under the 1982 Convention requires only that a judicial body be convinced that it has *prima facie* jurisdiction.[34] This begged the question as to whether an application for provisional measures was caught by the scope of Article 28 of Annex VI. This was considered to be unproblematic in the view of the judges, a position also taken by Judge Paik,[35] since the ITLOS Statute drew no distinction between the jurisdiction of the Tribunal in assessing provisional

[31] See especially *Fisheries Jurisdiction (United Kingdom* v. *Iceland)*, ICJ, Interim Protection, Order of 17 August 1972, para 11; *Fisheries Jurisdiction (Federal Republic of Germany* v. *Iceland)*, Interim Protection, Order of 17 August 1972, para 11; *Nuclear Tests (Australia* v. *France)*, ICJ, Interim Protection, Order of 22 June 1973, para 11; *Nuclear Tests (New Zealand* v. *France)*, ICJ, Interim Protection, Order of 22 June 1973, para 12; *Aegean Sea Continental Shelf Case (Greece* v. *Turkey)*, ICJ, Interim Protection, Order of 11 September 1976, para 13; *United States Diplomatic and Consular Staff in Tehran (United States of America* v. *Iran)*, ICJ, Provisional Measures, Order of 15 December 1979, para 9.

[32] *The 'Arctic Sunrise' Case*, para 56.

[33] Ibid., para 51.

[34] Ibid., Joint Separate Opinion of Judge Wolfrum and Judge Kelly, para 4.

[35] Ibid., Separate Opinion of Judge Paik, para 4.

measures as opposed to any other context. In their view, there was no ostensible reason as to why the default clause could not be applied to the present dispute and the Tribunal had duly missed an opportunity to expand both its own jurisprudence and that of international decision-making bodies generally.[36]

Strong criticism was nonetheless reserved for the Russian refusal to participate in the process, an approach that the Tribunal considered 'may hinder the regular conduct of the proceedings and affect the good administration of justice'.[37] Individual judges further noted their concerns that non-participation hampered the evidential base upon which to undertake their consideration of the issues,[38] and served to undermine both the position of the Respondent and the wider system of compulsory settlement established under the LOSC.[39] Unilateralism of this nature was clearly viewed in a dim light by ITLOS—especially since the Respondent had officially expressed clear faith in its legal position, which could have been swiftly tested before the Tribunal—and it has been suggested that a discernible punitive intent duly permeates the resulting Order.[40] Indeed, as noted below, a strikingly different stance was taken by the Tribunal in an action addressing a number of similar issues convened shortly before that in relation to the *Arctic Sunrise*, in which the respondent opted to rebut a distinctly flimsy claim brought against it, where non-appearance might otherwise have been a tempting option.[41]

14.2.3 Prompt Release and Provisional Measures

Given that Russia's refusal to participate provided no practical impediment to the continued judicial appraisal of the dispute, ITLOS ultimately ruled in favour of the Dutch application on 22 November 2013, ordering the immediate release of the *Arctic Sunrise* and its crew and the facilitation of their ability to leave Russian jurisdiction, contingent upon the payment of a bond of €3.6 million. As with other elements of the Order, however, the reasoning behind this decision is decidedly frugal and would have benefitted considerably from additional reflection—and, to a significant extent, a robust contribution in rebuttal on the part of the respondent.

---

[36] Ibid., at para 7.

[37] *The 'Arctic Sunrise' Case*, para 53.

[38] Ibid., Declaration of Judge Ad Hoc Anderson, para 2.

[39] Ibid., Joint Separate Opinion of Judge Wolfrum and Judge Kelly, para 5.

[40] Guilfoyle and Miles 2014, at 277–281.

[41] *The M/V Louisa Case (St. Vincent and the Grenadines* v. *Kingdom of Spain)*, ITLOS, Judgment of 28 May 2013. This is not to suggest that the action was vexatious—indeed, the dispute raises clear concerns over the procedural rights of arrested seafarers—merely that there was little basis for the dispute to be heard by that particular forum. Indeed, as Judge Cot wryly suggested in his dissenting opinion to the finding of jurisdiction by ITLOS, 'in applying to our Tribunal, the Applicant has come to the wrong address'.

As noted above, ITLOS is empowered under Article 290(5) LOSC to order provisional measures if it considers that the Annex VII body would have jurisdiction over the dispute and 'the urgency of the situation so requires'. The Tribunal ruled in the affirmative on both points; the first of which has been subsequently confirmed by the Annex VII tribunal itself.[42] The notion of 'urgency' being a relative concept, ITLOS observed that this provision must be read in conjunction with Article 290(1) LOSC, which emphasises the respective rights of the parties to the dispute and the need to prevent serious harm to the marine environment.[43] The latter issue appeared to be of most direct interest to the Tribunal, with the Netherlands having raised concerns that the vessel itself, a veteran icebreaker, required extensive maintenance to prevent its general condition from deteriorating which could, given that it lay impounded in Murmansk, potentially threaten Arctic waters with pollution. No further analysis of this position was forthcoming within the Order, however, and ITLOS appears to have accepted the Dutch submission *verbatim*, prompting the rather minimalist conclusion that 'the urgency of the case requires the prescription by the Tribunal of provisional measures'.[44]

In this respect, perhaps more than any other, the respondent was essentially the author of its own misfortune. By failing to provide any countervailing evidence that the *Arctic Sunrise* did not ultimately pose an environmental hazard, or that the national authorities were sufficiently equipped to address potential concerns, a considerable hurdle to the granting of provisional measures was duly removed by Russia itself. In marked contrast to this position, in rejecting a request for provisional measures in the *M/V Louisa* dispute, ITLOS was prepared to 'place on record the assurance given by Spain' that there was no threat of imminent harm and that the national authorities were able to respond appropriately should the vessel's condition deteriorate.[45] Interestingly, in that instance, the expert witness for the Applicant in raising such concerns had been accorded no opportunity to view the vessel in question, a position that further undermined the case for provisional measures. Conversely, in the *Arctic Sunrise* case, little first-hand evidence was adduced as to the supposedly troubling state of the vessel, yet this position was accepted uncritically by the Tribunal.

There may indeed be pressing reasons as to why an arresting state ought to be ordered as a provisional measure to surrender an impounded vessel due to environmental concerns—for instance, if it evidently lacks the resources or expertise to maintain it in safe condition or, hypothetically, if the authorities unreasonably insist upon securing a vessel with limited capacity to endure Arctic conditions in a noted

---

[42] *Arctic Sunrise Arbitration (Kingdom of the Netherlands* v. *Russian Federation)*, Arbitral Tribunal, Award on Jurisdiction, paras 70–78, http://www.pca-cpa.org/showpage.asp?pag_id=1556. Accessed 9 January 2015.

[43] *The 'Arctic Sunrise' Case*, para 80.

[44] Ibid., para 89.

[45] *The M/V Louisa Case (St. Vincent and the Grenadines* v. *Kingdom of Spain)*, ITLOS, Provisional Measures, Order of 23 December 2010, para 78.

cold-water port such as Murmansk. There was, however, no reasoned basis as to why the Russian authorities could be considered to have lacked the ability to effectively manage the *Arctic Sunrise* under these circumstances; the Tribunal merely observed that the vessel was within the possession of the national coastguard and a chain of command had been established thereto.[46] In refusing to participate in the proceedings, however, Russia forfeited the opportunity to subject such arguments to further scrutiny and it appears that the Tribunal had little inclination to do so on its behalf.[47]

Historical instances of non-participation before the ICJ appear to have accorded the defaulting state no operational advantage in the proceedings.[48] In this context, however, the Order appears to have reinforced a clear message that non-appearance can have a critical bearing on the narrative of provisional measures before ITLOS. This general message was endorsed by the Tribunal, although the two dissenting Judges each raised concerns on this point, with Judge Kulyk warning that a failure to consider the Russian documentation as sufficient confirmation of an assumption of environmental obligations might potentially undermine the principle of good faith on the part of ITLOS.[49] This is perhaps somewhat overplayed—the notion of 'security' was not expounded further in the Russian documentation pertaining to the arrest, and could have been so addressed had Russia engaged with the process. The prevailing jurisprudence of the Tribunal is nonetheless suggestive that, absent clear and contrary evidence, an unequivocal assertion of environmental stewardship over an impounded vessel by the arresting state is generally sufficient, since in the incontrovertible logic of Judge Paik in the *M/V Louisa* dispute, 'if and when pollution occurs, it is the Respondent that will suffer the most'.[50] While there was no intimation that the Russian authorities exhibited a negligent intent towards the vessel at the material time, it appears from the Order

46 Ibid., para 88.

47 This point was raised as a question to the Dutch legal team by Judge Golitsyn, for which it was considered, *inter alia*, that the Russian statements concerning the stewardship of the Arctic Sunrise during its period of detention were ambiguous, since they related only to responsibility for the 'security' of the vessel. Moreover, there was no indication that such measures were either final or pertained to the servicing of the vessel: *The 'Arctic Sunrise' Case (Kingdom of the Netherlands* v. *Russian Federation)*, ITLOS, Replies to Questions from the Tribunal, 7 November 2013, https://www.itlos.org/fileadmin/itlos/documents/cases/case_no.22/Response_questions_en.pdf. Accessed 9 January 2015. Again, it would appear that these issues could have been addressed in a relatively straightforward manner by Russia—in the same way that such assurances were taken seriously from Spain in the context of the *M/V Louisa* dispute—hence non-appearance was clearly to the detriment of the respondent's case in this instance.

48 It might be argued that, had the respondent entered an appearance in the *Aegean Sea Continental Shelf Case*, the ICJ could have further probed a Turkish declaration to the Court that the purported seismic surveying of the Aegean seabed was unlikely to cause irreparable and non-compensable harm. Nevertheless, the tenor of the judgment suggests that the Court was minded to have endorsed this proposition and that non-appearance did not deprive the judiciary of vital scope for further examination that might have influenced a marginal decision.

49 *The 'Arctic Sunrise' Case*, Dissenting Opinion of Judge Kulyk, para 10.

50 Ibid., Separate Opinion of Judge Paik, para 16.

that silence is nonetheless insufficient: effective environmental stewardship must be formally asserted in the context of provisional measures, and will seemingly not be otherwise presumed by the Tribunal.

Likewise, the question of the respective rights of the parties also had considerable resonance for the Tribunal, although its reasoning on this point was again skeletal, while the Respondent's failure to engage with the proceedings further undermined its position. In ordering the release of the vessel and crew,[51] the *Arctic Sunrise* case marked a new departure in the prompt release practice of the Tribunal. The LOSC prescribes a mechanism for the prompt release of a vessel in two clear instances, namely fisheries infractions under Article 73 LOSC and the violation of particular rules and procedures pertaining to the prevention, reduction and control of vessel-source pollution pursuant to Articles 220 and 226 LOSC. The circumstances of the *Arctic Sunrise* dispute accordingly lay outside these two fundamental premises, although there is no explicit position within the Convention that a similar process cannot in principle be applied in other contexts for the purposes of provisional measures. Nevertheless, the common denominator between the offences subject to the prompt release procedure under the LOSC is that they are to be addressed solely by financial penalties, as opposed to imprisonment or other sanctions.[52] Under these circumstances, if prompt release is ordered and the crew and/or vessel subsequently flee the jurisdiction, the coastal state is left in materially the same position had the legal process run its full and legitimate course. In contrast, for alternative offences that may include the possibility of incarceration, the provision of financial security may arguably fail to fully secure the rights of the arresting state in such an instance.

For this reason, Judge Jesus considered that the Order of the Tribunal potentially represents 'a back-door prompt release remedy' for which the precedential value of the decision ought to have merited clearer explanation.[53] Meanwhile, Judge Golitsyn considered that the decision fundamentally failed to protect the rights of the coastal state,[54] a position that would appear to have some foundation. Indeed, while Article 290 allows the Tribunal to award appropriate provisional measures, it would have arguably been on safer ground in expanding the principles of prompt release to instances of nautical offences that solely carry financial penalties.[55] The effect of the Order was therefore to truncate the criminal investigation into the

[51] *The 'Arctic Sunrise' Case*, para 92.

[52] Articles 73(3) and 230(1) and (2) LOSC.

[53] *The 'Arctic Sunrise' Case*, Separate Opinion of Judge Jesus, para 7. These concerns notwithstanding, Judge Jesus concurred with the general decision to release the vessel and the non-Russian members of the crew.

[54] Ibid., Dissenting Opinion of Judge Golitsyn, paras 43–47.

[55] For example, in November 2014 the Spanish authorities arrested the *Arctic Sunrise* following a number of clashes between activists and the offshore oil industry. The vessel was impounded and charged with breaches of nautical rules, a series of offences punishable solely by fines. Greenpeace Ship Arctic Sunrise Detained in Spain, *The Guardian*, 19 November 2014, http://www.theguardian.com/environment/2014/nov/19/greenpeace-ship-arctic-sunrise-detained-in-spain. Accessed 9 January 2015.

boarding of the *Prirazlomnaya*, which as noted below presented a genuine case to answer, thereby impinging upon the rights of the arrested state. Again, however, the future interpretation of this point may be based on the degree to which the *Arctic Sunrise* is viewed as a special case on default. To this end, it may be questioned whether a future panel would be as generously minded where the arresting state enters a robust defence of its entitlement to exercise the due process of its marine criminal jurisdiction.

On 18 December 2013, a general amnesty bill adopted by the Russian Duma to celebrate the twentieth anniversary of the Russian Constitution was amended to include the arrested *Prirzlomnaya* activists. The *Arctic Sunrise* itself was finally and somewhat unexpectedly released from detention by the Russian authorities on 6 June 2014.[56] In March 2014, petitions by the *Prirazlomnaya* activists were submitted to the European Court of Human Rights, alleging violations of Articles 5 and 10 of the European Convention on Human Rights.[57] This development, as well as the ongoing examination of the dispute by the Annex VII Tribunal, raises the question as to the general position of protest activism at sea, to which this article now turns.

14.3 Platforms and Protest Activism

14.3.1 Offshore Installations and the Law of the Sea

Specific powers over offshore installations are conferred on the coastal state through Article 60 of the LOSC.[58] Under Article 60(2) LOSC, the coastal state has exclusive jurisdiction over installations and therefore controls access to these structures, as well as imposing criminal sanctions for breaching these rules. Reasonable safety zones may also be established around installations to ensure the safety of navigation and of the structures themselves.[59] Under Article 60(5) LOSC, the coastal state may determine the dimensions of the safety zone up to a maximum of 500 m as measured from each point of their outer edge, except as authorised by 'generally accepted international standards or as recommended by the competent international organization', which is generally considered to be the International Maritime

[56] Greenpeace Arctic Sunrise: Russia 'Frees Protest Ship', *BBC News*, 6 June 2014, http://www.bbc.com/news/world-europe-27736927. Accessed 9 January 2015.

[57] The redacted petitions are reproduced on-line. Greenpeace, Applications to the European Court of Human Rights, http://www.greenpeace.org/international/en/campaigns/climate-change/arctic-impacts/Peace-Dove/Arctic-30/European-Court-of-Human-Rights/. Accessed 9 January 2015.

[58] This is based on the recognition that the coastal state exercises sovereign rights over the natural resources of the seabed and jurisdiction over the establishment and use of installations for the purpose of exploiting these resources pursuant to Article 58.

[59] Article 60(4) LOSC.

Organization (IMO). Notwithstanding a degree of agitation by coastal states, the IMO has resisted a general expansion of the 500 m limit for safety zones.[60] Nevertheless, state practice remains somewhat variable and a degree of creeping jurisdiction has been experienced in this regard, exemplified in the context of the *Prirazlomnaya*, whose safety zone exceeds the current standards by some 2500 m.

Where such a zone is lawfully designated, '[a]ll ships must respect these safety zones and shall comply with generally accepted international standards regarding navigation in the vicinity'.[61] In practice, breaching a safety zone will constitute a domestic criminal violation within most jurisdictions with an offshore industrial presence.[62] The LOSC accordingly establishes no general foundation for vessels to enter these areas, nor for unauthorised access to the rigs themselves. Nevertheless, if the 'vicinity' of an offshore platform is understood as encapsulating the remaining areas of the EEZ that are not pockmarked by installations and their accompanying safety zones, it would be a logical assumption that activists may assert a right to demonstrate in these waters, to the extent that such a right is forthcoming under general privileges accorded to foreign shipping within the EEZ as outlined below. This point was not explicitly addressed by ITLOS in the *Arctic Sunrise* dispute, although it was clearly within the contemplation of individual judges that the activists 'could invoke, among others, the freedom of expression as set out in the International Covenant on Civil and Political Rights whereas in the safety zone, depending on the factual situation, the exercise of such rights may have to yield to the safety interests of the operator of the platform'.[63] The general position that safety zones are in principle not to be freely entered remains intact, however, and was considered a fundamental basis by Judge Golitsyn as to why provisional measures may not have served the interests of the coastal state in the *Arctic Sunrise* case.[64]

Ultimately, however, offshore installations are likely to remain an attractive target for determined campaigners, which will generally provoke a defensive response from the coastal state in question. Under Article 58(2) LOSC, the exclusivity of flag state jurisdiction is broadly extended to issues arising within the EEZ; the breach of this was indeed an issue of particular consternation to the Dutch authorities in the *Arctic Sunrise* action. Indeed, the IMO has considered that reporting an infraction to the flag state is, in the first instance, the most appropriate course of action where a

---

[60] IMO NAV 56/20, 31 August 2010, at 14–17.

[61] Article 60(6) LOSC.

[62] This has also led to some divergent practices between jurisdictions, notably New Zealand which, in 2013 introduced a controversial amendment to the Crown Minerals Act 1981 to allow for the designation of 'specified non-interference zones' of 500 m within around individual vessels associated with permitted prospecting, mining or exploration. This exceeds the mandate of the LOSC, which prescribes no such position for support vessels.

[63] *The 'Arctic Sunrise' Case*, Joint Separate Opinion of Judge Wolfrum and Judge Kelly, para 13.

[64] Ibid., Dissenting Opinion of Judge Golitsyn, para 34.

safety zone has been violated.[65] Nevertheless, this appears to be subject to two broad exceptions operating in favour of the coastal state, although neither is without practical and legal difficulties. In the first instance, Article 111(2) LOSC establishes a right to hot pursuit in respect *inter alia* of violations of safety zones. This would seemingly extend to incursions by small boats launched from other ships which, under the doctrine of constructive presence, would justify the eventual arrest of the parent vessel if the conditions inherent in the exercise of hot pursuit have been lawfully followed.[66] The precise conditions regulating pursuit from inside a specific safety zone are not explicitly stated under the LOSC. However, Article 111(2) LOSC has been applied *mutatis mutandis* from the core principles established in Article 111(1) LOSC concerning pursuit from internal or archipelagic waters, the territorial sea or contiguous zone, specifying that pursuit must commence from within the zone in question. The implication is that hot pursuit in response to a violation of Article 60 must accordingly commence from within this zone to fulfil such criteria. As the *Arctic Sunrise* dispute amply illustrates, this may be a significant evidential burden for the arresting state to discharge. The non-participation of Russia deprived the Tribunal of vital evidence to assess the legitimacy of such an approach. In contrast, the testimony submitted by the Netherlands suggests strongly that, while the general position on hot pursuit from such zones may hold true, the precise conditions for its application were not made out in the present case.[67]

The second alternative is to invoke the law of piracy, as was controversially raised at the outset of the dispute, which would also override flag state jurisdiction. This option, especially when applied to environmental campaigners, generates particular legal and diplomatic obstacles for the arresting state, as was amply illustrated in the aftermath of the arrest of the 'Article 30' on this basis. Piracy is defined under Article 101 of the LOSC as:

> (a) any illegal acts of violence or detention, or any act of depredation, committed for private ends by the crew or the passengers of a private ship or a private aircraft, and directed:
>
> (i) on the high seas, against another ship or aircraft, or against persons or property on board such ship or aircraft;
> (ii) against a ship, aircraft, persons or property in a place outside the jurisdiction of any State;

[65] IMO Resolution A.671(16), Safety Zones and Safety of Navigation around Offshore Installations and Structures 19 October 1989. The Resolution expressly cites Article 60 LOSC as underpinning these considerations. Nevertheless, this Resolution was largely based on concerns over potential incursions into safety zones by fishing vessels, rather than the premeditated boarding of an installation as in the *Arctic Sunrise* case.

[66] This broad approach was asserted Judge Golitsyn, who observed that '[t]he Convention is quite clear in Article 111 LOSCon the right of hot pursuit that a mother ship is responsible for the activities of its boats or other craft as they work as a team.' *The 'Arctic Sunrise' Case*, Dissenting Opinion of Judge Golitsyn, para 35.

[67] See further Oude Elferink 2014, at 283.

(b) any act of voluntary participation in the operation of a ship or of an aircraft with knowledge of facts making it a pirate ship or aircraft;
(c) any act of inciting or of intentionally facilitating an act described in paras (a) or (b).

In this respect—and assuming that the unauthorised boarding of an oil platform qualifies as 'violence', 'detention or 'depredation', a connection that is by no means axiomatic—two particular impediments would appear to militate against a finding of piracy. First, the requirement of 'private ends' would need to be established, an issue that has proved to be notoriously controversial when applied against those with political or altruistic motivations. Commentators have expressed concerns that environmental activists ought not in principle to be considered piratical in motivation,[68] although a more inclusionary approach to the concept of private ends[69] has been favoured by national courts on the rare occasions in which protest cases have proceeded on a foundation of piracy. Indeed, the lack of state sanction for the actions of protestors was considered a determinative factor in the deliberations of both the Belgian Cour de Cassation[70] and the US Court of Appeals for the Ninth Circuit.[71] If current jurisprudence suggests that this might be less problematic for the arresting authorities than has traditionally been considered the case, it is still by no means certain that every jurisdiction would adopt this approach. Second, and perhaps rather more significantly, piracy must be directed against a 'ship or aircraft'. It is highly doubtful whether an installation that has been affixed to the seabed to the extent that the designation of a safety zone is necessary would ordinarily qualify as a 'ship'. No international court has as yet ruled upon the legal nature of an oil platform.[72] However, most domestic jurisdictions exclude

[68] See, for instance, Klein 2011, at 141.

[69] Such as that advanced by Guilfoyle, who argues that 'the words "for private ends" must be understood broadly. All acts of violence that lack state sanction are acts undertaken "for private ends".' Guilfoyle 2009, at 36–37.

[70] *Castle John and Nederlandse Stichting Sirius* v. *NV Mabeco and NV Parfin*, Belgium, Cour de Cassation, 19 December 1986, reproduced in 77 *International Legal Materials* 537. The Cour de Cassation considered that, in boarding a vessel allegedly laden with toxic waste on the high seas, Greenpeace had acted violently and 'in particular the pursuit by the applicant of the objects set out in its articles of association.' Ibid., at 540.

[71] *Institute of Cetacean Research and Others* v. *Sea Shepherd Conservation Society and Watson*, 9th Cir., 725 F.3d 940, 2013. In this instance, private ends included 'those pursued on personal, moral or philosophical grounds, such as Sea Shepherd's professed environmental goals. That the perpetrators believe themselves to be serving the public good does not render their ends public'. Ibid., at 944. This decision overturned a previous judgment that considered that piracy was not made out in this instance, albeit one based on flawed reasoning.

[72] This issue was fleetingly raised in an application for provisional measures before the ICJ, but the matter was ultimately settled by agreement. *Case Concerning Passage through the Great Belt (Finland* v. *Denmark*), ICJ, Provisional Measures, Order of 29 July 1991.

permanent seabed fixtures from the concept of a 'ship',[73] while the IMO expressly considers that drilling apparatus and other platforms are vessels only while in transit.[74] This provides some scope for piracy offences to be applied against oil platforms in certain circumstances—but not, it would clearly appear, in the particular context of the *Prirazlomnaya*.

A more specific basis for a coastal state to address incursions onto oil platforms would seem to be forthcoming from the Convention for the Suppression of Unlawful Acts against the Safety of Maritime Navigation 1988.[75] While the scope of this Convention is explicitly restricted to vessels 'of any type whatsoever not permanently attached to the sea-bed',[76] a widely-ratified Protocol to the Convention does, however, apply to fixed platforms[77] and creates a series of offence against such structures. Of most immediate relevance to at-sea protests is Article 2(1)(a) of the Protocol, which creates the offence of unlawfully and intentionally seizing or exercising control over a fixed platform 'by force or threat thereof or any other form of intimidation'. The nuances of this provision have not been tested by national or international courts and it nonetheless remains questionable whether the actions of Greenpeace would have met the requisite standards of force or intimidation had the *Prirazlomnaya* protest proceeded as planned.

14.3.2 Freedom of Speech at Sea

A final element of the case—and one that raises wider questions concerning the contemporary use of ocean space—involved the role of human rights considerations in framing the rationale for the protest itself and ensuring that the dispute between states did 'not infringe upon *[sic]* the enjoyment of individual rights and freedoms of the crew of the vessels concerned.'[78] At both the provisional measures stage and within the main proceedings of the Annex VII Tribunal, Greenpeace

---

[73] A small number of jurisdictions consider immovable property such as oil rigs to qualify as a 'ship', hence piracy may be a theoretical option for certain national courts. See, for example, Spain in Ley 21/1977 de 1 abril, Sobre aplicación de sanciones en los casos de contaminación marina provocada por vertidos desde buques y aeronaves, Article 1(3), reproduced at BOE-A-1977-8604.

[74] IMO Resolution A.671(16), Safety Zones and Safety of Navigation around Offshore Installations and Structures 19 October 1989.

[75] Convention for the Suppression of Unlawful Acts against the Safety of Maritime Navigation, 1678 UNTS 201 (hereinafter SUA Convention).

[76] Article 1(1)(a) SUA Convention.

[77] Protocol for the Suppression of Unlawful Acts against the Safety of Fixed Platforms Located on the Continental Shelf 2005, 1678 UNTS 304. Under Article 1(3) of this Protocol, it applies to 'an artificial island, installation or structure permanently attached to the sea-bed for the purpose of exploration or exploitation of resources or for other economic purposes.'

[78] *The 'Arctic Sunrise' Case*, para 87 (citing the Dutch position on the matter).

sought to join the litigation as an *amicus curiae*, purporting to draw the attention of both panels to the human rights considerations incumbent in the case. Ostensibly, the human rights dimension is barely addressed within the Order for provisional measures, although it has been suggested in some quarters that these considerations exercised a latent influence over the decision-making process.[79] As noted above, Judges Wolfrum and Kelly alluded to the possibility of the protestors invoking the ICCPR in support of certain elements of their activities, albeit with minimal discussion of the potential application of such norms in the present case. The clear rejection of both *amicus curiae* briefs suggests that such issues may remain secondary in importance to the more central—and, perhaps, less emotive—concerns raised by the Netherlands as to the freedom of navigation. A degree of attention may nonetheless be forthcoming from the European Court of Human Rights on this point in due course, however, which has expanded its activist tendencies towards the marine sphere in recent judgments.

The LOSC provides no specific guidance on the role of freedom of speech and assembly at sea, beyond a general rule of interpretation and through the residual rights established in the context of freedom of navigation. In the case of the former, Article 293(1) LOSC permits a court or tribunal faced with an interpretive question to apply both the LOSC as well as 'other rules of international law not incompatible with this Convention'. The Tribunal declined to articulate a clear statement as to the compatibility of pertinent human rights norms to the present dispute, although previous cases suggest that both ITLOS[80] and arbitral bodies[81] are prepared to do so where appropriate. In the meantime, it may be suggested that recourse to the European Court of Human Rights provides a more desirable means of raising these specific points, both in avoiding jurisdictional complications for a resulting tribunal and in addressing a more appropriate audience in the process.

Beyond the application of Article 293 LOSC, it may be suggested that there is considerable toleration for protest activities at sea under the 1982 Convention, albeit one that is contingent upon a balancing act with the rights of navigation of others and the overarching imperative of public safety at sea. In the context of the

---

[79] Guilfoyle and Miles 2014, at 284–287.

[80] Most notably, in the *M/V Saiga (No. 2) Case (St. Vincent and the Grenadines* v. *Guinea)*, ITLOS, Judgment on the Merits, 1 July 1999, ITLOS considered the extraneous context of the international rules governing the use of force, stating that '[a]lthough the Convention does not contain express provisions on the use of force in the arrest of ships, international law, which is applicable by virtue of article 293 of the Convention, requires that the use of force must be avoided as far as possible and, where force is unavoidable, it must not go beyond what is reasonable and necessary in the circumstances. Considerations of humanity must apply in the law of the sea, as they do in other areas of international law.' Ibid., para 155.

[81] In *Guyana and Suriname* the arbitral panel endorsed the approach of ITLOS in the *M/V Saiga (No. 2) Case* as a 'reasonable interpretation of Article 293' and accordingly rejected the submissions of Suriname that it had no jurisdiction to address alleged violations of the UN Charter and general international law. *Guyana and Suriname*, PCA Award, 17 September 2007, para 406, http://www.pca-cpa.org/showpage.asp?pag_id=1147. Accessed 9 January 2015.

Prirazlomnaya protest, within the EEZ (as is the case on the high seas[82]), the LOSC prescribes that a vessel may exercise freedom of navigation subject to an obligation to exercise 'due regard' to the rights and duties of the coastal state and compliance with rules and regulations that are not incompatible with the exercise of EEZ powers.[83] Therefore, there exists a right to conduct protest activities under the general principle of free navigation, provided that these conditions are met. This position has been reinforced by the IMO which, in May 2010, adopted a Resolution formally affirming 'the rights and obligations relating to legitimate and peaceful forms of demonstration, protest or confrontation' while simultaneously upholding the importance of vessel safety and condemning 'any actions that intentionally imperil human life, the marine environment, or property during demonstrations, protests or confrontations on the high seas'.[84] Resolution MSC.303(87) also calls upon protest vessels to refrain from actions that would violate international navigational standards and for governments to establish a clear jurisdictional basis to proceed against vessels that fail to heed this approach. Although the Resolution is ultimately vague as to the specific rights and obligations incumbent in maritime protest, it may be considered that it provides an additional political imperative for flag states to take disciplinary action against delinquent protest vessels upon the high seas. Through this measure, the IMO mandates compliance with global navigational rules as a minimum standard for protests at sea. It further appears that this position is reinforced within the margin of appreciation accorded to states under human rights norms to establish the boundaries of acceptable activism.

The current corpus of case-law addressing specifically nautical protest before the European Court of Human Rights is distinctly limited, but suggests that the Greenpeace petitions, if accepted by the Court, may encounter some turbulence in their appraisal of freedom of expression at sea. The Court has reaffirmed that marine space is little different from the terrestrial context in how the authorities should consider the legitimacy of such activities. It is clear from its jurisprudence that purported restrictions on access to marine areas by campaigners must be proportionate to the wider aim pursued by the state in question. In perhaps the leading case to date, *Women On Waves and Others* v. *Portugal*,[85] a Dutch NGO that had intended to conduct a family planning campaign in Portuguese ports was banned from the entirety of the national territorial sea, primarily due to concerns that the vessels would be used to facilitate abortions, a practice that was still illegal in Portugal at the time. Although no evidence of law-breaking was adduced, warships

[82] Article 87(1) LOSC.

[83] Article 58(3) LOSC. This position is different within the territorial sea, whereby a foreign vessel must exhibit innocent passage, for which protest activities may be considerably more restricted in scope. Similarly internal waters are subject to the exclusive sovereignty of the coastal state.

[84] Resolution MSC.303(87): Assuring Safety During Demonstrations, Protests or Confrontations on the High Seas.

[85] *Women On Waves and Others* v. *Portugal*, ECtHR, No. 31276/05, 9 February 2009.

were deployed to prevent the applicants from disembarking at any point within the territorial sea. The Court considered this response to be a violation of their Article 10 ECHR rights, since the Portuguese authorities had other, less intrusive, means at their disposal to address the perceived problem posed by the activists including, if the allegations as to their intentions were correct, the possibility of seizing medication and equipment proscribed under national law.[86]

Moreover, the Court held that there was no legal basis under the Convention to ban foreign campaigners from a zone of maritime jurisdiction, since the territorial sea was considered fundamentally to be:

> un espace public et ouvert de par sa nature meme, contrairement aux locaux d'une administration ou d'un ministère.[87]

While this decision would, at face value, suggest a broad toleration for nautical protest, it may be considered that the situation is rather more nuanced. Indeed, perhaps more problematic from the standpoint of Greenpeace's Article 10 arguments is a precedent that lies rather closer to home. In *Drieman and Others v. Norway*,[88] four Greenpeace activists were convicted of a series of public order offences, and a dinghy was impounded by the Norwegian courts, following a series of altercations between protestors and a whaling vessel in the Norwegian EEZ. The Norwegian Supreme Court reduced the fines that had been levied against the applicants by the municipal authorities, but upheld the confiscation order and rejected claims of a violation of Articles 10 and 11 ECHR. The European Court of Human Rights declined the application as manifestly ill-founded, with the measures adopted by Norway considered to have been supported by relevant and sufficient reasons and underpinned by a rationale for public maritime safety that was necessary in a democratic society.[89] Moreover, the Court reiterated that national policies to restrict obstructive protest 'must be allowed a wide margin of appreciation' and it was accordingly 'not persuaded by the applicants' argument that the proscribed conduct should be assimilated to an incident of navigation'.[90]

The combined effect of *Women On Waves* and *Drieman* suggests that, absent a reasonable basis to presume intended misconduct, a state cannot preclude access to its maritime jurisdiction to activists per se, although localised restrictions on movement may be imposed where necessary to safeguard public safety and the

---

[86] Ibid., para 41.

[87] Ibid., para 40. This stands in striking contrast to a recent decision of the US courts which, in restraining purported protest activities in Alaskan offshore waters, stated that 'the high seas are not a public forum … Greenpeace USA has no audience at sea'. *Shell Offshore Inc.* v. *Greenpeace Inc.*, 9th Cir., 709 F.3d 1281, 2013, at 1291 (*per* Tashima J.). This is a surprising conclusion, given the comparative strength of the First Amendment and its associated jurisprudence. It is also patently incorrect given the principle of freedom of navigation enshrined under the LOSC. While the Court may have been justified in preventing disruptive access to oil rigs, rights to navigate in these waters and conduct protest activities in conjunction with the LOSC would surely remain intact.

[88] *Drieman and Others* v. *Norway*, ECtHR, No. 33678/96, 4 May 2000.

[89] Ibid., para 10.

[90] Ibid.

legitimate rights of others. Nevertheless, this does not equate to an automatic right to maritime access in all cases. Freedom of speech may be upheld even where campaigners are refused entry to marine areas, although *Drieman* mandates that an effective alternative basis to espouse their views must be maintained. In the context of the *Prirazlomnaya* dispute, the Russian authorities considered the boarding of the platform unjustified since Greenpeace had been granted an opportunity to contribute to appropriate Arctic governance fora concerning the broad regulation of oil and gas installations in the High North. The extent to which these opportunities have provided a realistic platform to inform debate on the pursuit of Arctic hydrocarbons will be seemingly constitute a significant question in any future deliberations by the Court in assessing a potential breach of the Convention.

14.4 Concluding Remarks

The order for provisional measures by ITLOS in the *Arctic Sunrise* case marks the end of the beginning for a dispute that raises pressing questions concerning elements of free navigation, as well as the burgeoning international jurisprudence on the legal parameters of protest actions at sea. As with other such orders, which are debated and delivered in comparative haste and are not designed to address the specific merits of the dispute,[91] the reasoning of the Tribunal in the present case is decidedly brief and not entirely consistent with elements of previous decisions. The order in many respects represents a missed opportunity on the part of ITLOS to expand its procedural jurisprudence, not least concerning the specific rules on default as elaborated under Part VI of the LOSC, while conversely the projected extension of aspects of the prompt release mechanism could be construed as excessive.

Individual elements of the order present some cause for unease, notably the uncritical acceptance of the Dutch submission as to the alleged environmental imperatives for provisional measures, while the decision itself strikes a generous balance in favour of the flag state in the context of an ongoing and legitimate (if somewhat politicised) criminal investigation by the coastal state. It remains to be seen whether elements of this approach will be followed by ITLOS in subsequent cases, or whether the *Arctic Sunrise* will be viewed in its unique context of default by the respondent state. The underlying message of the order is nevertheless that non-appearance before the Tribunal can significantly undermine the position of the defaulting state; it remains an exercise in conjecture as to whether provisional measures would have been as freely ordered in this case had the respondent mounted a meaningful defence of its legal interests. Meanwhile, the position of

[91] Nevertheless, this issue did have some bearing on the order, with Judge Jesus considering that 'there are some matters of substance that a court or tribunal dealing with a request for provisional measures cannot abstain from addressing'. *The 'Arctic Sunrise' Case*, Separate Opinion of Judge Jesus, para 15.

Russia in the dispute remains a cause for wider concern: the national authorities have responded to the incident by ignoring international judicial institutions and adjusting domestic law to allow for a more robust security presence aboard offshore platforms such as the *Prirazlomnaya*.[92]

The *Arctic Sunrise* case also provides scope for further judicial appraisal of the human rights issues involved in protest actions at sea, an issue that has been developed piecemeal by national and regional courts to date. These elements were addressed peripherally within this order on an official basis, although as the Separate Opinion of Judges Wolfrum and Kelly demonstrates, they nonetheless played a role in the contemplation of individual judges. The arbitral panel may opt to follow the lead of ITLOS in this regard and focus specifically on the navigation-related elements of the dispute, for which there are important questions to answer. Issues of free speech at sea might be more appropriately addressed by the European Court of Human Rights in this instance, although there is a case for suggesting that such entitlements may be viewed more conservatively than a number of campaign groups have argued thus far; international maritime law considers that protest actions within clearly designated safety zones ought to be tempered by the demands of public security at sea. In the meantime the *Arctic Sunrise*, still bearing the Dutch flag, was arrested in November 2014 by the Spanish authorities, following a series of clashes during a protest against oil exploration. Questions over the exercise of free speech rights at sea—and the involvement of the Netherlands in their resolution—accordingly look set to continue for some considerable time.

References

Bastmeijer K (2009) Protecting Polar wilderness: just a western philosophical idea or a useful concept for regulating human activities in the Polar Regions? Yearb Polar Law 1:73–91

Churchill R (2015) Dispute settlement for the law of the sea: survey for 2013. Int J Mar Coast Law 30:1–53

Doby D (2013) Whale wars: how to end violence on the high seas. J Marit Law Commer 44:135–168

Guilfoyle D (2009) Shipping interdiction and the law of the sea. Cambridge University Press, Cambridge

Guilfoyle D, Miles CA (2014) Provisional measures and the MV *Arctic Sunrise*. Am J Int Law 108:271–287

[92] In April 2014, as a direct result of the *Prirazlomnaya* incident, new legislation was adopted to facilitate the use of private military contractors to guard Arctic installations. Федеральный закон Российской Федерации от 20 апреля 2014 О внесении изменений в отдельные законодательные акты Российской Федерации по вопросу создания ведомственной охраны для обеспечения безопасности объектов топливно-энергетического комплекса г. N 75-ФЗ [Federal Law of April 20, 2014 on Amendments to Certain Legislative Acts of the Russian Federation on the Establishment of Departmental Security to Ensure the Safety of the Fuel and Energy Complexes, N 75-FZ]. Under Article 4 of this Law, companies have the right to establish 'departmental security' to protect, *inter alia*, offshore oil rigs.

Kanehara A (2011) So-called eco-piracy and interventions by NGOs to protest against scientific research whaling on the high seas: an evaluation of the Japanese position. In: Symmons CR (ed) Selected contemporary issues in the law of the sea. Brill, Leiden, pp 195–219

Klein N (2011) Maritime security and the law of the sea. Oxford University Press, Oxford

Mead D (2010) The new law of peaceful protest: rights and regulation in the human rights act era. Hart, Oxford

Mossop J (2012) The security challenge posed by scientific permit whaling and its opponents in the Southern Ocean. In: Hemmings AD, Rothwell DR, Scott KN (eds) Antarctic security in the twenty-first century: legal and policy perspectives. Routledge, Abingdon, pp 307–326

Oude Elferink AG (2014) The *Arctic Sunrise* incident: a multi-faceted law of the sea case with a human rights dimension. Int J Mar Coast Law 29:244–289

Plant G (1983) Civilian protest vessels and the law of the sea. Neth Yearb Int Law 14:133–163

Plant G (2002) International law and direct action at sea: twenty years on. Neth Yearb Int Law 33:75–117

Teulings J (2011) Peaceful protests against whaling on the high seas—A human-rights based approach. In: Symmons CR (ed) Selected contemporary issues in the law of the sea. Brill, Leiden, pp 221–251

Table of Cases*

INTERNATIONAL

Ad hoc Arbitrations

Chamizal case (Mexico v. USA), 1911 147 n. 143, 148 n. 151
Charles van Bokkelen Case (USA v. Haiti), 1888 148 n. 151
Clipperton Island Arbitration (Mexico v. France), 1931 147 n. 143
Samoan Claims (Germany, Great Britain and USA), 1902 148 n. 151

European Court of Human Rights

A and Others v. United Kingdom, Case No.3455/05 (2009) 204, 205, 206 n. 47, 213 n. 75, n. 77
Aksoy v. Turkey, Case No. 21987/93 (1996) 215
Al-Saadoon and Mufdhi v. UK, Case No. 61498/08 150 n. 157
Albert and Le Compte v. Belgium, Case No. 7299/75, 1983 150 n. 157
Aspects Of The Laws On The Use Of Languages In Education In Belgium' v. Belgium, Case Nos. 1474/62, 1677/62, 1691/62, 1769/63, 1994/63, 2126/64 (1968) 213 n. 76, n. 78
Beer and Reagan v. Germany, Case No. 28934/95, 1999 173 n. 82, 190 n. 186
Brannigan and McBride v. United Kingdom, Case Nos. 14553/89 and 14554/89 (1993) 212–213, 214 n. 81, 215
Brogan and Others v. United Kingdom, Case Nos. 11209/84, 11234/84, 11266/84, 11386/85 (1988) 214 n. 83
Cossey v. UK, Case No. 10843/84 (1990) 133 n. 65
Drieman and Others v. Norway, Case No. 33678/96 (2000) 381, 382
Dudgeon v. UK, Case No. 7525/76, 1981 133 n. 69
E.B. v. France, Case No. 43546/02 (2008) 132 n. 58
Elezi v. Germany, Case No. 26771/03 (2008) 348

* The Table of Cases was compiled by Ms C.C. Diepeveen, Middelburg, The Netherlands, e-mail: cdiep@zeelandnet.nl.

M. Ambrus and R.A. Wessel (eds.), *Netherlands Yearbook of International Law 2014*, Netherlands Yearbook of International Law 45, DOI 10.1007/978-94-6265-060-2

Feldbrugge v. Netherlands, Case No. 8562/79, 1986 150 n. 157
Goodwin v. UK, Case No. 28957/95 (2002) 132 n. 57
Greek Case (Denmark, Norway, Sweden and the Netherlands v. Greece), Case Nos. 3321/67, 3322/67, 3323/67 and 3344/67 (1969) 204, 205, 206
Handyside v. United Kingdom, Case No. 5493/72 (1976) 213 n. 78, 214
Hatton and others v. UK, Case No. 36022/97 (2003) 132 n. 58
Hirst v. UK, Case No. 74025/01 (2005) 131 n. 52
Ireland v. the United Kingdom, Case No. 5310/71 (1978) 203 n. 30
Loizidou v. Turkey, Case No. 15318/89 (1995) 132 n. 57, 140 n. 103
Marckx v. Belgium, Case No. 6833/74 (1979) 209 n. 60
Matthews v. UK, Case No. 24833/94 (1999) 131 n. 45
Meftah v. France, Case No. 32911/96 (2002) 131 n. 51
Mothers of Srebrenica and Others v. The Netherlands, Case No, 65542/12, 2013 174–175
Murray v. United Kingdom, Case No. 14310/88 (1994) 203 n. 30, 215 n. 87
Öcalan v. Turkey, Case No. 46221/99, (2005) 133 n. 69
Öztürk v. Germany, Case No. 8544/79 (1984) 133 n. 64
R.R. v. Poland, Case No. 27617/04 (2011) 132 n. 58
Schalk and Kopf v. Austria, Case No. 30141/04 (2010) 132 n. 57
Soering v. UK, Case No.14038/88, (1989) 150 n. 158
Tyrer v. UK, Case No. 5856/72 (1978) 131 n. 45, 132 n. 57, 133 n. 66
Űner v. The Netherlands, Case No. 46410/99 (2006) 229 n. 39
Vo v. France, Case No. 53924/00 (2004) 132 n. 57
Waite and Kennedy v. Germany, Case No. 26083/94, (1999) 173 n. 82, 174, 176, 190
Women On Waves and Others v. Portugal, Case No. 31276/05 (2009) 380–381

Inter-American Court on Human Rights

Advisory Opinions

Effect of Reservations on the Entry Into Force of the American Convention on Human Rights, 1982 140 n. 103
Juridical Status and Human Rights of the Child, 2002 133 n. 68, 146 n. 135, n. 139
Juridical Status and Human Rights of Undocumented Migrants, 2003 146 n. 135, n. 139 'Other Treaties' Subject to the Advisory Jurisdiction of the Court, 1982 140 n. 103
Restrictions to the Death Penalty, 1983 140 n. 103
Right to Information on Consular Assistance (Mexico v. USA), 1999 129 n. 38, 131 n. 46, n. 50, 133 n. 64, n. 66, n. 68, n. 69, 146 n. 135, n. 139, n. 140

Judgments

Bámaca Velásquez v. Guatemala, 2000 131 n. 48
Caesar v. Trinidad and Tobago, 2005 129 n. 38, 131 n. 50, 132 n. 54, 140 n. 103
Gómez Paquiyauri and others (on behalf of Gómez Paquiyauri and Gómez Paquiyauri) v. Peru, 2004 133 n. 66, n. 68, 146 n. 135, n. 139, n. 140
Mapiripán Massacre v. Colombia, 2005 132 n. 58

Mayagna (Sumo) Awas Tingni Community v. Nicaragua, 2001 131 n. 47, 133 n. 66, n. 68
Roach and Pinkerton, Case No. 9647, 1987 218 n. 98
Sawhoyamaxa Indigenous Community of the Enxet-Lengua People v. Paraguay, 2006 133 n. 68
Serrano Cruz and Serrano Cruz v. El Salvador, 2004 146 n. 135, n. 139, n. 140
'Street Children' (Villagrán Morales et al.) v. Guatemala, 1999 133 n. 66, n. 68, 146 n. 135, n. 139, n. 140
Tibi v. Ecuador, 2004 146 n. 140
Villa García and others v. Colombia, 2006 146 n. 135, n. 139
Yakye Axa Indigenous Community v. Paraguay, 2005 132 n. 58, 133 n. 66, n. 68, 146 n. 140

International Centre for Settlement of Investment Disputes
ADF Inc. v. USA, Case No. ARB(AF)/00/1, 2003 132 n. 58
Ambiente Ufficio SpA and others v. Argentina, Case No. ARB/08/9, 2013 143 n. 123
ATA Construction, Industrial and Trading Company v. Jordan, Case No. ARB/08/2, 2010 128 n. 33, 150 n. 155
Daimler Financial Services AG v. Argentina, Case No. ARB/05/1, 2012 131 n. 48, 144 n. 126
Jan de Nul NV and Dredging International NV v. Egypt, Case No. ARB/04/13, 2008 128 n. 32
MCI Power Group LC and New Turbine Incorporated v. Ecuador, Case No. ARB/03/6, 2007 128 n. 34
Mondev International Limited v. USA, Case No. ARB(AF)/99/2, 2002 128 n. 33, 131 n. 48, 132 n. 58, 133 n. 67, 141 n. 111, 150 n. 155
Siemens AG v. Argentina, Case No. ARB/02/8, 2014 143 n. 123, n. 124
Waste Management Inc. v. Mexico, Case No. ARB(AF)/00/3, 2004 132 n. 58, 133 n. 67

International Court of Justice
Advisory Opinions
Difference Relating to Immunity from Legal Process of a Special Rapporteur of the Commission on Human Rights, 1998 173
Effect of Awards of Compensation Made by the United Nations Administrative Tribunal, 1954 186
Legal Consequences for States of the Continued Presence of South Africa in Namibia (SouthWest Africa), 1971 130 n. 45, 132 n. 58, 143 n. 124
Western Sahara Case, 1975 130 n. 44
Interim Protection Orders
Aegean Sea Continental Shelf Case (Greece v. Turkey), 1976 369 n. 31, 372 n. 48
Fisheries Jurisdiction (Germany v. Iceland), 1972 369 n. 31

Fisheries Jurisdiction (United Kingdom v. Iceland), 1972 369 n. 31
Nuclear Tests (Australia v. France), 1973 369 n. 31
Nuclear Tests (New Zealand v. France), 1973 369 n. 31
Judgments
Aegean Sea Continental Shelf (Greece v. Turkey) Case, 1978 130 n. 44, n. 45, 132 n. 58, 133 n. 62, 141 n. 111, 142 n. 115, n. 117, 143 n. 122, n. 124
Ambatielos case (Greece v. UK), 1952 147 n. 143
Anglo-Norwegian Fisheries Case (United Kingdom v. Norway), 1951 24
Application of the Convention on the Prevention and Punishment of the Crime of Genocide (Bosnia and Herzegovina v. Serbia and Montenegro), 2007 150 n. 154
Armed Activities on the Territory of the Congo (Congo Democratic Republic v. Uganda), 2005 295
Asylum Case (Colombia v. Peru), 1950 77 n. 53
Avena and Other Mexican Nationals (Mexico v. USA), 2004 148 n. 149
Barcelona Traction case (Belgium v. Spain), 1970 292 n. 33
Gabčíkovo-Nagymaros Project (Hungary/Slovakia), 1997 113, 130 n. 45, 131 n. 47, 132 n. 58, 133 n. 63, 139, 141 n. 111, 150 n. 153, n. 156, n. 159
Jurisdictional Immunities of the State (Germany v. Italy: Greece intervening), 2012 and 2013 111 n. 87, 163 n. 35
Kasikili/Sedudu Island (Botswana v. Namibia), 1999 130 n. 44, 142 n. 114, 143 n. 125, 147, 148 n. 146
Libya/Chad Territorial Dispute (LibyanArab Jamahariya/Chad), 1994 147 n. 144, 148 n. 149
Military and Paramilitary Activities in and against Nicaragua (Nicaragua v. United States), 1984 300
Minquiers and Ecrehos (France v. UK), 1953 130 n. 44
Navigational and Related Rights Dispute (Costa Rica v. Nicaragua), 2009 130 n. 44, 131 n. 45, 132 n. 58, 141 n. 111, 142 n. 122, 143 n. 124
Oil Platforms Case (Iran v. USA), 2003 147 n. 144, 148 n. 149
Pulp Mills on the River Uruguay (Argentina v. Uruguay), 2010 114
Right of Passage over Indian Territory (Portugal v. India), 1960 130 n. 44
South West Africa Cases (Ethiopia v. South Africa; Liberia v. South Africa), 1966 313 n. 7
South-West Africa (Second Phase) (Liberia and Ethiopia v. South Africa), 1966 150 n. 154
Sovereignty over Pulau Ligitan and Pulau Sipadan (Indonesia/Malaysia), 2002 148 n. 149
Temple of Preah Vihear (Cambodia v. Thailand), 1962 130 n. 44
United States nationals in Morocco, (France v. USA), 1952 130 n. 44, 135 n. 77
Whaling in the Antarctic Case (Australia v. Japan: New Zealand Intervening), 2014 362 n. 8

Provisional Measures
Passage through the Great Belt Case (Finland v. Denmark), 1991 377 n. 72
United States Diplomatic and Consular Staff in Tehran (United States v. Iran), 1979 369 n. 31

International Criminal Court for the Former Yugoslavia
Prosecutor v. Milosevic, Case No. IT-02-54-AR73.4, 21 October 2003 334
Prosecutor v. Seselj, Case No. IT-03-67-T
13 November 2013 353 n. 40
13 December 2013 342
Prosecutor v. Stakic (Prijedor), Case No. IT-97-24, 22 March 2006 27 n. 24

International Tribunal for the Law of the Sea
Arctic Sunrise Case (Netherlands v. Russia), Provisional Measures Order, 22 November 2013 359, 362, 365–374, 378–379, 382–383
M/V Louisa Case (St. Vincent and the Grenadines v. Spain), 23 December 2010 370 n. 41, 371, 372
M/V Saiga(No. 2) Case (St. Vincent and the Grenadines v. Guinea), 1 July 1999 379 n. 80

Permanent Court of Arbitration
Boundary Dispute between Argentina and Chile (Argentina v. Chile), 1994 130 n. 44
Delimitation of Maritime Boundary between Guinea-Bissau and Senegal (Guinea Bissau v. Senegal), 1989 130–131 n. 45
Grisbådarna Case (Norway v. Sweden), 1909 130 n. 44, 135 n. 77
Guyana and Suriname Case, 17 September 2007 379 n. 81
Iron Rhine Arbitration (Belgium v. Netherlands), 2005 129 n. 38, 131 n. 45, 132 n. 58, 141 n. 111
Island of Palmas Case (or Miangas) (Netherlands v. USA), 1928 128, 134
North Atlantic Coast Fisheries Case (Great Britain v. USA), 1910 130 n. 44, 135 n. 77

Permanent Court of International Justice
Advisory Opinions
Nationality Decrees Issued in Tunis and Morocco, 1923 141 n. 111

Special Tribunal for Lebanon
Prosecutor v. Ayyash et al.
Case No. STL-11-01/I, 16 February 2011 337
Case No. STL-11-01/T/TC, 16 January 2014 340

UNCITRAL Arbitration
GAMI Investment Inc. v. Mexico, 2004 132 n. 58, 133 n. 67
Merrill & Ring Forestry LP v. Canada, 2010 132 n. 58, 133 n. 67

United Nations Human Rights Committee
Franz Nahlik v. Austria, Case No. 608/1995 (1996) 314 n. 11
Judge v. Canada, Case No. No. 829/1998, 2002 132 n. 58
Landinelli Silva v. Uruguay, Case No. 34/1978 (1981) 215 n. 92

WTO Appellate Body

EC–Large Civil Aircraft, Case No. WT/DS316/AB/R, 2011 147 n. 142

USA—Import Prohibition of Certain Shrimp and Shrimp Products, Case No. WT/DS58/AB/R, 1998 132 n. 58, 141 n. 111

NATIONAL

Belgium

Court of Cassation

Castle John and Nederlandse Stichting Sirius v. NV Parfin, 1986 377

Court of Appeal Brussels

Manderlier v. United Nations and Belgium, 1969 173

Siedler v. Western European Union, 2003 174 n. 86

Canada

Supreme Court

Attorney General v. Ward [1993] 222 n. 3

Italy

Corte Constitutionale

Judgment No. 236/2014 110 n. 86

Ferrini Corte di Cassazione (Sezioni Unite)

Judgment No. 5044, 6 November 2003 110

Netherlands

Supreme Court

Mothers of Srebrenica v. The Netherlands and the United Nations, 13 April 2012 163 n. 33, n. 36

Court of Appeal

Mothers of Srebrenica v. The Netherlands and the United Nations, 20 March 2010 175

Somali piracy case (Dhow), 18 February 2014 349 n. 30

Sweden

Stockholm Chamber of Commerce Arbitration Institute (SCC Intitute)

RosInvest Company UK Limited v. Russian Federation, Case No. V079/2005 [2007] 131 n. 47, 140 n. 105, 141 n. 108

United Kingdom

House of Lords

Horvath v. Secretary of State for the Home Department [2001] 222 n. 3

M, Re, King v. Bristow Helicopters Limited [2002] 132 n. 58

Court of Appeal

R (on the application of Khan) v. Secretary of State for Foreign and Commonwealth Affairs [2014] 333 n. 2

United States

Supreme Court

Adarand Construction v. Pena [1995] 315 n. 14

Fischer v. University Texes at Austin et al [2013] 315, 328

Gratz v. Bollinger [2003] 327 n. 68
Grutter v. Bollinger [2003] 317, 326
Snepp v. United States [1980] 216 n. 93
Court of Appeal
Institute of Cetacean Research and Others v. Sea Shephard Conservation Society and Watson [2013 and 2014] 361 n. 4, 362 n. 8, 377
Marvin R Broadbent et al. v. Organization of American States et al. [1980] 189 n. 183
Shell Offshore Inc. v. Greenpeace Inc. [2013] 381 n. 87
District Court New York
Amici Curiae in Georges et al. v. United Nations et al. [2014] 163 n. 31, 166 n. 43
Brzak v. United Nations [2010] 176 n. 95
Georges et al. v. United Nations et al. [2013] 161 n. 17
LaVenture v. United Nations et al. [2014] 161 n. 17
Petit Homme Jean-Robert et al. v. United Nations [2014] 161 n. 17

Index*

A
Absence, of accused from trials, 340
Access
to asylum procedures, human right of, 236–237, 242
Accountability
for international law violations, 289
mechanisms for, 295–296
of international officials, 85
and IO's, 7–8, 184
Accountability gap
and IO's, 13
in private claims against UN, 157, 164, 172, 184
Accused
absence from trial, 340
rights of, international criminal justice, 334 n. 6, 345–346
Activism
at sea, 359, 360–361
and freedom of speech, 378–382, 383
legal responses to, 361–362, 364
against oil exploration activities, 359, 362–364
Adaptive flexibility, 271
Addis, Adeno, 6, 12
Adjudication
international, 287, 291–292
by commissions of inquiry, 290–295
impact of commissions of inquiry on, 295–306
selectivity appearance of, 306
Adversarial legal systems, 331–332
fairness aura of, 346–347
in international criminal justice, 333, 335, 336, 339
and preparedness for trial, 349
Affirmative action measures, 313 n. 8, 313 n. 9
and non-discrimination principle, 321–322
as temporary objects, 6, 11–12
time limits for, 317–318, 326–327
in United States, 328
see also Non-discrimination norm/principle; Temporary measures, in human rights treaties
African Charter on Human and Peoples Rights, derogation provision absent from, 202 n. 26, 218 n. 98
African Convention governing the Specific Aspects of Refugee Problems in Africa (1969), Art. 5, 231 n. 52
Agamben, A., 319 n. 36, 320 n. 40
Agrippa, 125 n. 10
Akande, D., 305 n. 99
Altruistic legal regimes, 207–208
of human rights law, 209, 210–211, 212–213, 218, 219
rules and standards in, 212
Alvarez, A., 167, 178, 184, 291, 294 n. 43
Alvarez, Jose Enrique, 172
American Convention on Human Rights (ACHR)
Art. 27, 217
on derogation of human rights, 201, 202, 217

* The Index was compiled by Ms C.C. Diepeveen, Middelburg, The Netherlands, e-mail: cdiep@zeelandnet.nl and Ms I.S. Bosschieter, Stitswerd, The Netherlands, e-mail: pierke@isbnindex.nl.

M. Ambrus and R.A. Wessel (eds.), *Netherlands Yearbook of International Law 2014*, Netherlands Yearbook of International Law 45, DOI 10.1007/978-94-6265-060-2

interpretation of, 146
Ammoun, Judge, 313 n. 7
Antarctic
Japanese whaling in, activism against, 361, 362 n. 8
Anti-terrorism legislation, in United Kingdom in, 204–205
Antonetti, Judge, 353 n. 40
Appeals, 353
interlocutory, 352 n. 37
Applicable law, determination of, commissions of inquiry on, 293
Arab Charter of Human Rights, on derogation of human rights, 201, 202
Arbitration
by commissions of inquiry, 290–291
human rights considerations in, 379
by Netherlands against Russia over *Arctic Sunrise*, 359, 362, 364, 365–374, 382–383
human rights considerations, 378–379, 382, 383
provisional measures in, 365–366, 369–374
Arctic region
claims to continental shelves of 11, 363 n. 11
EU concerns on environmental protection of, 363 n. 13
oil exploration activities in, activism against, 359, 362–364
Arctic Sunrise dispute, 359, 362–365
arbitration procedures, 359, 362, 364, 365–374, 382–383
human rights considerations, 378–379, 382, 383
piracy charges, 376–378
Articles on the Responsibility of International Organizations (ARIO), 183
Asselt, Harro van, 6, 9–10
Astronomical time, 94
Asylum
policies, EU harmonization of, 240
procedures
human right of access to, 236–237, 242
length of, 242–243
see also Protection
Atemporality, in concept of law, 93, 95, 96, 97–98, 99, 116
Atkin, Lord, 334 n. 6
Atrocities, occurrence of, 342
Attacks
terrorist
imminence of, 205
and normalcy, 320
Australia, Racial Discrimination Act 1975, 313 n. 8
Authority, delegations of, by courts, 208

B

Bagshaw, S., 238 n. 81
Bahrain commission of inquiry, 296
Bali Action Plan (2007), 267
Bartolus de Sassoferato, 110
Bassouini, M.C., 303, 305 n. 100, 309
Behavioural international law, state behaviour and, 43, 46, 50, 51, 53, 60–61, 62–63
Bill on Administrative Measures concerning National Security (*Wet Bestuurlijke Maatregelen Nationale Veiligheid*), 83
Bindingness, of commission of inquiry outcomes, 290–291, 292, 294, 296
Bohlander, Michael, 8, 13, 15
Bookey, B., 190
Bosnia and Herzegovina, refugees returning to, 240 n. 89
Bossuyt, Marc, 313 n. 9, 321
Boutros Ghali, Boutros, 107
Boutruche, T., 305 n. 100
Boyd, William, 280
Brölmann, C., 141
Brown, Gordon, 297
Brundtland Commission, 112
Brunnée, J., 260 n. 21
Buchan, R., 292

C

Cambodia, Extra-ordinary Chambers in the Courts of, 333 n. 5, 343
Canada, notification of withdrawal from Kyoto Protocol, 266, 271
Cancún Agreements, 267–268
Capotorti, Francesco, 324 n. 59
Cassese, Antonio, 337
Central Claims Commissions (UN), 187–188
Certainty, legal, 79, 84, 354
Change
concept of, 121, 123, 125–127, 133
passage of time and, 122–123
and temporariness, 21
universality of, 126
see also Legal change
Chesterman, Simon, 75
Chetail, V., 227
Chilcot, John, 297
Chilcot Inquiry (UK involvement in Iraq conflict), 297, 299

Choice, individual, 325 n. 61
Cholera claims
  and diplomatic protection against UN, 177
  as private law claims, 165–166, 175
  UN handling of, 160, 161–162, 184
    and international human rights laws, 180–181
    local claims review boards and, 171–172
    and rule of law, 179–180
  see also Private law claims
Cholera epidemic (Haiti)
  seen as human rights violation, 181–183, 186
  UN responsibility for, 158–160
Chowdhury, S.R., 209 n. 61
Chrysippus, 125
Churchill, R., 367
Cicero, 97
Claims commissions, of UN, 169–171, 182–183
Climate change
  international legal regime on, 255, 256
    flexibility in, 257–272
    research input, 256–257, 260–262
  as temporary object, 6, 9–10
Climate change law, 255, 256
  flexibility in, 257–272, 278–282
  legal pluralism in, 273–278, 281–282
  research input, 256–257, 260–262, 271–272
Clyde, Lord, 222 n. 3
Codex Alimentarius Commission, 35–36
Coles, G., 230
Commissions of inquiry (CoIs), 288–289
  creation of, 15
  establishment of, 306, 308
  impact on international legal adjudication, 289
  temporariness of, 8, 13, 287, 288, 289, 306–309
  as temporary adjudicative bodies, 290–295
Compliance
  with climate change treaties, 269–271
  with ideal theory, 323 n. 55
Compliance pull, 29–30
The Concept of Law (Hart), 199
Concurring vote, 23–24
Conflict of rights, and human rights derogation, 200
Consent, of states, to external authority/scrutiny, 300–301
Consistency, principle of, 180
Constitution, of Holy Roman Empire, 102
Constructivism, state behaviour and, 43, 50, 51, 52–53, 60, 62
Consuetudo (state practice), 109
Contemporaneity, in treaties interpretation, 124, 129, 130, 133, 134–138, 140, 142, 148, 152
Continuity
  international law and, 82
  international rule of law and, 79–81
Contract law, individualist regime of, 207
Convention for the Suppression of Unlawful Acts against the Safety of Maritime Navigation (1988), 378
  Protocol for the Suppression of Unlawful Acts against the Safety of Fixed Platforms Located on the Continental Shelf (2005), 378 n. 77
    Art. 2(1)(a), 378
Convention on the Elimination of all Forms of Discrimination of Women (CEDAW)
  Art. 4, 314 n. 10, 318 n. 33
  Art. 4(1), 320 n. 41
  Committee
    on equality, 324 n. 58, 325 n. 60
    on temporary measures, 326 n. 65
  non-discrimination norm in, 322
  temporary measures in, 313–314, 318, 320
Convention on the Elimination of All Forms of Racial Discrimination (CERD)
  Art. 1(4), 314 n. 10, 320 n. 41
  implementation of, in Australia, 313 n. 8
  non-discrimination norm in, 322
  temporary measures in, 313–314, 320
Convention on the Law of the Sea (UN, 1982), 362
  Annex VI, Art. 28, 368–369
  Annex VII arbitral proceedings, 364, 365
  Art. 15, 366
  Art. 56, 365
  Art. 58, 367, 374 n. 58
  Art. 58(1), 365
  Art. 58(2), 375
  Art. 60, 365, 374, 376
  Art. 73, 373
  Art. 74, 366
  Art. 80, 365
  Art. 83, 366
  Art. 87(1), 365
  Art. 101, 376–377
  Art. 111(1), 376
  Art. 111(2), 376
  Art. 220, 373
  Art. 226, 373
  Art. 283, 368 n. 30

Art. 287, 365
Art. 290, 369
Art. 290(1), 365, 371
Art. 290(5), 366, 371
Art. 293(1), 379
Art. 297(1), 367, 368
Art. 297(2) and (3), 367
Art. 298, 366, 367
Art. 309, 366, 367
Art. 310, 366, 367
on freedom of speech, 379–380
on offshore installations, 374–375
Russian Declaration upon ratification of, 366–367, 368
on seizure/arrest of ships, 371–373
Coordinated Universal Time, 95
Copenhagen Accord (2009), 260
Corpus Iuris Civilis, 97
Corte di Cassazione (Italy), 110–111
Costs, of affirmative action programs, 327
Cot, Judge, 370 n. 41
Counterterrorism policies, sunset clauses and, 81, 83
Courts
delegations of authority by, 208, 212
see also International courts/tribunals
Covenant of the League of Nations, 106
Crawford, James, 87
Criddle, E.J., 6, 11, 211 n. 68
Crimes, breaching safety zones of offshore installations, 375
Crimes against humanity, 344 n. 24
Criminal investigations, into boarding of *Priazlomnaya* oil platform, 373–374
Criminal justice, *see* International criminal justice
Criminal tribunals, temporariness of, 8, 13
Critical mass notion, 330 n. 77
Cultures, legal, 354
Customary international law, 345
equality norm as, 313
refugee law, 225
Customary law, persistent objector rule in, 24–25

D

Damaška, Mirjan, 341, 352
D'Amoto, Anthony, 30
Darfur commission of inquiry, 291, 292, 293, 299, 304–305
Dayton Peace Agreement (1995), 237, 238, 240
Annex 7, 240 n. 89
De juri belli ac pacis (Grotius), 101
De Vattel, Emer, 99, 134
Defences, in international criminal proceedings, 349, 350
Denmark, claim to Arctic continental shelve by, 363 n. 11
Depledge, Joanna, 263
Derogation of human rights, 248 n. 131
in emergencies, 197, 198–199
judging of, 201–202
protection of human rights through, 200
in Refugee Convention, 247–248, 251
regimes of, 199
standards for, 199–200
adjudication of, 200, 202–203, 204–206, 214, 215
rule-making authority on, 202, 203, 206–219
treaty clauses on, 198, 201–202, 209–210, 248, 320 n. 39
Developed-developing countries dichotomy, in international climate change regime, 267–268, 276, 277
Dicey, A.V., 72
Diplomatic protection, 177
Disclosure, in international criminal procedures, 342–343, 349, 350
Discrimination, 313 n. 9
prohibition of, 216, 320 n. 39, 321
see also Affirmative action measures; Non-discrimination norm/principle
Displacements, as goal of war, 234
Dispute settlement, inter-state, 291, 292 n. 30
Djeffal, Christian, 7
Dogger Bank inquiry (1904), 290
Domestic courts
role in customary international law, 110
UN legal immunity and, 158–159, 163, 168, 172–173, 174–175, 184–185, 189–191
Durban Platform on a Future Climate Agreement, 267
Durieux, J.-F., 6, 10, 230, 231, 233
Dworkin, Ronald, 115, 312, 324
Dynamic approach, in treaties interpretation, *see* Evolutive/dynamic approach

E

Economic rights, 198
Edwards, A., 244, 245, 248 n. 130
Efficiency, in international criminal justice, 345–346, 349, 352

Ellis, E., 315 n. 15
Emergencies
  defining of, 211
  derogation of human rights in, 197, 198–199
    judging of, 201–202, 204–205, 206 n. 47
  judging of, by international courts/tribunals, 216–217
  refugee influxes causing of, 251
  special/temporary measures in
    and equality, 314–315, 319
    and norms, 319–320
  as temporary objects, 6, 11
Emission reductions
  scientific research influences on, 271–272
  trade in, 268–269, 275, 277
Endurantism, 126, 127, 128, 133, 151
Enforcement, school in compliance theory, 270
Environment law
  influence of international investment law on, 31
  international, 256, 259. *see also* Climate change law
Environmental activism
  at sea, 359, 360–361
    and freedom of speech, 378–382, 383
    legal responses to, 361–362, 364, 376–377
    against oil exploration activities, 359, 362–364
Environmental stewardship, 371–373
Equality
  and affirmative action measures, 12
  and non-discrimination principle, 315 n. 15
  norm in international law, 312–313
  notion, 315–316, 318, 322–325, 326, 329
  and temporary measures in human rights treaties, 311, 314–315, 316, 319, 320, 321–322, 323, 329–330
Erga omnes nature, of human rights obligations, 292 n. 33
Ertük, Yakin, 299
Eser, A., 333 n. 1
Eternal Peace of 1686, 102
Ethnic cleansing
  reversal of, through repatriation, 234–235, 240 n. 89
Europe, refugee crisis from Yugoslavia break-up in, 232–235, 236, 237–240
European Coal and Steel Community, 77, 86
European Communities, Measures Concerning Meat and Meat Products, 30
European Convention on Human Rights (ECHR)
  Art. 5, 374
  Art. 6, 343
  Art. 10, 374, 381
  Art. 11, 381
  on derogation of human rights, 201, 202, 204
  interpretation of, 146
  Protocol 15, 214–215
European Court of Human Rights (ECtHR)
  altruism in jurisprudence of, 209, 212–213
  on deportation of settled migrants, 229 n. 39
  on human rights derogations, 204–206, 215
  and legal immunity of IO's, 173–175
  margin of appreciation doctrine of, 200, 201, 213–216, 217
  on maritime activism, 380–382, 383
European Union
  emissions trading system of, 277
  European Parliament Resolutions on oil exploration in Arctic waters, 363, 364 n. 14
  migration and asylum policies of, harmonization of, 240
  Temporary Protection Directive, 221, 241–245, 249
    Art. 6, 243
    Art. 6(1), 244
    Art. 17(2), 242
    Art. 19, 243 n. 104
    Art. 21, 243
    Art. 22, 243
Evidence
  collection of, 346 n. 26
  control over, 349
  disclosure of, 349, 350
  in international criminal procedure, 333–334, 350
  of potential environmental hazards, 371
  standards of, for commissions of inquiry, 304–305
Evolutive/dynamic approach
  in treaties interpretation, 108, 124, 131, 133–134, 137–138, 139–141, 150, 152
    evolution of facts in, 132
    evolution of law in, 132–133
    intertemporal law and, 131–132
    limits to, 150–151
    use of generic terms in, 141–143
Exception notion, 314, 320 n. 40
  and temporary/special measures, 319
Exclusion, of late additional evidence, 350

Exclusive Economic Zones (EEZs), state jurisdiction over, 375–376, 381
Exdurantism, 127–128, 133–134, 151
Experimentation, in climate change regime, 274–275
Expertise
of commission of inquiry members, 299, 305–306, 309
of judges, 337, 339–340
Expressions, referring, 142
Exxon Valdez disaster (1989), 363

F
Fact-finding, by commissions of inquiry, 289–290
Factual equality, 324
Fairness
procedural, 298, 339 n. 16, 341
in adversarial systems, 346–347
and commissions of inquiry, 303–306, 309
in international criminal justice, 334 n. 6, 342, 343, 345–346, 354, 207–208
Fiduciary law, altruism of, 207–208
Finnemore, Martha, 50
Fish, Jörg, 102
Fitzmaurice, G., 124, 129, 130, 143, 144
Fitzpatrick, Joan, 226, 228, 233, 234 n. 63, 235, 236, 237, 239, 241, 244
Fitzpatrick Hartman, J., 225
Flexibility
of commissions of inquiry, 308
in principle of sustainable development, 114–115
in UN climate change regime, 258–272, 278–282
Fluxus, in concept of law, 95, 96, 104–105, 108, 109, 110, 111, 115
Formality, of judicial bodies, 295–296
Fox-Decent, Evan, 211 n. 68
Framework Convention on Climate Change (United Nations), 61, 255, 257, 259, 271, 275
alternatives for, 276–277, 281, 282
Art. 2, 275
Art. 4(2)(d), 262
Art. 4(2)(f), 262 n. 38
Art. 7(2)(a), 262
classification/differentiation of Parties to, 266–268, 272, 279, 281
compliance with, 270
Conference of Parties, 259–260, 261, 262, 271, 279–280
decision-making of, 260, 272, 278–279
Rules of Procedure of, 260 n. 22, 279 n. 151
entry into force, 265
implementation of, 268
review and amendment of, 262–265, 271, 280
Subsidiary Body for Scientific and Technological Advice, 260, 261
withdrawal provisions, 266
Franco-Dutch War (1672–1678), 103
Frank, Thomas, 29–30, 36
Freedom
of navigation, 367, 380
of speech, at sea, 378–382, 383
Frisch, Max, 123
Frulli, M., 293 n. 35, 306

G
Galbraith, Jean, 9, 14–15
Gaza conflicts, commissions of inquiry on, 292 n. 30, 296, 298, 299
Gender, sexual orientation as category of, 344 n. 24
General Agreement of Tariffs and Trade (GATT), as temporary regime, 47
Generic terms, 141–142
Geneva Convention (1949), 69
Georgopoulos, Th., 132
German Code on Measurement Units and Measurement of Time, 95
Germany
legal system in, 351
temporary protection of Bosnian refugees ended by, 237–238
Gersen, Jacob, 46
Ginsburg, Ruth, 315–316, 327–328, 329 n. 75, 329 n. 76
Global governance
institutional change in, 19, 20
inter-institutional interactions, 20, 29
norm creation in, 19, 20
Global legal pluralism, 273
Global public goods, 274 n. 119
Global regulatory space, 14
dynamics within, 27–30
and gravitational pull, 30–31, 32–33
evaluation of, 36–37
of private parties, 34–36
inter-institutional interactions, 31–32
and regulatory capture, 34–36
and tunnel vision, 33–34
permanence in, 32–33

Goldstone, Richard, 58–59, 298
Golitsyn, Judge, 368 n. 30, 372 n. 47, 373, 376 n. 66
Goodwin-Gill, G.S., 223 n. 6, 225
Greenhouse gas emissions, reductions of, 268–269, 271–272
Greenland, claim to Arctic continental shelve by, 363 n. 11
Greenpeace
  action against Russian oil exploration in Arctic region, 359, 364
    human rights emphasis in, 378–379
  activism at sea, 360
    in Norwegian Exclusive Economic Zone, 381
    'Save the Arctic' campaign, 363
  Dutch registration of protest ships of, 362
Gross, Orin, 214 n. 81, 215 n. 90
Grotius, Hugo, 97, 101, 134
Guilfoyle, D., 377 n. 69

H

Haas, Peter, 261
Hague Convention for the Peaceful Settlement of Disputes (1899), 289–290, 291
Hague Peace Conference (1899), 289
Haiti
  cholera epidemic
    seen as human rights violation, 181–183, 186
    UN peacekeepers source of, 158–160
  government of, diplomatic protection against UN, 177
  Status of Forces Agreement with UN, 161–163, 165, 169–171, 176, 182–183
  see also Cholera claims
Halling, M., 190
Hamilton, Alexander, 211
Harm, environmental, 371
Hart, H.L.A., 199, 202
Hathaway, J.C., 227
Helfer, Laurence, 258, 266
Helgesen, J.E., 131
Helmersen, S.T., 142
Henderson, Christian, 8, 13, 15
Heraclitus of Ephesus, 122, 125
Herweg, Fabian, 50
Hezbollah, 340
Higgins, R., 128, 140, 143, 148, 299
High Commissioner for Refugees (UNHCR), *see* UNHCR
High-Level Panel Report on Threats, Challenges and Change, 107–108
Hirschman, Albert, 47
Historical institutionalism, state behaviour and, 43, 49–50, 51, 52, 60, 62–63
Hobbes, Thomas, 125 n. 11
Holy Roman Empire, constitution of, 102
Hot pursuit rights, 376
Huber's dictum, 128, 129, 134, 135
Human Development report, 106–107
Human rights
  derogation of
    in emergencies, 6, 11, 197, 198–199
      judging of, 201–202
    human rights protection through, 200
    regimes of, 199
    standards for, 199–200
      adjudication of, 200, 202–203, 204–206, 214, 215
      rule-making authority on, 202, 203, 206–219
    treaty clauses on, 198, 201–202, 209–210, 248, 320 n. 39
  freedom of speech, at sea, 378–382, 383
  to health, 181–182
  to life, 181
  non-derogable, 203 n. 36
  obligations
    erga omnes nature of, 292 n. 33
    of states, 208–209, 210
  to protest/demonstrate, 375, 378–382, 383
  to seek asylum, 236–237, 242
  to water, 181–182
Human rights law (HRL), 198
  adoption of emergency measures and, 11–12
  altruistic legal regime of, 209, 210–211, 212–213, 218, 219
  derogation concept in, 248 n. 131
  equality as core concept in, 312–313
  individualistic legal regime of, 208–209, 210, 218
  influence of international investment law on, 31
  legal standards in, 206–207
  as source of international criminal procedure, 343–344
  transforming regulatory space applicable to, 35
  violations, commissions of inquiry on, 292, 293, 298
  violations of, cholera outbreak seen as, 181–183
Human rights treaties
  on derogation of human rights, 198, 201–202, 209–210

equality in, 312
limitation clauses in, 198
temporary measures in, 313–314, 317–320
and equality, 311, 314–315, 316, 319, 320, 321–322, 323, 329–330
predictability requirement, 327–328
Humanitarian emergencies, temporary regime and, 45
Humanity, crimes against, 344 n. 24
Hunt, David, 334
Hurwitz, A., 230, 231, 233

I

Ideal theories, 322–323
Identity, concept of, 121, 123, 125–127
Imminence, of terrorist attacks, 205
Impartiality, of commissions of inquiry, 296, 298–299
In absentia trials, 340
Incremental change
gravitational pull and, 14
not recognizing of, 24, 25, 29
and regulatory capture, 34–35
and tunnel vision, 33
Independent Panel of Experts on the Cholera Outbreak in Haiti (UN), 167
India, Constitution, Art. 14, 313 n. 8
Indictments, 335 n. 8
admission of, 351
Indigenous peoples, special rights of, 317
Individualistic legal regimes, 207–208
in human rights law, 208–209, 210, 218
rules and standards in, 212
Informality, of commissions of inquiry, 295–299, 308
Institute de Droit International (IDI), 134
institutional change, in global governance, 19, 20
Institutional pluralism, 273
Interaction, inter-institutional, 20, 29, 31–32
Inter-American Court on Human Rights, margin of appreciation doctrine application by, 217–218
International Cocoa Agreement, as temporary regime, 46
International Code for Ships Operating in Polar Waters (IMO, 2017), 363 n. 11
International Court of Justice (ICJ)
on human rights obligations, *erga omnes* nature of, 292 n. 33
non-appearance regime, 369, 372
provisional measures of, 27
on state immunities, 110–111
Statute of
Art. 38, 344, 346
Art. 38(1), 333
Art. 38(1)(b), on source of customary law, 109
Art. 38(1)(c), on general principles of law, 111–112
Art. 53, 369
Art. 53–61, 303 n. 85
on term concurring vote, 23–24
on UN immunity, 164
International courts/tribunals
adjudication of human rights derogations by, 200, 202–203, 204–206, 214, 215
delegation of rule-making authority on human rights derogations by, 197, 201, 202–203, 213–214, 216–218, 219
disclosure regime of, 342–343, 349, 350
establishment of, 301, 302, 354–355
political influences on, 342
and human rights law, 344
temporary, 288
International Covenant on Civil and Political Rights (ICCPR)
Art. 4, 203
Art. 9, 365
Art. 12(2), 365
Art. 40(4), 203
delegation of rule-making in, 203
on derogation of human rights, 201, 202. *see also* Siracusa Principles
slavery prohibition in, 209
temporary measures in, 314 n. 11
International Covenant on Economic, Social and Cultural Rights (ICESCR), 181
International Criminal Court for Former Yugoslavia, 86
International Criminal Court (ICC)
Assembly of State Parties, 333
permanence of, 27, 288
referrals to, resulting from commissions of inquiry, 302
Rome Statute of
influence of ICTY and ICTR on, 58–60
power of Prosecutor in, 59
Statute of, 354
Art. 7(3), 344 n. 24
Art. 13(b), 301 n. 76
Art. 39–64, 303 n. 85
International criminal justice, 331–333
adversarial system in, 333, 335, 336, 339
criticism of system of, 333–336, 340, 342–343, 354–355

judge-led system in, 333, 336, 338, 339
preference for, 346–353
procedural fairness in, 334 n. 6, 342, 343, 345–346, 354
purposes of, 342, 343
recommendations for reform of, 336 n. 10, 337
sources of
general international law, 344–345
human rights law, 343–344
temporariness in, 336, 340, 354
International Criminal Tribunal for Rwanda (ICTR), as temporary regime, 47, 48, 58
International Criminal Tribunal for the Former Yugoslavia (ICTY), 27
Completion Strategy, 334 n. 6
evidence rules of, 333–334
as temporary regime, 47, 48, 58
International Dairy Federation (IDF), 35–36
International human rights law, *see* Human rights law (HRL)
International Humanitarian Fact Finding Commission (IHFFC), 288, 307
International humanitarian law, *see* Law of armed conflict
International investment agreements (IIA), 31
International investment law, and gravitational pull, 31
International law
change in, 13–14, 31, 76–77
langue of, 22–25, 29, 33
as replacement of the old, 22, 29
normative engagement and, 26
obscuring historical heritage and, 26
political dimensions to, 25
on climate change, 255, 256
flexibility in, 257–272, 278–282
legal pluralism in, 273–278, 281–282
research input in, 256–257, 260–262, 271–272
continuity and, 82
customary, 223, 225, 345
definitions of, 109
equality norm as, 313
formation of, 109
persistent objector rule in, 24–25
relationship between time and, 77
role of domestic courts in, 110
treaty interpretation and, 147–150
violations of, 110
environmental, 256, 259
flexibility mechanisms in, 257, 258
general principles of, 111–112
making/developing of
by commissions of inquiry, 293–294, 295
delegated, 271, 278
informal, 256
materialisation of, 112
positivist view of, 99–100
roles of, 19, 20, 68
seen as a process, 105
as source of international criminal justice, 344–345
stability in, 4, 12–13, 20, 68, 70, 77
sunset clauses adopted in, 86
temporariness in, 4–16, 19, 20, 21, 282
comparative concept and, 27–28
langue and, 22–23
paradigms in, 115–116
of atemporality, 93, 95, 96, 97–98, 99, 116
of fluxus, 95, 96, 104–106, 108, 109, 110, 111, 115
of temporality, 98–99, 100–104, 108, 111, 114
relationality and, 26–27
violations
accountability for, 289, 295–296
commissions of inquiry on, 292, 293–294, 297–298
see also Environment law; Human rights law; Refugee law
International Law Association (ILA), concerns about LCRB, 171–172
International Law Commission (ILC), adoption of ARIO by, 183
International legal adjudication, 287, 291–292
commissions of inquiry as temporary bodies of, 290–295
of human rights derogations, 200, 202–203, 204–206, 214, 215
impact of commissions of inquiry on, 289, 295–306
selectivity appearance of, 306
International legal system, structure of, and overlapping normativity, 28
International legislature, absence of, 4
International Maritime Organization (IMO), 374–375
Resolutions
Assuring Safety During Demonstrations, Protests or Confrontations on the High Seas (2010), 380
on Safety Zones and Safety of Navigation around Offshore Installations and Structures (1989), 376 n. 65, 378

International organisations
accountability gap of, 7–8, 13
accountability in, 184
constituent treaties of, interpretation of, 140–141
legal immunity of, 7–8, 172–176, 184–186
human rights approach to, 173–174
state-centered approach to, 176
permanence in, 21
rule of law applying to, 178
and temporariness, 21
International rule of law
continuity and, 79–81
definitions of, 72, 75
elements of, 75–76
implementation of, 74–75
importance of, 76
and IO's, 178
legal certainty and, 79
permanence and, 78
predictability and, 78–79
promotion of, 75, 81
relationship with time, 76–78, 88–89
roles of, 68–69
and temporariness, 78, 85–87, 88–89
and UN, 178–180
see also Rule of law
International Telecommunications Union (ITU), 95
International treaty bodies, *see* International tribunals/courts
International Tribunal for the Law of Sea
arbitration of Netherlands against Russia at, 359, 362, 364, 365–374, 382–383
human rights considerations, 378–379, 382, 383
on human rights, 379 n. 80
jurisdiction of, 365–368, 369–370
Intertemporal law
concept of, 128
and evolutive interpretation, 131–132
and non-retroactivity, 147, 150
and process of interpretation, 129, 134–138, 145, 151
Intra-generational justice, 114
IPCC (Intergovernmental Panel on Climate Change), 260–261
reports of, 256–257
Island of Palmas dictum, 128, 129, 134, 135
Israel
Gaza conflicts, commissions of inquiry on, 292 n. 30, 296, 298, 299, 292 n. 30
Lebanon intervention (2006), commission of inquiry on, 292 n. 30
Italy, Corte di Cassazione, 110–111
Ius gentium, concept of, 97

J
Jacobs, F.G., 145
Japan
Antarctic whaling by, activism against, 361, 362 n. 8
Jesus, Judge, 368, 373, 382 n. 91
Judge-led systems, 331, 347
in international criminal justice, 333, 336, 338, 339
preference for, 346–353
Judges
in commissions of inquiry, 299
investigating, 343
lay, 347–348
qualifications/expertise of, 337, 339–340
role of, 347
in common-law systems, 353 n. 39
in international criminal procedures, 349, 351–352
rule/law-making powers of, 333
Judgments, delivery and drafting of, 352–353
Judicial bodies, 291
commissions of inquiry as, 291
formality of, 295–296
see also Adjudication
Judicial review, of state conduct, 301
Jurisdiction
of International Tribunal for the Law of Sea of, 365–368, 369–370
over exclusive economic zones (EEZs), 375–376, 381
over offshore installations, 374–375
over territorial waters, 380 n. 83, 381
Jurisdictional immunity, *see* Legal immunity
Jury, role of, 346, 347
Jus cogens norms, 150, 163
Jus Gentium Methodo Scientifica Pertractum (Wolff), 99
Just societies, 323
Justice, 339 n. 16

K
Kant, Immanuel, 101
Kelly, Judge, 368, 369, 379, 383
Kennedy, Duncan, 21–22, 206–207, 208
Kingsburry, Benedict, 37
Kjaerum, M., 233, 236, 250–251
Klein, P., 140
Koremenos, Barbara, 45, 49

Koskenniemi, Martti, 276
Kosovo crisis, refugees resulting from, 240–241
Krisch, Nico, 273, 280
Kuhn, Thomas, 96
Kulyk, Judge, 368 n. 30, 372
Kumm, Mattias, 76
Kyoto Protocol (1997), 259, 271
  Art. 3(9), 263, 264
  Art. 21(7), 264
  classification/differentiation of Parties to, 266–268, 272, 279, 281
  Clean Development Mechanism (CDM), 259, 267, 269
  compliance with, 270–271
  entry into force, 265
  implementation of, 268–269
  negotiations on follow-up agreement to, 267
  review and amendment of, 263, 264, 271, 280
  as temporary regime, 46, 61–62
  withdrawal provisions, 266, 271

L

Langue, notion of, 21–23, 29
Lauterpacht, Hersch, 4, 134
Law
  and atemporality, 93, 95, 96, 97–98, 99, 116
  general principles of, 112
  relationship with time, 70–71, 76–78, 88–89, 95–96
  and temporality, 95, 96, 98–99, 100–104, 108, 111, 114
Law enforcement operations, exclusion from arbitration tribunal jurisdiction of, 366–367, 368
Law of armed conflict
  classification of conflicts in, commissions of inquiry on, 293
  influence of international investment law on, 31
  violations of
    commissions of inquiry on, 292, 293–294, 298
    duty to investigate, 299
Law of nations, 97–101
Law-making
  delegated, 271, 278
  informal, 256
  by treaty bodies, 260 n. 21
  see also Rule-making
Lawyers
  in commissions of inquiry, 299
  relationship with time, 95
Lay involvement, in criminal procedures, 347–348
League of Nations International Committee of Intellectual Cooperation, 106
Lebanon
  Code of Criminal Procedure, 340
    Art. 180 and 181, 338–339
    Art. 255–260, 338–339
  Israeli intervention in (2006), inquiry on, 292 n. 30, 298 n. 66
  legal system in, 338
  see also Special Tribunal for Lebanon
Legal certainty, 79, 84, 354
Legal change
  international law and, 13–14, 31, 76–77
    langue of, 22–25, 29, 33
    as replacement of the old, 22, 29
      normative engagement and, 26
      obscuring historical heritage and, 26
      political dimensions to, 25
  permanence in, 21
  political dimensions to, 25
  process of interaction in, 20
  treaty conflicts and, 23
Legal consciousness, 22
Legal cultures, 354
Legal immunity
  of European Space Agency, 174
  of IO's, 7–8, 172–176, 184–186
    human rights approach to, 173–174
    state-centered approach to, 176
  of states, 185
  of UN
    and cholera claims, *see* Cholera claims
    and claims arising from operational necessity, 166–167
    and domestic courts, 158–159, 162–163, 168, 172–173, 174–175, 184–186, 189–191
    human rights approach to, 176, 190
    and Mothers of Srebrenica claims, 163–164, 166, 174–175, 184
    and private law claims, 157, 159, 160–161, 164, 165–166, 175
      provisions for settlement of, 164–165
    and review of policy and political matters, 161, 165, 167
    state-centered approach to, 177–178
Legal pluralism, 273, 276, 280

in international climate change regime, 273–278, 281–282
Legal predictability
in international law, 20
pragmatism and, 10–11, 15
Legal procedures
fairness in, 298
and commissions of inquiry, 303–306, 309
Legal realism, 105
Legal scholars, and temporariness, 7
Legal systems, 341
adversarial, 331–332
fairness aura of, 346–347
in international criminal justice, 333, 335, 336
and preparedness for trial, 349
in climate change regime, 275
injurious conduct regulation by, 199
judge-led, 331, 347
in international criminal procedure, 333, 336
preference for, 346–353
relationships between, 273, 280
rules and standards in, 206–208, 212
Legg, A., 217 n. 95
Legitimacy, 29–30
Leibniz's Law of Identity, 126
Letelier and Moffitt commission of inquiry (1988), 290–291
Lex aeterna, concept of, 97
Lincoln, Abraham, 319
Linderfalk, U., 139 n. 97, 142
Local claims review boards (LCRB), 183
cholera claims and, 171–172
Lump sum settlements, 177

M

Macdonald, R.S.J., 205 n. 46, 248 n. 131
Maine inquiries, 288, 289
Majority voting
in climate change regimes, 279
disadvantages of, 263
Managerial school in compliance theory, 270
Mandates, of commissions of inquiry, 297–299, 308–309
Margin of appreciation doctrine, 200, 201, 213–216, 217–218, 219
Maritime protests, *see* Activism, at sea
Market mechanisms, in international climate change policies, 269
Markovits, Daniel, 207
Mavi Marmara incident (2010), 361 n. 6
Maxim par in parem non habit imperium, 110
McKinnon Wood, Hugh, 163
Means flexibility, 271
Media coverage, of activism at sea, 360
Members, of commissions of inquiry, 299, 305–306, 309
Merkouris, Panos, 7, 12
Merrills, J.G., 290, 291
Middle East, refugee crises in, 245
Minilateralism, 276
Minks, Simon, 349 n. 30
Minorities
repatriation of, 240 n. 89
special rights of, 317
MINUSTAH, *see* United Nations Stabilisation Mission in Haiti
Montreal Protocol on Substances that Deplete the Ozone Layer, 61
Mothers of Srebrenica claims, 163–164, 166, 174–175, 184
Muntarbhorn, Vitit, 299

N

Natural law, 97–101
Naturalisation, of refugees, 227 n. 32
Navigation, freedom of, 367, 380
Necessity
of human rights derogations, 199, 205, 206
for use of emergency powers, 319
Netherlands
arbitration against Russia over *Arctic Sunrise*, 359, 362, 364, 365–374, 382–383
human rights considerations, 378–379, 382, 383
protest vessels registered in, legal consequences of, 361–362
New Zealand, Crown Minerals Act (1981), 375 n. 62
Nì Aolaìn, Fionnuala, 214 n. 81
Noll, G., 234 n. 63
Nollkaemper, A., 191
Non-compliance, advantages of, 269–270
Non-derogable human rights, 203 n. 36
Non-discrimination norm/principle, 313 n. 7, 315, 321
equality notion equated with, 322, 323, 324
suspension of, 320
violations of, 317, 321–322.
see also Affirmative action measures; Equality

Non-ideal theories, 323, 327
Non-intervention principle, and commissions of inquiry, 300–303
Non-participation, in arbitration proceedings, 359, 366, 368–370, 371, 372, 376, 382
Non-refoulement rule of refugee law, 223
Non-retroacivity, intertemporal law and, 147, 150
Non-state actors
  in climate change law, 256
  in climate change regime, 256, 274
Normalcy, and terrorist attacks, 320
Norms
  categories of, 112
  creation of, in global governance, 19, 20
  customary
    of equality, 313
    in refugee law, 225
  for derogation of human rights, 199
  and exceptions, 314, 319–320
  peremptory, of human rights, 198
  suspension of, 320 n. 39
Norway, Greenpeace protests in Exclusive Economic Zone of, 381
Nuclear Non-Proliferation Treaty
  temporariness of, 45
    turning permanent, 49
Nuremberg Military Tribunal
  legitimacy of, 69
  temporariness of, 86

O

Objector rule, persistent, in international law, 24–25
Obligations
  of states
    in climate change law, 279
    human rights, 208–209, 210, 292 n. 33
      equality norm, 312
      non-discrimination principle, 321
    in refugee law, 225–226
      cessation of, 229–232
O'Connor, Sandra Day, 317–318, 326
Oda, Judge, 148
Offshore installations
  breaching of safety zones around, 375
  jurisdiction over, 374–375
  piracy against, possibility of, 377–378
  unauthorized boarding of, 363–364, 377–378
Ogata, Sadako, 233, 234–235
Oil exploration
  in Arctic region, activism against, 359, 362–364
Oil platforms, *see* Offshore installations
Opening statements, purpose of, 352
Opinio iuris sive necessitatis, 109
Opportunities, equality of, 315–316, 318, 322–325, 326, 329
Ostrom, Elinor, 273

P

Palestinian Territories
  Gaza conflicts, commissions of inquiry on, 292 n. 30, 296, 298, 299
Paradoxes, 122, 125
Parole, notion of, 22
Peace, notion of, in peace treaties, 101–104
Peace treaties, notion of peace in, 101–104
Peace Treaty Concerning the Termination of the Crimea War (1856), 103
Peace Treaty of Nijmegen, 103
Perdurantism, 126–127, 128, 133–134, 151
Peremptory norms, of human rights, 198
Perluss, D., 225
Permanence
  as closed to chance, 21
  in global regulatory space, 32–33
  in international criminal justice, needs for, 336–337
  of international organizations, 21
  international rule of law and, 78
Permanent Court of International Justice, Statute of, drafting of, 112
Permanent institutions, change and, 9, 13–14
Permanent international legal regimes, influenced by temporary legal regimes, 41, 42–43, 48–52, 69–70
Perpetual Peace (Kant), 101
Persistence, concept of, 121, 122, 123, 125, 133
Persistent objector rule, in international law, 24–25
Personal time, 94
Piracy proceedings/charges, against maritime activism, 361, 364, 365, 376–378
Pluralism, *see* Legal pluralism
Political influences
  on climate change debate, 261, 276, 277
  on international criminal procedure, 333, 342, 354
Politics, influences of, on climate change research, 261
Ponte, Carla del, 299

Porter Commission of inquiry (Uganda), 294–295
Portugal, actions against Women on Waves, 380–381
Positive measures in human rights treaties, *see* Temporary measures, in human rights treaties
Pragmatism
  legal predictability and, 10–11, 15
  temporary issues and, 5, 16
Precautionary principle, WTO and, 30
Predictability
  international rule of law and, 78–79
  as requirement for temporary measures, 327–328
  temporary issues and, 5, 12, 13, 16
  see also Stability
Preferential treatments, *see* Temporary measures, in human rights treaties
Principles
  of sovereignty, 112
  of sustainable development, 112–115
Prirazlomnaya oil platform
  Greenpeace's boarding of, 363–364
    criminal investigations in, 373–374
  safety zone of, 375
Private ends concept, 377
Private law claims
  cholera claims as, 165–166, 175
  and legal immunity of UN, 157, 159, 160–161, 164–166, 175
  against UN
    settling of, 183–184
    solutions for handling of, 187–191
      Central Claims Commissions, 187–188
      ombudsperson, 188
      role for domestic courts, 189–191
Private parties, in global regulatory space, 34–36
Procedural fairness, 298, 339 n. 16, 341
  and commissions of inquiry, 303–306, 309
  in international criminal justice, 334 n. 6, 342–346, 351
Procedures
  arbitration
    non-participation in, 359, 366, 368–370, 371, 372, 376, 382
    provisional measures in, 365–366, 369–374
  domestic criminal, 341, 343
    lay involvement in, 347–348
  international criminal, 331–333, 342
    adversarial system of, 333, 335, 336, 339
    criticism of, 333–336, 340, 342–343, 354–355
    human rights law as source of, 343–344
    international law as source of, 344–345
    judge-led system of, 333, 336, 338, 339
      preference for, 346–353
    purposes of, 342, 343
    recommendations for reform of, 336 n. 10, 337
Prohibitions
  of discrimination, 216
  of slavery, 209
  of torture, 211 n. 68
Proof, *see* Evidence
Proportionality, of anti-terrorism measures, 205
Prosecution, role in international criminal procedures, 349, 350
Protection
  for refugees, 222–223, 224–225. *see also* Surrogate protection for refugees
    cessation of, 228–232, 237–240, 245–246, 249, 250–251
    solidarity in regimes of, 241, 251–252
    temporary, 221, 226, 232–240, 241–247, 249–250
Protest
  rights to, 375
    at sea, 378–382, 383
Provisional measures, in arbitration proceedings, 365–366, 369–374
Provisional Protocol for the Application of the General Agreement of Trade and Tariffs (GATT), 27
Prusso-Austrian Peace Treaty (1866), 103
Public goods, global, 274 n. 119
Putin, Vladimir, 364

Q

Quasi-judicial bodies, 291

R

Ranchordás, Sophie, 7, 12–13
Rashkow, B., 175
Rational design theory, state behaviour and, 43, 45–46, 49, 51, 52, 59–60, 62
Rawls, John, 322–323
Reasonable suspicion, 304
Rechtsstaat, 72, 79

Red Crusader inquiry (1961), 290
Referring expressions, 142
Refugee Convention (1951), 221, 223, 224, 225
Art. 1A, 242
Art. 1A(2), 224 n. 13
Art. 1B, 224 n. 13
Art. 1C(5), 224 n. 13, 228, 229, 231, 239, 246, 251
Art. 9, 248
Art. 33, 223 n. 5
Art. 34, 227 n. 31
changed to permanent regime, 223 n. 5, 227 n. 31, 56–58
derogation possibilities in, 247–248, 251
Preamble, 223 n. 8
Protocol (1967), 224
as example of temporary regime turning permanent, 48
refugee status in, 226–227
cessation of, 228–232, 245–246, 249, 250–251
State Parties, 225 n. 18
convention implementation by, 230
obligations of, 225–226
and temporary protection mechanisms, 232, 234 n. 66, 236–237, 239–240, 242–245, 247, 250
temporariness of, 55–56
Refugee law (IRL), 221, 222–225
derogation concept in, 247–248
and temporary protection mechanisms, 250
Refugees
definition, 224
naturalisation of, 227 n. 32
repatriation of, 229
status/protection of, 224–225, 226–227
cessation of, 228–232, 237–240, 245–246, 249, 250–251
prima facie recognition of, 242 n. 102
solidarity in regimes for, 241, 251–252
temporariness of, 6, 10
temporary, 221, 222, 225, 226, 228–230, 232–240, 241–247, 249–250
Regulatory capture, 34–36
Regulatory regimes, 199
Regulatory space, notion of, 28–29
Relevance, determining of, 147
Repatriation
of refugees, 229, 243
after the Yugoslav war, 238–239
integration favoured over, 230
minority returns, 240 n. 89
as reversal of ethnic cleansing, 234–235
voluntariness of, 246, 251.
see also Voluntary repatriation doctrine
Report of the High-Level Panel on Threats, Challenges and Change, 107–108
Research
input into climate change law, 256–257, 260–262, 271–272
on international criminal justice, 345
Reservations, to climate change treaties, 265
Responsibility to Protect concept (R2P), 292–293
application of, 306
Rights
of accused, procedural; *see also* Fairness in international criminal justice, 334 n. 6, 345–346
of parties to arbitration, 373
special, of minorities/indigenous peoples, 317
of states, to hot pursuit, 376
of victims, 335
see also Human rights
The Rise and Fall of Classical Legal Thought (Kennedy), 21–23
River paradox, 122, 125
Rome Conference, 58–60
Rome Statute, *see* International Criminal Court (ICC), Statute of
Rule of law
conceptions of, 72–73
definitions of, 68
dynamics of, 73–74
groups of addressees, 74
in non-Western countries, 75
principle of consistency and, 180
promotion of, 73, 88
roles of, 87–88
suspension of, in state of emergency, 319
temporary rules and, 84–85
see also International rule of law
Rule-making authority for derogation of human rights standards, 202, 203, 206–219
Rules
in human rights regimes, 211
and standards, 206–208, 212
Russia
arbitration of Netherlands over *Arctic Sunrise* against, 359, 362, 364, 365–374, 382–383
human rights considerations, 378–379, 382, 383

arrest of *Arctic Sunrise* by, 364–365
oil exploration activities in Arctic region by, 363–364
Rwanda commission of inquiry, 302

S

Safety
assessment of, 239, 246
zones around offshore installations, 374–375
violations of, 375, 376
Sands, Ph., 140
Saussarian semiotics, 21–22
Schauer, F., 218 n. 98
Schmidt, Klaus, 50
Schmitt, Carl, 314 n. 12, 319 n. 36
Schrijver, N., 187
Science, *see* Research
Sea
environmental activism at, 359, 360–361
legal responses to, 361–362, 364
against oil exploration activities, 361–362, 364
freedom of speech at, 378–382, 383
law of, *see* Convention on the Law of the Sea
Sea Shepherd Conservation Society activism, 361, 362 n. 8, 377, n. 71
Security, notion of, 106–108, 372
Self-preservation
of states, human rights derogations for purpose of, 200, 203, 210, 216–217
September 11 terrorist attacks, 320
Sexual orientation, as category of gender, 344 n. 24
Shaffer, Gregory, 274, 277
Shany, Y., 211 n. 67
Sheeran, S.P., 206 n. 47
Ship paradox, 125
Ships
arrests/seizure of, 364–365, 383
Dutch registration of, 361–362
and environmental stewardship, 371–373
legality of, 376
release of, 373, 374
Sikkink, Kathryn, 35, 50
Simmons, John, 323 n. 55
Siracusa Principles on the Limitation and Derogation Provisions in the International Covenant on Civil and Political Rights, 203 n. 36, 210 n. 64
Slavery prohibition, 209
Sluiter, G., 336 n. 10, 346 n. 27
Social acceleration, 104
Social rights, 198
Social time, 94
Societies, just, 323
Solidarity, in refugee protection regimes, 241, 251–252
Sorensen, R., 126
Sovereignty
principle of, 112
of states, and non-intervention principle, 300–303
'space-time worms', 127, 128, 134, 144, 151
Spain, *Arctic Sunrise* arrested by, 373 n. 55, 383
Special measures, *see* Temporary measures, in human rights treaties
Special notion, 318–319
Special Tribunal for Lebanon (STL), 337–340
procedures at, 335
Rules of Procedure and Evidence, 340
Rule 145, 338, 339, 340
Statute
Art. 9(1), 339
Art. 20(2), 338, 339
Art. 22, 340
Art. 28(2), 340
Speech
freedom of, at sea, 378–382, 383
Srebrenica, failure of Dutch peacekeepers in, 163–164, 166
Stability
in international law, 4, 12–13, 20, 68, 70, 77
see also Predictability
'stage theory', 127
Standards
ex post application of, 207
of human rights, 344
of human rights derogation, 201–202
adjudication of, 125, 200, 202–203, 204–206, 214
application of, 199–200
rule-making authority on, 202, 203, 206–219
and legal regimes, 207–208
of proof, for commissions of inquiry, 304–305
of reasonable conduct, 199
for refugee protection, 225
State immunities, exceptions in, 110–111
State practice (*consuetudo*), 109

States
behaviour theories of
initial design of temporary regimes, 51–52
preference for temporary regimes
behavioural international law approach to, 46
fewer procedural barriers, 46–47
greater willingness to accept, 47–48
rational design approach to, 43, 45–46
when temporary regimes turn permanent
behavioural international law approach to, 43, 46, 50, 51, 53, 60–61, 62–63
constructivist approach to, 43, 50, 51, 52–53, 60, 62
historical institutionalist approach to, 43, 49–50, 51, 52, 60, 62–63
rational design approach to, 43, 45–46, 49, 51, 52, 59–60, 62
classification/differentiation of, in climate change regime, 266–268, 272, 279, 281
conduct of, judicial review of, 301
consent of, to external authority/scrutiny, 300–301
derogations of human rights by, 197, 201
rule-making authority on, 202, 203, 206–219
for self-preservation, 200, 203, 210, 216–217
dispute settlement between, 291, 292 n. 30
jurisdiction of
over exclusive economic zones (EEZs), 375–376
over offshore installations, 374–375
legal immunity of, 185
obligations of
in climate change law, 279
of human rights, 208–209, 210
equality norm, 312
non-discrimination principle, 321
in refugee law, 225–226
cessation of, 229–232
protection for refugees provided by, 222–223
sovereignty of, and non-intervention principle, 300–305
Suárez, Francisco, 97
Substantive equality, 324
Sunset clauses
benefits of, 83–85
counterterrorism policies and, 81, 83
definition of, 83
development of rule of law and, 84
in international law, 86
Surrogate protection for refugees, 222
Suspicion, reasonable, 304
Sustainable development, principle of, 112–115
Syria commission of inquiry, 293, 298, 299, 301, 304, 305
Systemic pluralism, 273

T

Tanaka, Judge, 313 n. 7
Taylor, Kate Nancy, 7–8, 13
Technological cooperation, advantages of, 276–277
Temporality, in concept of law, 95, 96, 98–99, 100–104, 108, 111, 114
Temporariness
of commissions of inquiry, 8, 13, 287, 288, 289, 306–309
of criminal tribunals, 8, 13
in international criminal justice, 336, 340, 354
in international law, 4–16, 19, 20, 21, 282
comparative concept and, 27–28
langue and, 22–23
paradigms in, 115–116
of atemporality, 93, 95, 96, 97–98, 99, 116
of fluxus, 95, 96, 104–106, 108, 109, 110, 111, 115
of temporality, 98–99, 100–104, 108, 111, 114
relationality and, 26–27
in international organizations, 21
international rule of law and, 78, 85–87, 88–89
legal scholars and, 7
of Nuclear Non-Proliferation Treaty, 45
turning permanent, 49
of Nuremberg Military Tribunal, 86
of Refugee Convention (1951), 55–56
of refugee status, 6, 10
views of change and, 21
see also Atemporality; Temporality; Temporary objects; Temporary subjects; Time
Temporary adjudicative bodies, commissions of inquiry, 290–295
Temporary international legal regimes
criticism on, 85

deliberate, 42
examples of, 81–82
General Agreement of Tariffs and Trade (GATT), 47
International Cocoa Agreement, 46
International Criminal Tribunal for Rwanda (ICTR), 47, 48, 58
International Criminal Tribunal for the Former Yugoslavia (ICTY), 47, 48, 58
international criminal tribunals, 87, 88
Kyoto Protocol (1997), 46, 61–62
Nuclear Non-Proliferation Treaty, 45, 49
Nuremberg Military Tribunal, 69, 86
Refugee Convention (1951), 55–56
truth commissions, 85
UNHCR, 48, 54–55
factors favouring use of, 44–47
influence on permanent legal regimes, 41, 42–43, 48–52, 69–70
case studies, 54–63
initial design of
state behaviour theories and, implications of, 51, 53–54
as temporary subjects, 9
willingness to accept, 47–48
see also Sunset clauses
Temporary measures, 329
in emergencies, 319–320
in human rights treaties, 313–314, 317–320
and equality, 311, 314–315, 316, 319, 320, 321–322, 323, 329–330
predictability requirement, 327–328
time limits for, 316, 317–318, 326–327, 329, 330
Temporary national legal regimes
as response to emergencies, 82–83
used as consensusgathering mechanisms, 83–84
see also Sunset clauses
Temporary objects, 4–5, 16
examples of, 6–7
influence on international law, 9–13
international law as, 7
Temporary protected status (United States), 226 n. 22
Temporary protection mechanisms for refugees, 221, 226, 232–237, 241
cessation of, 237–240, 243, 244–247
EU Directive on, 221, 241–245, 249
usefulness of, 249–250
Temporary refuge norm, 225
Temporary subjects, 3, 5, 16
examples of, 8–9
influence on international law, 13–15
Termination
of refugee status/protection, 228–232, 237–240, 245–246, 249, 250–251
of temporary measures, 316, 326–327, 329, 330
Termination clauses, *see* Sunset clauses
Territorial waters, jurisdiction over, 380 n. 83, 381
Terrorism
temporary rules for, 83
as threat to security, 107
Terrorismusbekämpfungsgesetz, 83
Terrorist attacks
imminence of, 205
and normalcy, 320
Teulings, J., 360 n. 3
Texas, affirmative action programs in, 328
Textor, Johan Wolfgang, 100–101, 109
Theories
ideal, 322–323
non-ideal, 323, 327
A Theory of Justice (Rawls), 322, 323
Theseus, 125
Thirlway, H., 130, 143, 144
Thirty Years War, 102
Tiger inquiry (1917), 290
Time
change and passage of, 122–123
concept of, 121, 123, 125–127
as dimension of refugee status, 222, 228–230
international standards concerning, 95
limits, for temporary measures, 316, 317–318, 326–327, 329, 330
relationship with law, 70–71, 76–78, 88–89, 95–96
understanding of, 94–95
'time-slices', 127, 144, 145
Tonkin, H., 305 n. 99
Torture, prohibition of, 211 n. 68
Trade, in emissions, 269, 275, 277
Transformative flexibility, 271
Transparency requirement, for temporary measures, 327–328
Treaties
compliance with, 269–270
derogation clauses in, 198, 201–202, 209–210, 248
entry into force, 265
environmental, interpretation of, 140

human rights, 198
interpretation of, 140, 145–146
interpretation of
contemporaneity in, 124, 129, 130, 133, 134–138, 140, 142, 148, 152
effects of time on, 122–123
evolutive/dynamic approach in, 108, 124, 131, 133–134, 137–138, 139–141, 150, 152
evolution of facts in, 132
evolution of law in, 132–133
and intertemporal law, 131–132
limits to, 150–151
use of generic terms in, 141–143
and intentions of the parties, 143–144, 149
and intertemporal law, 129, 134–138, 145, 151
linguistics in, 132 n. 59, 141–142
and 'time-will' of parties, 140, 142, 143–144, 145–147, 149
law-making by bodies of, 260 n. 21
refugee, 223
revision of, 23–24
Treaty law, allowing change in, 7, 12
Treaty of Berlin (1878), 103
Treaty of Muenster, 103
Treaty of Osnabrück, 102, 103
Treaty of Paris (1856), 103
Treaty of Paris (1951), 77
Trials
in absentia, 340
opening statements and pre-trial briefs in, 351–352
preparedness for, 349
rights to speedy, 345–346
Truth commissions, 85
Tubantia inquiry (1921), 290
Tunnel vision, 33–34
Turkel Commission of inquiry (Israel), 296

U
UNFCCC, *see* Framework Convention on Climate Change (United Nations)
UN-Haiti SOFA, 161–163, 165, 169–171
UNHCR, 223–224
changed to permanent regime, 57–58
on standards for refugee protection, 225
on temporary protection mechanisms, 221, 232 n. 57, 233, 234–237, 241, 244, 245–247, 249–250
as temporary regime, 48, 54–55
on termination of refugee status, 229–230, 238–239, 245–246
on voluntary repatriation, 230–231, 246
United Kingdom
anti-terrorism legislation in, 204–205
inquiry into involvement in Iraq conflict, 297, 299
United Nations
Charter
Art. 1, 312
Art. 2, 112
Art. 2(7), 300, 301 n. 76, 302
Art. 27, 22
Art. 104, 162
Art. 105, 162
Chapter VII powers, 302
equality in, 312
immunity in, 162–163
security in, 106
claims commissions of, 169–171, 182–183
climate change regime, flexibility in, 258–272
Development Programme, 106–107
diplomatic protection against, 177
enhancing accountability of, 183–184
General Assembly, Resolutions, No. 2329 (XXII, 1967) Question of methods of fact-finding, 309
General Convention
Section 2, 162, 168, 173
Section 29, 160, 164–165, 167, 168, 169–170, 173, 179, 184, 189–190
Section 30, 176–177
Haiti cholera claims
handling of, 160, 161–162, 184
international human rights laws and, 180–181
rule of law and, 179–180
High Commissioner for Refugees, *see* UNHCR
Human Rights Committee
on derogation of human rights, 203, 204
on equality, 312
on positive measures/affirmative action, 313 n. 9, 314 n. 11, 320 n. 41
Human Rights Council, commissions of inquiry of, 296–297, 298, 302, 303
ICESCR and, 182
Independent Panel of Experts on the Cholera Outbreak in Haiti, 167
legal immunity of
and claims arising from, operational necessity, 166–167

domestic courts and, 158–159, 163, 168, 172–173, 174–175, 184–185, 189–191
human rights approach to, 176, 190
and Mothers of Srebrenica claims, 163–164, 174–175, 184
and private law claims, 157, 159, 160–161, 164, 165–166, 175
provisions for settlement of, 164–165
and review of policy and political matters, 161, 165, 167
state-centered approach to, 177–178
local claims review boards (LCRB), cholera claims and, 171–172
lump sum settlements of, 177
MINUSTAH, *see* United Nations Stabilisation Mission in Haiti
Petition of Relief to, of cholera victims, 160
private law claims against
settling of, 183–184
solutions for handling of, 187–191
Central Claims Commissions, 187–188
ombudsperson, 188
role for domestic courts, 189–191
Resolution 61/39, 75
rule of law applying to, 178–180
Secretary-General
commissions of inquiry of, 297
on international rule of law, 75
on rule of law, 178–179
waiving of immunity by, 162 n. 27
Security Council
commissions of inquiry of, 297
international criminal tribunals established by, 301 n. 76
powers of, 302–303
Resolutions
No.752 (1992) Bosnia and Herzegovina, 235 n. 67
No.827 (1993) International Criminal Tribunal for the former Yugoslavia (ICTY), 301 n. 76
No.955 (1994) Establishment of the International Criminal Tribunal for Rwanda (ICTR) and adoption of the Statute of the Tribunal, 301 n. 76
No.1636 (2005) Middle East, 303
security and, 106, 107
Status of Force Agreements, 169–170
Status of Forces Agreement with Haiti, 161–163, 165, 169–171, 176, 182–183
United Nations Stabilisation Mission in Haiti (MINUSTAH)
claims against, 169–171
criticism against, 186–187
immunity of, 162–163
source of cholera outbreak, 158–160
United States
affirmative action programs in, 328
immigration law, 226 n. 22
Universal Declaration of Human Rights, 236
Art. 14(1), 236 n. 75
Universal Declaration on Race and Racial Prejudice (UNESCO, 1982), 313 n. 7
Unjust societies, 323
Urgency, assessments of, 371
Uruena, Rene, 9, 13–14, 15
USA Patriot Act, sunset clauses adopted in, 83

V

Verdirame, G., 188
Victims
in international criminal justice, increased role of, 335, 346 n. 26
Vienna Convention on the Law of Treaties (VCLT), 23
Art. 4, 147
Art. 31
rules of interpretation in, 108, 123, 124, 137–138, 151
evolutive/dynamic approach in, 139, 145–146
reflecting customary international law, 147–150
Art. 32
rules of interpretation in, 108, 123
reflecting customary international law, 148–150
Draft Article 56, rules of interpretation in, 135–137, 138
Draft Article 68, 137
Vietnam, refugees from, 225
Voluntary repatriation doctrine, 230–232
Von Bismarck, Otto, 103
Von Clausewitz, Carl, 101–102

W

Waldock, Humphrey, 135, 136–138
Waldron, Jeremy, 74
Wars, displacement as goal of, 234
Weber, Max, 112
Weingast, Barry, 80, 81

Welfare, equality of, 316, 324–325
Wellens, K., 170
Westphalian Peace, 102–103
Wet Bestuurlijke Maatregelen Nationale Veiligheid (Bill on Administrative Measures concerning National Security), 83
Wiersema, A., 260 n. 21
Witnesses
  questioning of, 338–339
  reliability of, 305
  written statements of, admissibility of, 334 n. 6
Wolff, Christian, 99–100
Wolfrum, Judge, 368, 369, 379, 383
Women on Waves activism, 380–381
World Bank, promotion of rule of law by, 73
World Commission on Environment and Development, 112
World Summit Outcome document, 306
World Trade Organization
  precautionary principle and, 30
  SPS Agreement, Art. 3, 35 n63

Y
Yamin, Farhana, 263
Young, Oran, 272
Yugoslav commission of inquiry, 293–294, 302
Yugoslav Truth and Reconciliation Commission, 85–86
Yugoslavia
  break-up of
    refugee crisis resulting from, 232–235, 236, 237–238
    repatriation of refugees after, 238–240
  Kosovo refugees fleeing to former states of, 241

Z
Zouche, Richard, 100

MIX
Papier aus verantwortungsvollen Quellen
Paper from responsible sources
FSC® C105338
FSC
www.fsc.org

If you have any concerns about our products,
you can contact us on
ProductSafety@springernature.com

In case Publisher is established outside the EU,
the EU authorized representative is:
Springer Nature Customer Service Center GmbH
Europaplatz 3, 69115 Heidelberg, Germany

Printed by Libri Plureos GmbH
in Hamburg, Germany